CCNA Security
210-260
Official Cert Guide

OMAR SANTOS, CISSP 463598

JOHN STUPPI, CCIE NO. 11154

Cisco Press
800 East 96th Street
Indianapolis, IN 46240

CCNA Security 210-260
Official Cert Guide

Omar Santos

John Stuppi

Copyright© 2015 Pearson Education, Inc.

Published by:
Cisco Press
800 East 96th Street
Indianapolis, IN 46240 USA

Printed in the United States of America

5   16

Library of Congress Control Number: 2015938283

ISBN-13: 978-1-58720-566-8

ISBN-10: 1-58720-566-1

Warning and Disclaimer

This book is designed to provide information about the CCNA Security Implementing Cisco Network Security (IINS) 210-260 exam. Every effort has been made to make this book as complete and as accurate as possible, but no warranty or fitness is implied.

The information is provided on an "as is" basis. The authors, Cisco Press, and Cisco Systems, Inc. shall have neither liability nor responsibility to any person or entity with respect to any loss or damages arising from the information contained in this book or from the use of the discs or programs that may accompany it.

The opinions expressed in this book belong to the authors and are not necessarily those of Cisco Systems, Inc.

Trademark Acknowledgments

All terms mentioned in this book that are known to be trademarks or service marks have been appropriately capitalized. Cisco Press or Cisco Systems, Inc., cannot attest to the accuracy of this information. Use of a term in this book should not be regarded as affecting the validity of any trademark or service mark.

Special Sales

For information about buying this title in bulk quantities, or for special sales opportunities (which may include electronic versions; custom cover designs; and content particular to your business, training goals, marketing focus, or branding interests), please contact our corporate sales department at corpsales@pearsoned.com or (800) 382-3419.

For government sales inquiries, please contact governmentsales@pearsoned.com.

For questions about sales outside the U.S., please contact international@pearsoned.com.

Feedback Information

At Cisco Press, our goal is to create in-depth technical books of the highest quality and value. Each book is crafted with care and precision, undergoing rigorous development that involves the unique expertise of members from the professional technical community.

Readers' feedback is a natural continuation of this process. If you have any comments regarding how we could improve the quality of this book, or otherwise alter it to better suit your needs, you can contact us through email at feedback@ciscopress.com. Please make sure to include the book title and ISBN in your message.

We greatly appreciate your assistance.

Publisher: Paul Boger

Associate Publisher: Dave Dusthimer

Business Operation Manager, Cisco Press: Jan Cornelssen

Acquisitions Editor: Denise Lincoln

Managing Editor: Sandra Schroeder

Senior Development Editor: Christopher Cleveland

Senior Project Editor: Tonya Simpson

Copy Editor: Keith Cline

Technical Editors: Scott Bradley, Panos Kampanakis

Editorial Assistant: Vanessa Evans

Cover Designer: Mark Shirar

Composition: Bronkella Publishing

Indexer: Erika Millen

Proofreader: Chuck Hutchinson

Americas Headquarters
Cisco Systems, Inc.
San Jose, CA

Asia Pacific Headquarters
Cisco Systems (USA) Pte. Ltd.
Singapore

Europe Headquarters
Cisco Systems International BV
Amsterdam, The Netherlands

Cisco has more than 200 offices worldwide. Addresses, phone numbers, and fax numbers are listed on the Cisco Website at **www.cisco.com/go/offices.**

CCDE, CCENT, Cisco Eos, Cisco HealthPresence, the Cisco logo, Cisco Lumin, Cisco Nexus, Cisco StadiumVision, Cisco TelePresence, Cisco WebEx, DCE, and Welcome to the Human Network are trademarks; Changing the Way We Work, Live, Play, and Learn and Cisco Store are service marks; and Access Registrar, Aironet, AsyncOS, Bringing the Meeting To You, Catalyst, CCDA, CCDP, CCIE, CCIP, CCNA, CCNP, CCSP, CCVP, Cisco, the Cisco Certified Internetwork Expert logo, Cisco IOS, Cisco Press, Cisco Systems, Cisco Systems Capital, the Cisco Systems logo, Cisco Unity, Collaboration Without Limitation, EtherFast, EtherSwitch, Event Center, Fast Step, Follow Me Browsing, FormShare, GigaDrive, HomeLink, Internet Quotient, IOS, iPhone, iQuick Study, IronPort, the IronPort logo, LightStream, Linksys, MediaTone, MeetingPlace, MeetingPlace Chime Sound, MGX, Networkers, Networking Academy, Network Registrar, PCNow, PIX, PowerPanels, ProConnect, ScriptShare, SenderBase, SMARTnet, Spectrum Expert, StackWise, The Fastest Way to Increase Your Internet Quotient, TransPath, WebEx, and the WebEx logo are registered trademarks of Cisco Systems, Inc. and/or its affiliates in the United States and certain other countries.

All other trademarks mentioned in this document or website are the property of their respective owners. The use of the word partner does not imply a partnership relationship between Cisco and any other company. (0812R)

About the Authors

Omar Santos is the technical leader for the Cisco Product Security Incident Response Team (PSIRT). He mentors and leads engineers and incident managers during the investigation and resolution of security vulnerabilities in all Cisco products. Omar has been working with information technology and cybersecurity since the mid-1990s. Omar has designed, implemented, and supported numerous secure networks for Fortune 100 and 500 companies and for the U.S. government. Prior to his current role, he was a technical leader within the World Wide Security Practice and the Cisco Technical Assistance Center (TAC), where he taught, led, and mentored many engineers within both organizations.

Omar is an active member of the security community, where he leads several industry-wide initiatives and standards bodies. His active role helps businesses, academic institutions, state and local law enforcement agencies, and other participants that are dedicated to increasing the security of the critical infrastructure.

Omar is the author of several books and numerous white papers, articles, and security configuration guidelines and best practices. Omar has also delivered numerous technical presentations at many conferences and to Cisco customers and partners, in addition to many C-level executive presentations to many organizations.

John Stuppi, CCIE No. 11154 (Security), is a technical leader in the Cisco Security Solutions (CSS) organization at Cisco, where he consults Cisco customers on protecting their network against existing and emerging cybersecurity threats. In this role, John is responsible for providing effective techniques using Cisco product capabilities to provide identification and mitigation solutions for Cisco customers who are concerned with current or expected security threats to their network environments. Current projects include helping customers leverage DNS and NetFlow data to identify and subsequently mitigate network-based threats. John has presented multiple times on various network security topics at Cisco Live, Black Hat, and other customer-facing cybersecurity conferences. In addition, John contributes to the Cisco Security Portal through the publication of white papers, security blog posts, and cyber risk report articles. Before joining Cisco, John worked as a network engineer for JPMorgan and then as a network security engineer at Time, Inc., with both positions based in New York City. John is also a CISSP (#25525) and holds an Information Systems Security (INFOSEC) professional certification. In addition, John has a BSEE from Lehigh University and an MBA from Rutgers University. John lives in Ocean Township, New Jersey (a.k.a. the "Jersey Shore") with his wife, two kids, and dog.

About the Technical Reviewers

Scott Bradley is a network engineer dedicated to customer success. He began building knowledge and experience in Cisco technology more than 15 years ago when he first started in the Technical Assistance Center (TAC). Over time, thousands of customers have been assisted by his knowledge of internetworking in routing, switching, and security, and his ability to provide network design, implementation, and troubleshooting service. Scott has enjoyed being an escalation resource to the Catalyst and Nexus switching group, a technical trainer, and an early field trial software and hardware tester.

Currently, he is an active member of the Applied Security Intelligence Team, testing security-related software and hardware and writing applied mitigation bulletins and white papers. He works closely with the Cisco Product Security Incident Response Team (PSIRT), consulting on security advisories.

Scott lives with his wife, Cathy, in Santa Cruz, California, where he enjoys gardening, hiking, and riding bicycles.

Panos Kampanakis is part of the Security Research and Operations teams at Cisco Systems, providing early-warning intelligence, threat, and vulnerability analysis and proven Cisco mitigation solutions to help protect networks. He holds a CCIE and other certifications. He has extensive experience in network and IT security and cryptography. He has written numerous research publications and security-related guides and white papers. Panos has often participated in the development and review of Cisco certification exam material. He also presents in Cisco conferences, teaching customers about security best practices, identification, and mitigation techniques. In his free time, he has a passion for basketball (and never likes to lose).

Dedications

From Omar

I would like to dedicate this book to my lovely wife, Jeannette, and my two beautiful children, Hannah and Derek, who have inspired and supported me throughout the development of this book.

I also dedicate this book to my father, Jose; and in memory of my mother, Generosa. Without their knowledge, wisdom, and guidance, I would not have the goals that I strive to achieve today.

From John

I would like to dedicate this book to my wife, Diane, and my two wonderful children, Tommy and Allison, who have had to put up with more (than usual!) late night and weekend hours with me on my laptop during the development of this book.

I also want to dedicate this book as a thank you to those friends and family who provided inspiration and support through their genuine interest in the progress of the book.

Finally, I want to thank Omar for convincing me to help him as a co-author on this book. Although the process was arduous at times, it was a blessing to be able to work together on this effort with someone as dedicated, intelligent, and motivated as Omar.

Acknowledgments

We would like to thank the technical editors, Scott Bradley and Panos Kampanakis, for their time and technical expertise. They verified our work and contributed to the success of this book.

We would like to thank the Cisco Press team, especially Denise Lincoln and Christopher Cleveland, for their patience, guidance, and consideration. Their efforts are greatly appreciated.

Finally, we would like to acknowledge the Cisco Security Research and Operations teams. Several leaders in the network security industry work there, supporting our Cisco customers under often very stressful conditions and working miracles daily. They arc truly unsung heroes, and we are all honored to have had the privilege of working side by side with them in the trenches when protecting customers and Cisco.

Contents at a Glance

Contents

Command Syntax Conventions

The conventions used to present command syntax in this book are the same conventions used in the IOS Command Reference. The Command Reference describes these conventions as follows:

- **Boldface** indicates commands and keywords that are entered literally as shown. In actual configuration examples and output (not general command syntax), boldface indicates commands that are manually input by the user (such as a **show** command).

- *Italic* indicates arguments for which you supply actual values.

- Vertical bars (|) separate alternative, mutually exclusive elements.

- Square brackets ([ ]) indicate an optional element.

- Braces ({ }) indicate a required choice.

- Braces within brackets ([{ }]) indicate a required choice within an optional element.

Introduction

Congratulations! If you are reading this, you have in your possession a powerful tool that can help you to

- Improve your awareness and knowledge of network security
- Increase your skill level related to the implementation of that security
- Prepare for the CCNA Security certification exam

When writing this book, we did so with you in mind, and together we will discover the critical ingredients that make up the recipe for a secure network and work through examples of how to implement these features. By focusing on both covering the objectives for the CCNA Security exam and integrating that with real-world best practices and examples, we created this content with the intention of being your personal tour guides as we take you on a journey through the world of network security.

The CCNA Security Implementing Cisco Network Security (IINS) 210-260 exam is required for the CCNA Security certification. The CCNA Security exam tests your knowledge of securing Cisco routers and switches and their associated networks, and this book prepares you for that exam. This book covers all the topics listed in Cisco's exam blueprint, and each chapter includes key topics and preparation tasks to assist you in mastering this information. The CD that accompanies this book also includes bonus videos to assist you in your journey toward becoming a CCNA in Security. Of course, the CD included with the printed book also includes several practice questions to help you prepare for the exam.

About the CCNA Security Implementing Cisco Network Security (IINS) 210-260 Exam

Cisco's objective of the CCNA Security exam is to verify the candidate's understanding, implementation, and verification of security best practices on Cisco hardware and software. The focus points for the exam (which this book prepares you for) are as follows:

- **Cisco routers and switches**
    - Common threats, including blended threats, and how to mitigate them
    - The lifecycle approach for a security policy
    - Understanding and implementing network foundation protection for the control, data, and management planes
    - Understanding, implementing, and verifying *AAA (authentication, authorization, and accounting)*, including the details of TACACS+ and RADIUS
    - Understanding and implementing basic rules inside of Cisco *Access Control Server (ACS)* Version 5.x, including configuration of both ACS and a router for communications with each other

- Standard, extended, and named access control lists used for packet filtering and for the classification of traffic
- Understanding and implementing protection against Layer 2 attacks, including CAM table overflow attacks, and VLAN hopping

- **Cisco firewall technologies**

  - Understanding and describing the various methods for filtering implemented by firewalls, including stateful filtering. Compare and contrast the strengths and weaknesses of the various firewall technologies.
  - Understanding the methods that a firewall may use to implement *Network Address Translation (NAT)* and *Port Address Translation (PAT)*.
  - Understanding, implementing, and interpreting a zone-based firewall policy through *Cisco Configuration Professional (CCP)*.
  - Understanding and describing the characteristics and defaults for interfaces, security levels, and traffic flows on the *Adaptive Security Appliance (ASA)*.
  - Implementing and interpreting a firewall policy on an ASA through the GUI tool named the *ASA Security Device Manager (ASDM)*.

- **Intrusion prevention systems**

  - Comparing and contrasting *intrusion prevention systems (IPS)* versus *intrusion detection systems (IDS)*, including the pros and cons of each and the methods used by these systems for identifying malicious traffic
  - Describing the concepts involved with IPS included true/false positives/negatives
  - Configuring and verifying IOS-based IPS using CCP

- **VPN technologies**

  - Understanding and describing the building blocks used for *virtual private networks (VPNs)* today, including the concepts of symmetrical, asymmetrical, encryption, hashing, *Internet Key Exchange (IKE)*, *public key infrastructure (PKI)*, authentication, Diffie-Hellman, certificate authorities, and so on
  - Implementing and verifying IPsec VPNs on IOS using CCP and the *command-line interface (CLI)*
  - Implementing and verifying *Secure Sockets Layer (SSL)* VPNs on the ASA firewall using ASDM

As you can see, it is an extensive list, but together we will not only address and learn each of these, but we will also have fun doing it.

You can take the exam at Pearson VUE testing centers. You can register with VUE at http://www.vue.com/cisco/.

CCNA Security Exam

Table I-1 lists the topics of the CCNA Security exam and indicates the parts in the book where these topics are covered.

Table I-1 *CCNA Security Exam Topics*

Exam Topic	Part
1.0 Security Concepts	
1.1 Common Security Principles	
1.1.a Describe Confidentiality, Integrity, Availability (CIA)	Chapter 1
1.1.b Describe SIEM technology	Chapter 1
1.1.c Identify common security terms	Chapter 1
1.1.d Identify common network security zones	Chapter 1
1.2 Common Security Threats	
1.2.a Identify Common network attacks	Chapter 2
1.2.b Describe Social Engineering	Chapter 2
1.2.c Identify Malware	Chapter 2
1.2.d Classify the vectors of Data Loss/Exfiltration	Chapter 2
1.3 Cryptography Concepts	
1.3.a Describe Key Exchange	Chapter 5
1.3.b Describe Hash Algorithm	Chapter 5
1.3.c Compare & Contrast Symmetric and Asymmetric Encryption	Chapter 5
1.3.d Describe Digital Signatures, Certificates and PKI	Chapter 5
1.4 Describe network topologies	
1.4.a Campus Area Network (CAN)	Chapter 1
1.4.b Cloud, Wide Area Network (WAN)	Chapter 1
1.4.c Data Center	Chapter 1
1.4.d Small office/Home office (SOHO)	Chapter 1
1.4.e Network security for a virtual environment	Chapter 1
2.0 Secure Access	
2.1 Secure management	
2.1.a Compare In-band and out of band	Chapter 11
2.1.b Configure secure network management	Chapter 11
2.1.c Configure and verify secure access through SNMP v3 using an ACL	Chapter 11
2.1.d Configure and verify security for NTP	Chapter 11
2.1.e Use SCP for file transfer	Chapter 11

Exam Topic	Part
2.2 AAA Concepts	
2.2.a Describe RADIUS & TACACS+ technologies	Chapter 3
2.2.b Configure administrative access on a Cisco router using TACACS+	Chapter 3
2.2.c Verify connectivity on a Cisco router to a TACACS+ server	Chapter 3
2.2.d Explain the integration of Active Directory with AAA	Chapter 3
2.2.e Describe Authentication & Authorization using ACS and ISE	Chapter 3
2.3. 802.1X Authentication	
2.3.a Identify the functions 802.1X components	Chapter 4
2.4. BYOD	
2.4.a Describe the BYOD architecture framework	Chapter 4
2.4.b Describe the function of Mobile Device Management (MDM)	Chapter 4
3. VPN	
3.1. VPN Concepts	
3.1.a Describe IPSec Protocols and Delivery Modes (IKE, ESP, AH, Tunnel mode, Transport mode)	Chapter 6
3.1.b Describe Hairpinning, Split Tunneling, Always-on, NAT Traversal	Chapter 6
3.2. Remote Access VPN	
3.2.a Implement basic Clientless SSL VPN using ASDM	Chapter 8
3.2.b Verify clientless connection	Chapter 8
3.2.c Implement basic AnyConnect SSL VPN using ASDM	Chapter 8
3.2.d Verify AnyConnect connection	Chapter 8
3.2.e Identify Endpoint Posture Assessment	Chapter 8
3.3 Site-to-Site VPN	
3.3.a Implement an IPSec site-to-site VPN with pre-shared key authentication on Cisco routers and ASA firewalls	Chapter 7
3.3.b Verify an IPSec site-to-site VPN	Chapter 7
4.0. Secure Routing & Switching	
4.1 Security on Cisco Routers	
4.1.a Configure multiple privilege levels	Chapter 11
4.1.b Configure IOS Role-based CLI Access	Chapter 11
4.1.c Implement IOS Resilient Configuration	Chapter 11

Exam Topic	Part
4.2 Securing Routing Protocols	
4.2.a Implement routing update authentication on OSPF	Chapter 13
4.3 Securing the Control Plane	
4.3.a Explain the function of Control Plane Policing	Chapter 13
4.4 Common Layer 2 Attacks	
4.4.a Describe STP attacks	Chapter 9
4.4.b Describe ARP Spoofing	Chapter 9
4.4.c Describe MAC spoofing	Chapter 9
4.4.d Describe CAM Table (MAC Address Table) Overflows	Chapter 9
4.4.e Describe CDP/LLDP Reconnaissance	Chapter 9
4.4.f Describe VLAN Hopping	Chapter 9
4.4.g Describe DHCP Spoofing	Chapter 9
4.5 Mitigation Procedures	
4.5.a Implement DHCP Snooping	Chapter 9
4.5.b Implement Dynamic ARP Inspection	Chapter 9
4.5.c Implement Port Security	Chapter 9
4.5.d Describe BPDU Guard, Root Guard, Loop Guard	Chapter 9
4.5.e Verify mitigation procedures	Chapter 9
4.6 VLAN Security	Chapter 9
4.6.a Describe the security implications of a PVLAN	Chapter 9
4.6.b Describe the security implications of a Native VLAN	Chapter 9
5.0 Cisco Firewall Technologies	**Chapter 14**
5.1 Describe operational strengths and weaknesses of the different firewall technologies	Chapter 14
5.1.a Proxy firewalls	Chapter 14
5.1.b Application firewall	Chapter 14
5.1.c Personal firewall	Chapter 14
5.2 Compare Stateful vs. Stateless Firewalls	
5.2.a Operations	Chapter 16
5.2.b Functions of the state table	Chapter 16

Exam Topic	Part
5.3 Implement NAT on Cisco ASA 9.x	
5.3.a Static	Chapter 16
5.3.b Dynamic	Chapter 16
5.3.c PAT	Chapter 16
5.3.d Policy NAT	Chapter 16
5.3 e Verify NAT operations	Chapter 16
5.4 Implement Zone Based Firewall	
5.4.a Zone to zone	Chapter 15
5.4.b Self zone	Chapter 15
5.5 Firewall features on the Cisco Adaptive Security Appliance (ASA) 9.x	
5.5.a Configure ASA Access Management	Chapter 16
5.5.b Configure Security Access Policies	Chapter 16
5.5.c Configure Cisco ASA interface security levels	Chapter 16
5.5.d Configure Default Modular Policy Framework (MPF)	Chapter 16
5.5.e Describe Modes of deployment (Routed firewall, Transparent firewall)	Chapter 16
5.5.f Describe methods of implementing High Availability	Chapter 16
5.5.g Describe Security contexts	Chapter 16
5.5.h Describe Firewall Services	Chapter 16
6.0 IPS	
6.1 Describe IPS Deployment Considerations	Chapter 17
6.1.a Network Based IPS vs. Host Based IPS	Chapter 17
6.1.b Modes of deployment (Inline, Promiscuous - SPAN, tap)	Chapter 17
6.1.c Placement (positioning of the IPS within the network)	Chapter 17
6.1.d False Positives, False Negatives, True Positives, True Negatives	Chapter 17
6.2 Describe IPS Technologies	
6.2.a Rules/Signatures	Chapter 17
6.2.b Detection/Signature Engines	Chapter 17
6.2.c Trigger Actions/Responses (drop, reset, block, alert, monitor/log, shun)	Chapter 17
6.2.d Blacklist (Static & Dynamic)	Chapter 17

Exam Topic	Part
7.0 Content and Endpoint Security	Chapter 18
7.1 Describe Mitigation Technology for Email-based Threats	
7.1.a SPAM Filtering, Anti-Malware Filtering, DLP, Blacklisting, Email Encryption	Chapter 18
7.2 Describe Mitigation Technology for Web-based Threats	
7.2.a Local & Cloud Based Web Proxies	Chapter 18
7.2.b Blacklisting, URL-Filtering, Malware Scanning, URL Categorization, Web Application Filtering, TLS/SSL Decryption	Chapter 18
7.3 Describe Mitigation Technology for Endpoint Threats	
7.3.a Anti-Virus/Anti-Malware	Chapter 19
7.3.b Personal Firewall/HIPS	Chapter 19
7.3.c Hardware/Software Encryption of local data	Chapter 19

About the *CCNA Security 210-260 Official Cert Guide*

This book maps to the topic areas of the CCNA Security exam and uses a number of features to help you understand the topics and prepare for your exam.

Objectives and Methods

This book uses several key methodologies to help you discover the exam topics for which you need more review, to help you fully understand and remember those details, and to help you prove to yourself that you have retained your knowledge of those topics. So, this book does not try to help you pass the exams only by memorization, but by truly learning and understanding the topics. This book is designed to assist you in the exam by using the following methods:

- Using a conversational style that reflects the fact that we wrote this book as if we made it just for you, as a friend, discussing the topics with you, one step at a time
- Helping you discover which exam topics you may want to invest more time studying, to really "get it"
- Providing explanations and information to fill in your knowledge gaps
- Supplying three bonus videos (on the CD) to reinforce some of the critical concepts and techniques that you have learned from in your study of this book
- Providing practice questions to assess your understanding of the topics

Book Features

To help you customize your study time using this book, the core chapters have several features that help you make the best use of your time:

- **"Do I Know This Already?" quiz:** Each chapter begins with a quiz that helps you determine how much time you need to spend studying that chapter.

- **Foundation Topics:** These are the core sections of each chapter. They explain the concepts for the topics in that chapter.

- **Exam Preparation Tasks:** After the "Foundation Topics" section of each chapter, the "Exam Preparation Tasks" section lists a series of study activities that you should do when you finish the chapter. Each chapter includes the activities that make the most sense for studying the topics in that chapter:

  - **Review All the Key Topics:** The Key Topic icon appears next to the most important items in the "Foundation Topics" section of the chapter. The "Review All the Key Topics" activity lists the key topics from the chapter, along with their page numbers. Although the contents of the entire chapter could be on the exam, you should definitely know the information listed in each key topic, so you should review these.

  - **Complete the Tables and Lists from Memory:** To help you memorize some lists of facts, many of the more important lists and tables from the chapter are included in a document on the CD. This document lists only partial information, allowing you to complete the table or list.

  - **Define Key Terms:** Although the exam is unlikely to ask a "define this term" type of question, the CCNA exams do require that you learn and know a lot of networking terminology. This section lists the most important terms from the chapter, asking you to write a short definition and compare your answer to the glossary at the end of the book.

  - **Command Reference to Check Your Memory:** Review important commands covered in the chapter.

- **CD-based practice exam:** The companion CD contains an exam engine that enables you to review practice exam questions. Use these to prepare with a sample exam and to pinpoint topics where you need more study.

How This Book Is Organized

This book contains 19 core chapters. Chapter 20 includes some preparation tips and suggestions for how to approach the exam. Each core chapter covers a subset of the topics on the CCNA Security exam. The core chapters are organized into parts. They cover the following topics:

Part I: Fundamentals of Network Security

- **Chapter 1, "Networking Security Concepts":** This chapter covers the need for and the building blocks of network and information security, threats to our networks today, and fundamental principles of secure network design.

- **Chapter 2, "Common Security Threats":** This chapter covers the current state of network security in terms of the types of threats organizations face on behalf of malicious actors. It provides coverage of different threat landscape topics and common attacks such as distributed denial-of-service (DDoS) attacks, social engineering, malware identification tools, data loss, and exfiltration.

Part II: Secure Access

- **Chapter 3, "Implementing AAA in Cisco IOS":** This chapter covers the role of Cisco Secure ACS and the Cisco Identity Services Engine (ISE), along with the two primary protocols used for authentication RADIUS and TACACS. It also covers configuration of a router to interoperate with an ACS server and configuration of the ACS server to interoperate with a router. The chapter also covers router tools to verify and troubleshoot router-to-ACS server interactions.

- **Chapter 4, "Bring Your Own Device (BYOD)":** This chapter covers different subjects focused on the topic of BYOD. It provides a description of the BYOD concept and an overview of a BYOD architecture framework. This chapter covers the fundamentals of mobile device management (MDM), its function, and the deployment options.

Part III: Virtual Private Networks (VPN)

- **Chapter 5, "Fundamentals of VPN Technology and Cryptography":** This chapter covers what VPNs are and why we use them and the basic ingredients of cryptography. This chapter also covers the concepts, components, and operations of the *public key infrastructure (PKI)* and includes an example of putting the pieces of PKI to work.

- **Chapter 6, "Fundamentals of IP Security":** This chapter covers the concepts, components, and operations of IPsec and how to configure and verify IPsec.

- **Chapter 7, "Implementing IPsec Site-to-Site VPNs":** This chapter covers planning and preparing to implement an IPsec site-to-site VPN and implementing and verifying the IPsec site-to-site VPN.

- **Chapter 8, "Implementing SSL VPNs Using Cisco ASA":** This chapter covers the functions and use of SSL for VPNs, configuring SSL clientless VPN on the ASA, and configuring the full SSL AnyConnect VPN on the ASA.

Part IV: Secure Routing and Switching

- **Chapter 9, "Securing Layer 2 Technologies":** This chapter covers VLANs and trunking fundamentals, spanning-tree fundamentals, and common Layer 2 threats and how to mitigate them.

- **Chapter 10, "Network Foundation Protection":** This chapter covers securing the network using the network foundation protection (NFP) approach, the management plane, the control plane, and the data plane.

- **Chapter 11, "Securing the Management Plane on Cisco IOS Devices":** This chapter covers management traffic and how to make it more secure and the implementation of security measures to protect the management plane.

- **Chapter 12, "Securing the Data Plane in IPv6":** This chapter covers IPv6 (basics, configuring, and developing a security plan for IPv6).

- **Chapter 13, "Securing Routing Protocols and the Control Plane":** This chapter covers different subjects focused on the control plane of the network device. It provides details on how to secure the control plane of network infrastructure devices. This chapter explains the function of control plane policing (CoPP), control plane protection (CPPr), and how to secure IP routing protocols.

Part V: Cisco Firewall Technologies and Intrusion Prevention System Technologies

- **Chapter 14, "Understanding Firewall Fundamentals":** This chapter covers firewall concepts and the technologies used by them, the function of *Network Address Translation (NAT)*, including its building blocks, and the guidelines and considerations for creating and deploying firewalls.

- **Chapter 15, "Implementing Cisco IOS Zone-Based Firewalls":** This chapter covers the operational and functional components of the IOS zone-based firewall and how to configure and verify the IOS zone-based firewall.

- **Chapter 16, "Configuring Basic Firewall Policies on Cisco ASA":** This chapter covers the *Adaptive Security Appliance (ASA)* family and features, ASA firewall fundamentals, and configuring the ASA.

- **Chapter 17, "Cisco IPS Fundamentals":** This chapter compares intrusion *prevention systems (IPS)* to *intrusion detection systems (IDS)* and covers how to identify malicious traffic on the network, manage signatures, and monitor and manage alarms and alerts.

Part VI: Content and Endpoint Security

- **Chapter 18, "Mitigation Technologies for E-Mail-Based and Web-Based Threats":** This chapter covers the different mitigation technologies for e-mail-based and web-based threats. It covers the Cisco Email Security Appliances (ESA), Cisco cloud e-mail security, Cisco Cloud Web Security (CWS), the Cisco Web Security Appliance (WSA), and the Cisco Content Security Management Appliance (SMA). Cisco has added advanced malware protection (AMP) to the ESA and WSA to enable security administrators to detect and block malware and perform continuous analysis and retrospective alerting. Both the ESA and WSA use cloud-based security intelligence to allow protection before, during, and after an attack. This chapter covers these technologies and solutions in detail. It details mitigation technologies such as spam and antimalware filtering, data loss prevention (DLP), blacklisting, e-mail encryption, and web application filtering.

- **Chapter 19, "Mitigation Technology for Endpoint Threats":** This chapter provides details of the different mitigation technologies available for endpoint threats. It covers introductory concepts of endpoint threats to advanced malware protection capabilities provided by Cisco security products. This chapter covers the different antivirus and antimalware solutions, personal firewalls and host intrusion prevention systems (HIPS), Cisco AMP for endpoints, and hardware and software encryption of endpoint data.

Part VII: Final Preparation

- **Chapter 20, "Final Preparation":** This chapter identifies tools for final exam preparation and helps you develop an effective study plan.

Appendixes

- **Appendix A, "Answers to the 'Do I Know This Already?' Quizzes":** Includes the answers to all the questions from Chapters 1 through 19.

- **Appendix B, "CCNA Security 210-260 (IINS) Exam Updates":** This appendix provides instructions for finding updates to the exam and this book when and if they occur.

- **Glossary:** The glossary contains definitions for all the terms listed in the "Define Key Terms" sections at the conclusions of Chapters 1 through 19.

CD-Only Appendixes

- **Appendix C, "Memory Tables":** This CD-only appendix contains the key tables and lists from each chapter, with some of the contents removed. You can print this appendix and, as a memory exercise, complete the tables and lists. The goal is to help you memorize facts that can be useful on the exams. This appendix is available in PDF format on the CD; it is not in the printed book.

- **Appendix D, "Memory Tables Answer Key":** This CD-only appendix contains the answer key for the memory tables in Appendix C. This appendix is available in PDF format on the CD; it is not in the printed book.

- **Appendix E, "Study Planner":** This spreadsheet provides major study milestones where you can track your progress through your study.

- **Glossary:** The glossary contains definitions for all the terms listed in the "Define Key Terms" sections at the conclusions of Chapters 1 through 19.

Premium Edition eBook and Practice Test

This Cert Guide contains a special offer for a 70 percent discount off the companion CCNA Security 210-260 Official Cert Guide Premium Edition eBook and Practice Test. The Premium Edition combines an eBook version of the text with an enhanced Pearson IT Certification Practice Test. By purchasing the Premium Edition, you get access to two eBook versions of the text: a PDF version and an EPUB version for reading on your tablet, eReader, or mobile device. You also get an enhanced practice test that contains an additional two full practice tests of unique questions. In addition, all the practice test questions are linked to the PDF eBook, allowing you to get more detailed feedback on each question instantly. To take advantage of this offer, you need the coupon code included on the paper in the CD sleeve. Just follow the purchasing instructions that accompany the code to download and start using your Premium Edition today.

This chapter covers the need for and the building blocks of network and information security, threats to our networks today, and fundamental principles of secure network design. It provides in-depth coverage of the following topics:

Confidentiality, integrity, availability (CIA)

Common security terms

Common network security zones

Describe different network topologies, such as

Campus-area network (CAN)

Cloud, wide-area network (WAN)

Data center

Small office/home office (SOHO)

CHAPTER 1

Networking Security Concepts

Although network security has been considered important for quite some time, especially for those of us who have spent a large portion of our careers in the network security field, there has been a surge in public interest over the past year or so due to events that have impacted even the least technically savvy person. It seems as if we cannot go a full week lately without hearing that credit card data or personally identifiable information (PII) has inadvertently been leaked (more accurately, stolen) from banks, retail stores, and the like by malicious actors.

Security has become more complex than ever as the motives and capabilities of threat actors continue to evolve while allowing the miscreants to often stay (at least) one step ahead of those of us in the network security space. In addition, the concept of *location of data* is becoming blurred by concepts of cloud computing and content-data networks and global load balancing. As we strive to empower employees around the world with ubiquitous access to important data, it is increasingly important to remain constantly vigilant about protecting data and the entities using it (individuals, businesses, governments, and so on).

This chapter covers the fundamental building blocks of network security (implementing and improving), an essential topic that you are ready to master now that you better understand its importance.

"Do I Know This Already?" Quiz

The "Do I Know This Already?" quiz helps you determine your level of knowledge of this chapter's topics before you begin. Table 1-1 details the major topics discussed in this chapter and their corresponding quiz questions.

Table 1-1   "Do I Know This Already?" Section-to-Question Mapping

Foundation Topics Section	Questions
Understanding Network and Information Security Basics	1–5
Recognizing Current Network Threats	6–7
Applying Fundamental Security Principles to Network Design	8–10

1. Which security term refers to a person, property, or data of value to a company?
   a. Risk
   b. Asset
   c. Threat prevention
   d. Mitigation technique

2. Which asset characteristic refers to risk that results from a threat and lack of a countermeasure?

   a. High availability

   b. Liability

   c. Threat prevention

   d. Vulnerability

3. Which three items are the primary network security objectives for a company?

   a. Revenue generation

   b. Confidentiality

   c. Integrity

   d. Availability

4. Which data classification label is usually *not* found in a government organization?

   a. Unclassified

   b. Classified but not important

   c. Sensitive but unclassified

   d. For official use only

   e. Secret

5. Which of the following represents a physical control?

   a. Change control policy

   b. Background checks

   c. Electronic lock

   d. Access lists

6. What is the primary motivation for most attacks against networks today?

   a. Political

   b. Financial

   c. Theological

   d. Curiosity

7. Which type of an attack involves lying about the source address of a frame or packet?

   a. Man-in-the-middle attack

   b. Denial-of-service attack

   c. Reconnaissance attack

   d. Spoofing attack

8. Which two approaches to security provide the most secure results on day one?

   a. Role based

   b. Defense in depth

   c. Authentication

   d. Least privilege

9. Which of the following might you find in a network that is based on a defense-in-depth security implementation? (Choose all that apply.)

    a. Firewall

    b. IPS

    c. Access lists

    d. Current patches on servers

10. In relation to production networks, which of the following are viable options when dealing with risk? (Choose all that apply.)

    a. Ignore it

    b. Transfer it

    c. Mitigate it

    d. Remove it

Foundation Topics

Understanding Network and Information Security Basics

Security is important, and the lack of it risks financial, legal, political, and public relations implications. This section covers some of the concepts, terms, and methodologies used in preparing for and working with secure networks.

Network Security Objectives

When considering networks, you can view them from different perspectives. For example, senior management might view the network as a business tool to facilitate the goals of the company. Network technicians (at least some) might consider their networks to be the center of the universe. End users might consider the network to be just a tool for them to get their job done, or possibly as a source for recreation.

Not all users appreciate their role in keeping data safe, and unfortunately the users of the network represent a significant vulnerability, in that they have usernames and passwords (or other credentials, such as one-time password token generators) that allow them access to the network. If a user is compromised or an unauthorized individual gains access to data, applications, or devices for which they should not have access, the security of the network may still fail as a result, even after you apply all the concepts that you learn in this book. So, an important point to remember is that the users' behaviors pose a security risk and that training users is a key part of a comprehensive security policy.

Confidentiality, Integrity, and Availability

Network security objectives usually involve three basic concepts:

- **Confidentiality:** There are two types of data: data in motion as it moves across the network; and data at rest, when data is sitting on storage media (server, local workstation, in the cloud, and so forth). Confidentiality means that only the authorized individuals/ systems can view sensitive or classified information. This also implies that unauthorized individuals should not have any type of access to the data. Regarding data in motion, the primary way to protect that data is to encrypt it before sending it over the network. Another option you can use with encryption is to use separate networks for the transmission of confidential data. Several chapters in this book focus on these two concepts.

- **Integrity:** Integrity for data means that changes made to data are done only by authorized individuals/systems. Corruption of data is a failure to maintain data integrity.

- **Availability:** This applies to systems and to data. If the network or its data is not available to authorized users—perhaps because of a *denial-of-service (DoS)* attack or maybe because of a general network failure—the impact may be significant to companies and users who rely on that network as a business tool. The failure of a system, to include data, applications, devices, and networks, generally equates to loss of revenue.

Perhaps thinking of these security concepts as the *CIA* "triad" might help you remember them: *confidentiality*, *integrity*, and *availability*.

Cost-Benefit Analysis of Security

Network security engineers must understand not only what they protect, but also from whom. *Risk management* is the key phrase that you will hear over and over, and although not very glamorous, it is based on specific principles and concepts related to both asset protection and security management.

What is an *asset*? It is anything that is valuable to an organization. These could be tangible items (people, computers, and so on) or intangible items (intellectual property, database information, contact lists, accounting info). Knowing the assets that you are trying to protect and their value, location, and exposure can help you more effectively determine the time and money to spend securing those assets.

A *vulnerability* is an exploitable weakness in a system or its design. Vulnerabilities can be found in protocols, operating systems, applications, and system designs. Vulnerabilities abound, with more discovered every day.

A *threat* is any potential danger to an asset. If a vulnerability exists but has not yet been exploited or, more importantly, it is not yet publicly known, the threat is *latent* and not yet realized. If someone is actively launching an attack against your system and successfully accesses something or compromises your security against an asset, the threat is *realized*. The entity that takes advantage of the vulnerability is known as the malicious actor and the path used by this actor to perform the attack is known as the *threat agent* or *threat vector*.

A *countermeasure* is a safeguard that somehow mitigates a potential risk. It does so by either reducing or eliminating the vulnerability, or at least reduces the likelihood of the threat agent to actually exploit the risk. For example, you might have an unpatched machine on your network, making it highly vulnerable. If that machine is unplugged from the network and ceases to have any interaction with exchanging data with any other device, you have successfully mitigated all of those vulnerabilities. You have likely rendered that machine no longer an asset, though; but it is safer.

Note that thresholds apply to how we classify things. We do not spend more than the asset is worth to protect it because doing so makes no sense. For example, purchasing a used car for $200 and then spending $2000 on a secure garage facility so that nobody can harm the car or $1500 on an alarm system for that car seems to be a fairly silly proposition.

If you identify the data with the greatest value/worth, you usually automatically identify where the greatest effort to secure that information will be. Keep in mind, however, that beyond a company's particular view about the value of any data, regulatory entities might also be involved (government regulations or laws, business partner agreements, contractual agreements, and so forth).

Just accepting the full risk (the all-or-nothing approach) is not really acceptable. After all, you can implement security measures to mitigate the risk. In addition, those same security devices, such as firewalls and *intrusion prevention systems (IPS)*, can protect multiple devices simultaneously, thus providing a cost benefit. So, you can reduce risk by spending money on appropriate security measures, and usually do a good job of protecting an asset. You can never completely eliminate risk, so you must find the balance.

Table 1-2 describes a number of security terms and the appliances to which they relate.

Table 1-2   Security Terms

Vocabulary Term	Explanation
Asset	An asset is an item that is to be protected and can include property, people, and information/data that have value to the company. This includes intangible items such as proprietary information or trade secrets and the reputation of the company. The data could include company records, client information, proprietary software, and so on.
Vulnerability	A vulnerability is an exploitable weakness of some type. That exploitation might result from a malicious attack, or it might be accidentally triggered because of a failure or weakness in the policy, implementation, or software running on the network.
Threat	This is what you are protecting against. A threat is anything that attempts to gain unauthorized access to, compromise, destroy, or damage an asset. Threats are often realized via an attack or exploit that takes advantage of an existing vulnerability. Threats today come in many varieties and spread more rapidly than ever before. Threats can also morph and be modified over time, and so you must be ever diligent to keep up with them.
Risk	Risk is the potential for unauthorized access to, compromise, destruction, or damage to an asset. If a threat exists, but proper countermeasures and protections are in place (it is your goal to provide this protection), the potential for the threat to be successful is reduced (thus reducing the overall risk).
Countermeasure	A countermeasure is a device or process (a safeguard) that is implemented to counteract a potential threat, which thus reduces risk.

Classifying Assets

One reason to classify an asset is so that you can take specific action, based on policy, with regard to assets in a given class. Consider, for example, *virtual private networks (VPN)*. We classify (that is, identify) the traffic that should be sent over a VPN tunnel. By classifying data and labeling it (such as labeling "top secret" data on a hard disk), we can then focus the appropriate amount of protection or security on that data: more security for top secret data than for unclassified data, for instance. The benefit is that when new data is put into the system, you can classify it as confidential or secret and so on and it will then receive the same level of protection that you set up for that type of data. Table 1-3 lists some common asset classification categories.

Table 1-3   Asset Classifications

Governmental classifications	Unclassified
	Sensitive but unclassified (SBU)
	Confidential
	Secret
	Top secret
Private sector classifications	Public
	Sensitive
	Private
	Confidential
Classification criteria	Value
	Age
	Replacement cost
	Useful lifetime
Classification roles	Owner (the group ultimately responsible for the data, usually senior management of a company)
	Custodian (the group responsible for implementing the policy as dictated by the owner)
	User (those who access the data and abide by the rules of acceptable use for the data)

Table 1-4 describes the four classification levels used within the *Traffic Light Protocol (TLP)*. The TLP is a set of designations developed by the US-CERT division to ensure that sensitive information is shared with the correct audience. It employs four colors to indicate different degrees of sensitivity and the corresponding sharing considerations to be applied by the recipients. The CERT division, part of the Software Engineering Institute and based at Carnegie Mellon University (Pittsburgh, Pennsylvania), is a worldwide respected authority in the field of network security and cyber security.

Table 1-4   TLP Classification Levels

Color	When Should It Be Used?	How May It Be Shared?
RED	Sources may use TLP: RED when information cannot be effectively acted upon by additional parties, and could lead to impacts on a party's privacy, reputation, or operations if misused.	Recipients may not share TLP: RED information with any parties outside of the specific exchange, meeting, or conversation in which it is originally disclosed.
AMBER	Sources may use TLP: AMBER when information requires support to be effectively acted upon, but carries risks to privacy, reputation, or operations if shared outside of the organizations involved.	Recipients may only share TLP: AMBER information with members of their own organization who need to know, and only as widely as necessary to act on that information.

GREEN	Sources may use TLP: GREEN when information is useful for the awareness of all participating organizations as well as with peers within the broader community or sector.	Recipients may share TLP: GREEN information with peers and partner organizations within their sector or community, but not via publicly accessible channels.
WHITE	Sources may use TLP: WHITE when information carries minimal or no foreseeable risk of misuse, in accordance with applicable rules and procedures for public release.	TLP: WHITE information may be distributed without restriction, subject to copyright controls.

Source: https://www.us-cert.gov/tlp

Classifying Vulnerabilities

Understanding the weaknesses and vulnerabilities in a system or network is a huge step toward correcting the vulnerability or putting in appropriate countermeasures to mitigate threats against those vulnerabilities. Potential network vulnerabilities abound, with many resulting from one or more of the following:

- Policy flaws
- Design errors
- Protocol weaknesses
- Misconfiguration
- Software vulnerabilities
- Human factors
- Malicious software
- Hardware vulnerabilities
- Physical access to network resources

Cisco and others have created databases that categorize threats in the public domain. The *Common Vulnerabilities and Exposures (CVE)* is a dictionary of publicly known security vulnerabilities and exposures. A quick search using your favorite search engine will lead you to the website. There is also a *National Vulnerability Database (NVD)*, which is a repository of standards-based vulnerability information; you can do a quick search for it, too. (URLs change over time, so it is better to advise you to just do a quick search and click any links that interest you.)

Classifying Countermeasures

After a company has identified its assets and considered the risks involved to that asset from a threat against a vulnerability, the company can then decide to implement countermeasures to reduce the risk of a successful attack. Common control methods used to implement countermeasures include the following:

- **Administrative:** These consist of written policies, procedures, guidelines, and standards. An example would be a written *acceptable use policy (AUP)*, agreed to by each user on the network. Another example is a change control process that needs to be followed when making changes to the network. Administrative controls could involve items such as background checks for users, as well.

- **Physical:** Physical controls are exactly what they sound like, physical security for the network servers, equipment, and infrastructure. An example is providing a locked door between users and the wiring closet on any floor (where the switches and other gear exist). Another example of a physical control is a redundant system (for instance, an uninterruptible power supply).

- **Logical:** Logical controls include passwords, firewalls, intrusion prevention systems, access lists, VPN tunnels, and so on. Logical controls are often referred to as *technical controls*.

Not all controls are created equal, and not all controls have the same purpose. Working together, however, the controls should enable you to prevent, detect, correct, and recover, all while acting as a deterrent to a threat.

What Do We Do with the Risk?

You can deal with risk in several ways, one of which is eliminate, or at least minimize, it. For example, by not placing a web server on the Internet, you eliminate any risk of that nonexistent web server being attacked. (This does not work very well for companies that do want the web server.)

An option for avoiding the web server altogether is to transfer the risk to someone else. For example, instead of hosting your own server on your own network, you could outsource that functionality to a service provider. The service provider could take full responsibility (the risk) for attacks that might be launched against its server and provide a service level agreement and guarantees to the customer. Keep in mind, however, the possibility of risk must be assumed if the outsourcing entity (for example, the service provider) does not adequately eliminate risk effectively.

So, the service provider now has the risk. How does it handle it? It does exactly what you're learning in this book: It reduces risk by implementing appropriate countermeasures. By applying the correct patches and using the correct firewalls and *Internet service providers (ISP)* and other safeguards, they reduce their own risk. If risk is purely financial, insurance can be purchased that helps manage the risk. Attacks against networks today are primarily motivated by the desire for financial gain. As mentioned in the previous paragraph, the risk assumed by the service provider is not completely eliminated, which results in residual risk that your organization must understand and accept.

Another option is for a company to put up its own web server and just assume the risk. Unfortunately, if it takes no security precautions or countermeasures against potential threats, the risk could be high enough to damage the company and put it out of business. Most people would agree that this is not acceptable risk.

Recognizing Current Network Threats

Threats today are constantly changing, with new ones emerging. Moving targets are often difficult to zero in on, but understanding the general nature of threats can prepare you to deal with new threats. This section covers the various network threat categories and identifies some strategies to stay ahead of those threats.

Potential Attackers

We could devote an entire book to attacks that have been launched in the past 15 minutes somewhere in the world against a network resource, a section of critical infrastructure, or a desired set of proprietary data. Instead of trying to list the thousands of attacks that could threaten vulnerable networks, let's begin by looking at the types of adversaries that may be behind attacks:

- Terrorists
- Criminals
- Government agencies
- Nation states
- Hackers
- Disgruntled employees
- Competitors
- Anyone with access to a computing device (sad, but true)

Different terms are used to refer to these individuals, including *hacker/cracker* (criminal hacker), *script-kiddie*, *hactivist*, and the list goes on. As a security practitioner, you want to "understand your enemy." This is not to say that everyone should learn to be a hacker or write malware, because that is really not going to help. Instead, the point is that it is good to understand the motivations and interests of the people involved in breaking all those things you seek to protect. You also need to have a good understanding of your network and data environment to know what is vulnerable and what can be targeted by the malicious actors.

Some attackers seek financial gain (as mentioned previously). Others might want the notoriety that comes from attacking a well-known company or brand. Sometimes attackers throw their net wide and hurt companies both intended and unintended.

Back in the "old days," attacks were much simpler. We had basic intrusions, war dialing, and things like that. Viruses were fairly new. But it was all about notoriety. The Internet was in its infancy, and people sought to make names for themselves. In the late 1990s and early 2000s, we saw an increase in the number of viruses and malware, and it was about fame.

More recently, many more attacks and threats revolve around actual theft of information and damage with financial repercussions. Perhaps that is a sign of the economy, or maybe it is just an evolution of who is computer literate or incentivized to be involved. Attackers may also be motivated by government or industrial espionage.

Attack Methods

Most attackers do not want to be discovered and so they use a variety of techniques to remain in the shadows when attempting to compromise a network, as described in Table 1-5.

Table 1-5 Attack Methods

Action	Description
Reconnaissance	This is the discovery process used to find information about the network. It could include scans of the network to find out which IP addresses respond, and further scans to see which ports on the devices at these IP addresses are open. This is usually the first step taken, to discover what is on the network and to determine potential vulnerabilities.
Social engineering	This is a tough one because it leverages our weakest (very likely) vulnerability in a secure system (data, applications, devices, networks): the user. If the attacker can get the user to reveal information, it is much easier for the attacker than using some other method of reconnaissance. This could be done through e-mail or misdirection of web pages, which results in the user clicking something that leads to the attacker gaining information. Social engineering can also be done in person or over the phone.
	Phishing presents a link that looks like a valid trusted resource to a user. When the user clicks it, the user is prompted to disclose confidential information such as usernames/passwords.
	Pharming is used to direct a customer's URL from a valid resource to a malicious one that could be made to appear as the valid site to the user. From there, an attempt is made to extract confidential information from the user.
Privilege escalation	This is the process of taking some level of access (whether authorized or not) and achieving an even greater level of access. An example is an attacker who gains user mode access to a router and then uses a brute-force attack against the router, determining what the enable secret is for privilege level 15 access.
Back doors	When attackers gain access to a system, they usually want future access, as well, and they want it to be easy. A backdoor application can be installed to either allow future access or to collect information to use in further attacks.
	Many back doors are installed by users clicking something without realizing the link they click or the file they open is a threat. Back doors can also be implemented as a result of a virus or a worm (often referred to as *malware*).
Code execution	When attackers can gain access to a device, they might be able to take several actions. The type of action depends on the level of access the attacker has, or can achieve, and is based on permissions granted to the account compromised by the attacker. One of the most devastating actions available to an attacker is the ability to execute code within a device. Code execution could result in an adverse impact to the confidentiality (attacker can view information on the device), integrity (attacker can modify the configuration of the device), and availability (attacker can create a denial of service through the modification of code) of a device.

Attack Vectors

Be aware that attacks are not launched only from individuals outside your company. They are also launched from people and devices inside your company who have current, legitimate user accounts. This vector is of particular concern these days with the proliferation of organizations allowing employees to *bring your own device (BYOD)* and allowing it seamless access to data, applications, and devices on the corporate networks. For more information on BYOD, see Chapter 4, "Bring Your Own Device (BYOD)." Perhaps the user is curious, or maybe a back door is installed on the computer on which the user is logged in. In either case, it is important to implement a security policy that takes nothing for granted and to be prepared to mitigate risk at several levels.

You can implement a security policy that takes nothing for granted by requiring authentication from users before their computer is allowed on the network (for which you could use 802.1X and Cisco *Access Control Server [ACS]*). This means that the workstation the user is on must go through a profiling before being allowed on the network. You could use *Network Admission Control (NAC)* or an *Identity Service Engine (ISE)* to enforce such a policy. In addition, you could use security measures at the switch port, such as port security and others. We cover many of these topics, in great detail, in later chapters.

Man-in-the-Middle Attacks

A man-in-the-middle attack results when attackers place themselves in line between two devices that are communicating, with the intent to perform reconnaissance or to manipulate the data as it moves between them. This can happen at Layer 2 or Layer 3. The main purpose is eavesdropping, so the attacker can see all the traffic.

If this happens at Layer 2, the attacker spoofs Layer 2 MAC addresses to make the devices on a LAN believe that the Layer 2 address of the attacker is the Layer 2 address of its default gateway. This is called *ARP poisoning*. Frames that are supposed to go to the default gateway are forwarded by the switch to the Layer 2 address of the attacker on the same network. As a courtesy, the attacker can forward the frames to the correct destination so that the client will have the connectivity needed and the attacker now sees all the data between the two devices. To mitigate this risk, you could use techniques such as *dynamic Address Resolution Protocol (ARP) inspection (DAI)* on switches to prevent spoofing of the Layer 2 addresses.

The attacker could also implement the attack by placing a switch into the network and manipulating the *Spanning Tree Protocol (STP)* to become the root switch (and thus gain the ability to see any traffic that needs to be sent through the root switch). You can mitigate this through techniques such as root guard and other spanning-tree controls discussed later in this book.

A man-in-the-middle attack can occur at Layer 3 by a rogue router being placed on the network and then tricking the other routers into believing that the new router has a better path. This could cause network traffic to flow through the rogue router and again allow the attacker to steal network data. You can mitigate attacks such as these in various ways, including routing authentication protocols and filtering information from being advertised or learned on specific interfaces.

To safeguard data in motion, one of the best things you can do is to use encryption for the confidentiality of the data in transit. If you use plaintext protocols for management, such as Telnet or HTTP, an attacker who has implemented a man-in-the-middle attack can see the contents of your cleartext data packets, and as a result will see everything that goes across the attacker's device, including usernames and passwords that are used. Using management protocols that have encryption built in, such as *Secure Shell (SSH)* and *Hypertext Transfer Protocol Secure (HTTPS)*, is considered a best practice, and using VPN protection for cleartext sensitive data is also considered a best practice.

Other Miscellaneous Attack Methods

No standards groups for attackers exist, so not all the attacks fit neatly or clearly in one category. In fact, some attacks fit into two or more categories at the same time. Table 1-6 describes a few additional methods attackers might use.

Table 1-6   Additional Attack Methods

Method	Description
Covert channel	This method uses programs or communications in unintended ways. For example, if the security policy says that web traffic is allowed but peer-to-peer messaging is not, users can attempt to tunnel their peer-to-peer traffic inside of HTTP traffic. An attacker may use a similar technique to hide traffic by tunneling it inside of some other allowed protocol to avoid detection. An example of this is a backdoor application collecting keystroke information from the workstation and then slowly sending it out disguised as *Internet Control Message Protocol (ICMP)*. This is a covert channel.
	A covert channel is the legitimate use of a protocol, such as a user with a web browser using HTTP to access a web server, for illegitimate purposes, including cloaking network traffic from inspection.
Trust exploitation	If the firewall has three interfaces, and the outside interface allows all traffic to the *demilitarized zone (DMZ)* but not to the inside network, and the DMZ allows access to the inside network from the DMZ, an attacker could leverage that by gaining access to the DMZ and using that location to launch his attacks from there to the inside network. Other trust models, if incorrectly configured, may allow unintentional access to an attacker including active directory and *NFS (Network File System* in UNIX).
Brute-force (password-guessing) attacks	Brute-force (password-guessing) types of attacks are performed when an attacker's system attempts thousands of possible passwords looking for the right match. This is best protected against by specifying limits on how many unsuccessful authentication attempts can occur within a specified time frame. Password-guessing attacks can also be done through malware, man-in-the-middle attacks using packet sniffers, or by using key loggers.
Botnet	A botnet is a collection of infected computers that are ready to take instructions from the attacker. For example, if the attacker has the malicious backdoor software installed on 10,000 computers, from his central location, he could instruct those computers to all send TCP SYN requests or ICMP echo requests repeatedly to the same destination. To add insult to injury, he could also spoof the source IP address of the request so that reply traffic is sent to yet another victim. The attacker generally uses a covert channel to manage the individual devices that make up the botnet.

Method	Description
DoS and DDoS	Denial-of-service (DoS) attack and distributed denial-of-service (DDoS) attack. An example is using a botnet to attack a target system. If an attack is launched from a single device with the intent to cause damage to an asset, the attack could be considered a DoS attempt, as opposed to a DDoS. Both types of attacks want the same result, and whether it is called a DoS or DDoS attack just depends on how many source machines are used in the attack. A more advanced and increasingly popular type of DDoS attack is called a reflected DDoS (RDDoS) attack. An RDDoS takes place when the source of the initial (query) packets is actually spoofed by the attacker. The response packets are then "reflected" back from the unknowing participant to the victim of the attack; that is, the original (spoofed) source of the initial (query) packets.

Applying Fundamental Security Principles to Network Design

This section examines the holistic approach to improve the security posture of your network before, during, and after your network implementation.

Guidelines

You want some basic principles and guidelines in place in the early stages of designing and implementing a network. Table 1-7 describes such key guidelines.

Table 1-7   Guidelines for Secure Network Architecture

Guideline	Explanation
Rule of least privilege	This rule states that minimal access is only provided to the required network resources, and not any more than that. An example of this is an access list applied to an interface for filtering that says "deny all." Before this, specific entries could be added allowing only the bare minimum of required protocols, and only then between the correct source and destination addresses.
Defense in depth	This concept suggests that you have security implemented on nearly every point of your network. An example is filtering at a perimeter router, filtering again at a firewall, using IPSs to analyze traffic before it reaches your servers, and using host-based security precautions at the servers, as well. Additional methods that can be used to implement a defense-in-depth approach include using authentication and authorization mechanisms, web and e-mail security, content security, application inspection monitoring, traffic monitoring, and malware protection. The concept behind defense in depth is that if a single security technology fails, additional levels, or mechanisms, of security are still in place to protect the data, applications, and devices on the network.
Separation of duties	When you place specific individuals into specific roles, there can be checks and balances in place regarding the implementation of the security policy. Rotating individuals into different roles periodically will also assist in verifying that vulnerabilities are being addressed, because a person who moves into a new role will be required to review the policies in place.

Guideline	Explanation
Auditing	This refers to accounting and keeping records about what is occurring on the network. Most of this can be automated through the features of *authentication, authorization, and accounting (AAA)* (covered later in this book). When events happen on the network, the records of those events can be sent to an accounting server. When the separation-of-duties approach is used, those who are making changes on the network should not have direct access to modify or delete the accounting records that are kept on the accounting server.

Network Topologies

There exist a number of network topologies that depend on the size and type of each organization. Some organizations will have a presence of each of the following topologies while others may only utilize a subset of this list. Refer to the list that follows and Figure 1-1 through Figure 1-4 for a description and depiction of each of the different topologies that can make up an entire organization's network.

■ **Campus-Area Network (CAN):** A campus-area network, as illustrated in Figure 1-1, is the network topology used to provide connectivity, data, applications, and services to users of an organization that are physically located at the corporate office (headquarters). The CAN includes a module for each building in the campus, for the data center, for WAN Aggregation, and for the Internet Edge. Security with the Campus Area Network.

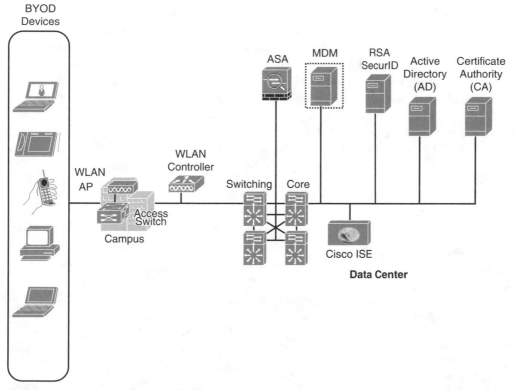

Figure 1-1   *Campus-Area Network Topology*

■ **Cloud, Wide-Area Network (WAN):** The cloud and WAN provide a logical and physical location for data and applications that an organization prefers to have moved off-site, as illustrated in Figure 1-2. This alleviates an organization from having to expend resources to operate, maintain, and manage the services that have been previously located within the organization's purview.

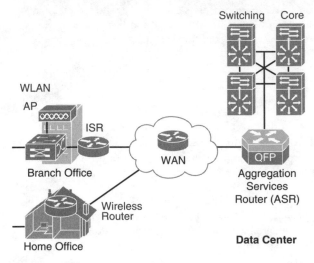

Figure 1-2   *Cloud/WAN Topology*

■ **Data Center:** The Data Center network contains the Unified Computing System (UCS) servers, voice gateways, and CUCM servers supporting the VoIP environment, all of which is provided network connectivity by a series of Nexus switches, as illustrated in Figure 1-3. The entire Data Center network is protected by a set of firewalls at the edge that filters all traffic ingressing and egressing the Data Center.

■ **Small office/Home office (SOHO):** The remote SOHO site will provide connectivity to the SOHO users through the use of WAN routers that find their way back to the WAN Aggregation module in the CAN via MPLS WANs, as illustrated in Figure 1-4. Within the SOHO, users are provided network connectivity through the presence of access switches.

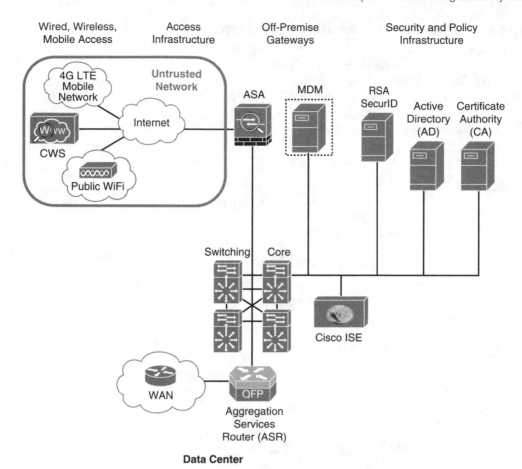

Figure 1-3 *Data Center Topology*

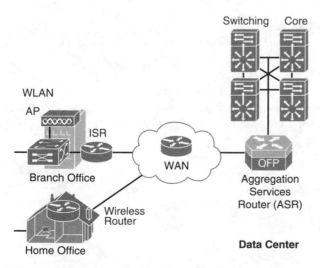

Figure 1-4 *Branch Office/Home Office Topology*

Network Security for a Virtual Environment

Today's data center environments must be designed to significantly reduce administrative overhead and improve flexibility and operational efficiency. Critical security functions must be able to dynamically scale to protect assets as business demands change. Cisco has created technologies and products such as the Application Centric Infrastructure (ACI) ecosystem and the Cisco ASAv (virtual ASA) to provide security solutions for today's data center demands. For example, ACI provides a centralized application-level policy engine for physical, virtual, and cloud infrastructures. The Cisco ASAv provides detailed visibility and control of application and services within the virtual environment.

Figure 1-5 illustrates a high-level data center environment with multiple network connections, and it defines the concept of east-west versus north-south traffic.

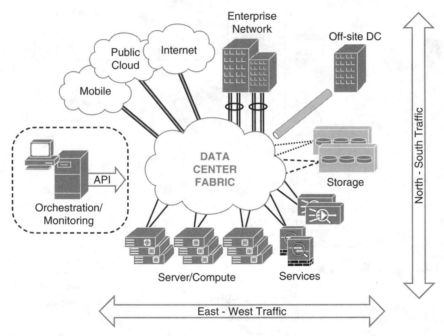

Figure 1-5 *High-level Data Center Environment and Traffic Definitions*

Figure 1-6 shows a virtualized data center where multiple software applications (such as VMWare, KVM, Xen) are used to divide one physical server into multiple isolated virtual environments. In this example physical firewalls are deployed to provide protection and segmentation to the data center from the rest of the corporate network.

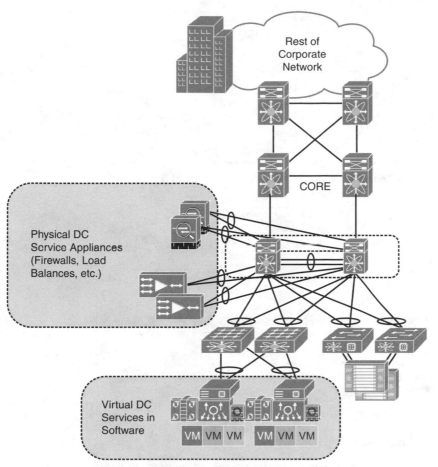

Figure 1-6 *Virtualized Data Center Topology*

The challenge of using physical firewalls and other security appliances in a virtualized environment is that sometimes the traffic does not leave the physical server (often referred to as bare metal). Subsequently, a virtual security solution is needed. Figure 1-7 demonstrates how a security administrator can provide detailed visibility and control of application and services within the virtual environment by deploying the Cisco ASAv.

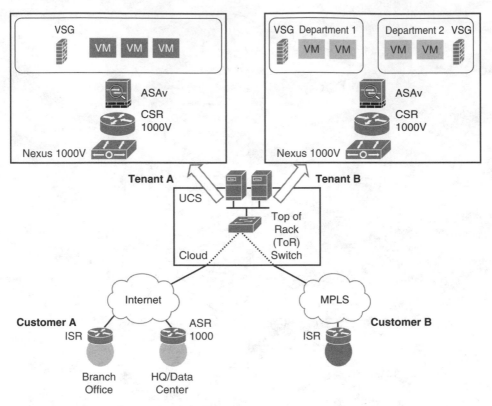

Figure 1-7   *Virtual Security Solution*

How It All Fits Together

This book explains how to implement security products from Cisco to mitigate or reduce the amount of risk that our companies and customers face. If there were a single magic button that we could press that both allowed the functionality we need and provided adequate security at the same time, that button would be a hot seller. Unfortunately, no magic button exists. However, what we do have are solid principles and guidelines that we can use to implement security on our networks today.

As you work through the rest of this book, keep in mind the concepts of confidentiality, data integrity, and availability (remember, CIA) for every single concept discussed. For example, the section on VPNs focuses on the different types of VPNs and how to implement them. You even learn how configure one of them. It is easy to get wrapped up in the details of how to do this or how to do that, but what you want to look at is which aspects of CIA a specific technology implements. In the case of VPNs, they protect the data with encryption, and so the concept of confidentiality applies. VPNs can also hash, which implements data integrity. If you are reading this book in hard-copy format, you might want to take three highlighters, one for each of the letters in CIA, and mark the technologies that address these exact issues as you encounter them in your reading of this book.

By keeping your mind open to the reasons for each and every technology we discuss, you can more easily build an overall fortress of security that everybody wants for mission-critical networks.

Exam Preparation Tasks

Review All the Key Topics

Review the most important topics from this chapter, denoted with a Key Topic icon. Table 1-8 lists these key topics.

Table 1-8   Key Topics

Key Topic Element	Description	Page Number
Section	Confidentiality, Integrity, and Availability	6
Table 1-2	Security Terms	8
Table 1-3	Asset Classifications	9
List	Classifying countermeasures	11
Section	Man-in-the-Middle Attacks	14
Table 1-6	Additional Attack Methods	15
Table 1-7	Guidelines for Secure Network Architecture	16
Section	Network Topologies	17

Complete the Tables and Lists from Memory

Print a copy of Appendix C, "Memory Tables" (found on the CD), or at least the section for this chapter, and complete the tables and lists from memory. Appendix D, "Memory Tables Answer Key," also on the CD, includes completed tables and lists so that you can check your work.

Define Key Terms

Define the following key terms from this chapter, and check your answers in the glossary:

asset, BYOD, brute-force (password-guessing) attacks, CERT, RDDoS, risk, threat, Traffic Light Protocol (TLP), vulnerability

This chapter covers the current state of network security in terms of the types of threats organizations face on behalf of malicious actors. It covers the following topics:

Distributed denial-of-service (DDoS) attacks

Social engineering

Malware identification tools

Data loss and exfiltration

CHAPTER 2

Common Security Threats

"Do I Know This Already?" Quiz

The "Do I Know This Already?" quiz helps you determine your level of knowledge of this chapter's topics before you begin. Table 2-1 details the major topics discussed in this chapter and their corresponding quiz questions.

Table 2-1 "Do I Know This Already?" Section-to-Question Mapping

Foundation Topics Section	Questions
Network Security Threat Landscape	1
Distributed Denial-of-Service Attacks	2–3
Social Engineering Methods	4–6
Malware Identification Tools	7–9
Data Loss and Exfiltration Methods	10

1. Which of the following is not a motivation of malicious actors?

    a. Disruption

    b. Bug bounty awards

    c. Financial

    d. Geopolitical

2. Which of the following is not considered a type of DDoS attack?

    a. Directed

    b. Cached

    c. Reflected

    d. Amplified

3. Why is UDP the "protocol of choice" for reflected DDoS attacks?

    a. There are more application choices when using UDP.

    b. UDP requires a three-way handshake to establish a connection.

    c. UDP is much more easily spoofed.

    d. TCP cannot be used in DDoS attacks.

4. Which of the following is leveraged in social engineering?

   a. Software vulnerabilities

   b. Human nature

   c. Protocol violations

   d. Application issues

5. Which of the following is not a form of social engineering?

   a. Phone scams

   b. Phishing

   c. Denial of service (DoS)

   d. Malvertising

6. Which of the following is not a valid defense against social engineering?

   a. Two-factor authentication

   b. Information classification

   c. Infrastructure hardening

   d. Physical security

7. Which tool provides the most granular information to help in the identification of malware?

   a. NetFlow

   b. Syslog

   c. Packet capture

   d. Server logs

8. NetFlow provides which of the following?

   a. Detailed data about each packet on the network

   b. Troubleshooting messages about the network devices

   c. Information on the types of traffic traversing the network

   d. Network names of routers, end hosts, servers

9. Which of the following is not used for identification of malware on the network?

   a. NetFlow

   b. IPS events

   c. Routing Information Base (RIB)

   d. Packet captures

10. Which type of data is not often attractive to malicious actors?

   a. Personally identifiable information (PII)

   b. Training schedules

   c. Credit and debit card data

   d. Intellectual property (IP)

Foundation Topics

Network Security Threat Landscape

Today's threat landscape is both complex and ever-changing. This makes working in network security a challenging yet never boring experience! This section provides a look at the motivations behind network attacks, who is being targeted, and how organizations can protect themselves.

With so many organizations and, more importantly, devices connected to the Internet, it is no surprise that there is no lack of sources of network threats and an abundance of malicious threat actors looking to take advantage of these threats. So, what are the motivations behind all of these threat actors?

- **Financial:** There are several different means in which attackers can make financial gains through their malicious actions. They can compromise a *point-of-sale (PoS)* system at a retail organization and siphon off millions of credit/debit cards, which can subsequently be sold on the online black market. Threat actors can also penetrate financial organizations for the sole purpose of compromising user accounts and transferring money to accounts of their choosing.

- **Disruption:** Unfortunately, many individuals and groups exist solely to cause disruption to the core business of many organizations and institutions. This disruption is created for several reasons:

    - To protest the actions, decisions, or behaviors of an enterprise

    - To serve as a distraction while the malicious actors plant something within the network to be leveraged at a future point in time

    - To gain media attention for the actions of the malicious group or individual

- **Geopolitical:** Not surprisingly, there are groups affiliated with certain nation states that leverage the Internet to engage in cyber warfare. In addition, there are groups of malicious actors, with no direct connection to any individual nation, who use the Internet to launch attacks against countries who they believe do not have their best interests at heart or whose ideals conflict with those of the malicious actors.

Distributed Denial-of-Service Attacks

Denial-of service (DoS) and *distributed DoS (DDoS)* attacks have been around for quite some time now, but there has been heightened awareness of them over the past few years. The reason for this increased attention is in large part due to the attacks that took place against the financial services sector in the fall of 2012 and spring of 2013.

DDoS attacks can generally be divided into the following three categories:

- **Direct:** Direct DDoS attacks occur when the source of the attack generates the packets, regardless of protocol, application, and so on, that are sent directly to the victim of the attack.

- **Reflected:** Reflected DDoS attacks occur when the sources of the attack are sent spoofed packets that appear to be from the victim, and then the sources become unwitting participants in the DDoS attacks by sending the response traffic back to the intended victim. UDP is often used as the transport mechanism because it is more easily spoofed due to the lack of a three-way handshake. For example, if the attacker (A) decides he wants to attack a victim (V), he will send packets (for example, *Network Time Protocol [NTP]* requests) to a source (S) who thinks these packets are legitimate. The source (S) then responds to the NTP requests by sending the responses to the victim (V), who was never expecting these NTP packets from source (S) (see Figure 2-1).

- **Amplification:** Amplification attacks are a form of reflected attacks in which the response traffic (sent by the unwitting participants) is made up of packets that are much larger than those that were initially sent by the attacker (spoofing the victim). An example of this is when DNS queries are sent and the DNS responses are much larger in packet size than the initial query packets. The end result is that the victim gets flooded by large packets for which it never actually issued queries.

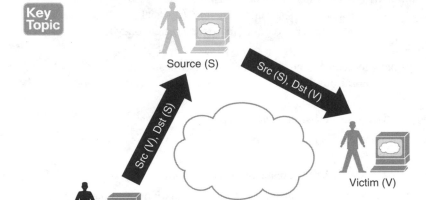

Figure 2-1   *Reflected DDoS Attack*

Social Engineering Methods

Malicious actors employ social engineering by relying on the human element of networking to find and create holes in the fortress known as cyber security.

Social engineering is evolving so rapidly that technology solutions, security policies, and operational procedures alone cannot protect critical resources. Even with these safeguards, hackers commonly manipulate employees into compromising corporate security. Victims might unknowingly reveal the sensitive information needed to bypass network security, or even unlock workplace doors for strangers without identification. Although attacks on human judgment are immune to even the best network defense systems, companies can mitigate the risk of social engineering with an active security culture that evolves as the threat landscape changes.

Social Engineering Tactics

Common forms of social engineering include the following:

- **Phishing:** Phishing elicits secure information through an e-mail message that appears to come from a legitimate source such as a service provider or financial institution. The e-mail message may ask the user to reply with the sensitive data, or to access a website to update information such as a bank account number.

- **Malvertising:** This is the act of incorporating malicious ads on trusted websites, which results in users' browsers being inadvertently redirected to sites hosting malware.

- **Phone scams:** It is not uncommon for someone to call up an employee and attempt to convince employees to divulge information about themselves or others within the organization. An example is a miscreant posing as a recruiter asking for names, e-mail addresses, and so on for members of the organization and then using that information to start building a database to leverage for a future attack, reconnaissance mission, and so forth.

Defenses Against Social Engineering

A security-aware culture must include ongoing training that consistently informs employees about the latest security threats, as well as policies and procedures that reflect the overall vision and mission of corporate information security. This emphasis on security helps employees understand the potential risk of social-engineering threats, how they can prevent successful attacks, and why their role within the security culture is vital to corporate health. Security-aware employees are better prepared to recognize and avoid rapidly changing and increasingly sophisticated social-engineering attacks, and are more willing to take ownership of security responsibilities.

Official security policies and procedures take the guesswork out of operations and help employees make the right security decisions. Such policies include the following:

- **Password management:** Guidelines such as the number and type of characters that each password must include how often a password must be changed, and even a simple declaration that employees should not disclose passwords to anyone (even if they believe they are speaking with someone at the corporate help desk) will help secure information assets.

- **Two-factor authentication:** Authentication for high-risk network services such as modem pools and VPNs should use two-factor authentication rather than fixed passwords.

- **Antivirus/antiphishing defenses:** Multiple layers of antivirus defenses, such as at mail gateways and end-user desktops, can minimize the threat of phishing and other social-engineering attacks.

- **Change management:** A documented change-management process is more secure than an ad hoc process, which is more easily exploited by an attacker who claims to be in a crisis.

- **Information classification:** A classification policy should clearly describe what information is considered sensitive and how to label and handle it.

- **Document handling and destruction:** Sensitive documents and media must be securely disposed of and not simply thrown out with the regular office trash.

- **Physical security:** The organization should have effective physical security controls such as visitor logs, escort requirements, and background checks.

Malware Identification Tools

One of the thorns in the side of every security conscious person today is having the ability to identify malware either as it attempts to get on the network or subsequent to the malware already being present. Several factors make this identification particularly difficult:

- The sheer amount of malware that exists and is created on a daily basis is almost incomprehensible. The creation of new malware often results in the rendering useless of signature-based detection tools.

- Malware is often embedded in otherwise-trusted applications and sent over protocols that are traditionally allowed through firewalls and access lists.

- Organizations have limited resources (both human and technology) to keep up with the massive amounts of traffic that traverse the network. The volume of network traffic, both good and bad, has become so large that it is almost too much for any one organization to keep up.

- The increasing use of encryption has, not surprisingly, added another layer of complexity for organizations trying to gain visibility into malicious traffic residing on the network.

Methods Available for Malware Identification

While by no means an exhaustive list, the following tools and technologies provide network administrators with the ability to identify the existence of malware on the network:

- **Packet captures:** Collecting, storing, and analyzing the raw packets that are traversing the network is certainly one way of inspecting traffic for the presence of malware. Although packet captures provide the most granular look into the traffic that is on the network, one primary hurdle in the use of packet capture for malware identification is the fact that you are looking for the proverbial "needle in a haystack" due to the volume of data generated by packet captures.

- **Snort:** Snort is an open source intrusion detection and prevention technology developed by the founder of Sourcefire (now a part of Cisco). The speed, power, and performance of Snort have made it the most popular *intrusion detection/prevention system (IDS/IPS)* technology in the world. The Snort engine consists of threat identification, detection, and prevention components that combine to reassemble traffic, prevent evasions, detect threats, and output information about advanced threats while minimizing false positives and missing legitimate threats (false negatives).

- **NetFlow:** Packet capture is often referred to as micro-analytical in terms of the granularity of data being analyzed, but NetFlow data is considered more of a macro-analytical approach. The use of NetFlow data collection consists of the creation of buckets or flows of data that are based on a set of predefined parameters such as source IP address, source port, destination IP address, destination port, IP protocol, ingress interface, and *type of service (ToS)*. Each time one of these parameters differs, a new flow is created. Flows are stored locally on the device for a configured time interval, after which time the flows are exported to external collectors. Although NetFlow data will not provide the same details sometimes needed for the identification of malware on the network, it can serve as an excellent tool in the toolbox to help trace back evidence of a compromise once some of the details of the malware become known to network security administrators.

- **IPS events:** When using IPS devices on your network, it is possible to leverage the alarms triggered on the IPS device as an emergency flare that network traffic should be further analyzed for the presence of malware. Often, IPS devices have signatures for specific strains of malware, which, when triggered, can be an indication that malicious traffic exists on the network.

- **Advanced Malware Protection:** Cisco *Advanced Malware Protection (AMP)* is designed for Cisco FirePOWER network security appliances. It provides visibility and control to protect against highly sophisticated, targeted, zero-day, and persistent advanced malware threats. AMP helps to identify inconspicuous attacks by continuously analyzing and monitoring files after they've entered the network, utilizing retrospective security alerts to help administrators take action during and after an attack, and provides multi-source indications of compromise to aid in the correlation of discrete events for better detection.

- **NGIPS:** The Cisco FirePOWER *next-generation intrusion prevention system (NGIPS)* solution provides multiple layers of advanced threat protection at high inspection throughput rates. The NGIPS threat protection solution is centrally managed through the Cisco FireSIGHT Management Center and can be expanded to include additional features such as AMP, application visibility and control, and URL filtering.

Data Loss and Exfiltration Methods

Major network attacks are now conducted by sophisticated, well-funded teams that can evade corporate security measures and steal millions of records from all types of organizations all over the world. Traditional security measures are good at identifying suspect traffic that is coming inbound, but many organizations lack the visibility into traffic that is leaving their internal networks. This outbound traffic, if being controlled by malicious actors with a foothold inside the corporate network, often includes company trade secrets, customer data, or other proprietary information that should not be seen by anyone outside of the organization. Having this type of traffic leave the corporation, unbeknownst to those who are responsible for it, places the organization at significant risk for compromised intellectual property, loss of sensitive customer and financial data, and high costs from disrupted operations and remediation efforts.

Several types of data are particularly attractive to the miscreants of the cyber (under) world:

- **Intellectual property (IP):** This consists of any type of data or documentation that is the property of an organization and has been created or produced by employees of the organization. IP often refers to the designs, drawings, and documents that support the development, sale, and support of an organization's products.

- **Personally identifiable information (PII):** This is the type of information that has, unfortunately, been talked about in the press all too often lately when we hear about data breaches. This information includes names, dates of birth, addresses, and *Social Security numbers (SSN)*.

- **Credit/debit cards:** In addition to PII, which is often stolen/compromised during data breaches, credit and debit card information (the information contained on the magnetic stripe or within the embedded chip in chip and pin cards) is extremely desired by the malicious actors.

It is paramount for every organization, no matter what size, vertical or not, or whether they are publicly or privately held, to make every effort to protect their data assets. This involves a combination of clearly communicated and effective security policies, employee education, and the technologies to help ensure that the security policies put in place can be enforced.

Summary

This chapter discussed a number of topics that comprise the current state of network security.

The chapter summarized reasons why malicious actors exist and what motivates them to attack our networks. The chapter then covered some of the methods used by these actors, including DDoS attacks and the use of social engineering. Next, the chapter provided an overview of some tools and techniques that can help network administrators identify the existence of malware used by malicious actors on their network. The chapter concluded with a brief look at the types of data that these malicious actors are looking to exfiltrate from your networks.

Exam Preparation Tasks

Review All the Key Topics

Review the most important topics from this chapter, denoted with a Key Topic icon. Table 2-2 lists these key topics.

Table 2-2   Key Topics

Key Topic Element	Description	Page Number
List	Description of DDoS attacks	27
Figure 2-1	Reflected DDoS Attack	28
List	A listing of some common forms of social engineering	29
Section	Defenses Against Social Engineering	29
List	A list of tools and technologies that provide network administrators with the ability to identify the existence of malware on the network	30
List	A description of several types of data that are particularly attractive to the miscreants of the cyber (under) world	31

Complete the Tables and Lists from Memory

Print a copy of Appendix C, "Memory Tables," (found on the CD) or at least the section for this chapter, and complete the tables and lists from memory. Appendix D, "Memory Tables Answer Key," also on the CD, includes completed tables and lists so that you can check your work. This chapter does not have any applicable tables.

Define Key Terms

Define the following key terms from this chapter, and check your answers in the glossary:

direct DDoS attacks, reflected DDoS attacks, amplification DDoS attacks, phishing, malvertising, Snort, NGIPS, Advanced Malware Protection (AMP), personally identifiable information (PII)

This chapter covers the following topics:

Cisco Secure ACS, RADIUS, and TACACS

Configuring routers to interoperate with an ACS server

Configuring the ACS server to interoperate with a router

Verifying and troubleshooting router-to-ACS server interactions

CHAPTER 3

Implementing AAA in Cisco IOS

The challenge, however, is that most companies have many network devices. If a single administrator needs access to ten different routers, and you are using the local database only for the username and password of that administrator (remember, the local database means the running configuration on that specific router), you must create that same user account ten different times, once on each router. If he ever needs to change the password, it also requires going back to all those ten devices and manually changing it on each one. This solution does not scale well in environments with multiple administrators and many devices.

A solution to this is to have a centralized database where all the usernames and passwords are kept for authentication and what the individual users are allowed to do (the *authorization* portion of AAA). This is primarily what the *Access Control Server (ACS)* can provide. It is a two-part process. The first part is to configure on the ACS server information about the users and their passwords and what those users are allowed to do. The second part is to tell the router that it should refer any of its decisions about authentication or authorization to the ACS server.

One other note about the word *users*. Often when we refer to the management plane, and we refer to users, those users are very likely administrators who need access to the *command-line interface (CLI)* or the web management console via HTTP/HTTPS. Also be aware that end users will not need CLI access, but will need access to network services and to have their packets allowed through the router. You can use the ACS server to authenticate either type of user, and you can call on it for authorization for these users. In addition, you can use the ACS server as a destination for logging (called accounting), noting which users access the system and what they do while there.

"Do I Know This Already?" Quiz

The "Do I Know This Already?" quiz helps you determine your level of knowledge of this chapter's topics before you begin. Table 3-1 details the major topics discussed in this chapter and their corresponding quiz questions.

Table 3-1 "Do I Know This Already?" Section-to-Question Mapping

Foundation Topics Section	Questions
Cisco Secure ACS, RADIUS, and TACACS	1–3
Configuring Routers to Interoperate with an ACS Server	4–6
Configuring the ACS Server to Interoperate with a Router	7–8
Verifying and Troubleshooting Router-to-ACS Server Interactions	9–10

1. Which of the following are most likely to be used for authentication of a network administrator accessing the CLI of a Cisco router? (Choose all that apply.)

    a. TACACS+

    b. Diameter

    c. RADIUS

    d. ACS

2. Which of the following allows for granular control related to authorization of specific Cisco IOS commands that are being attempted by an authenticated and authorized Cisco router administrator?

    a. RADIUS

    b. Diameter

    c. TACACS+

    d. ISE

3. Which devices or users would be clients of an ACS server? (Choose all that apply.)

    a. Routers

    b. Switches

    c. VPN users

    d. Administrators

4. On the router, what should be created and applied to a vty line to enforce a specific set of methods for identifying who a user is?

    a. RADIUS server

    b. TACACS+ server

    c. Authorization method list

    d. Authentication method list

5. What is the minimum size for an effective TACACS+ group of servers?

    a. 1

    b. 2

    c. 5

    d. 6

6. With what can you configure AAA on the router? (Choose all that apply.)

    a. ACS

    b. CCP

    c. CLI

    d. TACACS+

7. Which statement is true for ACS 5.x and later?

    a. User groups are nested in network device groups.

    b. Authorization policies can be associated with user groups that are accessing specific network device groups.

    c. There must be at least one user in a user group.

    d. User groups can be used instead of device groups for simplicity.

8. Where in the ACS do you go to create a new group of administrators?

    a. Users and Identity Stores > Identity Groups

    b. Identity Stores > Identity Groups

    c. Identity Stores and Groups > Identity Groups

    d. Users and Groups > Identity Groups

9. From the router, which method tests the most about the ACS configuration, without forcing you to log in again at the router?

    a. ping

    b. traceroute

    c. test aaa

    d. telnet

10. Which of the following could likely cause an ACS authentication failure, even when the user is using the correct credentials? (Choose all that apply.)

    a. Incorrect secret on the ACS

    b. Incorrect IP address of the ACS configured on the router

    c. Incorrect routing

    d. Incorrect filtering between the ACS and the router

Foundation Topics

Cisco Secure ACS, RADIUS, and TACACS

This section discusses how you can use a centralized authentication server such as ACS and the protocols it uses to communicate with its clients, which are routers and switches. This information is relevant to both certification and for the implementation of AAA using ACS.

Why Use Cisco ACS?

Most midsize and large companies using Cisco equipment are also going to use ACS servers so that they can centrally manage the users and control what those users are authorized to do. By configuring users locally on the ACS server, and then having the dozens or hundreds of routers and switches act as clients to the ACS server, you can use the Cisco ACS server as a central clearinghouse for the authentication of users. This way, you can create a user account one time on the ACS server, and configure the routers and switches to use the ACS server for any type of user, whether an administrator trying to access the router for configuration or an end user who just needs access through a router for some network application or service such as browsing the web. If all your network devices use the ACS server, you can avoid having to create that same user account on each of the individual routers' and switches' local database (in their running config).

Most companies using ACS servers have many users, and it is time-consuming to create all the user accounts manually in ACS. One convenient feature of an ACS server is that all the users do not have to be locally configured on the ACS server, either; instead, the ACS server can use an external database that already exists that contains the usernames and passwords. An example is Microsoft Active Directory, where all the users and their credentials are already in place. The chain of events goes something like this: A user connects to a router, and the router prompts the user for authentication. In this example, assume it is an administrator who wants CLI access to the router. The router being configured to use the ACS server prompts the user for his username and password. After getting the username and password, the router sends those credentials to the AAA server (in this case, the ACS server) and waits for a reply. At the ACS server, if it is configured to use an external database such as Microsoft Active Directory, the ACS server makes an inquiry out to Active Directory to validate whether the username and password that the user provided are accurate. If they are, Active Directory can indicate that to the ACS server, and the ACS server in turn can indicate that the credentials are correct back to the router, and then the router can provide the access to the user. If there were no Active Directory, the ACS server would consult its own local configuration to verify the username and password instead of handing it off to Active Directory. That's it in a nutshell. ACS could use multiple external databases for these lookups, and the basic concept is that if the users are already defined in some database, ACS can leverage that database and not have to re-create all users.

On What Platform Does ACS Run?

ACS has a few different flavors. They include older versions that can be installed on top of an existing Windows server, a dedicated physical appliance can be purchased from Cisco that is installed in a rack at the customer site and has ACS software preinstalled, and the most popular option moving forward is to install the ACS server logically in a VMware environment such as an ESXi server with ACS running as a virtual machine. Regardless of which implementation you choose, the core functionality of having a centralized database of users, along with authorization rules about what users are allowed to do, is the basic premise of ACS.

What Is ISE?

A product called *Identity Services Engine (ISE)* is an identity and access control policy platform that can validate that a computer meets the requirements of a company's policy related to virus definition files, service pack levels, and so on before allowing the device on the network. This solution leverages many AAA-like (authentication, authorization, and accounting) features, but is not a 100 percent replacement for ACS. For the near future, customers who want the features of ISE will likely use ACS for the authentication and authorization components and use ISE (in addition) for the posturing and policy-compliance checking for hosts.

Protocols Used Between the ACS and the Router

The next couple of sections discuss how to configure the router to forward authentication questions to the ACS server and examine how to tell the ACS server to work with the router. But right now, you need to understand the "language of love" used to communicate between the ACS server and the router (with a router acting as a client to the ACS server).

Two main protocols may be used between the ACS server and its client (such as a router that is using the ACS server to verify authentication requests): TACACS+ (pronounced TACK-AXE, you do not need to say the +) and RADIUS (pronounced RAY-D-US).

TACACS+ stands for *Terminal Access Control Access Control Server*, and that is why we just use the acronym. There have been earlier versions of TACACS+, which had slightly varying names, such as XTACACS and TACACS (without the plus). Because the only version now used is TACACS+, any time we refer to the term pronounced TACK-AXE, it is accepted and understood that we are referring to the currently implemented TACACS+ (even without saying the + at the end). TACACS+ is Cisco proprietary, which means its primary usage will likely be seen as a protocol used between a Cisco device and a Cisco ACS server. If you configure the router and the ACS server to use TACACS+, all the AAA packets that are sent between the router and the ACS server use the TACACS+ protocol, which encrypts each packet before it is sent on the network.

The other possible protocol that could be used between the router and the ACS server for the purpose of AAA services is RADIUS, which stands for *Remote Authentication Dial-In User Service*. RADIUS is an open standard, which means that not only ACS supports it but also that other vendors' implementations of AAA and their servers (such as Microsoft) can support communications with a client (such as a router) using this protocol. RADIUS encrypts only passwords, but not the whole packet being sent between the ACS server and the network device.

Protocol Choices Between the ACS Server and the Client (the Router)

Traditionally, and in common practice, if you are authenticating and authorizing administrators for command-line access, it is likely that you will configure TACACS+ on both the ACS server and the router for their communication with each other. A large reason for this is because TACACS+ has clearly defined and separate techniques and configurations for each aspect of AAA. For example, if you want to tell the router to check authorization for each individual command before allowing an administrator to put that command in, and only give the administrator a subset or portion of commands, TACACS+ and its authorization component allows extremely granular control in communicating which commands would be allowed. RADIUS, however, does not have the same level of granular control as TACACS+ command-by-command authorization.

If you are authenticating and authorizing end users who just want their packets to go through a network device (when authentication and authorization are required), it is likely that you are using RADIUS as the communications method between the ACS server on the router. You may configure the router and ACS server to use both TACACS+ and RADIUS simultaneously between the ACS server and its client, the router.

Table 3-2 compares these two protocols.

Table 3-2   TACACS+ Versus RADIUS

	TACACS+	RADIUS
Functionality	Separates AAA functions into distinct elements. Authentication is separate from authorization, and both of those are separate from accounting.	Combines many of the functions of authentication and authorization together. Has detailed accounting capability when accounting is configured for use.
Standard	Cisco proprietary, but very well known.	Open standard, and supported by nearly all vendors' AAA implementation.
L4 protocol	TCP.	UDP.
Confidentiality	*All* packets are encrypted between the ACS server and the router (which is the client).	Only the password is encrypted with regard to packets sent back and forth between the ACS server and the router.
Granular command by command authorization	This is supported, and the rules are defined on the ACS server about which commands are allowed or disallowed.	No explicit command authorization checking rules can be implemented.
Accounting	Provides accounting support.	Provide accounting support, and generally acknowledged as providing more detailed or extensive accounting capability than TACACS+.

Configuring Routers to Interoperate with an ACS Server

This section covers the detailed commands required for a router to use a central authentication server such as ACS. From the earlier discussion, you know that both the ACS server, which will have the usernames and passwords available to it, and the router that will be communicating with the ACS server need to be configured for them to work together. This section examines the router component.

The good news is that most of what you learned in the preceding chapter about AAA on the router still applies here. The biggest difference on the router is that in method lists, the router can be told to use the local database (which you now know is the running config on the local router) for verification of a username and password, or the router can be told to check with an ACS server to ask that server whether or not the username and password are valid.

On the router, you could use the CLI or *Cisco Configuration Professional (CCP)* for the configuration. Because you should know both (and you might need both depending on the certification environment), both methods are covered here. You first learn about the CLI version, followed by CCP. In this section, the configuration is based on a router that has not yet been set up for any type of AAA. Comments about each of the commands and what their purpose is are included. A few of these may be a review, too, because of the preceding chapter, but a little repetition will help reinforce these concepts.

Another key factor in any implementation is to have a plan, before beginning to configure the router. So, here is the plan. We want the router to implement the following:

- For administrators/users who are accessing the router via the vty lines, regardless of whether they are using Telnet or *Secure Shell (SSH)*, the router should check with a TACACS+ server (the ACS server using TACACS+ to communicate with this router) for the authentication check (username/password).

- Authenticated users need to be authorized to have access to a *command-line interface (CLI)* (EXEC) session, including the privilege level they should be placed into. The authorization check should be done by the router referring to the ACS server, using TACACS+.

Example 3-1 shows the configuration to implement these objectives.

Example 3-1 *Using the CLI to Configure IOS for Use with ACS*

```
! This command enables the configuration of the rest of the AAA
! If it is in the configuration, it doesn't need to be put in again.
! On most IOS systems, the default has aaa new-model disabled.
R1(config)# aaa new-model

! This authentication method list, when applied to a line such as the VTY
! lines will tell the router to prompt the user who is accessing that line
! for a username and password in order for that user to login.
! When the user supplies the username and password at the login prompt
! the router will send the credentials to a configured TACACS+ server
! and then the server can reply with a pass or fail message.
```

```
! This command indicates "group tacacs+" as the first method
! as there could be more than one server configured. If no ACS server
! responds
! after a short timeout the router will then try the second method in the
! method list which is "local" which means the router will then check the
! running
! config to see if there is a username and matching password
R1(config)# aaa authentication login AUTHEN_via_TACACS group tacacs+ local


! This next authorization method list, when applied to a line, will cause
! the router
! to check with the AAA server to verify that the user is authorized
! to gain access to the CLI. The CLI represents an Exec Shell.
! Not only can the ACS indicate to the router whether or not the user is
! authorized
! but it can also indicate what privilege level the user is placed into.
! Both the username and password will need to be created on the ACS server
! for the previous authentication method, and the authorization
! for a CLI will also need to be configured on that same ACS server.
! This authorization list will use one or more configured ACS servers
! via TACACS+, and if there are no servers that respond, then the router
! will check locally regarding whether the command is authorized for this
! user based on privilege level of the user, and privilege level of the
! command being attempted.
R1(config)# aaa authorization exec Author-Exec_via_TACACS group tacacs+ local


! It is important to note that before we apply either of these method lists
! to the VTY lines, we should create at least one local user as a backup
! in the event the ACS server is unreachable, or not yet configured.
! In the example below it will create a user on the local database of the
! router
! including a username, password as well as a privilege level for that user. It
! is highly recommended that you use strong passwords when configuring any user or
! device credentials.
R1(config)# username admin privilege 15 secret cisco


! Next we need to create a least one ACS server that the router should try
! to use
! via TACACS+. This is the equivalent of creating a server group of one.
! The password is used as part of the encryption of the packets, and
! whatever
! password we configure here, we also need to configure on the ACS server.
R1(config)# tacacs-server host 192.168.1.252 key cisco123


! Verifying that the IP addresses reachable is a test that can be done
! even before the full ACS configuration is complete on the AAA server
```

```
R1(config)# do ping 192.168.1.252

Type escape sequence to abort.
Sending 5, 100-byte ICMP Echos to 192.168.1.252, timeout is 2 seconds:
!!!!!
Success rate is 100 percent (5/5), round-trip min/avg/max = 8/13/28 ms

! Next, for the authentication method list and authorization method list
! to be used we would need to apply them. In the example below
! we are applying both method lists to the first five VTY lines.
R1(config)# line vty 0 4
R1(config-line)# authorization exec Author-Exec_via_TACACS
R1(config-line)# login authentication AUTHEN_via_TACACS
! users connecting to these vty lines will now be subject to both authentication
! and authorization, based on the lists that are applied to these lines
```

With the authentication and authorization method lists created and applied, you could attempt to log in through one of the five vty lines, and here is what you would expect: You should be prompted for username and password, the router should not be able to successfully contact the ACS server (because you have not configured the ACS part of it yet on that server), and then after a short timeout, the router would use the second method in each of its lists, which indicates to use the local database for the authentication and the authorization. Because you do have a local user with a password and a privilege level assigned to that user, it should work. By enabling a **debug**, and attempting to log in, you can see exactly what is happening, as shown in Example 3-2. If you are not connected to the device via the serial console, use the **terminal monitor** command to be able to see the debug messages in your screen.

Example 3-2   *Verifying AAA*

```
R1# debug tacacs
TACACS access control debugging is on

! Telnet to an IP address on the local router.
R1# telnet 10.0.0.1
Trying 10.0.0.1 ... Open

TPLUS: Queuing AAA Authentication request 102 for processing
TPLUS: processing authentication start request id 102
TPLUS: Authentication start packet created for 102()
TPLUS: Using server 192.168.1.252
TPLUS(00000066)/0/NB_WAIT/6812DC64: Started 5 sec timeout

User Access Verification
```

```
! Timing out on TACACS+ regarding authentication because no server is responding
TPLUS(00000066)/0/NB_WAIT/6812DC64: timed out
TPLUS(00000066)/0/NB_WAIT/6812DC64: timed out, clean up
TPLUS(00000066)/0/6812DC64: Processing the reply packet

! Now moving to the local database on the router
Username: admin
Password: cisco

! Timing out on TACACS+ regarding authorization due to no server responding.
TPLUS: Queuing AAA Authorization request 102 for processing
TPLUS: processing authorization request id 102
TPLUS: Protocol set to None .....Skipping
TPLUS: Sending AV service=shell
TPLUS: Sending AV cmd*
TPLUS: Authorization request created for 102(admin)
TPLUS: Using server 192.168.1.252
TPLUS(00000066)/0/NB_WAIT/6812DC64: Started 5 sec timeout
TPLUS(00000066)/0/NB_WAIT/6812DC64: timed out
TPLUS(00000066)/0/NB_WAIT/6812DC64: timed out, clean up
TPLUS(00000066)/0/6812DC64: Processing the reply packet
! After timing out, the router again uses its local database for
! authorization and appropriate privilege level for the user.

! If we exit, and change the debugs slightly, and do it again, it will give
! us yet another perspective.

R1# debug aaa authentication
AAA Authentication debugging is on
R1# debug aaa authorization
AAA Authorization debugging is on

Telnet
R1# telnet 10.0.0.1
Trying 10.0.0.1 ... Open

AAA/BIND(00000067): Bind i/f

! Notice it shows using the authentication list we assigned to the VTY
! lines
AAA/AUTHEN/LOGIN (00000067): Pick method list 'AUTHEN_via_TACACS'
! Not shown here, but indeed the ACS server is timing out, due to not yet
! being configured, which causes the second entry in the list "local" to be
! used.
```

```
User Access Verification

Username: admin
Password: cisco

! Now the authorization begins, using the method list we configured for the
! lines
AAA/AUTHOR (0x67): Pick method list 'Author-Exec_via_TACACS'

R1#
AAA/AUTHOR/EXEC(00000067): processing AV cmd=
AAA/AUTHOR/EXEC(00000067): processing AV priv-lvl=15
AAA/AUTHOR/EXEC(00000067): Authorization successful
R1#

!
```

So, what has happened so far? Table 3-3 describes the steps to configure the router for ACS.

Table 3-3   Configuring the Router to Use ACS via TACACS+

Task	How to Do It
Decide what the policy should be (for example, which vty lines should require authentication/authorization) and which methods (ACS, local, none) should be used.	This step is done way before you ever begin configuring the router, and is based on your security policy for your network. It is the concept of what you want to accomplish for authentication and authorization.
Enable the ability to configure AAA.	**aaa new-model** is not enabled by default. If you want to use the services of ACS, you must enable the feature of AAA as the very first step of configuration on a new router.
Specify the address of an ACS server to use.	Use the **tacacs-server host** command, including the IP address of the ACS server and the password.
Create a named method list for authentication and another for authorization, based on your policy.	Each method list is created in global configuration mode, specifying which methods this list uses, in order, from left to right.
Apply the method lists to the location that should use those methods.	In vty line configuration mode, specify the authentication and authorization method lists that you created in the preceding step.

Now that we have implemented the policy using the CLI, let's take a look at implementing a nearly identical policy but this time using CCP to implement it.

For this configuration, we have removed all AAA-related method lists and have left only the command **aaa new-model** as a starting point. The intent of this configuration using CCP is to familiarize you with the locations inside the *graphical user interface (GUI)* for you to configure the method lists for authentication and authorization and how to apply those to the vty lines.

In the configuration section of CCP, having selected the router that you want to configure, go to **Configure > Router > AAA > AAA Servers and Groups > Servers**, click the **Add** button, and provide the relevant information about your ACS server, as shown in Figure 3-1.

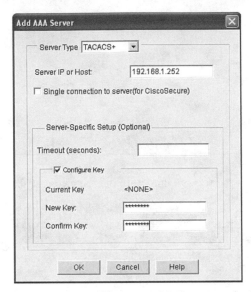

Figure 3-1   *Adding an ACS Server to the IOS Router via CCP*

You then click **OK** and any other confirmation buttons that are presented to apply this configuration to the router. Now that the router knows the IP address of the ACS server, and which protocol to use and the secret key used to encrypt the packets it sends to the server, the next step is to create the method lists. Just like at the CLI, you create one method list for authentication of logins and a second method list for authorization of the EXEC session. Each method list specifies that the ACS server should be used first, and if for whatever reason the ACS server fails to respond, the second method the router should use is the local configuration (the running config).

To create the method list for authentication, in CCP you go to **Configure > Router > AAA > Authentication Policies > Login**, click **Add**, and specify the details of the authentication method list, including its name and the methods from top to bottom that this method list will call on. The dialog looks similar to what Figure 3-2 shows.

From within the pop-up window, the **Add** button enables you to add the individual methods to be used by this method list. There is also the option of moving the methods up or down based on the order you want this method list to call on. As before, you would click the **OK** button and any other confirmation buttons you are prompted with until the configuration is delivered to the router.

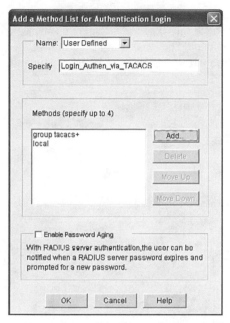

Figure 3-2 *Creating an Authentication Method List*

Now that your authentication method list is created, you can see this list and any other authentication lists that have been created on this same screen, as shown in Figure 3-3. This includes the methods, in order, from left to right.

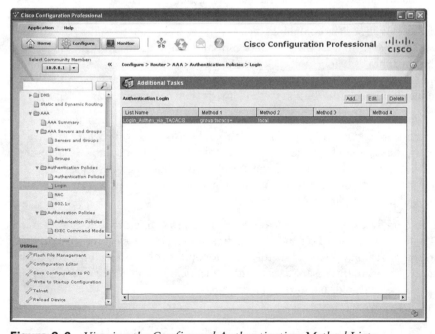

Figure 3-3 *Viewing the Configured Authentication Method Lists*

Now that you have created your authentication method list, you also need to create an authorization method list based on your policy. Again for this example, we are implementing the same exact policy we did earlier from the command line. To create the authorization method list, go to **Configure > Router > AAA > Authorization Policies > EXEC Command Mode** and click **Add**, as shown in Figure 3-4.

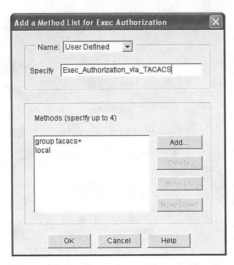

Figure 3-4 *Creating a New Authorization Method List*

Using a similar process as you did with the first method list, you choose **User Defined** (meaning that you are not going to set this method as the global default, but instead are only creating a method list that will not be used until this method list is associated somewhere else in the configuration, such as configured on a vty line). In addition to naming the authorization method list, you also click the **Add** button from this pop-up to select the individual methods to be used. Just as before, you click the **OK** button and any other confirmation buttons presented until CCP finally delivers the configuration to the router, at which point you can see a summary of your authorization method list, as shown in Figure 3-5.

At this point, with a method list configured for authentication and a second method list configured for authorization, it is time to put those method lists to work. Now what does that mean? Currently, those method lists are just wasting space in the configuration. If you want those method lists to be used, you need to specifically apply those methods lists. Based on the policy, you want the method list for authentication and the method list for authorization to both be applied to the vty lines of the router.

To apply the method lists, we leave the AAA section and go to **Configure > Router > Router Access > VTY**. From there, click **Edit** and use the drop-down box to select the method lists that we want to use. The only method lists that exist for authentication and authorization are the ones that you create. In this case, we select the authentication and authorization method lists that we previously created, as shown in Figure 3-6.

Figure 3-5 *List of Authorization Method Lists Configured on the Router*

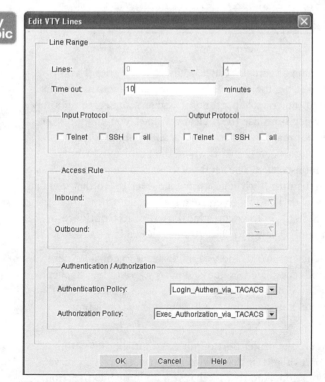

Figure 3-6 *Applying the Newly Created Method Lists*

You click **OK** and then click any confirmation buttons presented until CCP deploys the configuration to the router. Once it deploys the configuration, it shows you a summary of how your vty lines are configured, as shown in Figure 3-7.

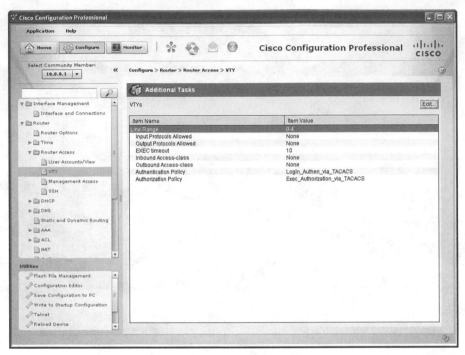

Figure 3-7   *Summary of vty Configuration, Showing the Method Lists Applied*

At this point in the configuration, you might actually cause yourself some grief if you accidentally log out. If you are connected via the console port, you might be okay because you have not applied the method list to the console port. But if you are connected remotely using Telnet or *Secure Shell (SSH)*, which both use the logical vty lines, you might not be able to reconnect if the ACS server is not reachable (because it is not configured yet) and the router falls back to the local configuration, and that is where the problem is. We have not yet created a local user in this demonstration. The secret is to make sure there is at least one locally configured user with administrative privileges (privilege level 15) so that you can always get back into the router. You saw earlier how to create a user account from the CLI. You should also do the equivalent here in CCP. To create a local user, go to **Configure > Router > Router Access > User Accounts/View** and click **Add**, as shown in Figure 3-8.

This user account should have a difficult password, and you might want to consider not giving this username a name that might be recognized or guessed at by a would-be attacker. After you've added the information, including the privilege level 15 access, click **OK** and any other confirmation pop-up confirmation messages until CCP delivers the configuration to the router.

So, now you have seen how to configure the router portion for AAA integration within ACS server using TACACS+. The second part of getting AAA working between an ACS server and a router is to configure the ACS portion. And that is what you do in the next section.

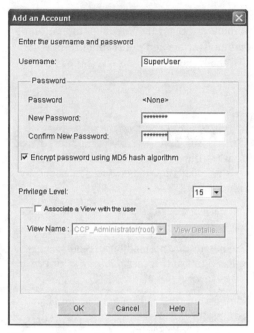

Figure 3-8   *Adding a Local User with Privilege Level 15*

Configuring the ACS Server to Interoperate with a Router

This section covers the GUI on the ACS server, which enables it to communicate with a client, such as a router.

Before examining the configuration of the ACS server itself, let's first review a few things. The ACS server has literally thousands of bells and whistles and options that may be configured and tuned. The goal in this section is to make sure that you are comfortable with the basic concept that the ACS server can be a centralized clearinghouse for user authentication/authorization and a repository for accounting records of what those users actually did. From an administrator's perspective, this includes which administrator issued which commands on which devices.

One challenge that large organizations face is having several administrators with different areas of responsibility. For example, one administrator may be responsible for the perimeter routers that are running zone-based firewall services. A different administrator might be responsible for the routers that are providing *virtual private network (VPN)* services, and the list goes on. In situations such as these, it is unwise to give every administrator full administrative rights to every single router. Instead, it makes sense to provide access only to those individuals who need it. For example, administrators who manage the perimeter routers should not have access, or at least full access, to the VPN devices that they do not manage. In this light, ACS can group the routers together into logical organizations called *device groups*. This way, you put specific routers into a group, and then on the ACS put the administrators who are currently responsible for those routers into a user group and assign that group an authorization role that includes administrative rights of full access for that specific group of routers. This scenario does require a bit more effort for the initial configuration of ACS, but after it is set up, you can just add new administrators and put them into specific groups within ACS, and they automatically receive the rights and access levels they need.

Table 3-4 describes the key components for this type of configuration.

Table 3-4   Key Components for Configuring ACS

Component of ACS	How It Is Used
Network device groups	Groups of network devices, normally based on routers or switches with similar functions/devices managed by the same administrators.
Network devices (ACS clients/ routers/switches)	The individual network devices that go into the device groups.
Identity groups (user/admin groups)	Groups of administrators, normally based on users who will need similar rights and access to specific groups of network devices.
User accounts	Individual administrator/user accounts that are placed in identity groups.
Authorization profiles	These profiles control what rights are permitted. The profile is associated with a network device group and a user/administrator identity group.

For the demonstration here, we create the following:

- Device group for border routers
- A single router that belongs to the device group
- Two groups, an Admin group and a Monitor group
- Two users (an administrator belonging to the Admin group and a help desk account belonging to the Monitor group)
- Two authorization policies (the first stating that members of the Admin group who are accessing devices in the device group should get full privilege level 15 access, the second policy stating that users who are members of the Monitor group will only have privilege level 1 access to the devices in the device group)

So, with this policy in mind, the first thing is to open a browser window from your local computer to the IP address that is running the ACS server. The URL is https://*a.b.c.d*/ acsadmin, where *a.b.c.d* is the actual IP address of your server. On a new installation of ACS, the default password is default. Initially, the ACS server is using an SSL self-signed certificate, and you may get a pop-up asking you whether you want to confirm your session to this device, even though your browser does not trust the certificate. You need to agree and continue if you want to manage the ACS server.

A newly installed ACS also requires proper licensing. The licensing information is provided along with the purchased product. Evaluation licenses are also available for individuals interested in evaluating the product. Contacting your Cisco representative to obtain the software is probably the easiest way to get it, and with your Cisco.com account you can register online for an evaluation license.

The first step is to create a device group. You do so by navigating to **Network Resources > Network Device Groups > Device Type** and clicking **Create**, as shown in Figure 3-9.

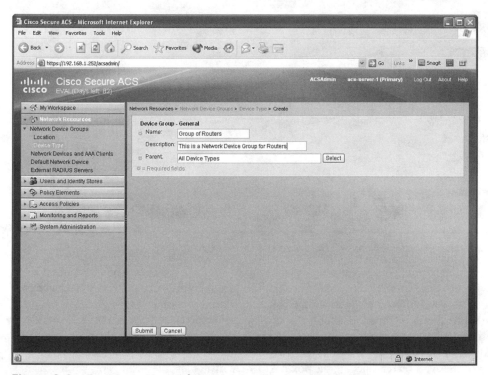

Figure 3-9   *Creating a Network Device Group*

After adding information about this group, click **Submit** to implement the new network device group. The problem with this device group is that by default there are no network devices in it. To fix that, we add as an example a single router (the router we configured earlier) to be included in this network device group on the ACS server. This is done by navigating to **Network Resources > Network Devices and AAA Clients** and clicking **Create**, as shown in Figure 3-10.

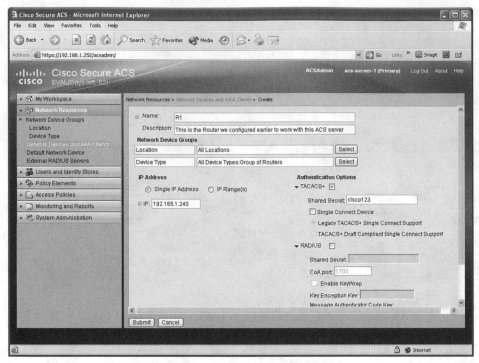

Figure 3-10   *Adding a Network Device to the Device Group*

In this dialog box, you click the **Select** button to the right of the device type and select the device group created from the previous step. In addition to that, you configure the name that the ACS server will know the router by. This name does not have to match the real name of the router, but it is a good idea for it to match so that someone looking at the ACS would know which client (the router) is being referred to in the configuration of the ACS. The IP address of this client (the router) is the reachable address of the router from the perspective of the ACS server. Clicking the box next to TACACS+ lets the ACS server know which protocol to expect from this client, and having the correct password (the one that matches the password configured earlier on the router) is also required for successful communication. After reviewing the information to confirm it is accurate, click **Submit**.

So, we have created a network device group, and added router R1 as the first network device (ACS client) in this group. The next step is to create a user group, and then create some users in those groups. The two groups we are going to create are an Admin group and a Monitor group. To create these groups, navigate to **Users and Identity Stores > Identity Groups** and click **Create**, as shown in Figure 3-11.

Complete the dialog box by providing the name of the group you are going to create, and then click **Submit**. You could repeat this process for any additional groups. For this discussion, we create two groups: one named Admin and the other named Monitor. After you click **Submit**, a summary of your existing groups displays, as shown in Figure 3-12.

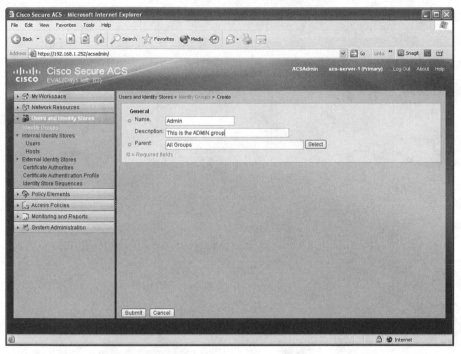

Figure 3-11 *Creating User Groups*

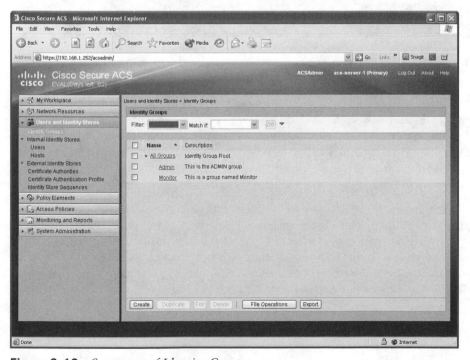

Figure 3-12 *Summary of Identity Groups*

These new groups have no users in them by default and have no special permissions by default. The first step to fixing that is to create a couple user accounts and place at least one user account into each group. To create individual users, navigate to **Users and Identity Stores > Internal Identity Stores > Users** and click **Create**, as shown in Figure 3-13.

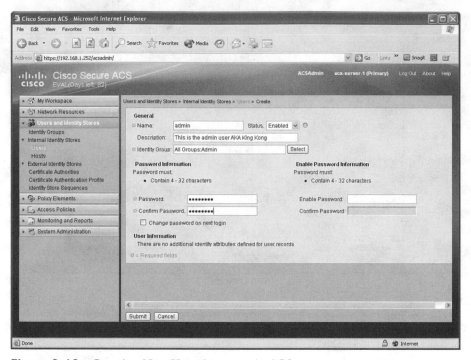

Figure 3-13 *Creating New User Accounts in ACS*

After entering in the name of this user, and a description (if desired), click the **Select** button from this pop-up window to select which user group you want this user to be a member of. It also specifies the password for this administrator. After verifying the details are correct, click **Submit**. In this scenario, we are creating one user named admin that belongs to the Admin group, and a second user named help-desk that belongs to the Monitor group. After you click **Submit**, a summary of your configured users configured on the ACS server displays, as shown in Figure 3-14.

The next step is to configure authorization policies that give full access to users in the Admin group who are trying to access routers in the network device group we created. We also want to give limited access to users in the Monitor group who are trying to access the same devices. We can do this with authorization policies. To create and assign the reservation policies, first navigate to **Access Policies > Access Services > Default Device Admin > Authorization** and click **Create**, as shown in Figure 3-15.

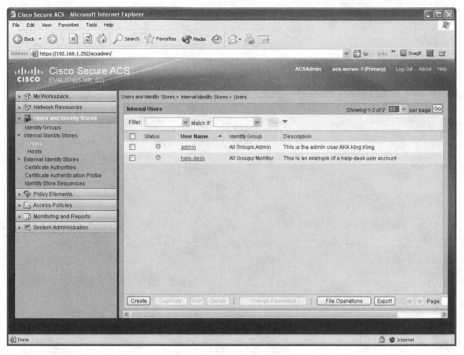

Figure 3-14   *Users Created on the ACS Server*

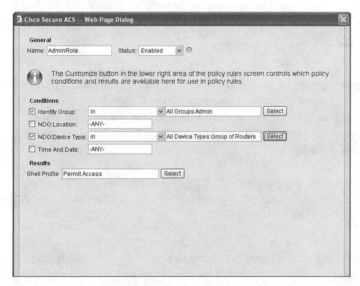

Figure 3-15   *Creating an Authorization Policy*

In the dialog box, indicate the name of this policy, called in this example AdminRole, and check the box next to the conditions next to identity group, and click the **Select** button to choose the Admin group created earlier. Use the same process, checking that box next to NDG Device Type (NDG stands for *network device group*) and then using the **Select** button, to indicate the device belongs to the group of routers device group that was created earlier.

This is setting up a condition so that if a user who is a member of the Admin group is attempting to access a device that is a member of the specific router group, then as a result we can provide specific access based on a custom shell profile that we can create. To do that, click the **Select** button next to the Shell Profile option, and you are presented with the screen shown in Figure 3-16. Shell profiles are used for authorization purposes and associated with an authorization policy (AdminRole in this example).

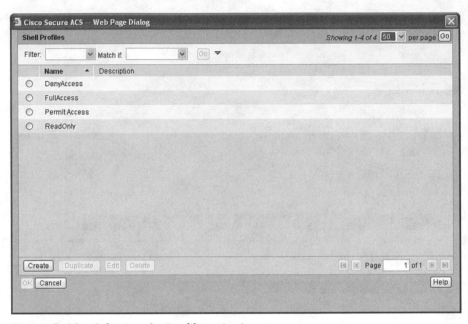

Figure 3-16   *Selecting the Profile to Assign*

You could assign one of the preconfigured profiles, or you could create your own profile and assign it to this group of users. To create a custom profile, click the **Create** button, and from the new window that is brought up, name the profile in the dialog box provided, and then display the Common Tasks tab and change the default privilege level to **Static**, and assign the privilege level of **15**, as shown in Figure 3-17.

> **NOTE**   The higher the privilege level, the more privileges a user has to configure and access information in the device.

Click **Submit**, and then confirm any dialog boxes presented to you from ACS until the configuration is applied. By using these steps, any users in the Admin group accessing any of the devices in the specified device group will not only be able to authenticate but also be automatically authorized for and placed into privilege level 15 after successfully authenticating on those routers. We repeat this process for the Monitor group, assigning a static privilege level of 1.

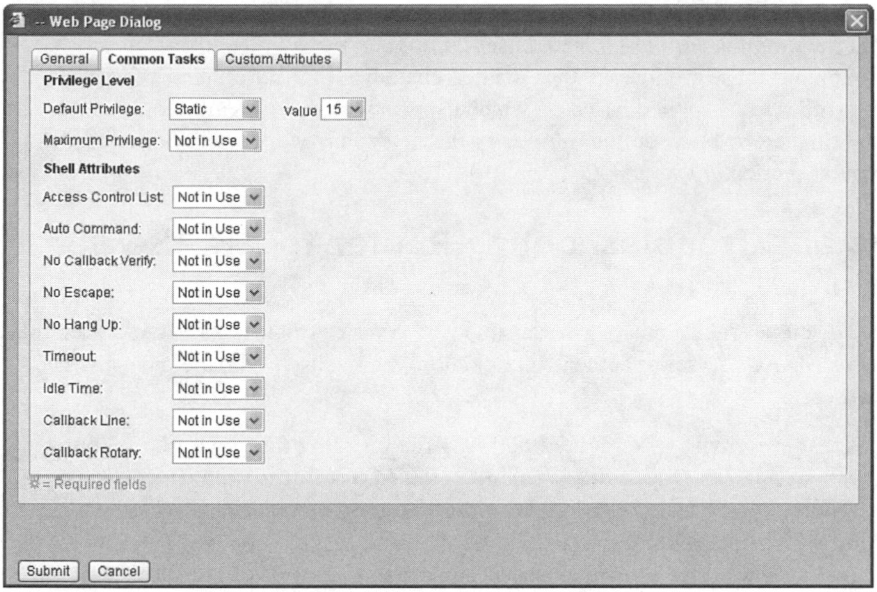

Figure 3-17 *Creating a Custom Authorization Profile*

After saving the changes, you can view a summary of the authorization profiles in this same location. Figure 3-18 shows two custom authorization profiles. One applies to admin users in the Admin group accessing devices in the router group, and the other applies to help desk users who are members of the Monitor group accessing the same devices.

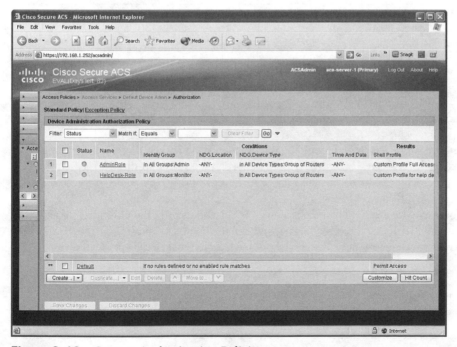

Figure 3-18 *Custom Authorization Policies*

In this section, we created device groups and added individual routers, or a least one in this case, to that device group. We also created user groups and put users (in this case, at least one per group) into those groups. We then created custom authorization profiles that indicate which profiles to be applied based on which users in which groups are accessing which devices. The final piece to the puzzle is to verify that it actually works. Let's do that right now in the next section.

Verifying and Troubleshooting Router-to-ACS Server Interactions

This section discusses the commands that enable you to verify/troubleshoot AAA when the router is using the ACS server to authenticate or authorize the users who are trying to connect to the router.

The chances that everything is configured perfectly the very first time on both the router and the ACS server to allow the router to call upon the ACS server for authentication of users and authorization of users are not very good. The good news is that after some practice and good documentation skills implementing ACS and Cisco router configurations, your ability will improve. Whether you are experienced or brand new to ACS, the tools covered right now will prove helpful in troubleshooting and verifying the configuration.

Back at the router, one of the first things you might want to do if you have not done so already is verify that you have reachability between the router and the ACS server. You might want to consider using ping to verify the connectivity, as shown in Example 3-3.

Example 3-3   *Verifying Basic Connectivity*

```
R1# ping 192.168.1.252

Type escape sequence to abort.
Sending 5, 100-byte ICMP Echos to 192.168.1.252, timeout is 2 seconds:
!!!!!
Success rate is 100 percent (5/5), round-trip min/avg/max = 16/21/32 ms
R1#
```

If the ping was not successful, it could be due to access control filtering that is denying *Internet Control Message Protocol (ICMP)* between the router and the ACS server, the ACS server may physically be powered off or its network cable may be disconnected, the ACS server may be connected to a switch port that is misconfigured and is in the wrong VLAN, or it may be a general routing issue or the network is not fully converged or able to route correctly. Verifying the basic routing and connectivity is a fantastic start, and after that is in place, here is the very next tool you should use, called **test** (see Example 3-4).

Key Topic

Example 3-4   *Testing AAA Between the Router and the ACS*

```
R1# test aaa group tacacs+ admin cisco123 legacy
Attempting authentication test to server-group tacacs+ using tacacs+
User was successfully authenticated.
```

In the syntax for the AAA test, we include the group (in this case, a group of one TACACS+ server and a username and the password for that user). The keyword **legacy** is also used as part of the syntax for the test. This is a cool tool because it enables you to verify that the ACS to router authentication component is working, before testing your authentication method list with Telnet. Another great thing to do when troubleshooting is to look at the reports on the ACS server that may indicate a reason as to why a problem occurred. You can find these reports by navigating to **Monitoring & Reports > Reports > Favorites**. Figure 3-19 shows an example.

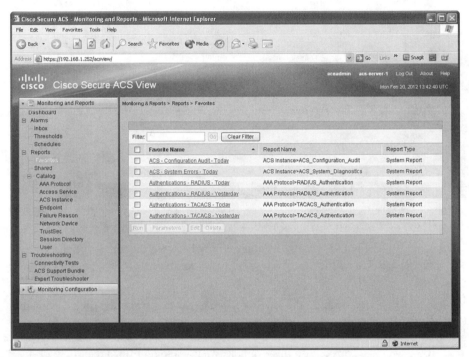

Figure 3-19   *Reporting Options from Within ACS*

From here, click the **Authentications – TACACS – Today** link for information and indications as to why errors may be occurring, as shown in Figure 3-20.

One common occurrence is that after the reports are looked at, there are no error messages about the ACS client (the router) that we believe is trying to use the ACS, yet the authentication test still fails. In cases such as these, you want to verify no filters are blocking the traffic from the router to the ACS and vice versa, and verify that in the router config it has the correct IP address of the ACS server. If the router does not have the correct IP address of the ACS server, there will never be any records on the ACS server about that misconfigured router.

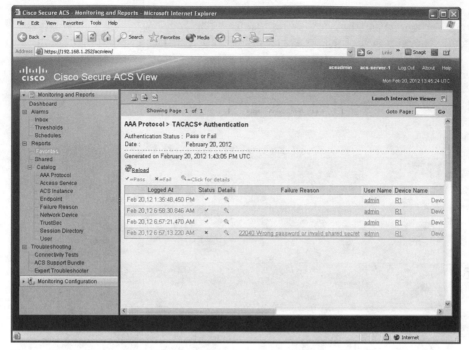

Figure 3-20 *Detailed Error Messages from ACS*

Now that we know we have functional AAA connectivity between the router and the server, let's test the method lists for authentication and authorization that we placed on the vty lines.

A simple Telnet to that router can do the job. It is often easier to start on the router, perhaps from a console port, and telnet back to that same router. A Telnet session, regardless of its source, should trigger the authentication, and with some **debug** commands in place, we can verify that ACS is working correctly. In this example, we use a login from a remote workstation and look at the **debug** messages on the console of the router, as shown in Example 3-5.

Example 3-5 *Using* **debug** *Commands to Verify Functionality*

```
! Verifying what debugging is currently in place on the router
R1# show debug
General OS:
  TACACS access control debugging is on
  AAA Authentication debugging is on
  AAA Authorization debugging is on

! on a remote machine, we telnet and authenticate as the user admin, and
! simply view the debug output on the console of the router receiving the
! telnet session

R1#
AAA/BIND(00000083): Bind i/f
```

```
! the session came in on a VTY line, which triggered the authentication
! method list associated with that line
AAA/AUTHEN/LOGIN (00000083): Pick method list 'Login_Authen_via_TACACS'
TPLUS: Queuing AAA Authentication request 131 for processing
TPLUS: processing authentication start request id 131
TPLUS: Authentication start packet created for 131()
TPLUS: Using server 192.168.1.252

! Sending a TACACS+ request to contact the server
TPLUS(00000083)/0/NB_WAIT/68BD742C: Started 5 sec timeout
TPLUS(00000083)/0/NB_WAIT: socket event 2
TPLUS(00000083)/0/NB_WAIT: wrote entire 33 bytes request
TPLUS(00000083)/0/READ: socket event 1
TPLUS(00000083)/0/READ: Would block while reading
TPLUS(00000083)/0/READ: socket event 1
TPLUS(00000083)/0/READ: read entire 12 header bytes (expect 16 bytes data)
R1#
TPLUS(00000083)/0/READ: socket event 1
TPLUS(00000083)/0/READ: read entire 28 bytes response

! Router got a message back from ACS
! Router will now prompt the user for their username
TPLUS(00000083)/0/68BD742C: Processing the reply packet
TPLUS: Received authen response status GET_USER (7)
R1#
TPLUS: Queuing AAA Authentication request 131 for processing
TPLUS: processing authentication continue request id 131
TPLUS: Authentication continue packet generated for 131
TPLUS(00000083)/0/WRITE/68BD742C: Started 5 sec timeout
TPLUS(00000083)/0/WRITE: wrote entire 22 bytes request
TPLUS(00000083)/0/READ: socket event 1
TPLUS(00000083)/0/READ: read entire 12 header bytes (expect 16 bytes data)
TPLUS(00000083)/0/READ: socket event 1
TPLUS(00000083)/0/READ: read entire 28 bytes response
TPLUS(00000083)/0/68BD742C: Processing the reply packet

! Router will now prompt user for the user password
TPLUS: Received authen response status GET_PASSWORD (8)
R1#
TPLUS: Queuing AAA Authentication request 131 for processing
TPLUS: processing authentication continue request id 131
TPLUS: Authentication continue packet generated for 131
TPLUS(00000083)/0/WRITE/68BD742C: Started 5 sec timeout
TPLUS(00000083)/0/WRITE: wrote entire 25 bytes request
TPLUS(00000083)/0/READ: socket event 1
TPLUS(00000083)/0/READ: read entire 12 header bytes (expect 6 bytes data)
```

```
TPLUS(00000083)/0/READ: socket event 1
TPLUS(00000083)/0/READ: read entire 18 bytes response
TPLUS(00000083)/0/68BD742C: Processing the reply packet


! The ACS server said YES to the username/password combination.
TPLUS: Received authen response status PASS (2)


! The router now begins the authorization process for the user
! using the authorization methods in the list associated with the VTY lines
AAA/AUTHOR (0x83): Pick method list 'Exec_Authorization_via_TACACS'
TPLUS: Queuing AAA Authorization request 131 for processing
TPLUS: processing authorization request id 131
TPLUS: Protocol set to None .....Skipping
TPLUS: Sending AV service=shell
TPLUS: Sending AV cmd*
TPLUS: Authorization request created for 131(admin)
TPLUS: using previously set server 192.168.1.252 from group tacacs+
TPLUS(00000083)/0/NB_WAIT/68BD742C: Started 5 sec timeout
TPLUS(00000083)/0/NB_WAIT: socket event 2
TPLUS(00000083)/0/NB_WAIT: wrote entire 57 bytes request
TPLUS(00000083)/0/READ: socket event 1
TPLUS(00000083)/0/READ: Would block while reading
TPLUS(00000083)/0/READ: socket event 1
TPLUS(00000083)/0/READ: read entire 12 header bytes (expect 18 bytes data)
TPLUS(00000083)/0/READ: socket event 1
TPLUS(00000083)/0/READ: read entire 30 bytes response
TPLUS(00000083)/0/68BD742C: Processing the reply packet


! Got the reply from the ACS server saying yes to authorization
! and that the user should be placed at privilege level 15
TPLUS: Processed AV priv-lvl=15
TPLUS: received authorization response for 131: PASS
AAA/AUTHOR/EXEC(00000083): processing AV cmd=
AAA/AUTHOR/EXEC(00000083): processing AV priv-lvl=15
AAA/AUTHOR/EXEC(00000083): Authorization successful
R1#


R1# show users
    Line       User      Host(s)          Idle      Location
   2 vty 0     admin     idle             00:00:51 10.0.0.25


! We could do the same test again, except this time, login as the user
! "help-desk"
! The results will be nearly identical, with the exception that the user
! will be provided with an exec shell (CLI) at privilege level 1
```

```
R1#
AAA/BIND(00000084): Bind i/f
AAA/AUTHEN/LOGIN (00000084): Pick method list 'Login_Authen_via_TACACS'
TPLUS: Queuing AAA Authentication request 132 for processing
TPLUS: processing authentication start request id 132
TPLUS: Authentication start packet created for 132()
TPLUS: Using server 192.168.1.252
TPLUS(00000084)/0/NB_WAIT/68793774: Started 5 sec timeout
TPLUS(00000084)/0/NB_WAIT: socket event 2
TPLUS(00000084)/0/NB_WAIT: wrote entire 33 bytes request
TPLUS(00000084)/0/READ: socket event 1
TPLUS(00000084)/0/READ: Would block while reading
TPLUS(00000084)/0/READ: socket event 1
TPLUS(00000084)/0/READ: read entire 12 header bytes (expect 16 bytes data)
R1#
TPLUS(00000084)/0/READ: socket event 1
TPLUS(00000084)/0/READ: read entire 28 bytes response
TPLUS(00000084)/0/68793774: Processing the reply packet
TPLUS: Received authen response status GET_USER (7)
R1#
TPLUS: Queuing AAA Authentication request 132 for processing
TPLUS: processing authentication continue request id 132
TPLUS: Authentication continue packet generated for 132
TPLUS(00000084)/0/WRITE/68793774: Started 5 sec timeout
TPLUS(00000084)/0/WRITE: wrote entire 26 bytes request
TPLUS(00000084)/0/READ: socket event 1
TPLUS(00000084)/0/READ: read entire 12 header bytes (expect 16 bytes data)
TPLUS(00000084)/0/READ: socket event 1
TPLUS(00000084)/0/READ: read entire 28 bytes response
TPLUS(00000084)/0/68793774: Processing the reply packet
TPLUS: Received authen response status GET_PASSWORD (8)
R1#
TPLUS: Queuing AAA Authentication request 132 for processing
TPLUS: processing authentication continue request id 132
TPLUS: Authentication continue packet generated for 132
TPLUS(00000084)/0/WRITE/68793774: Started 5 sec timeout
TPLUS(00000084)/0/WRITE: wrote entire 25 bytes request
TPLUS(00000084)/0/READ: socket event 1
TPLUS(00000084)/0/READ: read entire 12 header bytes (expect 6 bytes data)
TPLUS(00000084)/0/READ: socket event 1
TPLUS(00000084)/0/READ: read entire 18 bytes response
TPLUS(00000084)/0/68793774: Processing the reply packet
TPLUS: Received authen response status PASS (2)
AAA/AUTHOR (0x84): Pick method list 'Exec_Authorization_via_TACACS'
TPLUS: Queuing AAA Authorization request 132 for processing
TPLUS: processing authorization request id 132
```

```
TPLUS: Protocol set to None .....Skipping
TPLUS: Sending AV service=shell
TPLUS: Sending AV cmd*
TPLUS: Authorization request created for 132(help-desk)
TPLUS: using previously set server 192.168.1.252 from group tacacs+
TPLUS(00000084)/0/NB_WAIT/68793774: Started 5 sec timeout
TPLUS(00000084)/0/NB_WAIT: socket event 2
TPLUS(00000084)/0/NB_WAIT: wrote entire 61 bytes request
TPLUS(00000084)/0/READ: socket event 1
TPLUS(00000084)/0/READ: Would block while reading
TPLUS(00000084)/0/READ: socket event 1
TPLUS(00000084)/0/READ: read entire 12 header bytes (expect 17 bytes data)
TPLUS(00000084)/0/READ: socket event 1
TPLUS(00000084)/0/READ: read entire 29 bytes response
TPLUS(00000084)/0/68793774: Processing the reply packet
TPLUS: Processed AV priv-lvl=1
TPLUS: received authorization response for 132: PASS
AAA/AUTHOR/EXEC(00000084): processing AV cmd=
AAA/AUTHOR/EXEC(00000084): processing AV priv-lvl=1
AAA/AUTHOR/EXEC(00000084): Authorization successful
R1#

R1# show users
    Line       User      Host(s)          Idle      Location
  2 vty 0   help-desk   idle          00:01:24 10.0.0.25
! the show users command displays information about all logged in users. In this
! example, the help desk is logged in from a host with the IP address 10.0.0.25.
```

Exam Preparation Tasks

Review All the Key Topics

Review the most important topics from this chapter, denoted with a Key Topic icon. Table 3-5 lists these key topics.

Table 3-5   Key Topics

Key Topic Element	Description	Page Number
Section	Why Use Cisco ACS?	38
Section	Protocols Used Between the ACS and the Router	39
Table 3-2	TACACS+ Versus RADIUS	40
Example 3-1	Using the CLI to Configure IOS for Use with ACS	41
Table 3-3	Configuring the Router to Use ACS via TACACS+	45
Figure 3-6	Applying the Newly Created Method Lists	49
Table 3-4	Key Components for Configuring ACS	52
Example 3-4	Testing AAA Between the Router and the ACS	60

Complete the Tables and Lists from Memory

Print a copy of Appendix C, "Memory Tables," (found on the CD) or at least the section for this chapter, and complete the tables and lists from memory. Appendix D, "Memory Tables Answer Key," also on the CD, includes completed tables and lists so that you can check your work.

Define Key Terms

Define the following key terms from this chapter, and check your answers in the glossary:

ACS, RADIUS, TACACS+, AAA server, authentication method list, authorization method list

Command Reference to Check Your Memory

This section includes the most important configuration and EXEC commands covered in this chapter. To see how well you have memorized the commands as a side effect of your other studies, cover the left side of Table 3-6 with a piece of paper, read the descriptions on the right side, and see whether you remember the commands.

Table 3-6 Command Reference

Command	Description
aaa new-model	Enable the configuration of method lists and other AAA-related elements, including the use of ACS.
test aaa group tacacs+ *admin cisco123* **legacy**	Allow verification of the authentication function working between the AAA client (the router) and the ACS server (the AAA server).
aaa authentication login *MYLIST1* **group tacacs+ local**	Create an authentication method list that, when applied elsewhere in the configuration, requests the services of an ACS server via TACACS+, and if no server responds, the next method local (which is the local router configuration) is checked to verify the credentials of the user.
aaa authorization exec *MYLIST2* **group tacacs+ none**	Create an authorization method list that, when applied to a vty line, requests the services of an ACS server (via TACACS+). If no server responds, the second method "none" is used. This results in no username prompt being provided to the user, and authentication is not required.
tacacs-server host *192.168.1.252* **key** *cisco123*	Places a server into the group of ACS servers the router can use for TACACS+ requests. It includes the IP address and the secret used to encrypt packets between this router (the client) and the ACS server.

This chapter covers the following topics:

BYOD concept

BYOD architecture framework

Mobile device management (MDM)

Function of MDM

MDM deployment options (On-premise MDM, cloud-based MDM)

CHAPTER 4

Bring Your Own Device (BYOD)

"Do I Know This Already?" Quiz

The "Do I Know This Already?" quiz allows you to assess if you should read the entire chapter. If you miss no more than one of these self-assessment questions, you might want to move ahead to the "Exam Preparation Tasks." Table 4-1 lists the major headings in this chapter and the "Do I Know This Already?" quiz questions covering the material in those headings so you can assess your knowledge of these specific areas. The answers to the "Do I Know This Already?" quiz appear in Appendix A.

Table 4-1 "Do I Know This Already?" Section-to-Question Mapping

Foundation Topics Section	Questions
Bring Your Own Device Fundamentals	1
BYOD Architecture Framework	2–7
Mobile Device Management	8–10

1. Which of the following is not a business driver for a BYOD solution?

   a. Need for employees to work anywhere and anytime

   b. Increase in the type of devices needed and used by employees to connect to the corporate network

   c. The lack of IPv4 address space

   d. Fluidity of today's work schedules

2. Which component provides Wi-Fi access for employees in home offices, branch offices, and on the corporate campus?

   a. WLAN controllers (WLC)

   b. Cisco AnyConnect Client

   c. Wireless access points (AP)

   d. Identity Services Engine (ISE)

3. The Identity Services Engine (ISE) provides which of the following?

   a. Access, authentication, accounting

   b. Authentication, authorization, accounting

   c. Access, authorization, accounting

   d. Authentication, authorization, access

4. Which of the following is not enabled through the use of the Cisco AnyConnect Client?

   a. 802.1X

   b. VPN

   c. AAA

   d. Posture checking

5. The purpose of the RSA SecurID server/application is to provide what?

   a. Authentication, authorization, accounting (AAA) functions

   b. One-time password (OTP) capabilities

   c. 802.1X enforcement

   d. VPN access

6. The purpose of the certificate authority (CA) is to ensure what?

   a. BYOD endpoints are posture checked

   b. BYOD endpoints belong to the organization

   c. BYOD endpoints have no malware installed

   d. BYOD users exist in the corporate LDAP directory

7. What is the primary purpose of the Integrated Services Routers (ISR) in the BYOD solution?

   a. Provide connectivity in the home office environment back to the corporate campus

   b. Provide WAN and Internet access for users on the corporate campus

   c. Enforce firewall-type filtering in the data center

   d. Provide connectivity for the mobile phone environment back to the corporate campus

8. Which is not a function of mobile device management (MDM)?

   a. Enforce strong passwords on BYOD devices

   b. Deploy software updates to BYOD devices

   c. Remotely wipe data from BYOD devices

   d. Enforce data encryption requirements on BYOD devices

9. Which is not an advantage of an On-Premise MDM solution?

   a. Higher level of control over the BYOD solution

   b. Ease of deployment and operation of the BYOD solution

   c. Ability to meet regulatory requirements

   d. Security of the overall BYOD solution

10. Which is not an advantage of a cloud-based MDM solution?

   a. Scalability of the MDM solution

   b. Security of the overall MDM solution

   c. Flexibility in deploying the MDM solution

   d. Speed of deployment of MDM solution

Foundation Topics

This chapter focuses on the phenomenon known as *bring your own device (BYOD)*, and includes overview of BYOD, a high-level description of a BYOD architecture, and a discussion on a management approach for BYOD devices known as *mobile device management (MDM)*.

Bring Your Own Device Fundamentals

The concept of BYOD brings with it the constant challenge for network and security administrators, engineers, and management. This challenge is to provide seamless connectivity for users bringing their own network-connected devices while also maintaining an appropriate security posture. The organization must provide a level of security that meets the organization's security policies and ensures that network devices, systems, and data do not get compromised through the proliferation of vulnerable devices starting with the devices brought in by employees from "the outside."

It is no longer a "nice to have" to enable an organization's users to use their own devices both on the corporate network and remotely—home, hotels, coffee shops, and so on—through the use of encrypted *virtual private networks (VPN)*. Employees not only demand but, in today's business landscape, legitimately need to be able to use their devices to connect to and from any network-enabled location in the world.

Following are a number of business reasons that are driving the need for BYOD solutions:

■ **Wide variety of consumer devices:** It seems like every day there is a new vendor, a new device, or a new version of an existing device that requires connectivity to the Internet. And that's just what I see in my own house! It used to be simple when we had PCs that remained "fixed" to our desks at work, each one with a direct connection, via an Ethernet cable, to the corporate network. Now we have laptops, smartphones, and tablets, all of which not only require connectivity to the network but which also get carried throughout the office and to and from home, all while having connectivity to the Internet in some fashion.

■ **Blurred lines between work and play:** The term *9 to 5* used to signify the rigid start and end times of our (well, for those of us old enough to be working back then) traditional 8-hour work day. Obviously, times have changed and, not only have the start and end times changed, but we don't even necessarily have a defined work "day." We work on our commute to work, we work during lunch, we work on our commute home, we work at nights, and we work while watching our kids play baseball, softball, basketball, and ice hockey on the weekends! Heck, some of us even work while on vacation—now that sounds like an oxymoron.

■ **Connect me anytime, anywhere:** End users expect to be able to connect their devices whenever and wherever they may be regardless of whether they are "on the clock." These needs are satisfied by the continuing growth of wireless networks, 3G/4G mobile networks, and publicly available wireless networks at coffee shops, hotels, and so on.

BYOD Architecture Framework

There are many different ways to implement a BYOD solution, and each organization must decide on the level of openness and flexibility it wants to enable its employees in terms of the type of devices they can connect and the amount of access each of these devices will be granted. The bottom line, however, is that the organization's security policy must be leveraged to govern the level of access for BYOD devices, and then certain technologies will be used to ensure the security policy is managed and enforced.

The Cisco BYOD solution architecture leverages the Cisco Borderless Network Architecture and is based on the assumption that *best common practices (BCP)* are followed in network designs for campus, branch offices, Internet edge, and home office implementations.

Figure 4-1 shows a high-level view of the Cisco BYOD solution architecture. Each of the components of the Cisco BYOD solution is explained in detail in the following section.

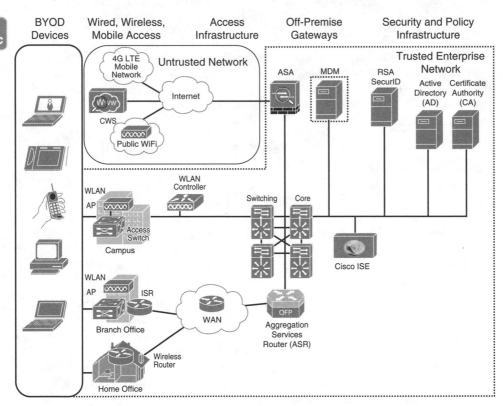

Figure 4-1 *High-Level BYOD Solution Architecture*

BYOD Solution Components

Each of the following components makes up the Cisco BYOD solution. See Figure 4-1 for an idea about where each respective Cisco component fits in topologically within the overall Cisco BYOD solution:

- **BYOD devices:** These are the corporate-owned and personally owned endpoints that require access to the corporate network regardless of their physical location. This physical location can be within the corporate campus, the branch office, the home office, or from a public location such as a coffee shop or hotel. BYOD devices include laptops, smartphones, tablets, e-readers, and notebooks.

- **Wireless access points (AP):** Cisco wireless APs provide wireless network connectivity to the corporate network for both corporate-owned and personally owned BYOD devices. These APs can be physically located in the corporate campus, the branch office environment, or in the home offices of the employees.

- **Wireless LAN (WLAN) controllers:** *Cisco WLAN controllers (WLC)* serve as a centralized point for the configuration, management, and monitoring of the Cisco WLAN solution. WLCs are used to implement and enforce the security requirements for the BYOD solution that map back to an organization's security policies. The WLC works with the Cisco *Identity Services Engine (ISE)* to enforce both authentication and authorization policies on each of the BYOD endpoints that require connectivity to the corporate network, both direct and remotely.

- **Identity Services Engine (ISE):** The Cisco ISE is a critical piece to the Cisco BYOD solution. It is the cornerstone of the *authentication, authorization, and accounting (AAA)* requirements for endpoint access, which are governed by the security policies put forth by the organization.

- **Cisco AnyConnect Secure Mobility Client:** The Cisco AnyConnect Client provides connectivity for end users who need access to the corporate network. For users within the corporate campus, branch, and home offices, the AnyConnect Client leverages 802.1X to provide secure access to the corporate network. For users who are using public Internet access (coffee shops, hotels, and so on), the AnyConnect Client provides secure VPN connectivity, including posture checking, for the user's BYOD device.

- **Integrated Services Routers (ISR):** Cisco ISRs will be used in the Cisco BYOD solution to provide WAN and Internet access for the branch offices and Internet access for home office environments. In addition, the ISR will provide both wired and WLAN connectivity in the branch office environments. Finally, the ISRs can be leveraged to provide VPN connectivity for mobile devices that are part of the BYOD solution.

- **Aggregation Services Routers (ASR):** Cisco Aggregation Services Routers (ASR) provide WAN and Internet access at the corporate campus and serve as aggregation points for all the branch and home office networks connecting back to the corporate campus for the Cisco BYOD solution.

- **Cloud Web Security (CWS):** Formerly ScanSafe, Cisco Cloud Web Security (CWS) provides enhanced security for all the BYOD solution endpoints while they access Internet websites using publicly available wireless hotspots and 3G, 4G, and 4G LTE mobile networks.

- **Adaptive Security Appliance (ASA):** The Cisco ASA provides all the standard security functions for the BYOD solution at the Internet edge. In addition to traditional firewall and *intrusion prevention system (IPS)* functions, the ASA also serves as a VPN termination point for mobile devices connecting over the Internet from home offices, branch offices, public wireless networks, and 3G/4G/4G LTE mobile networks.

> **NOTE**   The ASA serves as the primary VPN termination point in the program described here, but other platforms and technologies can provide VPN access in a BYOD solution.

- **RSA SecurID:** The RSA SecurID server provides *one-time password (OTP)* generation and logging for users that access network devices and other applications which require OTP authentication.

- **Active Directory:** The *Active Directory (AD)* server enforces access control to the network, to servers, and to applications. It restricts access to those users with valid authentication credentials.

- **Certificate authority:** The *certificate authority (CA)* server provides for, among other things, the onboarding of endpoints that meet certificate requirements for access to the corporate network. The CA server ensures that only devices with corporate certificates can access the corporate network.

Mobile Device Management

The function of mobile device managers, also known as *mobile device management (MDM)*, is to deploy, manage, and monitor the mobile devices that make up the Cisco BYOD solution. These devices consist not only of mobile phones, smartphones, and tablets but also notebooks, laptops, and any other user devices that connect back to the corporate network and that can physically be moved from the office to the home, hotels, and other remote locations offering public Internet connectivity. Specific functions provided by MDM include the following:

- Enforcement of a PIN lock (that is, locking a device after a set threshold of failed login attempts has been reached).

- Enforcement of strong passwords for all BYOD devices. Strong password policies can also be enforced by an MDM, reducing the likelihood of brute-force attacks.

- Detection of attempts to "jailbreak" or "root" BYOD devices, specifically smartphones, and then attempting to use these compromised devices on the corporate network. MDM can be used to detect these types of actions and immediately restrict a device's access to the network or other corporate assets.

- Enforcement of data encryption requirements based on an organization's security policies and regulatory requirements. MDM can ensure that only devices that support data encryption and have it enabled can access the network and corporate content.

- Provide the ability to remotely wipe a stolen or lost BYOD device so that all data is completely removed.

- Administration and execution of *data loss prevention (DLP)* for BYOD devices. DLP prevents authorized users from doing careless or malicious things with critical data.

MDM Deployment Options

Within the BYOD solution, there are generally two available options for deployment of MDM, as described in the sections that follow.

On-Premise MDM Deployment

In an on-premise deployment, MDM application software is installed on servers that are located within the corporate data center and are completely supported and maintained by the network staff of the corporation.

The benefits of having an on-premise MDM solution include greater control over management of the BYOD solution, a potentially higher degree of security, particularly with respect to intellectual property, and, depending on the vertical in which the organization resides, an easier means of meeting certain regulatory compliance.

The on-premise MDM solution diagram shown in Figure 4-2 consists of the following topology and network components:

■ **Data center:** In addition to the core and distribution layer switches, the data center consists of the Cisco ISE to enforce posture assessment and access control as well as DNS/ DHCP servers to provide DNS/DHCP services for network connectivity, a CA server to enable onboarding of endpoints that meet certificate requirements for access to the corporate network, and an AD server that restricts access to only those users with valid authentication credentials.

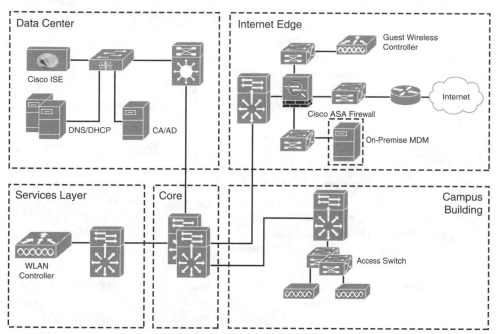

Figure 4-2   *Diagram of On-Premise MDM*

■ **Internet edge:** The Internet edge, in addition to providing connectivity to the public Internet, includes an ASA firewall to enforce security controls for all traffic going to and coming from the Internet. Also located in the Internet edge layer is a WLC, which is dedicated to any of the APs in the network to which guest users can connect. The last key component in the Internet edge layer is the on-premise MDM, which provides all the policies and profiles, digital certificates, applications, data, and configuration settings for all the BYOD devices that require connectivity to the corporate network.

■ **Services:** In Figure 4-2, this module contains the WLC for all APs to which the corporate users connect; however, any other network-based services required for the corporate network (for example, *Network Time Protocol [NTP]*) can potentially be found within the Services module.

■ **Core:** There are no other functions served by the Core module for the BYOD solution beyond what it normally provides. The Core serves as the main distribution and routing point for all network traffic traversing the corporate network environment.

■ **Campus building:** A distribution switch provides the main ingress/egress point for all network traffic entering and exiting from the campus environment. All users requiring network connectivity within the campus building do so through either hardwired connections to the access switches or via WLAN access to the corporate APs.

Cloud-Based MDM Deployment

In a cloud-based MDM deployment, MDM application software is hosted by a managed service provider who is solely responsible for the deployment, management, and maintenance of the BYOD solution.

The benefits of having a cloud-based MDM solution include a much more simplified solution from a customer perspective because the customer is no longer responsible for configuring, operating, and maintaining the MDM software. Giving up this control, however, brings with it some potential concerns with the overall security of the solution. The cloud-based solution also brings with it greater scalability, flexibility, and speed of deployment over an on-premise MDM solution.

The cloud-based MDM solution diagram shown in Figure 4-3 consists of the following topology and network components:

■ **Data Center:** In addition to the core and distribution layer switches, the data center consists of the Cisco ISE to enforce posture assessment and access control, in addition to DNS/DHCP servers to provide DNS/DHCP services for network connectivity, a CA server to enable onboarding of endpoints that meet certificate requirements for access to the corporate network, and an AD server that restricts access to only those users with valid authentication credentials.

■ **Internet edge:** The Internet edge, in addition to providing connectivity to the public Internet, includes an ASA firewall to enforce security controls for all traffic going to and coming from the Internet. Also located in the Internet edge layer is a WLC that is dedicated to any of the APs in the network to which guest users can connect.

■ **WAN:** The WAN module, which you didn't see within the on-premise MDM solution, serves three primary functions for the BYOD solution: (1) It provides MPLS VPN connectivity for the branch office back to corporate network, (2) Internet access for the branch office, and (3) access to the cloud-based MDM functionality. As with the on-premise solution, the cloud-based MDM provides all the policies and profiles, digital certificates, applications, data, and configuration settings for all of the BYOD devices that require connectivity to the corporate network.

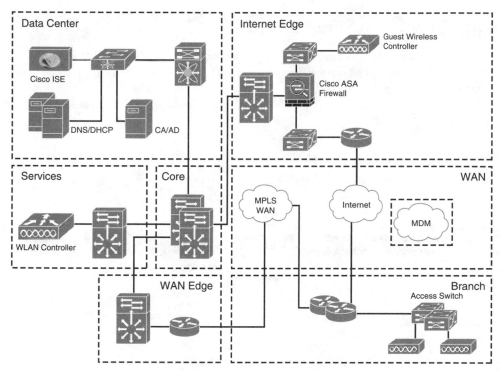

Figure 4-3 *Diagram of Cloud-Based MDM*

■ **WAN edge:** The primary function of the WAN edge is to serve as the ingress/egress point for the MPLS WAN traffic entering from and exiting to the branch office environment.

■ **Services:** In Figure 4-3, this module contains the WLC for all APs to which the corporate users connect; however, any other network-based services required for the corporate network (for example, NTP) can potentially be found within the Services module.

■ **Core:** There are no other functions served by the Core module for the BYOD solution beyond what it normally provides. The Core serves as the main distribution and routing point for all network traffic traversing the corporate network environment.

■ **Branch office:** In Figure 4-3, a pair of routers provides the main ingress/egress point for all network traffic entering and exiting from the branch office environment. All users requiring network connectivity within the branch office do so through either hardwired connections to the access switches or via WLAN access to the corporate APs.

Exam Preparation Tasks

This chapter covered the concept of bring your own device, some of the business drivers behind BYOD solutions, and an overview of the BYOD architecture, including several components that make up the BYOD solution. The chapter concluded with a description of the MDM function and provided two examples of MDM deployment models: on-premise and cloud-based.

Review All the Key Topics

Review the most important topics from this chapter, denoted with a Key Topic icon. Table 4-2 lists these key topics.

Table 4-2   Key Topics

Key Topic Element	Description	Page Number
Section	Bring Your Own Device Fundamentals	73
Section	BYOD Architecture Framework	74
Figure 4-1	High-Level BYOD Solution Architecture	74
Section	Mobile Device Management	76

Complete the Tables and Lists from Memory

Print a copy of Appendix C, "Memory Tables," (found on the CD) or at least the section for this chapter, and complete the tables and lists from memory. Appendix D, "Memory Tables Answer Key," also on the CD, includes completed tables and lists so that you can check your work. This chapter has no applicable tables.

Define Key Terms

Define the following key terms from this chapter, and check your answers in the glossary:

bring your own device (BYOD), BYOD devices, Identity Services Engine (ISE), Cisco AnyConnect Secure Mobility Client, mobile device management (MDM), on-premise MDM deployment, cloud-based MDM deployment

This chapter covers the following topics:

Understanding VPNs and why we use them

Cryptography basic components

Public key infrastructure

Putting the pieces of PKI to work

CHAPTER 5

Fundamentals of VPN Technology and Cryptography

Many organizations deploy *virtual private networks (VPN)* to provide data integrity, authentication, and data encryption to ensure confidentiality of the packets sent over an unprotected network or the Internet. VPNs are designed to avoid the cost of unnecessary leased lines. Understanding why VPNs are important and the underlying building blocks that make them work so well is the focus of this chapter.

"Do I Know This Already?" Quiz

The "Do I Know This Already?" quiz helps you determine your level of knowledge of this chapter's topics before you begin. Table 5-1 details the major topics discussed in this chapter and their corresponding quiz questions.

Table 5-1 "Do I Know This Already?" Section-to-Question Mapping

Foundation Topics Section	Questions
Understanding VPNs and Why We Use Them	1–4
Cryptography Basic Components	5–8
Public Key Infrastructure	9–16
Putting the Pieces of PKI to Work	17–18

1. What algorithms in a VPN provide the confidentiality? (Choose all that apply.)

    a. MD5

    b. SHA-1

    c. AES

    d. 3DES

2. A remote user needs to access the corporate network from a hotel room from a laptop. What type of VPN is used for this?

    a. Site-to-site VPN

    b. Dial-up VPN

    c. PPP VPN

    d. Remote-access VPN

3. Which type of VPN technology is likely to be used in a site-to-site VPN?

   a. SSL

   b. TLS

   c. HTTPS

   d. IPsec

4. Which two of the following are benefits of VPNs?

   a. Hashing

   b. Confidentiality

   c. Diffie-Hellman

   d. Data integrity

5. Which of the following are symmetrical encryption ciphers? (Choose all that apply.)

   a. SHA1

   b. AES

   c. RSA

   d. 3DES

6. What is the primary difference between a hash and Hashed Message Authentication Code (HMAC)?

   a. Keys

   b. MD5

   c. SHA1

   d. AES

7. What is used to encrypt the hash in a digital signature?

   a. Sender's public key

   b. Sender's private key

   c. Receiver's public key

   d. Receiver's private key

8. What are valid options to protect data in motion with or without a full VPN? (Choose all that apply.)

   a. TLS

   b. SSL

   c. HTTPS

   d. IPsec

9. Why is the public key in a typical public-private key pair referred to as public?

   a. Because the public already has it.

   b. Because it is shared publicly.

   c. Because it is a well-known algorithm that is published.

   d. The last name of the creator was publica, which is Latin for public.

10. What is the key component used to create a digital signature?

    a. Ink

    b. Public key

    c. Private key

    d. AES

11. What is the key component used to verify a digital signature?

    a. Sender's public key

    b. Receiver's public key

    c. AES

    d. One-time PAD

12. What is another name for a hash that has been encrypted with a private key?

    a. MD5

    b. SHA-1

    c. AES

    d. Digital signature

13. What are the primary responsibilities for a certificate authority (CA)? (Choose all that apply.)

    a. Verification of certificates

    b. Issuing identity certificates

    c. Maintaining client's private keys

    d. Tracking identity certificates

14. Which of the following is *not* a way for a client to check to see whether a certificate has been revoked?

    a. Look at the lifetime of the certificate itself

    b. CRL

    c. OSCP

    d. LDAP

15. Which of the following could be found in a typical identity certificate? (Choose all that apply.)

    a. CRL locations

    b. Validity date

    c. Public key of the certificate owner

    d. Serial number

16. Which standard format is used to request a digital certificate from a CA?

   a. PKCS#7

   b. PKCS#10

   c. LDAP

   d. TLS/SSL/HTTPS

17. When obtaining the initial root certificate, what method should be used for validation of the certificate?

   a. Sender's public key

   b. Telephone

   c. HTTPS/TLS/SSL

   d. Receiver's private key

18. Which method, when supported by both the client and the CA, is the simplest to use when implementing identity certificates on the client?

   a. PKCS#7

   b. PKCS#10

   c. SCEP

   d. LDAP

Foundation Topics

Understanding VPNs and Why We Use Them

This section examines the reasons why VPNs are so important and what types of VPNs are available to deploy and why a specific type of VPN is appropriate for a given business need.

What Is a VPN?

If we break down the term *virtual private network* into its individual components, we could say that a network allows connectivity between two devices. Those two devices could be computers on the same local-area network or could be connected over a wide-area network. In either case, a network is providing the basic connectivity between the two. The word *virtual* in VPN refers to a logical connection between the two devices. For example, one user may be connected to the Internet in Raleigh, North Carolina, and another user may be connected to the Internet in New York, and we could build a logical network, or virtual network, between the two devices using the Internet as our transport mechanism. The letter *P* in VPN refers to *private*. The virtual network we could create between our two users in Raleigh and New York would be private between those two parties. So, there are the basics for VPN, a virtual private network.

Unfortunately, if we did have a VPN established between two devices over the Internet, what would prevent an individual who had access to the packets from eavesdropping on the conversation? The answer is not much, by default. So, in addition to most VPNs, we add the ingredients of confidentiality and data integrity so that anyone who is eavesdropping cannot make sense of the data because it is encrypted, and they do not have the keys required to decrypt or unlock the data to see what the data actually is. The confidentiality provided by the encryption could also represent the *P* in VPNs. We also use integrity checking to make sure that our VPN is correctly seeing the packets as they were sent from the other side of the VPN and that they are not being altered or manipulated maliciously along the path.

Using the example of the user in New York and Raleigh, why would we ever want to use a VPN between the two? We do have other options for connectivity. We could purchase each user a dedicated WAN connection from New York to Raleigh. Each user could connect to his local side and communicate with each other over the dedicated link. One of the obvious problems with this is cost. It is much cheaper to connect the user to the Internet through a local service provider than to purchase a dedicated circuit that goes to only one other destination.

Another benefit of using a VPN is scalability. If 10 or 20 more new users need to connect to the corporate headquarters, we can provide users access to the Internet via their local service providers (*digital subscriber line [DSL]*, cable modem, and so on). Leveraging the single Internet connection from the headquarters site, we could then simply build logical VPNs using the Internet for the connectivity.

5

Types of VPNs

Based on the definition of a virtual private network, the following could be considered VPN technologies:

- **IPsec:** Implements security of IP packets at Layer 3 of the OSI model, and can be used for site-to-site VPNs and remote-access VPNs.

- **SSL:** Secure Sockets Layer implements security of TCP sessions over encrypted SSL tunnels of the OSI model, and can be used for remote-access VPNs (as well as being used to securely visit a web server that supports it via HTTPS).

- **MPLS:** Multiprotocol Label Switching and MPLS Layer 3 VPNs are provided by a service provider to allow a company with two or more sites to have logical connectivity between the sites using the service provider network for transport. This is also a type of VPN (called *MPLS L3VPN*), but there is no encryption by default. IPsec could be used on top of the MPLS VPN to add confidentiality (through encryption) and the other benefits of IPsec to protect the Layer 3 packets. MPLS L3VPNs are not the primary type of VPNs we focus on for the rest of this chapter and book. The primary VPNs that provide encryption, data integrity, authentication of who the peer is on the other end of the VPN, and so on use IPsec or SSL.

Two Main Types of VPNs

There are two major categories into which VPNs could be placed: remote-access and site-to-site. The following are details about each, including when they might be used:

- **Remote-access VPNs:** Some users might need to build a VPN connection from their individual computer to the corporate headquarters (or to the destination they want to connect to). This is referred to as a *remote-access VPN connection*. Remote-access VPNs can use IPsec or *Secure Sockets Layer (SSL)* technologies for their VPN. Many Cisco customers use the Cisco AnyConnect client for remote access SSL VPNs. SSL VPN use is more prevalent, even though the Cisco AnyConnect client also supports IPsec (IKEv2).

- **Site-to-site VPNs:** The other main VPN implementation is by companies that may have two or more sites that they want to connect securely together (likely using the Internet) so that each site can communicate with the other site or sites. This implementation is called a *site-to-site VPN*. Site-to-site VPNs traditionally use a collection of VPN technologies called *IPsec*.

Figure 5-1 shows an example of site-to-site and remote-access VPNs. The Cisco ASA in the Raleigh, North Carolina, corporate headquarters is configured to accept remote-access SSL VPN connections, in addition to a site-to-site tunnel with a branch in San Jose, California.

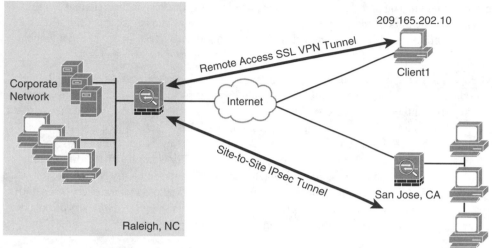

Figure 5-1 *Example of Remote-Access and Site-to-Site VPNs*

Main Benefits of VPNs

The main benefits of using either remote-access or site-to-site VPNs include the following:

- Confidentiality
- Data integrity
- Authentication
- Antireplay protection

We take a closer look at each of these four items right now.

Confidentiality

Confidentiality means that only the intended parties can understand the data that is sent. Any party that eavesdrops may see the actual packets, but the contents of the packet or the payload are scrambled (also called *cipher text*) and meaningless to anyone who cannot unlock or decrypt the data.

Consider the practical example shown in Example 5-1.

Example 5-1 *A Secret Message, Encrypted*

```
Tp uijt jt uif tfdsfu nfttbhf.   Ju jt fbtz up ef-fodszqu jg zpv lopx uif lfz.
```

Take a moment and see whether you can figure out what the message means, and imagine that this is the payload of a packet being sent over a VPN and that you have intercepted the packet and are trying to understand or make sense of it. The major goal of a VPN is confidentiality, and it is accomplished by the sender encrypting the data or the packet that needs to be protected and then sending it over the VPN. The receiver of the packet or data then faces the same challenge as the eavesdropper, in that the data must be decrypted to make sense out of it. The algorithms and formulas for encrypting data are publicly available and are well known. The part that makes the message secret is the key or "secret" that is used to encrypt the data. If the sender and the receiver both know the key that is used, they can encrypt and decrypt information back and forth using the same key or keys, and anyone in the middle who does not know the key or keys that were used cannot decrypt.

Going back to the encrypted message, if a "symmetric" algorithm was used, then if I gave you the key that I used to encrypt it, you could use that same key to decrypt it. So, here's the key (pun intended) for the encrypted example: Every letter in the encrypted message is one off of the real letter in the alphabet. So, take each letter, and replace it with the letter before it in the alphabet and you will have decrypted the message. The purpose of this exercise is to demonstrate the concept of how confidentiality is implemented through some type of an encryption process, and how having the keys comes in handy for the person who is decrypting. An encryption algorithm that uses the same key or keys for encryption and the exact same key or keys for decryption is an example of a *symmetrical* encryption algorithm. Example 5-2 shows the decrypted message from Example 5-1.

Example 5-2 *Results of Secret Message When Using the Correct "Key"*

```
"So this is the secret message.   It is easy to de-encrypt if you know the key."
```

Data Integrity

If two devices are communicating over a VPN, another important factor about the data that is being sent is to make sure it is accurate from end to end. If an attacker injects bits or data into the packets of a VPN session, data integrity could suffer if the modification of the data goes undetected.

Authentication

A VPN tunnel is fantastic in that you can encrypt data and verify that data has not been modified while in transit. But what if you have established a VPN connection, also called a VPN tunnel, directly to the attacker's computer? Being able to validate or authenticate the device that you are connected to is an important aspect of a good VPN. You can authenticate the peer at the other end of the VPN tunnel in several different ways, including the following:

- Pre-shared keys used for authentication only
- Public and private key pairs used for authentication only
- User authentication (in combination with remote-access VPNs)

Antireplay Protection

If an attacker watches your VPN traffic and captures it with the intent to replay it back and fool one of the VPN peers into believing that the peer trying to connect is a legitimate peer, an attacker might be able to build a VPN pretending to be a different device. To solve that, most implementations of VPNs have an antireplay functionality built in. This just means that once a VPN packet has been sent and accounted for, that exact same VPN packet is not valid the second time in the VPN session.

Cryptography Basic Components

You now know that confidentiality is a function of encryption, data integrity is a function of hashing, and authentication is the process of proving the identity of the other side of the tunnel. Now it is time to take a look at how those methods are implemented and the choices you have for each.

This section discusses the basic components of cryptography, including algorithms for hashing, encryption, and key management, which may be used by VPNs.

 ## Ciphers and Keys

Understanding the terminology is a large part of understanding any technology, so let's begin with some fundamentals.

Ciphers

A *cipher* is a set of rules, which can also be called an *algorithm*, about how to perform encryption or decryption. Literally hundreds of encryption algorithms are available, and there are likely many more that are proprietary and used for special purposes such as government and national security.

Common methods that ciphers use include the following:

- **Substitution:** This type of cipher substitutes one character for another. The example earlier used a simple cipher that substituted each letter from the alphabet with the previous letter of the alphabet. To make it more challenging, we could have shifted more than just a single character and only chose certain letters to substitute. The exact method of substitution could be referred to as the *key*. If both parties involved in the VPN understand the key, they can both encrypt and decrypt data.

- **Polyalphabetic:** This is similar to substitution, but instead of using a single alphabet, it could use multiple alphabets and switch between them by some trigger character in the encoded message.

- **Transposition:** This uses many different options, including the rearrangement of letters. For example, if we have the message "This is secret," we could write it out (top to bottom, left to right) as shown in Example 5-3.

Example 5-3   *Transposition Example*

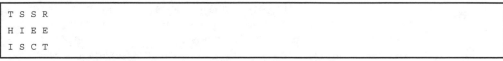

```
T S  S R
H I  E E
I S  C T
```

We then encrypt it as RETCSIHTSSEI, which is starting at the top right and going around like a clock, spiraling inward. To know how to encrypt/decrypt this correctly, we need the correct key.

Keys

The key in Example 5-3 refers to the instructions for how to reassemble the characters. In this case, it begins at the top-right corner and moves clockwise and spirals inward.

A *one-time pad (OTP)* is a good example of a key that is only used once. Using this method, if we want to encrypt a 32-bit message, we use a 32-bit key, also called the *pad*, which is used one time only. Each bit from the pad is mathematically computed with a corresponding bit from our message, and the results are our cipher text, or encrypted content. The key in this case is the one-time use pad. The pad must also be known by the receiver if he wants to decrypt the message. (Another use of the acronym OTP is for a user's one-time password, which is a different topic than the OTP.)

Block and Stream Ciphers

Encryption algorithms can operate on blocks of data at a time, or bits and bytes of data, based on the type of cipher. Let's compare the two methods.

Block Ciphers

A block cipher is a *symmetric* key (same key to encrypt and decrypt) cipher that operates on a group of bits called a *block*. A block cipher encryption algorithm may take a 64-bit block of plain text and generate a 64-bit block of cipher text. With this type of encryption, the same key to encrypt is also used to decrypt. Examples of symmetrical block cipher algorithms include the following:

- Advanced Encryption Standard (AES)
- Triple Digital Encryption Standard (3DES)
- Blowfish
- Digital Encryption Standard (DES)
- International Data Encryption Algorithm (IDEA)

Block ciphers may add padding in cases where there is not enough data to encrypt to make a full block size. This might result is a very small amount of wasted overhead, because the small padding would be processed by the cipher along with the real data.

Stream Ciphers

A *stream cipher* is a *symmetric* key cipher (same key to encrypt as decrypt), where each bit of plaintext data to be encrypted is done 1 bit at a time against the bits of the key stream, also called a *cipher digit stream*. The resulting output is a ciphertext stream. Because a cipher stream does not have to fit in a given block size, there may be slightly less overhead than a block cipher that is requiring padding to complete a block size.

Symmetric and Asymmetric Algorithms

As you build your vocabulary, the words *symmetric* and *asymmetric* are important ones to differentiate. Let's look at the options of each and identify which of these requires the most CPU overhead and which one is used for bulk data encryption.

Symmetric

As mentioned previously, a *symmetric* encryption algorithm, also known as a *symmetrical cipher*, uses the same key to encrypt the data and decrypt the data. Two devices connected via a VPN both need the key or keys to successfully encrypt and decrypt the data that is protected using a symmetric encryption algorithm. Common examples of symmetric encryption algorithms include the following:

- DES
- 3DES
- AES
- IDEA
- RC2, RC4, RC5, RC6
- Blowfish

Symmetrical encryption algorithms are used for most of the data that we protect in VPNs today. The reason we use symmetrical to encrypt the bulk of our data is because it is much faster to use a symmetrical encryption algorithm and takes less CPU for the same symmetrical encryption algorithm than it would for an asymmetrical algorithm. As with all encryption, the more difficult the key, the more difficult it is for someone who does not have the key to intercept and understand the data. We usually refer to keys with VPNs by their length. A longer key means better security. A typical key length is 112 bits to 256 bits. The minimum key length should be at least 128 bits for symmetrical encryption algorithms to be considered fairly safe. Again, bigger is better.

Asymmetric

An example of an *asymmetric* algorithm is public key algorithms. There is something magical about them. Instead of using the same key for encrypting and decrypting, we use two different keys that mathematically work together as a pair. Let's call these keys the *public key* and *private key*. Together they make a *key pair*. Let's put these keys to use with an analogy.

Imagine a huge shipping container that has a special lock with two keyholes (one large keyhole and one smaller keyhole). With this magical shipping container, if we use the small keyhole with its respective key to lock the container, the only way to unlock it is to use the big keyhole with its larger key. Another option is to initially lock the container using the big key in the big keyhole, and then the only way to unlock it is to use the small key in the small keyhole. (I told you it was magic). This analogy explains the interrelationship between the public key and its corresponding private key. (I'll let you decide which one you want to call the big key and which one you want to call the little key.) There is a very high CPU cost when using key pairs to lock and unlock data. For that reason, we use asymmetric algorithms sparingly. Instead of using them to encrypt our bulk data, we use asymmetric algorithms for things such as authenticating a VPN peer or generating keying material that we could use for our symmetrical algorithms. Both of these tasks are infrequent compared to encrypting all the user packets (which happens consistently).

One reason this is called *public key cryptography* is that we allow one of these keys to be published and available to anyone who wants to use it (the public key). The other key in the key pair is the private key, and this private key is known only to the device that owns the public-private key pair. An example of using a public-private key pair is visiting a secure website. In the background, the public-private key pair of the server is being used for security of the session. Your PC has access to the public key, and the server is the only one that knows its private key.

Examples of asymmetrical algorithms include the following:

- **RSA:** Named after Rivest, Shamir, and Adleman, who created the algorithm. The primary use of this asymmetrical algorithm today is for authentication. It is also known as *public key cryptography standard (PKCS) #1*. The key length may be from 512 to 2048, and a minimum size for good security is at least 1024. Regarding security, bigger is better.

- **DH:** Diffie-Hellman key exchange protocol. DH is an asymmetrical algorithm that allows two devices to negotiate and establish shared secret keying material (keys) over an untrusted network. The interesting thing about DH is that although the algorithm itself is asymmetrical, the keys generated by the exchange are symmetrical keys that can then be used with symmetrical algorithms such as *Triple Digital Encryption Standard (3DES)* and *Advanced Encryption Standard (AES)*.

- **ElGamal (second character is an L):** This asymmetrical encryption system is based on the DH exchange.

- **DSA:** Digital Signature Algorithm was developed by the U.S. National Security Agency.

- **ECC:** Elliptic Curve Cryptography.

Asymmetrical algorithms require more CPU processing power than a symmetrical algorithm. Asymmetrical algorithms, however, are more secure. A typical key length used in asymmetrical algorithms can be anywhere between 2048 and 4096. A key length that is shorter than 2048 is considered unreliable or not as secure as a longer key.

A commonly used asymmetrical algorithm used for authentication is RSA (as in RSA digital signatures).

Hashes

Hashing is a method used to verify data integrity. A cryptographic hash function is a process that takes a block of data and creates a small fixed-sized hash value. It is a one-way function, meaning that if two different computers take the same data and run the same hash function, they should get the same fixed-sized hash value (for example, perhaps a 12-bit long hash). (*Message digest 5 algorithm [MD5]* is an example.) It is not possible (at least not realistically) to generate the same hash from a different block of data. This is referred to as *collision resistance*. The result of the hash is a fixed-length small string of data, and is sometimes referred to as the *digest*, *message digest*, or simply the *hash*.

An example of using a hash to verify integrity is the sender running a hash algorithm on each packet and attaching that hash to the packet. The receiver runs the same hash against the packet and compares his results against the results the sender had (which were attached to the packet, as well). If the hash generated matches the hash that was sent, we know that the entire packet is intact. If a single bit of the hashed portion of the packet is modified, the hash calculated by the receiver will not match, and the receiver will know that the packet had a problem, specifically with the integrity of the packet.

The three most popular types of hashes are as follows:

- **Message digest 5 (MD5):** This creates a 128-bit digest.
- **Secure Hash Algorithm 1 (SHA-1):** This creates a 160-bit digest.
- **Secure Hash Algorithm 2 (SHA-2):** Options include a digest between 224 bits and 512 bits.

With encryption and cryptography, and now hashing, bigger is better, and more bits equals better security.

Hashed Message Authentication Code

Hashed Message Authentication Code (HMAC) uses the mechanism of hashing, but it kicks it up a notch. Instead of using a hash that anyone can calculate, it includes in its calculation a secret key of some type. Then only the other party who also knows the secret key and can calculate the resulting hash can correctly verify the hash. When this mechanism is used, an attacker who is eavesdropping and intercepting packets cannot inject or remove data from those packets without being noticed because he cannot recalculate the correct hash for the modified packet because he does not have the key or keys used for the calculation.

Digital Signatures

When you sign something, it often represents a commitment to follow through, or at least prove that you are who you say you are. In the world of cryptography, a digital signature provides three core benefits:

- Authentication
- Data integrity
- Nonrepudiation

Digital Signatures in Action

One of the best ways to understand how a digital signature operates is to remember what you learned in the previous sections about public and private key pairs, hashing, and encryption. Digital signatures involve each of these elements. Here's the play by play. Bob and Lois are two devices that want to establish a VPN connection to each other, and to do so they want to use digital signatures to verify each other to make sure they are talking to the right device. Both the devices want to verify each other, but for simplicity will focus on one device: Bob wanting to prove its identity to the other device Lois. (This could also be phrased as Lois asking Bob to prove Bob's identity.)

5

As a little setup beforehand, you should know that both Bob and Lois have generated public-private key pairs, and they both have been given digital certificates from a common *certificate authority (CA)*. A CA is a trusted entity that hands out digital certificates (more on that later). If you and I were to open a digital certificate, we would find the name of the entity (for example, Bob). We would find Bob's public key (which Bob gave to the CA when he applied for his digital certificate). There would also be a digital signature of the CA. Both Bob and Lois trust the CA and have both received their certificates. Okay, now back to the story.

Bob takes a packet and generates a hash. Bob then takes this small hash and encrypts it using Bob's private key. (Think of this as a shipping container, and we are using the small key in the small keyhole to lock the data.) We attach this encrypted hash to the packet and send it to Lois. There is a fancy name for this encrypted hash: a *digital signature*.

When Lois receives this packet, she looks at the encrypted hash that was sent and decrypts it using Bob's public key. (Think of this as a big keyhole and the big key being used to unlock the data.) She then sets the decrypted hash off to the side for one moment and she runs the same hash algorithm on the packet she just received. If the hash she just calculated matches the hash she received (after she decrypted it using the sender's public key), she knows two things. She knows the only person who could have encrypted that was Bob with Bob's private key, and that data integrity on the packet is solid, because if 1 bit had changed the hash would not have matched. This process is called *authentication*, using digital signatures, and normally happens in both directions with an IPsec VPN tunnel if the peers are using digital signatures for authentication, referred to as *rsa-signatures* in the configuration.

One might ask, okay so how did Lois get Bob's key (Bob's public key) to begin with? The answer is that Bob and Lois also exchanged digital certificates, which contained each other's public keys. Bob and Lois do not just trust any certificates, but they do trust certificates that are digitally signed by a CA that they trust. This also implies that to verify digital signatures from the CA, both Bob and Lois would also need the CA's public key. Most browsers today have the built-in certificates and public keys for the mainstream CAs on the Internet today.

Key Management

Key management is huge in the world of cryptography. We have symmetric keys that can be used with symmetric algorithms such as hashing and encryption. We have asymmetric keys such as public-private key pairs that can be used with asymmetric algorithms such as digital signatures, among other things. We could say that the key to security with all of these algorithms that we have taken a look at is the keys themselves.

Key management deals with generating keys, verifying keys, exchanging keys, storing keys, and at the end of their lifetime, destroying keys. An example of why this is critical is if two devices that want to establish a VPN session send the encryption keys over at the beginning of their session in plain text. If that happens, an eavesdropper who sees the keys could go ahead and use them to change cipher text into understandable data, which would result in a lack of confidentiality within the VPN.

Keyspace refers to all the possible key values for a key. The bigger the key, the more secure the algorithm will be. The only negative of having an extremely long key is that the longer the key, the more the CPU is used for the decryption and encryption of data.

Next-Generation Encryption Protocols

The industry is always looking for new algorithms for encryption, authentication, digital signatures, and key exchange to meet escalating security and performance requirements. The U.S. government selected and recommended a set of cryptographic standards called Suite B because it provides a complete suite of algorithms that are designed to meet future security needs. Suite B has been approved for protecting classified information at both the secret and top secret levels. Cisco participated in the development of some of these standards. The Suite B *next-generation encryption (NGE)* includes algorithms for authenticated encryption, digital signatures, key establishment, and cryptographic hashing, as listed here:

- *Elliptic Curve Cryptography (ECC)* replaces RSA signatures with the ECDSA algorithm, and replaces the DH key exchange with ECDH. ECDSA is an elliptic curve variant of the DSA algorithm, which has been a standard since 1994. The new key exchange uses DH with P-256 and P-384 curves.

- AES in the *Galois/Counter Mode (GCM)* of operation.

- ECC Digital Signature Algorithm.

- SHA-256, SHA-384, and SHA-512.

IPsec and SSL

IPsec is a suite of protocols used to protect IP packets and has been around for decades. It is in use today for both remote-access VPNs and site-to-site VPNs. SSL is the new kid on the block in its application with remote-access VPNs. Let's take a closer look at both of these options.

IPsec

IPsec is a collection of protocols and algorithms used to protect IP packets at Layer 3 (hence the name of *IP Security [IPsec]*). IPsec provides the core benefits of confidentiality through encryption, data integrity through hashing and HMAC, and authentication using digital signatures or using a *pre-shared key (PSK)* that is just for the authentication, similar to a password. IPsec also provides antireplay support. We take a closer look at IPsec in a later chapter, but here's a good preview of the coming attractions:

- **ESP and AH:** The two primary methods for implementing IPsec. The acronyms stand for *Encapsulating Security Payload (ESP)*, which can do all the features of IPsec, and *Authentication Header (AH)*, which can do many parts of the IPsec objectives, except for the important one of encryption of the data. For that reason, we do not frequently see AH being used.

- **Encryption algorithms for confidentiality:** DES, 3DES, AES.

- **Hashing algorithms for integrity:** MD5, SHA.

- **Authentication algorithms:** Pre-shared keys (PSK), RSA digital signatures.

- **Key management:** An example would be *Diffie-Hellman (DH)*, which can be used to dynamically generate symmetrical keys to be used by symmetrical algorithms; PKI, which supports the function of digital certificates issued by trusted CAs; and *Internet Key Exchange (IKE)*, which does a lot of the negotiating and management for us for IPsec to operate.

SSL

Transmitting information over a public network needs to be secured through encryption to prevent unauthorized access to that data. An example is going online to do banking. Not only do you want to avoid an attacker seeing your usernames, passwords, and codes, you also do not want an attacker to be able to modify the packets in transit during a transaction with the bank. It would seem that this would be a perfect opportunity for IPsec to be used to encrypt the data and perform integrity checking and authentication of the server you are connected to. Although it is true that IPsec could do all of this, there is not an IPsec client or software currently running on everybody's computer. Even if there were, not everyone has a digital certificate or a PSK that they could successfully use for authentication.

You can still benefit from the concept of encryption and authentication by using a different type of technology. This additional option is called *Secure Sockets Layer (SSL)*. The convenient thing about SSL is that almost every web browser on every computer supports it, so almost anyone who has a computer can use it.

To use SSL, the user connects to an SSL server, which is a fancy way of saying a web server that supports SSL, by using HTTPS rather than HTTP. An easy way to remember is that the *S* means *secure*. Depending on whom you talk to, SSL may also be labeled as *Transport Layer Security* or *TLS*. To the end user such as you or I, it represents a secure connection to the server, and to the correct server.

Even if the users does not type in HTTPS, the website could redirect the user behind the scenes to the correct URL. Once there, the browser requests that the web server identify itself. (Be aware that all of this that is about to happen is occurring in the background and does not require user intervention.) The server sends the browser a copy of its digital certificate, which may also be called an SSL certificate. When the browser receives the certificate, it checks whether it trusts the certificate. The browser decides whether it is trusted by looking at the digital signature of the CA that is on the certificate; using the method for verifying a digital signature discussed earlier, the browser determines the certificate is valid based on the signature of the CA (or is not valid). (If the signature is not valid, or at least if our browser does not think the certificate is valid, a pop-up is usually presented to the user asking whether the user wants to proceed.) This is where user training is important and users should be trained never to continue or accept a certificate that the browser does not trust.) Assuming the certificate is trusted, the browser now has access to the server's public key contained in the certificate.

Most of the time, the server does not require the browser to prove who it is. Instead, the web server uses some type of user authentication, such as a username or password as required, to verify who the user is.

After the authentication has been done, several additional exchanges occur between the browser and the server as they establish the encryption algorithm they will use and the keys that they will use to encrypt and decrypt the data. You learn more about that exact process in the chapter on PKI.

As mentioned previously, understanding the terminology is important for you in mastering VPN technologies. Table 5-2 describes VPN components, their functions, and examples of their implementation. Some of these terms are a review, whereas others are new. These concepts and their functions are repeated throughout the chapters on these topics to assist you in learning and applying these concepts.

Table 5-2   VPN Components

Component	Function	Examples of Use
Symmetrical encryption algorithms	Use the same key for encrypting and decrypting data.	DES, 3DES, AES, IDEA
Asymmetrical encryption	Uses a public and private key. One key encrypts the data, and the other key in the pair is used to decrypt.	RSA, Diffie-Hellman
Digital signature	Encryption of hash using private key, and decryption of hash with the sender's public key.	RSA signatures
Diffie-Hellman key exchange	Uses a public-private key pair asymmetrical algorithm, but creates final shared secrets (keys) that are then used by symmetrical algorithms.	Used as one of the many services of IPsec
Confidentiality	Encryption algorithms provide this by turning clear text into cipher text.	DES, 3DES, AES, RSA, IDEA
Data integrity	Validates data by comparing hash values.	MD5, SHA-1
Authentication	Verifies the peer's identity to the other peer.	PSKs, RSA signatures

Public Key Infrastructure

This section covers the moving parts and pieces involved with the public key infrastructure. This section presumes that you've read the previous sections regarding VPN technologies.

Public and Private Key Pairs

A *key pair* is a set of two keys that work in combination with each other as a team. In a typical key pair, you have one public key and one private key. The public key may be shared with everyone, and the private key is not shared with anyone. For example, the private key for a web server is known only to that specific web server. If you use the public key to encrypt data using an asymmetric encryption algorithm, the corresponding private key is used to decrypt the data. The inverse is also true. If you encrypt with the private key, you then decrypt with the corresponding public key. Another name for this asymmetric encryption is *public key cryptography* or *asymmetric key cryptography*. The uses for asymmetric algorithms are not limited to only authentication as in the case of the digital signature discussed in the previous sections, but that is one example of an asymmetrical algorithm.

RSA Algorithm, the Keys, and Digital Certificates

Keys are the secrets that allow cryptography to provide confidentiality. Let's take a closer look at the keys involved with RSA and how they are used.

Who Has Keys and a Digital Certificate?

With RSA digital signatures, with both parties intending on authenticating the other side, each party has a public-private key pair. Going back to the analogy in the previous sections, let's use two computers named Bob and Lois. They both generated their own public-private key pair, and they both enrolled with a *certificate authority (CA)*. That CA took each of their public keys and their names and IP addresses and created individual digital certificates, and the CA issued these certificates back to Bob and Lois, respectively. The CA also digitally signed each certificate.

How Two Parties Exchange Public Keys

When Bob and Lois want to authenticate each other, they send each other their digital certificates (or least a copy of them). Upon receiving the other party's digital certificate, they both verify the authenticity of the certificate by checking the signature of a CA that they currently trust. (When you talk about trusting a certificate authority, it really means that you know who the CA is and can verify that certificate authority's digital signature, by knowing the public key of that CA.)

Now that Bob and Lois both have each other's public keys, they can authenticate each other. This normally happens inside of a VPN tunnel in both directions (when RSA signatures are used for authentication). For the purpose of clarity, we focus on just one of these parties (for example, the computer Bob) proving its identity to computer Lois.

Creating a Digital Signature

Bob takes some data, generates a hash, and then encrypts the hash with Bob's private key. (Note that the private key has not been shared with anyone else; not even Bob's closest friends have it.) This encrypted hash is inserted to the packet and sent to Lois. This encrypted hash is Bob's digital signature.

Lois, having received the packet with the digital signature attached, first decodes or decrypts the encrypted hash using Bob's public key. She sets the decrypted hash to the side for a moment and runs a hash against the same data that Bob did previously. If the hash that Lois generates matches the decrypted hash, which was sent as a digital signature from Bob, she has just authenticated Bob. The reason is because only Bob has the private key used for the creation of his digital signature.

Certificate Authorities

A certificate authority is a computer or entity that creates and issues digital certificates. Inside of a digital certificate is information about the identity of a device, such as its IP address, *fully qualified domain name (FQDN)*, and the public key of that device. The CA takes requests from devices that supply all of that information (including the public key generated by the computer that is making the request) and generates a digital certificate, which the CA assigns a serial number to and signs the certificate with its own digital signature (the CA's signature). Also included in the final certificate is a URL that other devices can check to see whether this certificate has been revoked and the validity dates for the certificate (which is similar to the expiration date of food products). Also in the certificate is the information about the CA that issued the certificate and several other parameters used by PKI.

By using a third-party trusted certificate authority, the computers Bob and Lois can receive and verify identity certificates from each other (and thousands of others), as long as the certificates are signed by a CA that is trusted by Bob and Lois. Commercial CAs charge a fee to issue and maintain digital certificates. One benefit of using a commercial CA server to obtain digital certificates for your devices is that most web browsers maintain a list of the more common trusted public CA servers, and as a result anyone using a browser can verify the identity of your web server by default without having to modify the web browser at all. If a company wants to set up its own internal CA and then configure each of the end devices to trust the certificates issued by its internal CA, no commercial certificate authority is required, but the scope of that CA is limited to the company and its managed devices, because any devices outside of the company would not trust the company's internal CA by default.

Root and Identity Certificates

A digital certificate can be thought of as an electronic document that identifies a device or person. It includes information such as the name of a person or organization, their address, and the public key of that person or device. There are different types of certificates, including root certificates (which identify the CA), and identity certificates, which identify devices such as servers and other devices that want to participate in PKI.

Root Certificate

A *root certificate* contains the public key of the CA server and the other details about the CA server. Figure 5-2 shows an example of one.

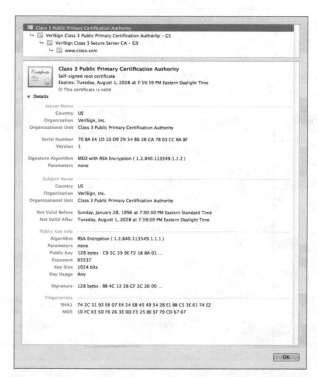

Figure 5-2 *Root Certificate Example*

The output in Figure 5-2 can be seen on most browsers, although the location might differ a bit depending on your browser vendor and version.

I recommend knowing the relevant parts of the certificate, including the following:

- **Serial number:** Issued and tracked by the CA that issued the certificate.

- **Issuer:** The CA that issued this certificate. (Even root certificates need to have their certificates issued from someone, perhaps even themselves.)

- **Validity dates:** The time window during which the certificate may be considered valid. If a local computer believes the date to be off by a few years, that same PC may consider the certificate invalid due to its own error about the time. Using *Network Time Protocol (NTP)* is a good idea to avoid this problem.

- **Subject of the certificate:** This includes the *organizational unit (OU)*, *organization (O)*, *country (C)*, and other details commonly found in an X.500 structured directory (more on that later in the chapter). The subject of the root certificate is the CA itself. The subject for a client's identity certificate is the client.

- **Public key:** The contents of the public key and the length of the key are often both shown. After all, the public key is public.

- **Thumbprint algorithm and thumbprint:** This is the hash for the certificate. On a new root certificate, you could use a phone to call and ask for the hash value and compare it to the hash value you see on the certificate. If it matches, you have just performed out-of-band (using the telephone) verification of the digital certificate.

Identity Certificate

An *identity certificate* is similar to a root certificate, but it describes the client and contains the public key of an individual host (the client). An example of a client is a web server that wants to support *Secure Sockets Layer (SSL)* or a router that wants to use digital signatures for authentication of a VPN tunnel. Figure 5-3 shows an example of an identity certificate.

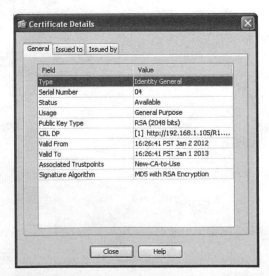

Figure 5-3 *Identity Certificate*

Using the Digital Certificates to Get the Peer's Public Key

In its basic components, any device that wants to verify a digital signature must have the public key of the sender. So, let's use an example of you and me. If we want to authenticate each other, and we both trust a common CA and have previously requested and received digital certificates (identity certificates) from the CA server, we exchange our identity certificates, which contain our public keys. We both verify the CA's signature on the digital certificate we just received from each other using the public key of the CA. In practice, this public key for the CA is built in to most of our browsers today for public CA servers. Once we verify each other's certificates, we can then trust the contents of those certificates (and most important, the public key). Now that you and I both have each other's public key, we can use those public keys to verify each other's digital signatures.

X.500 and X.509v3 Certificates

X.500 is a series of standards focused on directory services and how those directories are organized. Many popular network operating systems have been based on X.500, including Microsoft Active Directory. This X.500 structure is the foundation from which you see common directory elements such as CN=Bob (Common Name = CN), OU=engineering (organizational unit = OU), O=cisco.com (organization = O), and so on in an "org-chart" way, shaped like a pyramid. X.509 Version 3 is a standard for digital certificates that is widely accepted and incorporates many of the same directory and naming standards. A common protocol that is used to do lookups from a directory is called *Lightweight Directory Access Protocol (LDAP)*. A common use for this is having a digital certificate being used for authentication, and then based on the details of that certificate (for example, the OU=sales in the certificate itself), the user could be dynamically assigned the access rights that are associated with that group in Active Directory or some other LDAP accessible database. The concept is to define the rights in one place and then leverage that over and over again. An example is setting up Active Directory for the network and then using that to control what access is provided to each user after he or she authenticates.

As a review, most digital certificates contain the following information:

- **Serial number:** Assigned by the CA and used to uniquely identify the certificate
- **Subject:** The person or entity that is being identified
- **Signature algorithm:** The specific algorithm that was used for signing the digital certificate
- **Signature:** The digital signature from the certificate authority, which is used by devices that want to verify the authenticity of the certificate issued by that CA
- **Issuer:** The entity or CA that created and issued the digital certificate
- **Valid from:** The date the certificate became valid
- **Valid to:** The expiration date of the certificate
- **Key usage:** The functions for which the public key in the certificate may be used
- **Public key:** The public portion of the public and private key pair generated by the host whose certificate is being looked at
- **Thumbprint algorithm:** The hash algorithm used for data integrity

- **Thumbprint:** The actual hash
- **Certificate revocation list location:** The URL that can be checked to see whether the serial number of any certificates issued by the CA have been revoked

Authenticating and Enrolling with the CA

If you want to use a new CA as a trusted entity, and want to request and receive your own identity certificate from this CA, it is really a two-step process:

Step 1. The first step is to authenticate the CA server, or in other words trust the CA server. Unfortunately, if you do not have the public key for a CA server, you cannot verify the digital signature of the CA server. This is sort of like the chicken and the egg story, because you need the public key, which can be found in the root's CA certificate, but you cannot verify the signature on a certificate until you have the public key.

To get the ball rolling, you could download the root certificate and then use an out-of-band method, such as making a telephone call, to validate the root certificate. This can be done after downloading the root certificate and looking at the hash value, calling the administrators for the root CA and asking them to verbally tell you what the hash is. If the hash that they tell you over the phone matches the hash that you see on the digital certificate (and assuming that you called the right phone number and talked with the right people), you then know that the certificate is valid, and you can then use the public key contained in a certificate to verify future certificates which are signed by that CA. This process of getting the root CA certificate installed is often referred to as authenticating the CA. Current web browsers automate this process for well-known CAs.

Step 2. After you have authenticated the root CA and have a known good root certificate for that CA, you can then request your own identity certificate. This involves generating a public-private key pair and including the public key portion in any requests for your own identity certificate. An identity certificate could be for a device or person. Once you make this request, the CA can take all of your information and generate an identity certificate for you, which includes your public key, and then send this certificate back to you. If this is done electronically, how do you verify the identity certificate you got is really from the CA server that you trust? The answer is simple because the CA has not only issued the certificate but it also signed the certificate. Because you authenticated the CA server earlier and you have a copy of its digital certificate with its public key, you can now verify the digital signature it has put on your own identity certificate. If the signature from the CA is valid, you also know that your certificate is valid and so you can install it and use it.

Public Key Cryptography Standards

Many standards are in use for the PKI. Many of them have *Public Key Cryptography Standards (PKCS)* numbers. Some of these standards control the format and use of certificates, including requests to a CA for new certificates, the format for a file that is going to be the new identity certificate, and the file format and usage access for certificates. Having the standards in place helps with interoperability between different CA servers and many different CA clients.

Here are a few standards you should become familiar with, which include protocols by themselves and protocols used for working with digital certificates:

- **PKCS#10**: This is a format of a certificate request sent to a CA that wants to receive its identity certificate. This type of request would include the public key for the entity desiring a certificate.

- **PKCS#7**: This is a format that can be used by a CA as a response to a PKCS#10 request. The response itself will very likely be the identity certificate (or certificates) that had been previously requested.

- **PKCS#1**: RSA Cryptography Standard.

- **PKCS#12**: A format for storing both public and private keys using a symmetric password-based key to "unlock" the data whenever the key needs to be used or accessed.

- **PKCS#3**: Diffie-Hellman key exchange.

Simple Certificate Enrollment Protocol

The process of authenticating a CA server, generating a public-private key pair, requesting an identity certificate, and then verifying and implementing the identity certificate can be a several-step process. Cisco, in association with a few other vendors, developed the *Simple Certificate Enrollment Protocol (SCEP)*, which can automate most of the process for requesting and installing an identity certificate. Although it is not an open standard, it is supported by most Cisco devices and makes it convenient to get and install both root and identity certificates, as you see in action later in this chapter.

Revoked Certificates

If you decommission a device that has been assigned an identity certificate, or if the device assigned a digital certificate has been compromised and you believe that the private key information is no longer "private," you could request from the CA that the previously issued certificate be revoked. This poses a unique problem. Normally when two devices authenticate with each other, they do not need to contact a CA to verify the identity of the other party. This is because the two devices already have the public key of the CA and can validate the signature on a peer's certificate without direct contact with the CA. So here's the challenge: If a certificate has been revoked by the CA, and the peers are not checking with the CA each time they try to authenticate the peers, how does a peer know whether the certificate it just received has been revoked? The answer is simple: It is to check and see. A digital certificate contains information on where an updated list of revoked certificates can be obtained. This URL could point to the CA server itself or to some other publicly available resource on the Internet. The revoked certificates are listed based on the serial number of the certificates, and if a peer has been configured to check for revoked certificates, it adds this check before completing the authentication with a peer. If a *certificate revocation list (CRL)* is checked, and the certificate from the peer is on that list, the authentication stops at that moment. The three basic ways to check whether certificates have been revoked are as follows, in order of popularity:

■ **Certificate revocation list (CRL):** This is a list of certificates, based on their serial numbers, that had initially been issued by a CA but have since been revoked and as a result should not be trusted. A CRL could be very large, and the client would have to process the entire list to verify the certificate is not on the list. A CRL can be thought of as the naughty list. This is the primary protocol used for this purpose, compared to OSCP and AAA. A CRL could be accessed by several protocols, including LDAP and HTTP. A CRL could also be obtained via SCEP.

■ **Online Certificate Status Protocol (OCSP):** This is an alternative to CRLs. Using this method, a client simply sends a request to find the status of a certificate and gets a response without having to know the complete list of revoked certificates.

■ **Authentication, authorization, and accounting (AAA):** Cisco AAA services also provide support for validating digital certificates, including a check to see whether a certificate has been revoked. Because this is a proprietary solution, this is not often used in PKI.

Uses for Digital Certificates

Digital certificates aren't just for breakfast anymore. They can be used for clients who want to authenticate a web server to verify they are connected to the correct server using *HTTP Secure (HTTPS)*, *Transport Layer Security (TLS)*, or *Secure Sockets Layer (SSL)*. For the average user who does not have to write these protocols, but simply benefits from using them, they are all effectively the same, which is HTTP combined with TLS/SSL for the security benefits. This means that digital certificates can be used when you do online banking from your PC to the bank's website. It also means that if you use SSL technology for your remote-access VPNs you can also use digital certificates for authenticating the peers (at each end) of the VPN.

You can also use digital certificates with the protocol family of IPsec, which can also use digital certificates for the authentication portion.

Digital certificates can also be used with protocols such as 802.1X, which involves authentication at the edge of the network before allowing the user's packets and frames to progress through the network. An example is a wireless network, controlling access and requiring authentication, using digital certificates for the PCs/users, before allowing them in on the network.

PKI Topologies

There is not a one-size-fits-all solution for PKI. In small networks, a single CA server may be enough, but in a network with 30,000 devices, a single server may not provide the availability and fault tolerance required. To answer these issues, let's investigate the options available to us for implementation of the PKI, using various topologies, including single and hierarchical. Let's start off with the single CA and expand from there.

Single Root CA

If you have one trusted CA, and you have tens of thousands of customers who want to authenticate that CA and request their own identity certificates, there might be too large of a demand on a single server even though a single CA does not have to be directly involved in the day-to-day authentication that happens between peers. To offload some of the workload from a single server, you could publish CRLs on other servers. At the end of the day, it still makes sense to have at least some fault tolerance for your PKI, which means more than just a single root CA server.

Hierarchical CA with Subordinate CAs

One of our options to support fault tolerance and increased capacity is to use intermediate or subordinate CAs to assist the root CA. The root CA is the king of the hill. The root CA delegates the authority (to the subordinate CAs) to create and assign identity certificates to clients. This is called a *hierarchical PKI topology*. The root CA signs the digital certificates of its subordinate or intermediate CAs, and the subordinate CAs are the ones to issue certificates to clients. For a client to verify the "chain" of authority, a client needs both the subordinate CA's certificate and the root certificate. The root certificate (and its public key) is required to verify the digital signature of the subordinate CA, and the subordinate CA's certificate (and its public key) is required to verify the signature of the subordinate CA. If there are multiple levels of subordinate CAs, a client needs the certificates of all the devices in the chain from the root all the way to the CA that issued the client's certificate.

Cross-Certifying CAs

Another approach to hierarchical PKIs is called *cross-certifying*. With cross-certification, you could have a CA with a horizontal trust relationship over to a second CA so that clients of either CA could trust the signatures of the other CA.

Putting the Pieces of PKI to Work

This section covers how to implement these components in an actual production network.

We have taken a look at the ingredients for the recipe called PKI, the public key infrastructure. Both the *Adaptive Security Appliance (ASA)* and Cisco routers can use digital certificates. Let's take a look at installing digital certificates on the ASA, using the *Adaptive Security Device Manager (ASDM)*. Figure 5-4 shows the main Device Dashboard of ASDM.

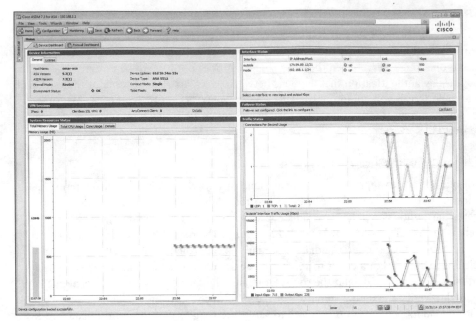

Figure 5-4 *Using the ASDM to Manage the ASA Firewall*

ASA's Default Certificate

The ASA is going to use a self-signed digital certificate by default. It needs this to support an administrator connecting to the firewall to support the ASDM, and for the ability to support any SSL VPN clients that you will be configuring in a later chapter. The problem with a self-signed certificate is that no browsers or other devices will have the ASA listed as a trusted CA, and HTTPS connections to the ASA, such as an administrator who wants to run ASDM, will receive a warning message that the certificate is not trusted.

If you do not want to use a self-signed certificate, but instead want to use a certificate from a CA server on the Internet, you must install a root certificate (of the CA you are going to trust) and then request an identity certificate.

Viewing the Certificates in ASDM

In the Device Management section of ASDM, you have options for configuring and viewing both identity certificates and root certificates. You could also find these options under the VPN sections of the Configuration menu. Figure 5-5 shows this section of the ASDM.

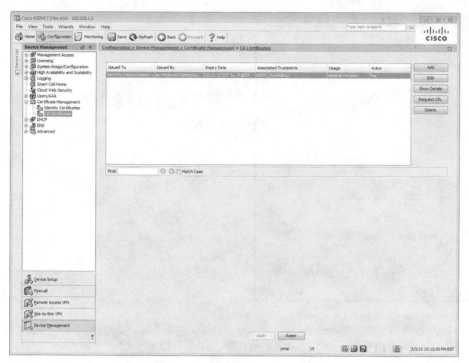

Figure 5-5 *Viewing Current CA Certificates*

Adding a New Root Certificate

If you want to add a new root certificate, click **Add**, and then you have options to install a root certificate from a file, or you could paste in the information or use SCEP. If you want to use the manual method from a file or through cut and paste, your CA vendor provides the file or instructions for obtaining the file for its root CA certificate. In this example, I have a CA that supports SCEP, so that is the option I chose, as shown in Figure 5-6.

When you add a new root certificate, you are also adding details about how you are going to work with that CA. By clicking the **More Options** button, you can answer questions about the CRL and specify other details about which protocols to be used for certificate verification for this firewall to use when dealing with certificates issued by this CA, as shown in Figure 5-7.

After you install a root certificate and verify it is valid by calling the CA and comparing the hash they give you against the hash for the certificate installed, you then can request your own identity certificate and follow a similar process to install it.

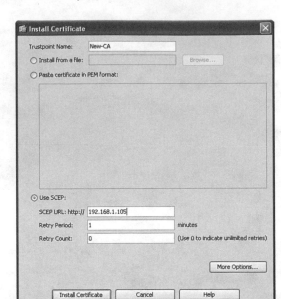

Figure 5-6 *Adding a New Root Certificate*

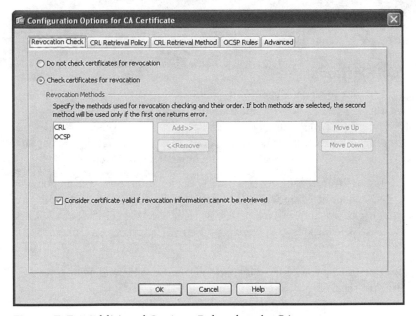

Figure 5-7 *Additional Options Related to the CA*

Easier Method for Installing Both Root and Identity Certificates

An easier option than manually installing the root certificate file is to use SCEP and install the root certificate, generate a new key pair, and request your identity certificate all using SCEP.

For this, you could begin in the Identity Certificate area in ASDM. Click **Add**, assign a name you want to associate with the new CA, and then click the **Add a New Identity Certificate** radio button. From here, if you want to use a brand new key pair in conjunction with this CA (that will be putting your public key into your digital certificate), click **New** (next to the key pair option), assign the key pair a name and the size of the key to use, and then click the **Generate Now** button, as shown in Figure 5-8.

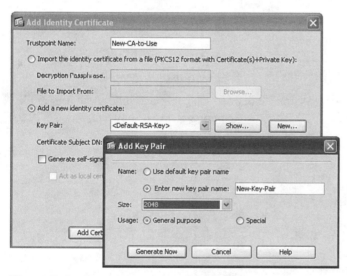

Figure 5-8 *Generating a New Key Pair*

After you click **Generate Now**, a public-private key pair is generated and the public key portion of it is sent to the CA as part of the SCEP certificate request process. The equivalent CLI command that could be used to generate the new key pair is shown in Example 5-4.

Example 5-4 *Generating a New Key Pair*

```
Keith-asa1(config)# crypto key generate rsa label My-Key-Pair modulus 2048 noconfirm
```

After the key pair is generated, and before clicking the **Add Certificate** button, you can specify the details of the CA server and how to reach that CA server by clicking the **Advanced** button, as shown in Figure 5-9.

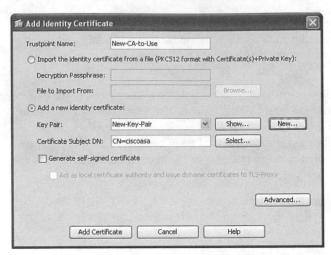

Figure 5-9   *Specifying What Key Pair to Use and the Option of Advanced*

Using the options presented by the Advanced button, you can specify the enrollment mode of SCEP and the IP address of the CA server that supports SCEP, as shown in Figure 5-10.

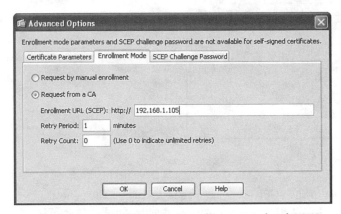

Figure 5-10   *Specifying the Enrollment Mode of SCEP*

Once the enrollment method and IP address are configured, click the **OK** button, and then click the **Add Certificate** button.

Example 5-5 shows the equivalent CLI commands to authenticate and enroll with a new CA via SCEP.

Example 5-5   *Authenticating and Enrolling with a New CA via SCEP*

```
! Create the name that you want the ASA to reference the CA by
Keith-asa1(config)# crypto ca trustpoint New-CA-to-Use


! Specify which key-pair will be used for the public portion that will go
! into the digital certificate. Below the new key pair we created is specified.
Keith-asa1(config-ca-trustpoint)# keypair New-Key-Pair
```

```
! Specify what the certificate may be used for. (Both SSL and IPsec)
Keith-asa1(config-ca-trustpoint)# id-usage ssl-ipsec


! Specify whether or not the fully qualified domain name (fqdn) will be
! required
! Keith-asa1(config-ca-trustpoint)# no fqdn


! Specify the x.500 common name (CN)
Keith-asa1(config-ca-trustpoint)# subject-name CN=ciscoasa


! Specify where the CA server can be reached.  HTTP must be running on the
! CA server.
Keith-asa1(config-ca-trustpoint)# enrollment url http://192.168.1.105
Keith-asa1(config-ca-trustpoint)# exit


! Retrieve and install the root certificate.  The "nointeractive" won't
! prompt the user for additional information.
Keith-asa1(config)# crypto ca authenticate New-CA-to-Use nointeractive


! Request and install the identity certificate from the CA.  The "noconfirm"
! will avoid prompting the user for additional confirmation messages.
Keith-asa1(config)# crypto ca enroll New-CA-to-Use noconfirm
```

If the SCEP-capable CA server is reachable, and configured correctly, a success message appears, as shown in Figure 5-11.

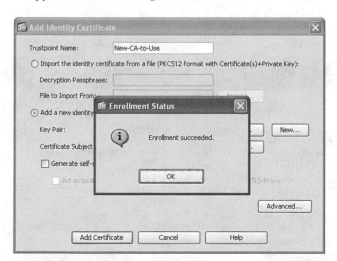

Figure 5-11   *Enrollment Succeeded Message*

To see the details of the new certificate, highlight the certificate and click **Show Details** (see Figure 5-12).

Figure 5-12 *Details of the Identity Certificate*

Notice the details that are found in most digital certificates, including serial number, CRL, and the validity dates.

NOTE   The serial number on a certificate from a public PKI server is much longer than the one issued by my internal CA server used in my lab.

We have discussed the concepts of using PKI, and also taken a look at an example using an ASA. To make sure you understand all components of PKI, review Table 5-3.

Table 5-3   Key PKI Components

Component	Description
RSA digital signatures	Using its private key to encrypt a generated hash, a digital signature is created. The receiver uses the public key of the sender to validate the digital signature and verify the identity of the peer.
Digital certificate	File that contains the public key of the entity, a serial number, and the signature of the CA that issued the certificate
Public and private keys	Used as a pair to encrypt and decrypt data in an asymmetrical fashion.
Certificate authority	The CA's job is to fulfill certificate requests and generate the digital certificates for its clients to use. It also maintains a list of valid certificates that have been issued, and maintains a CRL listing any revoked certificates.

Component	Description
X.509v3	A common certificate format used today.
Subordinate CA/ RA	Assistant to the CA, which can issue certificates to clients. Clients need both the certificates from the root and the subordinate to verify signatures all the way to the root. Used in a hierarchical PKI topology.
PKCS	Public Key Cryptography Standards, agreed to and implemented by vendors who want the ability to have compatibility with other devices in the PKI.

5

Exam Preparation Tasks

Review All the Key Topics

Review the most important topics from this chapter, denoted with a Key Topic icon. Table 5-4 lists these key topics.

Table 5-4 Key Topics

Key Topic Element	Description	Page Number
Section	What Is a VPN?	87
Figure 5-1	Example of Remote-Access and Site-to-Site VPNs	88
List	Main benefits of VPNs	89
List	VPN technologies	89
Section	Ciphers and Keys	91
Section	Symmetric and Asymmetric Algorithms	92
Section	Hashes	94
Section	Hashed Message Authentication Code	95
Section	Digital Signatures	95
Section	IPsec and SSL	97
Section	Public and Private Key Pairs	99
Section	RSA Algorithm, the Keys, and Digital Certificates	99
Section	Certificate Authorities	100
Section	Root and Identity Certificates	101
List	Certificate components	102
Section	X.500 and X.509v3 Certificates	103
List	What goes in to a digital certificate	103
Section	Authenticating and Enrolling with the CA	104
Section	Public Key Cryptography Standards	105
Section	Simple Certificate Enrollment Protocol	105
Section	Revoked Certificates	105
Section	PKI Topologies	106
Example 5-4	Generating a New Key Pair	111
Example 5-5	Authenticating and Enrolling with a New CA via SCEP	112
Table 5-3	Key PKI Components	114

Complete the Tables and Lists from Memory

Print a copy of Appendix C, "Memory Tables," (found on the CD) or at least the section for this chapter, and complete the tables and lists from memory. Appendix D, "Memory Tables Answer Key," also on the CD, includes completed tables and lists so that you can check your work.

Define Key Terms

Define the following key terms from this chapter, and check your answers in the glossary:

VPN, SSL, IPsec, 3DES, AES, MD5, SHA1, hash, HMAC, digital signature, symmetrical, asymmetrical, key, PKI, CA, subordinate CA, root certificate, identity certificate, PKCS#7, PKCS#12, RSA, digital signature, public key, X.509v3, CRL, SCEP, LDAP

Command Reference to Check Your Memory

This section includes the most important configuration and EXEC commands covered in this chapter. To see how well you have memorized the commands as a side effect of your other studies, cover the left side of Table 5-5 with a piece of paper, read the descriptions on the right side, and see whether you remember the commands.

Table 5-5   Command Reference

Command	Description
crypto key generate rsa	Generate a public-private key pair on the ASA
crypto ca authenticate	Retrieve and installs the root certificate via SCEP
crypto ca enroll	Request and installs an identity certificate via SCEP

This chapter covers the following topics:

IPsec concepts, components, and operations

Configuring and verifying IPsec

CHAPTER 6

Fundamentals of IP Security

IP Security (IPsec) is one of the most mature VPN standards in the industry. The secret of IPsec is that it is not locked in to one specific protocol or even one set of protocols. As technology advances, so can the protocols that are being used by IPsec. The goal of IPsec is quite simple: to provide confidentiality, data integrity, and authentication of the *virtual private network (VPN)* peer and provide antireplay support. It implements all of these to Layer 3 packets individually, protecting each one as it is sent from one end of the VPN tunnel until it reaches the other end.

This chapter presumes that you have read the previous chapters, and we build based on that.

"Do I Know This Already?" Quiz

The "Do I Know This Already?" quiz helps you determine your level of knowledge of this chapter's topics before you begin. Table 6-1 details the major topics discussed in this chapter and their corresponding quiz questions.

Table 6-1 "Do I Know This Already?" Section-to-Question Mapping

Foundation Topics Section	Questions
IPsec Concepts, Components, and Operations	1–10
Configuring and Verifying IPsec	11

1. Which technology is a primary method that IPsec uses to implement data integrity?
   a. MD5
   b. AES
   c. RSA
   d. DH

2. What are the source and destination addresses used for an encrypted IPsec packet?
   a. Original sender and receiver IP addresses
   b. Original sender's and outbound VPN gateway's addresses
   c. Sending and receiving VPN gateways
   d. Sending VPN gateway and original destination address in the packet

3. Which phase is used for private management traffic between the two VPN peers?
   a. IPsec
   b. IKE Phase 1
   c. IKE Phase 2
   d. IKE Phase 3

4. Which of the following are negotiated during IKE Phase 1?

   a. Hashing

   b. DH group

   c. Encryption

   d. Authentication method

5. What method is used to allow two VPN peers to establish shared secret keys and to establish those keys over an untrusted network?

   a. AES

   b. SHA

   c. RSA

   d. DH

6. Which of the following is *not* part of the IKE Phase 1 process?

   a. Negotiation of the IKE Phase 1 protocols

   b. Running DH

   c. Authenticating the peer

   d. Negotiating the transform set to use

7. How is the negotiation of the IPsec (IKE Phase 2) tunnel done securely?

   a. Uses the IKE Phase 1 tunnel

   b. Uses the IPsec tunnel

   c. Uses the IKE Phase 2 tunnel

   d. Uses RSA

8. What are the two main methods for authenticating a peer as the last step of IKE Phase 1? (Choose all that apply.)

   a. RSA signatures, using digital certificates to exchange public keys

   b. PSK (pre-shared key)

   c. DH Group 2

   d. TCP three-way handshake

9. Which component acts as an if-then statement, looking for packets that should be encrypted before they leave the interface?

   a. **crypto isakmp policy**

   b. **crypto map**

   c. **crypto ipsec transform-set**

   d. **crypto access-list** (access list used for cryptography)

10. What is true about symmetrical algorithms and symmetrical crypto access lists used on VPN peers?

   a. Symmetrical algorithms use the same secret (key) to lock and unlock the data. Symmetrical ACLs between two VPN peers should symmetrically swap the source and destination portions of the ACL.

   b. Symmetrical algorithms like RSA use the same secret (key) to lock and unlock the data. Symmetrical ACLs between two VPN peers should symmetrically swap the source and destination portions of the ACL.

   c. Symmetrical algorithms use the same secret (key) to lock and unlock the data. Symmetrical ACLs between two VPN peers should be identical.

   d. Symmetrical algorithms use the same secret (key) to lock and unlock the data. Symmetrical ACLs between two VPN peers require that only symmetrical algorithms be used for all aspects of IPsec.

11. Which one of the following commands reveal the ACLs, transform scts, and peer information and indicate which interface is being used to connect to the remote IPsec VPN peer?

   a. show crypto map

   b. show crypto isakmp policy

   c. show crypto config

   d. show crypto ipsec sa

6

Foundation Topics

IPsec Concepts, Components, and Operations

This section examines the moving parts and pieces involved with IPsec. This section presumes that you've read the previous chapters and already have an understanding of VPN technologies and *public key infrastructure (PKI)*.

The Goal of IPsec

To best understand how IPsec operates, let's take a look at a simple topology that we can use as a framework for this entire chapter, shown here in Figure 6-1.

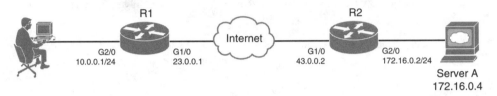

Figure 6-1 *IPsec Example Topology*

IPsec has four fundamental goals, as shown in Table 6-2.

Table 6-2 IPsec Goals and the Methods Used to Implement Them

Goal	Method That Provides the Feature
Confidentiality	Encryption
Data integrity	Hashing
Peer authentication	Pre-shared keys, RSA digital signatures
Antireplay	Integrated into IPsec, basically applying serial numbers to packets

The goals can be described as follows:

- **Confidentiality:** Provided through encryption changing clear text into cipher text.

- **Data integrity:** Provided through hashing and/or through *Hashed Message Authentication Code (HMAC)* to verify that data has not been manipulated during its transit across the network.

- **Authentication:** Provided through authenticating the VPN peers near the beginning of a VPN session using *pre-shared keys (PSK)* or digital signatures (leveraging digital certificates). Authentication can also be done continuously through the use of an HMAC, which includes a secret known only to two ends of the VPN.

- **Antireplay protection:** When VPNs are established, the peers can sequentially number the packets, and if a packet is attempted to be replayed again (perhaps by an attacker), the packet will not be accepted because the VPN device believes it has already processed that packet.

From our topology, we could decide that any traffic from the 10.0.0.0 network on the far left that needs to go to the 172.16.0.0 network on the far right should first be encrypted by R1, which would then send the protected packets over the Internet until they reach R2. The cloud between R1 and R2 represents an untrusted network, such as the Internet. R2 then decrypts each packet and sends the traffic on to its final destination, which may be a PC or server on the 172.16.0.0 network. The protected packets could be encrypted, hashed, and kept track of to provide the four major benefits previously listed.

The Internet Key Exchange (IKE) Protocol

IPsec uses the *Internet Key Exchange (IKE)* protocol to negotiate and establish secured site-to-site or remote access *virtual private network (VPN)* tunnels. IKE is a framework provided by the *Internet Security Association and Key Management Protocol (ISAKMP)* and parts of two other key management protocols, namely Oakley and *Secure Key Exchange Mechanism (SKEME)*.

In IKE Phase 1 IPsec peers negotiate and authenticate each other. In Phase 2 they negotiate keying materials and algorithms for the encryption of the data being transferred over the IPsec tunnel.

There are two versions of IKE:

- **IKEv1:** Defined in RFC 2409, *The Internet Key Exchange*
- **IKE version 2 (IKEv2):** Defined in RFC 4306, *Internet Key Exchange (IKEv2) Protocol*

IKEv2 enhances the function of performing dynamic key exchange and peer authentication. IKEv2 simplifies the key exchange flows and introduces measures to fix vulnerabilities present in IKEv1. Both IKEv1 and IKEv2 protocols operate in two phases. IKEv2 provides a simpler and more efficient exchange.

Phase 1 in IKEv2 is IKE_SA, consisting of the message pair IKE_SA_INIT. IKE_SA_INIT is used to initiate the IKE negotiation. IKE_SA is comparable to the IKEv1 Phase 1. The *security association (SA)* is the keying material used to encrypt packets over the VPN tunnel. The attributes of the IKE_SA phase are defined in the key exchange policy. The second phase in IKEv2 is CHILD_SA. The first CHILD_SA (Phase 2 SA) is the IKE_AUTH message pair. This phase is comparable to the IKEv1 Phase 2. Additional CHILD_SA message pairs can be sent for rekey and informational messages. The CHILD_SA attributes are defined in the data policy.

Differences from IKEv1 include the following:

- IKEv1 Phase 1 has two possible exchanges: main mode and aggressive mode. There is a single exchange of a message pair for IKEv2 IKE_SA.
- IKEv2 has a simple exchange of two message pairs for the CHILD_SA. IKEv1 uses at least a three-message pair exchange for Phase 2.

6

The Play by Play for IPsec

Let's start the play-by-play discussion assuming that both routers have been correctly configured to be VPN peers and that they have default routes pointing to the Internet and that they were both just powered up. With a site-to-site VPN, as shown in our topology, each of the peers could also be called a *VPN gateway*, which is serving the customers on the 10.0.0.0/24 and 172.16.0.0/24 networks. The two routers will become IPsec *peers* with each other to form the IPsec tunnel over the Internet.

The first thing the router on the left (R1) is going to do, if it has been told to encrypt and protect traffic that is sourced from the 10.0.0.0 network and destined for the 172.16.0.0 network, is wait for that traffic to show up. Let's say a user on the 10.0.0.0 network sends a packet to a server on the 172.16.0.0 network, and now R1 sees this packet and needs to encrypt it and protect it before sending it on its way. Unfortunately, the router has not yet established any VPN tunnels between itself and the router on the far right. So, if traffic did show up at R1 and it needed to be encrypted based on the policy, R1 would initiate negotiations with the router on the right. In this case, R1 would be the initiator of the VPN.

Step 1: Negotiate the IKEv1 Phase 1 Tunnel

What these two routers first negotiate is something called an *Internet Key Exchange (IKE)* Phase 1 tunnel. This can be done in one of two modes: main mode or aggressive mode. Main mode uses more packets for the process than aggressive mode, but main mode is considered more secure. Most current VPN implementations default to using main mode. This first tunnel (the IKE Phase 1 tunnel) is used between the two routers to speak directly to each other. This tunnel (once established) is not going to be used to forward user packets, but rather only to protect management traffic related to the VPN between the two routers. Packets such as a keepalive message to verify that the VPN tunnel is still working are an example of traffic that these two routers send across the IKE Phase 1 tunnel directly to each other.

Because the router on the left (R1) first received traffic that needed to be encrypted and there was no IKE Phase 1 tunnel in place, the router on the left becomes the initiator for the negotiations. The initiator sends over all of its configured/default parameters that it is willing to use for the IKE Phase 1 tunnel. Five basic items need to be agreed upon between the two VPN devices/gateways (in this case, the two routers) for the IKE Phase 1 tunnel to succeed, as follows:

- **Hash algorithm:** This could be *message digest 5 algorithm (MD5)* or *Secure Hash Algorithm (SHA)* on most devices.

- **Encryption algorithm:** This could be *Digital Encryption Standard (DES)* (bad idea, too weak), *Triple DES (3DES)* (better) or *Advanced Encryption Standard (AES)* (best) with various key lengths. (Longer is better for keys.)

- **Diffie-Hellman (DH) group to use:** The DH "group" refers to the modulus size (length of the key) to use for the DH key exchange. Group 1 uses 768 bits, group 2 uses 1024, and group 5 uses 1536. More secure DH groups are part of the *next-generation encryption (NGE)*:

  - **Group 14 or 24:** Provides 2048-bit DH

  - **Groups 15 and 16:** Support 3072-bit and 4096-bit DH

- **Group 19 or 20:** Supports the 256-bit and 384-bit ECDH groups, respectively

  The purpose of DH is to generate shared secret keying material (symmetric keys) that may be used by the two VPN peers for symmetrical algorithms, such as AES. It is important to note that the DH exchange itself is asymmetrical (and is CPU intensive), and the resulting keys that are generated are symmetrical.

- **Authentication method:** Used for verifying the identity of the VPN peer on the other side of the tunnel. Options include a *pre-shared key (PSK)* used only for the authentication or RSA signatures (which leverage the public keys contained in digital certificates).

- **Lifetime:** How long until this IKE Phase 1 tunnel should be torn down. (The default is one day, listed in seconds.) This is the only parameter that does not have to exactly match with the other peer to be accepted. If all other parameters match and the lifetime is different, they agree to use the smallest lifetime between the two peers. A shorter lifetime is considered more secure because it gives an attacker less time to calculate keys used for a current tunnel.

How to Remember the Five Items Negotiated in IKE Phase 1

As a handy way to recall the five pieces involved in the negotiation of the IKE Phase 1 tunnel, you might want to remember that the two devices HAGLE over IKE Phase 1:

H: Hash

A: Authentication method

G: DH group (a stretch, but it works)

L: Lifetime of the IKE Phase 1 tunnel

E: Encryption algorithm to use for the IKE Phase 1 tunnel

Who Begins the Negotiation?

The initiator sends over all of its IKE Phase 1 policies, and the other VPN peer looks at all of those policies to see whether any of its own policies match the ones it just received. If there is a matching policy, the recipient of the negotiations sends back information about which received policy matches, and they use that matching policy for the IKE Phase 1 tunnel.

Step 2: Run the DH Key Exchange

Now having agreed to the IKE Phase 1 policy of the peer, the two devices run the DH key exchange. They use the DH group (DH key size for the exchange) they agreed to during the negotiations, and at the end of this key exchange, they both have symmetrical keying material (which is a fancy way of saying they both have the same secret keys that they can use with symmetrical algorithms).

DH, as you learned in a previous chapter, allows two devices that do not yet have a secure connection to establish shared secret keying material (keys that can be used with symmetrical algorithms, such as AES).

Step 3: Authenticate the Peer

The last piece of IKE Phase 1 is to validate or authenticate the peer on the other side. For authentication, they use whatever they agreed to in the initial HAGLE, and if they successfully authenticate with each other, we now have an IKE Phase 1 tunnel in place between the two VPN gateways. This tunnel is bidirectional, meaning that either device can send or receive on that IKE Phase 1 tunnel. The authentication could be done either using a PSK or using RSA digital signatures (depending on what they agreed to use in Step 1).

What About the User's Original Packet?

Now here is the challenge: After all the work that went in to building the IKE Phase 1 tunnel, this tunnel is used only as a management tunnel so that the two routers can securely communicate with each other directly. This IKE Phase 1 tunnel is not used to encrypt or protect the end user's packets. To protect the end user's packets, (which is the entire goal for IPsec), the two VPN devices build a second tunnel for the sole purpose of encrypting the end-user packets. This second tunnel is called the IKE Phase 2 tunnel; it is also commonly referred to as (drum roll, please) the IPsec tunnel. This IKE Phase 2 tunnel is the tunnel used to protect the end-user packets as those packets cross untrusted networks between the VPN peers.

Leveraging What They Have Already Built

The two routers, with a beautiful IKE Phase 1 tunnel in place, can use that IKE Phase 1 tunnel to securely negotiate and establish the IPsec or IKE Phase 2 tunnel. In my years of working with students, this is where the confusion sometimes creeps in, because during the configuration the students say to themselves, "Didn't I already specify the details for encryption and hashing? Why is it asking for them again in the configuration?" The answer is that we have to set up specific commands to specify the IKE Phase 1 policies, and we set up a different set of similar commands for the IKE Phase 2 policy (including the component called a *transform set*).

Immediately after the IKE Phase 1 tunnel is established (the two different modes to set up the IKE Phase 1 tunnel are main mode, which takes more packets, or aggressive mode, which takes fewer packets and is considered less secure), the routers immediately begin to establish the IKE Phase 2 tunnel.

The IKE Phase 1 tunnel is their management tunnel. The entire conversation and negotiation of the IKE Phase 2 tunnel are completely done in private because of the IKE Phase 1 tunnel protection the negotiated traffic. The IKE Phase 2 tunnel includes the hashing and encryption algorithms. The name of the mode for building the IKE Phase 2 tunnel is called Quick mode.

Now IPsec Can Protect the User's Packets

Once the IKE Phase 2 tunnel is built, the routers can then begin to encrypt the user's traffic and send those encrypted packets directly to the peer on the far side. From the Internet's perspective, it looks like packets sourced from the IP address of R1 are being sent to the IP address of R2. The encrypted payload of these packets contains the original IP addresses and contents of the user who is forwarding a packet to a server or vice versa. If these packets are eavesdropped upon, the eavesdropper sees the IP addresses involved between the two routers; the payload (the original packets) has been encrypted and encapsulated inside, and is cipher text and unreadable to the individual who does not have the symmetric keys to decrypt the contents.

Traffic Before IPsec

If the packet is captured before IPsec is used, as it crosses the cloud (untrusted network), the eavesdropper sees the packet as it appears in Figure 6-2.

```
Internet Protocol, Src: 10.0.0.25 (10.0.0.25), Dst: 172.16.0.4 (172.16.0.4)
   Version: 4
   Header length: 20 bytes
 ▷ Differentiated Services Field: 0x00 (DSCP 0x00: Default; ECN: 0x00)
   Total Length: 58
   Identification: 0x3aed (15085)
 ▷ Flags: 0x02 (Don't Fragment)
   Fragment offset: 0
   Time to live: 127
   Protocol: TCP (0x06)
 ▷ Header checksum: 0x0aa4 [correct]
   Source: 10.0.0.25 (10.0.0.25)
   Destination: 172.16.0.4 (172.16.0.4)
Transmission Control Protocol, Src Port: ssslog-mgr (1204), Dst Port: telnet (23), Seq: 4, Ack: 18, Len: 18
   Source port: ssslog-mgr (1204)
   Destination port: telnet (23)
   [Stream index: 0]
   Sequence number: 4      (relative sequence number)
   [Next sequence number: 22     (relative sequence number)]
   Acknowledgement number: 18     (relative ack number)
   Header length: 20 bytes
 ▷ Flags: 0x18 (PSH, ACK)
   Window size: 64223
 ▷ Checksum: 0x0247 [validation disabled]
 ▷ [SEQ/ACK analysis]
Telnet
   Command: Do Suppress Go Ahead
   Command: Will Terminal Type
   Command: Will Negotiate About Window Size
 ▷ Suboption Begin: Negotiate About Window Size
   Command: Suboption End
```

Before IPsec, all the original IP, TCP, and Application Header information and payload are in plain text.

An eavesdropper would be able to see an entire telnet conversation between client and server.

Figure 6-2 *Plain Text, Before IPsec*

In this figure, any eavesdropper can see and determine the entire conversation between the client and the server. Because Telnet offers no encryption capabilities on its own, the attacker could learn the username and password used for initiation of this Telnet session and each command the Telnet user issued and its results.

Traffic After IPsec

After you configure R1 and R2 to become VPN peers/gateways, and tell them that all packets between the two networks of 10.0.0.0/24 and 172.16.0.0/24 should be protected by IPsec, R1 and R2 negotiate and build their VPN tunnels (IKE Phase 1 and IKE Phase 2), and then any traffic from either network and destined for the other is protected. Let's consider the packet shown in the earlier figure. When R1 sees this same packet heading out to 172.16.0.4, and because its source IP address is on the 10.0.0.0/24 network, R1 uses the IKE Phase 2 tunnel and encrypts the packet and encapsulates the encrypted packet with a new IP header that shows the source IP address as R1 and the destination address as R2. The Layer 4 protocol would show as being *Encapsulating Security Payload (ESP)*, which is reflected in the IP header as protocol #50. When R2 receives this, R2 de-encapsulates the packet, sees that it is ESP, and then proceeds to decrypt the original packet. Once decrypted, R2 forwards the plaintext packet to the server at 172.16.0.4. The encrypted packet, as it crosses over the untrusted network between R1 and R2, appears, as shown Figure 6-3.

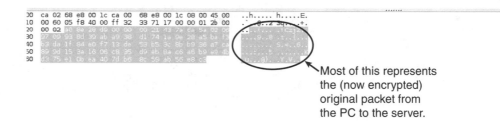

Only the new Layer 3 IP header and Layer 4 ESP header can be seen in plain text. The content of the original packet from the PC to the server is now protected as cipher text as the payload of this IPsec packet.

Most of this represents the (now encrypted) original packet from the PC to the server.

Figure 6-3 *Encrypted Packet Crossing the Internet*

Summary of the IPsec Story

In summary, the VPN peers/gateways negotiate the IKE Phase 1 tunnel using aggressive or main mode, and then use Quick mode to establish the IKE Phase 2 tunnel. They use the IKE Phase 2 tunnel to encrypt and decrypt user packets. Behind the scenes, the IKE Phase 2 tunnel really creates two one-way tunnels: one from R1 to R2 and one from R2 to R1. The end user does not see the process in any detail, and end users do not know the encryption is even being applied to their packets. So, we could say we have one IKE Phase 1 bidirectional tunnel used for management between the two VPN peers and two IKE Phase 2 unidirectional tunnels used for encrypting and decrypting end-user packets. These tunnels are often referred to as the security agreements between the two VPN peers. Many times, these agreements are called *security associations (SA)*. Each SA is assigned a unique number for tracking.

Configuring and Verifying IPsec

Now that we have taken a look at the building blocks for IPsec, let's apply what you have learned to the topology introduced at the beginning of the chapter in Figure 6-1.

Tools to Configure the Tunnels

In the CCNA Security courseware, *Cisco Configuration Professional (CCP)* is used to configure the VPN tunnels, including both IKE Phase 1 and IKE Phase 2. We use CCP here, but you also learn the *command-line interface (CLI)* equivalent for each of the commands, which are annotated to let you know what each command does.

Start with a Plan

The first thing to plan is what protocols to use for IKE Phase 1 and IKE Phase 2 and to iden-tify which traffic should be encrypted.

From the earlier topology, let's agree to encrypt any traffic from the 10.0.0.0/24 network behind R1 if those packets are going to 172.16.0.0/24 behind R2 and packets in the other direction from 172.16.0.0/24 to 10.0.0.0/24.

For IKE Phase 1, let's use the following:

H: For hashing, we can use MD5 (128 bits) or SHA-1 (160 bits). Let's go for MD5 for IKE Phase 1.

A: Authentication. We can use PSKs or digital certificates. Let's start off with PSKs (a password really) for authentication.

G: For DH group, we can use 1, 2, or 5 on most routers. Let's use group 2 in this example. If your router supports group 14 or higher, the higher DH group should be used because it is more secure.

L: Lifetime defaults to one day. Let's set the lifetime for the IKE Phase 1 to 21600 seconds (6 hours).

E: Encryption of the IKE Phase 1 can be DES, 3DES, or some flavor of AES. Let's use 128-bit AES.

Now for Phase 2, we also need to decide on hashing and encryption at a minimum. We can use the defaults for lifetime. For hashing, let's use SHA (just to see the difference between the hashing here and the hashing protocol in IKE Phase 1). Let's also use AES-256 in IKE Phase 2. The policies used for IKE Phase 2 are called transform sets.

Applying the Configuration

With all of that in mind, let's start the configuration on R1. Using CCP, select R1 from the drop-down menu and navigate to **Configure > Security > VPN > Site-to-Site VPN**. From there, you verify that the **Create a Site-to-Site VPN** option is selected, and then click the **Launch the Selected Task** button, as shown in Figure 6-4.

6

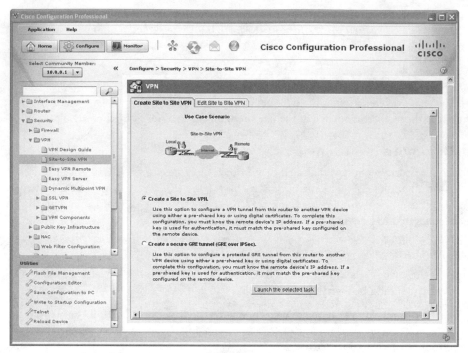

Figure 6-4   *Using CCP to Configure IPsec VPN Site-to-Site Tunnels*

Next, you are prompted to either use Quick Setup or the Step by Step Wizard. Quick Setup uses the defaults for IKE Phase 1 and IKE Phase 2 that are built in to CCP. If you want to customize the policies, choose the **Step by Step Wizard**, as shown in Figure 6-5, and then click **Next**.

From the interface drop-down list, select the interface on R1 that will be facing the Internet (this is also the interface facing toward its peer, R2), and configure the IP address of the peer (the reachable address over the Internet). In this case, R2's outside address is 43.0.0.2. Select the option for authenticating using a PSK and configure the key. (This needs to be the same key on both sides. For this example, we use the PSK of cisco123 for the IKE Phase 1 authentication.) After entering the data, review it to make sure it is accurate, as shown in Figure 6-6, and then click **Next** to continue.

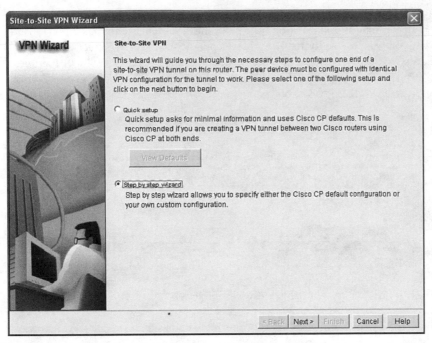

Figure 6-5   *Selecting the Step by Step VPN Wizard*

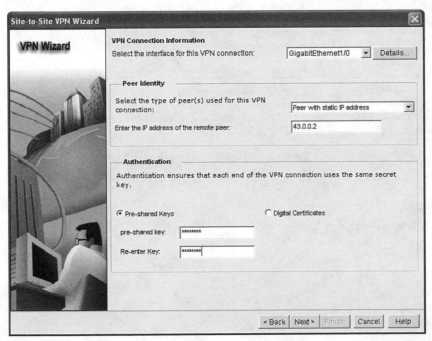

Figure 6-6   *Entering the Local Ethernet and Remote Peer Information, Including the PSK*

You are next asked for the IKE Phase 1 proposals you want to use. If you want to use the default, that is fine as long as you use it on both sides (both routers use the same policy) and it matches what you want to use for the IKE Phase 1 policy. We decided (earlier, you and I) that we would use MD5 for hashing, PSK for authentication, DH group 2, a 6-hour lifetime, and AES 128-bit key for encryption. After looking at the defaults, shown in Figure 6-7, you click **Add** to create a new IKE Phase 1 policy.

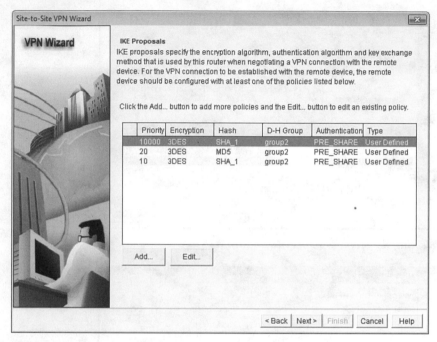

Figure 6-7   *Configuring the IKE Phase 1 Policy Within CCP*

After clicking the **Add** button, you put in your desired IKE Phase 1 policies, as shown in Figure 6-8, and click **OK**.

After creating your new IKE Phase 1 policy, you still need to select it (highlight it) before clicking **Next**. The CCP creates its default policy by default, along with your new policy. After highlighting the new policy (priority 2 in the example, as shown in Figure 6-9), click **Next** to continue.

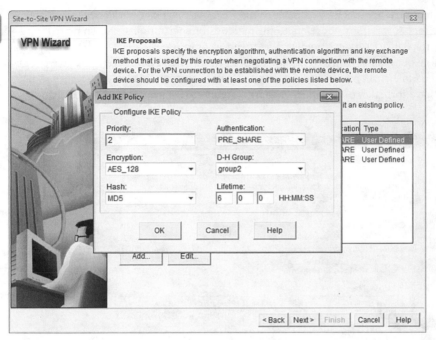

Figure 6-8   *Entering Custom IKE Phase 1 Policies*

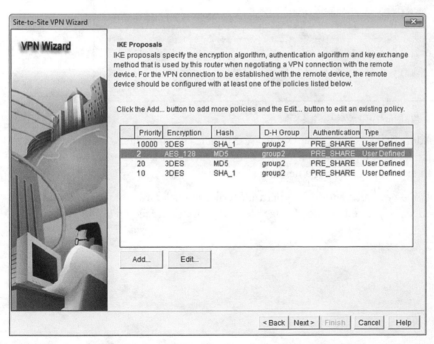

Figure 6-9   *Highlight the New Policy You Created Before Clicking Next*

The next screen that appears looks similar to the first, but this box has the title Transform Set near the top. A transform set refers to the methods of encryption and hashing that you want to use for the IKE Phase 2 tunnels. We do not want to use the defaults, but rather we want to follow our plan of using AES-256 and SHA for the IKE Phase 2 tunnels. (We could have used the same exact protocols, but I wanted you to see the distinction between the options we have for either tunnel independently.) Figure 6-10 shows the default transform set.

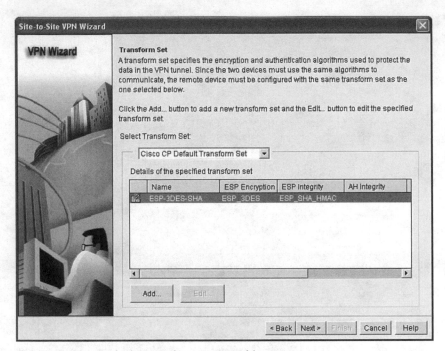

Figure 6-10   *Default Transform Set Used by CCP*

By clicking **Add**, you can specify the IKE Phase 2 policies of your choice. Remember that whatever you choose here, you also need to configure on the other router, as well. Figure 6-11 shows an example of creating a new transform set.

After entering the new information for your transform set, click **OK**, and then verify your new transform set is selected before clicking **Next** to continue, as shown in Figure 6-12.

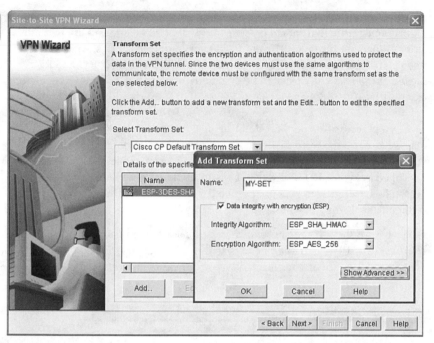

Figure 6-11 *Creating a New Transform Set (IKE Phase 2 Policy)*

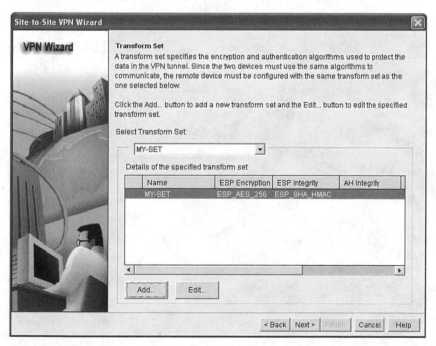

Figure 6-12 *Selecting the New Transform Set*

The wizard then asks what traffic should be encrypted. Because we are on R1, we should focus only on outbound traffic that should be encrypted. (It is R2's responsibility to make sure that the correct inbound traffic to R1 from R2 is encrypted). To do this, we use an access list as the classifier or identifier of what traffic should be encrypted. R1's and R2's classifying *access control lists (ACL)* should be symmetrical, in that if R1 says to encrypt all packets that are from 10.0.0.0/24 and going to 172.16.0.0/24, R2 should say that it will encrypt all packets from 172.16.0.0/24 that are destined for 10.0.0.0/24. That is what is meant by having *symmetrical* access lists on the VPN peers in a site-to-site VPN. (It is just a bad coincidence that we also use the word *symmetrical* to describe algorithms like AES that these peers will be using.) An ACL that has been created to identify which traffic should be encrypted is called a *crypto ACL*. Note that a crypto ACL is not applied directly to any interface, but instead it is referenced by a policy called *a crypto map* (discussed soon). The crypto map is directly applied to an interface.

From R1's perspective, we should "protect," which means use IPsec on packets with a source address from the 10.0.0.0/24 network and that also have a destination address in the 172.16.0.0/24 network. So, we fill in the wizard as shown in Figure 6-13 and click **Next** to continue.

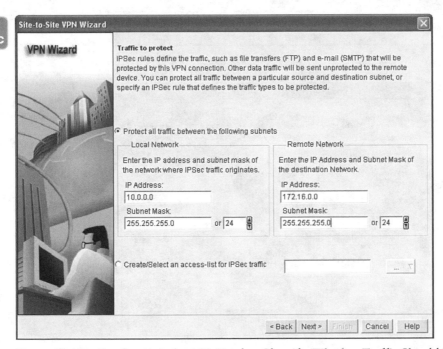

Figure 6-13 *Configuring the ACL Used to Classify Whether Traffic Should Be Protected by IPsec*

Packets that are not matched for IPsec protection will be forwarded as normal packets, without any IPsec encapsulation or encryption applied. When you click the **Next** button, a summary displays of the IKE policies (IKE Phase 1) and transform sets (IKE Phase 2) that it will implement on the router. Note that CCP likes to implement the default IKE Phase 1, along with the custom IKE Phase 1 policy, so both will end up in the configuration. The policy also specifies the authentication method we selected earlier in the wizard (PSK), and which network's traffic should be protected. (The traffic to protect is from the outbound perspective. In this case, R1's outbound traffic is from the 10.0.0.0/24 to the 172.16.0.0/24 network.) Figure 6-14 shows this summary table. If everything is correct, click **Finish** to deliver the configuration to the router.

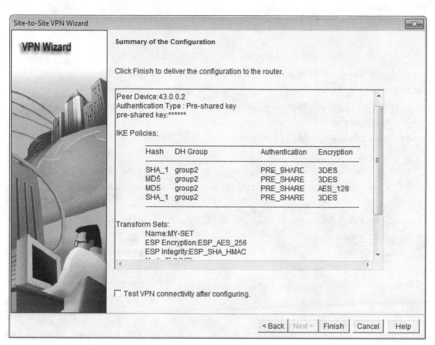

Figure 6-14 *Summary of the VPN Wizard Configuration*

Based on your preference settings, CCP may show you the CLI equivalent of the configuration it is about to deploy or may just deploy it when you click **Finish**. You can control these settings in the preference settings for CCP.

Viewing the CLI Equivalent at the Router

Example 6-1 shows the CLI equivalent that is implemented on R1 from the configuration we did in CCP on R1.

Example 6-1 *The CLI Equivalent Commands to Implement IPsec VPNs*

```
! This implements our IKE Phase 1 policy. The default policy that CPP
! implements is its policy #1, (which has higher priority than a higher
! numbered policy, including our policy #2.)
R1(config-isakmp)# crypto isakmp policy 2
R1(config-isakmp)# authentication pre-share
R1(config-isakmp)# encr aes 128
R1(config-isakmp)# hash md5
R1(config-isakmp)# group 2
R1(config-isakmp)# lifetime 21600
```

```
R1(config-isakmp)# exit
! Note: I like to remove the default policy from CCP for IKE Phase 1, and
! for that reason, I have not replicated it here.


! This specifies that the PSK of cisco123 should be used as a key for the
! authentication of IKE Phase 1 with peer 43.0.0.2.
R1(config)# crypto isakmp key cisco123 address 43.0.0.2


! Access list that identifies any traffic from the 10.0.0.0/24 network
! and destined for the 172.16.0.0/24 network. An ACL used for cryptography
! is often referred to as a "crypto ACL". This ACL will not be directly
! applied to an interface, but rather it will be called on or "referenced"
! within the crypto map, later in this configuration.
R1(config)# access-list 100 permit ip 10.0.0.0 0.0.0.255 172.16.0.0 0.0.0.255


! The IKE Phase 2 transform set that says SHA and AES 256 should be used.
R1(config)# crypto ipsec transform-set MY-SET esp-sha-hmac esp-aes 256


! Tunnel mode is the default, and means that R1 will take any outbound
! packets matching the access list, encrypt them and then re-encapsulate
! them inside of an IPsec packet, which is then forwarded to the peer (R2)
! on the other side of the VPN tunnel. Whenever customer traffic is going
! through a VPN router, it will need to be in tunnel mode to work.
! Transport mode is the other option, and it is used only when the transit
! traffic is directly from and to the endpoints of the VPN tunnel (such as
! R1 and R2 talking amongst themselves). Because we are encrypting traffic
! for the end users, tunnel mode (the default) will be used.
R1(cfg-crypto-trans)# mode tunnel


R1(cfg-crypto-trans)# exit


! The crypto map is a big "if-then" statement. It is applied to the outside
! (Internet facing) interface, and then it watches for traffic.
! If outbound traffic matches the ACL, then the router knows the packet
! should be encrypted, encapsulated into an IPsec header (usually protocol
! 50, which is ESP and stands for Encapsulating Security Payload), and then
! sent to the IP address of the peer on the other side (R2) who would
! decrypt and forward the plain text packet to the device on network
! 172.16.0.0/24 "ipsec-isakmp" means that we want the router to automatically
! negotiate the IKE Phase 2 tunnel, using isakmp, which stands for Internet
! Security Association Key Management Protocol. In short, it means automate
! the process, so the administrator doesn't manually have to configure all
! keys for encryption. The "1" represents sequence number 1. If we had
! 5 different IPsec peers, we could use 5 different sequence numbers in the
! same crypto map to organize our policies based on the sequence number and
! corresponding peer we would be using IPsec with.
```

```
R1(config)# crypto map SDM_CMAP_1 1 ipsec-isakmp

! This tells the crypto map to pay attention to ACL 100 to see if traffic
! should be encrypted or not
R1(config-crypto-map)# match address 100
! If the traffic matches the ACL, then R1 should use the transform-set
! named MY-SET to negotiate the IKE Phase 2 tunnel, with the peer at
! 43.0.0.2
! If the IKE Phase 1 tunnel isn't present, it will trigger the negotiation
! of that first. If the IKE Phase 2 is already in place, the router will
! use the existing tunnel for the encryption and transmission of the
! customer's packet
R1(config-crypto-map)# set transform-set MY-SET
R1(config-crypto-map)# set peer 43.0.0.2
R1(config-crypto-map)# exit

! Applying the crypto map to the interface, is what activates our policy,
! and tells the router to start paying attention in looking for interesting
! traffic (which is the traffic that matches the ACLs referenced in the
! crypto map).
R1(config)# interface GigabitEthernet1/0
R1(config-if)# crypto map SDM_CMAP_1
R1(config-if)# exit
%CRYPTO-6-ISAKMP_ON_OFF: ISAKMP is ONcom
```

Completing and Verifying IPsec

When you click **Finish**, the CCP shows you the status of the VPN tunnel, as shown in Figure 6-15. The reason the tunnel is down is because the other side is not yet configured.

To configure R2, we could select R2 from within CCP and follow the same process. A short-cut that CCP has provided is the ability to use the Generate Mirror button from R1's CCP, and then modify and apply that mirror image of the VPN-related configuration to R2. Figure 6-16 shows the result of clicking the **Generate Mirror** button.

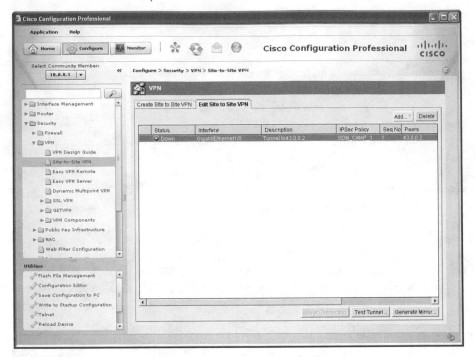

Figure 6-15 *Results of Finishing the VPN Wizard*

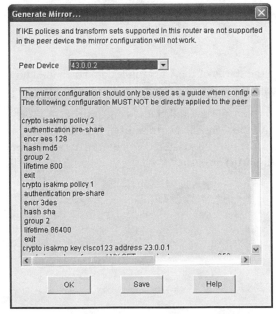

Figure 6-16 *Generating a Mirror of the VPN as a Guideline for the Remote Peer*

We could then take this file, edit it, and apply it to R2. Example 6-2 shows an edited file that is appropriate for R2.

Example 6-2 *Edited Mirrored VPN Configuration Appropriate for R2*

```
crypto isakmp policy 2
 authentication pre-share
 encr aes 128
 hash md5
 group 2
 lifetime 21600
 exit


crypto isakmp key cisco123 address 23.0.0.1
crypto ipsec transform-set MY-SET esp-sha-hmac esp-aes 256
 mode tunnel
 exit

ip access-list extended SDM_1
 permit ip 172.16.0.0 0.0.0.255 10.0.0.0 0.0.0.255
 exit

crypto map SDM_CMAP_1 1 ipsec-isakmp
 match address SDM_1
 set transform-set MY-SET
 set peer 23.0.0.1
 exit

interface g1/0
crypto map SDM_CMAP_1
end
```

If you are using CCP and apply this directly to the CLI of R2, be sure to refresh or redis-
cover R2 via CCP to reflect the changes. Saving the changes to NVRAM is also recommended after a working solution has been implemented. After generating some traffic from
a device on the 10.0.0.0/24 network that is destined for 172.16.0.0/24, the outbound traffic
on R1 should trigger encryption, which triggers IKE Phase 1 and Phase 2 to build their tunnels and then begin forwarding the traffic. The successful ping of a device in the 10.0.0.0/24
network to a device in the 172.16.0.0 network, along with the status being shown from CCP,
confirms that the VPN tunnel is working, as shown in Figure 6-17.

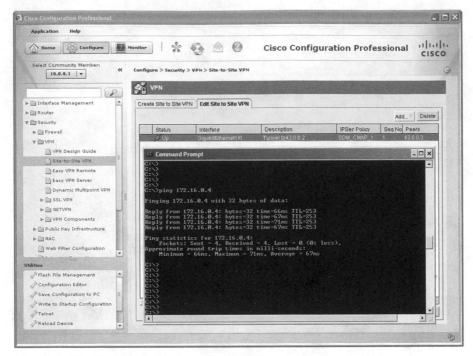

Figure 6-17 *Verifying the Tunnel Is Working*

Subsequent user packets use the newly formed IKE Phase 2 (IPsec) tunnel for the lifetime of that tunnel. From the command line, you could use the following to verify the IPsec, as well, as shown in Example 6-3.

Example 6-3 *Verifying the IPsec VPN from the CLI*

```
! Verify the IKE Phase 1 policies in place on the router
R1# show crypto isakmp policy

Global IKE policy
Protection suite of priority 2
        encryption algorithm:    AES - Advanced Encryption Standard (128 bit keys).
        hash algorithm:          Message Digest 5
        authentication method:   Pre-Shared Key
        Diffie-Hellman group:    #2 (1024 bit)
        lifetime:                21600 seconds, no volume limit

! Show the details of the crypto map, and where it is applied, showing
! the contents of the IKE Phase 2 transform sets, learning the ACLs
! involved for the VPN, who the current peer is, and more.
R1# show crypto map
Crypto Map "SDM_CMAP_1" 1 ipsec-isakmp
        Description: Tunnel to43.0.0.2
        Peer = 43.0.0.2
```

```
        Extended IP access list 100
            access-list 100 permit ip 10.0.0.0 0.0.0.255 172.16.0.0 0.0.0.255
        Current peer: 43.0.0.2
        Security association lifetime: 4608000 kilobytes/3600 seconds
        Responder-Only (Y/N): N
        PFS (Y/N): N
        Transform sets={
                MY-SET:  { esp-256-aes esp-sha-hmac  } ,
        }
        Interfaces using crypto map SDM_CMAP_1:
                GigabitEthernet1/0


! See the details for the IKE Phase 1 tunnel that is in place


R1# show crypto isakmp sa detail
Codes: C - IKE configuration mode, D - Dead Peer Detection
       K - Keepalives, N - NAT-traversal
       T - cTCP encapsulation, X - IKE Extended Authentication
       psk - Preshared key, rsig - RSA signature
       renc - RSA encryption
IPv4 Crypto ISAKMP SA


C-id  Local       Remote      I-VRF      Status Encr Hash Auth DH Lifetime Cap.


1001  23.0.0.1    43.0.0.2               ACTIVE aes  md5  psk  2  00:04:05
        Engine-id:Conn-id =  SW:1


! See the details for the IKE Phase 2 tunnels that are in place.  There is
! one inbound Security Association (SA) and one outbound. They both have
! different SA numbers used for tracking these sessions.
! ESP is used, and it provides all the services desirable from IPsec.
! The other option is Authentication Header (AH) which isn't used because
! it doesn't support any encryption algorithms.
R1# show crypto ipsec sa
<Note: less relevant content removed>
interface: GigabitEthernet1/0
    Crypto map tag: SDM_CMAP_1, local addr 23.0.0.1
! Shows what traffic is being encrypted.  All IP traffic between
! 10.0.0.0/24 and 172.16.0.0/24
   local  ident (addr/mask/prot/port): (10.0.0.0/255.255.255.0/0/0)
   remote ident (addr/mask/prot/port): (172.16.0.0/255.255.255.0/0/0)


! IKE Phase 1 uses UDP port 500 to negotiate and set up the IKE Phase 1
! tunnel
   current_peer 43.0.0.2 port 500
```

6

```
      #pkts encaps: 29, #pkts encrypt: 29, #pkts digest: 29
      #pkts decaps: 29, #pkts decrypt: 29, #pkts verify: 29


! From R1's perspective, the local side is its G1/0, and R2 is at 43.0.0.2
      local crypto endpt.: 23.0.0.1, remote crypto endpt.: 43.0.0.2
      path mtu 1500, ip mtu 1500, ip mtu idb GigabitEthernet1/0


! An SPI is a Security Parameter Index.  It is a fancy way of tracking
! a specific Security Association (SA) between itself and a peer.
! Think of it as a serial number (unique) for each SA.
      current outbound spi: 0x48A3CF57(1218694999)
! PFS stands for Perfect Forward Secrecy, and it is the ability for IKE
! Phase 2 to run the DH algorithm again, instead of using the keys
! generated during the DH from IKE Phase 1.   This feature is off by
! default for most platforms.
      PFS (Y/N): N, DH group: none


! The IPsec or IKE Phase 2 is really two tunnels.   There is one for
! traffic from R1 to R2.   There is another from R2 to R1.   They have
! different SPIs, but together, these two unidirectional tunnels make up
! the "IPsec" tunnel.
! Encapsulating Security Payload (ESP) is the primary method used by IPsec.
! The other option is to use Authentication Header (AH), but it doesn't
! have the ability to encrypt, and isn't often used for that reason.   AH
! also breaks when going through Network Address Translation (NAT).
! Here is the inbound SA used by R1 to receive encrypted user packets from
! R2.
      inbound esp sas:
       spi: 0xE732E3A0(3878871968)
         transform: esp-256-aes esp-sha-hmac ,
         in use settings ={Tunnel, }
         conn id: 1, flow_id: SW:1, sibling_flags 80000046, crypto map:
          SDM_CMAP_1
         sa timing: remaining key lifetime (k/sec): (4388080/3230)
         IV size: 16 bytes
! Here is the built in anti-replay support
         replay detection support: Y
         Status: ACTIVE
! We aren't using AH, so there are no Security Associations (SAs) for AH.
      inbound ah sas:


! Here is the Outbound SA used by R1 to send encrypted user packets to R2.
      outbound esp sas:
       spi: 0x48A3CF57(1218694999)
         transform: esp-256-aes esp-sha-hmac ,
         in use settings ={Tunnel, }
```

```
        conn id: 2, flow_id: SW:2, sibling_flags 80000046, crypto map: SDM_
         CMAP_1
        sa timing: remaining key lifetime (k/sec): (4388079/3230)
        IV size: 16 bytes
        replay detection support: Y
        Status: ACTIVE


     outbound ah sas:


! Another way of seeing that the encryption and decryption is working.
R1# show crypto engine connections active
Crypto Engine Connections

  ID  Type    Algorithm        Encrypt  Decrypt IP-Address
   1  IPsec   AES256+SHA             0       29 23.0.0.1
   2  IPsec   AES256+SHA            29        0 23.0.0.1
1001  IKE     MD5+AES               0        0 23.0.0.1
```

6

Exam Preparation Tasks

Review All the Key Topics

Review the most important topics from this chapter, denoted with a Key Topic icon. Table 6-3 lists these key topics.

Table 6-3   Key Topics

Key Topic Element	Description	Page Number
Section	The Goal of IPsec	122
Section	The Play by Play for IPsec	124
Text	How to remember the five items negotiated in IKE Phase 1	125
Section	Now IPsec Can Protect the User's Packets	127
Section	Traffic After IPsec	127
Section	Summary of the IPsec Story	128
Section	Start with a Plan	129
Figure 6-8	Entering Custom IKE Phase 1 Policies	133
Figure 6-11	Creating a New Transform Set (IKE Phase 2 Policy)	135
Figure 6-13	Configuring the ACL Used to Classify Whether Traffic Should Be Protected by IPsec	136
Example 6-1	The CLI Equivalent Commands to Implement IPsec VPNs	137
Example 6-2	Edited Mirrored VPN Configuration Appropriate for R2	141
Example 6-3	Verifying the IPsec VPN from the CLI	142

Complete the Tables and Lists from Memory

Print a copy of Appendix C, "Memory Tables," (found on the CD) or at least the section for this chapter, and complete the tables and lists from memory. Appendix D, "Memory Tables Answer Key," also on the CD, includes completed tables and lists so that you can check your work.

Define Key Terms

Define the following key terms from this chapter, and check your answers in the glossary:

IKE Phase 1, IKE Phase 2, transform set, DH group, lifetime, authentication, encryption, hashing, DH key exchange

Command Reference to Check Your Memory

This section includes the most important configuration and EXEC commands covered in this chapter. To see how well you have memorized the commands as a side effect of your other studies, cover the left side of Table 6-4 with a piece of paper, read the descriptions on the right side, and see whether you remember the commands.

Table 6-4   Command Reference

Command	Description
crypto map *mymap 1* ipsec-isakmp	Generate or edit a crypto map named MYMAP, sequence number 1, and request the services of ISAKMP.
crypto isakmp policy *3*	Enter IKE Phase 1 configuration mode for policy number 3.
show crypto map	Verify which components are included in the crypto map, including the ACL, the peer address, the transform set, and where the crypto map is applied.
crypto ipsec transform set *myset*	This is the beginning sequence to creating an IKE Phase 2 transform set named MYSET. This is followed by the HMAC (hashing with authentication) and encryption method (3DES, or AES preferably) that you want to use.

6

This chapter covers the following topics:

Planning and preparing IPsec site-to-site VPNs

Implementing and verifying IPsec site-to-site VPNs in Cisco IOS routers

Implementing and verifying IPsec site-to-site VPNs in Cisco ASA 5500-X series next-generation firewalls

CHAPTER 7

Implementing IPsec Site-to-Site VPNs

In the previous chapters, you learned about the benefits of *virtual private networks (VPN)* and the protocols and methods used to implement those benefits, such as encryption for confidentiality, hashing for data integrity, and authentication for peer verification. You have also seen examples of these protocols, such as *Triple Digital Encryption Standard (3DES)* and *Advanced Encryption Standard (AES)* for encryption, *message digest 5 algorithm (MD5)* and *Secure Hash Algorithm (SHA)* for data integrity, and *pre-shared keys (PSK)* or RSA signatures (also known as digital signatures) used for authentication.

In this chapter, we look at a case study and implement a VPN site-to-site tunnel using IOS routers as the VPN peers to provide the security the customer is looking for.

"Do I Know This Already?" Quiz

The "Do I Know This Already?" quiz helps you determine your level of knowledge of this chapter's topics before you begin. Table 7-1 details the major topics discussed in this chapter and their corresponding quiz questions.

Table 7-1   "Do I Know This Already?" Section-to-Question Mapping

Foundation Topics Section	Questions
Planning and Preparing an IPsec Site-to-Site VPN	1–6
Implementing and Verifying an IPsec Site-to-Site VPN	7–10
Implementing and Verifying an IPsec Site-to-Site VPN in a Cisco ASA 5500-X Series Next-Generation Firewalls	11–14

1. Which of the following could be part of both an IKEv1 Phase 1 and IKEv1 Phase 2 policy? (Choose all that apply.)

    a. MD5

    b. AES

    c. RSA

    d. DH

2. How is it possible that a packet with a private Layer 3 destination address is forwarded over the Internet?

   a. It is encapsulated into another packet, and the Internet only sees the outside valid IP destination address.

   b. It cannot be sent. It will always be dropped.

   c. The Internet does not filter private addresses, only some public addresses, based on policy.

   d. NAT is used to change the destination IP address before the packet is sent.

3. What is the method for specifying the IKEv1 Phase 2 encryption method?

   a. Crypto ACLs

   b. **crypto isakmp policy**

   c. **crypto ipsec transform-set**

   d. RSA signatures

4. Which of the following potentially could be negotiated during IKEv1 Phase 2? (Choose all that apply.)

   a. Hashing

   b. DH group

   c. Encryption

   d. Authentication method

5. Which of the DH groups is the most prudent to use when security is of the utmost importance?

   a. 1

   b. 2

   c. 5

   d. 6

6. Which of the following is never part of an IKEv1 Phase 2 process?

   a. Main mode

   b. Specifying a hash (HMAC)

   c. Running DH (PFS)

   d. Negotiating the transform set to use

7. Which encryption method will be used to protect the negotiation of the IPsec (IKEv1 Phase 2) tunnel?

   a. The one negotiated in the transform set.

   b. The one negotiated for the IKEv1 Phase 2 tunnel.

   c. The one negotiated in the ISAKMP policy.

   d. There is no encryption during this time; that is why DH is used.

8. Which is the most secure method for authentication of IKEv1 Phase 1?

   a. RSA signatures, using digital certificates to exchange public keys

   b. PSK

   c. DH group 5

   d. Symmetrical AES-256

9. Which component is not placed directly in a crypto map?

   a. Authentication policy

   b. ACL

   c. Transform set

   d. PFS

10. Which of the following would cause a VPN tunnel using IPsec to never initialize or work correctly? (Choose all that apply.)

    a. Incompatible IKEv1 Phase 2 transform sets

    b. Incorrect pre-shared keys or missing digital certificates

    c. Lack of interesting traffic

    d. Incorrect routing

11. Which of the following IKE versions are supported by the Cisco ASA? (Choose all that apply.)

    a. IKEv1

    b. IKEv2

    c. IKEv3

    d. IKEv4

12. What is the purpose of NAT exemption?

    a. To bypass NAT in the remote peer

    b. To bypass NAT for all traffic not sent over the IPsec tunnel

    c. To bypass NAT for traffic in the VPN tunnel

    d. To never bypass NAT in the local or remote peer

13. Which of the following commands are useful when troubleshooting VPN problems in the Cisco ASA? (Choose all that apply.)

    a. **show isakmp sa detail**

    b. **debug crypto ikev1 | ikev2**

    c. **show crypto ipsec sa detail**

    d. **show vpn-sessiondb**

14. (True or False) The Cisco ASA cannot be configured with more than one IKEv1 or IKEv2 policy.

    a. True

    b. False

Foundation Topics

Planning and Preparing an IPsec Site-to-Site VPN

In this section, we use a case study to identify a customer's needs for VPN services and plan out the details to implement the VPN. This section builds on the information learned in the previous chapters about VPNs.

Customer Needs

For this scenario, let's say you and I have a customer with offices in New York and Raleigh, North Carolina. The office in New York has a local area network and a single router, R1, that connects to the Internet. Router 2 (R2) is used to provide Internet access for the site in Raleigh. Figure 7-1 is a topology diagram of this network.

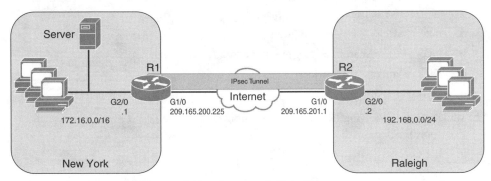

Figure 7-1   *Company Network Topology with Two Sites*

The site in New York has file servers that contain sensitive customer data, and the users at the site in Raleigh will need access to that data. In addition, users in New York need the ability to securely access some of the computers in Raleigh that have file sharing services enabled. Both sites are using private IP addresses for the LAN that cannot be forwarded directly over the Internet.

The customer has asked us for a recommendation to allow file services between the two offices that can be done securely. The customer also wants to ensure that the data as it is being sent over the networks does not become altered or corrupted in transit. The customer is also concerned about a possible attacker, who is on the Internet at some location other than the offices at New York or Raleigh being able to fool one of the routers by pretending to be the other router and connecting to the network. At the current time, the company does not need additional remote access to the networks other than directly between the two sites.

You and I go back to our office and consider the customer's network and requirements. As we consider the VPN options that provide security, we remember that IPsec can perform the following:

- **Confidentiality:** Using symmetrical encryption algorithms such as 3DES, IDEA, AES, and so on to encrypt clear text into cipher text.

- **Data integrity:** Using hashing algorithms such as MD5 or SHA and *Hashed Message Authentication Code (HMAC)* to verify that data has not been manipulated during its transit across the network.

- **Authentication:** Done by authenticating the VPN peers near the beginning of a VPN session, using PSKs or digital signatures (leveraging digital certificates).

- **Hiding the private address space from the Internet:** Because IPsec's *Encapsulation Security Protocol (ESP)* in tunnel mode encrypts and encapsulates the original packet, and then places a new IP header before forwarding the packet, the Internet sees only the packet as being from the global IP address of one router and destined to the global address of the second router.

IPsec uses two methods for encryption: tunnel and transport mode. If IPsec tunnel mode is used, the IP header and the payload are encrypted. When transport mode is used, only the packet payload is encrypted.

IPsec technologies and methods look like a perfect fit for the customer. Before we go too much further, you want to verify that the Internet connection for R1 and R2 are working, and that R1 and R2 have reachability to each other. You can do so with a simple ping to the global address of R2 from R1. If there is filtering of *Internet Control Message Protocol (ICMP)*, which is used by the ping utility, it does not necessarily mean that the IPsec will not work, as the protocols for IPsec may still be allowed between the routers. Table 7-2 shows the critical protocols that we may need between R1 and R2.

Table 7-2 Protocols That May Be Required for IPsec

Protocol/Port	Who Uses It	How It Is Used
UDP port 500	IKEv1 Phase 1	IKEv1 Phase 1 uses UDP:500 for its negotiation.
UDP port 4500	NAT-T (NAT Traversal)	If both peers support NAT-T, and if they detect that they are connecting to each other through a *Network Address Translation (NAT)* device (translation is happening), they may negotiate that they want to put a fake UDP port 4500 header on each IPsec packet (before the ESP header) to survive a NAT device that otherwise may have a problem tracking an ESP session (Layer 4 protocol 50).
Layer 4 Protocol 50	ESP	IPsec packets have the Layer 4 protocol of ESP (IP Protocol #50), which is encapsulated by the sender and decapsulated by the receiver for each IPsec packet. ESP is normally used instead of *Authentication Header (AH)*. The ESP header is hidden behind a UDP header if NAT-T is in use.
Layer 4 protocol 51	AH	AH packets have the Layer 4 protocol of AH (IP Protocol #51). We do not normally use AH (as opposed to ESP) because AH lacks any encryption capability for user data.

If R1 and R2 have access lists applied inbound on their outside interfaces (G1/0), we would want to ensure that we are allowing the required protocols between the global (Internet) IP addresses of the two routers. Each router needs to believe it could reach the remote networks through specific routes, or at a minimum, a default route. If the router does not have a route, it will not try to forward a packet, and will not trigger any crypto maps that are looking for the interesting traffic. The routing decision happens before IPsec is implemented.

7

Planning IKEv1 Phase 1

With the connectivity verified, our first planning step is to choose the components to use for the IKEv1 Phase 1 tunnel. (Remember our HAGLE options from a previous chapter.) Table 7-3 lists some of our choices for IKEv1 Phase 1.

Table 7-3 IKEv1 Phase 1 Policy Options

Function	Strong Method	Stronger Method
Hashing	MD5, 128-bit	SHA1, 160-bit
Authentication	Pre-shared Key (PSK)	RSA-Sigs (digital signatures)
Group # for DH key exchange	1,2,5	IKE Groups 14 and 24 use 2048-bit DH. Groups 15 and 16 use 3072-bit and 4096-bit DH. Groups 19 and 20 support the 256-bit and 384-bit ECDH groups, respectively.
Lifetime	86400 seconds (1 day, default)	Shorter than 1 day, 3600
Encryption	3DES	AES-128 (or 192, or 256)

For the customer, we decide that we will use the stronger options, and will use the following for the IKEv1 Phase 1 policy:

- **Hashing:** SHA
- **Authentication:** RSA-Sigs (which require PKI to be used)
- **DH group:** 5
- **Lifetime:** 3600 seconds
- **Encryption:** AES-256

We also note that all of these parameters are to be used for the IKEv1 Phase 1 policy, which we specify using the command **crypto isakmp policy**.

Planning IKEv1 Phase 2

For IKEv1 Phase 2, which is the actual tunnel that will be used to protect the user's packets, we have the elements listed in Table 7-4 to plan for.

Table 7-4 IKEv1 Phase 2 Policy Options

Item to Plan	Implemented By	Notes
Peer IP addresses	Crypto map	Having a known reachable IP address for the VPN peer is critical for the traditional IPsec site-to-site tunnel to negotiate and establish the VPN (both phases).
Traffic to encrypt	Crypto ACL, which is referred to in the crypto map	Extended ACL that is not applied to an interface but is referenced in the crypto map. This should *only* reference outbound (egress) traffic, which should be protected by IPsec. Traffic not matching the crypto ACL will not be encrypted, but will be sent as a normal packet.

Item to Plan	Implemented By	Notes
Encryption method	Transform set, which is referred to in the crypto map	DES, 3DES, AES are all options. IKEv1 Phase 2 does not need to be the same method as Phase 1. The method does need to match the peer's policy (transform sets) for Phase 2.
Hashing (HMAC) method	Transform set, which is referred to in the crypto map	MD5 and SHA HMACs may be used, and need to match the Phase 2 policy of the peer.
Lifetime (time, or data)	Global configuration command: **crypto ipsec security-association lifetime** ...	Lifetime for Phase 2 should match between the peers. If both use the default lifetime (by not specifying a lifetime), both peers would have compatible lifetime policies. The lifetime can be specified as number of seconds or number of kilobytes.
Perfect Forward Secrecy (PFS) (run DH again or not)	Crypto map	DH is run during IKEv1 Phase 1, and Phase 2 reuses that same keying material that was generated. If you want Phase 2 to rerun the DH, it is called Perfect Forward Secrecy (PFS), and you must choose a DH group number 1, 2, or 5 for Phase 2 to use.
Which interface used to peer with the other VPN device	Crypto map applied to the outbound interface	From a routing perspective, this is the interface of a VPN peer that is closest to the other peer, where outbound IPsec packets are leaving the router and inbound IPsec packets are coming into the router.

For our customer, we document and decide to implement the following for IKEv1 Phase 2:

- **VPN Peer global IP addresses:** R1=209.165.200.225 R2=209.165.201.1
- **Traffic to protect:** Bidirectional traffic between 172.16.0.0/16 (R1's local network) and 192.168.0.0/24 (R2's local network).
- **Encryption:** AES-192 (just to mix it up a bit, default for AES is 128)
- **HMAC:** SHA
- **Lifetime:** Default
- **Outside interfaces of routers:** G1/0 (on both)
- **PFS:** Group 2

With our plan in place, our next step is to implement the IPsec tunnel. If you have not done so already, I would like you to write out, on a piece of paper, our plans for both IKEv1 Phase 1 and IKEv1 Phase 2. By doing this, you have a resource you can look at, without turning the pages back and forth, as we implement the IPsec together.

Implementing and Verifying an IPsec Site-to-Site VPN in Cisco IOS Devices

In this section, we take the information from our planning in the previous section to implement, verify, and troubleshoot the VPN using a combination of *Cisco Configuration Professional (CCP)* and the *command-line interface (CLI)*.

In earlier chapters, we discussed important resources such as *Network Time Protocol (NTP)* and *certificate authorities (CA)*. Because we chose to implement RSA-Signatures for this customer, we want to implement NTP as one of our first steps. This is because when exchanging certificates during IKEv1 Phase 1, if R1 thinks the year is 2040, and the certificate it just received from R2 is listed as being valid from 2012 through 2016, R1 will reject the certificate as not being valid, and IKEv1 Phase 1 will not end well. (If IKEv1 Phase 1 does not work, IKEv1 Phase 2 does not have a chance either.) So for this implementation, we use a service provider on the simulated Internet (in our customer's topology) that will provide both NTP and CA services at the address of 3.3.3.3 (in the simulated Internet portion of the topology diagram).

Let's synchronize the time on both R1 and R2 with the service provider's NTP server, as shown in Figure 7-2.

Figure 7-2 *Configuring the Router to Use NTP Services*

The same process would be repeated for the other router as well. NTP can take up to 15 minutes to synchronize. Another item to be aware of is that NTP servers deliver time based on *coordinated universal time (UTC)*, and setting the local time zone on your router is important so that correct offset from UTC is reflected on the local router. To verify that the time is synchronized with the time server, at the CLI of the router we can use the commands shown in Example 7-1.

Example 7-1   *Verifying NTP Status*

```
R1# show ntp status
Clock is unsynchronized, stratum 16, no reference clock
nominal freq is 250.0000 Hz, actual freq is 249.9999 Hz, precision is 2**24
reference time is D2C15194.71E5E637 (14:11:32.444 UTC Wed Jan 18 2012)
clock offset is 0.0000 msec, root delay is 0.00 msec
root dispersion is 0.00 msec, peer dispersion is 0.00 msec
loopfilter state is 'CTRL' (Normal Controlled Loop), drift is 0.000000085 s/s
system poll interval is 64, last update was 1518 sec ago.

! Note the above indicates the time isn't synchronized.
! We can check to see if the router has the NTP server configured with the
! following:


R1# show ntp association

  address         ref clock      st    when    poll reach  delay  offset    disp
~3.3.3.3          .INIT.         16     -       64     0  0.000   0.000 16000.
* sys.peer, # selected, + candidate, - outlyer, x falseticker, ~ configured


! Based on this output, we know that it has information to use the 3.3.3.3
! server
! It may take anywhere from 5 to 15 minutes for
! the synchronization to happen.    After verifying the configuration, and
! waiting about 5 minutes, we can then issue the verification commands
! again and see that the synchronization is complete.
R1# show ntp status
Clock is synchronized, stratum 3, reference is 3.3.3.3
nominal freq is 250.0000 Hz, actual freq is 249.9999 Hz, precision is 2**24
reference time is D2C15854.6F453DAE (14:40:20.434 UTC Wed Jan 18 2012)
clock offset is 0.0029 msec, root delay is 0.01 msec
root dispersion is 0.95 msec, peer dispersion is 0.06 msec
loopfilter state is 'CTRL' (Normal Controlled Loop), drift is 0.000000097 s/s
system poll interval is 64, last update was 251 sec ago.
```

7

Our next task, in preparation for the IPsec, is to generate key pairs on R1 and R2, configure them to use a CA, have them authenticate the CA (get the root certificate), and then enroll with the CA (request their own identity certificates). The CA is at 3.3.3.3 and supports *Simple Certificate Enrollment Protocol (SCEP)*. From R1 and R2, the process is the same, and the commands used for R1 are shown in Example 7-2.

Example 7-2   *Preparing for and Obtaining Digital Certificates*

```
! Specify the domain-name that will be included with the key pair you
! are about to generate
! Note: if you have already created a key-pair to be used with SSH
! you don't need to create a separate key-pair.  You can use the same
! key pair for both purposes if desired.
R1(config)# ip domain name cisco.com
R1(config)# crypto key generate rsa
The name for the keys will be: R1.cisco.com
Choose the size of the key modulus in the range of 360 to 2048 for your
   General Purpose Keys. Choosing a key modulus greater than 512 may take
   a few minutes.
! The larger the key the better.  Using a minimum length of 1024 is a best
! practice
How many bits in the modulus [512]: 1024
% Generating 1024 bit RSA keys, keys will be non-exportable...[OK]

! Specify the CA that you would like to use, and the URL to be used to
! reach that CA
R1(config)# crypto pki trustpoint CA
R1(ca-trustpoint)# enrollment URL http://3.3.3.3
R1(ca-trustpoint)# exit

! Request the root certificate through "authenticating" the CA
R1(config)# crypto pki authenticate CA
Certificate has the following attributes:
       Fingerprint MD5: B1AF5247 21F35FE3 0200F345 7C20FBA0
       Fingerprint SHA1: F5BB33E3 1CB5D633 0DF720DF 8C72CD48 E744CF5B

% Do you accept this certificate? [yes/no]: yes
Trustpoint CA certificate accepted.

! Request an Identity certificate for this router, via SCEP and the
! "enroll" option
R1(config)# crypto pki enroll CA
%
% Start certificate enrollment ..
% Create a challenge password. You will need to verbally provide this
   password to the CA Administrator in order to revoke your certificate.
   For security reasons your password will not be saved in the configuration.
   Please make a note of it.

! Specifying the challenge password that can be used in the event you need to
! ask the CA to revoke this certificate in the future
Password: SuperSecret!23
```

```
Re-enter password: SuperSecret!23


% The subject name in the certificate will include: R1.cisco.com


! The next 2 items are optional elements that may be included in the certificate
% Include the router serial number in the subject name? [yes/no]: no
% Include an IP address in the subject name? [no]: no
Request certificate from CA? [yes/no]: yes
% Certificate request sent to Certificate Authority
% The 'show crypto pki certificate verbose CA' command will show the fingerprint.


CRYPTO_PKI:  Certificate Request Fingerprint MD5: E8E01D26 862C811C 32CB3FCF 858BAF5F
CRYPTO_PKI:  Certificate Request Fingerprint SHA1: E3133B07 07DEA5FD BC6A1D64 DBC9F71F
  3CACA767
%PKI-6-CERTRET: Certificate received from Certificate Authority


! We would repeat this process on the other router, R2
```

After we have digital certificates on both routers, we can configure the IKEv1 Phase 1 policy. This can be done in CCP by navigating to **Configure > Security > VPN > Site-to-Site
VPN**, as shown in Figure 7-3.

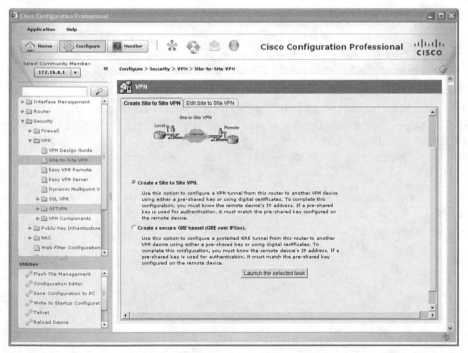

Figure 7-3 *Using the Site-to-Site VPN Wizard in CCP*

Using the **Launch the Selected Task** button to continue, we choose the **Step-by-Step Wizard** (in contrast to Quick Setup), and then click the **Next** button. We have the opportunity to begin entering the information we collected earlier about the interfaces to use and the policies to implement, as shown in Figure 7-4.

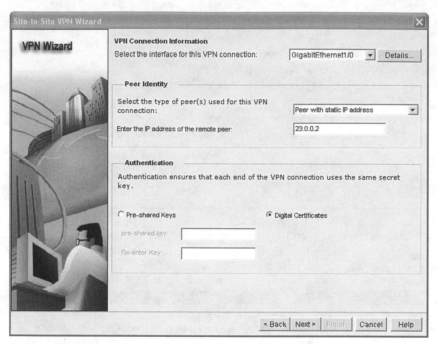

Figure 7-4 *Supplying the Wizard with the Information from Our Design for This Customer*

Notice that this time, because of our policy, we select the **Digital Certificates** radio button instead of using pre-shared keys for the authentication. After clicking **Next**, we are presented with the default IKEv1 Phase 1 policy, which is built in to CCP. To add a new policy, click the **Add** button and enter the details for the IKEv1 Phase 1 policy per the plan, as shown in Figure 7-5.

After you click **OK**, highlight the new policy, and then click **Next** to advance to the IKEv1 Phase 2 policy information. Once there, click **Add** and enter the IPsec/IKEv1 Phase 2 options that we planned earlier, as shown in Figure 7-6.

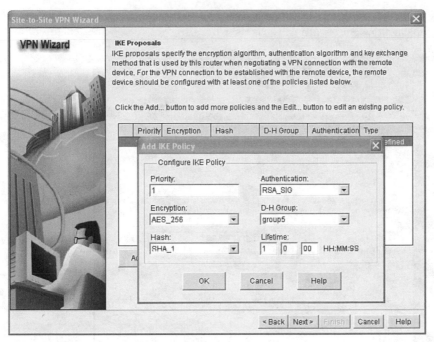

Figure 7-5 *Entering the IKEv1 Phase 1 Policy Details*

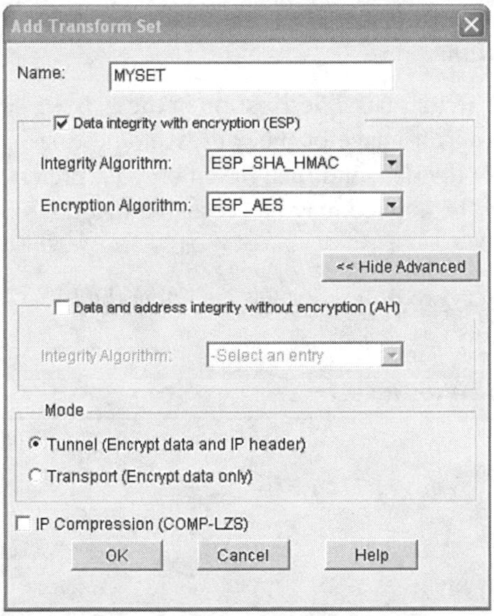

Figure 7-6 *Configuring the IKEv1 Phase 2/Transform Set Details*

Unfortunately, the options for setting up PFS for IKEv1 Phase 2 are not integrated in the wizard. Let's finish the wizard, to confirm the ACL information, by clicking **OK** for the transform set, clicking the transform set to highlight it, and clicking **Next** to continue. In the next window, we specify which traffic to encrypt. Remember that this is from the local router's perspective of outbound traffic that it should apply IPsec to. Figure 7-7 shows an example of implementing our crypto ACLs via the wizard.

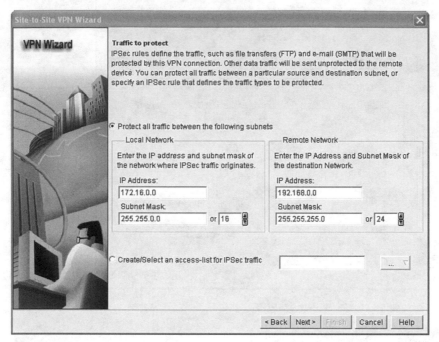

Figure 7-7 *Configuring the Crypto ACL Information*

On R1, the ACL matches on traffic from 172.16.0.0/16 that has a destination in the 192.168.0.0/24 network. The ACL on R2 must be a mirror image of the source and destination networks. When you click **Next**, a summary is provided, and then based on your preference settings in CCP, the actual commands about to be applied may be presented in a final window before you approve them to be delivered.

Example 7-3 shows the CLI implementation of the crypto policy for R1, including the PFS (which the wizard did not offer).

Example 7-3 *CLI Implementation of the Crypto Policy for R1*

```
R1(config)# crypto isakmp policy 1
R1(config-isakmp)# encr aes 256
R1(config-isakmp)# group 5
R1(config-isakmp)# lifetime 3600
R1(config-isakmp)# authentication rsa-sig
R1(config-isakmp)# hash sha


! To verify the configuration:
R1# show crypto isakmp policy

Global IKEv1 policy
Protection suite of priority 1
```

```
        encryption algorithm:    AES - Advanced Encryption Standard (256 bit keys).
        hash algorithm:          Secure Hash Standard
        authentication method:   Rivest-Shamir-Adleman Signature
        Diffie-Hellman group:    #5 (1536 bit)
        lifetime:                3600 seconds, no volume limit
! Note, that a show running-config, would only show configured items in the
! policy if they were different from the default.   Here is a snippet from
! the show run:

crypto isakmp policy 1
 encr aes 256
 group 5
 lifetime 3600


! Because the authentication and hash are using the defaults, they are not
! shown even though we put them in the configuration.   (interesting to know)


! We won't need a pre-shared key, because we are using digital signatures/
! certificates for the IKEv1 Phase 1 authentication.


! Next we can create our transform-set, and crypto ACL, which will be
! placed inside the crypto map.   The crypto map will be applied to the
! interface of the router.



! Transform set details the encryption and HMAC to use
R1(config)# crypto ipsec transform-set MYSET esp-aes esp-sha-hmac
R1(cfg-crypto-trans)# exit


! Crypto ACL identifies which traffic (outbound) should be encrypted
R1(config)# access-list 100 permit ip 172.16.0.0 0.0.255.255 192.168.0.0 0.0.0.255


! The crypto map contains the if/then statement to decide to encrypt or
! not to encrypt a packet on its way out
R1(config)# crypto map MYMAP 1 ipsec-isakmp
R1(config-crypto-map)# match address 100
R1(config-crypto-map)# set peer 209.165.201.1
R1(config-crypto-map)# set transform-set MYSET


! Here is the PFS part that we are adding manually, as the wizard didn't
! support this feature
R1(config-crypto-map)# set pfs group2
R1(config-crypto-map)# exit


! Applying the crypto map to the interface is what allows the entire IPsec
! function to be triggered.   That is why it is important that the router
```

```
! has at least a default route (if not a more specific route) out of this
! interface to reach the remote network for which the router is providing
! IPsec support.
! When the router considers forwarding traffic out the interface, that is
! what triggers the decision to encrypt or not.   If the traffic matches
! the crypto ACL in the crypto map, the router will encrypt the original
! packet, encapsulate the encrypted packet into a new packet with ESP as
! the L4 header, and the peer's global IP address as the new L3 header.
! If no IPsec SA (tunnel) is in place yet, this will also trigger the
! negotiations to build the tunnel, including the IKEv1 Phase 1 if it is not
! already in place.
R1(config)# interface GigabitEthernet1/0
R1(config-if)# crypto map MYMAP
R1(config-if)# exit
```

After the appropriate compatible configuration has been placed on R2, we should be able to
encrypt traffic between the two networks using IPsec.

Troubleshooting IPsec Site-to-Site VPNs in Cisco IOS

When you implement a new VPN, there may be a problem or two. So, let's walk through
the verification of the tunnel, and if we discover it not working, I will show you some of my
favorite commands to assist in the troubleshooting process.

Let's first of all verify our configuration so that we can confirm that what we have running
on the router is what we configured, starting with Example 7-4.

Example 7-4   *Verifying the IPsec Configuration*

```
! This verifies the IKEv1 Phase 1 policy or policies in place.   The lower
! the number of the policy, the higher its priority.

R1# show crypto isakmp policy

Global IKEv1 policy
Protection suite of priority 1
        encryption algorithm:   AES - Advanced Encryption Standard (256 bit keys).
        hash algorithm:         Secure Hash Standard
        authentication method:  Rivest-Shamir-Adleman Signature
        Diffie-Hellman group:   #5 (1536 bit)
        lifetime:               3600 seconds, no volume limit

! Next is my favorite command, as it shows virtually all of the rest of the
! config including the transform set and crypto ACLs involved, and where
! the crypto map is applied
R1# show crypto map
Crypto Map "MYMAP" 1 ipsec-isakmp
        Peer = 209.165.201.1
```

```
Extended IP access list 100
    access-list 100 permit ip 172.16.0.0 0.0.255.255 192.168.0.0
        0.0.0.255
Current peer: 209.165.201.1
Security association lifetime: 4608000 kilobytes/3600 seconds
Responder-Only (Y/N): N
PFS (Y/N): Y
DH group:  group2
Transform sets={
        MYSET:  { esp-aes esp-sha-hmac  } ,
}
Interfaces using crypto map MYMAP:
        GigabitEthernet1/0
```

Armed with this information, a packet from the 172.16.0.0 network destined to the 192.168.0.0 network should trigger the IPsec process. We can test this without even leaving the router console. Because R1 is connected to the 172.16.0.0 network, we can craft a ping request sourced from that network (interface g1/0) and destined for the 192.168.0.2 address or R2, as shown in Example 7-5.

Example 7-5   *Interesting Traffic to Trigger IPsec*

```
R1# ping 192.168.0.2 source g1/0

Type escape sequence to abort.
Sending 5, 100-byte ICMP Echos to 192.168.0.2, timeout is 2 seconds:
Packet sent with a source address of 209.165.200.225
U.U.U
Success rate is 0 percent (0/5)
R1#
```

The ping is being replied to with U.U.U messages. The *U* represents an ICMP unreachable message being sent to us from one of the Internet routers (probably our directly connected one). If our policy was not applied correctly, it may be possible that we are trying to send packets to 192.168.0.2, and when the service providers see these packets, they are denying them because they are addresses in the RFC 1918 address space (which are not being allowed on the Internet). If the packet had been successfully encapsulated into IPsec's Layer 4 protocol 50 (ESP), the Internet would have seen a packet destined to the Layer 3 global address of 209.165.201.1, sourced from the global address of R1.

Let's begin the troubleshooting! We may want to go to R2 and do the same **show** commands we did on R1. If R2 is not accessible via the CLI at the moment, we could also do some additional testing at R1 using **debug** commands specifically for IPsec Phase 1 and Phase 2. For IKEv1 Phase 1 debugging, we could use the commands shown in Example 7-6.

Example 7-6 *Debug Used for Troubleshooting IKEv1 Phase 1*

```
! debug the IKEv1 Phase 1 process
R1# debug crypto isakmp
Crypto ISAKMP debugging is on


! Generate interesting traffic that should match the ACLs used in the crypto map
R1# ping 192.168.0.2 source g1/0


Type escape sequence to abort.
Sending 5, 100-byte ICMP Echos to 192.168.0.2, timeout is 2 seconds:
Packet sent with a source address of 209.165.200.225
U.U.U
Success rate is 0 percent (0/5)
```

With the debugging of IKEv1 Phase 1 on, and then using the ping again, we see no output from the debug. This implies that either IKEv1 Phase 1 is already up and does not need to be negotiated, or if it is currently not up, no interesting traffic is triggering it. This could be due to a down interface, a misapplied crypto map, or routing that is not trying to forward traffic out the interface that has the crypto map applied. Let's take a closer look, as shown in Example 7-7.

Example 7-7 *Troubleshooting by Verifying Configuration*

```
R1# show crypto map
Crypto Map "MYMAP" 1 ipsec-isakmp
        Peer = 209.165.201.1
        Extended IP access list 100
            access-list 100 permit ip 172.16.0.0 0.0.255.255 192.168.0.0 0.0.0.255
        Current peer: 209.165.201.1
        Security association lifetime: 4608000 kilobytes/3600 seconds
        Responder-Only (Y/N): N
        PFS (Y/N): Y
        DH group:  group2
        Transform sets={
                MYSET:  { esp-aes esp-sha-hmac  } ,
        }
        Interfaces using crypto map MYMAP:
                GigabitEthernet1/0


R1# show ip int brief
Interface          IP-Address     OK? Method Status                Protocol
FastEthernet0/0    unassigned     YES unset  administratively down down
GigabitEthernet1/0 209.165.200.225    YES manual  up                    up
GigabitEthernet2/0 172.16.0.1 YES manual  up                    up
```

```
! Just as before, the crypto map appears to be applied to the correct
! interface, and the interfaces are both up.    Let's next check to see if
! there is an IKEv1 Phase 1 tunnel already in place


R1# show crypto isakmp sa
IPv4 Crypto ISAKMP SA
dst             src             state           conn-id status



! The output of the above command indicates that there is no current IKEv1
! Phase 1 tunnel in place.    Let's check routing, to see if R1 would even
! try to forward packets to 192.168.0.2 through its G1/0 interface.


R1# show ip route
Codes: C - connected, S - static, R - RIP, M - mobile, B - BGP
       D - EIGRP, EX - EIGRP external, O - OSPF, IA - OSPF inter area
       N1 - OSPF NSSA external type 1, N2 - OSPF NSSA external type 2
       E1 - OSPF external type 1, E2 - OSPF external type 2
       i - IS-IS, su - IS-IS summary, L1 - IS-IS level-1, L2 - IS-IS
          level-2
       ia - IS-IS inter area, * - candidate default, U - per-user static route
       o - ODR, P - periodic downloaded static route


Gateway of last resort is 209.165.200.226 to network 0.0.0.0

C    172.16.0.0/16 is directly connected, GigabitEthernet2/0
     209.165.200.0/24 is subnetted, 1 subnets
C       209.165.200.0 is directly connected, GigabitEthernet1/0
S*   0.0.0.0/0 [1/0] via 209.165.200.226


! The show IP route output indicates that R1 would use its G1/0 interface
! to use the default gateway of 209.165.200.226   We know that the internet router
! is there, because we received the U messages earlier from him.

! Sometimes, when making configuration changes regarding IPsec,
! the VPN device may become confused   If there is no VPN traffic working,
! I have found that removing and re-applying the crypto map on the
! interface is often helpful in re-starting the IPsec process on the
! router.    Let's try that next on R1.
R1# conf t
Enter configuration commands, one per line.  End with CNTL/Z.
R1(config)# int g1/0
R1(config-if)# no crypto map MYMAP
R1(config-if)# crypto map MYMAP
%CRYPTO-6-ISAKMP_ON_OFF: ISAKMP is OFF
R1(config-if)# crypto map MYMAP
```

7

```
R1(config-if)#
%CRYPTO-6-ISAKMP_ON_OFF: ISAKMP is ON
R1(config-if)#

! I see that ISAKMP turned itself off, when the map was removed and was
! turned back on when the map was replaced, based on the console messages.
! ISAKMP stands for Internet Security Association Key Management Protocol
! Now let's try the ping again.

! Debugging is still on.

R1# show debug

Cryptographic Subsystem:
  Crypto ISAKMP debugging is on


R1# ping 192.168.0.2 source g1/0

Type escape sequence to abort.
Sending 5, 100-byte ICMP Echos to 192.168.0.2, timeout is 2 seconds:
Packet sent with a source address of 209.165.200.225
U.U.U
Success rate is 0 percent (0/5)
R1#
```

Same result as before. So, why are we going through the pain of troubleshooting? Because this is a skill that you deserve to have, and by going through it together, it will make your skills better for the real world. Before we go too much further, let's pause and examine our test ping. A common mistake people make is assuming the VPN should come up, even if there is no interesting traffic (matching the crypto ACLs).

In our ping, we are sourcing the ping from the G1/0 interface (this interface is not the one in the 172.16.0.0/16 network), and therefore as a result the packet is not matching the crypto access control list (ACL). The router does not think it should apply IPsec to it, so it sends the ping out as a plain text. The original source and destination IP addresses have not changed, which would cause the service provider to deny that traffic.

Armed with the knowledge that our test ping had an issue, let's leave the debug on and try the ping, as shown in Example 7-8.

Example 7-8   *Test Ping Using the Correct Source Interface and Associated IP Address*

```
R1# ping 192.168.0.2 source g2/0

! Although there is lots of interesting output, I will point out the
! more relevant information regarding our troubleshooting
```

```
Sending 5, 100-byte ICMP Echos to 192.168.0.2, timeout is 2 seconds:


! Note the correct source address, important if we want to match the crypto
! acls
Packet sent with a source address of 172.16.0.1

ISAKMP:(0): SA request profile is (NULL)
ISAKMP: Created a peer struct for 209.165.201.1, peer port 500
ISAKMP: New peer created peer = 0x6A76F7A0 peer_handle = 0x80000005
ISAKMP: Locking peer struct 0x6A76F7A0, refcount 1 for isakmp_initiator
ISAKMP: local port 500, remote port 500
ISAKMP: set new node 0 to QM_IDLE
ISAKMP:(0):insert sa successfully sa = 66570618
ISAKMP:(0):Can not start Aggressive mode, trying Main mode.
ISAKMP:(0):No pre-shared key with 209.165.201.1!
ISAKMP:(0): constructed NAT-T vendor-rfc3947 ID
ISAKMP:(0): constructed NAT-T vendor-07 ID
ISAKMP:(0): constructed NAT-T vendor-03 ID
ISAKMP:(0): constructed NAT-T vendor-02 ID
ISAKMP:(0):Input = IKEv1_MESG_FROM_IPSEC, IKEv1_SA_REQ_MM
ISAKMP:(0):Old State = IKEv1_READY  New State = IKEv1_I_MM1


ISAKMP:(0): beginning Main Mode exchange

! R1 is the initiator, and so he is sending the first packet, trying
! to negotiate a compatible IKEv1 Phase 1 policy with R2
ISAKMP:(0): sending packet to 209.165.201.1 my_port 500 peer_port 500 (I) MM_NO_STATE
ISAKMP:(0):Sending an IKEv1 IPv4 Packet.
ISAKMP (0): received packet from 209.165.201.1 dport 500 sport 500 Global (I)
  MM_NO_STATE
ISAKMP:(0):Notify has no hash. Rejected.
ISAKMP (0): Unknown Input IKEv1_MESG_FROM_PEER, IKEv1_INFO_NOTIFY:  state =
  IKEv1_I_MM1
ISAKMP:(0):Input = IKEv1_MESG_FROM_PEER, IKEv1_INFO_NOTIFY
ISAKMP:(0):Old State = IKEv1_I_MM1  New State = IKEv1_I_MM1


! This line below is bad news.  IKEv1 Phase 1 failed.
%CRYPTO-6-IKMP_MODE_FAILURE: Processing of Informational mode failed with peer at
  209.165.201.1

! And our pings didn't make it either (no VPN tunnel working yet).
.....
Success rate is 0 percent (0/5)

! The IKEv1 Phase 1 tunnel has a state of MM_NO_STATE which is not good
! We want to see a state of QM_IDLE, meaning the IKEv1 Phase 1 is up, in the
! output of the following command, that shows the state of the IKEv1 Phase 1
```

```
! tunnel

R1# show crypto isakmp sa
IPv4 Crypto ISAKMP SA
dst                 src             state          conn-id status
209.165.201.1       209.165.200.225      MM_NO_STATE          0 ACTIVE
```

Perhaps R2 is not configured correctly. If IKEv1 Phase 1 had completed, we could investigate IKEv1 Phase 2, but due to Phase 1 failing, that is the first thing to check on R2. If the IKEv1 Phase 1 policy matches on R2, we would also want to verify that R2 has a digital certificate to use with the RSA-Signatures. Let's look at R2's policy, as shown in Example 7-9.

Example 7-9   *Verifying the Configuration on R2*

```
R2# show crypto isakmp policy
Global IKEv1 policy
Protection suite of priority 1
        encryption algorithm:    Three key triple DES
        hash algorithm:          Secure Hash Standard
        authentication method:   Rivest-Shamir-Adleman Signature
        Diffie-Hellman group:    #5 (1536 bit)
        lifetime:                3600 seconds, no volume limit

! Based on the output, it appears the encryption algorithm for R2's IKEv1
! Phase 1 is set for 3DES, and R1 was set for AES 256.  That is a problem.
! Let's make the change on R2, enable debugging, and see if we get a better
! result.

! Change the policy on R2
R2(config)# crypto isakmp policy 1
R2(config-isakmp)# encryption aes 256
R2(config-isakmp)# end

! Enable debug of IKEv1 Phase 1 and issue the ping from R2 to trigger the
! crypto ACLs (which are in the crypto map, which is applied to the
! interface)
R2# debug crypto isakmp
Crypto ISAKMP debugging is on

R2# ping 172.16.0.1 source g2/0

Type escape sequence to abort.
Sending 5, 100-byte ICMP Echos to 172.16.0.1, timeout is 2 seconds:
Packet sent with a source address of 192.168.0.2

ISAKMP:(0): SA request profile is (NULL)
ISAKMP: Created a peer struct for 209.165.200.225, peer port 500
```

```
ISAKMP: New peer created peer = 0x6816E21C peer_handle = 0x80000006
ISAKMP: Locking peer struct 0x6816E21C, refcount 1 for isakmp_initiator
ISAKMP: local port 500, remote port 500
ISAKMP: set new node 0 to QM_IDLE
ISAKMP:(0):insert sa successfully sa = 671E34DC


! The two modes for IKEv1 Phase 1 are aggressive, or main.   R2 is going to
! use main mode.
ISAKMP:(0):Can not start Aggressive mode, trying Main mode.


! R2 won't be needing a pre-shared key with R1 for authentication, due to
! it using digital signatures
ISAKMP:(0):No pre-shared key with 209.165.200.225!
ISAKMP:(0): constructed NAT-T vendor-rfc3947 ID
ISAKMP:(0): constructed NAT-T vendor-07 ID
ISAKMP:(0): constructed NAT-T vendor-03 ID
ISAKMP:(0): constructed NAT-T vendor-02 ID
ISAKMP:(0):Input = IKEv1_MESG_FROM_IPSEC, IKEv1_SA_REQ_MM
ISAKMP:(0):Old State = IKEv1_READY  New State = IKEv1_I_MM1


ISAKMP:(0): beginning Main Mode exchange
ISAKMP:(0): sending packet to 209.165.200.225 my_port 500 peer_port 500 (I)
  MM_NO_STATE
ISAKMP:(0):Sending an IKEv1 IPv4 Packet.
ISAKMP (0): received packet from 209.165.200.225 dport 500 sport 500 Global (I)
  MM_NO_STATE
ISAKMP:(0):Input = IKEv1_MESG_FROM_PEER, IKEv1_MM_EXCH
ISAKMP:(0):Old State = IKEv1_I_MM1  New State = IKEv1_I_MM2


ISAKMP:(0): processing SA payload. message ID = 0
ISAKMP:(0): processing vendor id payload
ISAKMP:(0): vendor ID seems Unity/DPD but major 69 mismatch
ISAKMP (0): vendor ID is NAT-T RFC 3947
ISAKMP : Scanning profiles for xauth ...


! Looks like these two peers have found a compatible policy.  It is the
! contents of the policy that need to be compatible, not the literal policy
! priority number  The debug shows the word "transform" but should not be
! confused with IKEv1 Phase 2 which occurs only after IKEv1 Phase 1 (whose
! policy is shown below) is complete.
ISAKMP:(0):Checking ISAKMP transform 1 against priority 1 policy
ISAKMP:        encryption AES-CBC
ISAKMP:        keylength of 256
ISAKMP:        hash SHA
ISAKMP:        default group 5
ISAKMP:        auth RSA sig
```

```
ISAKMP:        life type in seconds
ISAKMP:        life duration (basic) of 3600
! The peers have agreed on the IKEv1 Phase 1 policy.
ISAKMP:(0):atts are acceptable. Next payload is 0
ISAKMP:(0):Acceptable atts:actual life: 0
ISAKMP:(0):Acceptable atts:life: 0
ISAKMP:(0):Basic life_in_seconds:3600
ISAKMP:(0):Returning Actual lifetime: 3600
ISAKMP:(0)::Started lifetime timer: 3600.


ISAKMP:(0): processing vendor id payload
ISAKMP:(0): vendor ID seems Unit.y/DPD but major 69 mismatch
ISAKMP (0): vendor ID is NAT-T RFC 3947
ISAKMP:(0):Input = IKEv1_MESG_INTERNAL, IKEv1_PROCESS_MAIN_MODE
ISAKMP:(0):Old State = IKEv1_I_MM2  New State = IKEv1_I_MM2
! Next 40 or so lines include getting the certificate from the other side,
! so that this router will have a copy of the peer's public key, and
! performing RSA authentication with the peer.
ISAKMP (0): constructing CERT_REQ for issuer cn=CA
ISAKMP:(0): sending packet to 209.165.200.225 my_port 500 peer_port 500 (I)
  MM_SA_SETUP
ISAKMP:(0):Sending an IKEv1 IPv4 Packet.
ISAKMP:(0):Input = IKEv1_MESG_INTERNAL, IKEv1_PROCESS_COMPLETE
ISAKMP:(0):Old State = IKEv1_I_MM2  New State = IKEv1_I_MM3


ISAKMP (0): received packet from 209.165.200.225 dport 500 sport 500 Global (I)
  MM_SA_SETUP
ISAKMP:(0):Input = IKEv1_MESG_FROM_PEER, IKEv1_MM_EXCH
ISAKMP:(0):Old State = IKEv1_I_MM3  New State = IKEv1_I_MM4


ISAKMP:(0): processing KE payload. message ID = 0
ISAKMP:(0): processing NONCE payload. message ID = 0
ISAKMP:(1004): processing CERT_REQ payload. message ID = 0
ISAKMP:(1004): peer wants a CT_X509_SIGNATURE cert
ISAKMP:(1004): peer wants cert issued by cn=CA
 Choosing trustpoint CA as issuer
ISAKMP:(1004): processing vendor id payload
ISAKMP:(1004): vendor ID is Unity
ISAKMP:(1004): processing vendor id payload
ISAKMP:(1004): vendor ID is DPD
ISAKMP:(1004): processing vendor id payload
ISAKMP:(1004): speaking to another IOS box!
ISAKMP:received payload type 20
ISAKMP (1004): His hash no match - this node outside NAT
ISAKMP:received payload type 20
ISAKMP (1004): No NAT Found for self or peer
```

```
ISAKMP:(1004):Input = IKEv1_MESG_INTERNAL, IKEv1_PROCESS_MAIN_MODE
ISAKMP:(1004):Old State = IKEv1_I_MM4  New State = IKEv1_I_MM4


ISAKMP:(1004):Send initial contact
ISAKMP:(1004):My ID configured as IPv4 Addr, but Addr not in Cert!
ISAKMP:(1004):Using FQDN as My ID
ISAKMP:(1004):SA is doing RSA signature authentication using id type ID_FQDN
ISAKMP (1004): ID payload
        next-payload : 6
        type         : 2
        FQDN name    : R2.cisco.com
        protocol     : 17
        port         : 500
        length       : 20
ISAKMP:(1004):Total payload length: 20
ISAKMP (1004): constructing CERT payload for hostnam.e=R2.cisco.com
ISAKMP:(1004): using the CA trustpoint's keypair to sign
ISAKMP:(1004): sending packet to 209.165.200.225 my_port 500 peer_port 500 (I)
  MM_KEY_EXCH
ISAKMP:(1004):Sending an IKEv1 IPv4 Packet.
ISAKMP:(1004):Input = IKEv1_MESG_INTERNAL, IKEv1_PROCESS_COMPLETE
ISAKMP:(1004):Old State = IKEv1_I_MM4  New State = IKEv1_I_MM5


ISAKMP (1004): received packet from 209.165.200.225 dport 500 sport 500 Global (I)
  MM_KEY_EXCH
ISAKMP:(1004): processing ID payload. message ID = 0
ISAKMP (1004): ID payload
        next-payload : 6
        type         : 2
        FQDN name    : R1.cisco.com
        protocol     : 17
        port         : 500
        length       : 20
ISAKMP:(0):: peer matches *none* of the profiles
ISAKMP:(1004): processing CERT payload. message ID = 0
ISAKMP:(1004): processing a CT_X509_SIGNATURE cert
ISAKMP:(1004): peer's pubkey is cached
ISAKMP:(1004): Unable to get DN from certificate!
ISAKMP:(1004): Cert presented by peer contains no OU field.
ISAKMP:(0):: peer matches *none* of the profiles
ISAKMP:(1004): processing SIG payload. message ID = 0
ISAKMP:(1004):SA authentication status:
        authenticated

! The IKEv1 Phase 1 authentication completed successfully
ISAKMP:(1004):SA has been authenticated with 209.165.200.225
```

7

```
ISAKMP: Trying to insert a peer 209.165.201.1/209:165.200.225/500/,  and inserted
   successfully 6816E21C.
ISAKMP:(1004):Input = IKEv1_MESG_FROM_PEER, IKEv1_MM_EXCH
ISAKMP:(1004):Old State = IKEv1_I_MM5  New State = IKEv1_I_MM6


ISAKMP:(1004):Input = IKEv1_MESG_INTERNAL, IKEv1_PROCESS_MAIN_MODE
ISAKMP:(1004):Old State = IKEv1_I_MM6  New State = IKEv1_I_MM6


ISAKMP:(1004):Input = IKEv1_MESG_INTERNAL, IKEv1_PROCESS_COMPLETE
ISAKMP:(1004):Old State = IKEv1_I_MM6  New State = IKEv1_P1_COMPLETE


! Now that IKEv1 Phase 1 is complete, IKEv1 Phase 2 (quick mode) can begin.
ISAKMP:(1004):beginning Quick Mode exchange, M-ID of -534639709
ISAKMP:(1004):QM Initiator gets spi
ISAKMP:(1004): sending packet to 209.165.200.225 my_port 500 peer_port 500 (I) QM_IDLE
ISAKMP:(1004):Sending an IKEv1 IPv4 Packet.
ISAKMP:(1004):Node -534639709, Input = IKEv1_MESG_INTERNAL, IKEv1_INIT_QM
ISAKMP:(1004):Old State = IKEv1_QM_READY  New State = IKEv1_QM_I_QM1
ISAKMP:(1004):Input = IKEv1_MESG_INTERNAL, IKEv1_PHASE1_COMPLETE


ISAKMP:(1004):Old State = IKEv1_P1_COMPLETE  New State = IKEv1_P1_COMPLETE


ISAKMP (1004): received packet from 209.165.200.225 dport 500 sport 500 Global (I)
   QM_IDLE
ISAKMP: set new node -325744431 to QM_IDLE
ISAKMP:(1004): processing HASH payload. message ID = -325744431
ISAKMP:(1004): processing NOTIFY PROPOSAL_NOT_CHOSEN protocol 3
        spi 3138923289, message ID = -325744431, sa = 671E34DC
ISAKMP:(1004): deleting spi 3138923289 message ID = -534639709
ISAKMP:(1004):deleting node -534639709 error TRUE reason "Delete Larval"
ISAKMP:(1004):deleting node -325744431 error FALSE reason "Informational (in) state 1"
ISAKMP:(1004):Input = IKEv1_MESG_FROM_PEER, IKEv1_INFO_NOTIFY
ISAKMP:(1004):Old State = IKEv1_P1_COMPLETE  New State = IKEv1_P1_COMPLETE


! Bad news, the IKEv1 Phase 2 (the IPsec tunnel) didn't come up and allow the
! pings to work.   All 5 pings are lost.   The missing 3 periods are
! embedded  in the debug messages above.
..
Success rate is 0 percent (0/5)
R2#
```

With IKEv1 Phase 1 working, let's focus on IKEv1 Phase 2 and see whether we can resolve the problem (because the pings did not make it through) by comparing the IKEv1 Phase 2 components on both R1 an R2, as shown in Example 7-10.

Key
Topic

Example 7-10   *Troubleshooting IKEv1 Phase 2, the IPsec Tunnel*

```
R1# show crypto map
Crypto Map "MYMAP" 1 ipsec-isakmp
        Peer = 209.165.201.1
        Extended IP access list 100
            access-list 100 permit ip 172.16.0.0 0.0.255.255 192.168.0.0
                0.0.0.255
        Current peer: 209.165.201.1
        Security association lifetime: 4608000 kilobytes/3600 seconds
        Responder-Only (Y/N): N
        PFS (Y/N): Y
        DH group:  group2
        Transform sets={
                MYSET:  { esp-aes esp-sha-hmac  } ,
        }
        Interfaces using crypto map MYMAP:
                GigabitEthernet1/0


! Let's check the other router
R2# show crypto map
Crypto Map "MYMAP" 1 ipsec-isakmp
        Peer = 209.165.200.225
        Extended IP access list 100
            access-list 100 permit ip 192.168.0.0 0.0.0.255 172.16.0.0
                0.0.255.255
        Current peer: 209.165.200.225
        Security association lifetime: 4608000 kilobytes/3600 seconds
        Responder-Only (Y/N): N
        PFS (Y/N): N
        Transform sets={
                MYSET:  { esp-aes esp-sha-hmac  } ,
        }
        Interfaces using crypto map MYMAP:
                GigabitEthernet1/0



! Based on the output, it looks like R1 is configured to use PFS group 2,
! and R2 isn't. Let's correct this on R2, and retry the ping.


R2(config)# crypto map MYMAP 1 ipsec-isakmp
R2(config-crypto-map)# set pfs group2
R2(config-crypto-map)# end


! Now let's try that ping
R2# ping 172.16.0.1 source g2/0
```

7

```
Type escape sequence to abort.
Sending 5, 100-byte ICMP Echos to 172.16.0.1, timeout is 2 seconds:
Packet sent with a source address of 192.168.0.2
.!!!!
Success rate is 80 percent (4/5), round-trip min/avg/max = 32/38/44 ms
R2#

! The first ping may have timed out before the IPsec tunnel (Phase 2) had been
! established, but the rest of the pings and future pings can take
! advantage of the existing tunnel and should work.

R2# ping 172.16.0.1 source g2/0 repeat 500

Type escape sequence to abort.
Sending 500, 100-byte ICMP Echos to 172.16.0.1, timeout is 2 seconds:
Packet sent with a source address of 192.168.0.2
!!!!!!!!!!!!!!!!!!!!!!!!!!!!!!!!!!!!!!!!!!!!!!!!!!!!!!!!!!!!!!!!!!!!!!!!
!!!!!!!!!!!!!!!!!!!!!!!!!!!!!!!!!!!!!!!!!!!!!!!!!!!!!!!!!!!!!!!!!!!!!!!!
!!!!!!!!!!!!!!!!!!!!!!!!!!!!!!!!!!!!!!!!!!!!!!!!!!!!!!!!!!!!!!!!!!!!!!!!
!!!!!!!!!!!!!!!!!!!!!!!!!!!!!!!!!!!!!!!!!!!!!!!!!!!!!!!!!!!!!!!!!!!!!!!!
!!!!!!!!!!!!!!!!!!!!!!!!!!!!!!!!!!!!!!!!!!!!!!!!!!!!!!!!!!!!!!!!!!!!!!!!
!!!!!!!!!!!!!!!!!!!!!!!!!!!!!!!!!!!!!!!!!!!!!!!!!!!!!!!!!!!!!!!!!!!!!!!!
!!!!!!!!!!!!!!!!!!!!!!!!!!!!!!!!!!!!!!!!!!!!!!!!!!!!!!!!!!!!!!!!!!!!!!!!
!!!!!!!!!!
Success rate is 100 percent (500/500), round-trip min/avg/max = 20/39/68 ms
R2#

! To verify the IKEv1 Phase 1 and 2 tunnels, we can use these commands:

R2# show crypto isakmp sa
IPv4 Crypto ISAKMP SA
dst              src              state        conn-id status
209.165.200.225      209.165.201.1        QM_IDLE          1004 ACTIVE
! QM_IDLE is the desired state for the output of the above command

R2# show crypto isakmp sa detail
Codes: C - IKEv1 configuration mode, D - Dead Peer Detection
       K - Keepalives, N - NAT-traversal
       T - cTCP encapsulation, X - IKEv1 Extended Authentication
       psk - Preshared key, rsig - RSA signature
       renc - RSA encryption
IPv4 Crypto ISAKMP SA

C-id  Local     Remote    I-VRF   Status Encr Hash Auth DH Lifetime Cap.

1004  209.165.201.1  209.165.200.225          ACTIVE aes  sha  rsig 5  00:55:54
```

```
! This verifies a functioning IKEv1 Phase 1 (QM_IDLE,ACTIVE) and the detail
! option reveals that the IKEv1 Phase 1 used RSA signatures for
! authentication, AES for encryption, SHA for hashing and DH group 5, with
! the remaining lifetime from what was initially agreed to by the peers.


! To verify the IPsec (IKEv1 Phase 2) tunnel, we can do so with the following
! command:

R2# show crypto ipsec sa

interface: GigabitEthernet1/0
    Crypto map tag: MYMAP, local addr 209.165.201.1

   protected vrf: (none)
   local  ident (addr/mask/prot/port): (192.168.0.0/255.255.255.0/0/0)
   remote ident (addr/mask/prot/port): (172.16.0.0/255.255.0.0/0/0)
   current_peer 209.165.200.225 port 500
     PERMIT, flags={origin_is_acl,}
    #pkts encaps: 504, #pkts encrypt: 504, #pkts digest: 504
    #pkts decaps: 504, #pkts decrypt: 504, #pkts verify: 504
    #pkts compressed: 0, #pkts decompressed: 0
    #pkts not compressed: 0, #pkts compr. failed: 0
    #pkts not decompressed: 0, #pkts decompress failed: 0
    #send errors 11, #recv errors 0

     local crypto endpt.: 209.165.201.1, remote crypto endpt.: 209.165.200.225
     path mtu 1500, ip mtu 1500, ip mtu idb GigabitEthernet1/0
     current outbound spi: 0x3BE5B517(1004909847)
     PFS (Y/N): Y, DH group: group2
! Inbound Security Association (SA/tunnel) from traffic coming from the
! other peer
     inbound esp sas:
      spi: 0x87F1D10A(2280771850)
        transform: esp-aes esp-sha-hmac ,
        in use settings ={Tunnel, }
        conn id: 9, flow_id: SW:9, sibling_flags 80000046, crypto map: MYMAP
        sa timing: remaining key lifetime (k/sec): (4558182/3257)
        IV size: 16 bytes
        replay detection support: Y
        Status: ACTIVE
! Not using AH, so no inbound AH SA
     inbound ah sas:


! Outbound Security Association (SA/tunnel) for traffic going to the other
! peer
```

7

```
  outbound esp sas:
    spi: 0x3BE5B517(1004909847)
        transform: esp-aes esp-sha-hmac ,
        in use settings ={Tunnel, }
        conn id: 10, flow_id: SW:10, sibling_flags 80000046, crypto map: MYMAP
        sa timing: remaining key lifetime (k/sec): (4558182/3257)
        IV size: 16 bytes
        replay detection support: Y
        Status: ACTIVE
! Not using AH, so no outbound AH SA
    outbound ah sas:




! These outputs have been detailed in earlier chapters, but it is relevant
! to know that there are 2 SA (security associations) with the IKEv1 Phase 2
! (IPsec). One SA for outbound to the other peer, and another for the
! inbound from that peer. We can also see the encrypt and decrypt count for
! each of the SAs.



! One more command that is useful in seeing a bird's eye view of the
! cryptography is this:
R2# show crypto engine connections active
Crypto Engine Connections


   ID  Type    Algorithm         Encrypt  Decrypt  IP-Address
    9  IPsec   AES+SHA                 0      504   209.165.201.1
   10  IPsec   AES+SHA               504        0   209.165.201.1
 1004  IKEv1   SHA+AES256              0        0   209.165.201.1
```

There are other alternative site-to-site VPN technologies:

■ Dynamic Multipoint VPN (DMVPN)

■ FlexVPN

DMVPN is a Cisco solution for deploying highly scalable IPsec site-to-site VPNs. DMVPN uses a centralized architecture to enable the network administrator to deploy granular access controls. It enables branch locations to communicate directly with each other over the Internet without requiring a permanent VPN connection between sites.

FlexVPN is a unified VPN solution that can be deployed over either public Internet connections or a private Multiprotocol Label Switching (MPLS) VPN network. FlexVPN is designed for the concentration of both site-to-site and remote access VPNs. One FlexVPN deployment can accept both types of connection requests at the same time. It uses dynamic routing protocols for redundancy and path/head-end selection.

Implementing and Verifying an IPsec Site-to-Site VPN in Cisco ASA

The Cisco *Adaptive Security Appliance (ASA)* supports both IKEv1 (Version 1) and IKEv2 (Version 2). IKEv2 supported in Cisco ASA Software Version 8.4 and later. This section covers how to implement and verify an IPsec site-to-site VPN in Cisco ASA. The topology shown in Figure 7-8 is used in this section. A new branch office in Chicago needs to connect to the New York office over an IPsec site-to-site VPN tunnel. A Cisco ASA is configured in the Chicago office to terminate the IPsec site-to-site VPN tunnel.

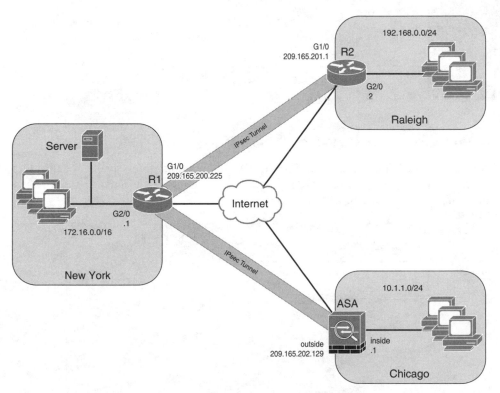

Figure 7-8   *Site-to-Site VPN Tunnel Between Cisco ASA and Cisco IOS Router*

There are many ways to set up a site-to-site tunnel through Cisco *Adaptive Security Device Manager (ASDM)*. The easiest way to define a new site-to-site connection is by following the IPsec VPN Wizard. Launch the wizard by choosing **Wizards > VPN Wizards > Site-to-Site VPN Wizard**. ASDM launches the IPsec VPN Wizard and provides a brief introduction of a site-to-site VPN tunnel, as shown in Figure 7-9.

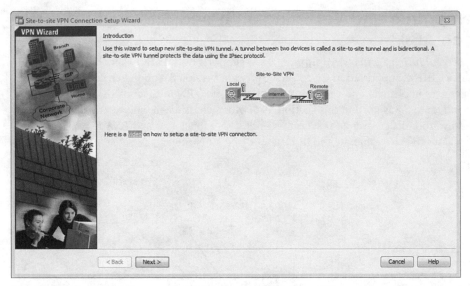

Figure 7-9 *ASDM Site-to-Site VPN Connection Setup Wizard Introduction Screen*

Click **Next** to start the configuration. The VPN Wizard prompts you to specify the IP address of the VPN peer and the interface used to access the peer (the interface that will be terminating the VPN tunnel), as shown in Figure 7-10.

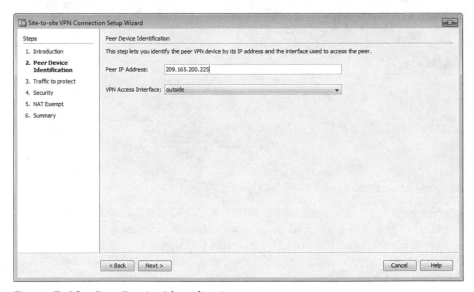

Figure 7-10 *Peer Device Identification*

In this example, the public IP address of the Cisco IOS router in New York is 209.165.200.225. The **outside** interface is selected from the VPN Access Interface drop-down menu. Click **Next**.

The screen shown in Figure 7-11 is displayed. Identify local and remote networks. Choose the hosts/subnets or networks to be used as the local and remote proxies during the IPsec negotiation.

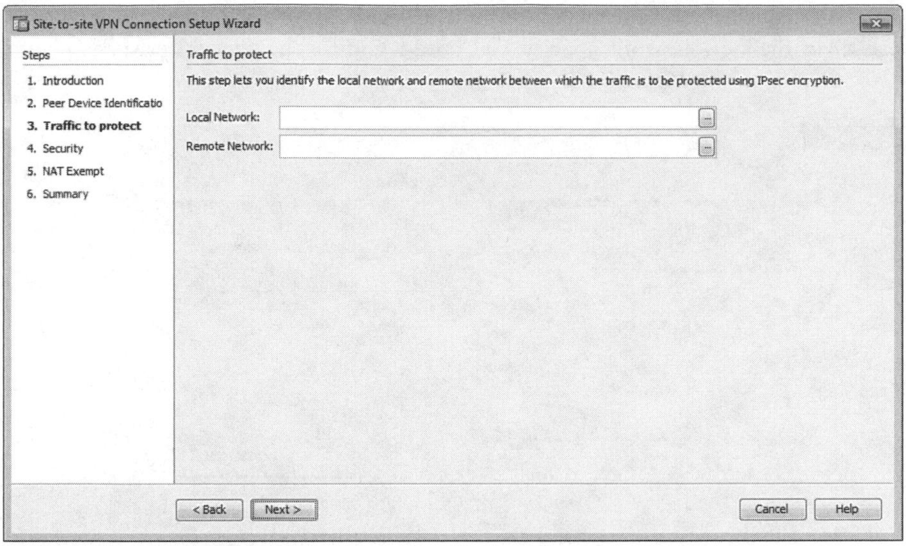

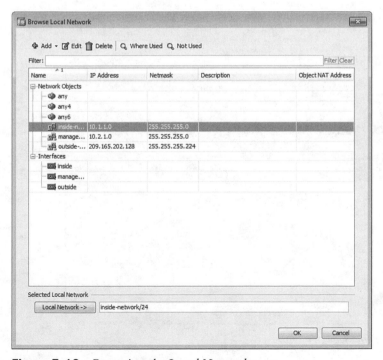

Figure 7-11   *Traffic to Protect*

The Cisco ASA recognizes all the local and remote networks if their routes are in the routing table. You can click the **...** button to see a list of the local networks, as shown in Figure 7-12. In this example, the inside network 10.1.1.0/24 is selected.

Figure 7-12   *Browsing the Local Networks*

Optionally, you may manually add an address in the IP Address field with the appropriate subnet mask. For the local network, specify **10.1.1.0/24**, and for the remote network, specify **172.16.0.0/16**, as shown in Figure 7-13.

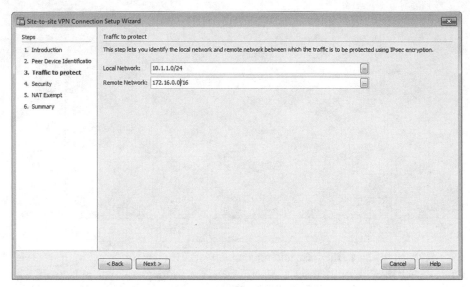

Figure 7-13   *Specifying the Local and Remote Networks*

After you specify the local and remote networks, click **Next**. The screen shown in Figure 7-14 is shown.

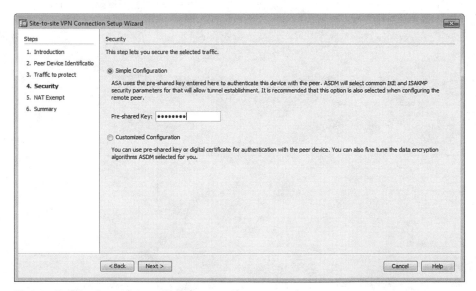

Figure 7-14   *Specifying the Security Options*

On this screen, you can specify the security parameters. You can choose the **Simple Configuration** option to use the commonly deployed IKE and ISAKMP security parameters. If you choose this option, you only need to specify the pre-shared key for the connection. You can choose the **Customized Configuration** if you want to customize the VPN policies. ASDM then permits you to choose the IKE version (1 or 2), local and remote pre-shared keys, IKE and IPsec proposals, and PFS. In this example, the simple configuration is used. Enter the pre-shared key to be used to authenticate the Cisco ASA with the VPN peer. Click **Next**. The screen shown in Figure 7-15 is displayed.

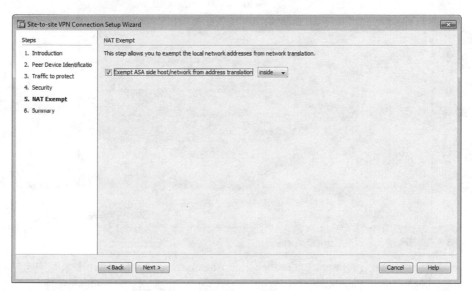

Figure 7-15   *Defining the NAT Exempt Policy*

The screen shown in Figure 7-15 allows you to define the NAT exempt policy. In most cases, you do not want to translate (that is, NAT) the addresses if traffic is traversing the VPN tunnel. ASDM allows you to check the **Exempt ASA Side Host/Network from Address Translation** check box with the **inside** interface selected to bypass address translation.

Click **Next** to verify your configuration in the resulting screen shown in Figure 7-16. This screen lists all the configuration parameters that will be sent to the Cisco ASA. Notice that the configuration wizard added numerous default options to the IKEv1 and IKEv2 IKE policies and IPsec proposals. You can customize these options by selecting the **Customized Configuration** in the VPN Wizard or by manually configuring the parameters, as you will learn later in this section.

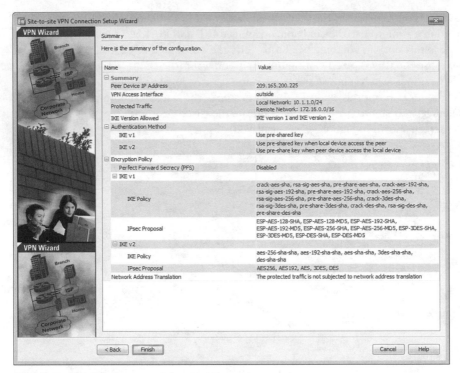

Figure 7-16 *Summary of the Configuration*

Click **Finish** to apply the configuration to the Cisco ASA. After the wizard finishes, you will be able to see the VPN connection profile for the new site-to-site tunnel to the 209.165.200.225 address (peer), as shown in Figure 7-16.

Example 7-11 shows all the commands sent to the Cisco ASA by ASDM.

Example 7-11 *Commands Sent to the Cisco ASA by ASDM*

```
! Crypto IPsec (Phase 2) IKEv1 and IKEv2 transform sets.
crypto ipsec ikev1 transform-set ESP-AES-128-SHA esp-aes esp-sha-hmac
crypto ipsec ikev1 transform-set ESP-AES-128-MD5 esp-aes esp-md5-hmac
crypto ipsec ikev1 transform-set ESP-AES-192-SHA esp-aes-192 esp-sha-hmac
crypto ipsec ikev1 transform-set ESP-AES-192-MD5 esp-aes-192 esp-md5-hmac
crypto ipsec ikev1 transform-set ESP-AES-256-SHA esp-aes-256 esp-sha-hmac
crypto ipsec ikev1 transform-set ESP-AES-256-MD5 esp-aes-256 esp-md5-hmac
crypto ipsec ikev1 transform-set ESP-AES-128-SHA-TRANS esp-aes esp-sha-hmac
crypto ipsec ikev1 transform-set ESP-AES-128-SHA-TRANS mode transport
crypto ipsec ikev1 transform-set ESP-AES-128-MD5-TRANS esp-aes esp-md5-hmac
crypto ipsec ikev1 transform-set ESP-AES-128-MD5-TRANS mode transport
crypto ipsec ikev1 transform-set ESP-AES-192-SHA-TRANS esp-aes-192 esp-sha-hmac
crypto ipsec ikev1 transform-set ESP-AES-192-SHA-TRANS mode transport
crypto ipsec ikev1 transform-set ESP-AES-192-MD5-TRANS esp-aes-192 esp-md5-hmac
crypto ipsec ikev1 transform-set ESP-AES-192-MD5-TRANS mode transport
crypto ipsec ikev1 transform-set ESP-AES-256-SHA-TRANS esp-aes-256 esp-sha-hmac
```

```
crypto ipsec ikev1 transform-set ESP-AES-256-SHA-TRANS mode transport
crypto ipsec ikev1 transform-set ESP-AES-256-MD5-TRANS esp-aes-256 esp-md5-hmac
crypto ipsec ikev1 transform-set ESP-AES-256-MD5-TRANS mode transport
crypto ipsec ikev1 transform-set ESP-3DES-SHA esp-3des esp-sha-hmac
crypto ipsec ikev1 transform-set ESP-3DES-MD5 esp-3des esp-md5-hmac
crypto ipsec ikev1 transform-set ESP-3DES-SHA-TRANS esp-3des esp-sha-hmac
crypto ipsec ikev1 transform-set ESP-3DES-SHA-TRANS mode transport
crypto ipsec ikev1 transform-set ESP-3DES-MD5-TRANS esp-3des esp-md5-hmac
crypto ipsec ikev1 transform-set ESP-3DES-MD5-TRANS mode transport
crypto ipsec ikev1 transform-set ESP-DES-SHA esp-des esp-sha-hmac
crypto ipsec ikev1 transform-set ESP-DES-MD5 esp-des esp-md5-hmac
crypto ipsec ikev1 transform-set ESP-DES-SHA-TRANS esp-des esp-sha-hmac
crypto ipsec ikev1 transform-set ESP-DES-SHA-TRANS mode transport
crypto ipsec ikev1 transform-set ESP-DES-MD5-TRANS esp-des esp-md5-hmac
crypto ipsec ikev1 transform-set ESP-DES-MD5-TRANS mode transport
crypto ipsec ikev2 ipsec-proposal DES
 protocol esp encryption des
 protocol esp integrity sha-1 md5
crypto ipsec ikev2 ipsec-proposal 3DES
 protocol esp encryption 3des
 protocol esp integrity sha-1 md5
crypto ipsec ikev2 ipsec-proposal AES
 protocol esp encryption aes
 protocol esp integrity sha-1 md5
crypto ipsec ikev2 ipsec-proposal AES192
 protocol esp encryption aes-192
 protocol esp integrity sha-1 md5
crypto ipsec ikev2 ipsec-proposal AES256
 protocol esp encryption aes-256
 protocol esp integrity sha-1 md5
!
! ASDM creates an access control list (ACL) named outside_cryptomap used to
! define the local and remote networks.
access-list outside_cryptomap extended permit ip 10.1.1.0 255.255.255.0 172.16.0.0
  255.255.0.0
!The ACL is then applied (matched) the crypto map
crypto map outside_map 1 match address outside_cryptomap
!
!The VPN peer is defined in the crypto map
crypto map outside_map 1 set peer 209.165.200.225
!
! The crypto map is configured with the IKEv1 transform set with several encryption
! algorithms. The highest security algorithm is picked first based on the peers
  proposals.
crypto map outside_map 1 set ikev1 transform-set ESP-AES-128-SHA ESP-AES-128-MD5
  ESP-AES-192-SHA ESP-AES-192-MD5 ESP-AES-256-SHA ESP-AES-256-MD5 ESP-3DES-SHA
```

7

```
   ESP-3DES-MD5 ESP-DES-SHA ESP-DES-MD5
!
!
! The crypto map is configured with the IKEv2 transform set
crypto map outside_map 1 set ikev2 ipsec-proposal AES256 AES192 AES 3DES DES
!
! the crypto map is applied to the outside interface
crypto map outside_map interface outside
!
!
! ASDM applies numerous default IKEv1 and IKEv2 policies
crypto ikev2 policy 1
 encryption aes-256
 integrity sha
 group 5 2
 prf sha
 lifetime seconds 86400
crypto ikev2 policy 10
 encryption aes-192
 integrity sha
 group 5 2
 prf sha
 lifetime seconds 86400
crypto ikev2 policy 20
 encryption aes
 integrity sha
 group 5 2
 prf sha
 lifetime seconds 86400
crypto ikev2 policy 30
 encryption 3des
 integrity sha
 group 5 2
 prf sha
 lifetime seconds 86400
crypto ikev2 policy 40
 encryption des
 integrity sha
 group 5 2
 prf sha
 lifetime seconds 86400
crypto ikev2 enable outside
crypto ikev1 enable outside
crypto ikev1 policy 10
 authentication crack
 encryption aes-256
```

```
 hash sha
 group 2
 lifetime 86400
crypto ikev1 policy 20
 authentication rsa-sig
 encryption aes-256
 hash sha
 group 2
 lifetime 86400
crypto ikev1 policy 30
 authentication pre-share
 encryption aes-256
 hash sha
 group 2
 lifetime 86400
crypto ikev1 policy 40
 authentication crack
 encryption aes-192
 hash sha
 group 2
 lifetime 86400
crypto ikev1 policy 50
 authentication rsa-sig
 encryption aes-192
 hash sha
 group 2
 lifetime 86400
crypto ikev1 policy 60
 authentication pre-share
 encryption aes-192
 hash sha
 group 2
 lifetime 86400
crypto ikev1 policy 70
 authentication crack
 encryption aes
 hash sha
 group 2
 lifetime 86400
crypto ikev1 policy 80
 authentication rsa-sig
 encryption aes
 hash sha
 group 2
 lifetime 86400
crypto ikev1 policy 90
```

7

```
 authentication pre-share
 encryption aes
 hash sha
 group 2
 lifetime 86400
crypto ikev1 policy 100
 authentication crack
 encryption 3des
 hash sha
 group 2
 lifetime 86400
crypto ikev1 policy 110
 authentication rsa-sig
 encryption 3des
 hash sha
 group 2
 lifetime 86400
crypto ikev1 policy 120
 authentication pre-share
 encryption 3des
 hash sha
 group 2
 lifetime 86400
crypto ikev1 policy 130
 authentication crack
 encryption des
 hash sha
 group 2
 lifetime 86400
crypto ikev1 policy 140
 authentication rsa-sig
 encryption des
 hash sha
 group 2
 lifetime 86400
crypto ikev1 policy 150
 authentication pre-share
 encryption des
 hash sha
 group 2
 lifetime 86400
!
! ASDM creates all the crypto ikev1 policies above by default.
! However, only the one that matches the peer's proposal will be used.
```

```
!
! The group policy for the tunnel is configured. The group policy name is
! GroupPolicy_209.165.200.225.
!
group-policy GroupPolicy_209.165.200.225 internal
group-policy GroupPolicy_209.165.200.225 attributes
 vpn-tunnel-protocol ikev1 ikev2
!
!
! The tunnel group is defined as type ipsec-l2l (which stands for IPsec Lan-to-Lan
! tunnel).
tunnel-group 209.165.200.225 type ipsec-l2l
!
! The group policy is applied to the tunnel group under the tunnel group general
! attributes.
tunnel-group 209.165.200.225 general-attributes
 default-group-policy GroupPolicy_209.165.200.225
!
! The pre-shared key is configured for both IKEv1 and IKEv2 by default.
tunnel-group 209.165.200.225 ipsec-attributes
 ikev1 pre-shared-key *****
 ikev2 remote-authentication pre-shared-key *****
 ikev2 local-authentication pre-shared-key *****
!
! nat is bypassed for the local and remote network communication over the site-to-site
! tunnel
nat (inside,outside) source static NETWORK_OBJ_10.1.1.0_24 NETWORK_OBJ_10.1.1.0_24
  destination static NETWORK_OBJ_172.16.0.0_16 NETWORK_OBJ_172.16.0.0_16 no-proxy-arp
  route-lookup
!
object network NETWORK_OBJ_10.1.1.0_24
 subnet 10.1.1.0 255.255.255.0
object network NETWORK_OBJ_172.16.0.0_16
 subnet 172.16.0.0 255.255.0.0
!
```

As you can see, ASDM sends numerous IKEv1 and IKEv2 policies and transform sets by default that can make the configuration very complicated. To avoid this, you can select the **Customized Configuration** in the VPN Wizard or manually configure the parameters on the Connection Profiles screen, as shown in Figure 7-17.

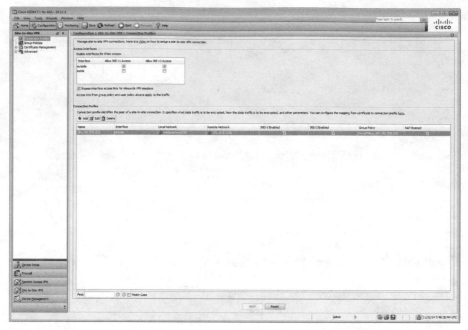

Figure 7-17   *Connection Profiles*

To edit the configuration, click the **Edit** button. The screen in Figure 7-18 is shown.

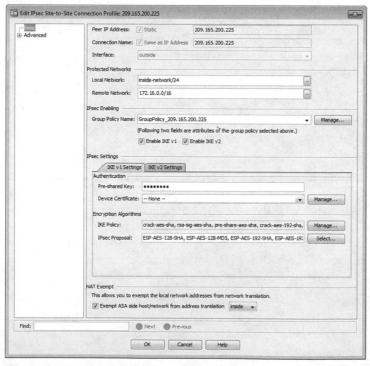

Figure 7-18   *Editing the IPsec Site-to-Site Connection Profile*

The Edit IPsec Site-to-Site Connection Profile dialog box lets you modify an IPsec site-to-site connection. These dialog boxes let you specify the peer IP address, specify a group policy name, select an interface, specify IKEv1 and IKEv2 peer and user authentication parameters, specify protected networks, and specify encryption algorithms.

To make the configuration simpler, you can navigate to the IPsec Settings, and under the IKEv1 Settings tab, you can specify the encryption algorithms that you want to use for this site-to-site tunnel. As you see, several default IKE policy encryption algorithms and IPsec proposal algorithms are selected. You can click the **Manage** button to open the Configure IKEv1 Policies dialog box, shown in Figure 7-19.

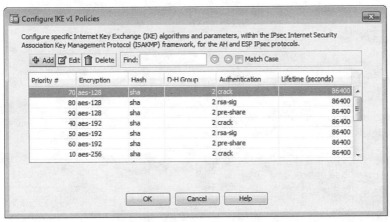

Figure 7-19 *Manually Configuring the IKEv1 Policies*

This screen allows you to manually add, edit, or delete the IKEv1 policies. In this example, we want to have a single IKE policy for the tunnel. The IKE policy is configured with pre-shared keys for authentication, the encryption algorithm is aes-256, the Diffie-Hellman Group is set to 2, the hashing algorithm is sha, and the lifetime is set to its default (86400 seconds), as shown in Figure 7-20.

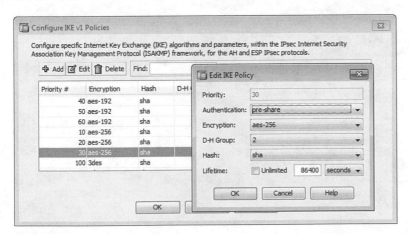

Figure 7-20 *Editing the IKE Policy*

Similarly, you can edit the IPsec proposals to specify one or more encryption algorithms to use for the IPsec IKEv1 policy. Edit the IPsec proposal by clicking the **Select** button. The dialog box shown in Figure 7-21 is displayed. This screen allows you to add, edit, or delete the IPsec proposals (transform sets) to be used in the Cisco ASA and to be assigned to the tunnel.

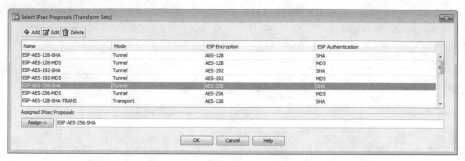

Figure 7-21 *Selecting the IPsec Proposals (Transform Sets)*

On the IKEv2 Settings tab, you can specify the authentication and encryption settings for IKEv2, as shown in Figure 7-22.

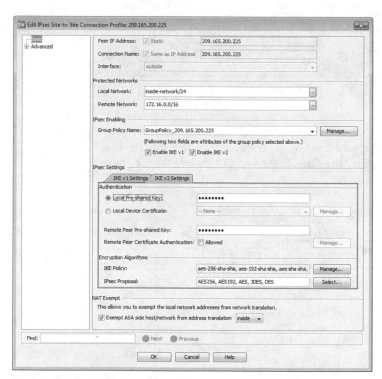

Figure 7-22 *IKEv2 Settings Tab*

Troubleshooting IPsec Site-to-Site VPNs in Cisco ASA

Similar to Cisco IOS devices, the Cisco ASA has several **show** commands that enable you to verify the configuration and the IKE and IPsec tunnel information. The following are some of the most useful **show** commands for troubleshooting IPsec implementations in the Cisco ASA:

- **show crypto isakmp stats:** Displays detailed information of both IKEv1 and IKEv2 transactions in the Cisco ASA

- **show crypto ikev1 stats:** Displays detailed information of IKEv1 transactions in the Cisco ASA

- **show crypto ikev2 stats:** Displays detailed information of IKEv2 transactions in the Cisco ASA

- **show isakmp sa:** Displays the IKEv1 and IKEv2 (Phase 1) runtime security association (SA) database

- **show isakmp sa detail:** Displays detailed information of the previous command

- **show crypto ipsec sa:** Displays the Phase 2 runtime SA database

- **show crypto ipsec sa detail:** Displays detailed information of the previous command

- **show vpn-sessiondb:** Displays the session database for any VPN connections terminated in the Cisco ASA

Example 7-12 shows the output of the **show crypto isakmp stats** after the site-to-site tunnel was established between the Cisco ASA and the remote router in New York.

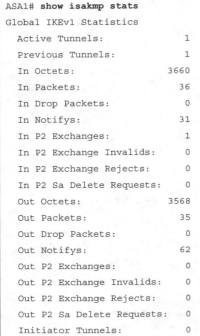

Example 7-12 *Output of the* **show isakmp stats** *Command*

```
ASA1# show isakmp stats
Global IKEv1 Statistics
  Active Tunnels:              1
  Previous Tunnels:            1
  In Octets:                3660
  In Packets:                 36
  In Drop Packets:             0
  In Notifys:                 31
  In P2 Exchanges:             1
  In P2 Exchange Invalids:     0
  In P2 Exchange Rejects:      0
  In P2 Sa Delete Requests:    0
  Out Octets:               3568
  Out Packets:                35
  Out Drop Packets:            0
  Out Notifys:                62
  Out P2 Exchanges:            0
  Out P2 Exchange Invalids:    0
  Out P2 Exchange Rejects:     0
  Out P2 Sa Delete Requests:   0
  Initiator Tunnels:           0
```

```
    Initiator Fails:              0
    Responder Fails:              0
    System Capacity Fails:        0
    Auth Fails:                   0
    Decrypt Fails:                0
    Hash Valid Fails:             0
    No Sa Fails:                  0


IKEV1 Call Admission Statistics
    Max In-Negotiation SAs:             200
    In-Negotiation SAs:                   0
    In-Negotiation SAs Highwater:         1
    In-Negotiation SAs Rejected:          0


Global IKEv2 Statistics
    Active Tunnels:                       0
    Previous Tunnels:                     0
    In Octets:                            0
    In Packets:                           0
    In Drop Packets:                      0
    In Drop Fragments:                    0
    In Notifys:                           0
    In P2 Exchange:                       0
    In P2 Exchange Invalids:              0
    In P2 Exchange Rejects:               0
    In IPSEC Delete:                      0
    In IKE Delete:                        0
    Out Octets:                           0
    Out Packets:                          0
    Out Drop Packets:                     0
    Out Drop Fragments:                   0
    Out Notifys:                          0
    Out P2 Exchange:                      0
    Out P2 Exchange Invalids:             0
    Out P2 Exchange Rejects:              0
    Out IPSEC Delete:                     0
    Out IKE Delete:                       0
    SAs Locally Initiated:                0
    SAs Locally Initiated Failed:         0
    SAs Remotely Initiated:               0
    SAs Remotely Initiated Failed:        0
    System Capacity Failures:             0
    Authentication Failures:              0
    Decrypt Failures:                     0
    Hash Failures:                        0
    Invalid SPI:                          0
```

```
    In Configs:                         0
    Out Configs:                        0
    In Configs Rejects:                 0
    Out Configs Rejects:                0
    Previous Tunnels:                   0
    Previous Tunnels Wraps:             0
    In DPD Messages:                    0
    Out DPD Messages:                   0
    Out NAT Keepalives:                 0
    IKE Rekey Locally Initiated:        0
    IKE Rekey Remotely Initiated:       0
    CHILD Rekey Locally Initiated:      0
    CHILD Rekey Remotely Initiated:     0

IKEV2 Call Admission Statistics
    Max Active SAs:             No Limit
    Max In-Negotiation SAs:          350
    Cookie Challenge Threshold:    Never
    Active SAs:                        0
    In-Negotiation SAs:                0
    Incoming Requests:                 0
    Incoming Requests Accepted:        0
    Incoming Requests Rejected:        0
    Outgoing Requests:                 0
    Outgoing Requests Accepted:        0
    Outgoing Requests Rejected:        0
    Rejected Requests:                 0
    Rejected Over Max SA limit:        0
    Rejected Low Resources:            0
    Rejected Reboot In Progress:       0
    Cookie Challenges:                 0
    Cookie Challenges Passed:          0
    Cookie Challenges Failed:          0
ASA1#
```

Example 7-13 shows the output of the **show crypto ipsec sa** command. Notice that the output is very similar to the Cisco IOS equivalent.

Example 7-13   *Output of the* **show crypto ipsec sa** *Command*

```
ASA1# show crypto ipsec sa
interface: outside
    Crypto map tag: outside_map, seq num: 1, local addr: 209.165.202.129

      access-list outside_cryptomap extended permit ip 10.1.1.0 255.255.255.0
        172.16.0.0 255.255.0.0
      local ident (addr/mask/prot/port): (10.1.1.0/255.255.255.0/0/0)
```

```
    remote ident (addr/mask/prot/port): (172.16.0.0/255.255.0.0/0/0)
    current_peer: 209.165.200.225

    #pkts encaps: 23, #pkts encrypt: 23, #pkts digest: 23
    #pkts decaps: 44, #pkts decrypt: 44, #pkts verify: 44
    #pkts compressed: 0, #pkts decompressed: 0
    #pkts not compressed: 0, #pkts comp failed: 0, #pkts decomp failed: 0
    #pre-frag successes: 0, #pre-frag failures: 0, #fragments created: 0
    #PMTUs sent: 0, #PMTUs rcvd: 0, #decapsulated frgs needing reassembly: 0
    #TFC rcvd: 0, #TFC sent: 0
    #Valid ICMP Errors rcvd: 0, #Invalid ICMP Errors rcvd: 0
    #send errors: 0, #recv errors: 0

    local crypto endpt.: 209.165.202.129/0, remote crypto endpt.: 209.165.200.225/0
    path mtu 1500, ipsec overhead 74(44), media mtu 1500
    PMTU time remaining (sec): 0, DF policy: copy-df
    ICMP error validation: disabled, TFC packets: disabled
    current outbound spi: D9E3D7F9
    current inbound spi : B5F956EC

inbound esp sas:
  spi: 0xB5F956EC (3053016812)
     transform: esp-aes-256 esp-sha-hmac no compression
     in use settings ={L2L, Tunnel, IKEv1, }
     slot: 0, conn_id: 16384, crypto-map: outside_map
     sa timing: remaining key lifetime (kB/sec): (4373999/3583)
     IV size: 16 bytes
     replay detection support: Y
     Anti replay bitmap:
      0x00000000 0x0000001F
outbound esp sas:
  spi: 0xD9E3D7F9 (3655587833)
     transform: esp-aes-256 esp-sha-hmac no compression
     in use settings ={L2L, Tunnel, IKEv1, }
     slot: 0, conn_id: 16384, crypto-map: outside_map
     sa timing: remaining key lifetime (kB/sec): (4374000/3583)
     IV size: 16 bytes
     replay detection support: Y
     Anti replay bitmap:
      0x00000000 0x00000001
```

Example 7-14 shows the output of the **show isakmp sa detail** command.

Example 7-14   *Output of the* **show isakmp sa detail** *Command*

```
ASA1# show isakmp sa detail
IKEv1 SAs:
   Active SA: 1
     Rekey SA: 0 (A tunnel will report 1 Active and 1 Rekey SA during rekey)
Total IKE SA: 1
1   IKE Peer: 209.165.200.225
     Type    : L2L             Role    : responder
     Rekey   : no              State   : MM_ACTIVE
     Encrypt : aes-256         Hash    : SHA
     Auth    : preshared       Lifetime: 86400
     Lifetime Remaining: 85921
There are no IKEv2 SAs
```

Example 7-15 shows the output of the **show vpn-sessiondb** command.

Example 7-15   *Output of the* **show vpn-sessiondb** *Command*

```
ASA1# show vpn-sessiondb
-------------------------------------------------------------------------
VPN Session Summary
-------------------------------------------------------------------------
                            Active : Cumulative : Peak Concur : Inactive
                            ---------------------------------------------
Site-to-Site VPN        :      1 :           1 :           1
  IKEv1 IPsec           :      1 :           1 :           1
-------------------------------------------------------------------------
Total Active and Inactive  :      1          Total Cumulative :       1
Device Total VPN Capacity  :    250
Device Load             :     0%
-------------------------------------------------------------------------


-------------------------------------------------------------------------
Tunnels Summary
-------------------------------------------------------------------------
                            Active : Cumulative : Peak Concurrent
                            ---------------------------------------------
IKEv1                   :      1 :           1 :            1
IPsec                   :      1 :           1 :            1
-------------------------------------------------------------------------
Totals                  :      2 :           2
-------------------------------------------------------------------------
ASA1#
```

Similar to Cisco IOS, there are several **debug** commands that are very helpful when trouble-shooting IPsec problems in the Cisco ASA. The four most important **debug** commands are the following:

■ **debug crypto ikev1|ikev2 [debug level 1-255]**

■ **debug crypto ipsec [debug level 1-255]**

■ **debug crypto ikev2 platform 2**

■ **debug crypto ikev2 protocol 2**

By default, the debug level is set to 1. You can increase the debug level up to 255 to get detailed logs. In most cases, however, setting the logging level to 127 provides enough information to determine the root cause of an issue.

> **NOTE**   If you have numerous of IPsec sessions established to a security appliance, enabling the **crypto ike** and **crypto ipsec** debugs can generate a lot of output. In Version 8.0 and later, the **crypto conditional** debug feature was introduced, which enables a user to debug an IPsec tunnel based on predefined conditions such as the peer's IP address, SPI values, or even the connection ID. For example, if you want to look at the **crypto isakmp** and **crypto ipsec** debugs for peer 209.165.200.225, enable the following commands:
>
> ```
> debug crypto isakmp 127
> debug crypto ipsec 127
> debug crypto condition peer 209.165.200.225
> ```

Exam Preparation Tasks

Review All the Key Topics

Review the most important topics from this chapter, denoted with a Key Topic icon. Table 7-5 lists these key topics.

Table 7-5   Key Topics

Key Topic Element	Description	Page Number
Table 7-2	Protocols That May be Required for IPsec	153
Table 7-3	IKEv1 Phase 1 Policy Options	154
Table 7-4	IKEv1 Phase 2 Policy Options	154
Example 7-3	CLI Implementation of the Crypto Policy for R1	162
Example 7-10	Troubleshooting IKEv1 Phase 2, the IPsec Tunnel	175
Example 7-11	Commands Sent to the Cisco ASA by ASDM	184
Examples 7-12 thru 7-15	Useful commands when troubleshooting IPsec problems in the Cisco ASA	193, 195, 197

Complete the Tables and Lists from Memory

Print a copy of Appendix C, "Memory Tables," (found on the CD) or at least the section for this chapter, and complete the tables and lists from memory. Appendix D, "Memory Tables Answer Key," also on the CD, includes completed tables and lists so that you can check your work.

Define Key Terms

Define the following key terms from this chapter, and check your answers in the glossary:

IKEv1 Phase 1, IKEv1 Phase 2, transform set, DH group, lifetime, authentication, encryption, hashing, DH key exchange, PFS

Command Reference to Check Your Memory

This section includes the most important configuration and EXEC commands covered in this chapter. To see how well you have memorized the commands as a side effect of your other studies, cover the left side of Table 7-6 with a piece of paper, read the descriptions on the right side, and see whether you remember the commands.

Table 7-6 Cisco IOS Command Reference

Command	Description
crypto map *MYMAP 1* ipsec-isakmp	Generate or edit a crypto map named MYMAP, sequence number 1, and request the services of ISAKMP.
crypto isakmp policy *3*	Enter IKEv1 Phase 1 configuration mode for policy number 3.
show crypto map	Verify what components are included in the crypto map, including the ACL, the peer address, the transform set, and where the crypto map is applied.
set peer *1.2.3.4*	Used inside a crypto map to indicate who the VPN peer should be.
match address *100*	Used inside a crypto map to indicate which ACL should be used to indicate interesting outbound traffic for the purpose of encryption.
crypto map *MYMAP*	Apply a crypto map to an interface.
crypto ipsec transform set *MYSET*	This is the beginning sequence to creating an IKEv1 Phase 2 transform set named MYSET. This is followed by the HMAC (hashing with authentication) and encryption method (3DES, or AES preferably) that you want to use.
crypto ipsec ikev1 transform-set *name*	Define the IKEv1 Phase 2 transform sets (encryption algorithms).
crypto ipsec ikev2 transform-set *name*	Define the IKEv2 Phase 2 transform sets (encryption algorithms).
crypto map *name*	Define the crypto map for the VPN tunnel in the Cisco ASA.
crypto ikev1 policy *number*	Define the IKEv1 Phase 1 policies.
crypto ikev2 policy *number*	Define the IKEv2 Phase 1 policies.
group-policy *name*	Define the VPN tunnel group name and the type of VPN tunnel that is configured (site-to-site or remote access VPN). The group policy is applied to the tunnel group under the tunnel group general attributes.
tunnel-group *name*	Define the tunnel group name and parameters. The group policy is applied to the tunnel group under the tunnel group general attributes.
nat	Define the NAT configuration in the ASA.
object network	
show isakmp stats	Display the ISAKMP (Phase 1) statistics.
show crypto ipsec sa	Display the IPsec Phase 2 SA information.
show isakmp sa detail	Display the ISAKMP (Phase 1) SA details.

Command	Description
show vpn-sessiondb	Display the VPN session database in the Cisco ASA. This command will show any VPN tunnels that are terminated in the Cisco ASA (including remote access and site-to-site VPN tunnels).
debug crypto isakmp	Troubleshoot ISAKMP (Phase 1) negotiation problems.
debug crypto ipsec	Troubleshoot IPsec Phase 2 negotiation problems.
debug crypto condition peer *ip-address*	Troubleshoot IPsec (Phase 1 and Phase 2) negotiation problems for a specific peer.

7

This chapter covers the following topics:

Functions and use of SSL for VPNs

Configuring SSL clientless VPNs on ASA

Configuring the Cisco ASA for remote-access SSL VPNs using the Cisco AnyConnect
Secure Mobility Client

CHAPTER 8

Implementing SSL VPNs Using Cisco ASA

Almost everybody is going mobile! This makes it convenient for users to be close to their data, but it also increases the challenge for the network administrator because the users are going to want access to their data and access to corporate data and resources from their mobile devices such as smartphones, laptops, and so on.

In the past, for secure remote access we traditionally installed IPsec *virtual private network (VPN)* client software on the end user's device, configured it, and then allowed them to use it to build a tunnel and after authenticating have access to corporate resources over that tunnel. The challenge with this is that the client software has to be preinstalled and configured on each machine.

Someone came up with the brilliant idea that using *Secure Sockets Layer (SSL)*, which is built in to nearly every browser and can communicate securely with the server on the other side, could be used to implement tunnels between the end users and corporate servers or even corporate networks. In addition, because browsers support SSL by default, we may not even need to install a client in every case, or if we do, we can bootstrap the entire process by initially communicating over SSL for security while we install a client. Long story short, bringing up thousands of users who need remote access can be done extremely quickly by leveraging the SSL that is built in to all of those customer devices.

This chapter explores the details of SSL and *Transport Layer Security (TLS)* and shows how to configure both the clientless flavor of SSL VPN and the full Cisco AnyConnect Secure Mobility Client.

"Do I Know This Already?" Quiz

The "Do I Know This Already?" quiz helps you determine your level of knowledge of this chapter's topics before you begin. Table 8-1 details the major topics discussed in this chapter and their corresponding quiz questions.

Table 8-1   "Do I Know This Already?" Section-to-Question Mapping

Foundation Topics Section	Questions
Functions and Use of SSL for VPNs	1–4
Configuring SSL Clientless VPNs on ASA	5–6
Configuring the Cisco ASA for Remote Access SSL VPNs Using the Cisco AnyConnect Secure Mobility Client	7–9

1. Which SSL solution is most appropriate for a remote user who is at a borrowed computer and needs access to a single server at the central office?

   a. SSL thin client

   b. SSL clientless VPN

   c. Cisco AnyConnect Secure Mobility Client SSL VPN client

   d. IPsec VPN client

2. Which of the following solutions assigns a virtual IP address to the remote user to use for traffic sent over the SSL VPN to the server?

   a. SSL thin client

   b. SSL clientless VPN

   c. Cisco AnyConnect Secure Mobility Client

   d. IPsec VPN client

3. What is the immediate cost savings when implementing SSL VPNs?

   a. No licensing is required on the server.

   b. No licensing is required on the clients.

   c. Easy deployment.

   d. SSL VPN licenses are significantly less expensive on the server than IPsec licenses.

4. How does an SSL client send the desired shared secret to the server?

   a. AES.

   b. Encrypts it with the server's public key.

   c. Encrypts it with the sender's public key.

   d. They use DH to negotiate the shared secret.

5. Which of the following is *not* part of configuring the clientless SSL VPN on the ASA?

   a. Launching the wizard

   b. Specifying the URL

   c. Configuring bookmarks

   d. Configuring a pool of IP addresses for the remote users to use

6. What may be the potential problem when enabling SSL VPNs on an interface on the ASA?

   a. ASDM is now disabled on that interface.

   b. ASDM must be additionally configured with a custom port.

   c. ASDM must be used with a different URL.

   d. ASDM is not affected because it does not connect on port TCP:443.

7. Which of the following steps is configured when setting up Cisco AnyConnect Secure Mobility Client on the ASA that would not be configured for clientless SSL VPN? (Choose all that apply.)

    a. NAT exemption

    b. Pool of addresses

    c. Connection profile

    d. Authentication method

8. Where does the ASA keep the copy of the Cisco AnyConnect Secure Mobility Client that may be deployed down to the client?

    a. On an HTTPS server only

    b. On flash

    c. On an SFTP server only

    d. On NVRAM

9. Which of the following are common issues that users experience when they cannot send or receive IP traffic over an SSL VPN tunnel? (Choose all that apply).

    a. Routing issues behind the ASA

    b. Access control lists blocking traffic

    c. Too much traffic for the VPN tunnel size

    d. Network Address Translation not being bypassed for VPN traffic

8

Foundation Topics

Functions and Use of SSL for VPNs

This section covers the alternative to IPsec for implementing secure VPN tunnels.

Is IPsec Out of the Picture?

SSL *virtual private networks (VPN)* and IPsec VPNs both have their pros and cons. The major benefit of using SSL for VPNs is that it is so darn easy to deploy because most popular browsers support SSL by default. IPsec, however, has a better security footprint than SSL, although they both do a terrific job. If a company has thousands of current clients deployed using IPsec, and it is working, there probably is not a compelling urgency to swap it out. The two technologies can both be configured on the same server, and clients, depending on the situation, can use either service. For example, if a user is at a kiosk or a borrowed computer and only needs access to one specific server, that user can open up a browser using the clientless VPN functionality and after authenticating have specific access to that one specific server. (This is where the clientless SSL VPN feature excels, when connections to only one or a few servers are needed and the full-tunneled Cisco AnyConnect Secure Mobility Client cannot be installed on the local computer.) When a user is done, she logs out, and the PC that she was using does not have a client installed or any software-installed remnants related to it. That same exact user, the next day on her own PC in a different city, may connect to the corporate network using the Cisco AnyConnect Secure Mobility Client full-blown SSL VPN client and gain full access to all the resources as a typical remote-access VPN user would. That same user could launch her IPsec VPN client (if it was installed and if the server was supporting IPsec) and build a tunnel to the corporate headquarters and have effectively the same features and feel that the Cisco AnyConnect Secure Mobility Client SSL VPN provided. Table 8-2 shows a comparison of IPsec versus SSL.

Table 8-2   Comparison of IPsec Versus SSL

	SSL	IPsec
Applications	Web-based applications, file sharing, e-mail (if not using full client). With the full Cisco AnyConnect Secure Mobility Client, all IP-based applications, similar to IPsec, are available.	All IP-based applications are available to the user. The experience is like being on the local network.
Ease of use	Very high.	Moderate. Can be challenging for nontechnical users, and deployment is more time-consuming.
Overall security	Moderate. Any device can initially connect.	Strong. Only specific devices with specific configurations, such as a VPN client, can connect.

SSL and TLS Protocol Framework

TLS and its predecessor SSL are cryptographic protocols that provide secure transactions on the Internet for things such as e-mail, web browsing, instant messaging, and so on. SSL as a protocol was originally developed by Netscape. Most online transactions that are browser based are secured by SSL or TLS. Both of these protocols provide confidentiality, integrity, and authentication services. These protocols are considered to be operating at the session layer and higher in the OSI logical model. They both can use the *public key infrastructure (PKI)* and digital certificates for authentication of the VPN endpoints and for establishing encryption keys that may be used. Similar to IPsec, these protocols use symmetric algorithms for bulk encryption, and asymmetric algorithms are used for the authentication and for the exchange of keys.

SSL 3.0 served as the basis of TLS 1.0. Both terms are casually, but perhaps incorrectly, referred to interchangeably by the average citizen on the street. Some implementations include the ability to switch to the other protocol if necessary, especially in the case of TLS, which can switch over to SSL if the client connection requires it. Fortunately for us, all of this is done behind the scenes and is transparent to the end user.

Table 8-3 compares these two protocols.

Table 8-3   Comparison Between SSL and TLS

SSL	TLS
Developed by Netscape in the 1990s	Standard developed by the *Internet Engineering Task Force (IETF)*
Starts with a secured channel and continues directly to security negotiations on a dedicated port	Can start with unsecured communications and dynamically switch to a secured channel based on the negotiation with the other side
Widely supported on client-side applications	Supported and implemented more on servers, compared to end-user devices
More weaknesses identified	Stronger implementation because of the standards process

From this point on, we use the term *SSL* to represent the concepts supported by either SSL or TLS in this chapter. Cisco SSL VPNs are really using TLS behind the scenes.

The Play by Play of SSL for VPNs

Security is important, and SSL VPNs can provide that security. We also know that SSL is used for most online transactions that require security. Before we jump in to the VPN portion, it is also important to understand the basics of how SSL works. If a customer was opening up a browser and going to connect to a banking server, or some other type of SSL device, here is what we would expect:

- The client initiates a connection to the server using the destination IP address of the server and the destination TCP port 443. The source IP address is the IP address of the client, and the source port is some random unused port number on the client machine greater than 1023.

- There is the standard three-way handshake, which is the normal process for TCP in establishing sessions.

- After the client initiates its request for the connection, the server responds, providing its digital certificate, which contains the server's public key.

- The client, upon receiving this digital certificate, has a big decision to make. That decision is whether to believe the credibility of the digital certificate that it just received from the SSL VPN server. This is where PKI comes into play. If the digital certificate is signed by a *certificate authority (CA)* that the client's browser trusts, and the validity dates for that certificate cause the client to believe that the time has not run out on that certificate, and if the client is checking a *certificate revocation list (CRL)* (and the serial number for the certificate is not on the CRL), the client can trust the certificate and extract the public key of the server out of the certificate.

- The client then generates a shared secret that it would like to use for encryption back and forth between itself and the server. The problem is now how to get this shared secret that the client wants to use sent securely over to the server? The answer is the client uses the public key of the server to encrypt the shared secret and send the encrypted secret to the server.

- The server decrypts the sent symmetric key using the server's own private key, and now both devices in the session know and can use the shared secret key.

- The key is then used to encrypt the SSL session.

Because SSL VPN provides network access to remote users, you have to consider the placement of the VPN termination devices. Before implementing the SSL VPN feature, ask the following questions:

- Should the Cisco ASA terminating the VPN be placed behind another firewall? If so, what ports should be opened in that firewall?

- Should the decrypted traffic be passed through another set of firewalls? If so, what ports should be allowed in those firewalls?

- Are there any proxy servers between the client and the Cisco ASAs?

NOTE If you have an HTTP 1.1 proxy server between the Cisco AnyConnect Secure Mobility Client and the server, your connection should succeed as long as the proxy server uses Basic and NTLM authentication. In the current implementation, Socks proxies are not supported.

SSL VPN Flavors

There are three different types of SSL VPN access methods. They are listed in Table 8-4, along with a description of each.

Table 8-4 Options for SSL VPN Implementation

	Clientless SSL VPN	Clientless SSL VPN with Plug-Ins for Some Port Forwarding	Full Cisco AnyConnect Secure Mobility Client SSL VPN Client
Other names	Web VPN.	Thin client.	Full SSL client.
Installed software on client	No client required.	Small applets and/or configuration required.	Full install of Cisco AnyConnect Secure Mobility Client required, but may be installed by initially connecting via the clientless option and securely installing it that way.
User experience	Feels like accessing resources (that are on the corporate network) through a specific browser window or hyperlink.	Some applications can be run locally with output redirected through the VPN. Includes the features of the clientless VPN to the left.	Full access to the corporate network. The local computer acts and feels like it is a full participant on the corporate network.
Servers that can be used	IOS with the correct software, and ASA with the correct licenses.	IOS with the correct software, and ASA with the correct licenses.	IOS with the correct software, and ASA with the correct licenses.
How the user looks from the corporate network	Traffic is proxied (*Port Address Translation [PAT]*) by the SSL server, as the users' packets enter the corporate network.	Traffic is proxied (PAT) by the SSL server as the users' packets enter the corporate network.	Clients are assigned their own virtual IP address to use while accessing the corporate network. Traffic is forwarded from the given IP address of the client into the corporate network.
Clients supported	Most SSL-capable computers.	Computers that support SSL and Java.	Most computers that support SSL.

SSL VPN support is provided for Windows, OS X, Linux, Apple's iOS, Android, and Windows Mobile with the appropriate licenses on the server, where the licenses are managed.

Configuring Clientless SSL VPNs on ASA

Using the Cisco *Adaptive Security Device Manager (ASDM)* on the Cisco *Adaptive Security Appliance (ASA)*, we walk through how to configure the clientless SSL VPN.

Using the SSL VPN Wizard

Wizards are prevalent in the ASA *graphical user interface (GUI)* management tool called the ASA Security Device Manager. Wizards come in handy when implementing configurations that have lots of little steps, which is the case with VPNs. So, as we've done in most of our chapters that include wizards and GUIs, we take a look at the configuration in ASDM, and then see the configuration from the *command-line interface (CLI)* before we finish the section.

Let's start by taking a look at the high-level tasks that may be used to implement the SSL clientless VPN:

- Find and launch the wizard for the SSL VPN inside the ASDM utility for the ASA.
- Configure the SSL VPN URL and interface.
- Configure user authentication.
- Configure user group policy.
- Configure bookmark lists.
- Verify that the configuration is what you intended, and verify it works.

Within ASDM, to launch the wizard, click the **Wizards** menu bar option, and from the drop-down list, select **VPN Wizards**. Then from the VPN Wizards drop-down list, select **Clientless SSL VPN Wizard**. This brings up the welcome page of the SSL VPN Wizard, shown in Figure 8-1.

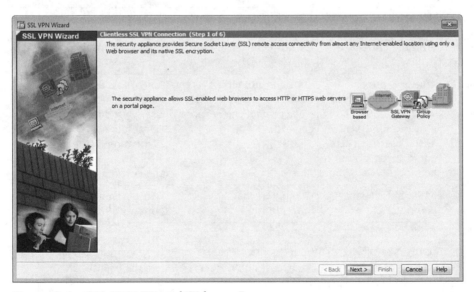

Figure 8-1 *SSL VPN Wizard Welcome Page*

When you click **Next** to continue, you are presented with a dialog box where you specify a connection profile to be associated with these users who are using clientless SSL VPNs, and the interface these users will be initially connecting to, which is normally the outside interface or a low-security interface on the ASA. In this example the connection profile name is NY-connection-profile. Figure 8-2 shows an example of this.

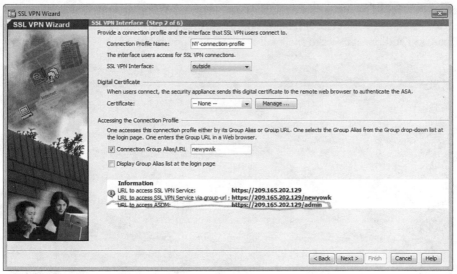

Figure 8-2 *Interface Configuration Page*

Digital Certificates

By default, a digital certificate is required to be used by the ASA acting as an SSL VPN server. It uses a self-signed digital certificate by default. In most production environments, the company applies for and implements a digital certificate signed by a well-known *public key infrastructure (PKI)* server so that clients connecting will also trust that common *certificate authority (CA)* server and not receive a warning about an unknown certificate. Also on the page shown in Figure 8-2, you indicate the URL that customers could use that would associate them with the correct group. For example, you may have many different SSL VPN groups, with different rights and different users as members of those groups, and handing out the correct URLs to use could make it easier for the initial connection. Another option that is available is to display all the groups from a drop-down list, from which the user could choose which group to connect to. From this page, click **Next** to continue.

Accessing the Connection Profile

If you are using ASDM to manage the ASA on the outside interface, pay special attention to the URL on this page. In this example the https://209.165.202.129/admin URL will be used for administration purposes. Both ASDM and SSL VPN connections are possible.

Authenticating Users

We specify how we are going to go about authenticating the individual users who are trying to connect. We have two general options. The first is that we could use an *authentication, authorization, and accounting (AAA)* server. Very likely, in a Cisco environment, this is an *Access Control Server (ACS)* (or *Identity Services Engine [ISE]*) server. The AAA server could be reached via RADIUS or TACACS+. In the case of authenticating users (end users, specifically SSL VPN users), if the ASA is using the AAA server, it will very likely use RADIUS because that is the recommended method for authentication. The other option is to use the local database, which just like on the router means the running configuration on the local device (in this case, the ASA's running config). At this point in the wizard, if you want to, you can add additional users to the local database, as shown in Figure 8-3.

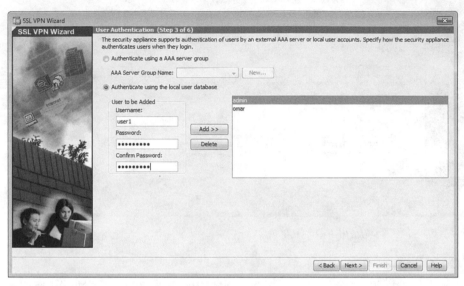

Figure 8-3 *Authentication Methods for SSL VPN Users*

When you click **Next** to continue, you are asked what group profile you want to use for these users. It is a lot easier to specify attributes and parameters based on a group and then put users into that group instead of individually assigning each user those attributes.

By default, all users belong to a default group, and that default group could be used by the SSL VPN users, as well. If you create a specific group for these users, any parameters assigned to the specific group override the default group policies and apply to those users. The pecking order is that the users inherit properties from their specific group, and a specific group inherits properties from the default group. If a conflict exists between these policies, any attributes assigned to the user win. If a conflict exists between a specific group and a default group, the attributes in the specific group win (or in other words, take precedence). Figure 8-4 shows an example of creating a specific group. The name of the new group policy is NY-Group-Policy.

When you click **Next**, you are prompted as to whether you want to provide these authenticated SSL VPN users with a convenient list of links/URLs that go to specific services on the corporate network (behind the ASA). Bookmarks can be created and reused for multiple groups. Figure 8-5 shows an example of managing the existing bookmarks and editing them.

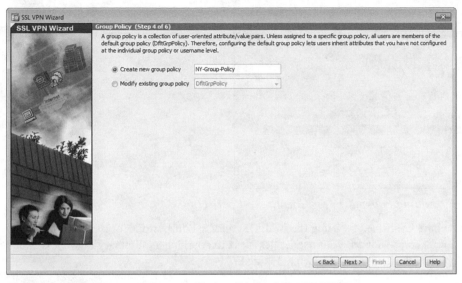

Figure 8-4 *Assigning a Specific Group for the SSL VPN Users*

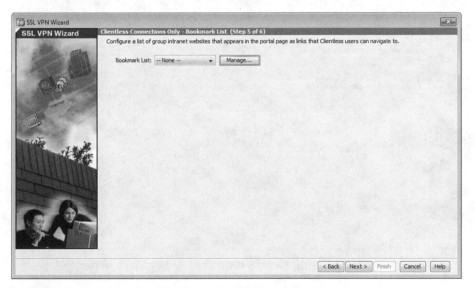

Figure 8-5 *Bookmarks to Be Provided for Your Users*

Click **Manage** to add new bookmarks for your VPN users, as shown in Figure 8-6.

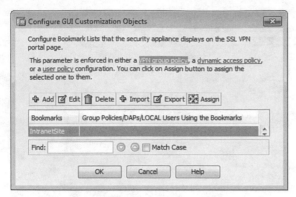

Figure 8-6   *Adding Bookmarks for Clientless VPN Users*

After you have confirmed by using the **Add**, **OK**, and/or **Edit** buttons for the bookmarks that you want to provide for your users, click **Next** to continue. A summary of what is about to be deployed is displayed, as shown in Figure 8-7.

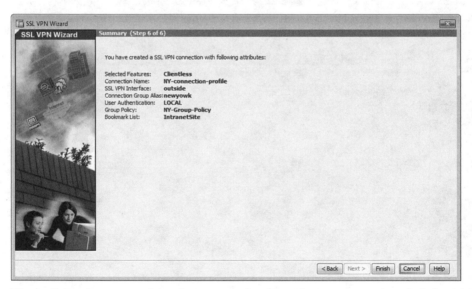

Figure 8-7   *Summary of Configuration Elements About to Be Deployed to the ASA Firewall*

When you click **Finish**, depending on how you have ASDM configured, it may prompt you for one more confirmation or display the CLI equivalent of what it is about to send.

Speaking of the CLI equivalent, Example 8-1 shows the CLI commands to implement the same policy we just used ASDM for.

Example 8-1 *Implementing a Clientless SSL VPN*

```
!  specifies  the creation of a local group
asa1(config)# group-policy NY-Group-Policy internal

! Specifies that it's using its own self signed certificate
! and enabling SSL VPN on the outside interface
asa1(config)# ssl trust-point ASDM_TrustPoint0 outside
asa1(config)# webvpn
asa1(config-webvpn)# enable outside
!  specifies the attributes for this local group, including the bookmarks
asa1(config-webvpn)# group-policy NY-Group-Policy attributes
asa1(config-group-policy)# vpn-tunnel-protocol ssl-clientless
asa1(config-group-policy)# webvpn
asa1(config-group-webvpn)# url-list value IntranetSite
asa1(config-group-webvpn)# exit
asa1(config-group-policy)# exit


!  specifies  a tunnel group for remote access, compared to site to site
asa1(config)# tunnel-group NY-connection-profile type remote-access

!  defines the attributes for this connection profile, including the group
!  policy to be used
asa1(config)# tunnel-group NY-connection-profile general-attributes
asa1(config-tunnel-general)# default-group-policy NY-Group-Policy

!  defines the URL that when connected will trigger what profile to use,
!  and that in turn controls what group profile should be applied

asa1(config-tunnel-general)# tunnel-group NY-connection-profile webvpn-attributes
asa1(config-tunnel-webvpn)# group-alias newyork enable
asa1(config-tunnel-webvpn)# group-url https://209.165.202.129/newyork enable
! The asa uses the outside IP address.
```

Logging In

For users to connect, they just point their browser to the HTTPS URL, which includes the IP address (or *Domain Name System [DNS]* resolvable name) and the SSL_VPN portion (based on our configuration). They are prompted for their username and password, and if successful, they are authenticated and provided the bookmarks you configured for that group. Those bookmarks could include not only HTTPS resources but also servers that are reachable via the *Common Internet File System (CIFS)* method. Users, in addition to the links provided by you, the administrator, could manually specify resources that they want to reach that are on the corporate networks behind the ASA. All of this can be controlled with the access controls that exist for VPN users on the ASA. Advanced topics, including granular control for the ASA, are in the CCNP Security curriculum, and what you learn here about VPNs and ASAs will assist in preparing you for that. Figure 8-8 shows the initial clientless SSL VPN login screen.

Figure 8-8   *User Interface for Logging In*

The user is presented with the bookmarks configured and the ability to enter an address manually at the top, using the drop-down menu to select the protocol to use, such as HTTP or CIFS (with the latter being used to reach file services being shared on the internal network). Figure 8-9 shows an example of what the user sees (based on your configuration) after authenticating.

Figure 8-9   *User Interface After Authenticating*

Seeing the VPN Activity from the Server

On the ASA ASDM, to verify the details of your current SSL VPN connections that are in place, navigate to **Monitoring > VPN > VPN Statistics > Sessions** to see the current VPN sessions. If there are many sessions, you can use the drop-down menu labeled **Filter By** to narrow down the output to just your VPN SSL remote-access clients. To see the details of a specific session, simply highlight it and click the **Details** button, as shown in Figure 8-10.

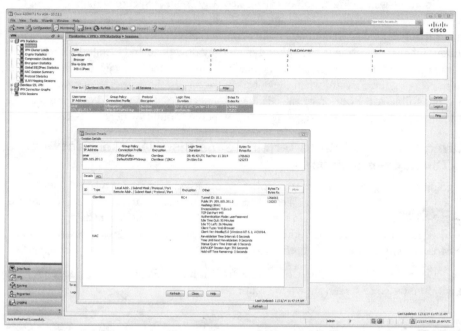

Figure 8-10   *Monitoring the Details of the SSL VPN Clients in ASDM*

As you can see from the output, it gives information about the user who authenticated (which is a user I just created and name omar), that user's source IP address on the Internet, what time the user logged in, how long the user has been logged in, the encryption method that is in use, and the type of client. In this case, the client happens to be an iPhone. (I mentioned that it is an iPhone because earlier I showed an example of connecting to the SSL server from a Windows machine with Internet Explorer, and when I snapped Figure 8-9, it happened to be while a mobile client was connected.) It is also worth noting that the encapsulation shown is TLS, but as I mentioned earlier, the common reference to this type of VPN is still called an *SSL clientless VPN*.

This client, while connected, can access a resource based on a reachable URL that is in a bookmark provided to them that goes to a resource on the internal network behind the ASA (or by using a manually entered URL).

Using the Cisco AnyConnect Secure Mobility Client

This section shows you how to implement a full-tunnel VPN using Cisco AnyConnect Secure Mobility Client and the SSL functionality.

Handwritten margin notes: "Types of SSL of ① IPsec: Connections: using VPN"

Handwritten top note: "SSL VPN: ① full client ② clientless"

Types of SSL VPNs

You might recall that we discussed three types of SSL VPN clients. In truth, the thin client, the one that may be using port redirection or have some plug-ins, is really just the SSL clientless VPN with a few extras features. So, really it boils down to two major choices for SSL, and that is SSL using the full-blown installed Cisco AnyConnect Secure Mobility Client software or using the clientless flavor, like the one we just configured in the previous section. Truth be told, if we were going to roll out the Cisco AnyConnect Secure Mobility Client to 1000 users, we would first probably set up the SSL clientless VPN for those users. We would configure the server so that when they initially connect, it prompts them to authenticate, and after successful authentication it can either dynamically download and install the client or present the option to install the client on the user's computer. Once the client is installed, we just use the client going forward when they need full access to the corporate network behind the ASA, but still have the option of the clientless connectivity if they need only limited access, instead of using the full Cisco AnyConnect Secure Mobility Client VPN client.

Configuring the Cisco ASA to Terminate the Cisco AnyConnect Secure Mobility Client Connections

We are going to configure the server to support remote users who are (or will be) using the Cisco AnyConnect Secure Mobility Client. This type of implementation can also be referred to as a *full-tunnel SSL VPN*. To begin the configuration, we click the **Wizards** option on the menu bar, select **VPN Wizards** from the drop-down list, and then select **Cisco AnyConnect Secure Mobility Client Wizard** from the next drop-down list.

Once we invoke the VPN Cisco AnyConnect Secure Mobility Client Wizard, we are presented with the welcome screen shown in Figure 8-11.

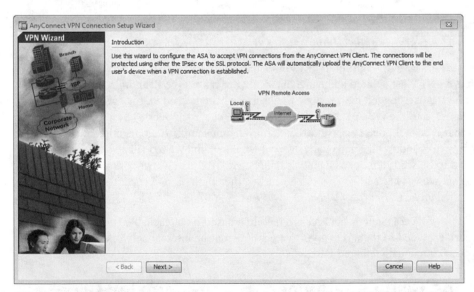

Figure 8-11 *The Cisco AnyConnect Secure Mobility Client VPN Wizard Welcome Screen*

The wizard asks what you want to name the connection profile that will support the Cisco AnyConnect Secure Mobility Client users and which interface you are expecting these users to connect on, as shown in Figure 8-12.

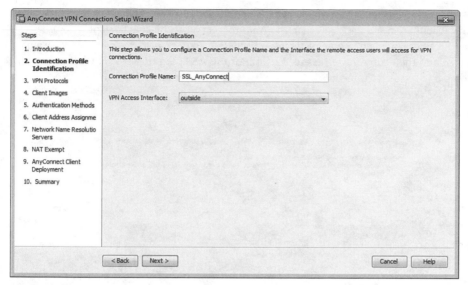

Figure 8-12   *Creating a Connection Profile for the Cisco AnyConnect Secure Mobility Client Users*

When you click **Next**, a dialog box asks what protocols you want to support and which digital certificate you want to use on the server. Again, it is best to have a digital certificate that has been issued by a CA that is part of PKI so that when clients connect they do not get a warning message about the certificate. Cisco AnyConnect Secure Mobility Client can support both SSL and IPsec. If you do not intend to use IPsec through the Cisco AnyConnect Secure Mobility Client, you can just uncheck the check box and it will not be supported. Figure 8-13 shows an example of this dialog box.

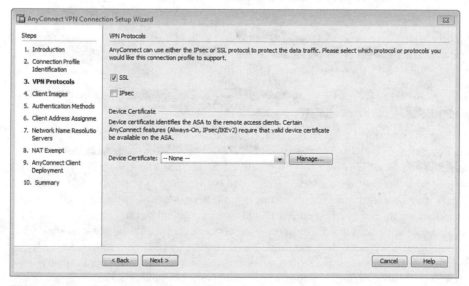

Figure 8-13   *Selecting the Protocols to Support and the Certificate to Use on the Server*

When you click **Next** to continue, you get to identify the Cisco AnyConnect Secure Mobility Client software packages that you want this server to be able to deploy to users. A new ASA may come with some of them on flash, but you can also download them from Cisco.com and then copy those files to the flash of the ASA. Figure 8-14 shows the options for adding a Cisco AnyConnect Secure Mobility Client software package to the ASA.

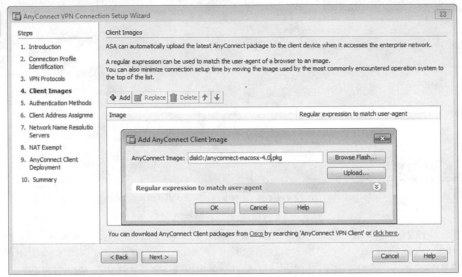

Figure 8-14 *Selecting the Cisco AnyConnect Secure Mobility Client Files to Place on the Flash of the ASA*

If the package file is already on the flash, the menus presented in Figure 8-14 allow you to tell the ASA which package (that already exists on the flash) to use.

After specifying the image files to use and clicking the **Next** button, you are presented with a dialog box asking how you want to authenticate users. Similar to the previous configuration, you can use a AAA server such as an ACS server, or you could use the local database on the ASA. Figure 8-15 shows an example of this dialog box.

The keyword LOCAL (in uppercase on the ASA) is the keyword from a AAA perspective on the ASA that represents the local database (the running config).

After adding any additional users to the local database, click **Next**. You are then presented with the questions about what IP address pool you want to use to assign internal addresses to the VPN clients. We didn't have this need before because SSL clientless VPN did not get their own IP addresses but were instead just proxied off the ASA. The pool of addresses that you specify may be a legitimate subnet of one of your networks or a completely made up pool of addresses. Be aware that whatever IP addresses you hand out to clients here should be reachable by the devices inside your corporate network. This could be accomplished with static routing for the network devices, policy-based routing by the network devices, or by creating a loopback interface (on a router) representing a subnet and including it in a dynamic routing protocol. Figure 8-16 shows an example of a pool being created.

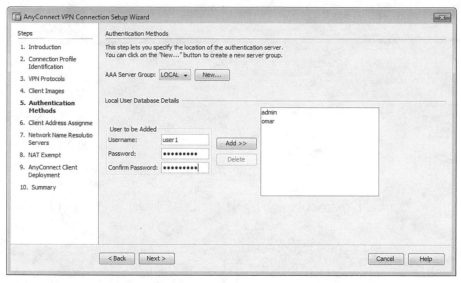

Figure 8-15   *Specifying the Authentication Method for SSL VPN Users*

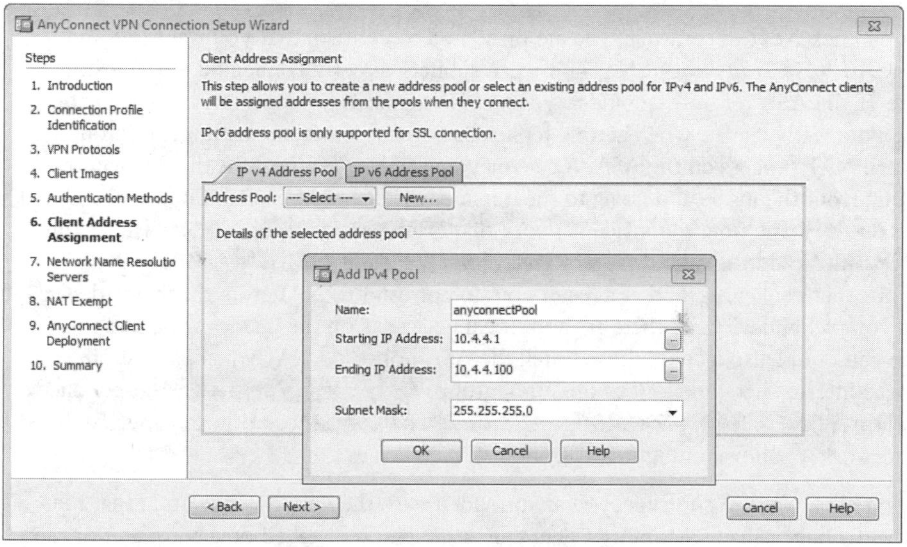

Figure 8-16   *Assigning a Pool for the Cisco AnyConnect Secure Mobility Clients*

Click **OK** to confirm your pool information. Then click **Next** to continue. At this point, you specify which DNS entries should be handed out to your clients and any NetBIOS name resolution servers (WINS) and a domain name that will primarily play a part in name resolution when the client uses DNSI (see Figure 8-17).

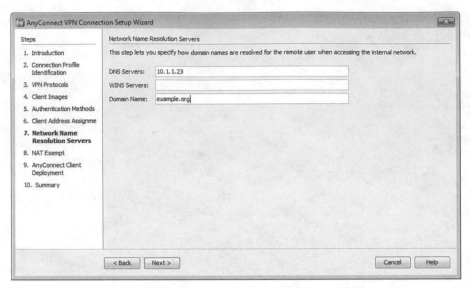

Figure 8-17   *DNS, WINS, and Domain Name Configuration to Be Given to AnyConnect Clients*

When you click **Next** to continue, you are prompted to confirm that you want to avoid *Network Address Translation (NAT)* between subnets directly connected to the inside interface of the ASA for traffic going to your VPN clients. The reason this is so critical is because your VPN clients, when getting replies back from servers, must not run through the normal NAT process on the ASA. A rule may be in place on the ASA that says all traffic coming from the inside and going to the outside world should be translated into a global address. If the traffic from the inside network that is going back to the VPN clients is translated, the source address is incorrect for what the VPN client is expecting. It also creates a couple of other challenges, and as a result you do not want to NAT from the inside devices back to your VPN devices. If there are additional networks on the inside, or behind the firewall, you could also include those to tell the ASA not to do NAT when packets are going from these internal networks out to this VPN group. To specify the NAT exemption, check the **Exempt VPN Traffic from Network Address Translation** check box and specify the inside network, as shown in Figure 8-18.

When you click **Next** to continue, you are provided with the window indicating that the Cisco AnyConnect Secure Mobility Client can either be preinstalled on a computer or the user can connect using SSL basic connectivity and then install the client from the server, as shown in Figure 8-19.

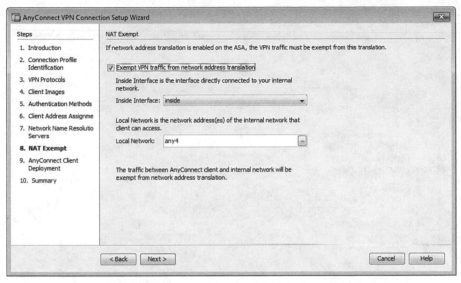

Figure 8-18 *Exemptions from NAT for Internal Traffic Going Back to the VPN Clients*

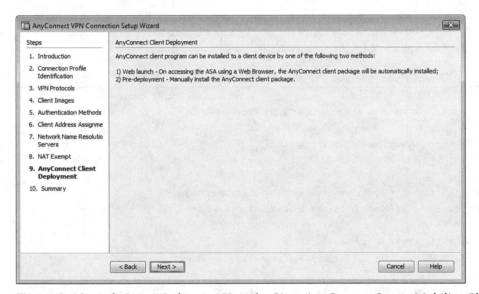

Figure 8-19 *Info Screen Indicating How the Cisco AnyConnect Secure Mobility Client May Be Installed*

Clicking **Next** one more time brings up the summary of what is about to be deployed to this ASA, as shown in Figure 8-20.

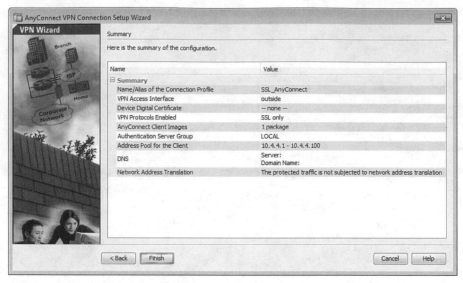

Figure 8-20 *Summary Screen for the AnyConnect Wizard*

After clicking **Finish,** depending on how ASDM is configured, you may have one or more dialog boxes to confirm the delivery of the configuration out to the ASA. Example 8-2 shows the CLI equivalent for the same configuration.

Example 8-2 *Configuring an SSL Cisco AnyConnect Secure Mobility Client VPN*

```
! For this example, to avoid the wrapping of some of the longer commands
! the firewall prompt has been omitted from the output below
! For use with the nat exemption, at the end of the config
object network NETWORK_OBJ_10.1.1.0_25
subnet 10.1.1.0 255.255.255.128


! Create the pool for the IP addresses it will be handing out
ip local pool anyconnectPool 10.4.4.1-10.4.4.100 mask 255.255.255.0


! Creates an internal group based on the name below
group-policy GroupPolicy_SSL_AnyConnectinternal


! Specifies the attributes of this group, that the protocol for transport
! will be SSL, specifies the DNS and Domain name to hand out.
group-policy GroupPolicy_SSL_AnyConnect attributes
  vpn-tunnel-protocol ssl-client
  dns-server value 10.1.1.23
  wins-server none
  default-domain value example.org
exit


! Specifies that SSL is enabled, and which packages from flash are available
```

```
! for client images
webvpn
 enable outside
 anyconnect image disk0:/anyconnect-macosx-4.0-k9.pkg 1

! Enables Anyconnect, and provides the group list (connection profile list)
! to users who are logging on, so they can initially select their "group"
  anyconnect enable
 tunnel-group-list enable

! Creates a tunnel group, and specifies the type of tunnel group it is
tunnel-group SSL_AnyConnect type remote-access

! Specifies what group policy should be used by this tunnel group,
! and what pool of IP addresses should be used for the users
tunnel-group SSL_AnyConnect general-attributes
  default-group-policy GroupPolicy_SSL_AnyConnect
  address-pool anyconnectPool

! Enables this URL (Alias) to be used to access the server
tunnel-group SSL_AnyConnectwebvpn-attributes
  group-alias SSL_AnyConnectenable

! provides the exception for NAT (if present) for VPN traffic from the inside
! network if it is going to the address range used by the AnyConnect clients.
! Note: the following is a single line that is shown as wrapped because
! is longer than the width of this page.
nat (inside,outside) 3 source static inside interface destination static
NETWORK_OBJ_10.1.1.0_25 NETWORK_OBJ_10.1.1.0_25 no-proxy-arp route-lookup
```

Groups, Connection Profiles, and Defaults

A great question that comes up quite a bit is this: Why do we have all these group connection profiles and default groups that seem to be interrelated? The answer is for flexibility. The connection profiles are responsible for the initial connection of the user (the end users only see these as groups, and they do not know all the details behind the scene), and two different connection profiles with two different URLs could use two different authentication methods. After you have authenticated users, you know who they are, and then you can associate group attributes with users' group memberships. In the CCNP Security curriculum, you have a greater opportunity to delve deeper into the workings of these components.

To log in initially to install the Cisco AnyConnect Secure Mobility Client, the customer opens a browser using HTTPS to the IP address of your ASA. The ASA prompts the user for which connection profile to use (displayed as Group to the user), as shown in Figure 8-21.

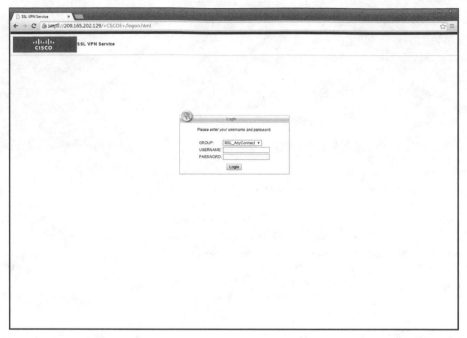

Figure 8-21 *Connecting to the ASA, with the Option to select the Connection Profile (Group)*

From the drop-down list, users can select the group, supply their credentials, and then click **Logon**.

One Item with Three Different Names

Now here is the interesting part. In the wizard, we created a connection profile called SSL_Cisco AnyConnect Secure Mobility Client. At the CLI, this is referred to as a tunnel group. From the user's perspective, the drop-down list is called Group. It is all referring to the same thing. It is important for you to understand the correlation between all of these and also to realize that it will be transparent to your users.

After the user authenticates, the ASA attempts to deliver and install the Cisco AnyConnect Secure Mobility Client software on the user's computer. A variety of methods can be used for the install, including ActiveX or Java. There are some minimum requirements at the workstation that is about to receive the installation. For full details of the current minimum requirements, visit Cisco.com for details about the latest version of Cisco AnyConnect Secure Mobility Client.

The installation looks slightly different on a Macintosh, but the concepts are the same in that the secure tunnel using SSL technology, along with an IP address being assigned to the customer, can allow them full tunnel access to the corporate network over the VPN.

Split Tunneling

One other option that applies to full-tunnel solutions for both Cisco AnyConnect Secure Mobility Client and IPsec remote-access clients is the ability to tell that remote device to send traffic over the IPsec or SSL tunnel only if the packets are destined to a specific sub-network or subnetworks at the headquarters' site. By doing this, the customer at a remote location can directly send out to the Internet to get responses from public servers and at the same time reach remote servers behind the ASA using the VPN. Without split tunneling, all IP traffic leaving the client's machine goes through the tunnel to the ASA (regardless of the destination), and if those resources being sought are not behind the ASA, the ASA also needs to be configured to NAT and redirect those requests out to the Internet. This causes double traffic, and the return path from the Internet server would come back to the ASA and then back through the tunnel to the client. A split tunnel addresses this issue by sending traffic down the VPN only if it is destined for specific networks located at the headquarter site. All other traffic is sent normally, outside the VPN. On the downside, a split tunnel is not considered to be as secure, because an attacker on the Internet may potentially have access to the remote machine, which in turn has access to the internal network through the VPN. By not allowing split tunneling, a corporation could perform additional security features on all the client's traffic, such as *intrusion prevention system (IPS)* and application inspection, before the client's traffic is sent in plain text out to the Internet.

To enable split tunneling on the ASA, navigate to **Configuration > Remote Access VPN > Network(Client) Access> Group Policies**. From there, edit the group policy by going to **Advanced > Split Tunneling**. From there, specify the networks for which you want to tunnel traffic. Anything not identified as traffic that should be tunneled is simply sent by the user through its natural path not inside the tunnel. An example is going to Cisco.com or some other web server, with the packets going in plain text to the user's default gateway and then onto the Internet toward that resource. Figure 8-22 shows an example of configuring split tunneling.

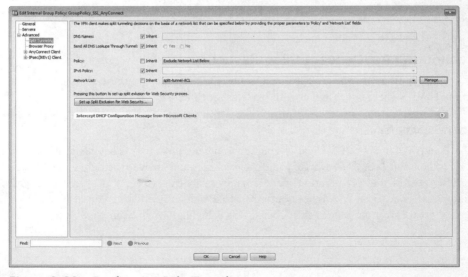

Figure 8-22 *Configuring Split Tunneling*

As clients establish VPN sessions, you are going to want the ability to identify who is connected. You can see this information from the Monitoring section of ASDM, in the same way you looked at the SSL clientless VPN connection information. Navigate to **Monitoring > VPN > VPN Statistics > Sessions**. From there, filter out which types of VPN connections you want to view. You can select an existing connection by clicking it, and then click the **Details** button to see more information.

Troubleshooting SSL VPN

The following sections discuss the troubleshooting steps that are available to help you in running the SSL VPN solution smoothly on the Cisco ASA.

Troubleshooting SSL Negotiations

If you have a user who is unable to connect to the Cisco ASA using SSL, follow these steps to isolate the SSL negotiation issues:

Step 1.   Verify that the user's computer can ping the Cisco ASA's outside IP address.

Step 2.   If the user's workstation can ping the address, issue the **show running all | include ssl** command on the Cisco ASA and verify that SSL encryption is configured.

Step 3.   If SSL encryption is properly configured, use an external sniffer to verify whether the TCP three-way handshake is successful.

> **NOTE**   AnyConnect clients will fail to establish connection if the Cisco ASAs are configured to accept connection with SSL Server Version 3. You must use TLSv1 for AnyConnect clients. Navigate to **Configuration > Remote Access VPN > Advanced > SSL Settings** to specify the SSL encryption type and version that you want to use.

Troubleshooting AnyConnect Client Issues

The following sections provide guidelines on troubleshooting the two most common AnyConnect VPN client issues and how to troubleshoot them.

Initial Connectivity Issues

If you use an AnyConnect VPN client in your environment and a user is having initial connectivity issues, run **debug webvpn svc** on the Cisco ASA and analyze the debug messages. You can fix most of the configuration-specific issues easily by looking at the error messages. For example, if your Cisco ASA is not configured to assign an IP address, you receive a "No assigned address" error message in the debugs. This is highlighted in Example 8-3.

Example 8-3 *Output of the* debug webvpn svc *Command*

```
ASA1# debug webvpn svc
CSTP state = HEADER_PROCESSING

http_parse_cstp_method()
...input: 'CONNECT /CSCOSSLC/tunnel HTTP/1.1'
webvpn_cstp_parse_request_field()
...input: 'Host: 209.165.200.226'
<snip>
Processing CSTP header line: 'X-DTLS-CipherSuite: AES256-SHA:AES128-SHA:DES-CBC3-SHA:
  DES-CBC-SHA'
Validating address: 0.0.0.0
CSTP state = WAIT_FOR_ADDRESS
webvpn_cstp_accept_address: 0.0.0.0/0.0.0.0
webvpn_cstp_accept_address: no address?!?
CSTP state = HAVE_ADDRESS
No assigned address
webvpn_cstp_send_error: 503 Service Unavailable
CSTP state = ERROR
```

The **debug webvpn svc** command has been replaced by **debug webvpn anyconnect** in recent versions of Cisco ASA.

Alternatively, you can enable an SVC-specific syslog on the Cisco ASA and look at the messages. For example, if the Cisco ASA does not assign an IP address to an AnyConnect client, you should see the "No address available for SVC connection" message, as shown in Example 8-4.

Example 8-4 *SVC Logging*

```
ASA1(config)# logging on
ASA1(config)# logging class svc buffered debugging
ASA1(config)# exit
ASA1# show logging
%ASA-3-722020: TunnelGroup <SSLVPNTunnel> GroupPolicy <AnyConnectGroupPolicy> User
  <sslvpnuser> IP <209.165.200.231> No address available for SVC connection
```

In addition, you can look at the AnyConnect VPN client logs in Windows Event Viewer. Choose **Start > Settings > Control Panel > Administrative Tools > Event Viewer > Cisco AnyConnect Secure Mobility Client** and review the logs. If an address is not being assigned, you should see an error message.

Traffic-Specific Issues

If you are able to connect but unable to successfully send traffic over the SSL VPN tunnel, look at the traffic statistics on the client to verify that traffic is being received and transmitted by the client. Detailed client statistics are available in all versions of AnyConnect (including mobile devices). If the client shows that traffic is being sent and received, check the Cisco ASA for received and transmitted traffic. If the Cisco ASA applies a filter, the filter name is shown, and you can look at the ACL entries to check whether your traffic is being dropped.

Common issues that users experience include the following:

- Routing issues behind the ASA—internal network unable to route packets back to the assigned IP addresses and VPN clients
- Access control lists blocking traffic
- Network Address Translation not being bypassed for VPN traffic

Exam Preparation Tasks

Review All the Key Topics

Review the most important topics from this chapter, denoted with a Key Topic icon. Table 8-5 lists these key topics.

Table 8-5   Key Topics

Key Topic Element	Description	Page Number
Section	Is IPsec Out of the Picture?	206
Table 8-2	Comparison of IPsec Versus SSL	206
Table 8-3	Comparison Between SSL and TLS	207
Section	The Play by Play of SSL for VPNs	207
Table 8-4	Options for SSL VPN Implementation	209
Figure 8-2	Interface Configuration Page	211
Figure 8-10	Monitoring the Details of the SSL VPN Clients in ASDM	217
Figure 8-14	Selecting the Cisco AnyConnect Secure Mobility Client Files to Place on the Flash of the ASA	220
Section	One Item with Three Different Names	226
Text	Troubleshooting AnyConnect initial connectivity issues	228
Text	Troubleshooting SSL VPN traffic-specific issues	230

Complete the Tables and Lists from Memory

Print a copy of Appendix C, "Memory Tables," (found on the CD) or at least the section for this chapter, and complete the tables and lists from memory. Appendix D, "Memory Tables Answer Key," also on the CD, includes completed tables and lists so that you can check your work.

Define Key Terms

Define the following key terms from this chapter, and check your answers in the glossary:

SSL, TLS, clientless SSL VPN, Cisco AnyConnect Secure Mobility Client full-tunnel VPN, PKI, digital certificate

8

This chapter covers the following topics:

VLAN and trunking fundamentals

Spanning-tree fundamentals

Common Layer 2 threats and how to mitigate them

CHAPTER 9

Securing Layer 2 Technologies

We often take for granted Layer 2 in the network because it just works. *Address Resolution Protocol (ARP)* and Layer 2 forwarding on Ethernet are all proven technologies that work very well. This certification, the CCNA Security, was built with the presumption that candidates would have a CCNA in routing/switching or equivalent knowledge. With this knowledge, your understanding of the details about VLANs, trunking, and inter-VLAN routing is presumed. However, so that you absolutely understand these fundamental concepts, this chapter begins with a review.

The first two sections of this chapter deal with ARP and DHCP. It is important to make sure that the basics are in place so that you can fully understand the discussion about protecting Layer 2 in the last section of this chapter, which covers the really important "stuff." That section focuses on just a few Layer 2–related security vulnerabilities and explains exactly how to mitigate threats at Layer 2. If you are currently comfortable with VLANs, trunking, and routing between VLANs, you might want to jump right to the last section.

"Do I Know This Already?" Quiz

The "Do I Know This Already?" quiz helps you determine your level of knowledge of this chapter's topics before you begin. Table 9-1 details the major topics discussed in this chapter and their corresponding quiz questions.

Table 9-1   "Do I Know This Already?" Section-to-Question Mapping

Foundation Topics Section	Questions
VLAN and Trunking Fundamentals	1, 6–7
Spanning-Tree Fundamentals	2
Common Layer 2 Threats and How to Mitigate Them	3–5, 8–10
CDP and LLDP	11
DHCP Snooping	12
Dynamic ARP Inspection	13

1. Which is the primary Layer 2 mechanism that allows multiple devices in the same VLAN to communicate with each other even though those devices are physically connected to different switches?

   a. IP address

   b. Default gateway

   c. Trunk

   d. 802.1D

2. How does a switch know about parallel Layer 2 paths?

   a. 802.1Q

   b. BPDU

   c. CDP

   d. NTP

3. When implemented, which of the following helps prevent CAM table overflows?

   a. 802.1w

   b. BPDU Guard

   c. Root Guard

   d. Port security

4. Which of the following is *not* a best practice for security?

   a. Leaving the native VLAN as VLAN 1

   b. Shutting down all unused ports and placing them in an unused VLAN

   c. Limiting the number of MAC addresses learned on a specific port

   d. Disabling negotiation of switch port mode

5. What is the default number of MAC addresses allowed on a switch port that is configured with port security?

   a. 1

   b. 5

   c. 15

   d. Depends on the switch model

6. Which two items normally have a one-to-one correlation?

   a. VLANs

   b. Classful IP networks

   c. IP subnetworks

   d. Number of switches

   e. Number of routers

7. What is a typical method used by a device in one VLAN to reach another device in a second VLAN?

   a. ARP for the remote device's MAC address

   b. Use a remote default gateway

   c. Use a local default gateway

   d. Use trunking on the PC

8. Which two configuration changes prevent users from jumping onto any VLAN they choose to join?

    a. Disabling negotiation of trunk ports

    b. Using something else other than VLAN 1 as the "native" VLAN

    c. Configuring the port connecting to the client as a trunk

    d. Configuring the port connecting to the client as an access port

9. If you limit the number of MAC addresses learned on a port to five, what benefits do you get from the port security feature? (Choose all that apply.)

    a. Protection for DHCP servers against starvation attacks

    b. Protection against IP spoofing

    c. Protection against VLAN hopping

    d. Protection against MAC address spoofing

    e. Protection against CAM table overflow attacks

10. Why should you implement Root Guard on a switch?

    a. To prevent the switch from becoming the root

    b. To prevent the switch from having any root ports

    c. To prevent the switch from having specific root ports

    d. To protect the switch against MAC address table overflows

11. Why should CDP be disabled on ports that face untrusted networks?

    a. CDP can be used as a DDoS vector.

    b. CDP can be used as a reconnaissance tool to determine information about the device.

    c. Disabling CDP will prevent the device from participating in spanning tree with untrusted devices.

    d. CDP can conflict with LLDP on ports facing untrusted networks.

12. Which of the following is not a true statement for DHCP snooping?

    a. DHCP snooping validates DHCP messages received from untrusted sources and filters out invalid messages

    b. DHCP snooping information is stored in a binding database.

    c. DHCP snooping is enabled by default on all VLANs.

    d. DHCP snooping rate-limits DHCP traffic from trusted and untrusted sources.

13. Which of the following is not a true statement regarding dynamic ARP inspection (DAI)?

    a. DAI intercepts, logs, and discards ARP packets with invalid IP-to-MAC address bindings.

    b. DAI helps to mitigate MITM attacks.

    c. DAI determines validity of ARP packets based on IP-to-MAC address bindings found in the DHCP snooping database.

    d. DAI is enabled on a per-interface basis.

Foundation Topics

VLAN and Trunking Fundamentals

You must understand the basics of how VLANs and trunking operate before you can learn to secure those features. This section reviews how VLANs and trunking are configured and how they operate.

Figure 9-1 serves as a reference for the discussion going forward. You might want to bookmark this page or take a moment to make a simple drawing of the topology. You will want to refer to this illustration often during the discussion.

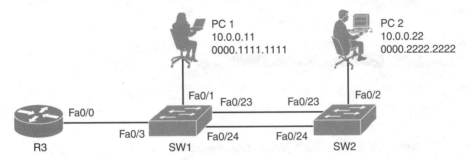

Figure 9-1   *Base Topology for Most of the Discussion in This Chapter*

What Is a VLAN?

One way to identify a local-area network is to say that all the devices in the same LAN have a common Layer 3 IP network address and that they also are all located in the same Layer 2 broadcast domain. A *virtual LAN (VLAN)* is another name for a *Layer 2 broadcast domain*. VLANs are controlled by the switch. The switch also controls which ports are associated with which VLANs. In Figure 9-1, if the switches are in their default configuration, all ports by default are assigned to VLAN 1, and that means all the devices, including the two users and the router, are all in the same broadcast domain, or VLAN.

As you start adding hundreds of users, you might want to separate groups of users into individual subnets and associated individual VLANs. To do this, you assign the switch ports to the VLAN, and then any device that connects to that specific switch port is a member of that VLAN. Hopefully, all the devices that connect to switch ports that are assigned to a given VLAN also have a common IP network address configured so that they can communicate with other devices in the same VLAN. Often, *Dynamic Host Configuration Protocol (DHCP)* is used to assign IP addresses from a common subnet range to the devices in a given VLAN.

If you want to move the two users in Figure 9-1 to a new common VLAN, you create the VLAN on the switches, and then assign the individual access ports that connect the users to the network to that new VLAN, as shown in Example 9-1.

Example 9-1 *Creating a New VLAN and Placing Switch Ports into That VLAN*

```
! Create the new VLAN
SW1(config)# vlan 10

! Assign the port as an access port belonging to VLAN 10
SW1(config-vlan)# interface fa0/1
SW1(config-if)# switchport mode access
SW1(config-if)# switchport access vlan 10

! Verify the VLAN exists, and that Fa0/1 has been assigned to it.
SW1(config-if)# do show vlan brief

VLAN Name                 Status           Ports
---- ------------------   --------------   --------------------------------
1    default              active           Fa0/2, Fa0/3, Fa0/4, Fa0/5
                                           Fa0/6, Fa0/7, Fa0/8, Fa0/9
                                           Fa0/10, Fa0/11, Fa0/12, Fa0/13
                                           Fa0/14, Fa0/15, Fa0/16, Fa0/17
                                           Fa0/18, Fa0/19, Fa0/20, Fa0/21
                                           Fa0/22, Fa0/23, Fa0/24, Gi0/1
                                           Gi0/2
10   VLAN0010             active           Fa0/1
<snip>

! Another way to verify the port is assigned the VLAN:
SW1# show vlan id 10
VLAN Name                 Status           Ports
---- ------------------   --------------   --------------------------------
10   VLAN0010             active           Fa0/1

! One more way to verify the same thing:
SW1# show interfaces fa0/1 switchport
Name: Fa0/1
Switchport: Enabled
Administrative Mode: static access
Operational Mode: static access
<snip>
Access Mode VLAN: 10 (VLAN0010)
<snip>
```

NOTE You would perform a similar configuration on SW2 with regard to creating VLAN 10 and assigning port Fa0/2 on SW2 as an access port in that VLAN.

Trunking with 802.1Q

One problem with having two users in the same VLAN but not on the same physical switch is how SW1 tells SW2 that a broadcast or unicast frame is supposed to be for VLAN 10. The answer is simple. For connections between two switches that contain ports in VLANs that exist in both switches, you configure specific trunk ports instead of configuring access ports. If the two switch ports are configured as trunks, they include additional information called a *tag* that identifies which VLAN each frame belongs to. 802.1Q is the standard protocol for this tagging. The most critical piece of information (for this discussion) in this tag is the VLAN ID.

Currently, the two users cannot communicate because they are in the same VLAN (VLAN 10), but the interswitch links (between the two switches) are not configured as trunks. To configure both sets of interfaces as trunks, you would specify the trunk method of 802.1Q and then turn on the feature, as shown in Example 9-2.

Example 9-2   *Configure Interfaces as Trunk Ports*

```
SW2(config)# interface range fa0/23-24
SW2(config-if-range)# switchport trunk encapsulation dot1q
SW2(config-if-range)# switchport mode trunk
SW2(config-if-range)#

! To verify the trunks:
SW2(config-if-range)# do show interface trunk

Port        Mode            Encapsulation  Status       Native vlan
Fa0/23      on              802.1Q         trunking     1
Fa0/24      on              802.1Q         trunking     1

Port        Vlans allowed on trunk
Fa0/23      1-4094
Fa0/24      1-4094

Port        Vlans allowed and active in management domain
Fa0/23      1,10
Fa0/24      1,10

Port        Vlans in spanning tree forwarding state and not pruned
Fa0/23      1,10
Fa0/24      none
SW2(config-if-range)#

! Another way to verify the trunk:
SW2# show interface fa0/23 switchport
Name: Fa0/23
Switchport: Enabled
Administrative Mode: trunk
```

```
Operational Mode: trunk
Administrative Trunking Encapsulation: dot1q
Operational Trunking Encapsulation: dot1q
Negotiation of Trunking: On
Access Mode VLAN: 1 (default)
Trunking Native Mode VLAN: 1 (default)
Administrative Native VLAN tagging: enabled
<snip>
```

Following the Frame, Step by Step

A broadcast frame sent from PC1 and received by SW1 would forward the frame over the trunk tagged as belonging to VLAN 10 to SW2. SW2 would see the tag, know it was a broadcast associated with VLAN 10, remove the tag, and forward the broadcast to all other interfaces associated with VLAN 10, including the switch port that is connected to PC2. These two core components (access ports being assigned to a single VLAN, and trunk ports that tag the traffic so that a receiving switch knows which VLAN a frame belongs to) are the core building blocks for Layer 2 switching, where a VLAN can extend beyond a single switch.

The Native VLAN on a Trunk

From the output in the earlier example, we verified our trunk interfaces between the two switches. One option shown in the output was a native VLAN. By default, the native VLAN is VLAN 1. So, what does this mean, and why do we care? If a user is connected to an access port that is assigned to VLAN 1 on SW1, and that user sends a broadcast frame, when SW1 forwards that broadcast to SW2, because the frame belongs to the native VLAN (and both switches agree to using the same native VLAN), the 802.1Q tagging is simply left off. This works because when the receiving switch receives a frame on a trunk port, if that frame is missing the 802.1Q tag completely, the receiving switch assumes that the frame belongs to the native VLAN (in this case, VLAN 1).

This is not a huge problem until somebody tries to take advantage of this, as discussed later in this chapter. In the meantime, just know that using a specific VLAN as the native VLAN (different from the default of VLAN 1) and never using that same VLAN for user traffic is a prudent idea.

So, What Do You Want to Be? (Asks the Port)

Trunks can be automatically negotiated between two switches, or between a switch and a device that can support trunking. Automatic negotiation to determine whether a port will be an access port or a trunk port is risky because an attacker could potentially negotiate a trunk with a switch; then the attacker could directly access any available VLANs simply by illegally tagging the traffic directly from his PC.

Inter-VLAN Routing

Our two users (PC1 and PC2) communicate with each other, and they can communicate with other devices in the same VLAN (which is also the same IP subnet), but they cannot communicate with devices outside their local VLAN without the assistance of a default gateway. A router could be implemented with two physical interfaces: one connecting to an access port on the switch that is been assigned to VLAN 10, and another physical interface connected to yet a different access port that has been configured for yet a different VLAN. With two physical interfaces and a different IP address on each, the router could perform routing between the two VLANs.

The Challenge of Using Physical Interfaces Only

So here is the problem: What if you have 50 VLANs? Purchasing 50 physical interfaces for the router would be pricey, let alone the fact that you would also be using 50 physical interfaces on the switch. One solution is to use a technique called *router-on-a-stick*. Consider Figure 9-1. R3 has one physical interface physically connected to the switch. So, from a physical topology perspective, it looks like the router is a lollipop, and that is where it gets its name. There are several video examples about router-on-a-stick and inter-VLAN routing available on the following YouTube channel: http://tinyurl.com/KeithBarker.

Using Virtual "Sub" Interfaces

To use one physical interface, we have to play a little game, where we tell the switch that we are going to do trunking out to the router, which from the switch perspective looks exactly like trunking to another switch. And on the router, we tell the router to pay attention to the 802.1Q tags, and assign frames from specific VLANs, based on the tags, to logical subinterfaces. Each subinterface has an IP address from different subnets, as shown in Example 9-3.

Example 9-3   *Configuring Router-on-a-Stick and Switch Support for the Router*

```
! Enable trunking on the switchport connected to the router
SW1(config)# interface fa 0/3
SW1(config-if)# switchport trunk encapsulation dot1q
SW1(config-if)# switchport mode trunk


! Move to R3:
! Make sure the physical interface isn't shutdown
R3(config)# interface fa 0/0
R3(config-if)# no shutdown


! Create a logical sub interface, using any number following the "0/0." (in the
! following we use "10" to correspond to VLAN 10)
R3(config-if)# interface fa 0/0.10


! Tell the router to process any dot1q frames tagged with VLAN ID 10 with this
! logical interface
R3(config-subif)# encapsulation dot1q 10
```

```
! Provide an IP address that is in the same subnet as other devices in VLAN 10
R3(config-subif)# ip address 10.0.0.1 255.255.255.0


! Verify that this router can ping devices in VLAN 10, namely PC1 and PC2
R3(config-subif)# do ping 10.0.0.11

Type escape sequence to abort.
Sending 5, 100-byte ICMP Echos to 10.0.0.11, timeout is 2 seconds:
!!!!!
Success rate is 100 percent (5/5), round-trip min/avg/max = 1/2/4 ms
R3(config-subif)# do ping 10.0.0.22

Type escape sequence to abort.
Sending 5, 100-byte ICMP Echos to 10.0.0.22, timeout is 2 seconds:
!!!!!
Success rate is 100 percent (5/5), round-trip min/avg/max = 1/2/4 ms
R3(config-subif)#
```

NOTE   The PC1 and PC2 computers need to configure R3's address of 10.0.0.1 as their default gateway if those computers want to use R3 to reach nonlocal networks (that is, VLANs other than VLAN 10).

You can repeat the process of creating additional subinterfaces on the router to support more VLANs until the router has a subinterface in every VLAN you want.

Spanning-Tree Fundamentals

This section discusses the basics of how the *Spanning Tree Protocol (STP)* can avoid loops at Layer 2 of the OSI model. It is important to understand how it works so that you can fully understand correct mitigation techniques.

This discussion references Figure 9-1 again.

Loops in Networks Are Usually Bad

Without STP, whenever we have parallel connections between Layer 2 devices, such as the connections between SW1 and SW2, we would have Layer 2 loops. Let's take a look at this using the network configured in the previous section. STP is on by default on most Cisco switches, but for the purposes of this discussion, assume that STP is not running, at least for now.

The Life of a Loop

If PC1 sends an ARP request into the network, SW1 receives it and knows that this frame belongs to VLAN 10 because of the access port it came in on, and forwards it out all other ports that are also assigned to VLAN 10, in addition to any trunk ports that are allowing

VLAN 10. By default, trunk ports allow all VLAN traffic. So, this broadcast is tagged as belonging to VLAN 10, and is sent down ports 23 and 24.

Just for a moment, let's follow just one of those ports. So, the traffic is being sent down port 23, and SW2 sees it and decides it needs to forward it out all other ports that are assigned to VLAN 10, which includes port number 2, which is an access port assigned to VLAN 10, and also the trunk port 24. So, now SW2 sends the same broadcast to SW1 on port 24. SW1 repeats the process and sends it out port 23, and there would be a loop. The loop happens in the other direction, as well. Besides having a loop, both switches become confused about which port is associated with the source MAC address of PC1. Because a looping frame is seen inbound on both ports 23 and 24, because of the loop going both directions, MAC address flapping occurs in the dynamically learned MAC address table of the switch. Not only does this lead to excessive and unnecessary forwarding of the ARP request to switch ports, it also could present a denial-of-service condition if the switch is unable to perform all of its functions as it is wasting resources due to this loop in the network.

The Solution to the Layer 2 Loop

STP, or 802.1D, was developed to identify parallel Layer 2 paths and block on one of the redundant paths so that a Layer 2 loop would not occur. A single switch with the lowest bridge ID becomes the *root bridge*, and then all the other nonroot switches determine whether they have parallel paths to the root and block on all but one of those paths. STP communicates using *bridge protocol data units (BPDU)*, and that is how negotiation and loop detection are accomplished.

Example 9-4, which contains annotations, allows you to both review how STP operates and see the commands to verify it at the same time; it uses the topology from the beginning of this chapter.

Example 9-4 *STP Verification and Annotations*

```
SW1# show spanning-tree vlan 10


VLAN0010
! This top part indicates the Bridge ID of the root bridge, which is a combination
! of the Bridge Priority and Base MAC address. The switch with the lowest overall
! Bridge ID of all switches in the network becomes the Root Bridge.
! NOTE: If all switches in a network are enabled with default spanning-tree settings
! (default bridge priority is 32768), the switch with the lowest MAC
! address becomes the Root Bridge.
! This switch is claiming victory over the other switch (SW2)
! This is due to this switch having a lower bridge ID

  Spanning tree enabled protocol ieee
  Root ID    Priority    32778
             Address     0019.060c.9080
             This bridge is the root
             Hello Time   2 sec  Max Age 20 sec  Forward Delay 15 sec
```

```
! This is the output about the local switch.  Because this is the root
! switch,
! this information will be identical to the information above regarding the
! bridge ID, which is a combination of the Priority and Base MAC address
  Bridge ID  Priority    32778  (priority 32768 sys-id-ext 10)
             Address     0019.060c.9080
             Hello Time   2 sec  Max Age 20 sec  Forward Delay 15 sec
             Aging Time  300 sec


! This specifies the state of each interface, and the default costs associated
! with each interface if trying to reach the root switch. Because this
! switch
! is the root bridge/switch, the local costs are not relevant.
! This also shows the forwarding or blocking state.   All ports on the root
! switch
! will be forwarding, every time, for the VLAN for which it is the root bridge.
Interface           Role Sts Cost      Prio.Nbr Type
------------------- ---- --- --------- -------- --------------------------
Fa0/1               Desg FWD 19        128.3    P2p
Fa0/3               Desg FWD 19        128.5    P2p
Fa0/23              Desg FWD 19        128.25   P2p
Fa0/24              Desg FWD 19        128.26   P2p


! Road trip over to SW2, who didn't win the STP election
SW2# show spanning-tree vlan 10

! This first part identifies who the root is, and the cost for this switch to get
! to the root switch.   SW1 advertised BPDUs that said the cost to reach me (SW1)
! is 0, and then this switch SW2, added that advertised cost to its only local
! interface cost to get to 19 as the cost for this switch to reach the root
! bridge.
VLAN0010
  Spanning tree enabled protocol ieee
  Root ID    Priority    32778
             Address     0019.060c.9080
             Cost        19
             Port        25 (FastEthernet0/23)
             Hello Time   2 sec  Max Age 20 sec  Forward Delay 15 sec

! This part identifies the local switch STP information. If you compare the
! bridge ID of this switch, to the bridge ID of SW1 (the root switch), you
! will notice that the priority values are the same, but SW1's MAC address
! is slightly lower (".060c" is lower than ".0617"), and as a result has a lower
! Bridge ID, which caused
! SW1 to win the election for root bridge of the spanning tree for VLAN 10
  Bridge ID  Priority    32778  (priority 32768 sys-id-ext 10)
```

```
              Address       0019.0617.6600
              Hello Time    2 sec  Max Age 20 sec   Forward Delay 15 sec
              Aging Time    300 sec


! This is the port forwarding/blocking information for SW2.   SW2 received
! BPDUs from root bridge on both 23 and 24, and so it knew there was a
! loop. It decided to block on port 24.   The cost was the same on both
! ports, and STP used the advertised port priority of the sending switch,
! and chose the lower value. In STP lower is always preferred.   By
! default, lower numbered physical ports, have lower numbered port
! priorities.
Interface            Role Sts Cost       Prio.Nbr Type
-------------------- ---- --- --------- -------- --------------------------

Fa0/2                Desg FWD 19         128.4    P2p

Fa0/23               Root FWD 19         128.25   P2p

Fa0/24               Altn BLK 19         128.26   P2p


! The blocking on port 24 is also reflected in the output of the show
! commands for trunking.   Notice that port 23 is forwarding for both
! VLAN 1 and 10, while port 24 is not forwarding for either VLAN.
SW2# show interfaces trunk


Port        Mode           Encapsulation  Status      Native vlan
Fa0/23      on             802.1Q         trunking    1
Fa0/24      on             802.1Q         trunking    1


Port        Vlans allowed on trunk
Fa0/23      1-4094

Fa0/24      1-4094


Port        Vlans allowed and active in management domain
Fa0/23      1,10

Fa0/24      1,10


Port        Vlans in spanning tree forwarding state and not pruned
Fa0/23      1,10

Fa0/24      none
```

STP is on by default, and will have a separate instance for each VLAN. So, if you have five VLANs, you have five instances of STP. Cisco calls this default implementation *Per-VLAN Spanning Tree Plus (PVST+)*.

STP consists of the following port states:

- **Root Port:** The switch port that is closest to the root bridge in terms of STP path cost (that is, it receives the best BPDU on a switch) is considered the root port. All switches, other than the root bridge, contain one root port.

- **Designated:** The switch port that can send the best BPDU for a particular VLAN on a switch is considered the designated port.
- **Nondesignated:** These are switch ports that do not forward packets, so as to prevent the existence of loops within the networks.

STP Is Wary of New Ports

When an interface is first brought up and receives a link signal from a connected device, such as a PC or router that is connected, STP is cautious before allowing frames in on the interface. If another switch is attached, there is a possible loop. STP cautiously waits for 30 seconds (by default) on a recently brought up port before letting frames go through that interface; 15 seconds of that is the listening state, where STP is seeing whether any BPDUs are coming in. During this time, it does not record source MAC addresses in its dynamic table. The second half of the 30 seconds (15 more) is then still looking for BPDUs, but STP also begins to populate the MAC address table with the source MAC addresses it sees in frames. This is called the *learning state*. After listening and learning have completed (full 30 seconds), the switch can begin forwarding frames. If a port is in a blocking state at first, an additional 20-second delay might occur as the port determines that the parallel path is gone, before moving to listening and learning.

For most administrators and users, this delay is too long. When configured, enhancements to STP, including the PortFast feature, can tell the switch to bypass the listening and learning stage and go right to forwarding. This leaves a small window for a loop if a parallel path is injected in the network.

Improving the Time Until Forwarding

Cisco had some proprietary improvements to the 802.1D (traditional STP) that allowed faster convergence in the event of a topology change and included many features such as the PortFast, UplinkFast, and BackboneFast. Many of these features were used in a newer version of STP called *Rapid Spanning Tree* (also known as 802.1w). Enabling PortFast for traditional STP and configuring Rapid Spanning Tree globally are shown in Example 9-5.

Example 9-5   *Configuring PortFast, Then Rapid Spanning Tree*

```
! PortFast can be enabled locally per interface
SW2(config)# interface fa0/2
SW2(config-if)# spanning-tree portfast
%Warning: portfast should only be enabled on ports connected to a single
 host. Connecting hubs, concentrators, switches, bridges, etc... to this
 interface  when portfast is enabled, can cause temporary bridging loops.
 Use with CAUTION

%Portfast has been configured on FastEthernet0/2 but will only
 have effect when the interface is in a non-trunking mode.
SW2(config-if)#

! or PortFast could be enabled globally
SW2(config)# spanning-tree portfast default
```

```
%Warning: this command enables portfast by default on all interfaces. You
 should now disable portfast explicitly on switched ports leading to hubs,
 switches and bridges as they may create temporary bridging loops.

! To change the STP from 802.1D to 802.1w, it requires just this one command
SW2(config)# spanning-tree mode rapid-pvst

! The show command will display rstp, instead of the original ieee for the
! mode
SW2# show spanning-tree vlan 10

VLAN0010
  Spanning tree enabled protocol rstp
<snip>
```

Common Layer 2 Threats and How to Mitigate Them

This section discusses many security threats that focus on Layer 2 technologies, and addresses how to implement countermeasures against those risks. This is relevant to the "security" portion of the CCNA Security certification.

Disrupt the Bottom of the Wall, and the Top Is Disrupted, Too

Everything at Layer 3 and higher is encapsulated into some type of Layer 2 frame. If the attacker can interrupt, copy, redirect, or confuse the Layer 2 forwarding of data, that same attacker can also disrupt any type of upper-layer protocols that are being used.

Layer 2 Best Practices

Let's begin with best practices for securing your switches and then discuss in more detail which best practice mitigates which type of attack.

Best practices for securing your infrastructure, including Layer 2, include the following:

- Select an unused VLAN (other than VLAN 1) and use that for the native VLAN for all your trunks. Do not use this native VLAN for any of your enabled access ports.

- Avoid using VLAN 1 anywhere, because it is a default.

- Administratively configure access ports as access ports so that users cannot negotiate a trunk and disable the negotiation of trunking (no *Dynamic Trunking Protocol [DTP]*).

- Limit the number of MAC addresses learned on a given port with the *port security* feature.

- Control spanning tree to stop users or unknown devices from manipulating spanning tree. You can do so by using the BPDU Guard and Root Guard features.

- Turn off *Cisco Discovery Protocol (CDP)* on ports facing untrusted or unknown networks that do not require CDP for anything positive. (CDP operates at Layer 2 and may provide attackers information we would rather not disclose.)

- On a new switch, shut down all ports and assign them to a VLAN that is not used for anything else other than a parking lot. Then bring up the ports and assign correct VLANs as the ports are allocated and needed.

To control whether a port is an access port or a trunk port, you can revisit the commands used earlier in this chapter, including the ones shown in Example 9-6.

Example 9-6 *Administratively Locking Down Switch Ports*

```
SW2(config)# interface fa0/2


! Specifies that this is an access port, not a trunk, and specifies VLAN
! association
SW2(config-if)# switchport mode access
SW2(config-if)# switchport access VLAN 10


! Disables the ability to negotiate, even though we hard coded the port as
! an access port.   This command disables DTP, which otherwise is still on
! by default, even for an interface configured as an access port.
SW2(config-if)# switchport nonegotiate



SW2(config-if)# interface fa 0/23
! Specifies the port as a trunk, using dot1q
SW2(config-if)# switchport trunk encapsulation dot1q
SW2(config-if)# switchport mode trunk

! Specify a VLAN that exists, but isn't used anywhere else, as the native
! VLAN
SW2(config-if)# switchport trunk native vlan 3



! Disables the ability to negotiate, even though we hard coded the port as
! a trunk
SW2(config-if)# switchport nonegotiate

! Note, negotiation packets  are still being sent unless we disable -
! negotiation
```

Do Not Allow Negotiations

The preceding example prevents a user from negotiating a trunk with the switch, maliciously, and then having full access to each of the VLANs by using custom software on the computer that can both send and receive dot1q tagged frames. A user with a trunk established could perform "VLAN hopping" to any VLAN he desired by just tagging frames with the VLAN of choice. Other malicious tricks could be done, as well, but forcing the port to an access port with no negotiation removes this risk.

Layer 2 Security Toolkit

Cisco has many tools for protecting Layer 2, including those described in Table 9-2.

Table 9-2   Toolkit for Layer 2 Security

Tool	Description
Port security	Limits the number of MAC addresses to be learned on an access switch port, as covered later in this chapter.
BPDU Guard	If BPDUs show up where they should not, the switch protects itself, as covered in this chapter.
Root Guard	Controls which ports are not allowed to become root ports to remote root switches, as covered in this chapter.
Dynamic ARP inspection	Prevents spoofing of Layer 2 information by hosts.
IP Source Guard	Prevents spoofing of Layer 3 information by hosts.
802.1X	Authenticates users before allowing their data frames into the network.
DHCP snooping	Prevents rogue DHCP servers from impacting the network.
Storm control	Limits the amount of broadcast or multicast traffic flowing through the switch.
Access control lists	Traffic control to enforce policy. Access control is covered in another chapter.

The key Layer 2 security technologies we focus on in CCNA Security include port security, BPDU Guard, Root Guard, DHCP snooping, and access lists. The other topics from the table you can save for your *CCNP* Security studies.

Specific Layer 2 Mitigation for CCNA Security

With a review of the switching technologies and how they operate now in mind, let's take a specific look at implementing security features on our switches.

BPDU Guard

No loops

When you enable BPDU Guard, a switch port that was forwarding stops and disables the port if a BPDU is seen inbound on the port. A user should never be generating legitimate BPDUs. This configuration, applied to ports that should only be access ports to end stations, helps to prevent another switch (that is sending BPDUs) from being connected to the network. This could prevent manipulation of your current STP topology. Example 9-7 shows the implementation of BPDU Guard.

Example 9-7   *Implementing BPDU Guard on a Switch Port*

```
SW2(config-if)# interface fa 0/2
SW2(config-if)# spanning-tree bpduguard enable

! Verify the status of the switchport
```

```
SW2# show interface fa0/2 status

Port        Name            Status      Vlan    Duplex  Speed  Type
Fa0/2                       connected   10      a-full  a-100  10/100BaseTX
SW2#
```

A port that has been disabled because of a violation shows a status of err-disabled. To bring the interface back up, issue a **shutdown** and then a **no shutdown** in interface configuration mode.

You can also configure the switch to automatically bring an interface out of err-disabled state, based on the reason it was placed there and how much time has passed before bringing the interface back up. To enable this for a specific feature, follow Example 9-8.

Example 9-8   *Configuring the Switch to Automatically Restore Err-Disabled Ports*

```
SW2(config)# errdisable recovery cause bpduguard

! err-disabled ports will be brought back up after 30 seconds of no bpdu
! violations
SW2(config)# errdisable recovery interval 30

! You can also see the timeouts for the recovery

SW2# show errdisable recovery
ErrDisable Reason           Timer Status
-----------------           -------------
arp-inspection              Disabled
bpduguard                   Enabled
<snip>

Timer interval: 30 seconds
Interfaces that will be enabled at the next timeout:

SW2#
```

Root switch will stay root switch

Root Guard

Your switch might be connected to other switches that you do not manage. If you want to prevent your local switch from learning about a new root switch through one of its local ports, you can configure Root Guard on that port, as shown in Example 9-9. This will also help in preventing tampering of your existing STP topology.

Example 9-9   *Controlling Which Ports Face the Root of the Spanning Tree*

```
SW1(config)# interface fa 0/24
SW1(config-if)# spanning-tree guard root
%SPANTREE-2-ROOTGUARD_CONFIG_CHANGE: Root guard enabled on port
   FastEthernet0/24.
```

Port Security

How many MAC addresses should legitimately show up inbound on an access port?

Port security controls how many MAC addresses can be learned on a single switch port. This feature is implemented on a port-by-port basis. A typical user uses just a single MAC address. Exceptions to this may be a virtual machine or two that might use different MAC addresses than their host, or if there is an IP phone with a built-in switch, which may also account for additional MAC addresses. In any case, to avoid a user connecting dozens of devices to a switch that is then connected to their access port, you can use port security to limit the number of devices (MAC addresses) on each port.

This also protects against malicious applications that may be sending thousands of frames into the network, with a different bogus MAC address for each frame, as the user tries to exhaust the limits of the dynamic MAC address table on the switch, which might cause the switch to forward all frames to all ports within a VLAN so that the attacker can begin to sniff all packets. This is referred to as a *CAM table overflow attack. Content-addressable memory (CAM)* is a fancy way to refer to the MAC address table on the switch.

Port security also prevents the client from depleting DHCP server resources, which could have been done by sending thousands of DHCP requests, each using a different source MAC address. DHCP spoofing attacks take place when devices purposely attempt to generate enough DHCP requests to exhaust the number of IP addresses allocated to a DHCP pool.

With the port security feature, the default violation action is to shut down the port. Alternatively, we can configure the violation response to be to "protect," which will not shut down the port but will deny any frames from new MAC addresses over the set limit. The "restrict" action does the same as protect but generates a syslog message, as well.

To implement port security, follow Example 9-10.

Example 9-10 *Implementing Port Security*

```
SW2(config-if)# interface fa 0/2


! Enable the feature per interface
SW2(config-if)# switchport port-security


! Set the maximum to desired number.  Default is 1. If we administratively
! set the maximum to 1, the command won't show in the running configuration
! because the configuration matches the default value. It is handy to know
! this behavior, so you won't be surprised by what may seem to be a missing
! part of your configuration.
SW2(config-if)# switchport port-security maximum 5


! Set the violation action.  Default is err-disable. Protect will simply
! not allow
! frames from MAC addresses above the maximum.
SW2(config-if)# switchport port-security violation protect
```

```
! This will cause the dynamic mac addresses to be placed into running
! -config to save them to startup config, use copy run start
SW2(config-if)# switchport port-security mac-address sticky


! To verify settings, use this command
SW2# show port-security
Secure Port  MaxSecureAddr  CurrentAddr  SecurityViolation  Security Action
                (Count)       (Count)        (Count)
---------------------------------------------------------------------------
    Fa0/2           5              1              0              Protect
---------------------------------------------------------------------------
Total Addresses in System (excluding one mac per port)    : 0
Max Addresses limit in System (excluding one mac per port) : 6144


! This can also provide additional information about port security:


SW2# show port-security interface fa0/2
Port Security            : Enabled
Port Status              : Secure-up
Violation Mode           : Protect
Aging Time               : 0 mins
Aging Type               : Absolute
SecureStatic Address Aging : Disabled
Maximum MAC Addresses    : 5
Total MAC Addresses      : 1
Configured MAC Addresses : 0
Sticky MAC Addresses     : 1
Last Source Address:Vlan : 0000.2222.2222:10
Security Violation Count : 0
```

For a video demonstration of port security, see the video on that topic that accompanies this book.

 ## CDP and LLDP

Cisco Systems introduced the *Cisco Discovery Protocol (CDP)* in 1994 to provide a mechanism for the management system to automatically learn about devices connected to the network. CDP runs on Cisco devices (routers, switches, phones, and so on) and is also licensed to run on some network devices from other vendors. Using CDP, network devices periodically advertise their own information to a multicast address on the network, making it available to any device or application that wishes to listen and collect it.

Over time, enhancements have been made to discovery protocols to provide greater capabilities. Applications (such as voice) have become dependent on these capabilities to operate properly, leading to interoperability problems between vendors. Therefore, to allow interworking between vendor equipment, it has become necessary to have a single, standardized discovery protocol. Cisco has been working with other leaders in the Internet and IEEE community to develop a new, standardized discovery protocol, 802.1AB (Station and Media Access Control Connectivity Discovery, or *Link Layer Discovery Protocol [LLDP]*). LLDP, which defines basic discovery capabilities, was enhanced to specifically address the voice application; this extension to LLDP is called LLDP-MED or LLDP (for *Media Endpoint Devices*).

As mentioned previously, a recommended best practice is to disable CDP on any ports facing untrusted or unknown networks that do not require CDP. CDP operates at Layer 2 and can provide attackers with information (for example, device types, hardware and software versions, VLAN and IP address details, and so on) that you would rather not disclose. Example 9-11 details the configuration steps necessary to disable CDP on a global and per interface basis.

In the same way it is recommended to disable CDP, it is also a best practice to disable LLDP in areas of the network that it is not needed. Example 9-11 also includes the configuration steps necessary to disable LLDP on a global basis.

Example 9-11 *Disabling CDP*

```
! Disable CDP on Interface Fa1/0/24
sw2(config)# interface fa1/0/24
sw2(config-if)# no cdp ?
  enable  Enable CDP on interface
sw2(config-if)# no cdp enable
! Disable CDP Globally on switch
sw2(config)# no cdp run
sw2(config)# exit
sw2#
! Verify CDP has been disabled
sw2(config)# do show cdp
% CDP is not enabled
! Confirm LLDP is enabled on switch
sw2# show lldp

Global LLDP Information:
    Status: ACTIVE
    LLDP advertisements are sent every 30 seconds
    LLDP hold time advertised is 120 seconds
    LLDP interface reinitialisation delay is 2 seconds
sw2#
! Disable LLDP on a global basis
sw2# conf t
Enter configuration commands, one per line.  End with CNTL/Z.
sw2(config)# no lldp run
sw2(config)# exit
! Confirm LLDP has been disabled
sw2# show lldp
% LLDP is not enabled
sw2#
```

DHCP Snooping

DHCP snooping is a security feature that acts like a firewall between untrusted hosts and trusted DHCP servers. The DHCP snooping feature performs the following activities:

- Validates DHCP messages received from untrusted sources and filters out invalid messages.
- Rate-limits DHCP traffic from trusted and untrusted sources.
- Builds and maintains the DHCP snooping binding database, which contains information about untrusted hosts with leased IP addresses.
- Utilizes the DHCP snooping binding database to validate subsequent requests from untrusted hosts

Other security features, such as *dynamic ARP inspection (DAI)*, which is described in the next section, also use information stored in the DHCP snooping binding database.

DHCP snooping is enabled on a per-VLAN basis. By default, the feature is inactive on all VLANs. You can enable the feature on a single VLAN or a range of VLANs.

As mentioned previously, DHCP spoofing attacks take place when devices purposely attempt to generate enough DHCP requests to exhaust the number of IP addresses allocated to a DHCP pool.

The DHCP snooping feature determines whether traffic sources are trusted or untrusted. An untrusted source may initiate traffic attacks or other hostile actions. To prevent such attacks, the DHCP snooping feature filters messages and rate-limits traffic from untrusted sources.

The following steps are required to implement DHCP snooping on your network:

Step 1. Define and configure the DHCP server. Configuration of this step does not take place on the switch or router and is beyond the scope of this book.

Step 2. Enable DHCP snooping on at least one VLAN. By default, DHCP snooping is inactive on all VLANs.

Step 3. Ensure that DHCP server is connected through a trusted interface.

By default, the trust state of all interfaces is untrusted.

Step 4. Configure the DHCP snooping database agent. This step ensures that database entries are restored after a restart or switchover.

Step 5. Enable DHCP snooping globally.

The DHCP snooping feature is not active until you complete this step.

Example 9-12 provides the configuration details necessary to implement DHCP snooping to mitigate the effects of DHCP spoofing attacks.

Example 9-12 *Configuring DHCP Snooping*

```
! Enable DHCP Snooping Globally
sw2(config)# ip dhcp snooping
! Enable DHCP Snooping on VLAN 10
sw2(config)# ip dhcp snooping vlan 10
! Configure Interface Fa1/0/24 as a Trusted interface
sw2(config)# interface fa1/0/24
sw2(config-if)# ip dhcp snooping trust
! Configure the DHCP snooping database agent to store the bindings at a given location
sw2(config)# ip dhcp snooping database tftp://10.1.1.1/directory/file
sw2(config)# exit
sw2#
! Verify DHCP Snooping Configuration
sw2# show ip dhcp snooping
Switch DHCP snooping is enabled
DHCP snooping is configured on following VLANs:
10
DHCP snooping is operational on following VLANs:
none
DHCP snooping is configured on the following L3 Interfaces:

Insertion of option 82 is enabled
   circuit-id default format: vlan-mod-port
   remote-id: 000f.90df.3400 (MAC)
Option 82 on untrusted port is not allowed
Verification of hwaddr field is enabled
Verification of giaddr field is enabled
DHCP snooping trust/rate is configured on the following Interfaces:

Interface            Trusted    Allow option    Rate limit (pps)
-------------------- -------    ------------    ----------------
FastEthernet1/0/24   yes        yes             unlimited
  Custom circuit-ids:
```

Dynamic ARP Inspection

ARP provides IP communication within a Layer 2 broadcast domain by mapping an IP address to a MAC address. For example, Host B wants to send information to Host A but does not have the MAC address of Host A in its *Address Resolution Protocol* (ARP) cache. Host B generates a broadcast message for all hosts within the broadcast domain to obtain the MAC address associated with the IP address of Host A. All hosts within the broadcast domain receive the ARP request, and Host A responds with its MAC address.

ARP spoofing attacks and ARP cache poisoning can occur because ARP allows a gratuitous reply from a host even if an ARP request was not received. After the attack, all traffic from the device under attack flows through the attacker's computer and then to the router, switch, or host.

An ARP spoofing attack can target hosts, switches, and routers connected to your Layer 2 network by poisoning the ARP caches of systems connected to the subnet and by intercepting traffic intended for other hosts on the subnet. Figure 9-2 shows an example of ARP cache poisoning.

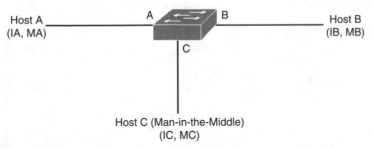

Host A
(IA, MA)

A   B

Host B
(IB, MB)

C

Host C (Man-in-the-Middle)
(IC, MC)

Figure 9-2 *ARP Cache Poisoning*

Hosts A, B, and C are connected to the switch on interfaces A, B, and C, all of which are on the same subnet. Their IP and MAC addresses are shown in parentheses; for example, Host A uses IP address IA and MAC address MA. When Host A needs to communicate to Host B at the IP layer, it broadcasts an ARP request for the MAC address associated with IP address IB. When the switch and Host B receive the ARP request, they populate their ARP caches with an ARP binding for a host with the IP address IA and a MAC address MA; for example, IP address IA is bound to MAC address MA. When Host B responds, the switch and Host A populate their ARP caches with a binding for a host with the IP address IB and the MAC address MB.

Host C can poison the ARP caches of the switch for Host A, and Host B by broadcasting forged ARP responses with bindings for a host with an IP address of IA (or IB) and a MAC address of MC. Hosts with poisoned ARP caches use the MAC address MC as the destination MAC address for traffic intended for IA or IB. This means that Host C intercepts that traffic. Because Host C knows the true MAC addresses associated with IA and IB, it can forward the intercepted traffic to those hosts by using the correct MAC address as the destination. Host C has inserted itself into the traffic stream from Host A to Host B, which is the topology of the classic man-in-the middle attack.

DAI is a security feature that validates ARP packets in a network. DAI intercepts, logs, and discards ARP packets with invalid IP-to-MAC address bindings. This capability protects the network from some man-in-the-middle attacks.

DAI determines the validity of an ARP packet based on valid IP-to-MAC address bindings stored in a trusted database, the DHCP snooping binding database. As described in the previous section, this database is built by DHCP snooping if DHCP snooping is enabled on the VLANs and on the switch. If the ARP packet is received on a trusted interface, the switch forwards the packet without any checks. On untrusted interfaces, the switch forwards the packet only if it is valid.

You can configure DAI to drop ARP packets when the IP addresses in the packets are invalid or when the MAC addresses in the body of the ARP packets do not match the addresses specified in the Ethernet header

Example 9-13 provides the configuration details necessary to implement DAI to mitigate the effects of ARP spoofing attacks.

Example 9-13   *Configuring Dynamic ARP Inspection (DAI)*

```
! Enable DAI on VLAN 10
sw2(config)# ip arp inspection vlan 10
sw2(config)# exit
! Verify DAI Configuration for VLAN 10
sw2# show ip arp inspection vlan 10

Source Mac Validation      : Disabled
Destination Mac Validation : Disabled
IP Address Validation      : Disabled


 Vlan     Configuration    Operation   ACL Match           Static ACL
 ----     -------------    ---------   ---------           ----------
   10     Enabled          Inactive


 Vlan    ACL Logging      DHCP Logging      Probe Logging
 ----    -----------      ------------      -------------
   10    Deny             Deny              Off
! Configure Interface Fa1/0/24 as a Trusted DAI Interface
sw2(config)# interface fa1/0/24
sw2(config-if)# ip arp inspection trust
sw2(config-if)# exit
sw2(config)# exit
sw2# show ip arp inspection interfaces
 Interface        Trust State     Rate (pps)     Burst Interval
 --------------   -----------     ----------     --------------
 Fa1/0/1          Untrusted              15                   1
 Fa1/0/2          Untrusted              15                   1
! output removed for brevity
 Fa1/0/23         Untrusted              15                   1
 Fa1/0/24         Trusted              None                 N/A
```

Exam Preparation Tasks

Review All the Key Topics

Review the most important topics from this chapter, denoted with a Key Topic icon. Table 9-3 lists these key topics.

Table 9-3   Key Topics

Key Topic Element	Description	Page Number
Section	What Is a VLAN?	236
Example 9-1	Creating a New VLAN and Placing Switch Ports into That VLAN	237
Section	Trunking with 802.1Q	238
Example 9-2	Configure Interfaces as Trunk Ports	238
Section	The Native VLAN on a Trunk	239
Section	Inter-VLAN Routing	240
Example 9-3	Configuring Router-on-a-Stick and Switch Support for the Router	240
Example 9-5	Configuring PortFast, Then Rapid Spanning Tree	245
List	Layer 2 best practices	246
Example 9-6	Administratively Locking Down Switch Ports	247
Table 9-2	Toolkit for Layer 2 Security	248
Section	BPDU Guard	248
Section	Root Guard	249
Text	Port security	250
Example 9-10	Implementing Port Security	250
Section	CDP and LLDP	251
Example 9-11	Disabling CDP	252
Section	DHCP Snooping	253
Example 9-12	Configuring DHCP Snooping	254
Section	Dynamic ARP Inspection	254
Example 9-13	Configuring Dynamic ARP Inspection (DAI)	256

9

Complete the Tables and Lists from Memory

Print a copy of Appendix C, "Memory Tables," (found on the CD) or at least the section for this chapter, and complete the tables and lists from memory. Appendix D, "Memory Tables Answer Key," also on the CD, includes completed tables and lists so that you can check your work.

Review the Port Security Video Included with This Book

Watch the video, and if possible practice the port security commands, including the commands to verify port security. If you do not have access to simulated or practice gear, verify that you can write out the commands, on paper, without assistance.

Define Key Terms

Define the following key terms from this chapter, and check your answers in the glossary:

access port, trunk port, inter-VLAN routing, router-on-a-stick, STP, Root Guard, port security, BPDU Guard, CDP, LLDP, DHCP snooping, dynamic ARP inspection

Command Reference to Check Your Memory

This section includes the most important configuration and EXEC commands covered in this chapter. To see how well you have memorized the commands as a side effect of your other studies, cover the left side of Table 9-4 with a piece of paper, read the descriptions on the right side, and see whether you remember the commands.

Table 9-4   Command Reference

Command	Description
switchport mode access	Assign a switch port as an access port
switchport access vlan *10*	Control the VLAN assignment for the device connecting to this port, and associate that device with a single specific VLAN of 10
show interfaces *fa0/1* switchport	Verify the current configuration and operating status of a switch port
switchport trunk encapsulation dot1q	Specify the trunking encapsulation to be used, if doing trunking
switchport mode trunk	Specify that this port should be a trunk
switchport trunk native vlan *3*	Specify the native VLAN should be 3, if the port is acting as a trunk port
switchport nonegotiate	Disable negotiation between the switch and the device connected to the device related to trunking
spanning-tree bpduguard enable	Protect the switch port against being connected on this port to another device that is generating any type of BPDUs

Command	Description
spanning-tree guard root	Protect this switch port against believing the root bridge is reachable via this port
switchport port-security	Protect the switch (on this port at least) against a MAC address table flooding attack (CAM table overflow) and prevent a DHCP starvation attack from being launched from the device connected to this port
no cdp enable	Disable CDP on a per-interface basis
no cdp run	Disable CDP globally on the switch
ip dhcp snooping	Enable DHCP snooping globally on the switch
ip dhcp snooping vlan 10	Enable DHCP snooping on VLAN 10
ip dhcp snooping trust	Configure an interface as a trusted DHCP snooping interface
ip arp inspection vlan 10	Configure VLAN 10 for DAI
ip arp inspection trust	Configure an interface as a trusted DAI interface

9

This chapter covers the following topics:

Using Network Foundation Protection to secure networks

Understanding the management plane

Understanding the control plane

Understanding the data plane

CHAPTER 10

Network Foundation Protection

The network infrastructure primarily consists of routers and switches and their interconnecting cables. The infrastructure has to be healthy and functional if we want to be able to deliver network services reliably.

If we break a big problem down into smaller pieces, such as security and what an attacker might do, we can then focus on individual components and parts. By doing this, the work of implementing security becomes less daunting. That is what *Network Foundation Protection (NFP)* is all about: breaking the infrastructure down into smaller components and then systematically focusing on how to secure each of those components.

"Do I Know This Already?" Quiz

The "Do I Know This Already?" quiz helps you determine your level of knowledge of this chapter's topics before you begin. Table 10-1 details the major topics discussed in this chapter and their corresponding quiz questions.

Table 10-1 "Do I Know This Already?" Section-to-Question Mapping

Foundation Topics Section	Questions
Using Network Foundation Protection to Secure Networks	1–3
Understanding the Management Plane	4–5
Understanding the Control Plane	6–8
Understanding the Data Plane	9–10

1. Which of the following is not a core element addressed by NFP (Network Foundation Protection)?

   a. Management plane

   b. Control plane

   c. Data plane

   d. Executive plane

2. If you add authentication to your routing protocol so that only trusted authorized routers share information, which plane in the NFP are you securing?

   a. Management plane

   b. Control plane

   c. Data plane

   d. Executive plane

3. If you use authentication and authorization services to control which administrators can access which networked devices and control what they are allowed to do, which primary plane of NFP are you protecting?

   a. Management plane

   b. Control plane

   c. Data plane

   d. Executive plane

4. Which of the following is not a best practice to protect the management plane? (Choose all that apply.)

   a. HTTP

   b. Telnet

   c. HTTPS

   d. SSH

5. Which of the following is a way to implement role-based access control related to the management plane? (Choose all that apply.)

   a. Views

   b. AAA services

   c. Access lists

   d. IPS

6. What do CoPP and CPPr have in common? (Choose all that apply.)

   a. They both focus on data plane protection.

   b. They both focus on management plane protection.

   c. They both focus on control plane protection.

   d. They both can identify traffic destined for the router that will likely require direct CPU resources to be used by the router.

7. Which type of attack can you mitigate by authenticating a routing protocol? (Choose all that apply.)

   a. Man-in-the-middle attack

   b. Denial-of-service attack

   c. Reconnaissance attack

   d. Spoofing attack

8. What is a significant difference between CoPP and CPPr?

   a. One works at Layer 3, and the other works at Layer 2.

   b. CPPr can classify and act on more-specific traffic than CoPP.

   c. CoPP can classify and act on more-specific traffic than CPPr.

   d. One protects the data plane, and the other protects the management plane.

9. Which of the following enables you to protect the data plane?

   a. IOS zone-based firewall

   b. IPS

   c. Access lists

   d. Port security

10. DHCP snooping protects which component of NFP?

   a. Management plane

   b. Control plane

   c. Data plane

   d. Executive plane

10

Foundation Topics

Using Network Foundation Protection to Secure Networks

This section covers a strategic approach to hardening the network so that you can manage it and allow it to correctly maintain the routing tables, and most important, so that the network stays "healthy" and can forward traffic.

The Importance of the Network Infrastructure

Many pieces and parts make up a network, and even one simple component that is not working can cause a failure of the network. If a network does not work, revenue and productivity suffer. In a nutshell, if you have vulnerabilities such as weak passwords (or no passwords), software vulnerabilities, or misconfigured devices, that leaves the door open to attackers. The impact of a down network is huge; it normally affects the workforce and other systems and customers that rely on that network. The NFP framework is designed to assist you to logically group functions that occur on the network and then focus on specific security measures you can take with each of these functions.

The Network Foundation Protection Framework

For Cisco IOS routers and switches, the *Network Foundation Protection (NFP)* framework is broken down into three basic planes (also called sections/areas), each of which has a separate chapter dedicated to it later in this book:

- **Management plane:** This includes the protocols and traffic that an administrator uses between his workstation and the router or switch itself. An example is using a remote management protocol such as *Secure Shell (SSH)* to monitor or configure the router or switch. The management plane is listed here first because until the device is configured (which occurs in the management plane), the device will not be very functional in a network. If a failure occurs in the management plane, it may result in losing the ability to manage the network device altogether.

- **Control plane:** This includes protocols and traffic that the network devices use on their own without direct interaction from an administrator. An example is a routing protocol. A routing protocol can dynamically learn and share routing information that the router can then use to maintain an updated routing table. If a failure occurs in the control plane, a router might lose the capability to share or correctly learn dynamic routing information, and as a result might not have the routing intelligence to be able to route for the network.

- **Data plane:** This includes traffic that is being forwarded through the network (sometimes called transit traffic). An example is a user sending traffic from one part of the network to access a server in another part of the network; the data plane represents the traffic that is either being switched or forwarded by the network devices between clients and servers. A failure of some component in the data plane results in the customer's traffic not being able to be forwarded. Other times, based on policy, you might want to deny specific types of traffic that is traversing the data plane.

Interdependence

Some interdependence exists between these three planes. For example, if the control plane fails, and the router does not know how to forward traffic, this scenario impacts the data plane because user traffic cannot be forwarded. Another example is a failure in the management plane that might allow an attacker to configure devices and as a result could cause both a control plane and data plane failure.

Implementing NFP

You learn more about each of these three planes later in this chapter as well as in each of the subsequent chapters dedicated to each of the three planes individually. Before that, however, Table 10-2 describes security measures you can use to protect each of the three planes.

Table 10-2   Components of a Threat Control and Mitigation Strategy

Plane	Security Measures	Protection Objectives
Management plane	Authentication, authorization, accounting (AAA) Authenticated Network Time Protocol (NTP) Secure Shell (SSH) Secure Sockets Layer/Transport Layer Security (SSL/TLS) Protected syslog Simple Network Management Protocol Version 3 (SNMPv3) Parser views	Authenticate and authorize any administrators. Protect time synchronization by using authenticated NTP. Use only encrypted remote-access protocols such as SSH for CLI and SSL/TLS for GUI tools, and use secure versions of SNMP. If plaintext tools are used (such as syslog or Telnet), they should be protected by encryption protocols such as IPsec or should be used out of band (a separate network just for management traffic). A parser "view" is a way to limit what a specific individual, based on his role, can do on the router.
Control plane	Control Plane Policing (CoPP) and Control Plane Protection (CPPr) Authenticated routing protocol updates	The control plane tools can be implemented to limit the damage an attacker can attempt to implement directly at one of the router's IP addresses (traffic addressed directly to the router, which the router must spend CPU resources to process). Routing protocol updates should be authenticated to remove the possibility of an attacker manipulating routing tables by putting a rogue router running the same routing protocol on your network. The attacker could be doing reconnaissance to learn the routes, or the attacker could be attempting to manipulate the resulting data plane by changing the routing on the network.

10

Plane	Security Measures	Protection Objectives
Data plane	Access control lists (ACL) Layer 2 controls, such as private VLANs, Spanning Tree Protocol (STP) guards IOS IPS, zone-based firewall	ACLs, when applied as filters on interfaces, can control which traffic (transit traffic) is allowed on the data plane. At Layer 2, by protecting the infrastructure there, you can avoid a rogue switch from becoming the root of your spanning tree, which would affect the data plane at Layer 2. Firewall filtering and services can also control exactly what traffic is flowing through your network. An example is using an IOS zone-based firewall to implement policy about the data plane and what is allowed.

As you might have noticed, NFP is not a single feature but rather is a holistic approach that covers the three components (that is, planes) of the infrastructure, with recommendations about protecting each one using a suite of features that you can implement across your network.

A command-line utility called **auto secure** implements security measures (several in each category) across all three of the planes. You will see the equivalent of **auto secure** in *Cisco Configuration Professional (CCP)*, the *graphical user interface (GUI)* tool that you can use to manage routers) in the next chapter.

When implementing the best practices described by NFP, does that mean your network is going to be up forever and not have any problems? Of course not. If the network is designed poorly, with no fault tolerance, for example, and a device fails (because of a mechanical or software failure or a physical problem or because cables were removed), if you do not have the failovers in place to continue to move traffic, your data plane is going to suffer. Other factors, such as lack of change control or an administrator accidentally putting in the incorrect configuration, are, of course, ongoing potential opportunities for the network to stop functioning.

Understanding the Management Plane

This section examines what you can do to protect management access and management protocols used on the network.

First Things First

As mentioned earlier, the management plane is covered first in this discussion. After all, without a configured router (whether configured through the console port or through an IP address with a secure remote-access tool such as SSH), the network device is not much good without a working configuration that either an administrator or some other type of management system such as *Cisco Security Manager (CSM)* has put in place. (A basic Layer 2 switch with all ports in the same VLAN would be functional, but this is unlikely to be the desired configuration for that device.)

Best Practices for Securing the Management Plane

To secure the management plane, adhere to these best practices:

- Enforce password policy, including features such as maximum number of login attempts and minimum password length.

- Implement *role-based access control (RBAC)*. This concept has been around for a long time in relation to groups. By creating a group that has specific rights and then placing users in that group, you can more easily manage and allocate administrators. With RBAC, we can create a role (like a group) and assign that role to the users who will be acting in that role. With the role comes the permissions and access. Ways to implement RBACs include using *Access Control Server (ACS)* and CLI parser views (which restrict the commands that can be issued in the specific view the administrator is in). Custom privilege level assignments are also an option to restrict what a specific user may do while operating at that custom privilege level.

- Use AAA services, and centrally manage those services on an ACS server. With AAA, a network router or switch can interact with a centralized server before allowing any access, before allowing any command to be entered, and while keeping an audit trail that identifies who has logged in and what commands they executed while there. Your policies about who can do what can be configured on the central server, and then you can configure the routers and switches to act as clients to the server as they make their requests asking whether it is okay for a specific user to log in or if it is okay for a specific user to issue a specific command.

- Keep accurate time across all network devices using secure *Network Time Protocol (NTP)*.

- Use encrypted and authenticated versions of SNMP, which includes Version 3 (and some features from Version 2).

- Control which IP addresses are allowed to initiate management sessions with the network device.

- Lock down syslog. Syslog is sent in plain text. On the infrastructure of your network, only permit this type of traffic between the network device's IP address and the destinations that the network device is configured to send the syslog messages to. In practice, not too many people are going to encrypt syslog data, although it is better to do so. Short of doing encryption, we could use an *out-of-band (OOB)* method to communicate management traffic between our network devices and the management stations. An example is a separate VLAN that user traffic never goes on to, and using that separate VLAN just for the management traffic. If management traffic is sent in-band, which means the management traffic is using the same networks (same VLANs, for instance), all management traffic needs to have encryption, either built in or have it protected by encryption (such as using IPsec).

- Disable any unnecessary services, especially those that use *User Datagram Protocol (UDP)*. These are infrequently used for legitimate purposes, but can be used to launch *denial-of-service (DoS)* attacks. Following are some services that should be disabled if they are not needed:

  - TCP and UDP small services

  - Finger

10

- BOOTP

- DHCP

- Maintenance Operation Protocol (MOP)

- DNS resolution

- Packet assembler/disassembler (PAD)

- HTTP server and Secure HTTP (HTTPS) server

- CDP

- LLDP

You learn more about management plane security in Chapter 11, "Securing the Management Plane on Cisco IOS Devices."

Understanding the Control Plane

This section reviews what you can do to protect network devices in the event of attacks involving traffic directed *to* (nontransit traffic) the network device itself.

The route processor, the CPU on a router, can only do so much. So, whenever possible, the router is going to cache information about how to forward packets (transit packets going from one device on the network to some other device). By using cached information when a packet shows up that needs to be forwarded, the CPU has to expend little effort. Forwarding of traffic is the data plane, and that is what really benefits from using cached information.

So, what has that got to do with the control plane? If a packet, such as an *Open Shortest Path First (OSPF)* or *Enhanced Interior Gateway Routing Protocol (EIGRP)* routing advertisement packet, is being sent to an IP on the router, it is no longer a transit packet that can be simply forwarded by looking up information in a route cache of some type. Instead, because the packet is addressed to the router itself, the router has to spend some CPU cycles to interpret the packet, look at the application layer information, and then potentially respond. If an attacker sends thousands of packets like these to the router, or if there is a *botnet* of hundreds of thousands of devices, each configured to send these types of packets to the router, the router could be so busy just processing all these requests that it might not have enough resources to do its normal work. Control plane security is primarily guarding against attacks that might otherwise negatively impact the CPU, including routing updates (which are also processed by the CPU).

Best Practices for Securing the Control Plane

Table 10-3 describes three ways to implement security of the control plane.

Table 10-3   Three Ways to Secure the Control Plane

Feature	Explanation
CoPP	Control plane policing. You can configure this as a filter for any traffic destined to an IP address on the router itself. For example, you can specify that management traffic, such as SSH/HTTPS/SSL and so on, can be rate-limited (policed) down to a specific level or dropped completely. This way, if an attack occurs that involves an excessive amount of this traffic, the excess traffic above the threshold set could simply be ignored and not have to be processed directly by the CPU. Another way to think of this is as applying quality of service (QoS) to the valid management traffic and policing to the bogus management traffic. This is applied to a logical control plane interface (not directly to any Layer 3 interface) so that the policy can be applied globally to the router.
CPPr	Control plane protection. This allows for a more detailed classification of traffic (more than CoPP) that is going to use the CPU for handling. The three specific subinterfaces that can be classified are (1) Host subinterface, which handles traffic to one of the physical or logical interfaces of the router; (2) Transit subinterface, which handles certain data plane traffic that requires CPU intervention before forwarding (such as IP options); and Cisco (3) Express Forwarding (CEF)-Exception traffic (related to network operations, such as keepalives or packets with Time-To-Live [TTL] mechanisms that are expiring) that has to involve the CPU. The benefit of CPPr is that you can rate-limit and filter this type of traffic with a more fine-toothed comb than CoPP. This is also applied to a logical control plane interface, so that regardless of the logical or physical interface on which the packets arrive, the router processor can still be protected.
Routing protocol authentication	Most routing protocols support authentication. If you use authentication, a rogue router on the network will not be believed by the authorized network devices (routers). The attacker may have intended to route all the traffic through his device, or perhaps at least learn details about the routing tables and networks.

10

Using CoPP or CPPr, you can specify which types of management traffic are acceptable at which levels. For example, you could decide and configure the router to believe that SSH is acceptable at 100 packets per second, syslog is acceptable at 200 packets per second, and so on. Traffic that exceeds the thresholds can be safely dropped if it is not from one of your specific management stations. You can specify all those details in the policy.

You learn more about control plane security in Chapter 13, "Securing Routing Protocols and the Control Plane."

Although not necessarily a security feature, *Selective Packet Discard (SPD)* provides the ability to prioritize certain types of packets (for example, routing protocol packets and Layer 2 keepalive messages, which are received by the *route processor [RP]*). SPD provides priority of critical control plane traffic over traffic that is less important or, worse yet, is being sent maliciously to starve the CPU of resources required for the RP.

Understanding the Data Plane

This section covers the methods available for implementing policy related to traffic allowed *through* (transit traffic) network devices.

For the data plane, this discussion concerns traffic that is going *through* your network device rather than *to* a network device. This is traffic from a user going to a server, and the router is just acting as a forwarding device. This is the data plane. Table 10-4 describes some of the prevalent ways to control the data plane (which may be implemented on an IOS router).

Table 10-4　Protecting the Data Plane

Feature	Explanation
ACLs used for filtering	There are many types of ACLs and many ways to apply them for filtering. Note that an ACL can be used as a classification mechanism used in other features, such as an IOS firewall, identifying traffic for control plane protection, identifying who is allowed to connect to a vty line, where SNMP is allowed, and so on. In the discussion of protecting the data plane, we focus primarily on ACLs applied directly to interfaces for the purpose of filtering.
IOS firewall support	The firewall features on an IOS router have grown over the years. The older technology for implementing a firewall on IOS routers was called *context-based access control (CBAC)*. CBAC has been replaced with the more current zone-based firewall on the IOS.
IOS IPS	IOS IPS is a software implementation of an *intrusion prevention system (IPS)* that is overlaid on top of the existing routing platform, to provide additional security. IOS IPS uses signature matches to look for malicious traffic. When an alert goes off because of a signature match, the router can prevent the packet from being forwarded, thus preventing the attack from reaching the final destination.
TCP Intercept	This tool enables the router to look at the number of half-formed sessions that are in place and intervene on behalf of the destination device. This can protect against a destination device from a SYN-flood attack that is occurring on your network. The zone-based firewall on an IOS router includes this feature.
Unicast Reverse Path Forwarding	*Unicast Reverse Path Forwarding (uRPF)* can mitigate spoofed IP packets. When this feature is enabled on an interface, as packets enter that interface the router spends an extra moment considering the source address of the packet. It then considers its own routing table, and if the routing table does not agree that the interface that just received this packet is also the best egress interface to use for forwarding to the source address of the packet, it then denies the packet. This is a good way to limit IP spoofing.

Best Practices for Protecting the Data Plane

To secure the data plane, adhere to these best practices:

■ Block unwanted traffic at the router. If your corporate policy does not allow TFTP traffic, just implement ACLs that deny traffic that is not allowed. You can implement ACLs inbound or outbound on any Layer 3 interface on the router. With extended ACLs, which can match based on the source and/or destination address, placing the ACL closer to the source saves resources because it denies the packet before it consumes network bandwidth and before route lookups are done on a router that is filtering inbound rather than outbound. Filtering on protocols or traffic types known to be malicious is a good idea.

■ Reduce the chance of DoS attacks. Techniques such as TCP Intercept and firewall services can reduce the risk of SYN-flood attacks.

■ Reduce spoofing attacks. For example, you can filter (deny) packets trying to enter your network (from the outside) that claim to have a source IP address that is from your internal network.

■ Provide bandwidth management. Implementing rate-limiting on certain types of traffic can also reduce the risk of an attack (*Internet Control Message Protocol [ICMP]*, for example, which would normally be used in small quantities for legitimate traffic).

■ When possible, use an IPS to inhibit the entry of malicious traffic into the network.

Additional Data Plane Protection Mechanisms

Normally, for data plane protection we think of Layer 3 and routers. Obviously, if traffic is going through a switch, a Layer 2 function is involved, as well. Layer 2 mechanisms that you can use to help protect the data plane include the following:

■ Port security to protect against MAC address flooding and *CAM (content-addressable memory)* overflow attacks. When a switch has no more room in its tables for dynamically learned MAC addresses, there is the possibility of the switch not knowing the destination Layer 2 address (for the user's frames) and forwarding a frame to all devices in the same VLAN. This might give the attacker the opportunity to eavesdrop.

■ *Dynamic Host Configuration Protocol (DHCP)* snooping to prevent a rogue DHCP server from handing out incorrect default gateway information and to protect a DHCP server from a starvation attack (where an attacker requests all the IP addresses available from the DHCP server so that none are available for clients who really need them).

■ *Dynamic ARP inspection (DAI)* can protect against *Address Resolution Protocol (ARP)* spoofing, ARP poisoning (which is advertising incorrect IP-to-MAC address mapping information), and resulting Layer 2 man-in-the-middle attacks.

■ IP Source Guard, when implemented on a switch, verifies that IP spoofing is not occurring by devices on that switch.

See Chapter 9, "Securing Layer 2 Technologies," for more information on the above Layer 2 Security mechanisms.

You learn more about data plane security in Chapter 12, "Securing the Data Plane."

10

Exam Preparation Tasks

Review All the Key Topics

Review the most important topics from this chapter, denoted with a Key Topic icon. Table 10-5 lists these key topics.

Table 10-5   Key Topics

Key Topic Element	Description	Page Number
List	The Network Foundation Protection (NFP) framework	264
Table 10-2	Components of a Threat Control and Mitigation Strategy	265
List	Best practices for securing the management plane	267
Table 10-3	Three Ways to Secure the Control Plane	269
Table 10-4	Protecting the Data Plane	270
List	Best practices for protecting the data plane	271
List	Additional data plane protection mechanisms	271

Complete the Tables and Lists from Memory

Print a copy of Appendix C, "Memory Tables," (found on the CD) or at least the section for this chapter, and complete the tables and lists from memory. Appendix D, "Memory Tables Answer Key," also on the CD, includes completed tables and lists so that you can check your work.

Define Key Terms

Define the following key terms from this chapter, and check your answers in the glossary:

management plane, control plane, data plane, NFP, Unicast Reverse Path Forwarding

This chapter covers the following topics:

Securing management traffic

Implementing security measures to protect the management plane

CHAPTER 11

Securing the Management Plane on Cisco IOS Devices

Accessing and configuring Cisco devices are common occurrences for an administrator. Malicious router management traffic from an unauthorized source can pose a security threat. For example, an attacker could compromise router security by intercepting login credentials (such as the username and password). This chapter introduces the concept of the *management plane* (which is a collection of protocols and access methods we use to configure, manage, and maintain a network device) and examines how to protect it.

"Do I Know This Already?" Quiz

The "Do I Know This Already?" quiz helps you determine your level of knowledge of this chapter's topics before you begin. Table 11-1 details the major topics discussed in this chapter and their corresponding quiz questions.

Table 11-1 "Do I Know This Already?" Section-to-Question Mapping

Foundation Topics Section	Questions
Securing Management Traffic	1–4, 6
Implementing Security Measures to Protect the Management Plane	5, 7–10

1. Which one of the following follows best practices for a secure password?

   a. ABC123!

   b. SlE3peR1#

   c. tough-passfraze

   d. InterEstIng-PaSsWoRd

2. When you connect for the first time to the console port on a new router, which privilege level are you using initially when presented with the command-line interface?

   a. 0

   b. 1

   c. 15

   d. 16

3. Which of the following is *not* impacted by a default login authentication method list?

   a. AUX line

   b. HDLC interface

   c. Vty line

   d. Console line

4. You are trying to configure a method list, and your syntax is correct, but the command is not being accepted. Which of the following might cause this failure? (Choose all that apply.)

   a. Incorrect privilege level

   b. AAA not enabled

   c. Wrong mode

   d. Not allowed by the view

5. Cisco recommends which version of Simple Network Management Protocol (SNMP) on your network if you need it?

   a. Version 1

   b. Version 2

   c. Version 3

   d. Version 4

6. How can you implement role-based access control (RBAC)? (Choose all that apply.)

   a. Provide the password for a custom privilege level to users in a given role

   b. Associate user accounts with specific views

   c. Use access lists to specify which devices can connect remotely

   d. Use AAA to authorize specific users for specific sets of permissions

7. Which of the following indirectly requires the administrator to configure a hostname?

   a. Telnet

   b. HTTP

   c. HTTPS

   d. SSH

8. What are the two primary benefits of using NTP along with a syslog server? (Choose all that apply.)

   a. Correlation of syslog messages from multiple different devices

   b. Grouping of syslog messages into summary messages

   c. Synchronization in the sending of syslog messages to avoid congestion

   d. Accurate accounting of when a syslog message occurred

9. Which of the following commands result in a secure bootset? (Choose all that apply.)

   a. secure boot-set

   b. secure boot-config

   c. secure boot-files

   d. secure boot-image

10. What is a difference between a default and named method list?

   a.   A default method list can contain up to four methods.

   b.   A named method list can contain up to four methods.

   c.   A default method list must be assigned to an interface or line.

   d.   A named method list must be assigned to an interface or line.

Foundation Topics

Securing Management Traffic

Fixing a problem is tricky if you are unaware of the problem. So, this first section starts by classifying and describing management traffic and identifying some of the vulnerabilities that exist. It also identifies some concepts that can help you to protect that traffic. This chapter then provides implementation examples of the concepts discussed earlier.

What Is Management Traffic and the Management Plane?

When you first get a new router or switch, you connect to it for management using a blue rollover cable that connects from your computer to the console port of that router or switch. This is your first exposure to the concept of management traffic. By default, when you connect to a console port, you are not prompted for a username or any kind of password. By requiring a username or password, you are taking the first steps toward improving what is called the *management plane* on this router or switch.

The management plane includes not only configuration of a system, but also who may access a system and what they are allowed to do while they are logged in to the system. The management plane also includes messages to or from a Cisco router or switch that is used to maintain or report on the current status of the device, such as a management protocol like *Simple Network Management Protocol (SNMP)*.

Beyond the Blue Rollover Cable

Using the blue rollover cable directly connected to the console port is fairly safe. Unfortunately, it is not very convenient to require the use of a console port when you are trying to manage several devices that are located in different buildings, or on different floors of the same building. A common solution to this problem is to configure the device with an IP address that you can then use to connect to that device remotely. It is at this moment that the security risk goes up. Because you are connecting over IP, it might be possible for an unauthorized person to also connect remotely. The management plane, if it were secure, would enable you to control who may connect to manage the box, when they may connect, what they may do, and report on anything that they did. At the same time, you want to ensure that all the packets that go between the device being managed and the computer where the administrator is sitting are encrypted so that anyone who potentially may capture the individual packets while going through the network could not interpret the contents of the packets (which might contain sensitive information about the configuration or passwords used for access).

Management Plane Best Practices

When implementing a network, remember the following best practices. Each one, when implemented, improves the security posture of the management plane for your network. In other words, each additional best practice, when put in place, raises the level of difficulty required on behalf of the attackers to compromise your device:

- **Strong passwords:** Make passwords very difficult to break. Whenever you use passwords, make them complex and difficult to guess. An attacker can break a password in several ways, including a dictionary and/or a brute-force attack. A dictionary attack automates the process of attempting to log in as the user, running through a long list of words (potential passwords); when one attempt fails, the attack just tries the next one (and so on). A brute-force attack does not use a list of words, but rather tries thousands or millions of possible character strings trying to find a password match (modifying its guesses progressively if it incorrectly guesses the password or stops before it reaches the boundary set by the attacker regarding how many characters to guess, with every possible character combination being tried). A tough password takes longer to break than a simple password.

- **User authentication and AAA:** Require administrators to authenticate using usernames and passwords. This is much better than just requiring a password and not knowing exactly who the user is. To require authentication using usernames and passwords, you can use a method for *authentication, authorization, and accounting (AAA)*. Using this, you can control which administrators are allowed to connect to which devices and what they can do while they are there, and you can create an audit trail (accounting records) to document what they actually did while they were logged in.

- **Login Password Retry Lockout:** The Login Password Retry Lockout feature allows system administrators to lock out a local AAA user account after a configured number of unsuccessful attempts by the user to log in using the username that corresponds to the AAA user account. A locked-out user cannot successfully log in again until the user account is unlocked by the administrator.

- **Role-based access control (RBAC):** Not every administrator needs full access to every device, and you can control this through AAA and custom privilege levels/parser views. For example, if there are junior administrators, you might want to create a group that has limited permissions. You could assign users who are junior administrators to that group; they then inherit just those permissions. This is one example of using RBAC. Another example of RBAC is creating a custom privilege level and assigning user accounts to that level. Regardless of how much access an administrator has, a change management plan for approving, communicating, and tracking configuration changes should be in place and used before changes are made.

- **Encrypted management protocols:** When using either in-band or out-of-band management, encrypted communications should be used, such as *Secure Shell (SSH)* or *Hypertext Transfer Protocol Secure (HTTPS)*. Out-of-band (OOB) management implies that there is a completely separate network just for management protocols and a different network for end users and their traffic. In-band management is when the packets used by your management protocols may intermingle with the user packets (considered less secure than OOB). Whether in-band or OOB, if a plaintext management protocol must be used,

11

such as Telnet or HTTP, use it in combination with a *virtual private network (VPN)* tunnel that can encrypt and protect the contents of the packets being used for management.

■ **Logging and monitoring:** Logging is a way to create an audit trail. Logging includes not only what administrators have changed or done but also system events that are generated by the router or switch because of some problem that has occurred or some threshold that has been reached. Determine the most important information to log, and identify logging levels to use. A logging level simply specifies how much detail to include in logging messages, and may also indicate that some less-serious logging messages do not need to be logged. Because the log messages may include sensitive information, the storage of the logs and the transmission of the logs should be protected to prevent tampering or damage. Allocate sufficient storage capacity for anticipated logging demands. Logging may be done in many different ways, and your logging information may originate from many different sources, including messages that are automatically generated by the router or switch and sent to a syslog server. A syslog server is a computer that is set up to receive and store syslog messages generated from network devices. If SNMP is used, preferably use Version 3 because of its authentication and encryption capabilities. You can use SNMP to change information on a router or switch, and you can also use it to retrieve information from the router or switch. An *SNMP trap* is a message generated by the router or switch to alert the manager or management station of some event.

■ **Network Time Protocol (NTP):** Use NTP to synchronize the clocks on network devices so that any logging that includes time stamps may be easily correlated. Preferably, use NTP Version 3, to leverage its ability to provide authentication for time updates. This becomes very important to correlate logs between devices in case there is ever a breach and you need to reconstruct (or prove in a court of law) what occurred.

■ **Secure system files:** Make it difficult to delete, whether accidentally or on purpose, the startup configuration files and the IOS images that are on the file systems of the local routers and switches. You can do so by using built-in IOS features discussed later in this chapter.

NOTE   Even though OOB management is usually preferred over in-band management, some management applications benefit from in-band management. For example, consider a network management application that checks the reachability of various hosts and subnets. To check this reachability, an application might send a series of pings to a remote IP address, or check the availability of various Layer 4 services on a remote host. To perform these "availability" checks, the network management application needs to send traffic across a production data network. Also, in-band network management often offers a more economical solution for smaller networks. Even if using in-band management, it should be a separate subnet/ VLAN, and one that only a select few people/devices have access to get to. This reduces your footprint for possible attack vectors.

Password Recommendations

Using passwords is one way to provide access. Using passwords alone is not as good as requiring a user ID or login name associated with the password for a user.

Here are some guidelines for password creation:

- It is best to have a minimum of eight characters for a password; bigger is better. This rule can be enforced by the local router if you are storing usernames and passwords on the router in the running config. The command security passwords min-length followed by the minimum password length enforces this rule on new passwords that are created, including the enable secret and line passwords on the vty, AUX, and console 0. Preexisting passwords will still operate even if they are less than the new minimum specified by the command.

- Passwords can include any alphanumeric character, a mix of uppercase and lowercase characters, and symbols and spaces. As a general security rule, passwords should not use words that may be found in a dictionary, because they are easier to break. Leading spaces in a password are ignored, but any subsequent spaces, including in the middle or at the end of a password, literally become part of that password and are generally a good idea. Another good practice is using special characters or even two different words (that are not usually associated with each other) as a passphrase when combined together. Caution should be used to not require such a complex password that the user must write it down to remember it, which increases the chance of it becoming compromised.

  Passwords in a perfect environment should be fairly complex and should be changed periodically. The frequency of requiring a change in passwords depends on your security policy. Passwords changed often are less likely to be compromised.

- From a mathematical perspective, consider how many possibilities someone would need to try to guess a password. If only capital letters are used, you have 26 possibilities for each character. If your password is one character long, that is 26^1, or 26 possible variants. If you have a two-character password, that is 26^2, or 676 possible variants. If you start using uppercase (26) and lowercase (26), numerals (10), and basic special characters (32), your starting set becomes 94 possible variants per character. Even if we look at using an eight-character password, that is 94^8 or 6,095,689,385,410,816 (6.1 quadrillion) possibilities.

Using AAA to Verify Users

Unauthorized user access to a network creates the potential for network intruders to gain information or cause harm or both. Authorized users need access to their network resources, and network administrators need access to the network devices to configure and manage them. AAA offers a solution for both. In a nutshell, the goal of AAA is to identify who users are before giving them any kind of access to the network, and once they are identified, only give them access to the part they are authorized to use, see, or manage. AAA can create an audit trail that identifies exactly who did what and when they did it. That is the

11

spirit of AAA. User accounts may be kept on the local database or on a remote AAA server. The *local database* is a fancy way of referring to user accounts that are created on the local router and are part of the running configuration.

AAA Components

Providing network and administrative access in a Cisco environment—regardless of whether it involves administrators managing the network or users getting access through network resources—is based on a modular architecture composed of the following three functional components:

- **Authentication:** Authentication is the process by which individuals prove that they are who they claim to be. The network environment has a variety of mechanisms for providing authentication, including the use of a username and password, token cards, and challenge and response. A common use is authenticating an administrator's access to a router console port, auxiliary port, or vty lines. An analogy is a bank asking you to prove that you are who you say you are before allowing you to make a transaction. As an administrator, you can control how a user is authenticated. Choices include referring to the local running configuration on the router to look for the username, going to an external server that holds the username and password information, and other methods. To specify the method to use, you create an authentication "method list" that specifies how to authenticate the user. There can be custom named method lists or default method lists. Examples of each are shown later in this chapter.

- **Authorization:** After the user or administrator has been authenticated, authorization can be used to determine which resources the user or administrator is allowed to access, and which operations may be performed. In the case of the average user, this might determine what hours that user is allowed on the network. In the case of an administrator, it could control what the administrator is allowed to view or modify. An analogy is a bank (after having already authenticated who you are) determining whether you are authorized to withdraw some amount of money (probably based on your balance in your account at the bank). You can create authorization method lists to specify how to authorize different users or groups of users on the network.

- **Accounting and auditing:** After being authenticated and possibly authorized, the user or administrator begins to access the network. It is the role of accounting and auditing to record what the user or administrator actually does with this access, what he accesses, and how long he accesses it. This is also known as *creating an audit trail*. An analogy is a bank documenting and debiting your account for the money you withdraw. You can create and assign accounting method lists to control what is accounted for and where the accounting records will be sent.

Options for Storing Usernames, Passwords, and Access Rules

Cisco provides many ways to implement AAA services for Cisco devices, many of which use a centralized service to keep usernames, passwords, and configured rules about who can access which resources. Over the years, there have been many names and access methods associated with the central server, including calling it an authentication server, AAA server, ACS server, TACACS server, or RADIUS server. These all refer to the same type of function:

a server that contains usernames, passwords, and rules about what may be accessed. A router or switch acts like a client to this server and can send requests to the server to verify the credentials of an administrator or user who is trying to access a local router or switch. The following list describes a few of these centralized server types:

- **Cisco Secure ACS Solution Engine:** This is a dedicated server that contains the usernames, their passwords, and other information about what users are allowed to access and when they are allowed to access. In the past, this was sold as a server appliance with the *Access Control Server (ACS)* software preinstalled. A router or switch becomes a client to the server. The router can be configured to require authentication from a user or administrator before providing access, and the router sends this request to the ACS server and lets the ACS server make the decision about allowing the user or administrator to continue. The protocol used between the router and the ACS server is normally TACACS+ if you are authenticating an administrator who is seeking command-line access to the network device (for example, the router). The protocol used between the router and the ACS server is normally RADIUS if you are authenticating an end user that is requesting access to the network (for example, an end user needs to successfully authenticate in order to access the network using a VPN connection). These are not hard-and-fast rules, and you can use either of the two protocols for similar features in many cases.

- **Cisco Secure ACS for Windows Server:** This software package may be used for user and administrator authentication. AAA services on the router or *network access server (NAS)* contact an external Cisco Secure ACS (running on a Microsoft Windows system). This is an older flavor of ACS, but may still be relevant to the certification exams.

- **Current flavors of ACS functionality:** The most common way that ACS services are implemented today is through a virtual machine running on some flavor of VMware. Another service to support similar services to ACS is called the Cisco *Identity Services Engine (ISE)*, which can be bundled in a single physical or logical device or appliance.

- **Self-contained AAA:** AAA services may be self-contained in the router itself. Implemented in this fashion, this form of authentication and authorization is also known as *local* authentication and authorization. The database that contains the usernames and passwords is the running configuration of the router or IOS device, and from a AAA perspective is referred to as the *local database* on the router. So, if you create a user locally on the router, you can also say that you created a user in the local database of the router. It is the same thing. In this case, because the router is acting as its own AAA server, you do not use TACACS+ or RADIUS as a protocol to connect to a remote ACS server, because you are not using an ACS server.

Authorizing VPN Users

One common implementation of AAA is its use in authenticating users accessing the corporate LAN through a remote-access IPsec VPN.

Let's see how authentication and authorization apply to users who are trying to access our network through a VPN. The first step is to authenticate users to find out who they are, and after we find out who they are, we can then control what they are authorized for. For example, if a user connects via a VPN, that user may or may not be allowed access to certain portions of the network based on who the user is and the privileges possessed by the user. This type of access is sometimes called *packet mode*, as in a user attempting to send packets through the network instead of trying to get a *command-line interface (CLI)* like an administrator would. A user connecting over a dial-up connection (older technology) could very likely be authenticated via a PPP connection using the same concepts. In either case, we authenticate the users by asking for their username and password, and then check the rules to see what they are authorized to access. If we use the remote *Access Control Server (ACS)* server for the authentication and authorization for an end user, we would very likely use the RADIUS protocol between the router and the AAA server.

AAA access control is supported using either a local username-password database or through a remote server (such as an ACS server). To provide access to a small group of network users, or as a backup in case the ACS server cannot be reached, a local security database can be configured in the router using the **username** command.

Router Access Authentication

Note that we must choose authentication first if we want to also use authorization for a user or administrator. We cannot choose authorization for a user without knowing who that user is through authentication first.

Typically, if we authenticate an administrator, we also authorize that administrator for what we want to allow him to do. Administrators traditionally are going to need access to the CLI. When an administrator is at the CLI, that interface is provided by something called an EXEC shell. If we want to authorize the router to provide this CLI, that is a perfect example of using AAA to first authenticate the user (in this case, the administrator) and then authorize that user to get a CLI prompt (the EXEC shell) and even place the administrator at the correct privilege level. This type of access (CLI) could also be referred to as *character mode*. Simply think of an administrator at a CLI typing in characters to assist you in remembering that this is "character" mode. With the administrator, we would very likely authenticate his login request and authorize that administrator to use an EXEC shell. If we were using a remote ACS server for this authentication and authorization of an administrator, we would very likely use TACACS+ (between the router and the ACS server) because it has the most granular control, compared with RADIUS, which is the alternative. TACACS+ and RADIUS are both discussed in another chapter of this book in greater detail.

Table 11-2 identifies some of the terms that refer to the type of access and the likely protocols used between the router acting as a client and the ACS server acting as the AAA server.

Table 11-2   AAA Components to Secure Administrative and Remote LAN Access

Access Type Mode	Mode	Where These Are Likely to Be Used	AAA Command Element
Remote administrative access Usually TACACS+ between the router and the ACS	Character (line or EXEC mode)	Lines: vty, AUX console, and tty	**login**, **enable**, **exec**
Remote network access end users Usually RADIUS between the router and the ACS	Packet (interface mode) such as an interface with PPP requiring authentication	Interfaces: async, group-async, BRI, PRI Other functionality: VPN user authentication	**ppp**, **network**, **vpn groups**

The AAA Method List

To make implementing AAA modular, we can specify individual lists of ways we want to authenticate, authorize, and account for the users. To do this, we create a *method list* that defines what resource will be used (such as the local database, an ACS server via TACACS+ protocol or an ACS server via RADIUS protocol, and so forth). To save time, we can create a default list or custom lists. We can create method lists that define the authentication methods to use, authorization method lists that define which authorization methods to use, and accounting method lists that specify which accounting method lists to use. A default list, if created, applies to the entire router or switch. A custom list, to be applied, must be both created and then specifically referenced in line or interface configuration mode. You can apply a custom list over and over again in multiple lines or interfaces. The type of the method list may be authentication, authorization, or accounting.

The syntax for a method list is as follows:

```
aaa type {default | list-name} method-1 [method-2 method-3 method-4]
```

The commands for a method list, along with their descriptions, are shown in Table 11-3.

Table 11-3   Method List Options

Command Element	Description
type	Identifies the type of list being created. Relevant options are **authentication**, **authorization**, or **accounting.**
default	Specifies the default list of methods to be used based on the methods that follow this argument. If you use the keyword **default**, a custom name is not used.
list-name	Used to create a custom method list. This is the name of this list, and is used when this list is applied to a line, such as to vty lines 0–4.

11

Command Element	Description
method	At least one method must be specified. To use the local user database, use the **local** keyword. A single list can contain up to four methods, which are tried in order, from left to right.
	In the case of an authentication method list, methods include the following:
	enable: The enable password is used for authentication. This might be an excellent choice as the last method in a method list. This way, if the previous methods are not available (such as the AAA server, which might be down or not configured), the router times out on the first methods and eventually prompts the user for the enable secret as a last resort.
	krb5: Kerberos 5 is used for authentication.
	krb5-telnet: Kerberos 5 Telnet authentication protocol is used when using Telnet to connect to the router.
	line: The line password (the one configured with the password command, on the individual line) is used for authentication.
	local: The local username database (running config) is used for authentication.
	local-case: Requires case-sensitive local username authentication.
	none: No authentication is used.
	group radius: A RADIUS server (or servers) is used for authentication.
	group tacacs+: A TACACS+ server (or servers) is used for authentication.
	group *group-name*: Uses either a subset of RADIUS or TACACS+ servers for authentication as defined by the **aaa group server radius** or **aaa group server tacacs+** command.

Role-Based Access Control

The concept of *role-based access control (RBAC)* is to create a set of permissions or limited access and assign that set of permissions to users or groups. Those permissions are used by individuals for their given roles, such as a role of administrator or a role of a help desk person and so on. There are different ways to implement RBAC, including creating custom privilege levels and creating parser views (coming up later in this section). In either case, the custom level or view can be assigned the permissions needed for a specific function or role, and then users can use those custom privilege levels or parser views to carry out their job responsibilities on the network, without being given full access to all configuration options.

Custom Privilege Levels

When you first connect to a console port on the router, you are placed into user mode. User mode is really privilege level 1. This is represented by a prompt that ends with **>**. When you move into privileged mode by typing the **enable** command, you are really moving into privilege level 15. A user at privilege level 15 has access and can issue all the commands that are attached to or associated with level 15 and below. Nearly all the configuration commands, and the commands that get us into configuration mode, are associated by default with privilege level 15.

By creating custom privilege levels (somewhere between levels 2 and 14, inclusive), and assigning commands that are normally associated with privilege level 15 to this new level, you can give this subset of new commands to the individual who either logs in at this custom level or to the user who logs in with a user account that has been assigned to that level.

Limiting the Administrator by Assigning a View

Working with individual commands and assigning them to custom privilege levels is tedious at best, and it is for that reason that method is not used very often. So, what can be done if we need users to have a subset of commands available to them, but not all of them? In Chapter 3, "Implementing AAA in Cisco IOS," we looked at how *Cisco Configuration Professional (CCP)* could restrict the visibility of the features in the navigation pane by using user profiles. This technique, however, did not protect the router against a user connecting with Telnet or SSH, and if that user had level 15 permissions, the router would once again be unprotected at the CLI.

A solution to this is to use *parser views*, also referred to as simply a *view*. You can create a view and associate it with a subset of commands. When the user logs in using this view, that same user is restricted to only being able to use the commands that are part of his current view. You can also associate multiple users with a singleview.

Encrypted Management Protocols

It is not always practical to have console access to the Cisco devices you manage. There are several options for remote access via IP connectivity, and the most common is an application called Telnet. The problem with Telnet is that it uses plain text, and anyone who gets a copy of those packets can identify our usernames and passwords used for access and any other information that goes between administrator and the router being managed (over the management plane). One solution to this is to not use Telnet. If Telnet must be used, it should only be used out of band, or placed within a VPN tunnel for privacy, or both.

Secure Shell (SSH) provides the same functionality as Telnet, in that it gives you a CLI to a router or switch; unlike Telnet, however, SSH encrypts all the packets that are used in the session. So, with SSH, if a packet is captured and viewed by an unauthorized individual, it will not have any meaning because the contents of each packet are encrypted, and the attacker or unauthorized person will not have the keys or means to decrypt the information. The encryption provides the feature of confidentiality (Remember that CIA triad from Chapter 1, "Networking Security Concepts"?)

11

With security, bigger really is better. With SSH, Version 2 is bigger and better than Version 1. Either version, however, is better than the unencrypted Telnet protocol. When you type in **ip ssh version 2** (to enable Version 2), the device may respond with "Version 1.99 is active." This is a function of a server that runs 2.0 but also supports backward compatibility with older versions. For more information, see RFC 4253, section 5.1. You should use SSH rather than Telnet whenever possible.

For *graphical user interface (GUI)* management tools such as CCP, use HTTPS rather than HTTP because, like SSH, it encrypts the session, which provides confidentiality for the packets in that session.

Using Logging Files

I still recall an incident on a customer site when a database server had a failed disk and was running on its backup. It was like that for weeks until they noticed a log message. If a second failure had occurred, the results would have been catastrophic. Administrators *should*, on a regular basis, analyze logs, especially from their routers, in addition to logs from other network devices. Logging information can provide insight into the nature of an attack. Log information can be used for troubleshooting purposes. Viewing logs from multiple devices can provide event correlation information (that is, the relationship between events occurring on different systems). For proper correlation of events, accurate time stamps on those events are important. Accurate time can be implemented through *Network Time Protocol (NTP)*.

Cisco IOS devices can send log output to a variety of destinations, including the following:

- **Console:** A router's console port can send log messages to an attached terminal (such as your connected computer, running a terminal emulation program).
- **vty lines:** *Virtual tty (vty)* connections (used by SSH and Telnet connections) can also receive log information at a remote terminal (such as an SSH or Telnet client). However, the **terminal monitor** command should be issued to cause log messages to be seen by the user on that vty line.
- **Buffer:** When log messages are sent to a console or a vty line, those messages are not later available for detailed analysis. However, log messages can be stored in router memory. This "buffer" area can store messages up to the configured memory size, and then the messages are rotated out, with the first in being the first to be removed (otherwise known as *first in, first out [FIFO]*). When the router is rebooted, these messages in the buffer memory are lost.
- **SNMP server:** When configured as an SNMP device, a router or switch can generate log messages in the form of SNMP traps and send them to an SNMP manager (server).
- **Syslog server:** A popular choice for storing log information is a syslog server, which is easily configured and can store a large volume of logs. Syslog messages can be directed to one or more syslog servers from the router or switch.

A syslog logging solution consists of two primary components: syslog servers and syslog clients. A syslog server receives and stores log messages sent from syslog clients such as routers and switches.

Not all syslog messages are created equal. Specifically, they have different levels of severity. Table 11-4 lists the eight levels of syslog messages. The higher the syslog level, the more detailed the logs. Keep in mind that more-detailed logs require a bit more storage space, and also consider that syslog messages are transmitted in clear text. Also consider that the higher levels of syslog logging consume higher amounts of CPU processing time. For this reason, take care when logging to the console at the debugging level.

Table 11-4   Syslog Severity Levels

Level	Name	Description
0	Emergencies	System is unusable.
1	Alerts	Immediate action needed.
2	Critical	Critical conditions.
3	Errors	Error conditions.
4	Warnings	Warning conditions.
5	Notifications	Normal, but significant conditions.
6	Informational	Informational messages.
7	Debugging	Highly detailed information based on current debugging that is turned on.

The syslog log entries contain time stamps, which are helpful in understanding how one log message relates to another. The log entries include severity level information in addition to the text of the syslog messages. Having synchronized time on the routers, and including time stamps in the syslog messages, makes correlation of the syslog messages from multiple devices more meaningful.

Understanding NTP

Network Time Protocol (NTP) uses UDP port 123, and it allows network devices to synchronize their time. Ideally, they would synchronize their time to a trusted time server. You can configure a Cisco router to act as a trusted NTP server for the local network, and in the same way, that trusted NTP server (Cisco router) could turn around and be an NTP client to a trusted NTP server either on the Internet or reachable via network connectivity. NTP Version 3 supports cryptographic authentication between NTP devices, and for this reason its use is preferable over any earlier versions.

One benefit of having reliable synchronized time is that log files and messages generated by the router can be correlated. In fact, if we had 20 routers, and they were all reporting various messages, and all had the same synchronized time, we could very easily correlate the events across all 20 routers if we looked at those messages on a common server. A common server that is often used is a syslog server.

Protecting Cisco IOS Files

Similar to the computers that we use every day, a router also uses an operating system. The traditional Cisco operating system on the router is called *IOS*, or sometimes *classic IOS*.

11

When a router first boots, it performs a power-on self-test and then looks for an image of IOS on the flash. After loading the IOS into RAM, the router then looks for its startup configuration. If for whatever reason an IOS image or the startup configuration cannot be found or loaded properly, the router will effectively be nonfunctional as far as the network is concerned.

To help protect a router from accidental or malicious tampering of the IOS or startup configuration, Cisco offers a resilient configuration feature. This feature maintains a secure working copy of the router IOS image and the startup configuration files at all times. Once enabled, the administrator cannot disable the features remotely (but can if connected directly on the console). The secure files are referred to as a *secure bootset*.

Implementing Security Measures to Protect the Management Plane

The first section of this chapter covered some best practices to protect the management plane. With that in mind, you can now leverage what you have learned and look at some practical examples of implementing those best practices. It requires both the understanding and implementation of these best practices to secure your networks.

Implementing Strong Passwords

The privileged EXEC secret (the one used to move from user mode to privileged mode) should not match any other password that is used on the system. Many of the other passwords are stored in plain text (such as passwords on the vty lines). If an attacker discovers these other passwords, he might try to use them to get into privileged mode, and that is why the enable secret should be unique. Service password encryption scrambles any plaintext passwords as they are stored in the configuration. This is useful for preventing someone who is looking over your shoulder from reading a plaintext password that is displayed in the configuration on the screen. Any new plaintext passwords are also scrambled as they are stored in the router's configuration.

Example 11-1 shows the use of strong passwords.

Example 11-1 *Using Strong Passwords*

```
! Use the "secret" keyword instead of the "password" for users
! This will create a secured password in the configuration by default
! The secret is hashed using the MD5 algorithm as it is stored in the
! -configuration
R1(config)# username admin secret CeyeSc01$24


! At a minimum, require a login and password for access to the console port
! Passwords on lines, including the console, are stored as plain text, by
! default, in the configuration
R1(config)# line console 0
R1(config-line)# password k4(1fmMsS1#
R1(config-line)# login
R1(config-line)# exit
```

```
! At a minimum, require a login and password for access to the VTY lines which
! is where remote users connect when using Telnet
! Passwords on lines, including the vty lines, are stored as plain text, by
! default, in the configuration
R1(config)# line vty 0 4
R1(config-line)# password 8wT1*eGP5@
R1(config-line)# login


! At a minimum, require a login and password for access to the AUX line
! and disable the EXEC shell if it will not be used
R1(config-line)# line aux 0
R1(config-line)# no exec
R1(config-line)# password 1wT1@ecP27
R1(config-line)# login
R1(config-line)# exit


! Before doing anything else, look at the information entered.
R1(config)# do show run | include username
username admin secret 5 $1$XJdX$9hqvG53z3lesP5BLOqggO.
R1(config)#
R1(config)# do show run | include password
no service password-encryption
 password k4(1fmMsS1#
 password 8wT1*eGP5@
 password 1wT1@ecP27
R1(config)#


! Notice that we cannot determine the admin user's password, since
! it is automatically hashed using the MD5 algorithm because of using
! the secret command, however, we can still see all the other plain text
! passwords.


! Encrypt the plain text passwords so that someone reading the configuration
! won't know what the passwords are by simply looking at the configuration.
R1(config)# service password-encryption


! Verify that the plain text passwords configured are now scrambled due to the
! command "service password-encryption"
R1(config)# do show run | begin line
line con 0
 password 7 04505F4E5E2741631A2A5454
 login
line aux 0
 no exec
 login
 password 7 075E36781F291C0627405C
```

11

```
line vty 0 4
 password 7 065E18151D040C3E354232
 login
!
end
```

User Authentication with AAA

Example 11-2 shows the use of method lists, both named and default.

Example 11-2   *Enabling AAA Services and Working with Method Lists*

```
! Enable aaa features, if not already present in the running configuration
R1(config)# aaa new-model


! Identify a AAA server to be used, and the password it is expecting with
! requests from this router. This server would need to be reachable and
! configured as a TACACS+ server to support R1's requests
R1(config)# tacacs-server host 50.50.4.101
R1(config)# tacacs-server key ToUgHPaSsW0rD-1#7


! configure the default method list for the authentication of character
! mode login (where the user will have access to the CLI)
! This default method list, created below has two methods listed "local"
! and "enable"
! This list is specifying that the local database (running-config) will
!  be used first to look for the username.  If the username isn't in the
! running-config, then it will go to the second method in the list.
! The second method of "enable" says that if the user account isn't found
! in the running config, then to use the enable secret to login.
! This default list will apply to all SSH, Telnet, VTY, AUX and Console
! sessions unless there is another (different) custom method list that is
! created and directly applied to one of those lines.
R1(config)# aaa authentication login default local enable


! The next authentication method list is a custom authentication
! method list named MY-LIST-1.This method list says that the first attempt
! to verify the user's name and password should be done through one of the
! tacacs servers (we have only configured one so far), and then if that server
! doesn't respond, use the local database (running-config), and if the
! username isn't in the running configuration to then use the enable secret
! for access to the device.  Note: this method list is not used until
! applied to a line elsewhere in the configuration, i.e. the default list
! configured previously is used unless MY-LIST-1 is specifically configured.
R1(config)# aaa authentication login MY-LIST-1 group tacacs local enable


! These next method lists are authorization method lists.
```

```
! We could create a default one as well, using the key
! word "default" instead of a name.    These custom method lists for
! authorization won't be used until we apply them
! elsewhere in the configuration, such as on a VTY line.
! The first method list called TAC1 is an authorization
! method list for all commands at user mode (called privilege level 1).
! The second method list called TAC15 is an
! authorization method list for commands at level 15 (privileged exec mode).
! If these method lists are applied to a line, such as the
! console or VTY lines, then before any commands
! are executed at user or privileged mode, the router will check
! with an ACS server that is one of the "tacacs+" servers, to see if the user
! is authorized to execute the command. If a tacacs+ server isn't
! reachable, then the router will use its own database of users (the local
! database) to determine if the user trying to issue the command
! is at a high enough privilege level to execute the command.
R1(config)# aaa authorization commands 1 TAC1 group tacacs+ local
R1(config)# aaa authorization commands 15 TAC15 group tacacs+ local

! The next 2 method lists are accounting method lists that will record the
! commands issued at level 1 and 15 if the lists are applied to a line, and
! if an administrator connects to this device via that line.
! Accounting method lists can have multiple methods, but can't log to the
! local router.
R1(config)# aaa accounting commands 1 TAC-act1 start-stop group tacacs+
R1(config)# aaa accounting commands 15 TAC-act15 start-stop group tacacs+

! Creating a user with level 15 access on the local router is a good idea,
! in the event the ACS server can't be
! reached, and a backup method has been specified as the local database.
R1(config)# username admin privilege 15 secret 4Je7*1swEsf

! Applying the named method lists is what puts them in motion.
! By applying the method lists to the VTY lines
! any users connecting to these lines will be authenticated by the
! methods specified by the lists that are applied
! and also accounting will occur, based on the lists that are applied.
R1(config)# line vty 0 4
R1(config-line)# login authentication MY-LIST-1
R1(config-line)# authorization commands 1 TAC1
R1(config-line)# authorization commands 15 TAC15
R1(config-line)# accounting commands 1 TAC-act1
R1(config-line)# accounting commands 15 TAC-act15

! Note: on the console and AUX ports, the default list will be applied,
! due to no custom method list being applied
! directly to the console or AUX ports.
```

11

Using **debug** as a tool to verify what you think is happening is a good idea. In Example 11-3, we review and apply AAA and perform a **debug** verification.

Example 11-3 *Another Example of Creating and Applying a Custom Method List to vty Lines*

```
! Creating the method list, which in this example has 3 methods.
! First the local database
! (if the username exists in the configuration, and if not
! then the enable secret (if configured),  and if not then no
! authentication required
! (none)
R2(config)# aaa authentication login MY-AUTHEN-LIST-1 local enable none

! Applying the method list to the VTY lines 0-4
R2(config)# line vty 0 4
R2(config-line)# login authentication MY-AUTHEN-LIST-1
R2(config-line)# exit

! Creating a local username in the local database (running-config)
R2(config)# username bob secret ciscobob

! Setting the password required to move from user mode to privileged mode
R2(config)# enable secret ciscoenable
R2(config)# interface loopback 0

! Applying an IP address to test a local telnet to this same local router
! Not needed if the device has another local IP address that is in use
R2(config-if)# ip address 2.2.2.2 255.255.255.0
R2(config-if)# exit

! Enable logging so we can see results of the upcoming debug
R2(config)# logging buffered 7
R2(config)# end

! Enabling debug of aaa authentication, so we can see what the router is
! thinking regarding aaa authentication
R2# debug aaa authentication
AAA Authentication debugging is on

R2# clear log
Clear logging buffer [confirm]

! Telnet to our own address
R2# telnet 2.2.2.2
```

```
Trying 2.2.2.2 ... Open

User Access Verification

Username: bob
AAA/BIND(00000063): Bind i/f
AAA/AUTHEN/LOGIN (00000063): Pick method list 'MY-AUTHEN-LIST-1'
Password: [ciscobob] password not shown when typing it in

R2>

! Below, after issuing the who command, we can see that bob is connected via line
! vty 0, and that from the debug messages above
! the correct authentication list was used.
R2>who
    Line        User       Host(s)              Idle        Location
   0 con 0                 2.2.2.2              00:00:00
*  2 vty 0      bob        idle                 00:00:00 2.2.2.2
R2> exit

! If we exit back out, and remove all the users in the local database,
! (including bob) then the same login authentication will fail on the first
! method of the "local" database (no users there), and will go to the second
! method in the list, which is "enable", meaning use the enable secret if
! configured.

! As soon as I supply a username, the router discovers that there are no
! usernames
! configured in running configuration (at least none that match the user
! who is trying to
! login), and fails on the first method "local" in the list
! It then tries the next method of just caring about the enable secret.

R2# telnet 2.2.2.2
Trying 2.2.2.2 ... Open
User Access Verification

AAA/BIND(00000067): Bind i/f
AAA/AUTHEN/LOGIN (00000067): Pick method list 'MY-AUTHEN-LIST-1'

! Note: bertha in not a configured user in the local database on the router
Username: bertha
Password: [ciscoenable} not shown while typing.  This is the enable secret we set.
AAA/AUTHEN/ENABLE(00000067): Processing request action LOGIN
AAA/AUTHEN/ENABLE(00000067): Done status GET_PASSWORD
```

11

```
R2>
AAA/AUTHEN/ENABLE(00000067): Processing request action LOGIN
AAA/AUTHEN/ENABLE(00000067): Done status PASS
R2> exit

! One more method exists in the method list we applied to the VTY lines.
! If the local fails, and the enable secret fails (because neither of these
! is configured on the router, then the third method in the method list
! 'MY-AUTHEN-LIST-1' will be tried. The third method we specified is none,
! meaning no authentication required, come right in.  After removing the
! enable secret, we try once more.


R2# telnet 2.2.2.2
Trying 2.2.2.2 ... Open


User Access Verification


AAA/BIND(00000068): Bind i/f
AAA/AUTHEN/LOGIN (00000068): Pick method list 'MY-AUTHEN-LIST-1'
Username: doesn't matter
R2>
AAA/AUTHEN/ENABLE(00000068): Processing request action LOGIN
AAA/AUTHEN/ENABLE(00000068): Done status FAIL - secret not configured
R2>
! No password was required.   All three methods of the method lists were
! tried.
! The first two methods failed, and the third of "none" was accepted.
```

Using the CLI to Troubleshoot AAA for Cisco Routers

One tool you can use when troubleshooting AAA on Cisco routers is the **debug** command. You may use three separate **debug** commands to troubleshoot the various aspects of AAA:

- **debug aaa authentication:** Use this command to display debugging messages for the authentication functions of AAA.

- **debug aaa authorization:** Use this command to display debugging messages for the authorization functions of AAA.

- **debug aaa accounting:** Use this command to display debugging messages for the accounting functions of AAA.

Each of these commands is executed from privileged EXEC mode. To disable debugging for any of these functions, use the **no** form of the command, such as **no debug aaa authentication**. If you want to disable all debugging, issue the **undebug all** command.

Example 11-4 shows an example of debugging login authentication, EXEC authorization, and commands at level 15 authorization. As shown in the example, you can use **debug** not only for verification, as in the preceding example, but also as a troubleshooting method.

Example 11-4   *Using* **debug** *Commands*

```
! R4 will have a loopback, so we can telnet to ourselves to test
R4(config-if)# ip address 4.4.4.4 255.255.255.0
R4(config-if)# exit


! Local user in the database has a privilege level of 15
R4(config)# username admin privilege 15 secret cisco


! This method list, if applied to a line, will specify local authentication
R4(config)# aaa authentication login AUTHEN_Loc local


! This next method list, if applied to a line, will require authorization
! before giving the administrator an exec shell.  If the user has a valid
! account in the running configuration, the exec shell will be created for
! the authenticated
! user, and it will place the user in their privilege level automatically
R4(config)# aaa authorization exec AUTHOR_Exec_Loc local


! This method list, if applied to a line, will require authorization for
! each and every level 15 command issued.  Because the user is at -
! privilege level 15 the router will say "yes" to any level 15 commands
! that may be issued by the user
R4(config)# aaa authorization commands 15 AUTHOR_Com_15 local


! Next we will apply the 3 custom method lists to vty lines 0-4, so that
! when anyone connects via these vty lines, they will be subject to the
! login authentication, the exec authorization, and the level 15 command
! authorizations for the duration of their session.


R4(config)# line vty 0 4
R4(config-line)# login authentication AUTHEN_Loc
R4(config-line)# authorization exec AUTHOR_Exec_Loc
R4(config-line)# authorization commands 15 AUTHOR_Com_15
R4(config-line)# exit
R4(config)#
R4(config)# do debug aaa authentication
AAA Authentication debugging is on
R4(config)# do debug aaa authorization
AAA Authorization debugging is on
R4(config)# exit


! Now test to see it all in action.
R4# telnet 4.4.4.4
Trying 4.4.4.4 ... Open
User Access Verification
```

Key
Topic

11

```
Username: admin
Password: [cisco] password not displayed when entering

! It  picked the login authentication list we specified
AAA/BIND(00000071): Bind i/f
AAA/AUTHEN/LOGIN (00000071): Pick method list 'AUTHEN_Loc'

! It picked the authorization list we specified for the exec shell
R4#
AAA/AUTHOR (0x71): Pick method list 'AUTHOR_Exec_Loc'
AAA/AUTHOR/EXEC(00000071): processing AV cmd=
AAA/AUTHOR/EXEC(00000071): processing AV priv-lvl=15
AAA/AUTHOR/EXEC(00000071): Authorization successful

! It picked the command level 15 authorization list, when we issued the
! configure terminal command, which is a level 15 command.
R4# config t
Enter configuration commands, one per line.  End with CNTL/Z.
R4(config)#
AAA/AUTHOR: auth_need : user= 'admin' ruser= 'R4' rem_addr= '4.4.4.4' priv= 15 list=
'AUTHOR_Com_15' AUTHOR-TYPE= 'command'
AAA: parse name=tty2 idb type=-1 tty=-1
AAA: name=tty2 flags=0x11 type=5 shelf=0 slot=0 adapter=0 port=2 channel=0
AAA/MEMORY: create_user (0x6A761F34) user='admin' ruser='R4' ds0=0 port='tty2'
rem_addr='4.4.4.4' authen_type=ASCII service=NONE priv=15 initial_task_id='0',
vrf= (id=0)
tty2 AAA/AUTHOR/CMD(1643140100): Port='tty2' list='AUTHOR_Com_15' service=CMD
AAA/AUTHOR/CMD: tty2(1643140100) user='admin'
tty2 AAA/AUTHOR/CMD(1643140100): send AV service=shell
tty2 AAA/AUTHOR/CMD(1643140100): send AV cmd=configure
tty2 AAA/AUTHOR/CMD(1643140100): send AV cmd-arg=terminal
tty2 AAA/AUTHOR/CMD(1643140100): send AV cmd-arg=<cr>
tty2 AAA/AUTHOR/CMD(1643140100): found list "AUTHOR_Com_15"
tty2 AAA/AUTHOR/CMD(1643140100): Method=LOCAL
AAA/AUTHOR (1643140100): Post authorization status = PASS_ADD
AAA/MEMORY: free_user (0x6A761F34) user='admin' ruser='R4' port='tty2'
rem_addr='4.4.4.4' authen_type=ASCII service=NONE priv=15 vrf= (id=0)
R4(config)#
! It made a big splash, with lots of debug output, but when you boil it all
! down it means the user was authorized to issue the configure terminal
! command.
```

There is also a **test aaa** command that is very useful when verifying connectivity with a remote ACS server.

This section walked you through the details of AAA using the command line with very exact examples because you need to understand how it works. Now that you have taken a look at how it works, you should know that you can also use CCP as a GUI to implement the AAA.

Let's take a moment to review where you can find the AAA elements inside CCP. In the configuration section, using the navigation pane on the left, go to **Configure > Router > AAA > AAA Summary**. You will see there an overview of what authentication policies have been created on a router and any authorization or accounting policies, as shown in Figure 11-1.

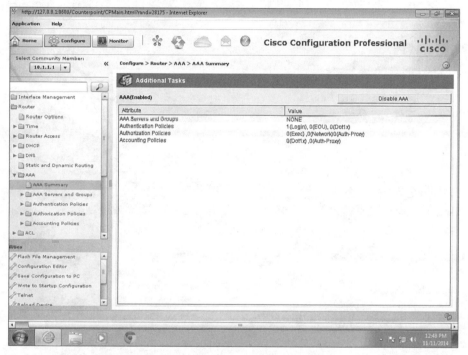

Figure 11-1 *Using CCP to View AAA Policies*

If you want to add, edit, or modify your authentication policies, you just navigate to **Configure > Router > AAA > Authentication Policies > Login**, as shown in Figure 11-2.

If you want to see which method lists were applied to your vty lines, just navigate to **Configure > Router > Router Access > VTY**, as shown in Figure 11-3.

11

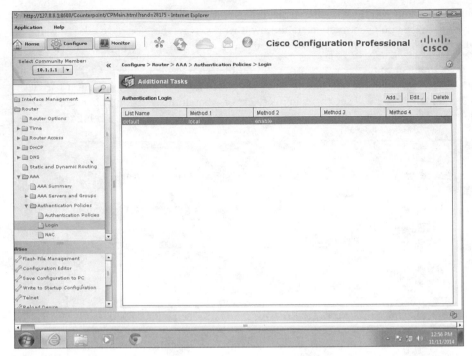

Figure 11-2 *Using CCP to See Method Lists for Login*

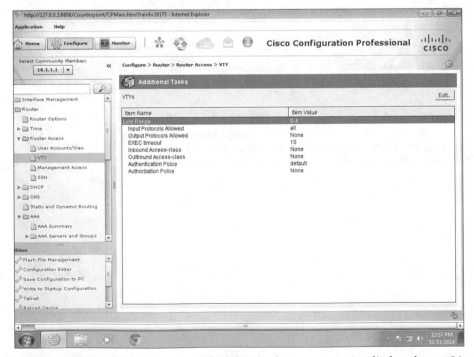

Figure 11-3 *Using CCP to See Which Methods Have Been Applied to the vty Lines*

From here, you can also modify which AAA policies are applied to vty lines by clicking **Edit**, which prompts the opening of an Edit VTY Lines dialog, as shown in Figure 11-4.

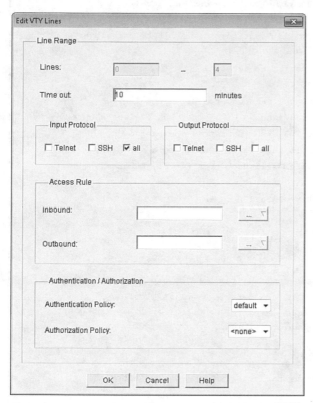

Figure 11-4 *Using CCP to Edit vty Line Properties, Including AAA Method Lists Applied*

RBAC Privilege Level/Parser View

You may implement RBAC through AAA, with the rules configured on an ACS server, but you may implement it in other ways, too, including creating custom privilege levels and having users enter those custom levels where they have a limited set of permissions, or creating a *parser view* (also sometimes simply called a *view*), which also limits what the user can see or do on the Cisco device. Each option can be tied directly to a username, so that once users authenticate they may be placed at the custom privilege level, or in the view that is assigned to them.

Let's implement a custom privilege level first, as shown in Example 11-5. The example includes explanations throughout.

Example 11-5 *Creating and Assigning Commands to a Custom Privilege Level*

```
! By default,  we use privilege level 1 (called user mode), and privilege
! level 15 (called privileged mode).   By creating custom levels, (between
! 1-15) and assigning commands to those levels, we are creating custom
! privilege levels
```

```
! A user connected at level 8, would have any of the new commands -
! associated with level 8, as well as any commands that have been custom
! assigned or defaulted to levels 8 and below.   A user at level 15 has
! access to all commands at level 15 and below.
! This configuration assigns the command "configure terminal" to privilege
! level 8
R2(config)# privilege exec level 8 configure terminal

! This configuration command assigns the password for privilege level 8
! the keyword "password" could be used instead of secret, but is less secure
! as the "password" doesn't use the MD5 hash to protect the password
! The "0" before the password, implies that we are inputting a non-hashed
! (to begin with) password.  The system will hash this for us, because we
! used the enable "secret" keyword.
R2(config)# enable secret level 8 0 NewPa5s123&
R2(config)# end
R2#
%SYS-5-CONFIG_I: Configured from console by console

! To enter this level, use the enable command, followed by the level you want
! to enter.   If no level is specified, the default level is 15
R2# disable
! Validate that user mode is really privilege level 1
R2> show privilege
Current privilege level is 1
! Context sensitive help shows that we can enter a level number after the
! word enable
R2> enable ?
  <0-15>  Enable level
  view    Set into the existing view
  <cr>


R2> enable 8
Password: [NewPa5s123&] ! note: password doesn't show when typing it in
R2# show privilege
Current privilege level is 8
! We can go into configuration mode, because "configure terminal" is at our
! level
R2# configure terminal
Enter configuration commands, one per line.  End with CNTL/Z.
! Notice we don't have further ability to configure the router, because
! level 8 doesn't include the interface configuration or other router -
! configuration commands.
R2(config)# ?
Configure commands:
  beep     Configure BEEP (Blocks Extensible Exchange Protocol)
```

```
call       Configure Call parameters
default    Set a command to its defaults
end        Exit from configure mode
exit       Exit from configure mode
help       Description of the interactive help system
license    Configure license features
netconf    Configure NETCONF
no         Negate a command or set its defaults
oer        Optimized Exit Routing configuration submodes
sasl       Configure SASL
wsma       Configure Web Services Management Agents
```

If we are requiring login authentication, we can associate a privilege level with a given user
account, and then when users authenticate with their username and password, they will automatically be placed into their appropriate privilege level. Example 11-6 shows an example of
this.

Example 11-6 *Creating a Local User and Associating That User with Privilege Level 8
and Assigning Login Requirements on the vty Lines*

```
! Create the user account in the local database (running-config) and
! associate that user with the privilege level you want that user to use.
R2(config)# username Bob privilege 8 secret Cisco123
R2(config)# line vty 0 4

! "login local" will require a username and password for access if the "aaa
! new-model" command is not present.   If we have set the aaa new-model,
! then we would also want to create a default or named method list that
! specifies we want to use the local database for authentication.
R2(config-line)# login local

! Note:  Once bob logs in, he would have access to privilege level 8 and
! below, (including all the normal show commands at level 1)
```

Implementing Parser Views

To restrict users without having to create custom privilege levels, you can use a *parser* view,
also referred to as simply a *view*. A view can be created with a subset of privilege level 15
commands, and when the user logs in using this view, that same user is restricted to only
being able to use the commands that are part of his current view.

To create a view, an enable secret password must first be configured on the router. AAA
must also be enabled on the router (**aaa new-model** command).

Example 11-7 shows the creation of a view.

11

Example 11-7 *Creating and Working with Parser Views*

```
! Set the enable secret, and enable aaa new-model (unless already in
! place)
R2(config)# enable secret aBc!2#&iU
R2(config)# aaa new-model
R2(config)# end


! Begin the view creation process by entering the "default" view, using the
! enable secret
R2# enable view
Password: [aBc!2#&iU] note password not shown when typed


R2#
%PARSER-6-VIEW_SWITCH: successfully set to view 'root'.
R2# configure terminal


! As the administrator in the root view, create a new custom view
R2(config)# parser view New_VIEW
%PARSER-6-VIEW_CREATED: view 'New_VIEW' successfully created.


! Set the password required to enter this new view
R2(config-view)# secret New_VIEW_PW


! Specify which commands you want to include as part of this view.
! commands "exec" refer to commands issued from the command prompt
! commands "configure" refer to commands issued from privileged mode
R2(config-view)# commands exec include ping
R2(config-view)# commands exec include all show
R2(config-view)# commands exec include configure


! This next line adds the ability to configure "access-lists" but nothing
! else
R2(config-view)# commands configure include access-list
R2(config-view)# exit
R2(config)# exit


! Test the view, by going to user mode, and then back in using the new view
R2# disable
R2>enable view New_VIEW
Password: [New_VIEW_PW] Password not shown when typed in


! Console message tells us that we are using the view
%PARSER-6-VIEW_SWITCH: successfully set to view 'New_VIEW'.


! This command reports what view we are currently using
```

```
R2# show parser view
Current view is 'New_VIEW'


! We can verify that the commands assigned to the view work
! Note: we only assigned configure, not configure terminal so we have to
! use the configure command, and then tell the router we are configuring
! from the terminal.  We could have assigned the view "configure terminal"
! to avoid this
R2# configure terminal
Enter configuration commands, one per line.  End with CNTL/Z.


! Notice that the only configuration options we have are for access-list,
! per the view
R2(config)# ?
Configure commands:
  access-list  Add an access list entry
  do           To run exec commands in config mode
  exit         Exit from configure mode
```

We could also assign this view to a user account, so that when users log in with their username and password, they are automatically placed into their view, as shown in Example 11-8.

Example 11-8 *Associating a User Account with a Parser View*

```
R2(config)# username Lois view New_VIEW secret cisco123
```

NOTE   This creation of a username and assigning that user to a view needs to be done by someone who is at privilege level 15.

SSH and HTTPS

Because Telnet sends all of its packets as plain text, it is not secure. SSH allows remote management of a Cisco router or switch, but unlike Telnet, SSH encrypts the contents of the packets to protect it from being interpreted if they fall into the wrong hands.

To enable SSH on a router or switch, the following items need to be in place:

■ Hostname other than the default name of router.

■ Domain name.

■ Generating a public/private key pair, used behind the scenes by SSH.

■ Requiring user login via the vty lines, instead of just a password. Local authentication or authentication using an ACS server are both options.

■ Having at least one user account to log in with, either locally on the router, or on an ACS server.

11

Example 11-9 shows how to implement these components, along with annotations and examples of what happens when the required parts are not in place. If you have a nonproduction router or switch handy, you might want to follow along.

Example 11-9 *Preparing for SSH*

```
! To create the public/private key pair used by SSH, we would issue the
! following command.   Part of the key pair, will be the hostname and the
! domain name.
! If these are not configured first, the crypto key generate command will
! tell you as shown in the next few lines.
Router(config)# crypto key generate rsa
% Please define a hostname other than Router.
Router(config)# hostname R1
R1(config)# crypto key generate rsa
% Please define a domain-name first.
R1(config)# ip domain-name cisco.com


! Now with the host and domain name set, we can generate the key pair
R1(config)# crypto key generate rsa
The name for the keys will be: R1.cisco.com
Choose the size of the key modulus in the range of 360 to 2048 for your
  General Purpose Keys. Choosing a key modulus greater than 512 may take
  a few minutes.


! Bigger is better with cryptography, and we get to choose the size for the
! modulus
! The default is 512 on many systems, but you would want to choose 1024 or
! more to improve security.   SSH has several flavors, with version 2 being
! more secure than version 1.   To use version 2, you would need at least a
! 1024 size for the key pair
How many bits in the modulus [512]: 1024
% Generating 1024 bit RSA keys, keys will be non-exportable...


R1(config)#
%SSH-5-ENABLED: SSH 1.99 has been enabled
! Note the "1.99" is based on the specifications for SSH from RFC 4253
! which indicate that an SSH server may identify its version as 1.99 to
! identify that it is compatible with current and older versions of SSH.


! Create a user in the local database
R1(config)# username Keith secret Ci#kRk*ks


! Configure the vty lines to require user authentication
R1(config)# line vty 0 4
R1(config-line)# login local
```

```
! Alternatively, we could do the following for the requirement of user
! authentication
! This creates a method list which points to the local database, and then
! applies that list to the VTY lines
R1(config)# aaa new-model
R1(config)# aaa authentication login Keith-List-1 local
R1(config)# line vty 0 4
R1(config-line)# login authentication Keith-List-1


! To test this we could SSH to ourselves from the local machine, or from
! another router that has IP connectivity to this router.


R1# ssh ?
  -c    Select encryption algorithm
  -l    Log in using this user name
  -m    Select HMAC algorithm
  -o    Specify options
  -p    Connect to this port
  -v    Specify SSH Protocol Version
  -vrf  Specify vrf name
  WORD  IP address or hostname of a remote system


! Note: one of our local IP addresses is 10.1.0.1
R1# ssh -l Keith 10.1.0.1


Password: <password for Keith goes here>


R1>
! to verify the current SSH session(s)
R1> show ssh
Connection Version Mode Encryption  Hmac       State           Username
0         2.0     IN   aes128-cbc  hmac-sha1  Session started Keith
0         2.0     OUT  aes128-cbc  hmac-sha1  Session started Keith
%No SSHv1 server connections running.
R1>
```

Perhaps you want to manage a router via HTTPS. If so, you can use CCP or a similar tool and implement HTTPS functionality, as shown in Example 11-10.

Example 11-10 *Preparing for HTTPS*

```
! Enable the SSL service on the local router.  If it needs to generate
! keys for this feature, it will do so on its own in the background.
R1(config)# ip http secure-server


! Specify how you want users who connect via HTTPS to be authenticated
R1(config)# ip http authentication ?
```

```
   aaa     Use AAA access control methods
   enable  Use enable passwords
   local   Use local username and passwords

R1(config)# ip http authentication local

! If you are using the local database, make sure you have at least one user
! configured in the running-config so that you can login.  To test, open
! a browser to HTTPS://a.b.c.d where a.b.c.d is the IP address on the
! router.
```

Implementing Logging Features

Logging is important as a tool for discovering events that are happening in the network and for troubleshooting. Correctly configuring logging so that you can collect and correlate events across multiple network devices is a critical component for a secure network.

Configuring Syslog Support

Example 11-11 shows a typical syslog message and how to control what information is included with the message.

Example 11-11 *Using Service Time Stamps with Syslog Events*

```
R4(config)# interface fa0/0
R4(config-if)# shut
%LINK-5-CHANGED: Interface FastEthernet0/0, changed state to administratively down
%LINEPROTO-5-UPDOWN: Line protocol on Interface FastEthernet0/0, changed state to down
R4(config-if)#

! If we add time stamps to the syslog messages, those time stamps can assist in
! correlating events that occurred on multiple devices

R4(config)# service timestamps log datetime
R4(config)# int fa0/0
R4(config-if)# no shutdown

! These syslog messages have the date of the event, the event (just after
! the %) a description, and also the level of the event (the first event in
! the example below is level 3 with the second event being level 5).
*Nov 22 12:08:13: %LINK-3-UPDOWN: Interface FastEthernet0/0, changed state to up
*Nov 22 12:08:14: %LINEPROTO-5-UPDOWN: Line protocol on Interface
  FastEthernet0/0, changed state to up
```

To configure logging, tell the CCP the address of your syslog server and what logging level you want to use. As a reminder, level 7, also known

at level 7 and lower. To configure logging, navigate to **Configure > Router > Logging**, as shown in Figure 11-5.

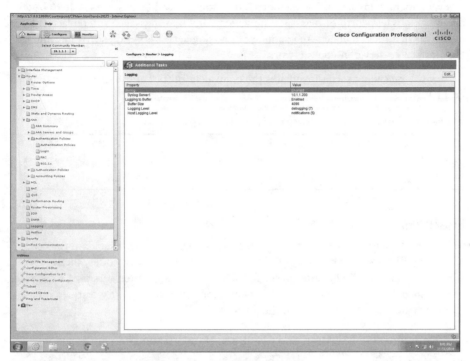

Figure 11-5 *Viewing the Logging Configuration*

To modify any of the logging settings, click the **Edit** button, as shown in Figure 11-6.

Figure 11-6 *Using CCP to Edit the Logging Settings*

In Figure 11-6, we have configured level 5 logging (notifications level) to a syslog server at the IP address of 10.1.1.200, and we have specified that the logging level to the buffer on the router is level 7 (debugging level). The memory buffer to hold syslog messages is 4096 bytes. Beyond the 4096 bytes' worth of messages in memory, any new messages will replace the oldest messages in a FIFO manner. An example of a syslog server is syslog software running on a PC or dedicated server in your network.

The CCP (for the preceding scenario) creates the equivalent output at the CLI, as shown in Example 11-12.

Example 11-12 *CLI Equivalent Generated by CCP*

```
logging 10.1.1.200
logging trap notifications
logging buffered 4096 debugging
```

SNMP Features

Simple Network Management Protocol (SNMP) has become a de facto standard for network management protocols. The intent of SNMP is to manage network nodes, such as network servers, routers, switches, and so on. SNMP versions range from version 1 to 3, with some intermediate steps in between. The later the version, the more security features it has. Table 11-5 describes some of the components of SNMP.

Table 11-5 Components of SNMPv1 and SNMPv2c Network Management Solutions

Component	Description
SNMP manager	An SNMP manager runs a network management application. This SNMP manager is sometimes called a *network management server (NMS)*.
SNMP agent	An SNMP agent is a piece of software that runs on a managed device (such as a server, router, or switch).
Management Information Base	Information about a managed device's resources and activity is defined by a series of *objects*. The structure of these management objects is defined by a managed device's *Management Information Base (MIB)*. This can be thought of as a collection of unique numbers associated with each of the individual components of a router.

An SNMP manager can send information to, receive requested information from, or receive unsolicited information (called a trap) from a managed device (a router). The managed device runs an SNMP agent and contains the MIB.

Even though multiple SNMP messages might be sent between an SNMP manager and a managed device, consider the three broad categories of SNMP message types:

- **GET:** An SNMP GET message is used to retrieve information from a managed device.
- **SET:** An SNMP SET message is used to set a variable in a managed device or to trigger an action on a managed device.

- **Trap:** An SNMP trap message is an unsolicited message sent from a managed device to an SNMP manager. It can be used to notify the SNMP manager about a significant event that occurred on the managed device.

Unfortunately, the ability to get information from or send configuration information to a managed device presents a potential security vulnerability. Specifically, if an attacker introduces a rogue NMS into the network, the attacker's NMS might be able to gather information about network resources by polling the MIBs of managed devices. In addition, the attacker might launch an attack against the network by manipulating the configuration of managed devices by sending a series of SNMP SET messages.

Although SNMP does offer some security against such an attack, the security integrated with SNMPv1 and SNMPv2c is considered weak. Specifically, SNMPv1 and SNMPv2c use *community strings* to gain read-only access/read-write access to a managed device. You can think of a community string much like a password. Also, be aware that multiple SNMP-compliant devices on the market today have a default read only community string of "public" and a default read-write community string of "private."

The security weaknesses of SNMPv1 and SNMPv2c are addressed in SNMPv3. SNMPv3 uses the concept of a security model and a security level:

- **Security model:** A security model defines an approach for user and group authentications.

- **Security level:** A security level defines the type of security algorithm performed on SNMP packets. Three security levels are discussed here:

  - **noAuthNoPriv:** The noAuthNoPriv (no authentication, no privacy) security level uses community strings for authentication and does not use encryption to provide privacy.

  - **authNoPriv:** The authNoPriv (authentication, no privacy) security level provides authentication using *Hashed Message Authentication Code (HMAC)* with *message digest algorithm 5 (MD5)* or *Secure Hash Algorithm (SHA)*. However, no encryption is used.

  - **authPriv:** The authPriv (authentication, privacy) security level offers HMAC MD5, or SHA authentication and also provides privacy through encryption. Specifically, the encryption uses the *Cipher Block Chaining (CBC) Data Encryption Standard (DES) (DES-56)* algorithm.

As summarized in Table 11-6, SNMPv3 supports all three of the previously described security levels. Notice that SNMPv1 and SNMPv2 support only the noAuthNoPriv security level.

Key Topic

Table 11-6   Security Models and Security Levels Supported by Cisco IOS

Security Model	Security Level	Authentication Strategy	Encryption Type
SNMPv1	noAuthNoPriv	Community string	None
SNMPv2c	noAuthNoPriv	Community string	None
SNMPv3	noAuthNoPriv	Username	None
	authNoPriv	MD5 or SHA	None
	authPriv	MD5 or SHA	CBC-DES (DES-56)

11

Through the use of the security algorithms, as shown in Table 11-6, SNMPv3 dramatically increases the security of network management traffic as compared to SNMPv1 and SNMPv2c. Specifically, SNMPv3 offers three primary security enhancements:

- **Integrity:** Using hashing algorithms, SNMPv3 can ensure that an SNMP message was not modified in transit.

- **Authentication:** Hashing allows SNMPv3 to validate the source of an SNMP message.

- **Encryption:** Using the CBC-DES (DES-56) encryption algorithm, SNMPv3 provides privacy for SNMP messages, making them unreadable by an attacker who might capture an SNMP packet.

To configure SNMP on the router is simple, especially with CCP. If you know the community strings to use, and the IP address of the SNMP manager, you can configure it on the router by navigating to **Configure > Router > SNMP** and from there use the **Edit** button to add, change, or remove any of the SNMP-related settings. CCP enables command-line editing through the Utilities menu, but currently the SNMP Properties window does not support the configuration of SNMPv3. You can configure the basic SNMPv1 information, as shown in Figure 11-7.

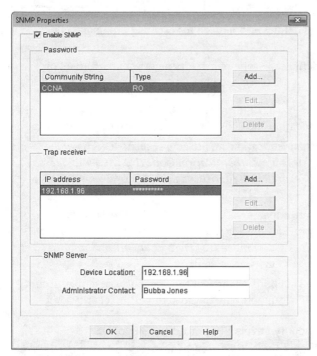

Figure 11-7   *Using CCP to Configure SNMPv1 Information*

The command-line output for this GUI would look similar to that shown in Example 11-13.

Example 11-13 *Output Created by CCP for Implementing SNMPv1*

```
snmp-server location 192.168.1.96
snmp-server contact Bubba Jones
snmp-server community CCNA RO
snmp-server host 10.1.0.26 trap cisK0tRap^
```

Example 11-14 shows the configuration for SNMPv3.

Example 11-14 *SNMPv3 Configuration*

```
! Enter global configuration mode
CCNA-Router# configure terminal
! Configure the community string along with an access-list to restrict access
CCNA-Router(config)# snmp-server community CCNA RO 99
! Create the IP Standard Access List defined in the previous step
CCNA-Router(config)# access-list 99 permit 192.168.1.0 /24
! Configure the v3 for no authentication (noauth)
CCNA-Router(config)# snmp-server group CCNA-group v3 noauth
! Configure a v3 user that resides in the v3 group
CCNA-Router(config)# snmp-server user CCNA-user CCNA-group v3
! Configure the community string and access-list to restrict SNMP to hosts in the
! 192.168.1.0/24 subnet
CCNA-Router(config)# snmp-server community CCNA RO 99
! Specify interface to be used for SNMP traps
CCNA-Router(config)# snmp-server trap-source FastEthernet0/1
! Specify the SNMP v3 server that will be allowed SNMP access
CCNA-Router(config)# snmp-server host 192.168.1.96 version 3 noauth CCNA-user
!
```

Configuring NTP

Because time is such an important factor, you should use *Network Time Protocol (NTP)* to synchronize the time in the network so that events that generate messages and time stamps can be correlated. You can use CCP to implement the NTP in addition to using the CLI. Let's take a look at both right now.

To configure the NTP, you first need to know what the IP address is of the NTP server you will be working with, and you also want to know what the authentication key is and the key ID. NTP authentication is not required to function, but is a good idea to ensure that the time is not modified because of a rogue NTP server sending inaccurate NTP messages using a spoofed source IP address.

Armed with the NTP server information, in CCP you go to **Configure > Router > Time > NTP and SNTP** and click **Add** and put in the information about the server you will be getting the time from. When done, you click **OK** to close the dialog box. It may take anywhere between 5 and 15 minutes for the router to synchronize its clock. In Figure 11-8, this router is being told that the NTP server is at 192.168.1.96, that it should source the NTP requests

11

from its IP address on its local Fast Ethernet 0/1 interface, and that it should use key number 1, and the password associated with that key. Note that the password is not visible in the figure. If multiple NTP servers are configured, the Prefer option is used to identify the preference of which NTP server to use.

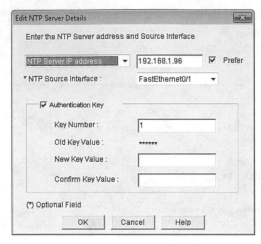

Figure 11-8 *Configuring a Router to Use an NTP Server*

NTP supports authentication on a Cisco router because the router supports NTPv3. Example 11-15 shows the effective equivalent syntax that is created and delivered to the router.

Example 11-15 *Using Authentication via Keys with NTPv3*

```
ntp authentication-key 1 md5 141411050D 7
ntp authenticate
ntp trusted-key 1
ntp update-calendar
ntp server 192.168.1.96 key 1 prefer source FastEthernet0/1
```

To verify the status on this router acting as an NTP client, you could use the commands from the CLI shown in Example 11-16.

Example 11-16 *Verifying Synchronization from the NTP Client*

```
CCNA-Router# show ntp status
Clock is synchronized, stratum 4, reference is 192.168.1.96
nominal freq is 250.0000 Hz, actual freq is 249.9980 Hz, precision is 2**24
reference time is D8147295.4E6FD112 (13:11:49.306 UTC Mon Nov 17 2014)
clock offset is -0.3928 msec, root delay is 83.96 msec
root dispersion is 94.64 msec, peer dispersion is 2.22 msec
loopfilter state is 'CTRL' (Normal Controlled Loop), drift is 0.000007749 s/s
system poll interval is 64, last update was 126 sec ago.
CCNA-Router#

CCNA-Router# show ntp association
```

```
   address          ref clock       st    when   poll reach  delay  offset    disp
*~192.168.1.96     208.75.89.4       3      49     64   377  1.341  -0.392   2.424
 * sys.peer, # selected, + candidate, - outlyer, x falseticker, ~ configured
CCNA-Router#
```

> **NOTE** NTP uses UDP port 123. If NTP does not synchronize within 15 minutes, you may want to verify that connectivity exists between this router and the NTP server that it is communicating to. You also want to verify that the key ID and password for NTP authentication are correct.

Secure Copy Protocol

The *Secure Copy (SCP)* feature provides a secure and authenticated method for copying device configurations or device image files. SCP relies on *Secure Shell (SSH)*, an application and protocol that provide a secure replacement for the Berkeley r-tools suite (Berkeley university's own set of networking applications). In addition, SCP requires that *authentication, authorization, and accounting (AAA)* authorization be configured so that the device can determine whether the user has the correct privilege level. Example 11-17 provides the procedure to configure a Cisco device for SCP server-side functionality. This configuration assumes that AAA has already been configured on the device.

Example 11-17   *SCP Configuration*

```
CCNA-Router# configure terminal
Enter configuration commands, one per line.  End with CNTL/Z.
CCNA-Router(config)# ip scp server enable
CCNA-Router(config)# exit
```

SCP enables a user with appropriate authorization to copy any file that exists in the Cisco *IOS File System (IFS)* to and from a device by using the **copy** command. An authorized administrator may also perform this action from a workstation.

Securing the Cisco IOS Image and Configuration Files

If a router has been compromised, and the flash file system and NVRAM have been deleted, there could be significant downtime as the files are put back in place before restoring normal router functionality. The Cisco Resilient Configuration feature is intended to improve the recovery time by making a secure working copy of the IOS image and startup configuration files (which are referred to as the *primary bootset*) that cannot be deleted by a remote user.

To enable and save the primary bootset to a secure archive in persistent storage, follow Example 11-18.

11

Example 11-18 *Creating a Secure Bootset*

```
! Secure the IOS image
R6(config)# secure boot-image
%IOS_RESILIENCE-5-IMAGE_RESIL_ACTIVE: Successfully secured running image


! Secure the startup-config
R6(config)# secure boot-config
%IOS_RESILIENCE-5-CONFIG_RESIL_ACTIVE: Successfully secured config archive
   [flash:.runcfg-20111222-230018.ar]


! Verify the bootset
R6(config)# do show secure bootset
IOS resilience router id FTX1036A13J


IOS image resilience version 12.4 activated at 23:00:10 UTC Thu Dec 22 2011
Secure archive flash:c3825-advipservicesk9-mz.124-24.T.bin type is image (elf) []
  file size is 60303612 bytes, run size is 60469256 bytes
  Runnable image, entry point 0x80010000, run from ram


IOS configuration resilience version 12.4 activated at 23:00:18 UTC Thu Dec 22 2011
Secure archive flash:.runcfg-20111222-230018.ar type is config
configuration archive size 1740 bytes


! Note: to undo this feature, (using the "no" option in front of the command)
! you must be connected via the console.  This prevents remote users from
! disabling the feature.
```

Exam Preparation Tasks

Review All the Key Topics

Review the most important topics from this chapter, denoted with a Key Topic icon. Table 11-7 lists these key topics.

Table 11-7   Key Topics

Key Topic Element	Description	Page Number
Section	Management Plane Best Practices	278
Section	AAA Components	282
Section	Options for Storing Usernames, Passwords, and Access Rules	282
Section	Router Access Authentication	284
Table 11-2	AAA Components to Secure Administrative and Remote LAN Access	285
Section	The AAA Method List	285
Table 11-3	Method List Options	285
Section	Limiting the Administrator by Assigning a View	287
Section	Encrypted Management Protocols	287
Section	Using Logging Files	288
Section	User Authentication with AAA	292
Section	Using the CLI to Troubleshoot AAA for Cisco Routers	296
Example 11-4	Using **debug** Commands	297
Example 11-5	Creating and Assigning Commands to a Custom Privilege Level	301
Section	Implementing Parser Views	303
Example 11-7	Creating and Working with Parser Views	304
Example 11-9	Preparing for SSH	306
Section	SNMP Features	310
Table 11-6	Security Models and Security Levels Supported by Cisco IOS	311
Example 11-14	SNMPv3 Configuration	313
Example 11-15	Using Authentication via Keys with NTPv3	314
Section	Secure Copy Protocol	315
Example 11-17	SCP Configuration	315
Example 11-18	Creating a Secure Bootset	316

11

Complete the Tables and Lists from Memory

Print a copy of Appendix C, "Memory Tables," (found on the CD) or at least the section for this chapter, and complete the tables and lists from memory. Appendix D, "Memory Tables Answer Key," also on the CD, includes completed tables and lists so that you can check your work.

Define Key Terms

Define the following key terms from this chapter, and check your answers in the glossary:

AAA, method list, custom privilege level, parser view, SSH, syslog, SNMP, NTP, secure bootset, Secure Copy (SCP)

Command Reference to Check Your Memory

This section includes the most important configuration and EXEC commands covered in this chapter. To see how well you have memorized the commands as a side effect of your other studies, cover the left side of Table 11-8 with a piece of paper, read the descriptions on the right side, and see whether you remember the commands.

Table 11-8   Command Reference

Command	Description
service password-encryption	Encrypt most plaintext passwords in the configuration.
aaa new-model	Enable AAA features.
aaa authentication login default local	Create a default method list for character mode login that will use the local database (running config) on the router or switch.
enable view	Enter the root parser view, from where you can create additional views. This requires that **aaa new-model** already be in place in the configuration.
privilege exec level 8 *show startup-config*	Assign a **show startup-config** command to a custom privilege level 8.
crypto key generate rsa	Create the public/private key pair required for SSH.
secure boot-image	Secure the IOS image on flash
aaa authentication *bubba* local enable	Create an authentication method list called bubba that will use the local database first, and if the username does not exist, will require the enable secret to allow login.
line console 0 login authentication bubba	Apply the method list named bubba to the console port.
ip scp server enable	Enable the SCP server on an IOS device.

Command	Description
snmp-server group *CCNA-group* **v3 noauth**	Configures SNMPv3 server group for no authentication (noauth)
snmp-server user *CCNA-user* *CCNA-group* **v3**	Configures an SNMPv3 user (CCNA-user) that resides in the SNMPv3 group (CCNA-group)
snmp-server host *192.168.1.96* **version 3 noauth** *CCNA-user*	Specify the SNMPv3 server (192.168.1.96) that will be allowed SNMP access

11

This chapter covers the following topics:

Understanding and configuring IPv6

Configuring IPv6 routing

Developing a security plan for IPv6

CHAPTER 12

Securing the Data Plane in IPv6

IPv6 is definitely in the future for those who will be working with IP. The prerequisite for CCNA Security is the CCNA in Routing/Switching. As a result, it is assumed that Security candidates are familiar with IPv6. To make certain that you are, this chapter explains how IPv6 works and how to configure it, and then you learn how to develop a security plan for IPv6. If you already feel comfortable with IPv6, you can go directly to the "Developing a Security Plan for IPv6" section, later in this chapter.

"Do I Know This Already?" Quiz

The "Do I Know This Already?" quiz helps you determine your level of knowledge of this chapter's topics before you begin. Table 12-1 details the major topics discussed in this chapter and their corresponding quiz questions.

Table 12-1 "Do I Know This Already?" Section-to-Question Mapping

Foundation Topics Section	Questions
Understanding and Configuring IPv6	1
Configuring IPv6 Routing	2
Developing a Security Plan for IPv6	3–10

1. Which of the following are the valid first four characters of a globally routable IPv6 address? (Choose all that apply.)

   a. 1234

   b. 2345   *range is between 2000   3FFF*

   c. 3456

   d. 4567

2. Which of the following are the valid first four characters of a link-local address?

   a. FE80

   b. FF02

   c. 2000

   d. 3000

3. What is the default method for determining the interface ID for a link-local address on Ethernet?

   a. EUI-64

   b. MAC address with FFFE at the end

   c. MAC address with FFFE at the beginning

   d. Depends on the network address being connected to

4. How many groups of four hexadecimal characters does an IPv6 address contain?

   a. 4

   b. 8

   c. 16

   d. 32

5. Which of the following routing protocols have both an IPv4 and IPv6 version? (Choose all that apply.)

   a. Routing Information Protocol

   b. Enhanced Interior Gateway Routing Protocol

   c. Open Shortest Path First

   d. Interior Gateway Routing Protocol

6. Which best practices apply to networks that run both IPv4 and IPv6? (Choose all that apply.)

   a. Physical security

   b. Routing protocol authentication

   c. Authorization of administrators

   d. Written security policy

7. Which of protocols, if abused, could impair an IPv6 network, but not IPv4? (Choose all that apply.)

   a. ARP

   b. NDP

   c. Broadcast addresses

   d. Solicited node multicast addresses

8. If a rogue IPv6 router is allowed on the network, which information could be incorrectly delivered to the clients on that network? (Choose all that apply.)

   a. IPv6 default gateway

   b. IPv6 DNS server

   c. IPv6 network address

   d. IPv6 ARP mappings

9. Why is tunneling any protocol (including IPv6) through another protocol a security risk? (Choose all that Apply.)

   a. The innermost contents of the original packets may be hidden from normal security filters.

   b. The tunnels, if they extend beyond the network perimeter, may allow undesired traffic through the tunnel.

   c. Functionality might need to be sacrificed when going through a tunnel.

   d. Quality of service, for the underlying protocol, might be compromised.

10. What is one method to protect against a rogue IPv6 router?

    a. Port security

    b. Static ARP entries

    c. DHCPv6

    d. RA guard

12

Foundation Topics

Understanding and Configuring IPv6

When compared to IPv4, both similarities and differences exist as to how IPv6 operates. Certification requires that you know the fundamentals of IPv6, and that is the focus of this section, which first reviews IPv6 basics and then shows you how to configure it.

Why IPv6?

Two good reasons to move to IPv6 are as follows:

- IPv6 has more address space available.
- We are running out of public IPv4 addresses.

For more than a decade, the requirement to implement IPv6 has been threatened as imminent. The lifetime of its predecessor (IPv4) was extended more than a decade because of features such as *Network Address Translation (NAT)*, which enables you to hide thousands of users with private IP addresses behind a single public IP address.

With IPv6, upper-layer applications still work like you are used to with IPv4. The biggest change is that we are doing a forklift upgrade to Layer 3 of the OSI model. Along with this change, there are some modifications as to how IPv6 interacts with the rest of the protocol stack and some modifications to its procedures for participating on the network.

Table 12-2 describes a few of the notable differences and some similarities between IPv4 and IPv6.

Table 12-2   IPv4 Versus IPv6

IPv4	IPv6
32-bit (4-byte) address supports 2^{32} or 4,294,967,296 addresses.	128-bit (16-byte) address supports 2^{128} (about 3.4 × 10^{38}) addresses [340 undecillion addresses altogether, or roughly 42 octillion addresses per person on the planet! Or 438 quintillion addresses per square inch of land on Earth. (Or *lots*!)]
You can use NAT to extend address space limitations.	Does not support NAT by design (and has plenty of addresses for everyone).
Administrators must use *Dynamic Host Configuration Protocol (DHCP)* or static configuration to assign IP addresses to hosts.	Hosts can use stateless address autoconfiguration to assign an IP address to themselves, but can also use DHCP features to learn more information, such as about *Domain Name System (DNS)* servers.
IPsec support is an optional add-on concept to protect IP packets through encryption, validating a peer, data integrity, and antireplay support.	IPsec is fully supported in IPv6. In fact, IPsec was supposed to be mandatory when using IPv6, however IPv6 does not actually require IPsec to be enabled for IPv6 to work.
An IPv4 header consists of multiple fields.	Simplified (but larger) IPv6 header, with options for header extensions as needed.

IPv4	IPv6
Uses broadcasts for several functions, including *Address Resolution Protocol (ARP)*.	Does not use any broadcasts and does not use ARP. Instead, it uses multicast addresses and *Neighbor Discovery Protocol (NDP* also called *ND)*. ND replaces ARP. Devices can automatically discover the IPv6 network address and many other housekeeping features such as discovering any routers on the network. ND uses IPv6's version of *Internet Control Message Protocol (ICMP)* as the workhorse behind most of its functions.
Both support common Layer 4 protocols such as TCP, UDP.	Both support common Layer 4 protocols such as TCP, UDP.
Both support common application layer protocols, such as HTTP, FTP, and so on, that are encapsulated in their respective Layer 4 protocols.	Both support common application layer protocols, such as HTTP, FTP, and so on, that are encapsulated in their respective Layer 4 protocols.
Both support common Layer 2 technologies, such as Ethernet standards and WAN standards.	Both support common Layer 2 technologies, such as Ethernet standards and WAN standards.
Both contain two parts in the IP address: the network on the left side of the address and the host part on the right side of the address.	Both contain two parts in the IP address: the network on the left side of the address and the host part on the right side of the address. In IPv6, the host part is also called the *host ID*.
Both use a network mask to identify which part of the address is the network (on the left) indicated by the mask bits that are on (or 1), and the rest of the bits to the right represent the host part of the IPv4 address.	Both use a network mask to identify which part of the address is the network (on the left) indicated by the mask bits that are on (or 1), and the rest of the bits to the right represent the host part or host ID or interface ID of the IPv6 address.

The Format of an IPv6 Address

Understanding the basic format of an IPv6 address is important for certification and for the actual implementation of IPv6. A few key details about IPv6 and its format are as follows:

- **Length:** IPv6 addresses are 128 bits (16 bytes) long.
- **Groupings:** IPv6 addresses are segmented into eight groups of four hex characters.
- **Separation of groups:** Each group is separated by a colon (:).
- **Length of mask:** Usually 50 percent (64 bits long) for network ID, which leaves 50 percent (also 64 bits) for interface ID (using a 64-bit mask).
- **Number of networks:** The network part is allocated by Internet registries 2^{64} (1.8×10^{19})

This allows room for billions of networks.

Hexadecimal only takes one character to represent 4 bits and is used to represent IPv6 addresses (4 bits at a time). Table 12-3 shows the conversion between decimal, binary, and hexadecimal.

Table 12-3 Conversion Charts Between Decimal, Binary, and Hexadecimal

Decimal	Binary	Hexadecimal
0	0000	0
1	0001	1
2	0010	2
3	0011	3
4	0100	4
5	0101	5
6	0110	6
7	0111	7
8	1000	8
9	1001	9
10	1010	A
11	1011	B
12	1100	C
13	1101	D
14	1110	E
15	1111	F

We can represent an IPv6 address the hard way or the easier way. The hard way is to type in every hexadecimal character for the IP address. In Example 12-1, we put in a 128-bit IPv6 address, typed in as 32 hexadecimal characters, and a 64-bit mask.

Example 12-1 *An IPv6 Address Configured the Hard Way*

```
R1(config-if)# ipv6 address 2001:0db8:0000:0000:1234:0000:0052:0001/64

! The output reflects how we could have used some shortcuts in representing
! the groups of zeros.
R1(config-if)# do show ipv6 interface brief
FastEthernet0/1          [up/up]
    FE80::C800:41FF:FE32:6
    2001:DB8::1234:0:52:1
R1(config-if)#
```

Understanding the Shortcuts

Example 12-1 shows the address being configured and the abbreviated address from the output of the **show** command. When inserting a group of four hexadecimal numbers, you can limit your typing a bit. For example, if any leading characters in the group are 0, you can omit them (just as the 0 in front of DB8 is in the second group from the left). In addition, if there are one or more consecutive groups of all 0s, you can input them as a double colon (::). The system knows that there should be eight groups separated by seven colons, and when it sees ::, it just looks at how many other groups are configured and assumes that the number of missing groups plus the existing groups that are configured totals eight. In the example, the first two groups of consecutive 0s are shortened in the final output. This shortcut may be done only once for any given IPv6 address. This example contains three groupings of 0s, and if you use the shortcut twice, the system will not know whether there should be four 0s after the DB8: and eight 0s (or two groups) after the 1234: or vice versa.

Did We Get an Extra Address?

Besides the IPv6 global address configured in Example 12-1, the system automatically con-figured for itself a second IPv6 address known as a *link-local* address that begins with FE80. A link-local address is an IPv6 address that you can use to communicate with other IPv6 devices on the same local network (local broadcast domain). If an IPv6 device wants to com-municate with a device that is remote, it needs to use its global and routable IPv6 address for that (not the link-local one). To reach remote devices, you also need to have a route to that remote network or a default gateway to use to reach the remote network.

The following section covers the other types of addresses that you will work with in IPv6 networks.

IPv6 Address Types

In IPv6, you must be familiar with several types of addresses. Some are created and used automatically; others you must configure manually. These address types include the following:

- **Link-local address:** Link-local addresses may be manually configured, but if they are not, they are dynamically configured by the local host or router itself. These always begin with the characters FE80. The last 64 bits are the host ID (also referred to as the *inter-face ID*), and the device uses the modified EUI-64 format (by default) to create that. The modified EUI-64 uses the MAC address (if on Ethernet; and if not on Ethernet, it bor-rows the MAC address of another interface), and realizes it is only 48 bits. To get to 64 bits for the host ID, it inserts four hexadecimal characters of FFFE, (which is the 16 more bits we need) and injects those into the middle of the existing MAC address to use as the 64-bit host ID. It also looks at the seventh bit from the left (of the original MAC address) and inverts it. If it is a 0 in the MAC address, it is a 1 in the host ID and vice versa. To see an example of this, look back at Example 12-1, at the output of the **show** command there, focusing on the address that begins with FE80.

- **Loopback address:** In IPv4, this was the 127 range of IP addresses. In IPv6, the address is ::1 (which is 127 0s followed by a 1).

12

- **All-nodes multicast address:** In IPv6, multicasts begin with FFxx: (where the x = some other hex number). The number 02 happens to designate a multicast address that is link-local in scope. There are other preset scopes, but you do not have to worry about them here. The IPv6 multicast group that all IPv6 devices join is FF02::1. If any device needs to send a packet/frame to all other local IPv6 devices, it can send the packet to the multicast address of FF02::1, which translates to a specific multicast Layer 2 address, and then all the devices that receive those frames continue to de-encapsulate those frames. If a device receives a frame, and the receiving device determines that the Layer 2 destination in the frame is not destined for itself and not destined for any multicast groups that the local device has joined, it discards the frame, instead of continuing to decapsulate it to find out what is inside (in the upper layers).

- **All-routers multicast address:** In addition to the multicast group address of FF02::1 that is joined by all devices configured for IPv6, routers that have had routing enabled for IPv6 also join the multicast group FF02::2. By doing so, any client looking for a router can send a request to this group address and get a response if there is a router on the local network. You might have noticed a pattern here: FF02 is just like 224.0.0.x in IPv4 multicast. 224.0.0.1 = all devices. 224.0.0.2 = all routers.

- **Unicast and anycast addresses (configured automatically or manually):** A global IPv6 address, unlike a link-local address, is routable and can be reached through one or more routers that are running IP routing and that have a correct routing table. Global IPv6 unicast addresses have the first four characters in the range of 2000 to 3FFF, and may be manually configured, automatically discovered by issuing a router solicitation request to a local router, or be learned via IPv6 *Dynamic Host Configuration Protocol (DHCP)*. An anycast address can be a route or an IP address that appears more than one time in a network, and then it is up to the network to decide the best way to reach that IP. Usually, two DNS servers, if they both use the same anycast address, are functional to the users, so that regardless of which DNS server that packets are forwarded to, the client gets the DNS response it needs.

- **Solicited-node multicast address for each of its unicast and anycast addresses:** When a device has global and link-local addresses, it joins a multicast group of FF02::1:FFxx:xxxx The x characters represent the last 24 bits of the host ID being used for the addresses. If a device needs to learn the Layer 2 address of a peer on the same network, it can send out a neighbor solicitation (request) to the multicast group that the device that has that address should have joined. This is the way IPv6 avoids using broadcasts.

- **Multicast addresses of all other groups to which the host belongs:** If a router has enabled IPv6 routing, it joins the FF02::2 group (all routers), as mentioned earlier. If a router is running RIPng (the IPv6 flavor), it joins the multicast group for RIPng, which is FF02::9, so that it will process updates sent to that group from other RIP routers. Notice again some similarities. RIPv2 in IPv4 uses 224.0.0.9 as the multicast address.

Example 12-2 shows the output for a router that has been enabled for IPv6 routing, RIPng, and has an IPv6 global address.

Example 12-2 *IPv6 Interface Information*

```
! MAC address, for reference, that is currently used on the Fa0/1
! interface
R1# show interfaces fa0/1 | include bia
  Hardware is i82543 , address is ca00.4132.0006 (bia ca00.4132.0006)


R1# show ipv6 interface fa0/1
FastEthernet0/1 is up, line protocol is up



! Link-local address, beginning with FE80::
! and using modified EUI-64 for the host ID
! Notice that CA from the MAC address is C8 in the host ID
! due to inverting the 7th bit for the modified EUI-64 formatting
  IPv6 is enabled, link local address is FE80::C000:41FF:FE32:6


! Global addresses have the first group range of 2000-3fff
  Global unicast address(es):
    2001:DB8::1234:0:52:1, subnet is 2001:DB8::/64


! Multicast begins with FFxx:
  Joined group address(es):


! Because we are enabled for IPv6 on this interface
    FF02::1


! Because we are enabled for IPv6 routing
    FF02::2


! Because we are enabled for RIPng
    FF02::9


! Because our link-local address ends in 32:0006
! This is a solicited node multicast group
    FF02::1:FF32:6


! Because our global address ends in 52:0001
! This is a solicited node multicast group
    FF02::1:FF52:1

<snip>
```

12

Configuring IPv6 Routing

To support multiple IPv6 networks and allow devices to communicate between those networks, you need to tell the routers how to reach remote IPv6 networks. You can do so through static routes, IPv6 routing protocols, and default routes. For the router to route any customer's IPv6 traffic, you need to enable unicast routing for IPv6 from global configuration mode. If you fail to do this, the router can send and receive its own packets, but it will not forward packets for others, even if it has the routes in its IPv6 routing table.

IPv6 can use the new and improved flavors of these dynamic routing protocols with their versions that support IPv6:

- RIP, called *RIP next generation (RIPng)*
- OSPFv3
- EIGRP for IPv6

One difference with the interior gateway routing protocols for IPv6 is that none of them support **network** statements. To include interfaces of the routing process, you use **interface** commands. For EIGRP, you also need to issue the **no shutdown** command in EIGRP router configuration mode. Example 12-3 shows the enabling of unicast routing and the configuring of IPv6 routing protocols.

Example 12-3   *Enabling IPv6 Routing and Routing Protocols*

```
! Enables IPv6 routing of other devices' packets
R1(config)#
ipv6 unicast-routing


! Enabling all 3 IGPs on interface Fa0/1
! Note: that in a production network, we would only need 1 routing protocol
! on a given interface.   If we did have multiple identical learned routes
! the Administrative Distance (same as in IPv4) would determine which
! routing protocols would be the "best" and be placed in the routing table.
R1(config)# int fa 0/1


! Enabling RIPng on the interface
! Simply create a new "name" for the process.  I called this one "MYRIP"
! Use the same name on all the interfaces on the local router where you
! want RIPng to be used on that same router.
R1(config-if)# ipv6 rip MYRIP enable


! Enabling OSPFv3 on the interface
! Syntax is the keywords ipv6 ospf, followed by the process ID (The process ID is
! locally assigned and can be a positive integer from 1 to 65535), then the
! area information
R1(config-if)# ipv6 ospf 1 area 0


! Enabling IPv6 EIGRP on the interface
```

```
R1(config-if)# ipv6 eigrp 1
R1(config-if)# exit

! Bringing the EIGRP routing process out of its default shutdown state
! Note: This is done in global (not interface) configuration mode.
! This is not needed for RIPng or OSPFv3
R1(config)# ipv6 router eigrp 1
R1(config-rtr)# no shutdown

! Verify which routing protocols are running
R1# show ipv6 protocol
IPv6 Routing Protocol is "connected"
IPv6 Routing Protocol is "rip MYRIP"
  Interfaces:
    FastEthernet0/1
  Redistribution:
    None
IPv6 Routing Protocol is "ospf 1"
  Interfaces (Area 0):
    FastEthernet0/1
  Redistribution:
    None
IPv6 Routing Protocol is "eigrp 1"
  EIGRP metric weight K1=1, K2=0, K3=1, K4=0, K5=0
  EIGRP maximum hopcount 100
  EIGRP maximum metric variance 1
  Interfaces:
    FastEthernet0/1
  Redistribution:
    None
  Maximum path: 16
  Distance: internal 90 external 170
```

The command **show ipv6 route** outputs the IPv6 routes the router knows how to reach, including the ones learned through dynamic routing protocols.

Moving to IPv6

Moving to IPv6 will be more of a transition or migration than a one-time event. As such, there are mechanisms in place to support coexistence between IPv4 and IPv6 including the ability for a router or network device to run both protocol stacks at the same time, and the ability to perform tunneling. A tunneling example would be when there are two isolated portions of the network that want to run IPv6, and between them, there is a big patch of IPv4 only. Tunneling would take the IPv6 packets and re-encapsulate them into IPv4 for transport across the IPv4 portion of the network. At the other end of the tunnel, the router would de-encapsulate the IPv6 from the IPv4 shell and then continue forwarding the IPv6 packet on toward its final destination.

12

Developing a Security Plan for IPv6

Most security risks associated with the older IPv4 are the same security risks associated with the newer IPv6. Now what does that mean to you? It means that you need to make sure that you have considered and implemented security controls to address both protocol stacks. This section discusses many security threats common to both IPv4 and IPv6 (and some specific to IPv6) and how to address them.

Best Practices Common to Both IPv4 and IPv6

For both protocol stacks, here are some recommended best practices, which is a great place to start your network configuration:

- **Physical security:** Keep the room where the router is housed free (safe) from electrostatic and magnetic interference. It should also be temperature and humidity controlled. There should be controlled and logged access to that physical room. Redundant systems for electricity that feed into the routers are part of this, as well.

- **Device hardening:** Disable services that are not in use and features and interfaces that are not in use. You learned about this concept in an earlier chapter with regard to *Cisco Configuration Professional (CCP)*. A great reference for these best practices is the Cisco Guide to Harden Cisco IOS Devices (http://www.cisco.com/c/en/us/support/docs/ip/access-lists/13608-21.html).

- **Control access between zones:** Enforce a security policy that clearly identifies which packets are allowed between networks (using either simple access list controls or more advanced controls such as stateful inspection that leverages firewall features on a router or a dedicated firewall appliance, all of which are covered extensively in other chapters in this book).

- **Routing protocol security:** Use authentication with routing protocols to help stop rogue devices from abusing the information being used in routing updates by your routers. You can find more information on this topic in Chapter 13, "Securing Routing Protocols and the Control Plane."

- **Authentication, authorization, and accounting (AAA):** Require AAA so that you know exactly who is accessing your systems, when they are accessing your systems, and what they are doing. You learned about AAA in earlier chapters. *Network Time Protocol (NTP)* is a critical part to ensure that time stamps reflect reality. Check log files periodically. All management protocols should be used with cryptographic services. *Secure Shell (SSH)* and *Hypertext Transfer Protocol Secure (HTTPS)* include these features. Place Telnet and HTTP inside of an encrypted *virtual private network (VPN)* tunnel to meet this requirement.

- **Mitigating DoS attacks:** *Denial of service* refers to willful attempts to disrupt legitimate users from getting access to the resources they intend to use. Although no complete solution exists, administrators can do specific things to protect the network from a DoS attack and to lessen its effects and prevent a would-be attacker from using a system as a source of an attack directed at other systems. These mitigation techniques include filtering based on bogus source IP addresses trying to come into the networks and vice versa. Unicast reverse path verification is one way to assist with this, as are access lists. Unicast reverse path verification looks at the source IP address as it comes into an interface, and then looks at the routing table. If the source address seen would not be reachable out of the same interface it is coming in on, the packet is considered bad, potentially spoofed, and is dropped.

■ **Have and update a security policy:** A security policy should be referenced and possibly updated whenever major changes occur to the administrative practices, procedures, or staff. If new technologies are implemented, such as a new VPN or a new application that is using unique protocols or different protocols than your current security policy allows, this is another reason to revisit the security policy. Another time a security policy might need to be updated is after a significant attack or compromise to the network has been discovered.

Threats Common to Both IPv4 and IPv6

The following threats and ways to mitigate them apply to both IPv4 and IPv6:

■ **Application layer attacks:** An attacker is using a network service in an unexpected or malicious way. To protect against this, you can place filters to allow only the required protocols through the network. This will prevent services that aren't supposed to be available from being accessed through the network. You can also use application inspection, done through the *Adaptive Security Appliance (ASA)* or the IOS zone-based firewall, or *intrusion prevention system (IPS)* functionality to identify and filter protocols that are not being used in their intended way. Being current on system and application patches will also help mitigate an application layer attack.

■ **Unauthorized access:** Individuals not authorized for access are gaining access to network resources. To protect against this, use AAA services to challenge the user for credentials, and then authorize that user for only the access they need. This can be done for users forwarding traffic through the network and for administrators who want to connect directly for network management. Accounting records can create a detailed record of the network activity that has taken place.

■ **Man-in-the-middle attacks:** Someone or something is between the two devices who believe they are communicating directly with each other. The "man in the middle" may be eavesdropping or actively changing the data that is being sent between the two parties. You can prevent this by implementing Layer 2 *dynamic ARP inspection (DAI)* and *Spanning Tree Protocol (STP)* guards to protect spanning tree. You can implement it at Layer 3 by using routing protocol authentication. Authentication of peers in a VPN is also a method of preventing this type of attack.

■ **Sniffing or eavesdropping:** An attacker is listening in on the network traffic of others. This could be done in a switched environment, where the attacker has implemented a *content-addressable memory (CAM)* table overflow, causing the switch to forward all frames to all other ports in the same VLAN. To protect against this, you can use switch port security on the switches to limit the MAC addresses that could be injected on any single port. In general, if traffic is encrypted as it is transported across the network, either natively or by a VPN, that is a good countermeasure against eavesdropping.

■ **Denial-of-service (DoS) attacks:** Making services that should be available unavailable to the users who should normally have the access/service. Performing packet inspection and rate limiting of suspicious traffic, physical security, firewall inspection, and IPS can all be used to help mitigate a DoS attack.

12

- **Spoofed packets:** Forged addressing or packet content. Filtering traffic that is attempting to enter the network is one of the best first steps to mitigating this type of traffic. Denying inbound traffic that is claiming to originate from inside the network will stop this traffic at the edge of the network. Reverse path checks can also help mitigate this type of traffic.

- **Attacks against routers and other network devices:** Turning off unneeded services and hardening the routers, similar to what the CCP security audit can do, will help the router be less susceptible to attacks against the router itself. Implement the techniques you learned in the NFP chapter to protect the control, management, and data planes.

The Focus on IPv6 Security

With IPv6, you do have a few advantages related to security. If an attacker issues a ping sweep of your network, he will not likely find all the devices via a traditional ping sweep to every possible address, so reconnaissance will be tougher for the attacker using that method (because there are potentially millions of addresses on each subnet [264 possibilities, or about 18 quintillion!]). Be aware, however, that this is a double-edged sword, because each device on an IPv6 network joins the multicast group of FF02::1. So, if the attacker has local access to that network, he could ping that local multicast group and get a response that lets him know about each device on the network. FF02::1 is local in scope, so the attacker cannot use this technique remotely; he would have to be on the local network.

The scanners and worms that used to operate in IPv4 will still very likely be able to operate in IPv6, but they will just use a different mechanism to do it. Customers unaware that IPv6 is even running on their workstations represent another security risk. They could be using IPv4 primarily but still have an active IPv6 protocol stack running. An attacker may leverage a newfound vulnerability in some aspect of IPv6 and then use that vulnerability to gain access to the victim's computer. Disabling an unused protocol stack (in this case, the unused IPv6 stack) would appropriately mitigate this risk.

New Potential Risks with IPv6

Any new feature or way of operating could be open to a new form of attack. Here is a list of features that are implemented differently or have slightly different methods than IPv4, and as a result, any manipulation of how the feature works could result in a compromise of the network:

- **Network Discovery Protocol:** Clients discover routers using NDP, and if a rogue router is present, it could pretend to be a legitimate router and send incorrect information to the clients about the network, the default gateway, and other parameters. This could also lead to a man-in-the-middle attack, where the rogue router now has the opportunity to see all packets from the hosts that are being sent to remote networks.

- **Neighbor cache resource starvation:** If an attacker attempts to spoof many IPv6 destinations in a short time, the router can get overwhelmed while trying to store temporary cache entries for each destination. The IPv6 Destination Guard feature blocks data traffic from an unknown source and filters IPv6 traffic based on the destination address. It populates all active destinations into the IPv6 first-hop security binding table, and blocks data traffic when the destination is not identified.

- **DHCPv6:** A rogue router that has fooled a client about being a router could also manipulate the client into using incorrect DHCP-learned information. This could cause a man-in-the-middle attack because the host could be using the address of the rogue router as the default gateway.

- **Hop-by-hop extension headers:** With IPv4, there were IP options that could be included in IP headers. Malicious use of these headers could cause excessive CPU utilization on the routers that receive or forward these packets, in addition to dictating the path the packet should take through the network. There are no IP options in IPv6; instead, there are IPv6 extensions, which can also be misused. One of the IPv6 extension headers is the Routing Header, type 0 (also referred to as RH0). RH0 can be used to identify a list of one or more intermediate nodes to be included on the path toward the final destination (think IP source routing). This can enable an attacker to dictate the path a packet can take through the network. By default, Cisco IOS disables the processing of RH type 0 headers on most of its current versions of IOS. You can find more information on the use of IPv6 extension headers in the Cisco.com document "IPv6 Extension Headers Review and Considerations" (http://tinyurl.com/ipv6ext-headers). As noted in this white paper, there is always the possibility that IPv6 traffic with a significant number of, or very long, extension headers is sent into the network maliciously to attempt to overwhelm the HW resources of the router. Regardless of the platform HW design, this provides for a *distributed DoS (DDoS)* attack vector, and security mechanisms should be put in place to reduce the risk of a DDoS attack. To protect the CPU from being overwhelmed by high rates of this type of traffic, Cisco routers implement rate limiting of packets that are diverted from the hardware to software path. This rate limiting reduces the chance that the CPU resources of the router will be depleted while trying to process the combination of extensions headers.

- **Packet amplification attacks:** Using multicast addresses rather than IPv4 broadcast addresses could allow an attacker to trick an entire network into responding to a request. An example is to send a neighbor solicitation request (which is part of the NDP) to the all-hosts multicast address of FF02::1, which would cause all devices to respond. Another example is if a packet is sent with the header extensions set so that a packet is just looped around the network until the *Time-To-Live (TTL)* mechanism expires, and perhaps injecting thousands of these to consume bandwidth and resources on the network devices forwarding them.

- **ICMPv6:** This protocol is used extensively by IPv6 as its NDP. Much potential harm may result from manipulation of this protocol by an attacker.

- **Tunneling options:** Tunneling IPv6 through IPv4 parts of a network may mean that the details inside the IPv6 packet might not be inspected or filtered by the IPv4 network. Filtering needs to be done at the edges of the tunnel to ensure that only authorized IPv6 packets are successfully sent end to end.

- **Autoconfiguration:** Because an IPv6 host can automatically configure an IP address for itself, any trickery by a rogue router could also cause the host's autoconfiguration to be done incorrectly, which could cause a failure on the network or a man-in-the-middle attack as the client tries to route all traffic through the rogue router.

- **Dual stacks:** If a device is running both IPv4 and IPv6 at the same time, but is aware of only one (or is primarily only using one), the other protocol stack, if not secured, provides a potential vector for an attacker to remotely access the device. Once access is obtained this way, the attacker could then change IP settings or other configuration options based on the end goal the attacker is trying to achieve.

12

■ **Bugs in code:** Any software has the potential to have bugs, including the software that is supporting the IPv6 features in the network or end-station devices.

IPv6 Best Practices

Implementing security measures at the beginning of a deployment improves the initial security posture instead of waiting until after an attack has occurred. IPv6 best practices include the following:

■ **Filter bogus addresses:** Drop, at the edge of your network, any addresses that should never be valid source or destination addresses. These are also referred to as *bogon addresses*.

■ **Filter nonlocal multicast addresses:** If you are not running multicast applications, you should never need multicast to be forwarded beyond a specific VLAN. Local multicast is often used by IPv6 (for example, in routing updates and neighbor discovery).

■ **Filter ICMPv6 traffic that is not needed on your specific networks:** Normal NDP uses ICMPv6 as its core protocol. A path's *maximum transmission unit (MTU)* is also determined by using ICMP. Outside of its normal functionality, you want to filter the unused parts of ICMP so that an attacker cannot use it against your network.

■ **Drop routing header type 0 packets:** Routing header 0, also known as *RH0*, may contain many intermediate next hops, and if followed an attacker could control the path of a packet through a network. The attacker could also use this to create an amplification attack that could loop until the TTL expires on the packet. Cisco routers, by default, drop packets with this type of header.

■ **Use manual tunnels rather than automatic tunnels:** If tunneling, do not use automatic tunnel mechanisms such as automatic 6to4, because you cannot control all of them. (They are dynamic.) With the manual tunnels, avoid allowing the tunnels to go through the perimeter of your network, as you will not have tight controls on the contents of the tunneled packets.

■ **Protect against rogue IPv6 devices:** There are a number of mechanisms available within IPv6 to help defend against the spoofing of IPv6 neighbors. These include the following:

■ **IPv6 first-hop security binding table:** This table is used to validate that the IPv6 neighbors are legitimate.

■ **IPv6 device tracking:** This feature provides the IPv6 neighbor table with the ability to immediately reflect changes when an IPv6 host becomes inactive.

■ **IPv6 port-based access list support:** Similar to IPv4 port access control lists (PACL), this feature provides access control on Layer 2 switch ports for IPv6 traffic.

■ **IPv6 RA Guard:** Provides the capability to block or reject rogue RA Guard messages that arrive at the network switch platform.

■ **IPv6 ND Inspection:** IPv6 ND inspection analyzes neighbor discovery messages to build a trusted binding table database, and IPv6 neighbor discovery messages that do not conform are dropped.

■ **Secure Neighbor Discovery in IPv6 (SeND):** Although platform support of SeND still remains limited, this feature defines a set of new ND options, and two new ND messages (*Certification Path Solicitation [CPS]* and *Certification Path Answer [CPA]*), to help mitigate the effects of the ND spoofing and redirection.

IPv6 Access Control Lists

As with IPv4, network administrators can use *access control lists (ACL)* on IOS devices to filter and restrict the types of IPv6 traffic that enters the network at ingress points. The configuration in Example 12-4 prevents unauthorized IPv6 packets on UDP port 53 (DNS) from entering the network from interface Gigabit 0/0. In this example, 2001:DB8:1:60::/64 represents the IP address space that is used by DNS servers that the network administrator is trying to protect, and 2001:DB8::100:1 is the IP address of the host that is allowed to access the DNS servers.

CAUTION   Be careful to ensure that all required traffic for routing and administrative access is allowed in the ACL before denying all unauthorized traffic.

Example 12-4   *IPv6 Access Control List*

```
CCNA-Router-1#
CCNA-Router-1# config t
Enter configuration commands, one per line.  End with CNTL/Z.
CCNA-Router-1(config)# ipv6  access-list IPv6-ACL
!
!Include explicit permit statements for trusted sources that
!require access on UDP port 53 (DNS)
!
CCNA-Router-1(config-ipv6-acl)# permit upd host 2001:DB8::100:1 2001:DB8:1:60::/64 eq
53
!
CCNA-Router-1(config-ipv6-acl)#  deny udp any 2001:DB8:1:60::/64 eq 53
!
! Allow IPv6 neighbor discovery packets, which
! include neighbor solicitation packets and neighbor
! advertisement packets
CCNA-Router-1(config-ipv6-acl)#  permit icmp any any nd-ns
CCNA-Router-1(config-ipv6-acl)#  permit icmp any any nd-na
!
!-- Explicit deny for all other IPv6 traffic
!
CCNA-Router-1(config-ipv6-acl)#  deny ipv6 any any
!
! Apply ACL to interface in the ingress direction
!
CCNA-Router-1(config-ipv6-acl)# interface GigabitEthernet0/0
CCNA-Router-1(config-if)# ipv6 traffic-filter IPv6-ACL in
CCNA-Router-1(config-if)# exit
CCNA-Router-1(config)# exit
CCNA-Router-1#
```

12

Exam Preparation Tasks

Review All the Key Topics

Review the most important topics from this chapter, denoted with a Key Topic icon. Table 12-4 lists these key topics.

Table 12-4 Key Topics

Key Topic Element	Description	Page Number
Table 12-2	IPv4 Versus IPv6	324
Example 12-1	An IPv6 Address Configured the Hard Way	326
List	Address types with IPv6	327
Example 12-2	IPv6 Interface Information	329
Example 12-3	Enabling IPv6 Routing and Routing Protocols	330
List	Best practices common to both IPv4 and IPv6	332
List	Threats common to both IPv4 and IPv6	333
List	New potential risks with IPv6	334
List	IPv6 best practices	336

Complete the Tables and Lists from Memory

Print a copy of Appendix C, "Memory Tables," (found on the CD) or at least the section for this chapter, and complete the tables and lists from memory. Appendix D, "Memory Tables Answer Key," also on the CD, includes completed tables and lists so that you can check your work.

Define Key Terms

Define the following key terms from this chapter, and check your answers in the glossary:

amplification attack, RS, RA, NS, NA, eavesdropping, man-in-the-middle attack, spoofing, EUI-64

Command Reference to Check Your Memory

This section includes the most important configuration and EXEC commands covered in this chapter. To see how well you have memorized the commands as a side effect of your other studies, cover the left side of Table 12-5 with a piece of paper, read the descriptions on the right side, and see whether you remember the commands.

Table 12-5 Command Reference

Command	Description
ipv6 address	Apply an IPv6 address to an interface
ipv6 unicast-routing	Enable the router to forward IPv6 packets on behalf of other devices
ipv6 ospf 1 area 0	Enable the interface for OSPF process 1, in area 0
ipv6 access-list	Enter mode to begin configuring an IPv6 ACL
ipv6 traffic-filter *IPv6-ACL* **in**	Apply IPv6 ACL in ingress direction on an interface

12

This chapter covers the following topics:

Securing the Control Plane

   The function of control plane policing

   The function of control plane protection

Securing Routing Protocols

   Routing update authentication on OSPF

   Routing update authentication on EIGRP

   Routing update authentication on RIP

   Routing update authentication on BGP

CHAPTER 13

Securing Routing Protocols and the Control Plane

"Do I Know This Already?" Quiz

The "Do I Know This Already?" quiz allows you to assess if you should read the entire chapter. If you miss no more than one of these self-assessment questions, you might want to move ahead to the "Exam Preparation Tasks." Table 13-1 lists the major headings in this chapter and the "Do I Know This Already?" quiz questions covering the material in those headings so you can assess your knowledge of these specific areas. The answers to the "Do I Know This Already?" quiz appear in Appendix A.

Table 13-1 "Do I Know This Already?" Section-to-Question Mapping

Foundation Topics Section	Questions
Securing the Control Plane	1–3
Control Plane Policing	4–6
Securing Routing Protocols	7–10

1. Control plane packets are handled by which of the following?

   a. Ingress Interface

   b. CPU

   c. Management Interface

   d. SNMP Interface

2. Which of the following functions is not handled by the control plane?

   a. BGP

   b. RSVP

   c. SSH

   d. ICMP

3. Which command provides information on receive adjacency traffic?

   a. show ip bgp

   b. show processes cpu

   c. show interfaces summary

   d. show ip cef

4. Control plane policing helps to protect the CPU by doing what?

   a. Diverting all control plane traffic to the data and management planes

   b. Filtering and rate-limiting traffic destined to the control plane

   c. Rate-limiting SNMP traffic to reduce the impact on the CPU

   d. Throttling all traffic ingressing the device during heavy traffic periods until the CPU performance has improved

5. In the following CoPP example, which traffic is being prevented from reaching the control plane?

```
Extended IP access list 123
    10 deny tcp 192.168.1.0 0.0.0.25 any eq telent
    20 deny udp 192.168.1.0 0.0.0.255 any eq domain
    30 permit tcp any any eq telnet
    40 permit udp any any eq domain
    50 deny ip any any
Class-map match-all PEARSON
    match access-group 123
policy-map Pearson_Example
    class Pearson
police 10000 5000 5000 conform-action DROP exceed-action drop
```

   a. Telnet traffic from the 192.168.1.0/24

   b. Telnet and DNS traffic from outside the 192.168.1.0./24 subnet

   c. Telnet and DNS traffic from the 192.168.1.0/24 subnet

   d. DNS traffic from the 192.168.1.0/24 subnet

6. Which of the following is not a subinterface that can be leveraged as part of control plane protection?

   a. Host subinterface

   b. Frame Relay subinterface

   c. CEF-Exception subinterface

   d. Transit subinterface

7. Which line in the following OSPF configuration will not be required for MD5 authentication to work?

```
interface GigabitEthernet0/1
 ip address 192.168.10.1 255.255.255.0
 ip ospf authentication message-digest
 ip ospf message-digest-key 1 md5 CCNA
 !
router ospf 65000
 router-id 192.168.10.1
 area 20 authentication message-digest
 network 10.1.1.0 0.0.0.255 area 10
 network 192.168.10.0 0.0.0.255 area 0
 !
```

   a. ip ospf authentication message-digest

   b. network 192.168.10.0 0.0.0.255 area 0

   c. area 20 authentication message-digest

   d. ip ospf message-digest-key 1 md5 CCNA

8. Which of the following pairs of statements is true in terms of configuring MD authentication?

   a. Interface statements (OSPF, EIGRP) must be configured; use of key chain in OSPF

   b. Router process (OSPF, EIGRP) must be configured; key chain in EIGRP

   c. Router process or interface statement for OSPF must be configured; key chain in EIGRP

   d. Router process (only for OSPF) must be configured; key chain in OSPF

9. Which of the following statements is true?

   a. RIPv1 supports cleartext authentication, and RIPv2 supports MD5 authentication.

   b. RIPv2 and OSPF make use of a key chain for authentication.

   c. RIPv2 and EIGRP both require router process configuration for authentication.

   d. RIPv2 and EIGRP both make use of a key chain for authentication.

10. What is needed to implement MD5 authentication for BGP?

   a. Interface and router process configuration

   b. Interface and key chain configuration

   c. Router process configuration

   d. Router process and key chain configuration

13

Foundation Topics

This chapter begins with a discussion of how to secure the control plane of a router, and specifically through the use of *control plane policing (CoPP)* and *control plane protection (CPPr)*. The chapter then covers the use of routing update authentication for the following routing protocols: *Routing Information Protocol (RIP)*, *Open Shortest Path First (OSPF)*, *Enhanced Interior Gateway Routing Protocol (EIGRP)*, and *Border Gateway Protocol (BGP)*.

Securing the Control Plane

Protection of the control plane of a network device is critical because the control plane ensures that the management (discussed in Chapter 11, "Securing the Management Plane on Cisco IOS Devices") and data (discussed in Chapter 12, "Securing the Data Plane in IPv6") planes are maintained and operational. If the control plane were to become unstable during a security incident, it can be impossible for you to recover the stability of the network.

Control plane packets are network device–generated or received packets that are used for the creation and operation of the network itself. From the perspective of the network device, control plane packets always have a receive destination IP address and are handled by the CPU in the network device route processor. Some examples of control plane functions include routing protocols (for example, BGP, OSPF, EIGRP), as well as protocols like *Internet Control Message Protocol (ICMP)* and the *Resource Reservation Protocol (RSVP)*.

Minimizing the Impact of Control Plane Traffic on the CPU

In many cases, you can disable the reception and transmission of certain types of packets on an interface to minimize the amount of CPU load that is required to process unneeded packets. These types of packets fall into a category known as process switched traffic. This traffic must be handled by the CPU and hence results in a performance impact on the CPU of the network device.

Process switched traffic falls into two primary categories:

- **Receive adjacency traffic:** This traffic contains an entry in the *Cisco Express Forwarding (CEF)* table whereby the next router hop is the device itself, which is indicated by the term *receive* in the **show ip cef** *command-line interface (CLI)* output. This indication is the case for any IP address that requires direct handling by the Cisco IOS device CPU, which includes interface IP addresses, multicast address space, and broadcast address space.

    Example 13-1 provides sample output generated when issuing the **show ip cef** command. Any of the IP addresses/subnets for which "receive" is listed as the Next Hop indicates that packets destined for this address space will end up hitting the control plane and CPU.

Example 13-1   show ip cef *Output*

```
CCNA-Router-1# show ip cef
Prefix              Next Hop            Interface
0.0.0.0/0           no route
0.0.0.0/8           drop
```

```
0.0.0.0/32              receive
10.2.2.0/24             192.168.10.2          GigabitEthernet0/1
127.0.0.0/8             drop
192.168.10.0/24         attached              GigabitEthernet0/1
192.168.10.0/32         receive               GigabitEthernet0/1
192.168.10.1/32         receive               GigabitEthernet0/1
192.168.10.2/32         attached              GigabitEthernet0/1
192.168.10.255/32       receive               GigabitEthernet0/1
192.168.15.0/24         attached              Loopback1
192.168.15.0/32         receive               Loopback1
192.168.15.1/32         receive               Loopback1
192.168.15.255/32       receive               Loopback1
192.168.30.0/24         192.168.10.2          GigabitEthernet0/1
192.168.100.0/24        attached              Loopback0
192.168.100.0/32        receive               Loopback0
192.168.100.1/32        receive               Loopback0
192.168.100.255/32      receive               Loopback0
192.168.200.0/24        192.168.10.2          GigabitEthernet0/1
224.0.0.0/4             drop

CCNA-Router-1#
```

- **Data plane traffic requiring special processing by the CPU**: Although this chapter focuses on control plane traffic, there is still a need to address certain data plane traffic (that is, traffic which has a destination beyond, or through, the network device in question). The following types of data plane traffic require special processing by the CPU resulting in a performance impact on the CPU:

  - **Access control list (ACL) logging**: ACL logging traffic consists of any packets that are generated due to a match (permit or deny) of an *access control entry (ACE)* on which the **log** keyword is used.

  - **Unicast Reverse Path Forwarding (Unicast RPF)**: Unicast RPF, used in conjunction with an ACL, can result in the process switching of certain packets.

  - **IP options**: Any IP packets with options included must be processed by the CPU.

  - **Fragmentation**: Any IP packet that requires fragmentation must be passed to the CPU for processing.

  - **Time-To-Live (TTL) expiry**: Packets that have a TTL value less than or equal to 1 require "Internet Control Message Protocol Time Exceeded (ICMP Type 11, Code 0)" messages to be sent, which results in CPU processing.

  - **ICMP unreachables**: Packets that result in ICMP unreachable messages due to routing, *maximum transmission unit (MTU)*, or filtering are processed by the CPU.

  - **Traffic requiring an ARP request**: Destinations for which an ARP entry does not exist require processing by the CPU.

  - **Non-IP traffic**: All non-IP traffic is processed by the CPU.

13

Control Plane Policing

Control plane policing (CoPP) can be used to identify the type and rate of traffic that reaches the control plane of the Cisco IOS device. Control plane policing can be performed through the use of granular classification ACLs, logging, and the use of the **show policy-map control-plane** command.

CoPP is a Cisco IOS-wide feature designed to allow users to manage the flow of traffic handled by the route processor of their network devices. CoPP is designed to prevent unnecessary traffic from overwhelming the route processor that, if left unabated, could affect system performance. Route processor resource exhaustion, in this case, refers to all resources associated with the punt path and route processors such as Cisco IOS process memory and buffers and ingress packet queues.

As just discussed, more than just control plane packets can punt and affect the route processor and system resources. Management plane traffic, as well as certain data plane exceptions IP packets and some services plane packets, may also require the use of route processor resources. Even so, it is common practice to identify the resources associated with the punt path and route processors as the control plane.

In Example 13-2, only Telnet and DNS traffic from trusted hosts (that is, devices in the 192.168.1.0/24 subnet) is permitted to reach the Cisco IOS device CPU. In addition, certain types of ICMP traffic destined to the network infrastructure (that is, devices with IP addresses in the 10.1.1.0/24 subnet) will be rate-limited to 5000 packets per second (pps).

NOTE   When constructing Access Control Lists (ACL) to be used for CoPP, traffic that is "permitted" translates to traffic that will be inspected by CoPP, and traffic that is "denied" translates to traffic that CoPP bypasses. Please refer to this white paper on CoPP: http://www.cisco.com/web/about/security/intelligence/coppwp_gs.html. Specifically, see the following excerpt from the section, "Access List Construction":

"There are several caveats and key points to keep in mind when constructing your access lists.

- The **log** or **log-input** keywords must never be used in access-lists that are used within MQC policies for CoPP. The use of these keywords may cause unexpected result in the functionality of CoPP.

- The use of the deny rule in access lists used in MQC is somewhat different to regular interface ACLs. Packets that match a deny rule are excluded from that class and cascade to the next class (if one exists) for classification. This is in contrast to packets matching a permit rule, which are then included in that class and no further comparisons are performed."

Example 13-2   *Control Plane Policing Configuration*

```
!
!
access-list 101 permit icmp any 10.1.1.0 0.0.0.255 echo
access-list 101 permit icmp any 10.1.1.0 0.0.0.255 echo-reply
access-list 101 permit icmp any 10.1.1.0 0.0.0.255 time-exceeded
access-list 101 permit icmp any 10.1.1.0 0.0.0.255 ttl-exceeded
access-list 123 deny   tcp 192.168.1.0 0.0.0.255 any eq telnet
```

```
access-list 123 deny    udp 192.168.1.0 0.0.0.255 any eq domain
access-list 123 permit tcp any any eq telnet
access-list 123 permit udp any any eq domain
access-list 123 deny    ip any any
!!
!
class-map match-all ICMP
 match access-group 101
class-map match-all UNDESIRABLE-TRAFFIC
 match access-group 123
!
policy-map COPP-INPUT-POLICY
 class UNDESIRABLE-TRAFFIC
  drop
 class ICMP
  police 50000 5000 5000 conform-action transmit  exceed-action drop
!
control-plane
 service-policy input COPP-INPUT-POLICY
!
```

To display the CoPP currently configured on the device, issue the **show policy-map control-plane** command, as demonstrated in Example 13-3.

Example 13-3 *Verifying the Control Plane Policing Configuration*

```
CCNA-Router-1# show policy-map control-plane

 Control Plane

  Service-policy input: COPP-INPUT-POLICY

    Class-map: UNDESIRABLE-TRAFFIC (match-all)
      0 packets, 0 bytes
      5 minute offered rate 0000 bps, drop rate 0000 bps
      Match: access-group 123
      drop


    Class-map: ICMP (match-all)
      0 packets, 0 bytes
      5 minute offered rate 0000 bps, drop rate 0000 bps
      Match: access-group 101
      police:
          cir 50000 bps, bc 5000 bytes, be 5000 bytes
        conformed 0 packets, 0 bytes; actions:
          transmit
        exceeded 0 packets, 0 bytes; actions:
          drop
```

13

```
        violated 0 packets, 0 bytes; actions:
          drop
        conformed 0000 bps, exceeded 0000 bps, violated 0000 bps

    Class-map: class-default (match-any)
      3 packets, 551 bytes
      5 minute offered rate 0000 bps, drop rate 0000 bps
      Match: any
CCNA-Router-1#
```

Control Plane Protection

Control plane protection (CPPr) is another feature, similar to control plane policing, that can help to mitigate the effects on the CPU of traffic that requires processing by the CPU.

CPPr can restrict traffic with finer granularity by dividing the aggregate control plane into three separate control plane categories known as *subinterfaces*. The three subinterfaces are as follows:

- Host subinterface
- Transit subinterface
- CEF-Exception subinterface

In addition to providing three more granular buckets in which to place packets destined to the device's control plane, the CPPr feature also additionally provides the following:

- **Port-filtering feature:** Enables the policing and dropping of packets that are sent to closed or nonlistening TCP or UDP ports
- **Queue-thresholding feature:** Limits the number of packets for a specified protocol that are allowed in the control-plane IP input queue

Securing Routing Protocols

By default, network devices send routing information to and from their routing peers in the clear, making this information visible to all interested parties. Failure to secure the exchange of routing information allows an attacker to introduce false routing information into the network. By using password authentication with routing protocols between routers, you can enhance the overall security of the network. However, because this authentication is sent as clear text, it can be simple for an attacker to subvert this security control.

If you add *message digest 5 algorithm (MD5)* hash capabilities to the authentication process, routing updates no longer contain cleartext passwords, and the entire contents of the routing update are more resistant to tampering. However, MD5 authentication is still susceptible to brute-force and dictionary attacks if weak passwords are chosen. You are advised to use passwords with sufficient randomization. Because MD5 authentication is much more secure when compared to password authentication, these examples are specific to MD5 authentication.

Implement Routing Update Authentication on OSPF

MD5 authentication for OSPF requires configuration at either the interface level, that is, for each interface in which OSPF will be used, or within the router OSPF process itself.

The authentication type must be the same for all routers and access servers in an area. The authentication password for all OSPF routers on a network must be the same if they are to communicate with each other via OSPF. Use the **ip ospf authentication-key** interface command to specify this password.

If you enable MD5 authentication with the **message-digest** keyword, you must configure a password with the **ip ospf message-digest-key** interface command.

To remove the authentication specification for an area, use the **no** form of this command with the **authentication** keyword.

Example 13-4 shows the portion of a configuration required to implement OSPF router authentication using MD5.

Example 13-4   *OSPF MD5 Authentication Configuration*

```
!
interface GigabitEthernet0/1
 ip address 192.168.10.1 255.255.255.0
 ip ospf authentication message-digest
 ip ospf message-digest-key 1 md5 CCNA
!
router ospf 65000
 router-id 192.168.10.1
 area 0 authentication message-digest
 network 10.1.1.0 0.0.0.255 area 10
 network 192.168.10.0 0.0.0.255 area 0
!
```

NOTE   The same configuration (with the exception of the interface IP address and router ID) must be identical on the other OSPF peer.

Implement Routing Update Authentication on EIGRP

The addition of authentication to your routers' EIGRP messages ensures that your routers accept routing messages only from other routers that know the same pre-shared key. Without this authentication configured, if someone introduces another router with different or conflicting route information on to the network, the routing tables on your routers could become corrupt and a denial-of-service attack could ensue. Thus, when you add authentication to the EIGRP messages sent between your routers, it prevents someone from purposely or accidentally adding another router to the network and causing a problem.

As with OSPF, MD5 authentication for EIGRP requires configuration at the interface level, that is, for each interface in which EIGRP will be used; however, there is no specific con-

13

figuration required within the router EIGRP process itself. In addition, unlike OSPF, EIGRP authentication also makes use of a key chain that is configured in global configuration mode. The key chain consists of a key number and a key string.

Example 13-5 shows the portion of a configuration required to implement EIGRP router authentication using MD5.

Example 13-5 *EIGRP MD5 Authentication Configuration*

```
!
key chain CCNA
 key 1
  key-string CCNA-SECURITY
!
!
interface Loopback0
 ip address 192.168.100.1 255.255.255.0
!
interface GigabitEthernet0/1
 ip address 192.168.10.1 255.255.255.0
 ip authentication mode eigrp 65000 md5
 ip authentication key-chain eigrp 65000 CCNA
!
router eigrp 65000
 network 192.168.10.0
 network 192.168.100.0
!
```

NOTE The same configuration (with the exception of the interface IP address) needs to be identical on the other EIGRP peer.

Implement Routing Update Authentication on RIP

The Cisco implementation of RIPv2 supports two modes of authentication: plaintext authentication and MD5 authentication. Plaintext authentication mode is the default setting in every RIPv2 packet, when authentication is enabled. Plaintext authentication should not be used when security is an issue because the unencrypted authentication password is sent in every RIPv2 packet.

NOTE RIP Version 1 (RIPv1) does not support authentication. If you are sending and receiving RIPv2 packets, you can enable RIP authentication on an interface.

As with both OSPF and EIGRP, MD5 authentication for RIPv2 requires configuration at the interface level (that is, for each interface in which RIP will be used). However, like EIGRP, no specific configuration is required within the router RIP process. Also, like EIGRP, RIPv2 authentication also makes use of a key chain, which is configured in global configuration mode. The key chain consists of a key number and a key string.

Example 13-6 shows the portion of a configuration required to implement RIPv2 router authentication using MD5.

Example 13-6 *RIPv2 MD5 Authentication Configuration*

```
!
key chain CCNA
 key 1
  key-string CCNA-SECURITY
 !


 !
interface Loopback0
 ip address 192.168.100.1 255.255.255.0
 !

 !
interface GigabitEthernet0/1
 ip address 192.168.10.1 255.255.255.0
 ip rip authentication mode md5
 ip rip authentication key-chain CCNA
 !
router rip
 version 2
 network 192.168.10.0
 network 192.168.100.0
 !
```

NOTE   The same configuration (with the exception of the interface IP address and network statements) needs to be identical on the other RIP peer.

Implement Routing Update Authentication on BGP

Peer authentication with MD5 creates an MD5 digest of each packet sent as part of a BGP session. Specifically, portions of the IP and TCP headers, TCP payload, and a secret key are used to generate the digest.

The created digest is then stored in TCP option Kind 19, which was created specifically for this purpose by RFC 2385. The receiving BGP speaker uses the same algorithm and secret key to regenerate the message digest. If the received and computed digests are not identical, the packet is discarded.

Peer authentication with MD5 is configured with the **password** option to the **neighbor** BGP router configuration command.

As shown in Example 13-7, MD5 authentication for BGP is much simpler than the other routing protocols (OSPF, EIGRP, RIPv2) that were discussed earlier. All that is required is one additional **neighbor** statement within the router BGP process.

13

Example 13-7 shows the portion of a configuration required to implement BGP router authentication using MD5.

Example 13-7 *BGP MD5 Authentication Configuration*

```
!
interface Loopback1
 ip address 192.168.15.1 255.255.255.0
!
interface GigabitEthernet0/1
 ip address 192.168.10.1 255.255.255.0
!
router bgp 65000
 bgp log-neighbor-changes
 network 192.168.15.0
 neighbor 192.168.10.2 remote-as 65100
 neighbor 192.168.10.2 password CCNA-SECURITY
!
```

NOTE   A similar configuration must be in place on the other BGP peer.

To verify that MD5 authentication is used between the BGP peers, issue the **show ip bgp neighbors | include Option Flags** command and look for **md5** in the output, as demonstrated in Example 13-8.

Example 13-8 *Verifying MD5 Authentication Between BGP Peers*

```
CCNA-Router-1#show ip bgp neighbors | include Option Flags
Option Flags: nagle, path mtu capable, md5, Retrans timeout
CCNA-Router-1#
```

Exam Preparation Tasks

This chapter looked at the types of network traffic that hits the control plane of network devices and how this traffic can impact the performance of the CPU of the device. The chapter then covered two features that help mitigate the effects of traffic that is processed by the control plane and hence the CPU. These features are control plane policing and control plane protection. The chapter concluded by covering the use of MD5 route authentication for each of the following routing protocols: OSPF, EIGRP, RIP, and BGP.

Review All the Key Topics

Review the most important topics from this chapter, denoted with a Key Topic icon. Table 13-2 lists these key topics.

Table 13-2   Key Topics

Key Topic Element	Description	Page Number
Example 13-1	**show ip cef** Output	344
Section	Control Plane Policing	346
Section	Control Plane Protection	348
Section	Securing Routing Protocols	348

Complete the Tables and Lists from Memory

Print a copy of Appendix C, "Memory Tables," (found on the CD) or at least the section for this chapter, and complete the tables and lists from memory. Appendix D, "Memory Tables Answer Key," also on the CD, includes completed tables and lists so that you can check your work. There are no applicable tables in this chapter.

Define Key Terms

Define the following key terms from this chapter, and check your answers in the glossary:

Control Plane, **show ip cef** command, control plane policing (CoPP), **show policy-map control-plan** command, control plane protection (CPPr), MD5 route authentication

This chapter covers the following topics:

Firewall concepts and technologies

Using Network Address Translation

Creating and deploying firewalls

CHAPTER 14

Understanding Firewall Fundamentals

The word *firewall* commonly describes systems or devices that are placed between a trusted and an untrusted network. A detailed understanding of how firewalls and their related technologies work is extremely important for all network security professionals. This knowledge helps you to configure and manage the security of your networks accurately and effectively.

Complete separation means that no network connectivity exists, which does not serve anyone very well. By allowing specific traffic through the firewall, you can implement a balance of the required connectivity and security. Traffic that may be identified as harmful is any traffic that compromises confidentiality, data integrity, or availability for the intended users.

Several network firewall solutions offer user and application policy enforcement that supplies protection for different types of security threats. These solutions often provide logging capabilities that enable the security administrators to identify, investigate, validate, and mitigate such threats.

In addition, several software applications can run on a system to protect only that host. These types of applications are known as *personal firewalls*. This section includes an overview of network and personal firewalls and their related technologies.

"Do I Know This Already?" Quiz

The "Do I Know This Already?" quiz helps you determine your level of knowledge of this chapter's topics before you begin. Table 14-1 details the major topics discussed in this chapter and their corresponding quiz questions.

Table 14-1 "Do I Know This Already?" Section-to-Question Mapping

Foundation Topics Section	Questions
Firewall Concepts and Technologies	1–4
Using Network Address Translation	5–6
Creating and Deploying Firewalls	7–8

1. Which firewall methodology requires the administrator to know and configure all the specific ports, IPs, and protocols required for the firewall?

   a. AGL

   b. Packet filtering

   c. Stateful filtering

   d. Proxy server

2. Which technology dynamically builds a table for the purpose of permitting the return traffic from an outside server, back to the client, in spite of a default security policy that says no traffic is allowed to initiate from the outside networks?

   a. Proxy

   b. NAT

   c. Packet filtering

   d. Stateful filtering

3. What does application layer inspection provide?

   a. Packet filtering at Layer 5 and higher

   b. Enables a firewall to listen in on a client/server communication, looking for information regarding communication channels

   c. Proxy server functionality

   d. Application layer gateway functionality

4. Which one of the following is true about a transparent firewall?

   a. Implemented at Layer 1

   b. Implemented at Layer 2

   c. Implemented at Layer 3

   d. Implemented at Layer 4 and higher

5. What is the specific term for performing Network Address Translation for multiple inside devices but optimizing the number of global addresses required?

   a. NAT-T

   b. NAT

   c. PAT

   d. PAT-T

6. What term refers to the internal IP address of a client using NAT as seen from other devices on the same internal network as the client?

   a. Inside local

   b. Inside global

   c. Outside local

   d. Outside global

7. Which of the following describes a rule on the firewall which will never be matched because of where the firewall is in the network?

   a. Orphaned rule

   b. Redundant rule

   c. Shadowed rule

   d. Promiscuous rule

8. What is the long-term impact of providing a promiscuous rule as a short-term test in an attempt to get a network application working?

   a. The promiscuous rule may be left in place, leaving a security hole.

   b. The rule cannot be changed later to more accurately filter based on the business requirement.

   c. It should be a shadowed rule.

   d. Change control documentation may not be completed for this test.

Foundation Topics

Firewall Concepts and Technologies

These concepts apply to IOS routers performing firewall services and to dedicated firewalls, which are purpose built for security. This section covers the concepts of firewalls, their strengths and weaknesses, and why they are used in specific situations. This information is used in nearly all networks where security is a concern.

Firewall Technologies

A firewall is a concept that can be implemented by a single device, a group of devices, or even simply software running on a device such as a host or a server. As mentioned in the introduction to this chapter, the function of a firewall primarily is to deny unwanted traffic from crossing the boundary of the firewall. For network traffic, this means that a firewall, in its basic form, could be implemented by the following:

- A router or other Layer 3 forwarding device that has an access list or some other method used to filter traffic that is trying to go between two of its interfaces. This is the primary method that is implemented by an IOS router (using firewall features) or the *Adaptive Security Appliance (ASA)* firewall.

- A switch that has two *virtual LANs (VLAN)* without any routing in between them, which would absolutely keep traffic from the two different networks separate (by not being able to have inter-VLAN communications).

- Hosts or servers that are running software that prevents certain types of received traffic from being processed and controls which traffic can be sent. This is an example of a software firewall.

Objectives of a Good Firewall

Here are some common properties that a good firewall should possess:

- **It must be resistant to attacks:** If a firewall can be brought down or compromised to the point where it allows unwanted access, it thus fails to implement policy correctly. If the firewall is a victim of a *denial-of-service (DoS)* attack, to the point where it cannot provide normal access for users, that is also problem. If there is some vulnerability that an attacker can leverage with an exploit, thus enabling the attacker to modify the firewall configuration, that (of course) is also a problem.

- **Traffic between networks must be forced through the firewall:** If multiple paths exist between network A and network B, and a firewall is controlling the traffic for these connections, but if there are alternative paths, the malicious traffic has the potential to avoid the firewall. So, if there are multiple paths, each of those paths should have the same firewall policy, and very likely will have the same firewall methodology at each point.

- **The firewall enforces the access control policy of the organization:** Many times, unfortunately, the tail wags the dog as new firewalls are put into place. Rules are made for that firewall about traffic allowed through the firewall, and then as a result we document the policy. What ideally should happen is that a policy would be created on paper first that identifies the business requirements for which traffic should be allowed through the firewall, and then the rules should be created and applied to the firewall to enforce that policy, in that order.

Firewall Justifications

Companies often make a significant investment in security, including the monies they spend on firewalls. Table 14-2 describes some of the items a firewall can help protect against.

Table 14-2 Protective Measures Provided by a Firewall

Reduces the Risk Of	Explanation
Exposure of sensitive systems to untrusted individuals	By hiding most of the functionality of a host or network device, and permitting only the minimum required connectivity to that given system, the firewall reduces the exposure for that system. An example is only allowing web traffic to a specific IP address of a web server on your *demilitarized zone (DMZ)*. Even if that web server has other services running, those services will not be available to users trying to access those services through the firewall.
Exploitation of protocol flaws	You can configure a firewall to inspect protocols to ensure compliance with the standards for that protocol at multiple layers of the protocol stack. It can also control the amount of time it will allow for a normal connection sequence before saying enough is enough. An example is only allowing a specific amount of time between a *Domain Name System (DNS)* request and the DNS reply. Another example is the three-way handshake for TCP and the firewall only allowing so much time for that to complete between a client on one side of the firewall and a server being accessed on the other side of the firewall.
Unauthorized users	By using authentication methods, a firewall could control which user's traffic is allowed through the firewall and be configured to block on all other traffic based on policy. For example, a firewall could leverage *authentication, authorization, and accounting (AAA)* services using its local configuration or an *Access Control Server (ACS)* server.
Malicious data	A firewall can detect and block malicious data, which would stop traffic from reaching the intended destination. This function could also be provided by an *intrusion prevention system (IPS)*.

We could hope that by just purchasing a firewall and putting it in place all of our security issues can be put to rest. It should be understood that having a firewall and implementing correctly the policies for an organization are mitigation steps for reducing risk but do not completely eliminate risk. In addition, firewalls do have some limitations, as described in Table 14-3.

Table 14-3   Potential Firewall Limitations

Limitation	Explanation
Configuration mistakes have serious consequences.	The firewall's job is to implement a policy. Based on a specific firewall you are dealing with, there are specific ways of implementing features such as *access control lists (ACL)*, packet inspection, *Network Address Translation (NAT)*, authentication, and so on. If the firewall rules are not implemented correctly, it might not do the job of implementing the policy as intended. It takes good technical gear and a good technical configuration on that gear for a successful policy implementation.
Not all network applications were written to survive going through the firewall.	If there is some type of custom application that simply will not work based on the combination of what the application is doing and what the current firewall rules in place are, the choice is to rewrite the application or make an exception in the firewall policy for the application.
Individuals who are forced to go through a firewall might try to engineer a way around it.	If there is a firewall policy, for example, that specifies no instant messaging file transfers are allowed, it might be possible for a user to circumvent that rule by getting creative. Options such as hiding the forbidden instant messaging file transfers inside of another protocol so that it looks like standard *Hypertext Transfer Protocol (HTTP)* or *Hypertext Transfer Protocol Secure (HTTPS)* is one thing they may try. This concept is called *tunneling* and can be done with a variety of protocols. A firewall that is capable of application layer inspection may be able to identify and prevent this type of malicious tunneling.
Latency being added by the firewall.	If a firewall is given a huge job of analyzing all the traffic, it might take a few milliseconds or more per packet for the analysis, and as a result some slight delay may be added to the overall network traffic delivery time.

The Defense-in-Depth Approach

Having just one single point of control/security for your entire network is not wise; if that one single point is misconfigured or fails to implement policy, the network is wide open to all the negative impact that the firewall is trying to prevent. One solution, which is really more an idea than a solution, is to use a defense-in-depth approach or what is known as a *layered approach* to security.

Let's take a look at an example of a defense-in-depth approach for an average company that has a web server that is publicly available to access. We, as the end user on the outside global Internet, open up a browser and type in the name of the server. Behind the scenes, our browser facilitates a DNS request to find out the IP address of that server. Once we have the IP address of the server, we initiate a *Transfer Control Protocol (TCP)* session with that server.

As our packets go over the Internet toward that company, the perimeter router at that company is their first line of defense. The router could be checking the source IP address of our packet to verify that it is not a spoofed source IP address (such as the IP address space that is internal to their company, which should never be in the Source IP Address field of the packet coming into their network). On the perimeter router, they also might have some limited ACLs that may immediately drop well-known malicious traffic right there at the edge of their network. Because our packet is not malicious (at least not according to the router), the packet is forwarded toward the corporate network and through the firewall, which is the second line of defense.

The firewall can do all sorts of things at this point before the packet is ever forwarded to the intended server. The firewall could pretend that it is the server and communicate back and forth with us for the three-way handshake to verify that we are not trying to do a SYN flood attack. The firewall could require us to authenticate before forwarding our traffic any further, and many other rules could be implemented on that firewall. Assuming we pass all the rules for that firewall, our packet is then forwarded to the server.

The connectivity between their firewall and their server is very likely going through a switch on the company's local network or wherever the server is hosted. That switch, in addition, could have filtering implemented as another layer of defense. The packets as they finally arrive at the server may or may not be processed by the server based on software firewall rules that are also running in software on the individual server.

So, although that explanation is a little bit involved, it is important for you to understand how you can use a defense-in-depth or layered approach to defend your network. In short, it cannot be just a single device protecting all of your network; it needs to be a team effort by nearly all the devices.

Another reason for this defense-in-depth approach is that not all attacks or malicious traffic is coming from outside networks. Much of it is sourced from internal devices that are already on the inside of the networks, such as end-user machines.

The goal of the firewall, or firewalls, is to reduce risk. It is part of an overall strategy for keeping the network up and keeping data reliable and available. Firewalls do not replace the need for other systems such as a backup or disaster recovery plans, which are additional pieces needed for overall business continuity.

 ## Firewall Methodologies

Network-based firewalls provide key features used for perimeter security. The primary task of a network firewall is to deny or permit traffic that attempts to enter or leave the network based on explicit preconfigured policies and rules. Firewalls are often deployed in several other parts of the network to provide network segmentation within the corporate infrastructure and also in data centers. The processes used to allow or block traffic may include the following:

- Simple packet-filtering techniques
- Proxy servers (also known as *application layer gateway [ALG]*)
- NAT
- Stateful inspection firewalls

- Transparent firewalls
- Next-generation context and application-aware firewalls

Let's take a closer look at each one of these, beginning with static packet filtering.

Static Packet Filtering

Static packet filtering is based on Layer 3 and Layer 4 of the OSI model. An example of a firewall technology that uses static packet filtering is a router with an ACL applied to one or more of its interfaces for the purpose of permitting or denying specific traffic. One of the challenges with static packet filtering is that the administrator must know exactly what traffic needs to be allowed through the firewall, which can be tricky if you have many users that need to access many servers.

Table 14-4 lists some of the advantages and disadvantages of static packet filtering.

Table 14-4 Advantages and Disadvantages of Packet Filters

Advantages	Disadvantages
Based on simple sets of permit or deny entries	Susceptible to IP spoofing. If the ACL allows traffic from a specific IP address, and someone is spoofing the source IP address, the ACL permits that individual packet.
Have a minimal impact on network performance	Does not filter fragmented packets with the same accuracy as nonfragmented packets.
Are simple to implement	Extremely long ACLs are difficult to maintain.
Configurable on most routers	Stateless (does not maintain session information for current flows of traffic going through the router).
Can perform many of the basic filtering needs without requiring the expense of a high-end firewall	Some applications jump around and use many ports, some of which are dynamic. A static ACL may be required to open a very large range of ports to support application that may only use a few of them.

Because packet filtering uses a simple rule set (a packet that comes in or out of an interface where there is an ACL applied for filtering), there is a check against the packet with the entries in the ACL from top to bottom. As soon as a match occurs, the ACL stops processing the rest of the list and implements the action against the packet, which is either a permit or deny. An extended ACL on a Cisco router can use many matching criteria against the Layer 3 and Layer 4 headers, including the following:

- Source IP address
- Destination IP address
- Source port
- Destination port
- TCP synchronization information

Application Layer Gateway

Application layer firewalls, which are also sometimes called *proxy firewalls* or *application gateways*, can operate at Layer 3 and higher in the OSI reference model. Most of these proxy servers include specialized application software that takes requests from a client, puts that client on hold for a moment, and then turns around and makes the requests as if it is its own request out to the final destination.

A proxy firewall acts as an intermediary between the original client and the server. No direct communication occurs between the client and the destination server. Because the application layer gateway can operate all the way up to Layer 7, it has the potential to be very granular and analytical about every packet that the client and server exchange and can enforce rules based on anything the firewall sees.

Table 14-5 lists the advantages and disadvantages of application layer gateways.

Table 14-5   Advantages and Disadvantages of Application Layer Gateways

Advantages	Disadvantages
Very tight control is possible, due to analyzing the traffic all the way to the application layer.	Is processor intensive because most of the work is done via software on the proxy server.
It is more difficult to implement an attack against an end device because of the proxy server standing between the attacker and potential victim.	Not all applications are supported, and in practice it might support a specific few applications.
Can provide very detailed logging.	Special client software may be required.
May be implemented on common hardware.	Memory and disk intensive at the proxy server. Could potentially be a single point of failure in the network, unless fault tolerance is also configured.

Stateful Packet Filtering

Stateful packet filtering is one of the most important firewall technologies in use today. It is called *stateful* because it remembers the state of sessions that are going through the firewall. Here is a great example. Suppose that you and I go to an amusement park, and halfway through the day we realize that we forgot something in the car. So, on our way out to retrieve the item, we wonder (at the gate) whether we have to pay to get back in. The nice person at the gate explains that she will stamp our hand with a code so that when we return we can show the code and they will let us back in for free. Let's say, for our example, that they also write our names on a list of people who were already on the inside and were going outside to the parking lot with the intention of returning. When we want to come back inside, the people at the gate check the list and see that we have already been on the inside and that we left temporarily. So, they allow us back in.

With a stateful packet-filtering device, for customers on the inside of the corporate network, as they are trying to reach resources on the outside public networks, their packets go to the firewalls on the way out. The firewalls take a look at the source IP address, destination IP address, the ports in use, and other layers for information and remember that information in what is known as a *stateful database* on the firewall (like writing the names down, from the amusement park example). It is called *stateful* because the firewall is remembering the state of the session (that it was on the way outside, including the ports and IP addresses involved). By default, this same firewall does not allow any traffic from the outside and untrusted networks back into the private trusted inside network. The exception to this is for return traffic that exactly matches the expected return traffic based on the stateful database information on the firewall. In short, the reply traffic goes back to the users successfully, but attackers on the outside trying to initiate sessions are denied by default.

Table 14-6 lists some advantages and disadvantages of stateful packet-filtering devices.

Table 14-6   Advantages and Disadvantages of Stateful Packet-Filtering Devices

Advantages	Disadvantages
Can be used as a primary means of defense by filtering unwanted or unexpected traffic	Might not be able to identify or prevent an application layer attack.
Can be implemented on routers and dedicated firewalls	Not all protocols contain tightly controlled state information, such as *User Datagram Protocol (UDP)* and *Internet Control Message Protocol (ICMP)*.
Dynamic in nature compared to static packet filtering	Some applications may dynamically open up new ports from the server, which if a firewall is not analyzing specific applications or prepared for this server to open up a new port, it could cause a failure of that application for the end user. If a firewall also supports application layer inspection, it may be able to predict and allow this inbound connection.
Provides a defense against spoofing and *denial-of-service (DoS)* attacks	Stateful technology, by itself, does not support user authentication. This, however, does not prevent a firewall that implements stateful packet filtering from also implementing authentication as an additional feature.

Application Inspection

An application inspection firewall can analyze and verify protocols all the way up to Layer 7 of the OSI reference model, but does not act as a proxy between the client and the server being accessed by the client. Table 14-7 lists some of the advantages of an application inspection firewall.

Table 14-7   Advantages of an Application Inspection Firewall

Feature	Explanation
Can see deeper into the conversations, to see secondary channels that are about to be initiated from the server	If an application is negotiating dynamic ports, and the server is about to initiate one of these dynamic ports to the client, the application inspection could have been analyzing that conversation and dynamically allowed that connection from the server to allow it through the firewall and to the client. This would allow the application to work for the client (through the firewall).

Feature	Explanation
Awareness of the details at the application layer	If there is a protocol anomaly that is a deviation from the standard, an application layer firewall could identify this and either correct the packet or deny the packet from reaching the destination.
Can prevent more kinds of attacks than stateful filtering on its own	Current firewalls today, such as the ASA and Cisco IOS zone-based firewall solutions, have packet filtering, stateful filtering, and application inspection capabilities in a single device. With the additional features, more types of traffic can be classified, then permitted or denied based on policy.

14

Transparent Firewalls

A transparent firewall is more about how we inject the firewall into the network as opposed to what technologies it uses for filtering. A transparent firewall can use packet-based filtering, stateful filtering, application inspection as we discussed earlier, but the big difference with transparent firewalls is that they are implemented at Layer 2.

Most traditional firewalls are implemented as a Layer 3 hop in the network (similar to a router hop), meaning that packets have to go through this device at Layer 3. In a Layer 3 firewall, each of the interfaces has an IP address on a different network, and traffic from one subnet to another that goes through the firewall has to pass the rules on the firewall.

With a transparent firewall, we still have two interfaces, but we do not assign IP addresses to those interfaces, and those two interfaces act more like a bridge (or a switch with two ports in the same VLAN). Traffic from one segment of a given subnet is going to be forced through the transparent firewall if those frames want to reach the second segment behind the firewall. A transparent firewall has a management IP address so that we can remotely access it, but that is all. Users accessing resources through the firewall will not be aware that it is even present, and one of the biggest advantages of using a transparent firewall is that we do not have to re-address our IP subnets to put a transparent firewall in-line on the network.

Even though this is implemented as a Layer 2 device, it still sees all packets that go between its interfaces, and it can still apply all the rules of a normal Layer 3 firewall related to permitting traffic, building a stateful database, and performing application inspection.

Next-Generation Firewalls

Next-generation firewalls (NGFW) provide threat-focused security services allowing for more comprehensive protection from known and advanced threats, including protection against targeted and persistent malware attacks. An example of an NGFW is the Cisco ASA with FirePOWER Services. It combines the classic ASA firewall with Sourcefire threat prevention and advanced malware protection in a single device.

The goal of NGFW is to maintain comprehensive visibility into users, mobile devices, client-side apps, *virtual machine (VM)*-to-VM communications, vulnerabilities, threats, and *uniform resource locators (URL)*.

Using Network Address Translation

Network Address Translation (NAT) is an important feature that is often implemented on firewalls. This section provides a detailed look at the options that exist for NAT. You can use NAT in combination with the other firewall features previously discussed.

Figure 14-1 serves as a reference point for this discussion.

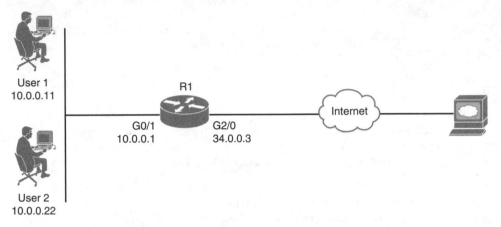

Figure 14-1   *Reference Diagram Used for This NAT Discussion*

NAT Is About Hiding or Changing the Truth About Source Addresses

It is really true: Lying is what NAT does for a living. Let's look at Figure 14.1. The two users are using private address space on the 10 network along with the G0/1 interface of the router. R1 is also connected to the Internet through a service provider through its G2/0 interface. From a security perspective (and a NAT perspective), the G0/1 interface connects to the "trusted" or "inside" network (from the company's perspective), and the G2/0 interface connects to the "untrusted" or "outside" network. Now the router itself does not have a problem with IP connectivity to the Internet because the router has a globally reachable IP address (34.0.0.3) in this example. The users are not so fortunate, however, because they are using private IP address space, and that kind of address is not allowed directly on the Internet by the service providers. So, if the users want to access a server on the Internet, they forward their packets to the default gateway, which in this case is R1, and if configured to do so, R1 modifies the IP headers in those packets and swaps out the original source IP addresses with either its own global address or a global address from a pool of global addresses (which R1 is responsible for managing, meaning that if a packet was destined to one of those addresses, the routing to those addresses on the Internet would forward the packets back to R1). These are global addresses assigned by the service provider for R1's use.

The primary device that does NAT is either a router or a firewall. NAT not only allows us to have thousands of users hide behind a single IP address (using *Port Address Translation [PAT]*, discussed momentarily), but it also offers protection of those users because the outside world does not know exactly which devices have been dynamically assigned to which IP addresses, so initiating a connection from the outside to an inside device is more difficult, (not even mentioning the ACLs that might prevent the packets from the outside making it back to the inside).

It is important to understand that NAT or PAT should not be considered as a security mechanism alone. The traffic is either allowed or denied by using ACLs.

Inside, Outside, Local, Global

Some terms that are used with NAT are often confusing, such as the words *inside*, *outside*, *local*, and *global*. Before looking at these words specifically, here are some options that you can do with NAT that will make these terms more meaningful.

You can translate the IP address of User 1 as its packets go out to the Internet. This is an example of something often referred to as *inside* NAT (performing translation for a packet coming from an inside host). You can also translate the source IP address of a device that lives on the outside as its packets come into your local network. This is commonly referred to as *outside* NAT. So, if you were going to do both inside NAT and outside NAT, for User 1 on the inside and Server A on the outside, the router would have to track all that information, including the source IP addresses on both sides and the translated addresses for both sides. To track all the addresses, the terms shown in Table 14-8 would apply to a single router performing all the NAT.

Table 14-8   NAT Terminology

NAT Term	Description
Inside local	The real IP configured on an inside host, such as User 1.
Inside global	The mapped/global address that the router is swapping out for the inside host during NAT. The outside world sees User 1 coming from this mapped/global address.
Outside local	If performing NAT on outside devices (outside NAT), this is the mapped address of the outside device (such as Server A) as it would appear to inside hosts. If not doing outside NAT on the router, this appears as the normal outside device's IP address to the inside devices.
Outside global	The real IP configured on an outside host, such as the IP on Server A.

Terms that we use are all about establishing a reference point. The *inside* and *outside* have to do with where an IP exists before we touch it. It is either inside our network and control or it is not. The *local* and *global* then have to do with the appearance of the address and may therefore be pre- or post-NAT manipulation. The inside local address as shown in Table 14-8 originated inside our control, and is what the address looks like locally on our network (pre-NAT). The same address post-NAT is inside global, again originating inside our network, but looking at it from a global perspective.

Example 14-1 shows the output for two static NAT entries. One is for User 1, and the other is for Server A. In this example, Server A is made to appear (mapped) as 10.0.0.3 to users on the inside. User 1 is made to appear (mapped) as 34.0.0.11 to users on the outside.

Example 14-1   *One Inside and One Outside Static NAT Translation*

```
R1# show ip nat translations
Pro Inside global      Inside local      Outside local      Outside global
--- ---                ---               10.0.0.3           45.1.2.3
--- 34.0.0.11          10.0.0.11         ---                ---
```

Besides the security provided by NAT, NAT is also used to allow communications between two networks that otherwise would have incompatible IP addressing (such as overlapping addresses), and with the use of PAT, we have been able to extend the lifetime of IPv4 for a least a decade longer than it should have been used (because it was running out of IP addresses).

Port Address Translation

Port Address Translation (PAT) is a subset of NAT, and it is still swapping out the source IP address as traffic goes through the NAT/PAT device, except with PAT everyone does not get their own unique translated address. Instead, the PAT device keeps track of individual sessions based on port numbers and other unique identifiers, and then forwards all packets using a single source IP address, which is shared. This is often referred to as *NAT with overload*; we are hiding multiple IP addresses on a single global address. When all those packets come back, they return to unique port numbers. Fortunately, the PAT device has been keeping track of which clients from which IP addresses initiated which sessions. So, referring to that table, the PAT device can rewrite the reply packet with all the correct information and return the packet to the client so that the client is not even aware that NAT/PAT even happened. Example 14-2 shows a router's NAT table when performing PAT for both User 1 and User 2 as they connect out to Server A using Telnet.

Example 14-2   *PAT Table for Both User 1 and User 2, Using the Same Global Address*

```
R1# show ip nat translations
Pro Inside global      Inside local      Outside local      Outside global
!  Note: source ports 56177 and 41300 are source port numbers that are
!  dynamically chosen by USER 1 and USER 2  respectively.
!  the destination port of 23 is the well-known port for telnet,  which is
!  what both PCs are  connecting to the server with.

! Entry for the translation for USER 1, to the global address of 34.0.0.3
! which is also the outside interface address of the router
tcp 34.0.0.3:56177     10.0.0.11:56177   45.1.2.3:23        45.1.2.3:23

! Entry for the translation for USER 2, mapped to the global address of
! 34.0.0.3
! It is sharing this mapping with USER 1. R1 is tracking all the addresses
! and ports involved, and knows which return packets from the server
! should be forwarded to which user, and on which ports.
tcp 34.0.0.3:41300     10.0.0.22:41300   45.1.2.3:23        45.1.2.3:23
```

As you see in the example, PAT preserves the same source port that the PCs chose to initially use. If by chance the PCs both initiate sessions to the same server and use identical source ports, the router dynamically uses a different source port for one of the sessions. This is perfectly okay because the PAT router keeps track of all the sessions and all the ports, and as long as the return traffic can be correctly forwarded to the correct PC, it provides the functionality desired. Dynamic port numbers are unlikely to be completely used because the range begins at 1024 and goes all the way to 65,535. If for some reason PAT cannot find an available port, and if multiple IP global addresses are available for PAT, the router can decide to move to the next available global IP address and start performing PAT using that. For instance, the router could be configured for PAT and reference a pool of global addresses to use rather than a single IP for use with PAT.

NAT Options

Table 14-9 describes the several flavors and options related to NAT configuration and deployment.

Table 14-9   NAT Deployment Options

Option	Description
Static NAT	This is a one-to-one permanent mapping. If you have 100 internal users and 100 global addresses, a one-to-one mapping can be done for every user, and every user would have a dedicated global address associated with his inside address. We do not usually have enough global addresses for each user. A typical use of a static mapping is this: We have a server on the inside of our network, or perhaps on a *demilitarized zone (DMZ)* interface off of our firewall, and we want to allow devices on the Internet access to that specific device. When you create a static mapping for that one server to a global IP address, that global IP address can be used in the *Domain Name System (DNS)* tables, and users on the Internet can reach our server by name (for example, www.server.com).
Dynamic NAT	Dynamic NAT involves having a pool of global addresses and only mapping those global addresses to inside devices when those inside devices have and need to go out to the Internet. For example, a printer on the inside network may not need to send packets out to the Internet, and as a result we will not use any global addresses (NAT or PAT) for that printer because the printer will never initiate traffic from the inside network going to the Internet. With dynamic NAT applied to inside hosts, after a period of time of a host not using a dynamically assigned IP address, the router or firewall performing the NAT reclaims that IP address and can use it for another device that might need it in the future.
Dynamic PAT (NAT with overload)	This is the feature that is used for most users who access the Internet. It combines the benefits of dynamically assigning global addresses only when needed, and it uses overload so that literally thousands of inside devices can be translated to the same global IP address, and as previously discussed, the router is tracking all ports and IP addresses in use to maintain the translation tables. The PAT global addresses include a single IP address that is already assigned to the outside interface of the router, a single global address dedicated for the use of PAT, or a pool of global addresses allocated for the use of PAT.

Option	Description
Policy NAT/PAT	Policy-based NAT is based on a set of rules, such as what is the source IP address, what is the destination IP address, and which ports are used that would qualify that packet to have NAT/PAT applied to it. Rules can be set up that only specific source IP addresses which are destined for specific destination addresses and/or specific ports will be translated, and that is what the *policy* part means. Traffic outside the policy is simply forwarded based on normal routing forwarding without translation.

Creating and Deploying Firewalls

Various rules and options apply to firewalls, but this section covers the best practices for implementing a firewall.

Firewall Technologies

We know that a firewall has a goal of separating two entities, and specifically controlling access between those two, such as two networks. Most commercial firewalls today can do packet filtering, application layer inspection, stateful packet filtering, NAT (in all its flavors), AAA functions, and perform *virtual private network (VPN)* services. A good example of a device such as this is the Cisco *Adaptive Security Appliance (ASA)*, which is a dedicated firewall appliance. Many of these same features can all be implemented in software and on top of an IOS router whose license, memory, and CPU can support it. A dedicated firewall appliance is considered more secure and therefore preferable to simply using a standalone router. A defense-in-depth approach suggests that perhaps you can run these features on more than a single device for the added levels of protection.

Firewall Design Considerations

Here is a partial list of best practices for firewall deployment:

- Firewalls should be placed at security boundaries, such as between two networks that have different levels of trust (from the perspective of your organization). An example is your internal network compared to the Internet.

- Firewalls should be a primary security device, but not the only security device or security measure on the network.

- A policy that starts with a "deny all" attitude and then specifically only permits traffic that is required is a better security posture than a default "permit all" attitude first and then denying traffic specifically not wanted.

- Leverage the firewall feature that best suits the need. For example, if you know you have thousands of users who need access to the Internet, you can implement dynamic NAT/PAT for those users, along with stateful filtering and deny all inbound traffic coming from the Internet. This stops users on the Internet from initializing sessions to your users because of the deny on the outside interface. It allows users to access the Internet because you are performing NAT dynamically for them. Return traffic coming back from the Internet is allowed into the firewall because the stateful filtering is being done and the firewall can dynamically allow the return traffic. If you want to allow only specific users access to the Internet, you can additionally enable AAA.

- Make sure that physical security controls and management access to the firewall devices, and the infrastructure that supports them such as cables and switches, are secure.

- Have a regularly structured review process looking at the firewall logs. Many tools enable you to review syslog messages and look for anomalies and messages that might indicate a need for further investigation.

- Practice change management for any configuration modification on the firewalls. AAA and proper documentation is important to have a record of which administrator made which changes and when they were made. The accounting records (or least a copy of these accounting records regarding changes) should be forwarded to at least one server that is out of the administrative control of the admin group. This protects the company from administrators who might make malicious (or innocent) changes to the configuration and cause a network problem and then try to delete the accounting logs.

Firewall Access Rules

As mentioned before, the appropriate method for implementing firewall rules is based on a policy. The policy (on paper) drives what the firewall configuration should be. You can implement many different types of access rules on a typical firewall, some of which are described in Table 14-10.

Table 14-10   Firewall Access Rules

Rule	Description
Rules based on service control	These rules are based on the types of services that may be accessed through the firewall, inbound or outbound. An example is that access to web servers, both HTTP or HTTPS, is allowed while all other types of traffic are denied.
Rules based on address control	These rules are based on the source/destination addresses involved, usually with a permit or deny based on specific entries in an access control list.
Rules based on direction control	These rules specify where the initial traffic can flow. For example, a rule might say that traffic from the inside going to the outside (which we could also call outbound traffic) is permitted. Traffic initiated from the outside going to inside resources (which we could call inbound traffic) would be denied. Note that stateful filtering, with its stateful database, could dynamically allow the return traffic back to the inside users. These types of rules could very easily be combined (and usually are) with various protocols/services (such as HTTP, HTTPS, and so on).
Rules based on user control	These rules control access based on knowing who the user is and what that user is authorized to do. This can be implemented via AAA services.
Rules based on behavior control	These rules control how a particular service is used. For example, a firewall may implement an e-mail filter to protect against spam.

Packet-Filtering Access Rule Structure

In the context of packet filtering, an ACL is applied to an interface either inbound or outbound on that interface. If applied inbound, all packets attempting to go through that interface must be permitted by the entries in the ACL. Access lists are processed in a top-down fashion. As soon as the firewall identifies a match from a single entry in the ACL, it then implements the action of permit or deny (based on what that entry in the ACL says to do) on the packet, and then the firewall moves on to the next packet and does the list again from top to bottom, or at least from the top until a match occurs. If there is no match in the ACL, the packet-filtering function assumes the worst and denies the packet.

Firewall Rule Design Guidelines

Regardless of which type of rules you choose to implement, here are some guidelines for the creation of those rules:

- Use a restrictive approach as opposed to a permissive approach for all interfaces and all directions of traffic. By using this as a starting point, you can then permit only traffic that you specify while denying everything else. This might take a little while to fine-tune because many administrators often discover additional required protocols for the functionality of their networks that may not have initially been considered, such as routing protocols, network management protocols, and so on.

- Presume that your internal users' machines may be part of the security problem. If you blindly trust all devices on the inside to access resources through the firewall, this may also include an attacker who has physical access to the building or malicious code that is unknown to the user running on one of his PCs.

- Be as specific as possible in your **permit** statements, such as avoiding the use of the keyword **any** or **all** IP protocols if possible.

- Recognize the necessity of a balance between functionality and security. Customers have a network for a reason, and they need to allow traffic through the firewalls to meet their business needs. At some point, you might need to point out a potential security weakness based on allowing something through your firewall but allow the traffic anyway based on the business need. It is usually up to someone higher up in the political food chain to make those final decisions.

- Filter bogus traffic, and perform logging on that traffic. Some packets should never be allowed into your network. For example, if your network is the 23.1.2.0/24 network, there should never be a packet that is entering your network (from a remote network) that (based on its source address) claims it is also from the 23.1.2.0/24 network. Traffic from the RFC 1918 private address space is unlikely to be legitimate traffic if coming in from the Internet. Bogus traffic, such as the two examples just provided, should be filtered at the edges of the network. Even if you think your service provider will deny the traffic, you should implement the same filtering on your perimeter routers as well.

- Periodically review the policies that are implemented on the firewall to verify that they are current and correct. Obsolete rules that are no longer in use should be removed or at least updated through documented change control.

Rule Implementation Consistency

For any changes that will be made to a firewall, a change control procedure should identify exactly what is going to be done, why it is going to be done, and the approval of the person in charge of making that authorization for the work to be done. The change control documentation should include what the possible impact might be to the network related to this change and what the restore procedure and timeframe would be in the event the changes need to be backed out.

Unfortunately, if there is not a consistent and well-considered process for implementing the rules, some negative results may follow regarding the rules that end up on the firewall that is supposed to be implementing the policy for the company. Table 14-11 describes some of these rules that may inadvertently show up.

Table 14-11   Results of Inconsistent or Ill-Considered Rule Implementation

Rule	Description
Rules that are too promiscuous	These types of rules allow more access than is necessary for the business requirement. Often, a rule may be implemented in an attempt to get a network application working, and the keyword of **any** is allowed for either the addresses or the IP keyword for the entire protocol stack. Unfortunately, if this rule is put in as a temporary test, and the application begins to work, it will be very difficult later in the production environment to narrow the scope of the access and still allow the application to function. Rules that are too promiscuous are significant holes in a security policy.
Redundant rules	ACLs are processed from top to bottom. If a rule is already in place as allowing a specific flow of traffic, a second rule for that does not need to be added to the control lists. Unfortunately, if an ACL is thousands of lines long, or is using object groups that are not understood by the administrator, additional unnecessary entries may be inadvertently added by the administrator. This does not necessarily cause an additional security risk, but it does create rules that are unnecessarily long (or at least longer).
Shadowed rules	A shadowed rule is basically incorrect order placement in the ACL. For example, if you want to deny a specific source IP address from going to a specific web server, and you add the entry for that to an ACL, one would think that that access is now filtered. However, access control entries are added by default to the bottom of an ACL. As a result, if a previous line specifically permits all web traffic to any web server, that entry permits this individual device to go to the specified web server before the new ACL entry is ever considered.
Orphaned rules	This most likely results from a configuration error that is referencing incorrect IP addresses that would never be seen by the firewall. For example, if an ACL intended to filter traffic from inside users includes a source IP address range that does not exist on the inside of the network, that ACL entry will never be matched. Orphaned rules are simply taking up space in the configuration and are never matched.
Incorrectly planned rules	This may result from an error that is made as the business requirements are being translated to the technical and logical controls that the firewall will implement. This may be due to a lack of understanding what protocols (and/or ports) are really used by the devices in the network with the applications in use.

Rule	Description
Incorrectly implemented rules	This results from an administrator implementing the incorrect port, protocol, or IP information on the firewall.

ACLs can be configured in Cisco IOS and Cisco ASA to permit or deny traffic. An ACL is a sequential list of rules that includes at least one **permit** statement and may also include one or more **deny** statements. The ACL has an identifier that can be a name or a number. ACL rules are often referred to as *access control entries (ACE)*. An ACL will not take effect until it is applied to an interface with the **ip access-group** command. They can also be configured to a *virtual terminal line (vty)* by using the **access-class** command or associated to other commands that use ACLs (such as crypto-maps in the case of IPsec tunnels).

As you can see, ACLs have many uses, therefore many Cisco IOS Software commands accept a reference to an ACL in their command syntax. For the purpose of the following example, the focus is on ACLs that are configured to allow or protect traffic traversing a Cisco IOS device. Example 14-3 includes an example of an ACL configured to allow HTTP (TCP port 80) and *Secure Shell (SSH)* (TCP port 22) traffic from the host with the IP address 10.1.1.8 (source) to a host with 192.168.1.10 (destination).

Example 14-3   *ACL Example*

```
ip access-list extended myACL
 permit tcp host 10.1.1.8 host 192.168.1.10 eq www
 permit tcp host 10.1.1.8 host 192.168.1.10 eq 22
!
interface GigabitEthernet0/0
 ip address 10.1.1.1 255.255.255.0
 ip access-group myACL in
```

In Example 14-3, the ACL name is myACL and includes two entries. One permits TCP port 80 traffic from 10.1.1.8 to the destination 192.168.1.10. The keyword **www** is used to specify port 80. The second entry allows SSH traffic from the same source to the same destination. Then the ACL is applied to the Gigabit Ethernet 0/0 interface with the **ip access-group** command. An ACL can be applied inbound (using the **in** keyword) or outbound (using the **out** keyword) on an interface. In Example 14-3, the ACL is applied inbound (**in**). Outbound ACLs process packets before they leave the Cisco IOS device. IP packets are routed to the egress interface and then processed by the outbound ACL.

You can only configure one ACL per interface, per protocol, and per direction. An ACL must include at least one **permit** statement; otherwise, all packets are denied because there is an explicit deny at the end of any ACL. The order that you configure each ACL entry (or ACE) is very important because ACLs are processed in the order that they were configured. After a match is found, no more criteria statements are checked. ACLs can control traffic through or to the Cisco IOS device, but not traffic originating from the Cisco IOS device.

Exam Preparation Tasks

Review All the Key Topics

Review the most important topics from this chapter, denoted with a Key Topic icon. Table 14-12 lists these key topics.

Table 14-12   Key Topics

Key Topic Element	Description	Page Number
List	The objectives of a good firewall	358
Table 14-3	Potential Firewall Limitations	360
Section	Firewall Methodologies	361
Section	Stateful Packet Filtering	363
Table 14-8	NAT Terminology	367
Table 14-9	NAT Deployment Options	369
List	Firewall design considerations	370
Table 14-10	Firewall Access Rules	371
List	Firewall rules design guidelines	372
Table 14-11	Results of Inconsistent or Ill-Considered Rule Implementation	373

Complete the Tables and Lists from Memory

Print a copy of Appendix C, "Memory Tables," (found on the CD) or at least the section for this chapter, and complete the tables and lists from memory. Appendix D, "Memory Tables Answer Key," also on the CD, includes completed tables and lists so that you can check your work.

Define Key Terms

Define the following key terms from this chapter, and check your answers in the glossary:

packet filtering, stateful filtering, transparent firewall, NAT, PAT

This chapter covers the following topics:

Cisco IOS Zone-Based Firewalls

Configuring and verifying Cisco IOS Zone-Based Firewalls

CHAPTER 15

Implementing Cisco IOS Zone-Based Firewalls

Cisco has implemented a stateful firewall feature set in Cisco IOS Software called *zone-based firewall (ZBF)*. ZBF has a predecessor called the *context-based access control (CBAC)*, which provided basic firewall features in Cisco IOS Software. ZBF allows the administrator to configure more granular firewall policies and introduces a default deny-all policy that prohibits traffic between firewall security zones until an explicit policy is configured. This chapter is all about understanding and implementing the ZBF feature on an IOS-based router.

"Do I Know This Already?" Quiz

The "Do I Know This Already?" quiz helps you determine your level of knowledge of this chapter's topics before you begin. Table 15-1 details the major topics discussed in this chapter and their corresponding quiz questions.

Table 15-1 "Do I Know This Already?" Section-to-Question Mapping

Foundation Topics Section	Questions
Cisco IOS Zone-Based Firewalls	1–4
Configuring and Verifying Cisco IOS Zone-Based Firewalls	5–8

1. Which zone is implied by default and does not need to be manually created?

    a. Inside

    b. Outside

    c. DMZ

    d. Self

2. If interface number 1 is in zone A, and interface number 2 is in zone B, and there are no **policy** or **service** commands applied yet to the configuration, what is the status of transit traffic that is being routed between these two interfaces?

    a. Denied

    b. Permitted

    c. Inspected

    d. Logged

3. When creating a specific zone pair and applying a policy to it, policy is being implemented on initial traffic in how many directions?

   a. 1

   b. 2

   c. 3

   d. Depends on the policy

4. What is the default policy between an administratively created zone and the self zone?

   a. Deny

   b. Permit

   c. Inspect

   d. Log

5. What is one of the added configuration elements that the Advanced security setting has in the ZBF Wizard that is not included in the Low security setting?

   a. Generic TCP inspection

   b. Generic UDP inspection

   c. Filtering of peer-to-peer networking applications

   d. NAT

6. Why is it that the return traffic, from previously inspected sessions, is allowed back to the user, in spite of not having a zone pair explicitly configured that matches on the return traffic?

   a. Stateful entries (from the initial flow) are matched, which dynamically allows return traffic.

   b. Return traffic is not allowed because it is a firewall.

   c. Explicit ACL rules need to be placed on the return path to allow the return traffic.

   d. A zone pair in the opposite direction of the initial zone pair (including an applied policy) must be applied for return traffic to be allowed.

7. What does the keyword *overload* imply in a NAT configuration?

   a. NAT is willing to take up to 100 percent of available CPU.

   b. PAT is being used.

   c. NAT will provide "best effort" but not guaranteed service, due to an overload.

   d. Static NAT is being used.

8. Which of the following commands shows the current NAT translations on the router?

   a. show translations

   b. show nat translations

   c. show ip nat translations

   d. show ip nat translations *

Foundation Topics

Cisco IOS Zone-Based Firewalls

This section examines the logic and structural components that make up the IOS-based *zone-based firewall (ZBF)*.

How Zone-Based Firewall Operates

With ZBFs, interfaces are placed into zones. Zones are created by the network administrator, using any naming convention that makes sense (although names such as inside, outside, and *demilitarized zone [DMZ]* are quite common). Then policies are specified as to what transit (user) traffic is allowed to be initiated (for example, from users on the inside destined to resources on the outside) and what action the firewall should take, such as inspection (which means to do stateful inspection of the traffic). After traffic is inspected, the reply traffic is allowed back through the firewall because of the stateful filtering feature. The policies are implemented in a single direction (for example, inside to outside). If you want to allow initial traffic in both directions, you create two unidirectional policies for traffic to be allowed and inspected from the inside to the outside, and also from the outside to the inside. You implement two separate policies because the policies themselves are unidirectional.

One benefit of this modular approach is that after policies are in place, if you add additional interfaces, all you need to do is add those interfaces to existing zones, and your policies will automatically be in place.

Specific Features of Zone-Based Firewalls

The ZBF major features include the following:

- Stateful inspection.
- Application inspection.
- Packet filtering.
- URL filtering.
- Transparent firewall (implementation method).
- Support for *virtual routing and forwarding (VRF)*.
- *Access control lists (ACL)* are not required as a filtering method to implement the policy.

Many of these features we have addressed in a previous chapter, and some of the concepts are new. Let's consider a few not yet discussed. *Uniform resource locator (URL)* filtering refers to the ability to control what traffic is permitted or denied (mostly denied) based on the URL that is trying to be accessed by the client. VRFs are virtual routing tables on a Cisco router that can be used to compartmentalize the routing tables on the router instead of keeping all the routes in the global (primary) routing tables. A transparent firewall is implemented at Layer 2 but can still perform analysis of traffic at Layer 3 and higher. You learn more about these details as you progress through this chapter.

nice way to explain trans. firewall

Zones and Why We Need Pairs of Them

A *zone* is a logical area where devices with similar trust levels reside. For example, we could define a DMZ for devices in the DMZ in an organization. A zone is created by the administrator, and then interfaces can be assigned to zones. A zone can have one or more interfaces assigned to it. Any given interface can belong to only a single zone. There is a default zone, called the *self zone*, which is a logical zone. For any packets directed to the router directly (the destination IP represents the packet is for the router), the router automatically considers that traffic to be entering the self zone. In addition, any traffic initiated by the router is considered as leaving the self zone. By default, any traffic to or from the self zone is allowed, but you can change this policy.

For the rest of the administrator-created zones, no traffic is allowed between interfaces in different zones. For interfaces that are members of the same zone, all traffic is permitted by default. So, here is the catch. If you want to allow traffic between two zones, such as between the inside zone (using interfaces facing the inside network) and the outside zone (interfaces facing the Internet or less trusted networks), you must create a policy for traffic between the two zones, and that is where a zone pair comes into play. A zone pair, which is just a configuration on the router, is created identifying traffic sourced from a device in one zone and destined for a device in the second zone. The administrator then associates a set of rules (the policy) for this unidirectional zone pair, such as to inspect the traffic, and then applies that policy to the zone pair.

A small company, with users on the inside network, with the only other connection being the Internet, might want to create two zones, one for the inside and one for the outside. Then they would assign the inside interface to the inside zone, and the outside interface to the outside zone. Then, a policy could be created that specifies that traffic that is initiated from the inside users and going out to the Internet should be inspected and that information should be placed in the stateful database. A zone pair identifying traffic from the inside to the outside would have the policy applied to it, letting it know that the stateful inspection should be done.

A larger company that has a public-facing server may have three interfaces and three zones. The zones may be inside, outside, and DMZ. Compared to the small company, this medium-sized company creates an additional zone pair (from outside to DMZ) and then applies a policy to that zone pair to allow outside users to access the servers on the DMZ.

Figure 15-1 shows an example of a medium-sized company with a DMZ.

15

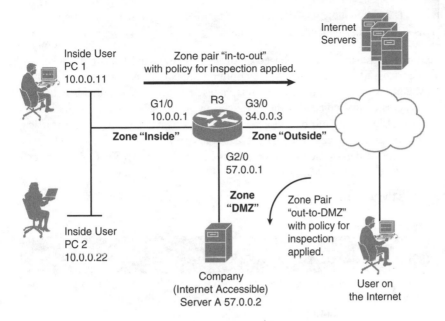

Figure 15-1 *Topology for This ZBF Discussion*

Putting the Pieces Together

Cisco uses a language called the *Cisco Common Classification Policy Language (C3PL)* for the implementation of the policy. This process has three primary components:

- **Class maps:** These are used to identify traffic, such as traffic that should be inspected. Traffic can be matched based on Layer 3 through Layer 7 of the OSI model, including application-based matching. Class maps can also refer to *access control lists (ACL)* for the purpose of identifying traffic or even call upon other class maps. Class maps can have multiple **match** statements. A class map can specify that all **match** statements have to match (which is a *match-all condition*) or can specify that matching any of the entries is considered a match (which is a *match-any condition*). A system-defined class map named class-default can be used that represents all traffic not matched in a more specific (administratively configured) class map.

- **Policy maps:** These are the actions that should be taken on the traffic. Policy maps call on the class maps for the classification of traffic. Policy maps with multiple sections are processed in order. The primary actions that can be implemented by the policy map are inspect (which means that stateful inspection should happen), permit (which means that traffic is permitted but not inspected), drop, or log.

- **Service policies:** This is where you apply the policies, identified from a policy map, to a zone pair. This step actually implements the policy.

If a policy map contains multiple actions, based on different class map–identified traffic, the policy map is processed from top to bottom, applying the actions as traffic matches the class maps. If a specific section of a policy map matches, the action is taken. If traffic does not match, the packet is compared against the next section of the policy map. If none of the sections match the traffic, the default behavior action is taken. The default policy for traffic that is trying to be initiated between two zones (starting in one zone and going to a device in another zone) is an implicit deny. (The exception to this default deny is traffic to or from the built-in "self" zone, which is allowed by default.)

Table 15-2 describes the actions that you may specify in a policy map.

Table 15-2   Policy Map Actions

Policy Action	Description	When to Use It
Inspect	Permit and statefully inspect the traffic	This should be used on transit traffic initiated by users who expect to get replies from devices on the other side of the firewall.
Pass	Permit/allow the traffic but do not create an entry in the stateful database	Traffic that does not need a reply. Also in the case of protocols that do not support inspection, this policy could be applied to the zone pair for specific outbound traffic, and be applied to a second zone pair for inbound traffic.
Drop	Deny the packet	Traffic you do not want to allow between the zones where this policy map is applied.
Log	Log the packets	If you want to see log information about packets that were dropped because of policy, you can add this option.

Service Policies

A service policy is applied to a zone pair. The zone pair represents a unidirectional flow of traffic between two zones. A specific zone pair can have only a single service policy assigned to it. Because the zone pair is unidirectional, the policy map applied to the zone pair (using the **service-policy** command) applies to traffic initiated in one zone going to the other zone in one direction. If reply traffic is desired, the **inspect** action in the policy map should be applied, which will allow stateful inspection, and the reply traffic from the servers will be dynamically allowed (because of the stateful database being referenced).

When a router receives a packet, it normally makes a routing decision and then forwards that packet on its way. If ZBF is configured, the router may or may not forward the packet, based on the stateful table and the policies that are in place. Table 15-3 describes the flow of traffic (packets) being routed between interfaces in various zones, depending on the configuration. This is a good table to commit to memory; it will assist anyone troubleshooting ZBFs. *Ingress* refers to a packet going into an interface of the router, and *egress* refers to a packet that is being sent out of an interface of the router.

Table 15-3   Traffic Interaction Between Zones

Ingress Interface Member of Zone	Egress Interface Member of Zone	Zone Pair Exists, with Applied Policy	Result
No	No	Does not matter	Traffic is forwarded.
No	Yes (any zone)	Does not matter	Traffic is dropped.
Yes (zone A)	Yes (zone A)	Does not matter	Traffic is forwarded.
Yes (zone A)	Yes (zone B)	No	Traffic is dropped.
Yes (zone A)	Yes (zone B)	Yes	Policy is applied. If policy is inspect or pass, the initial traffic is forwarded. If the policy is drop, the initial traffic is dropped.

15

If there is a zone pair that identifies traffic between two zones, and the policy is not applied to the zone pair, the default behavior is to drop traffic as if no zone pair even existed.

Before we go any further, I want to show you a configuration that includes the following ZBF components:

- Zones
- Interfaces that are members of zones
- Class maps that identify traffic
- Policy maps that use class maps to identify traffic and then specify the actions which should take place
- Zone pairs, which identify a unidirectional traffic flow, beginning from devices in one zone and being routed out an interface in a second zone
- Service policy, which associates a policy map with a zone pair

Now that you know all the pieces, it is time to take a look at the commands for the policy of allowing users on the inside to access the Internet (as shown earlier in Figure 15-1). Example 15-1 both shows and explains this.

Example 15-1   *Components That Make Up the ZBF*

```
! The class map "classifies" or "identifies" the traffic
! In this example, this class map will match on either TELNET traffic or
! any type of ICMP traffic
R3(config)# class-map type inspect match-any MY-CLASS-MAP
R3(config-cmap)# match protocol telnet
R3(config-cmap)# match protocol icmp
R3(config-cmap)# exit


! The policy map calls on a specific class map that it wants to use
! to identify which traffic the policy applies to, and then specifies the
```

```
! policy action.   In this example, it is to inspect the traffic
R3(config)# policy-map type inspect MY-POLICY-MAP
R3(config-pmap)# class type inspect MY-CLASS-MAP
R3(config-pmap-c)# inspect
R3(config-pmap-c)# exit
R3(config-pmap)# exit


! Next we create the security zones, they can be named whatever you want to
! name them.  In this example, I named them inside and outside.
R3(config)# zone security inside
R3(config-sec-zone)# exit
R3(config)# zone security outside
R3(config-sec-zone)# exit


! Create the zone-pair, specifying the zones and the direction (from where
! to where)
R3(config)# zone-pair security in-to-out source inside destination outside


! Use the service-policy command in zone-pair configuration mode to apply
! the policy map you want to use for traffic that matches this zone-pair
R3(config-sec-zone-pair)# service-policy type inspect MY-POLICY-MAP
R3(config-sec-zone-pair)# exit


! Configure the interfaces, so they become members of the respective zones
R3(config)# interface GigabitEthernet3/0
R3(config-if)# description Belongs to outside zone
R3(config-if)# zone-member security outside
R3(config-if)# exit
R3(config)# interface GigabitEthernet1/0
R3(config-if)# description  Belongs to inside zone
R3(config-if)# zone-member security inside
R3(config-if)# exit
R3(config)#
```

The preceding policy performs stateful inspection for traffic from the inside users for traffic going to the Internet if that traffic is Telnet traffic (which is TCP port 23) or is *Internet Control Message Protocol (ICMP)* traffic. ACLs can be used by the class map for matching and generic protocol matches such as *User Datagram Protocol (UDP)* or *Transfer Control Protocol (TCP)*. Application-specific matching adds the ability for the firewall to detect additional communication channels that may be initialized by the outside devices, such as in the case of inspecting FTP, where the server may initiate the data connection on a port mutually agreed to by the client and the FTP server.

The Self Zone

Traffic directed to the router itself (as opposed to traffic going through the router as transit traffic that is not destined directly to the router) involves the self zone. Traffic destined to the router, regardless of which interface is used, is considered to be going to the self zone. Traffic being sourced from the router is considered to be coming from the self zone. By default, all traffic to the self zone or from the self zone (which really means all traffic from the router or to the router) is allowed. However, if you want to create policies related to traffic to or from this self zone, you do it the same way by creating zone pairs and assigning a policy to the zone pair. Table 15-4 describes self zone traffic behavior.

Table 15-4   Self Zone Traffic Behavior

Source Traffic Member of Zone	Destination Traffic Member of Zone	Zone Pair Exists, with a Policy Applied	Result
Self	Zone A	No	Traffic is passed.
Zone A	Self	No	Traffic is passed.
Self	Zone A	Yes	Policy is applied.
Zone A	Self	Yes	Policy is applied.

Regarding the self zone, if there is a zone pair but no policy is applied, the default behavior is to forward all traffic (which is different from the traffic between manually created zones). When configuring a zone pair that includes the self zone, the administrator must allow management traffic to be allowed so as to prevent administrative connections from being denied.

Configuring and Verifying Cisco IOS Zone-Based Firewalls

This section examines configuring the IOS ZBF feature from both *Cisco Configuration Professional (CCP)* and the *command-line interface (CLI)*.

First Things First

As discussed earlier in this book, having a policy or a plan in place first is a good idea before you configure anything. Remember that the policy you implement on the firewall is supposed to reflect the business needs of the company. The previous section examined a basic implementation of ZBFs, and that Example 15-1 (in that section) is a fantastic reference.

You can use CCP for an easy walkthrough of the configuration of ZBF. We use the wizard for the configuration, and then we use the CLI for the verification. One thing you will notice is that the wizard adds a lot of additional configuration that may not apply directly to your network. One recommendation, if you are going to use CCP, is to use the wizards but take the recommended commands that CCP is about to apply and put those into a text editor. Edit out the pieces that are not needed or wanted, and then manually paste the configuration in after you have verified that it is perfect. For certification, it is recommended that you become familiar with interpreting a ZBF configuration, using CCP, to be able to determine what actions will be taken on a packet going through the firewall. As you will see in the section that follows, CCP will push many policy rules based on the setting chosen. For more granular policy control, you could configure ZBF using the CLI.

We use the same topology as shown earlier in the chapter (refer to Figure 15-1).

Using CCP to Configure the Firewall

In CCP, you select the router that you want to configure from the drop-down list and navigate to **Configure > Security > Firewall > Firewall**, as shown in Figure 15-2.

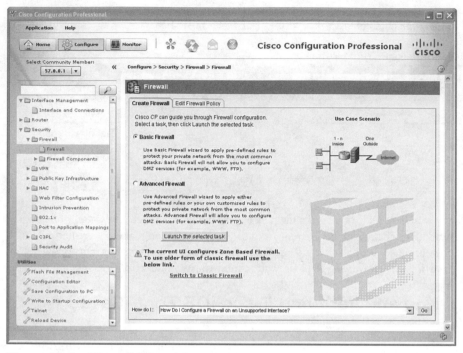

Figure 15-2　*Firewall Wizard Page in CCP*

The Basic Firewall option involves two interfaces, which are in different zones. The Advanced Firewall option enables you to apply predefined rules and allows you to configure a third zone such as a DMZ. The basic concept of a ZBF is that we're dealing with only two interfaces at a time. Each pair of interfaces has a zone pair for each direction for which you want to apply policy. Working with multiple interfaces and multiple zones is simply repeating the process focusing on one zone pair at a time, applying the policies you want to each zone pair.

There is an option to configure the older method of IOS-based firewall, which is the CBAC. You can select it by clicking the **Switch to Classic Firewall** link on this page. We are not going backward today, and so we click the **Launch of the Selected Task** button; and because the **Basic Firewall** radio button was selected, the wizard presents the welcome screen shown in Figure 15-3.

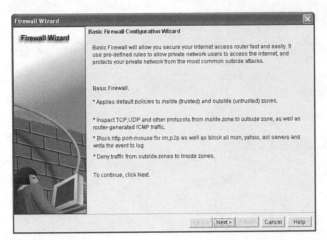

Figure 15-3 *Welcome Screen to Basic Firewall Wizard*

From here, click the **Next** button, at which point you are asked which interfaces are facing the trusted network and which interfaces are facing the untrusted network, as shown in Figure 15-4.

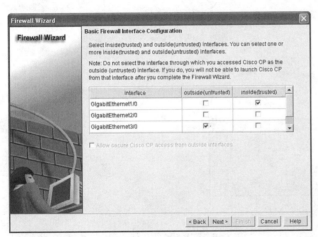

Figure 15-4 *Specifying Which Interfaces Connect to Trusted or Untrusted Networks*

Note that if an interface is not identified as being part of a zone, no traffic is allowed between the unspecified interface and interfaces in any other zones. In the preceding example, interface Gigabit Ethernet 2/0 cannot forward traffic to (route between) either of the other two interfaces. If that is your intention, you are okay. This configuration is such in this example for demonstration purposes only. After you click **Next**, you are given a notification that this interface is not a member of the zone, as shown in Figure 15-5.

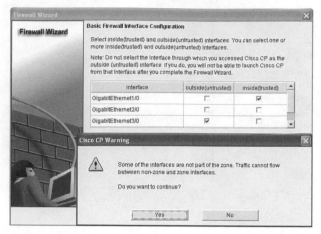

Figure 15-5   *Warning Message About an Interface Not Belonging to a Zone*

After you click **Yes** to continue, if your router supports *Call Manager Express (CME)*, even if it is not configured, you may be presented a warning message, as shown in Figure 15-6.

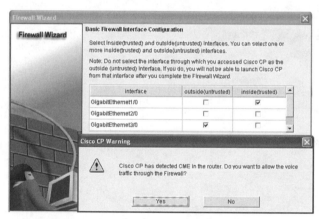

Figure 15-6   *Warning Message About CME*

If this CME is not applicable to your network, you can click the **No** button. If it is applicable, you can click **Yes**, and CCP will configure the additional policies to allow this traffic through the firewall. After answering this dialog box, you are next presented with a warning message letting you know that CCP cannot access this router through interfaces connected to the untrusted networks. In our case, that is G3/0, as indicated in the warning in Figure 15-7.

After you click the **OK** button, the wizard asks you which level of security you want to implement, as shown in Figure 15-8.

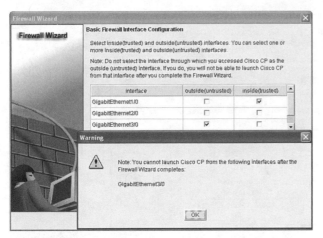

Figure 15-7 *Warning Message That Untrusted Interfaces Will Not Support CCP Access*

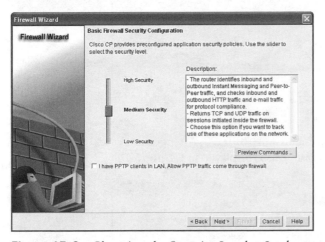

Figure 15-8 *Choosing the Security Level to Implement*

When configuring the ZBF Wizard, you can choose from three security levels:

- **High Security:** With this setting, the firewall identifies and drops instant messaging and peer-to-peer traffic. It does application inspection for web and e-mail traffic and drops noncompliant traffic. It does generic inspection of TCP and UDP applications.

- **Medium Security:** This is similar to the High Security option, but it does not check web and e-mail traffic for protocol compliance.

- **Low Security:** The router does not perform any application layer inspection. It does do generic TCP and UDP inspection.

It is important to note that the details of exactly what is implemented from each of these options are totally under the control of CCP. It is quite possible that in CCP any future updates may modify the details of all or any of these settings from the wizard. As the administrator of your network, it is up to you to confirm exactly what configurations will be applied to the router.

For this example, we chose the **Medium Security** option from the wizard. After you click **Next**, if a *Domain Name System (DNS)* server is not configured, the wizard asks you to provide the IP address of a DNS server for the router to use, as shown in Figure 15-9.

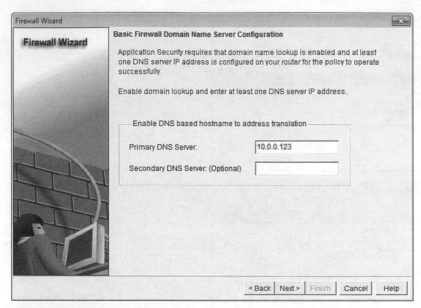

Figure 15-9   *Configuring a DNS Server*

In this example, the DNS server's IP address is 10.0.0.123. After you click **Next**, a summary of the features to be implemented is shown, as displayed in Figure 15-10.

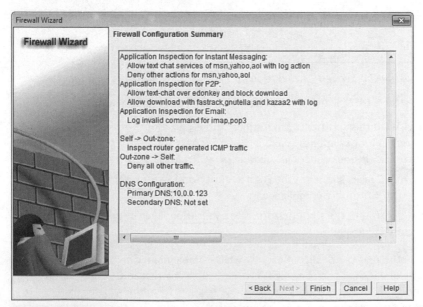

Figure 15-10   *Summary Page from ZBF Wizard*

After you click **Finish**, the wizard may provide one or more warnings about traffic that may be filtered by the policy and then delivers the configuration to the router.

Now for the interesting news. CCP created several pages of commands to implement the policy. Example 15-2 shows the literal commands that CCP created and applied.

Example 15-2 *Literal CLI Commands That the CCP Basic Zone-Based Firewall Creates*

```
! although this is an incredible amount of output, the basic concepts are
! the same as shown in more basic Example 15-1.

access-list 100 remark CCP_ACL Category=128
access-list 100 permit ip host 255.255.255.255 any
access-list 100 permit ip 127.0.0.0 0.255.255.255 any
access-list 100 permit ip 34.0.0.0 0.0.0.255 any
ip domain lookup
ip name-server 10.0.0.123
parameter-map type protocol-info yahoo-servers
 server name scs.msg.yahoo.com
 server name scsa.msg.yahoo.com
 server name scsb.msg.yahoo.com
 server name scsc.msg.yahoo.com
 server name scsd.msg.yahoo.com
 server name cs16.msg.dcn.yahoo.com
 server name cs19.msg.dcn.yahoo.com
 server name cs42.msg.dcn.yahoo.com
 server name cs53.msg.dcn.yahoo.com
 server name cs54.msg.dcn.yahoo.com
 server name ads1.vip.scd.yahoo.com
 server name radio1.launch.vip.dal.yahoo.com
 server name in1.msg.vip.re2.yahoo.com
 server name data1.my.vip.sc5.yahoo.com
 server name address1.pim.vip.mud.yahoo.com
 server name edit.messenger.yahoo.com
 server name messenger.yahoo.com
 server name http.pager.yahoo.com
 server name privacy.yahoo.com
 server name csa.yahoo.com
 server name csb.yahoo.com
 server name csc.yahoo.com
 exit
parameter-map type protocol-info aol-servers
 server name login.oscar.aol.com
 server name toc.oscar.aol.com
 server name oam-d09a.blue.aol.com
 exit
parameter-map type protocol-info msn-servers
```

```
  server name messenger.hotmail.com
  server name gateway.messenger.hotmail.com
  server name webmessenger.msn.com
  exit
class-map type inspect match-any ccp-cls-protocol-im
 match protocol ymsgr yahoo-servers
 match protocol msnmsgr msn-servers
 match protocol aol aol-servers
 exit
class-map type inspect edonkey match-any ccp-app-edonkeydownload
 match file-transfer
 exit
class-map type inspect match-any ccp-h323annexe-inspect
 match protocol h323-annexe
 exit
class-map type inspect http match-any ccp-http-blockparam
 match request port-misuse im
 match request port-misuse p2p
 match req-resp protocol-violation
 exit
class-map type inspect aol match-any ccp-app-aol-otherservices
 match service any
 exit
class-map type inspect match-all ccp-protocol-pop3
 match protocol pop3
 exit
class-map type inspect msnmsgr match-any ccp-app-msn
 match service text-chat
 exit
class-map type inspect match-any ccp-cls-icmp-access
 match protocol icmp
 match protocol tcp
 match protocol udp
 exit
class-map type inspect match-all ccp-icmp-access
 match class-map ccp-cls-icmp-access
 exit
class-map type inspect match-all ccp-protocol-imap
 match protocol imap
 exit
class-map type inspect match-any ccp-cls-insp-traffic
 match protocol cuseeme
 match protocol dns
 match protocol ftp
 match protocol https
 match protocol icmp
```

```
 match protocol imap
 match protocol pop3
 match protocol netshow
 match protocol shell
 match protocol realmedia
 match protocol rtsp
 match protocol smtp extended
 match protocol sql-net
 match protocol streamworks
 match protocol tftp
 match protocol vdolive
 match protocol tcp
 match protocol udp
 exit
class-map type inspect aol match-any ccp-app-aol
 match service text-chat
 exit
class-map type inspect edonkey match-any ccp-app-edonkey
 match file-transfer
 match text-chat
 match search-file-name
 exit
class-map type inspect kazaa2 match-any ccp-app-kazaa2
 match file-transfer
 exit
class-map type inspect fasttrack match-any ccp-app-fasttrack
 match file-transfer
 exit
class-map type inspect match-any ccp-h323-inspect
 match protocol h323
 exit
class-map type inspect match-any ccp-h323nxg-inspect
 match protocol h323-nxg
 exit
class-map type inspect match-all ccp-insp-traffic
 match class-map ccp-cls-insp-traffic
 exit
class-map type inspect edonkey match-any ccp-app-edonkeychat
 match search-file-name
 match text-chat
 exit
class-map type inspect match-any ccp-h225ras-inspect
 match protocol h225ras
 exit
class-map type inspect msnmsgr match-any ccp-app-msn-otherservices
 match service any
```

```
 exit
class-map type inspect ymsgr match-any ccp-app-yahoo-otherservices
 match service any
 exit
class-map type inspect http match-any ccp-app-httpmethods
 match request method bcopy
 match request method bdelete
 match request method bmove
 match request method bpropfind
 match request method bproppatch
 match request method connect
 match request method copy
 match request method delete
 match request method edit
 match request method getattribute
 match request method getattributenames
 match request method getproperties
 match request method index
 match request method lock
 match request method mkcol
 match request method mkdir
 match request method move
 match request method notify
 match request method options
 match request method poll
 match request method propfind
 match request method proppatch
 match request method put
 match request method revadd
 match request method revlabel
 match request method revlog
 match request method revnum
 match request method save
 match request method search
 match request method setattribute
 match request method startrev
 match request method stoprev
 match request method subscribe
 match request method trace
 match request method unedit
 match request method unlock
 match request method unsubscribe
 exit
class-map type inspect match-any ccp-skinny-inspect
 match protocol skinny
 exit
class-map type inspect match-all ccp-protocol-im
```

```
 match class-map ccp-cls-protocol-im
 exit
class-map type inspect match-any ccp-cls-protocol-p2p
 match protocol edonkey signature
 match protocol gnutella signature
 match protocol kazaa2 signature
 match protocol fasttrack signature
 match protocol bittorrent signature
 exit
class-map type inspect http match-any ccp-http-allowparam
 match request port-misuse tunneling
 exit
class-map type inspect gnutella match-any ccp-app-gnutella
 match file-transfer
 exit
class-map type inspect match-any ccp-sip-inspect
 match protocol sip
 exit
class-map type inspect match-all ccp-invalid-src
 match access-group 100
 exit
class-map type inspect ymsgr match-any ccp-app-yahoo
 match service text-chat
 exit
class-map type inspect pop3 match-any ccp-app-pop3
 match invalid-command
 exit
class-map type inspect imap match-any ccp-app-imap
 match invalid-command
 exit
class-map type inspect match-all ccp-protocol-p2p
 match class-map ccp-cls-protocol-p2p
 exit
class-map type inspect match-all ccp-protocol-http
 match protocol http
 exit
policy-map type inspect http ccp-action-app-http
 class type inspect http ccp-http-blockparam
  log
  reset
  exit
 class type inspect http ccp-app-httpmethods
  log
  reset
  exit
 class type inspect http ccp-http-allowparam
  log
```

```
   allow
   exit
  exit
 policy-map type inspect imap ccp-action-imap
  class type inspect imap ccp-app-imap
   log
   exit
  exit
 policy-map type inspect pop3 ccp-action-pop3
  class type inspect pop3 ccp-app-pop3
   log
   exit
  exit
 policy-map type inspect p2p ccp-action-app-p2p
  class type inspect edonkey ccp-app-edonkeychat
   log
   allow
   exit
  class type inspect edonkey ccp-app-edonkeydownload
   log
   allow
   exit
  class type inspect fasttrack ccp-app-fasttrack
   log
   allow
   exit
  class type inspect gnutella ccp-app-gnutella
   log
   allow
   exit
  class type inspect kazaa2 ccp-app-kazaa2
   log
   allow
   exit
  exit
 policy-map type inspect im ccp-action-app-im
  class type inspect aol ccp-app-aol
   log
   allow
   exit
  class type inspect msnmsgr ccp-app-msn
   log
   allow
   exit
  class type inspect ymsgr ccp-app-yahoo
   log
   allow
```

```
  exit
 class type inspect aol ccp-app-aol-otherservices
  log
  reset
  exit
 class type inspect msnmsgr ccp-app-msn-otherservices
  log
  reset
  exit
 class type inspect ymsgr ccp-app-yahoo-otherservices
  log
  reset
  exit
 exit
policy-map type inspect ccp-inspect
 class type inspect ccp-invalid-src
  drop log
  exit
 class type inspect ccp-protocol-http
  no drop
  inspect
  service-policy http ccp-action-app-http
  exit
 class type inspect ccp-protocol-imap
  no drop
  inspect
  service-policy imap ccp-action-imap
  exit
 class type inspect ccp-protocol-pop3
  no drop
  inspect
  service-policy pop3 ccp-action-pop3
  exit
 class type inspect ccp-protocol-p2p
  no drop
  inspect
  service-policy p2p ccp-action-app-p2p
  exit
 class type inspect ccp-protocol-im
  no drop
  inspect
  service-policy im ccp-action-app-im
  exit
 class type inspect ccp-insp-traffic
  no drop
  inspect
  exit
```

```
 class type inspect ccp-sip-inspect
  no drop
  inspect
  exit
 class type inspect ccp-h323-inspect
  no drop
  inspect
  exit
 class type inspect ccp-h323annexe-inspect
  no drop
  inspect
  exit
 class type inspect ccp-h225ras-inspect
  no drop
  inspect
  exit
 class type inspect ccp-h323nxg-inspect
  no drop
  inspect
  exit
 class type inspect ccp-skinny-inspect
  no drop
  inspect
  exit
 exit
policy-map type inspect ccp-permit
 class class-default
 exit
policy-map type inspect ccp-permit-icmpreply
 class type inspect ccp-icmp-access
  no drop
  inspect
  exit
 class class-default
  no drop
  pass
  exit
 exit
zone security in-zone
zone security out-zone
zone-pair security ccp-zp-out-self source out-zone destination self
 service-policy type inspect ccp-permit
 exit
zone-pair security ccp-zp-in-out source in-zone destination out-zone
 service-policy type inspect ccp-inspect
 exit
```

```
zone-pair security ccp-zp-self-out source self destination out-zone
 service-policy type inspect ccp-permit-icmpreply
 exit
interface GigabitEthernet3/0
 description $FW_OUTSIDE$
 zone-member security out-zone
 exit
interface GigabitEthernet1/0
 description $FW_INSIDE$
 zone-member security in-zone
 exit
```

Verifying the Firewall

You can verify the firewall from both the CCP and the command line. In the bonus material included with this book, there is a video on using CCP to interpret the configuration of a ZBF. This video reviews the concepts and walks you through the details of how and where to find all the components. Review the video and practice with CCP yourself to confirm that you can interpret a ZBF policy by navigating through and looking at the *graphical user interface (GUI)* of CCP.

To edit or verify the policy within CCP, navigate to **Configure > Security > Firewall > Firewall** and click **Edit**, as shown in Figure 15-11.

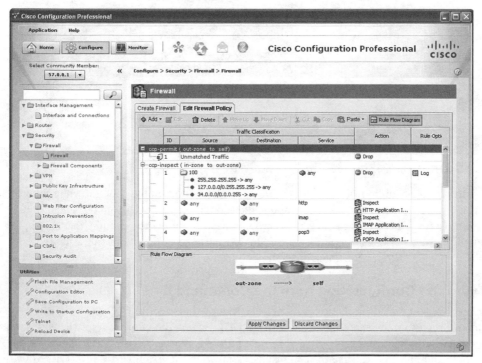

Figure 15-11 *Verifying the Firewall Configuration from Within CCP*

If logging is enabled and you are logging to a syslog server, you could verify any logged events by looking at those logs at the server.

The CCP Application menu contains a drop-down menu that enables you to set user preferences such as log level, show community at startup, and show CLI preview parameters. You can view log messages on the router under the Log Monitoring section by navigating to **Monitor > Router > Logging**.

To see the firewall status and current activity, you can use the Monitor feature within CCP. To access this, navigate to **Monitor > Security > Firewall Status** and select the options you want to monitor. Figure 15-12 shows an example of this feature.

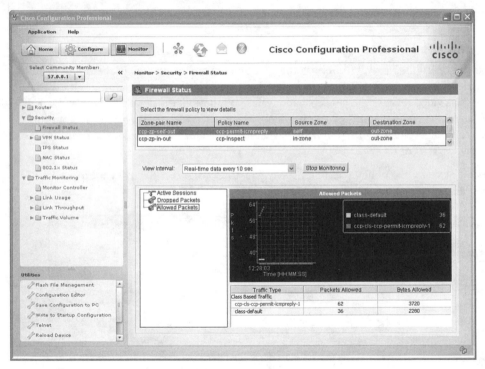

Figure 15-12   *Monitoring the Firewall Through CCP*

A button enables you to stop and start the monitoring (located on the page shown in Figure 15-12). The output shown in the figure about allowed packets and a custom class map is just an example from a customized firewall policy and may not reflect the defaults that are implemented by the ZBF Wizard. It is shown here for the purpose of demonstrating where to go in the GUI to monitor traffic going through the firewall.

Verifying the Configuration from the Command Line

For certification purposes, the focus of ZBFs is from the perspective of CCP. So, in preparation for the exam, be sure to practice with the GUI. Having the knowledge of the CLI is more relevant to a live environment, and for that purpose, it is also important to know. From the command line, you can use the commands as shown in the Example 15-3 to verify your ZBF components.

Example 15-3   *Verifying the Configuration from the Command Line*

```
R3# show class-map type inspect
 Class Map type inspect match-any ccp-cls-protocol-p2p (id 27)
   Match protocol edonkey signature
   Match protocol gnutella signature
   Match protocol kazaa2 signature
   Match protocol fasttrack signature
   Match protocol bittorrent signature

 Class Map type inspect match-any ccp-skinny-inspect (id 25)
   Match protocol skinny

 Class Map type inspect match-all ccp-insp-traffic (id 19)
   Match class-map ccp-cls-insp-traffic

 Class Map type inspect match-any ccp-h323nxg-inspect (id 18)
   Match protocol h323-nxg

 Class Map type inspect match-any ccp-cls-icmp-access (id 8)
   Match protocol icmp
   Match protocol tcp
   Match protocol udp

 Class Map type inspect match-any ccp-cls-protocol-im (id 1)
   Match protocol ymsgr yahoo-servers
   Match protocol msnmsgr msn-servers
   Match protocol aol aol-servers

 Class Map type inspect match-all ccp-protocol-pop3 (id 6)
   Match protocol pop3

 Class Map type inspect match-any ccp-h225ras-inspect (id 21)
   Match protocol h225ras

 Class Map type inspect match-any ccp-h323annexe-inspect (id 3)
   Match protocol h323-annexe

 Class Map type inspect match-any ccp-cls-insp-traffic (id 12)
   Match protocol cuseeme
   Match protocol dns
   Match protocol ftp
   Match protocol https
   Match protocol imap
   Match protocol pop3
   Match protocol netshow
```

15

```
      Match protocol shell
      Match protocol realmedia
      Match protocol rtsp
      Match protocol smtp extended
      Match protocol sql-net
      Match protocol streamworks
      Match protocol tftp
      Match protocol vdolive
      Match protocol tcp
      Match protocol udp

  Class Map type inspect match-all ccp-protocol-p2p (id 35)
     Match class-map ccp-cls-protocol-p2p

  Class Map type inspect match-any ccp-h323-inspect (id 17)
     Match protocol h323

  Class Map type inspect match-all ccp-protocol-im (id 26)
     Match class-map ccp-cls-protocol-im

  Class Map type inspect match-all ccp-icmp-access (id 9)
     Match class-map ccp-cls-icmp-access

  Class Map type inspect match-all ccp-invalid-src (id 31)
     Match access-group  100

  Class Map type inspect match-any ccp-sip-inspect (id 30)
     Match protocol sip

  Class Map type inspect match-all ccp-protocol-imap (id 11)
     Match protocol imap

  Class Map type inspect match-all ccp-protocol-http (id 36)
     Match protocol http


  R3#



  ! Note, although there is a lot of output, the objective is to understand
  ! the commands that allow you to see what is happening from the CLI
  ! In the example content below, we see the detailed information
  ! regarding a telnet session that is currently going through the firewall,
  ! as well as a PING that is being sent through the firewall.
  R3# show policy-map type inspect zone-pair ccp-zp-in-out sessions

  policy exists on zp ccp-zp-in-out
```

```
  Zone-pair: ccp-zp-in-out

   Service-policy inspect : ccp-inspect
<snip>

   Inspect

    Class-map: ccp-insp-traffic (match-all)
      Match: class-map match-any ccp-cls-insp-traffic
        Match: protocol cuseeme
          0 packets, 0 bytes
          30 second rate 0 bps
        Match: protocol dns
          0 packets, 0 bytes
          30 second rate 0 bps
        Match: protocol ftp
          0 packets, 0 bytes
          30 second rate 0 bps
        Match: protocol https
          0 packets, 0 bytes
          30 second rate 0 bps
        Match: protocol imap
          0 packets, 0 bytes
          30 second rate 0 bps
        Match: protocol pop3
          0 packets, 0 bytes
          30 second rate 0 bps
        Match: protocol netshow
          0 packets, 0 bytes
          30 second rate 0 bps
        Match: protocol shell
          0 packets, 0 bytes
          30 second rate 0 bps
        Match: protocol realmedia
          0 packets, 0 bytes
          30 second rate 0 bps
        Match: protocol rtsp
          0 packets, 0 bytes
          30 second rate 0 bps
        Match: protocol smtp extended
          0 packets, 0 bytes
          30 second rate 0 bps
        Match: protocol sql-net
          0 packets, 0 bytes
          30 second rate 0 bps
        Match: protocol streamworks
```

15

```
            0 packets, 0 bytes
            30 second rate 0 bps
        Match: protocol tftp
            0 packets, 0 bytes
            30 second rate 0 bps
        Match: protocol vdolive
            0 packets, 0 bytes
            30 second rate 0 bps
        Match: protocol tcp
            0 packets, 0 bytes
            30 second rate 0 bps
        Match: protocol udp
            0 packets, 0 bytes
            30 second rate 0 bps


    Inspect

        Number of Established Sessions = 2
        Established Sessions
          Session 673BBD00 (10.0.0.11:29333)=>(34.0.0.4:23) tacacs:tcp SIS_OPEN
            Created 00:02:20, Last heard 00:00:37
            Bytes sent (initiator:responder) [39:273572]
          Session 673BC100 (10.0.0.22:8)=>(34.0.0.4:0) icmp SIS_OPEN
            Created 00:00:40, Last heard 00:00:00
            ECHO request
            Bytes sent (initiator:responder) [69912:69912]


 <snip>
```

Implementing NAT in Addition to ZBF

You can add *Network Address Translation (NAT)* to the same router that is performing ZBF. The simplest way to implement NAT is to use the outside interface of the firewall and overload on that address (*Port Address Translation [PAT]*). All packets going through the firewall toward the Internet would appear to the Internet as coming from the single global address of the router. The router may have obtained its global IP address via *Dynamic Host Configuration Protocol (DHCP)* from the service provider, or it may be statically configured. You can verify the address by looking at the details of the interface to determine how the IP address was obtained and what the current IP address is.

To configure NAT, navigate to **Configure > Router > NAT**, and from there, launch the basic NAT Wizard, as shown in Figure 15-13.

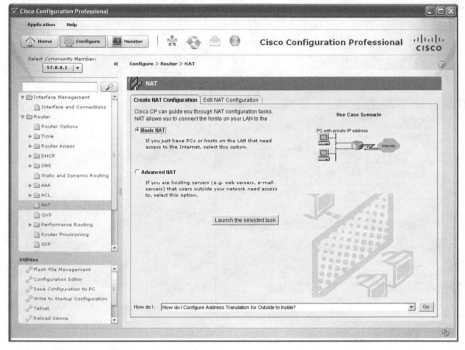

Figure 15-13 *Basic NAT Wizard*

If you have a DMZ or are hosting a server (on a third interface) and that server needs specific address translation so that users on the outside may access it, you could use the Advanced NAT Wizard to configure that in addition to the Basic NAT for the inside users. Basic NAT is just for inside users accessing outside resources.

For this example, we use the Basic NAT Wizard. When we click the **Launch the Selected Task** button, we are presented with the welcome screen for the Basic NAT Wizard, as shown in Figure 15-14.

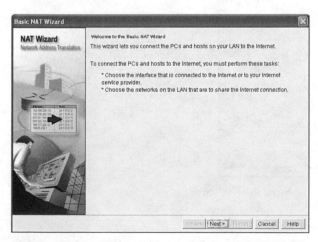

Figure 15-14 *Welcome Screen of the Basic NAT Wizard*

When we click **Next** to continue, the router needs to know which of our interfaces are connecting to the Internet. (This will be our untrusted interface if we have configured ZBF.) The wizard also wants to know which internal networks will be permitted to be translated as packets from devices on those networks are routed through the firewall and out toward the Internet. Figure 15-15 shows an example of selecting these interfaces.

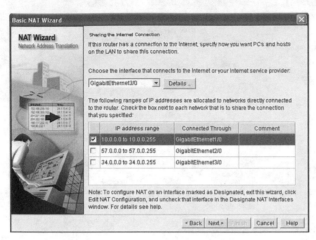

Figure 15-15 *Selecting the Appropriate Interfaces for NAT*

If we want to allow traffic from the DMZ network to also be translated to this single IP address on the outside interface of the router, we can just add it by placing a check in the check box next to that network address range.

When we click **Next** to continue, the wizard presents a summary of the configuration it is about to implement, as shown in Figure 15-16.

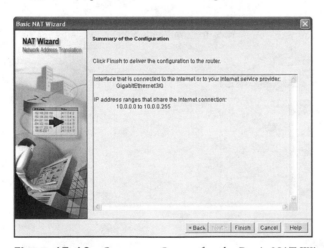

Figure 15-16 *Summary Screen for the Basic NAT Wizard*

Click the **Finish** button to continue. You can also implement NAT from the CLI. The configuration that we just implemented via CCP is implemented with the commands shown in Example 15-4.

Example 15-4 *Implementing NAT*

```
! The ACL is a classifier that is simply identifying (matching) on packets
! that have a source IP address from the 10.0.0.0/24 network.
R3(config)# access-list 2 permit 10.0.0.0 0.0.0.255


! The  next two commands tell the router which of its interfaces from a NAT
! perspective are connected to the inside versus the outside.
! The normal configuration is to translate packets coming from the inside
! that are going to be outside. This is also referred to as inside NAT
! notice also that the term NAT  is often used,  even when in reality
! we are using port address translation (PAT),  as is the case in this
! example
R3(config)# interface GigabitEthernet3/0
R3(config-if)# ip nat outside
R3(config-if)# exit
R3(config)# interface GigabitEthernet1/0
R3(config-if)# ip nat inside
R3(config-if)# exit


! this next rule says that if traffic matches access list number 2
! and the traffic is going to be routed out of the outside interface
! then the source IP address should be translated to the current IP address
! that is configured on the outside interface of the router.
! The overload keyword indicates  PAT,  and can support thousands of
! internal clients
R3(config)# ip nat inside source list 2 interface GigabitEthernet3/0 overload
```

Verifying Whether NAT Is Working

To verify the configuration, we could show the running configuration from the command line or view it inside CCP. To do the latter, navigate to **Configure > Router > NAT** and select the **Edit NAT Configuration** table. Figure 15-17 shows our current configuration.

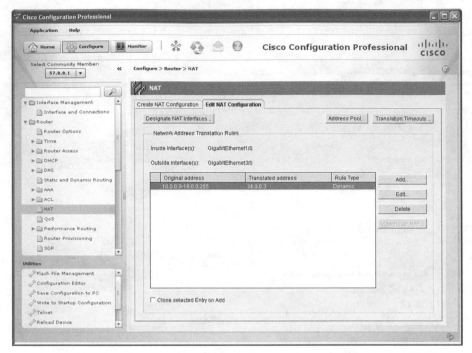

Figure 15-17 *Verifying Our NAT Configuration from Within CCP*

If you actually have traffic flowing through the router from the inside to the Internet, you should be able to see those translations, as shown in Example 15-5.

Example 15-5 *Viewing Existing Translations*

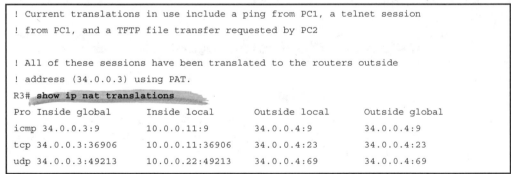

```
! Current translations in use include a ping from PC1, a telnet session
! from PC1, and a TFTP file transfer requested by PC2


! All of these sessions have been translated to the routers outside
! address (34.0.0.3) using PAT.
R3# show ip nat translations
Pro Inside global      Inside local      Outside local      Outside global
icmp 34.0.0.3:9        10.0.0.11:9       34.0.0.4:9         34.0.0.4:9
tcp 34.0.0.3:36906     10.0.0.11:36906   34.0.0.4:23        34.0.0.4:23
udp 34.0.0.3:49213     10.0.0.22:49213   34.0.0.4:69        34.0.0.4:69
```

Exam Preparation Tasks

Review All the Key Topics

Review the most important topics from this chapter, denoted with a Key Topic icon. Table 15-5 lists these key topics.

Table 15-5   Key Topics

Key Topic Element	Description	Page Number
Text	Overview of how the ZBF operates	379
List	Specific features of the ZBF	379
List	Putting the pieces together	381
Table 15-2	Policy Map Actions	382
Table 15-3	Traffic Interaction Between Zones	383
Example 15-1	Components That Make Up the ZBF	383
Table 15-4	Self Zone Traffic Behavior	385
List	ZBF Wizard configurable security levels	389
Example 15-4	Implementing NAT	407
Example 15-5	Viewing Existing Translations	408

Complete the Tables and Lists from Memory

Print a copy of Appendix C, "Memory Tables," (found on the CD) or at least the section for this chapter, and complete the tables and lists from memory. Appendix D, "Memory Tables Answer Key," also on the CD, includes completed tables and lists so that you can check your work.

Define Key Terms

Define the following key terms from this chapter, and check your answers in the glossary:

zones, zone pairs, class map type inspect, policy map type inspect, service policy, stateful inspection, PAT

Command Reference to Check Your Memory

This section includes the most important configuration and EXEC commands covered in this chapter. To see how well you have memorized the commands as a side effect of your other studies, cover the left side of Table 15-6 with a piece of paper, read the descriptions on the right side, and see whether you remember the commands.

Table 15-6   Command Reference

Command	Description
show class-map type inspect	Show ZBF-related class maps.
show policy-map type inspect	Show ZBF-related policy maps.
class-map type inspect match-any MY-CLASS-MAP	Create a ZBF-related class map that will be a match if *any* of its entries is a match.
policy-map type inspect MY-POLICY-MAP	Create a ZBF-related policy map.
class type inspect MY-CLASS-MAP	Used inside of a ZBF policy map to call on the classification services of a zone-based class map.
zone-pair security in-to-out source inside destination outside	Create a zone pair that identifies an initial unidirectional flow of traffic.
show ip nat translations	Show current active address translations occurring on the router.

This chapter covers the following topics:

The ASA appliance family and features

ASA firewall fundamentals

Configuring the ASA

CHAPTER 16

Configuring Basic Firewall Policies on Cisco ASA

Cisco over the years has had a dedicated firewall appliance. Many years ago, it was a device named the PIX. As technology improved, a new device was created that leveraged all the features of the PIX and added some new ones. This new device is the *Adaptive Security Appliance (ASA)*. It is pronounced as if you are saying the three individual letters of *A, S, A*. It is important to understand the basics of a device before you configure it, so that is what we do here in this chapter. You first learn the logic of what the ASA goes through as it makes its determination about forwarding or filtering, and then once you understand that, we configure and implement a security policy and verify the security policy with the built-in tool called Packet Tracer.

"Do I Know This Already?" Quiz

The "Do I Know This Already?" quiz helps you determine your level of knowledge of this chapter's topics before you begin. Table 16-1 details the major topics discussed in this chapter and their corresponding quiz questions.

Table 16-1 "Do I Know This Already?" Section-to-Question Mapping

Foundation Topics Section	Questions
The ASA Appliance Family and Features	1–3
ASA Firewall Fundamentals	4–7
Configuring the ASA	8–10

1. Which of the following features does the Cisco ASA provide? (Choose all that apply.)

    a. Simple packet filtering using standard or extended access lists

    b. Layer 2 transparent implementation

    c. Support for remote-access SSL VPN connections

    d. Support for site-to-site SSL VPN connections

2. Which of the following Cisco ASA models are designed for small and branch offices? (Choose all that apply.)

    a. 5505

    b. 5512-X

    c. 5555-X

    d. 5585-X with SSP10

3. When used in an access policy, which component could identify multiple servers?

    a. Stateful filtering

    b. Application awareness

    c. Object groups

    d. DHCP services

4. Which of the following is an accurate description of the word *inbound* as it relates to an ASA? (Choose all that apply.)

    a. Traffic from a device that is located on a high-security interface

    b. Traffic from a device that is located on a low-security interface

    c. Traffic that is entering any interface

    d. Traffic that is exiting any interface

5. When is traffic allowed to be routed and forwarded if the source of the traffic is from a device located off of a low-security interface if the destination device is located off of a high-security interface? (Choose all that apply.)

    a. This traffic is never allowed.

    b. This traffic is allowed if the initial traffic was inspected and this traffic is the return traffic.

    c. If there is an access list that is permitting this traffic.

    d. This traffic is always allowed by default.

6. Which of the following tools could be used to configure or manage an ASA? (Choose all that apply.)

    a. Cisco Security Manager (CSM)

    b. ASA Security Device Manager (ASDM)

    c. Cisco Configuration Professional (CCP)

    d. The command-line interface (CLI)

7. Which of the following elements, which are part of the Modular Policy Framework on the ASA, are used to classify traffic?

    a. Class maps

    b. Policy maps

    c. Service policies

    d. Stateful filtering

8. When you configure the ASA as a DHCP server for a small office, what default gateway will be assigned for the DHCP clients to use?

    a. The service provider's next-hop IP address.

    b. The ASA's outside IP address.

    c. The ASA's inside IP address.

    d. Clients need to locally configure a default gateway value.

9.   When you configure network address translation for a small office, devices on the Internet will see the ASA inside users as coming from which IP address?

   a.   The inside address of the ASA.

   b.   The outside address of the ASA.

   c.   The DMZ address of the ASA.

   d.   Clients will each be assigned a unique global address, one for each user.

10.   You are interested in verifying whether the security policy you implemented is having the desired effect. How can you verify this policy without involving end users or their computers?

   a.   Run the policy check tool, which is built in to the ASA.

   b.   The ASA automatically verifies that policy matches intended rules.

   c.   Use the Packet Tracer tool.

   d.   You must manually generate the traffic from an end-user device to verify that the firewall will forward it or deny it based on policy.

16

Foundation Topics

The ASA Appliance Family and Features

This section examines the various models and offerings for the ASA and many of the features provided by these firewalls.

Meet the ASA Family

The ASA family comes in many shapes and sizes, but they all provide a similar set of features. Typically, the smaller the number of the model represents a smaller capacity for throughput. The main standalone appliance model number begins with a 55, but there are also devices in the ASA family that go into a switch such as a 6500. Table 16-2 describes the various models of the ASA.

Table 16-2   Cisco ASA Models: Deployment and Usage

Cisco ASA 5500 Series Models	Usage
Cisco ASA 5505	Small offices and branch offices
Cisco ASA 5506-X	Small offices and branch offices
Cisco ASA 5510	Small offices and branch offices
Cisco ASA 5512-X	Small offices and branch offices
Cisco ASA 5515-X	Small offices and branch offices
Cisco ASA 5520	Medium-sized offices
	Internet-edge security appliances
Cisco ASA 5525-X	Medium-sized offices
	Internet-edge security appliances
Cisco ASA 5540	Medium-sized offices
	Internet-edge security appliances
Cisco ASA 5545-X	Medium-size offices
	Internet-edge security appliances
Cisco ASA 5550	Large enterprise
	Internet-edge security appliances
Cisco ASA 5555-X	Medium-sized offices
	Internet-edge security appliances
Cisco ASA 5585-X	Data center and large enterprise networks
Cisco ASA Services Module	Data center and large enterprise networks
Cisco ASAv	Virtual ASA used in many different environments

ASA Features and Services

Summing up the exact features of an ASA could take quite a while because most of the features discussed in the previous chapter related to firewalls and different implementations are included in ASA. ASA provides the following features:

■ **Packet filtering:** Simple packet filtering normally represents an access list. It is also true with regard to this feature that the ASA provides. The ASA supports both standard and extended access lists. The most significant difference between an access list on an ASA versus an access list on a router is that the ASA never ever uses a wildcard mask. Instead, if it needs to represent a mask related to a **permit** or **deny** statement in an access list, it just uses the real mask in the *access control list (ACL)*.

■ **Stateful filtering:** By default, the ASA enters stateful tracking information about packets that have been initially allowed through the firewall. Therefore, if you have an ACL applied inbound on the outside interface of the firewall that says deny everything, but a user from the inside makes a request to a server on the outside, the return traffic is allowed back in through the firewall (in spite of the ACLs that stops initial traffic from the outside) because of the stateful inspection that is done by default on the initial traffic from the client out to the server, which is now dynamically allowing the return traffic to come back in. This is probably the most significant and most used feature on the ASA. One way of thinking about stateful filtering is to imagine that the ASA is going to build a dynamic permit entry in a virtual ACL that will permit the return traffic. Suppose that you are sending a packet to a web server. Your source address is 10.4.4.4, and your source TCP port is 4444. The destination IP address of the server is 10.5.5.5, and the destination port is TCP 80 (web/HTTP). The ASA will (virtually, as this is just a way to consider it) remember this outbound session and expect to see a return packet from 10.5.5.5 destined to 10.4.4.4 (the client), and the source port is TCP:80 (for the return packet), and the destination port is TCP:4444 (again going back to the client). The "virtual" ACL, or state table, that is dynamically created by the ASA would say, "Please permit this packet (the return one) from the outside network to the inside network where the client is waiting for this reply."

■ **Application inspection/awareness:** The ASA can listen in on conversations between devices on one side and devices on the other side of the firewall. The benefit of listening in is so that the firewall can pay attention to application layer information. An example of this is a client on the inside of our network going to an FTP server on the outside. The client may open a connection from a source port of 6783 to the well-known FTP port of TCP:21. During the conversation between the client and the server, stateful inspection is inspecting traffic (and allowing reply traffic inbound from the outside networks) as long as the source IP address is the server and the source port is 21 (coming from the server back to the client) and the destination port is 6783. That is how stateful inspection works. Unfortunately, some applications, such as FTP, dynamically use additional ports. In the case of standard FTP, the client and the server negotiate the data connection, which is sourced from ports 20 at the server and destined for whatever port number was agreed to by the client. The challenge with this is that the initial packets for this data connection are initiated from the server on the outside. As a result, normal stateful filtering denies it (either by default rules or an ACL that is denying initial traffic from the outside). With application layer inspection, the ASA learns about the dynamic ports that were agreed to and dynamically allows the data connection to be initiated from the server that is on the outside going to the client on the inside.

- **Network Address Translation (NAT):** You learned about the benefits of NAT and *Port Address Translation (PAT)* earlier in this book, and it comes as no surprise that the ASA supports both of these. It supports inside and outside NAT, and both static and dynamic NAT and PAT, including Policy NAT, which is only triggered based on specific matches of IP addresses or ports. There is also the ability to perform NAT exemption (for example, specifying that certain traffic should not be translated). This comes in handy if you have NAT rules that say everybody who is going from the inside networks out to the Internet should be translated, but at the same time you have a *virtual private network (VPN)* tunnel to either a remote user or a remote network. Any traffic from the inside network going over the VPN tunnel in most cases should not be translated, so you set up an exemption rule that says traffic from the inside networks to the destinations that are reachable via the VPN tunnels should not be translated. The policy that indicates that traffic should not be translated is often referred to as *NAT zero*.

- **DHCP:** The ASA can act as a *Dynamic Host Configuration Protocol (DHCP)* server or client or both. This is a handy feature when implementing a firewall at a smaller office that might require getting a globally routable address from our service provider through DHCP and at the same time the ability to hand out addresses to the internal DHCP clients at that location.

- **Routing:** The ASA supports most of the interior gateway routing protocols, including *Routing Information Protocol (RIP)*, *Enhanced Interior Gateway Routing Protocol (EIGRP)*, and *Open Shortest Path First (OSPF)*. It also supports static routing.

- **Layer 3 or Layer 2 implementation:** The ASA can be implemented as a traditional Layer 3 firewall, which has IP addresses assigned to each of its routable interfaces. The other option is to implement a firewall as a transparent firewall, in which the actual physical interfaces receive individual IP addresses, but a pair of interfaces operate like a bridge. Traffic that is going across this two-port bridge is still subject to the rules and inspection that can be implemented by the ASA. The ASA can still perform application layer inspection and stateful filtering.

- **VPN support:** The ASA can operate as either the head-end or remote-end device for VPN tunnels. When using IPsec, the ASA can support remote-access VPN users and site-to-site VPN tunnels. When supporting *Secure Sockets Layer (SSL)*, it can support the clientless SSL VPN and the full AnyConnect SSL VPN tunnels (which hand out IP addresses to remote VPN users, similar to the IPsec remote VPN users). SSL is a very upcoming and popular option for VPNs and is only used for remote access, not for site-to-site VPNs.

- **Object groups:** An object group is a configuration item on the ASA that refers to one or more items. In the case of a network object group, it refers to one or more IP addresses or network address ranges. The benefit of an object group is that a single entry in an ACL could refer to an object group as the source IP or destination IP address in an individual access control entry (a single line of an ACL), and the ASA logically applies that entry against all the IP addresses that are currently in the object group. If an object group has four IP addresses in it, and we use that object group in a single entry of an ACL that permits TCP traffic to the object group, in effect we are allowing TCP traffic to each of those four IP addresses that are in the group. If we change the contents of the group, the dynamics of what that ACL permits or denies also change.

■ **Botnet traffic filtering:** A *botnet* is a collection of computers that have been compromised and are willing to follow the instructions of someone who is attempting to centrally control them (for example, 10,000 machines all willing [or so commanded] to send a flood of ping requests to the IP address dictated by the person controlling these devices). Often, users of these computers have no idea that their computers are participating in this coordinated attack. The ASA works with an external system at Cisco that provides information about the Botnet Traffic Filter Database and so can protect against this.

■ **Advanced malware protection (AMP):** The Cisco ASA provides *next-generation firewall (NGFW)* capabilities that combine traditional firewall features with thread and advanced malware protection in a single device. AMP allows an administrator to protect the network from known and advanced threats, including *advanced persistent threats (APT)* and targeted attacks.

■ **High availability:** By using two firewalls in a high-availability failover combination, you can implement protection against a single system failure.

■ **AAA support:** The use of *authentication, authorization, and accounting (AAA)* services, either locally or from an external server such as *Access Control Server (ACS)*, is supported.

ASA Firewall Fundamentals

This section covers the logic that is used by the ASA to provide firewall services, the various ways to manage the firewall, and the components used to implement policy.

ASA Security Levels

With the IOS *zoned-based firewall (ZBF)* discussed in a previous chapter, we placed interfaces into zones, and no traffic was allowed between zones until we specified a policy.

With the ASA, it works a bit differently. The ASA uses security levels associated with each routable interface. The security level is a number between 0 and 100. The bigger the number, the more trust you have for the network that the interface is connected to. For example, I would very likely give a value of 100 to the interface that is connected to my inside network because it is the most trusted network I am connected to. Be aware, though, that we are not just talking about the directly connected network, but also any packets that might come in to the firewall via this interface. So, if I have a firewall with an inside interface, and I have assigned the interface a security level of 100, and if there are 57 additional networks that all forward traffic to me through that single interface, they are all considered as coming in through a security 100 level interface. If your firewall is connected to an untrusted network, such as the Internet, which is not under your control, you very likely will assign for that interface a minimum security level of 0.

In addition to assigning security levels to interfaces, you also assign a name to the interface, such as *inside* on the interface that connects to your trusted inside network, or *outside* to label the interface that connects to the Internet. You do not have to use these names, but if you do not, your coworkers might laugh, and the rest of the world may wonder. In all seriousness, it makes sense to label them this way even though you are free to choose. Each of these interfaces is assigned an IP address, and the syntax for assigning an IP address is just the same as on a Cisco router. So, you do three things to make interfaces on the ASA operational:

- Assign a security level to the interface
- Assign a name to the interface
- Bring up the interface with the **no shutdown** command

Besides the inside and outside interfaces, it is typical to have at least one interface that is somewhere in between. The reason for this is you may have a web server that you want to make available out to the Internet, and the best practice for allowing users to access a resource on your network is to avoid placing your server on your internal private network, instead placing it on a separate network off of the firewall and allowing users from the outside the limited access they need to that server that lives off of this third interface of the firewall. A common name assigned to this third interface is the *demilitarized zone (DMZ)*. Besides an IP address for this interface and the name of DMZ, you also have to assign a security level. The security level for a DMZ type of interface off of the firewall is usually set to somewhere between 1 and 99. Let's choose 50 for the DMZ interface, as shown in Figure 16-1.

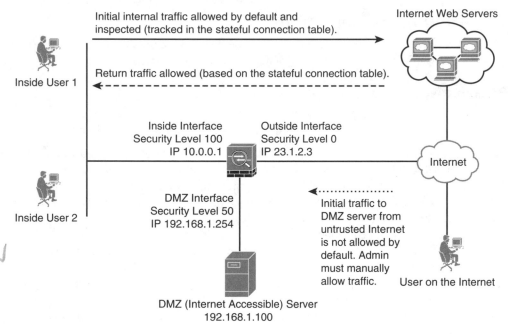

Figure 16-1 *Topology Example of a Firewall with a DMZ*

The Default Flow of Traffic

By default, and this is important, the ASA forwards traffic (assuming it has a route to know where to forward it) if the initial traffic is sourced from a device that lives off of its high-security interface (such as the inside at security 100, which is the highest) and if the destination of the packet is being routed out of an interface that has a lower security level. That is it in a nutshell. So, a user on the inside can initiate traffic to devices off of the DMZ because that is going from higher to lower security levels (100 to 50). The user on the inside can initiate traffic to a server that lives off of the outside interface because that initial traffic is also going from a higher security level to a lower security level. This is where the default stateful inspection happens, as initial traffic goes through the firewall. As a result of this inspection, when the server on the outside replies back to our inside client, the ASA dynamically allows that return traffic only because it is in the stateful table of the ASA that is expecting that return traffic. The same thing happens for return traffic from the DMZ back to the inside client, again because of the initial inspection.

So, you might ask, how is that a firewall? What is it stopping? The firewall, by default, is stopping all initial traffic that is trying to go from lower security levels to higher security levels. For example, a server on the outside is trying to start a conversation with the server on the DMZ network. Because the initial traffic came in on an interface at a security level of 0 and is trying to go uphill through an interface on the DMZ with the security level of 50, that traffic is denied by default. If we play this all the way through, servers from the outside cannot initialize traffic to the DMZ or to the inside. The DMZ devices could initialize traffic out to the outside (from high to low, 50 going to 0), but that same DMZ device could not initialize a conversation going to the inside (from low to high, 50 trying to go to 100). Think of it like water: The default policy is like a waterfall, in that it allows higher to go to lower. The stateful inspection determines whether the reply traffic (in response to the initial session) is allowed to make it back through. Figure 16-2 shows the initial traffic that will be permitted and the reply traffic that is being permitted because of the stateful filtering. Without any additional controls in place, this is the full extent of what the firewall allows.

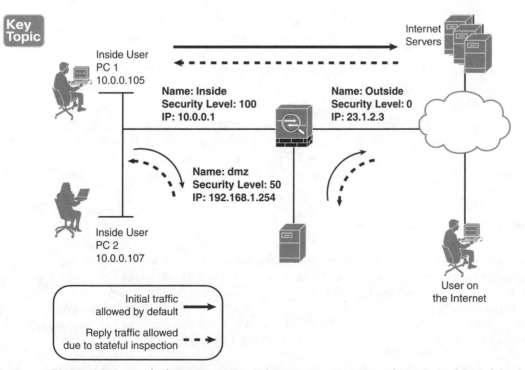

Figure 16-2 *Default Permissions and Return Traffic Allowed Because of Stateful Filtering*

By default, if two interfaces are both at the exact same security level, traffic is not allowed between those two interfaces. Also by default the ASA does not like to (meaning it will not) receive a packet on a specific interface and route the same packet out of the exact same interface (hairpin routing). You can change both of these default behaviors.

Tools to Manage the ASA

You can use several tools to manage an ASA, including the following:

- **Command-line interface (CLI):** Functions similar to IOS
- **ASA Security Device Manager (ASDM):** *Graphical user interface (GUI)* included with the ASA
- **Cisco Security Manager (CSM):** An enterprise (commercial grade) GUI tool that can manage most of your network devices, including routers, switches, and security appliances such as the ASA

Initial Access

On a brand new ASA without an IP address configured, you connect to the console port of the ASA. In the old days, most computers had an RS-232 type serial port, and we connected from that serial port on the computer using the blue rollover cable to the console port. In current times, we have moved to USB on the computers. Part of your equipment that you should carry with you is a USB-to-serial adapter so that you can connect from your USB port to the serial blue cable, which then connects to the console port on your network device (in this case, the ASA).

At the CLI, we have access to ROM Monitor, EXEC mode (both user and privileged), configuration mode, interface configuration mode, and several others. Context-sensitive help and navigation at the CLI is similar to the router, including the functions of enable, exit, Ctrl+Z, and so on. One difference worth noting is that if you scroll through multiple pages of output, you use the letter *Q* (for quit) to stop scrolling through the pages of output one page at a time.

ASDM is a configuration tool that is built in to (included with) the ASA firewall family. We use ASDM to implement and verify our security policy later in this chapter. It uses *Secure Sockets Layer (SSL)* to ensure secure communications and runs on a variety of Windows platforms. You can connect to up to five separate firewalls and switch between them conveniently from ASDM.

Packet Filtering on the ASA

We discussed the default flow of traffic, which allows initial traffic to flow from higher to lower security levels, and we also discussed why the reply traffic is allowed (because of the stateful filtering and the database created from the initial traffic flow). But what about individuals on the outside who need access to your web server on the DMZ? You need to allow that initial traffic if you want the customer to have access. To provide access, you can implement packet filtering ACLs on the interfaces. These work just like IOS router ACLs; there are both standard and extended lists, and they can be applied inbound and outbound to a given interface.

The word *inbound*, from a firewall perspective, could mean traffic that is trying to go uphill (from a low-security interface to a higher-security interface). By default, initial traffic in this direction is denied by the firewall. Reply traffic matching the database is allowed. Another use of the word *inbound* is as traffic is going into an interface. In this context, traffic from users on the inside of the network as they send traffic to the outside world is inbound to the inside interface. If there is a user or device on the outside network that is sending traffic to the inside network, those packets, as they reach the firewall's outside interface, are also inbound to that interface. Here's a quick summary:

- **Inbound to an interface:** Traffic that is going into an interface (any interface). This is also referred to as ingress traffic (from an interface perspective).

- **Inbound from a security level perspective:** Traffic that is being routed by the ASA from a lower-security interface to a higher-security interface, such as from the outside to the DMZ, from the outside to the inside, from the DMZ to the inside. This is from a high-level perspective of the firewall as a whole device.

- **Outbound to an interface:** Traffic that is exiting an interface (any interface) is also referred to as egress traffic (from an interface perspective).

- **Outbound from a security level perspective:** Traffic that is being routed by the ASA from a high-security interface to a lower-security interface, such as inside to DMZ, inside to outside, or DMZ to outside. This is from a high-level perspective of the firewall as a whole device.

Implementing a Packet-Filtering ACL

Now that we have that cleared up, let's return to the issue of a device on the outside needing to initiate a connection to a server on the DMZ. To make that happen, you use an ACL that specifically permits the traffic to the server from the outside. If the server will be accessed by the general public, the ACL specifies that any device has access through the firewall to the DMZ server as long as the destination IP address and port numbers match the server's address and services offered by the DMZ server. If the ACL is applied inbound on the outside interface, any permit entries inside the ACL allow traffic to be sourced on the lower-security interface and go to the higher-security interface such as the DMZ. One thing that a lot of people learned the hard way is that just like a router, there is an implicit **deny** at the end of an ACL. For outside users, this is no big deal, because previously they had no access to the DMZ, and after the ACL they are simply being allowed access to only that one server. The big challenge with ACLs comes into play when you apply them inbound on a high-security interface such as the inside interface. When you do that, the inside users can initiate connections through the firewall if there is an explicit **permit** statement allowing it. So, if you are using ACLs on each interface of the ASA, the security levels no longer control what the initial traffic flows may be. With ACLs, the initial traffic flow is completely controlled by the entries in that ACL, which are processed from top to bottom; and the stateful inspection, which is still being done dynamically, allows the return traffic to come back through the firewall regardless of any ACLs in place (related to the return traffic).

In short, everything you learned about ACLs in the previous chapter on that topic applies to ACLs on the ASA. The biggest implementation difference is that no wildcard masks are used on the ASA ACLs, but rather just normal masks.

Modular Policy Framework

For IOS ZBFs, class maps are used to identify traffic, policy maps are used to implement actions on that traffic, and the application of those policies is done with the service policy commands. On the IOS router, all of these features included the keywords **inspect** to differentiate them from normal class maps and policy maps and service policies.

On the ASA, you also use class maps to identify traffic, policy maps to identify the actions you are going to take on that traffic, and service policy commands to implement the policy. The service policies can attach the policy to a specific interface or can be applied globally, which would affect all interfaces on the ASA. One way to use the *Modular Policy Framework (MPF)* is to allow the ASA to perform application layer inspection on FTP traffic, to listen in and dynamically allow the data connection to commence from the server (as discussed earlier in this chapter). Another option is that you want to take the traffic destined for your servers and forward it to the *intrusion prevention system (IPS)* module that installs as a hardware add-on in your ASA in its option slot. Another example is that you want to prioritize the forwarding of voice traffic so that once again the class map looks for the voice traffic, the policy map says to give priority queuing to the voice traffic, and the service policy implements where that policy applies (either to a specific interface or all interfaces).

Class maps can identify traffic based on Layer 3 and Layer 4. (There are also application-specific class maps for Layers 5 to 7 that identify traffic based on application layer information, a discussion best saved for your CCNP Security training. For now, just stick with normal class maps at Layer 3 and Layer 4.) These Layer 3 and Layer 4 class maps can identify traffic using several different methods, including the following:

- Referring to an ACL
- Looking at the *differentiated services code point (DSCP)*/IP Precedence fields of the packet
- TCP or UDP ports
- IP Precedence
- *Real-time Transport Protocol (RTP)* port numbers
- VPN tunnel groups

The policy maps use the services of the class maps to identify traffic and then specify the actions to take on each class of traffic, which may include the following:

- Reroute the traffic to a hardware module such as the IPS module that is inside the ASA
- Perform inspection on that traffic (related to stateful filtering or application layer inspection/filtering)
- Give priority treatment to the forwarding of that traffic
- Rate-limit or police that traffic
- Perform advanced handling of the traffic

Where to Apply a Policy

You can apply a policy to a specific interface, and any given interface can have only one policy applied to it. You can also apply a policy globally, which means that all interfaces implement that policy. It is possible that an interface has a manually configured policy and an inherited global policy, at which point both policies are implemented (so long as no conflict of policy exists between the two).

Configuring the ASA

In this section, you use the ASDM GUI to implement and verify a security policy on an ASA firewall.

Beginning the Configuration

Now that you know the features and functions of the ASA and the core concepts of what it can do (for example, stateful filtering, packet filtering, NAT), it is time to put those concepts into practice.

Most of the time, you will be dealing with a firewall that is already configured and in a production network. If so, you just use the CLI, ASDM, or CSM (if your company owns CSM) to manage the device. However, if it is a brand new firewall and has no configuration, you want to establish a console port connection to it, power up the firewall, and set your terminal emulation program to connect through the serial cable using 9600 bits per second, no parity, 8 data bits, and 1 stop bit. In your terminal emulation program, you press the **Enter** key on your keyboard to initialize the CLI EXEC session to the ASA. With the console connection, if you watch the ASA power up, a Cisco ASA 5512-X boot looks similar to what is shown in Example 16-1.

Example 16-1 *Initial Boot of a Cisco ASA 5512-X*

```
CISCO SYSTEMS
Cisco BIOS Version:9B2C106A
Build Date:11/10/2011 09:59:37


CPU Type: Intel(R) Pentium(R) CPU       G6950  @ 2.80GHz, 2793 MHz
Total Memory:4096 MB(DDR3 1066)
System memory:624 KB, Extended Memory:3573 MB



PCI Device Table:
  Bus   Dev   Func   VendID   DevID   Class   IRQ
-------------------------------------------------------------
  00    00    00     8086     0040    Bridge Device
  00    06    00     8086     0043    PCI Bridge,IRQ=11
  00    16    00     8086     3B64    I/O Port Device,IRQ=11
  00    1A    00     8086     3B3C    USB Controller,IRQ=11
  00    1C    00     8086     3B42    PCI Bridge,IRQ=10
  00    1C    04     8086     3B4A    PCI Bridge,IRQ=10
```

```
00    1C    05    8086    3B4C    PCI Bridge,IRQ=11
00    1D    00    8086    3B34    USB Controller,IRQ=7
00    1E    00    8086    244E    PCI Bridge
00    1F    00    8086    3B16    Bridge Device
00    1F    02    8086    3B22    SATA DPA,IRQ=5
00    1F    03    8086    3B30    SMBus,IRQ=11
01    00    00    10B5    8618    PCI Bridge,IRQ=11
02    01    00    10B5    8618    PCI Bridge,IRQ=10
02    03    00    10B5    8618    PCI Bridge,IRQ=5
02    05    00    10B5    8618    PCI Bridge,IRQ=10
02    07    00    10B5    8618    PCI Bridge,IRQ=5
02    09    00    10B5    8618    PCI Bridge,IRQ=10
02    0B    00    10B5    8618    PCI Bridge,IRQ=5
02    0D    00    10B5    8618    PCI Bridge,IRQ=10
02    0F    00    10B5    8618    PCI Bridge,IRQ=5
03    00    00    8086    10D3    Ethernet,IRQ=10
04    00    00    8086    10D3    Ethernet,IRQ=5
05    00    00    8086    10D3    Ethernet,IRQ=10
07    00    00    8086    10D3    Ethernet,IRQ=10
08    00    00    8086    10D3    Ethernet,IRQ=5
09    00    00    8086    10D3    Ethernet,IRQ=10
0B    00    00    177D    0010    Cavium Encryption,IRQ=11
0C    00    00    8086    10D3    Ethernet,IRQ=11
0D    00    00    1A03    1150    PCI Bridge,IRQ=10
0E    00    00    1A03    2000    VGA,IRQ=10
FF    00    00    8086    2C61    Bridge Device
FF    00    01    8086    2D01    Bridge Device
FF    02    00    8086    2D10    Bridge Device
FF    02    01    8086    2D11    Bridge Device
FF    02    02    8086    2D12    Bridge Device
FF    02    03    8086    2D13    Bridge Device


Booting from ROMMON


Cisco Systems ROMMON Version (2.1(9)8) #1: Wed Oct 26 17:14:40 PDT 2011




Use BREAK or ESC to interrupt boot.
Use SPACE to begin boot immediately.


Launching BootLoader...
Boot configuration file contains 1 entry.


Loading disk0:/asa913-smp-k8.bin... Booting...
```

```
Platform ASA5512

Loading...
IO memory blocks requested from bigphys 32bit: 32540
?dosfsck 2.11, 12 Mar 2005, FAT32, LFN
Starting check/repair pass.
Starting verification pass.
/dev/sda1: 188 files, 286777/1005579 clusters
dosfsck(/dev/sda1) returned 0
Processor memory 1705463808, Reserved memory: 0

Total NICs found: 11
i82574L rev00 Gigabit Ethernet @ irq10 dev 0 index 06 MAC: c464.1339.86d9
i82574L rev00 Gigabit Ethernet @ irq10 dev 0 index 05 MAC: c464.1339.86dc
i82574L rev00 Gigabit Ethernet @ irq05 dev 0 index 04 MAC: c464.1339.86d8
i82574L rev00 Gigabit Ethernet @ irq05 dev 0 index 03 MAC: c464.1339.86db
i82574L rev00 Gigabit Ethernet @ irq10 dev 0 index 02 MAC: c464.1339.86d7
i82574L rev00 Gigabit Ethernet @ irq10 dev 0 index 01 MAC: c464.1339.86da
i82574L rev00 Gigabit Ethernet @ irq11 dev 0 index 00 MAC: c464.1339.86d6
ivshmem rev03 Backplane Data Interface    @ index 07 MAC: 0000.0001.0002
en_vtun rev00 Backplane Control Interface @ index 08 MAC: 0000.0001.0001
en_vtun rev00 Backplane Int-Mgmt Interface  @ index 09 MAC: 0000.0001.0003
en_vtun rev00 Backplane Ext-Mgmt Interface  @ index 10 MAC: 0000.0000.0000
Verify the activation-key, it might take a while...
Running Permanent Activation Key: 0xc02eda7a 0x30a99862 0xd992f9c8 0xd29cb818
  0x8c2fe5bd

Licensed features for this platform:
Maximum Physical Interfaces     : Unlimited      perpetual
Maximum VLANs                   : 100            perpetual
Inside Hosts                    : Unlimited      perpetual
Failover                        : Active/Active  perpetual
Encryption-DES                  : Enabled        perpetual
Encryption-3DES-AES             : Enabled        perpetual
Security Contexts               : 5              perpetual
GTP/GPRS                        : Enabled        perpetual
AnyConnect Premium Peers        : 100            perpetual
AnyConnect Essentials           : Disabled       perpetual
Other VPN Peers                 : 250            perpetual
Total VPN Peers                 : 250            perpetual
Shared License                  : Disabled       perpetual
AnyConnect for Mobile           : Enabled        perpetual
AnyConnect for Cisco VPN Phone  : Enabled        perpetual
Advanced Endpoint Assessment    : Enabled        perpetual
UC Phone Proxy Sessions         : 2              perpetual
Total UC Proxy Sessions         : 2              perpetual
```

```
Botnet Traffic Filter            : Disabled      perpetual
Intercompany Media Engine        : Enabled       perpetual
IPS Module                       : Enabled       perpetual
Cluster                          : Enabled       perpetual


This platform has an ASA 5512 Security Plus license.


Encryption hardware device : Cisco ASA-55xx on-board accelerator (revision 0x1)
                             Boot microcode       : CNPx-MC-BOOT-2.00
                             SSL/IKE microcode    : CNPx-MC-SSL-PLUS-T020
                             IPSec microcode      : CNPx-MC-IPSEC-MAIN-0026


Cisco Adaptive Security Appliance Software Version 9.1(3)

    **************************** Warning *****************************
    This product contains cryptographic features and is
    subject to United States and local country laws
    governing, import, export, transfer, and use.
    Delivery of Cisco cryptographic products does not
    imply third-party authority to import, export,
    distribute, or use encryption. Importers, exporters,
    distributors and users are responsible for compliance
    with U.S. and local country laws. By using this
    product you agree to comply with applicable laws and
    regulations. If you are unable to comply with U.S.
    and local laws, return the enclosed items immediately.


    A summary of U.S. laws governing Cisco cryptographic
    products may be found at:
    http://www.cisco.com/wwl/export/crypto/tool/stqrg.html


    If you require further assistance please contact us by
    sending email to export@cisco.com.
    **************************** Warning *****************************

This product includes software developed by the OpenSSL Project
for use in the OpenSSL Toolkit (http://www.openssl.org/)
Copyright (C) 1995-1998 Eric Young (eay@cryptsoft.com)
All rights reserved.
Copyright (c) 1998-2011 The OpenSSL Project.
All rights reserved.

This product includes software developed at the University of
California, Irvine for use in the DAV Explorer project
(http://www.ics.uci.edu/~webdav/)
Copyright (c) 1999-2005 Regents of the University of California.
```

Busybox, version 1.16.1, Copyright (C) 1989, 1991 Free Software Foundation, Inc.
51 Franklin St, Fifth Floor, Boston, MA 02110-1301   USA
Busybox comes with ABSOLUTELY NO WARRANTY.
This is free software, and you are welcome to redistribute it under the General
Public License v.2 (http://www.gnu.org/licenses/gpl-2.0.html)
See User Manual ("Licensing") for details.

DOSFSTOOLS, version 2.11, Copyright (C) 1989, 1991 Free Software Foundation, Inc.
59 Temple Place, Suite 330, Boston, MA 02111-1307
675 Mass Ave, Cambridge, MA 02139
DOSFSTOOLS comes with ABSOLUTELY NO WARRANTY.
This is free software, and you are welcome to redistribute it under the General
Public License v.2 (http://www.gnu.org/licenses/gpl-2.0.html)
See User Manual ("Licensing") for details.

grub, version 0.94, Copyright (C) 1989, 1991 Free Software Foundation, Inc.
59 Temple Place, Suite 330, Boston, MA 02111-1307
grub comes with ABSOLUTELY NO WARRANTY.
This is free software, and you are welcome to redistribute it under the General
Public License v.2 (http://www.gnu.org/licenses/gpl-2.0.html)
See User Manual ("Licensing") for details.

libgcc, version 4.3, Copyright (C) 2007 Free Software Foundation, Inc.
libgcc comes with ABSOLUTELY NO WARRANTY.
This is free software, and you are welcome to redistribute it under the General
Public License v.2 (http://www.gnu.org/licenses/gpl-2.0.html)
See User Manual ("Licensing") for details.

libstdc++, version 4.3, Copyright (C) 2007 Free Software Foundation, Inc.
libstdc++ comes with ABSOLUTELY NO WARRANTY.
This is free software, and you are welcome to redistribute it under the General
Public License v.2 (http://www.gnu.org/licenses/gpl-2.0.html)
See User Manual ("Licensing") for details.

Linux kernel, version 2.6.29.6, Copyright (C) 1989, 1991 Free Software
Foundation, Inc.)
51 Franklin St, Fifth Floor, Boston, MA 02110-1301   USA
Linux kernel comes with ABSOLUTELY NO WARRANTY.
This is free software, and you are welcome to redistribute it under the General
Public License v.2 (http://www.gnu.org/licenses/gpl-2.0.html)
See User Manual ("Licensing") for details.

module-init-tools, version 3.10, Copyright (C) 1989, 1991 Free Software
Foundation, Inc.

```
59 Temple Place, Suite 330, Boston, MA 02111-1307 USA
module-init-tools comes with ABSOLUTELY NO WARRANTY.
This is free software, and you are welcome to redistribute it under the General
Public License v.2 (http://www.gnu.org/licenses/gpl-2.0.html)
See User Manual ("Licensing") for details.


numactl, version 2.0.3, Copyright (C) 2008 SGI.
Author: Andi Kleen, SUSE Labs
Version 2.0.0 by Cliff Wickman, Christopher Lameter and Lee Schermerhorn
numactl comes with ABSOLUTELY NO WARRANTY.
This is free software, and you are welcome to redistribute it under the General
Public License v.2 (http://www.gnu.org/licenses/gpl-2.0.html)
See User Manual ("Licensing") for details.


pciutils, version 3.1.4, Copyright (C) 1989, 1991 Free Software Foundation, Inc.
51 Franklin St, Fifth Floor, Boston, MA 02110-1301  USA
pciutils comes with ABSOLUTELY NO WARRANTY.
This is free software, and you are Public License v.2
   (http://www.gnu.org/licenses/gpl-2.0.html)
See User Manual ("Licensing") for details.


qemu, version 0.12.5, Copyright (C) 1989, 1991 Free Software Foundation, Inc.
51 Franklin St, Fifth Floor, Boston, MA 02110-1301  USA
qemu comes with ABSOLUTELY NO WARRANTY.
This is free software, and you are welcome to redistribute it under the General
Public License v.2 (http://www.gnu.org/licenses/gpl-2.0.html)
See User Manual ("Licensing") for details.


qemu-KVM Inter-VM Shared Memory Patch, version 1.0,
Copyright (C) 2009 Cam Macdonell
qemu-KVM Inter-VM Shared Memory Patch comes with ABSOLUTELY NO WARRANTY.
This is free software, and you are welcome to redistribute it under the General
Public License v.2 (http://www.gnu.org/licenses/gpl-2.0.html)
See User Manual ("Licensing") for details.


readline, version 5.2, Copyright (C) 1989, 1991 Free Software Foundation, Inc.
59 Temple Place, Suite 330, Boston, MA 02111 USA
readline comes with ABSOLUTELY NO WARRANTY.
This is free software, and you are welcome to redistribute it under the General
Public License v.2 (http://www.gnu.org/licenses/gpl-2.0.html)
See User Manual ("Licensing") for details.


udev, version 146, Copyright (C) 1989, 1991 Free Software Foundation, Inc.
51 Franklin St, Fifth Floor, Boston, MA 02110-1301  USA
udev comes with ABSOLUTELY NO WARRANTY.
This is free software, and you are welcome to redistribute it under the General
```

```
Public License v.2 (http://www.gnu.org/licenses/gpl-2.0.html)
See User Manual ("Licensing") for details.

Cisco Adaptive Security Appliance Software, version 9.1,
Copyright (c) 1996-2013 by Cisco Systems, Inc.
Certain components of Cisco ASA Software, Version 9.1 are licensed under the GNU
Lesser Public License (LGPL) Version 2.1.  The software code licensed under LGPL
Version 2.1 is free software that comes with ABSOLUTELY NO WARRANTY.  You can
redistribute and/or modify such LGPL code under the terms of LGPL Version 2.1
(http://www.gnu.org/licenses/lgpl-2.1.html).  See User Manual for licensing
details.

                    Restricted Rights Legend

Use, duplication, or disclosure by the Government is
subject to restrictions as set forth in subparagraph
(c) of the Commercial Computer Software - Restricted
Rights clause at FAR sec. 52.227-19 and subparagraph
(c) (1) (ii) of the Rights in Technical Data and Computer
Software clause at DFARS sec. 252.227-7013.


                    Cisco Systems, Inc.
                    170 West Tasman Drive
                    San Jose, California 95134-1706


Reading from flash...
Flash read failed
ERROR: MIGRATION - Could not get the startup configuration.

Cryptochecksum (changed): d41d8cd9 8f00b204 e9800998 ecf8427e

INFO: Power-On Self-Test in process.
..........................................................
INFO: Power-On Self-Test complete.

INFO: Starting HW-DRBG health test...
INFO: HW-DRBG health test passed.

INFO: Starting SW-DRBG health test...
INFO: SW-DRBG health test passed.

Pre-configure Firewall now through interactive prompts [yes]?
```

At this point, to initially bootstrap the ASA, you can press **Enter** to tell the ASA that you want to use the interactive prompts for the initial setup. If you answer **no** to this, you can later run the **setup** command to return to this script. The objective here is to give the ASA enough basic information so that you can connect to it via ASDM and then use ASDM to configure the rest of it. As we work through this example, we look at both the configuration done through the ASDM and from the CLI. If you answer **yes**, we can supply the basic information needed for connectivity on the ASA by the ASDM, as shown in Example 16-2.

Example 16-2   *Running the Initial Setup Script on the ASA*

```
Pre-configure Firewall now through interactive prompts [yes]? yes
! By pressing the Enter key, the value in the brackets, such as the [yes}
! above will be accepted.


! The other option would be transparent mode (non-routed)
Firewall Mode [Routed]:


! Please use a password that is more secure than this example
Enable password [<use current password>]: Sup3rs3crtP4ss


!   pressing enter will accept the option presented in the brackets
Allow password recovery [yes]?
Clock (UTC):
  Year [2013]:
  Month [Mar]:
  Day [2]:
  Time [17:34:41]:


!  this will be the IP address on the logical interface VLAN1
!  remember all eight switch ports belong to this VLAN by default
!  we could use any of the eight ports to connect ASA to our network
!   it will name this interface "management", and give it a security level
!   of zero you will want to plan ahead of time regarding which IP address
!   to use
Management IP address: 192.168.1.254
Management network mask: 255.255.255.0
Host name: ASA1
Domain name: example.org


!  the ASA doesn't allow any ASDM/HTTPS  connections to it by default
!  it will ask for the address of your computer that you will be using
!  to access ASDM,  and allow that connection
IP address of host running Device Manager: 192.168.1.7


!  a summary is provided before asking you to confirm
The following configuration will be used:
Enable password: cisco123
Allow password recovery: yes
Clock (UTC): 12:34:41 Nov 2 2014
```

```
Firewall Mode: Routed
Management IP address: 192.168.1.254
Management network mask: 255.255.255.0
Host name: ASA1
Domain name: example.org
IP address of host running Device Manager: 192.168.1.7



!    if everything looks right you can type yes and press enter to implement
!    the changes
Use this configuration and write to flash? yes
INFO: Security level for "management" set to 0 by default.


!  it takes a few moments for the self signed certificate to be generated
!  by the ASA for use with SSL, so the warning below is only relevant
!  for the first few seconds, and then will be ok.
WARNING: http server is not yet enabled to allow ASDM access.
Cryptochecksum: 3001087b 2c98260b a4ed70b8 06b690d6


2052 bytes copied in 0.730 secs




Type help or '?' for a list of available commands.
ASA1>
```

As a good initial check to verify that connectivity is at least working from an IP perspective, you can ping a device on the local network (be sure to verify it is a device that is willing to respond to a ping request), as shown in Example 16-3.

Example 16-3 *Issuing an ICMP Echo Request (Ping) from the ASA*

```
ASA1# ping 192.168.1.100
Type escape sequence to abort.
Sending 5, 100-byte ICMP Echos to 192.168.1.100, timeout is 2 seconds:
!!!!!
Success rate is 100 percent (5/5), round-trip min/avg/max = 1/28/130 ms
ASA1#
```

Getting to the ASDM GUI

With that in place, the next thing to attempt is opening an HTTPS connection from a Windows PC (whose IP address you identified in the setup script). On the initial connection, your PC is given a digital certificate of the ASA, and unfortunately the certificate is self-signed by the ASA, and your browser will not by default trust that certificate. On a brand new ASA, you need to accept the certificate to get ASDM functionality. Later you can implement a *public key infrastructure (PKI)* signed certificate for the ASA. (For more information on digital certificates, see the chapter on PKI in this book.) After you accept the certificate, you are given the option of running ASDM as an applet directly from the ASA, or you can install the program on your local PC and launch it from there. Either way, when it is launched, ASDM prompts you for a username and password, which is quite interesting because you did not configure any usernames in the setup script. At this point, you just leave the username blank and supply the enable secret that was configured in the setup script. After you have authenticated, and the configuration is then downloaded from the ASA to ASDM, you are provided with the dashboard for the ASA, as shown in Figure 16-3.

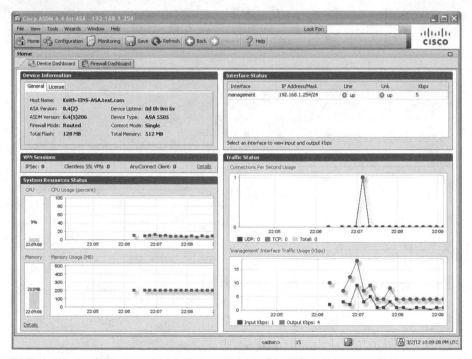

Figure 16-3   *Initial Dashboard Presented by the ASDM*

As shown in the figure, the dashboard shows the general information about the firewall, including the version of software, the model, the mode it is running in, and the memory size of flash and RAM. A tab shows current licensing information, as well. The dashboard also graphically represents information about VPN sessions, system resources, and traffic status. When you initially connect to the ASA, one of the options is to run the Startup Wizard. In our example, we chose to go directly to ASDM, but it is not too late; on the menu bar is an option labeled Wizards. By choosing that menu option and from the drop-down selecting **Startup Wizard**, you can launch the Startup Wizard to help you configure more of the basics to get your firewall up and running. Figure 16-4 shows the welcome screen for the wizard.

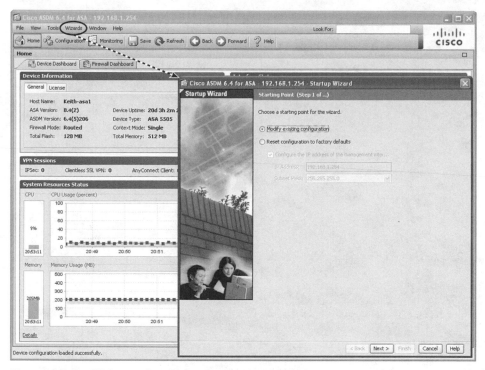

Figure 16-4 *Welcome Screen for the Startup Wizard*

When you click the **Next** button to continue, you are presented with the option to configure many of the components required for a functional firewall, including the IP addresses to use, the names of the interfaces, NAT configuration, and so forth. From an instructional perspective and certification-relevancy issue, I want to walk you through the configuration manually using the GUI (instead of the wizard) so that you will both know where to go in the interface and how to configure each item.

Configuring the Interfaces

The first order of business is to configure the interfaces. To do this, you click the **Configuration** button on the menu bar in the upper left and then navigate to **Configuration > Device Setup > Interfaces**, as shown in Figure 16-5.

Currently, we have one logical Layer 3 interface. It is interface VLAN 1, and it has been given the name of management with a security level of 0 and all of the eight switch ports belong to this VLAN as access ports by default. (This was done from the CLI setup script.) To create new switched virtual interfaces (the Layer 3 interfaces), you just click **Add** and specify the information for each of the interfaces one at a time. Figure 16-6 shows an example of this.

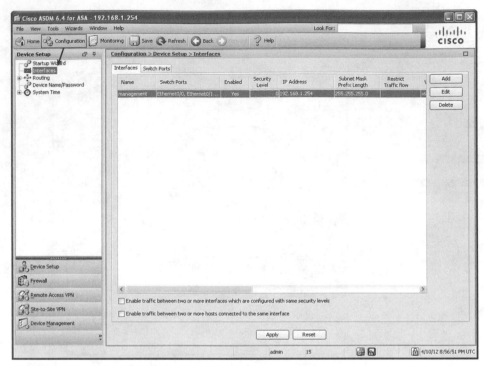

Figure 16-5   *Interface Configuration in ASDM*

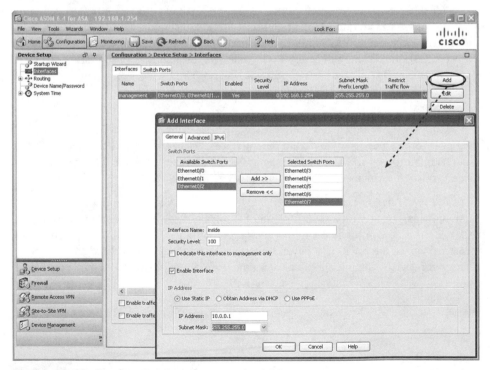

Figure 16-6   *Configuring Interfaces on the ASA*

Figure 16-6 shows creating a logical Layer 3 interface named inside, with a security level of 100 (which is pretty standard for your interface connected to your internal network). I also associated five of the ports that I intend to use for connecting internal users and devices as belonging to this new VLAN. By default, this creates a new VLAN using a VLAN number that does not currently exist on this firewall. If you click the **Advanced** tab, you can specify the exact number of the VLAN you want, as shown in Figure 16-7.

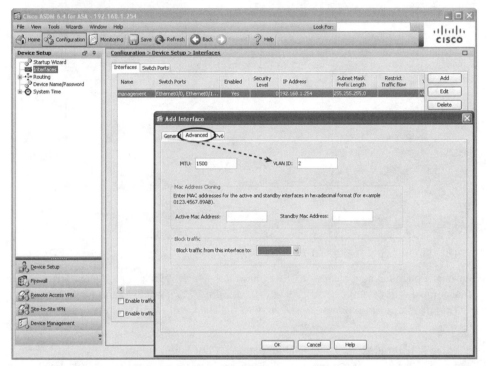

Figure 16-7   *Specifying the VLAN Number to Associate with the New Layer 3 Interface*

In this example, I use the VLAN number 2 for the inside. From this window, you can also specify the *maximum transmission unit (MTU)*, and some information that could be used for high-availability failover. You can also specify that traffic from this VLAN should never be forwarded to another interface, which can be selected from the drop-down list in the Block Traffic section.

The number of named interfaces you are allowed to use is governed by the license on the ASA. After you have configured your interfaces, you can apply the changes by clicking the **Apply** button (see Figure 16-8).

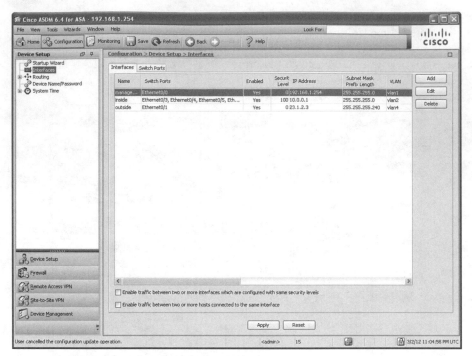

Figure 16-8   *Summary Screen for Adding New Interfaces*

The Summary page includes the name of the interface, which switch ports are associated with that logical interface, the security level, IP address, VLAN number, and more. If the information does not fit on one page, scrolling to the right will reveal the rest of the columns.

Earlier, we talked about the defaults related to an ASA not being willing to forward traffic between two interfaces if those two interfaces are both at the same security level. We also discussed that the ASA does not like to route a packet out the exact same interface that the packet came in on. To modify both these behaviors, you can place a check mark in each of the check boxes near the bottom of the screen shown in Figure 16-8.

The number of named interfaces that you can create is controlled by the license on the ASA. In our scenario, I want to have an inside interface, an outside interface, and a DMZ interface, so I reconfigure the name and security level of the current interface named management and use it as a DMZ interface, as shown in Figure 16-9.

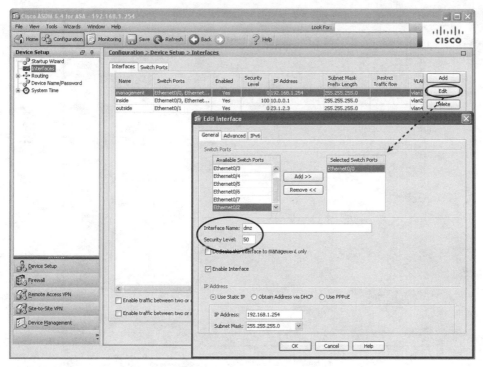

Figure 16-9 *Editing an Interface*

Changing the name of the interface does not change the security posture, but it makes sense to name the interfaces so that when you see them you will know where they connect. In addition, changing the security level (in our example to 50) is important because this interface has a higher security level than the outside but a lower security level than the inside. We could have changed the security level to any number between 1 and 99, inclusive, and achieved the same results. To implement these changes, you click the **OK** button to dismiss the pop-up windows, and click the **Apply** button to implement the changes on the ASA. In the process of making these changes, you may receive warnings from ASDM indicating that changing interface parameters, including security levels, may cause loss of connectivity (especially if you are disabling an interface that you are currently using to communicate with the ASA).

Because you are likely to run into this issue, you need to be aware of one more tweak for this configuration. On the Advanced tab shown in Figure 16-7, indicate that you are willing to block traffic from one of your interfaces so that it cannot be forwarded to another specific interface. An upgraded Plus license allows for three full-functioning interfaces. Figure 16-10 shows some restrictions in place in the Restrict Traffic Flow column. This figure shows restricting traffic from the outside to the inside. (This is an example only; in production, this configuration would not work too well for your users who are trying to get replies from servers on the outside.) I will not be leaving the restriction in place.

Figure 16-10 shows the final configuration.

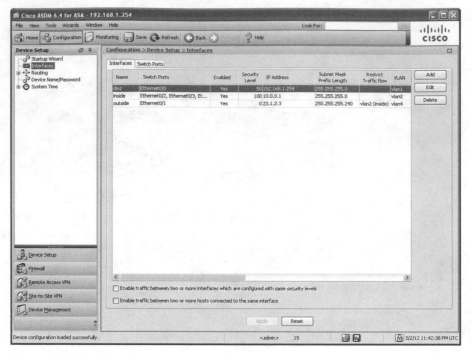

Figure 16-10   *Final Configuration of the Interfaces*

From the CLI, you can implement these same changes using the commands shown in Example 16-4.

Example 16-4   *Implementing Additional Firewall Interfaces*

```
ASA1(config)# configure terminal
ASA1(config)#

! Configure the logical Switched Virtual Interface (SVI, it is the Layer 3
! interface)
ASA1(config)# interface Vlan1

! Bring it out of shutdown state
ASA1(config-if)# no shutdown

! Add an optional description
ASA1(config-if)# description Connect to the dmz

! Give the interface a name
ASA1(config-if)# nameif dmz

! Give the interface a security level
ASA1(config-if)# security-level 50
```

```
! Give the interface an IP address
ASA1(config-if)# ip address 192.168.1.254 255.255.255.0
ASA1(config-if)# exit


! Repeat this process for the other interfaces
ASA1(config)# interface Vlan2
ASA1(config-if)# no shutdown
ASA1(config-if)# description Connects to my private network
ASA1(config-if)# nameif inside
ASA1(config-if)# security-level 100
ASA1(config-if)# ip address 10.0.0.1 255.255.255.0
ASA1(config-if)# exit
ASA1(config)#
ASA1(config)# interface Vlan4
ASA1(config-if)# no shutdown
ASA1(config-if)# description Connects to the Internet
ASA1(config-if)# no forward interface Vlan2
ASA1(config-if)# nameif outside
ASA1(config-if)# security-level 0
ASA1(config-if)# ip address 23.1.2.3 255.255.255.240
ASA1(config-if)# exit
ASA1(config)#


! Assign the access ports of the built in switch to the VLANs that you
! want them to belong to, repeat for all switch ports you intend to use.
ASA1(config)# interface Ethernet0/1
ASA1(config-if)# switchport access vlan 4
ASA1(config-if)# exit
ASA1(config)#)
ASA1(config)# interface Ethernet0/2
ASA1(config-if)# switchport access vlan 2
ASA1(config-if)# exit
ASA1(config)#
ASA1(config)# interface Ethernet0/3
ASA1(config-if)# switchport access vlan 2
ASA1(config-if)# exit
ASA1(config)#
ASA1(config)# interface Ethernet0/4
ASA1(config-if)# switchport access vlan 2
ASA1(config-if)# exit
ASA1(config)#
ASA1(config)# interface Ethernet0/5
ASA1(config-if)# switchport access vlan 2
ASA1(config-if)# exit
ASA1(config)#
ASA1(config)# interface Ethernet0/6
```

16

```
ASA1(config-if)# switchport access vlan 2
ASA1(config-if)# exit
ASA1(config)#
ASA1(config)# interface Ethernet0/7
ASA1(config-if)# switchport access vlan 2
ASA1(config-if)# exit


! To verify your work:
ASA1(config)# show run interface

! Note the E0/0 is assigned to VLAN 1 (the dmz interface) and because the
! default is for a port to be assigned to VLAN 1, there is no specific
! configuration that shows up in the interface belonging to VLAN 1
interface Ethernet0/0
!

! The rest of the ports are assigned to non-default VLANs, so they show up
! with the VLAN assignment in their configuration.
interface Ethernet0/1
 switchport access vlan 4
!
interface Ethernet0/2
 switchport access vlan 2
!
interface Ethernet0/3
 switchport access vlan 2
!
interface Ethernet0/4
 switchport access vlan 2
!
interface Ethernet0/5
 switchport access vlan 2
!
interface Ethernet0/6
 switchport access vlan 2
!
interface Ethernet0/7
 switchport access vlan 2
!
interface Vlan1
 description Connect to the dmz portion of my network
 nameif dmz
 security-level 50
 ip address 192.168.1.254 255.255.255.0
!
```

```
interface Vlan2
 description Connects to my private network
 nameif inside
 security-level 100
 ip address 10.0.0.1 255.255.255.0
!
interface Vlan4
 description Connects to the Internet
 no forward interface Vlan2
 nameif outside
 security-level 0
 ip address 23.1.2.3 255.255.255.240
ASA1(config)#
```

For the physical connectivity, you would use a patch cable from the appropriate port on the built-in eight-port switch to either a DMZ device, an inside device, or to the outside network device. For example, our server on the DMZ is connected with a patch cable to port 0/0 on the ASA. An inside host could be connected to any of the ports between 0/2 through 0/7 because all of those ports have been assigned to VLAN 2 (VLAN 2 is where the inside logical interface [the SVI] of the ASA is configured).

IP Addresses for Clients

Now that the ASA has its own IP addresses, you can configure it to hand out addresses to clients using DHCP by acting as a DHCP server. To do that, navigate to **Configuration > Device Management > DHCP > DHCP Server**, as shown in Figure 16-11.

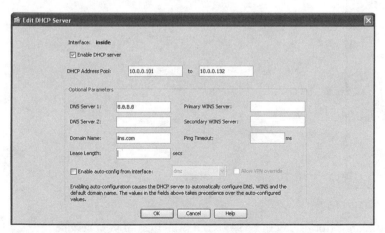

Figure 16-11   *Configuring the ASA to Be a DHCP Server*

By editing the properties of the inside interface and checking the check box that says you want to enable the DHCP service, you then also apply the pool of addresses that you want to hand out. The maximum size of the pool is 32 on the configuration shown for the ASA. You can also supply DNS and other related information. If we do not specify timeouts and lengths, it assumes the defaults for those values.

Example 16-5 shows the CLI equivalent result for the work we just did in ASDM.

Example 16-5 *Configuring the ASA as a DHCP Server for Inside Clients*

```
!  specifies the pool range, enables the feature and specifies the
!  interface
ASA1(config)# dhcpd address 10.0.0.101-10.0.0.132 inside
ASA1(config)# dhcpd enable inside
ASA1(config)# dhcpd dns 10.8.8.8  interface inside
ASA1(config)# dhcpd domain example.org interface inside
```

The ASA, by default, assigns itself as the default gateway for the DHCP clients to use.

Basic Routing to the Internet

The ASA needs to know how to forward traffic. Just like a router, ASAs can learn routes via dynamic routing protocols (*interior gateway protocols [IGP]* not *Border Gateway Protocol [BGP]*) from directly connected networks (which an ASA knows how to reach because it is directly connected) or default routes. If you want to look at or modify the routing table on the ASA, navigate to **Configuration > Device Setup > Routing**. From this location, you can view or manage static routes and dynamic routing protocols. If you want to add a static route such as a default route, you do that by clicking the **Static Routes** link and then clicking the **Add** button. From there, you use the drop-down menu to choose the interface where you are going to add this route. (This means the interface closest to the next hop where traffic will flow out of this interface to reach the destination network.) Figure 16-12 shows adding a static default route.

Figure 16-12 *Adding a Static Default Route*

The default gateway IP address (for use by the ASA) is the IP address of your service provider that is giving you access to the Internet. After you click **OK** and then **Apply**, the changes are sent to the ASA. Example 16-6 shows the CLI equivalent for these commands.

Example 16-6 *CLI Equivalent for Adding a Static Route*

```
! this tells the  ASA  that the default route will use the next hop of
! 23.1.2.7
! which is located off of the outside interface (on that same subnet)
ASA1(config)# route outside 0.0.0.0 0.0.0.0 23.1.2.7
```

NAT and PAT

16

Now that the ASA knows how to forward to the Internet and the DHCP clients on the inside know to use the ASA as their default gateway, we have a problem with the IP addresses the clients are using on the inside: They are all using private IP address space. Those packets will not be allowed on the Internet. Have no fear, because we know that the ASA can do *Network/Port Address Translation (NAT/PAT)*. To implement this, navigate to **Configuration > Firewall > NAT Rules** and click **Add** (see Figure 16-13).

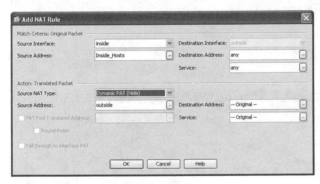

Figure 16-13 *Adding NAT Rules*

In the top half of the dialog box, you specify the source traffic (where the traffic will be coming from). I specified that the traffic will be coming into the inside interface from an object group that I created named Inside_Hosts. This interface allows you to dynamically create object groups by using the ellipsis button (...). It also asks about the exit interface that packet will have to be taking for the address translation to be used. The bottom half of the dialog box asks what you want to translate the IP address to. If you want to translate the addresses to the outside interface (meaning you are going to use PAT and the global address that is on the outside interface of the ASA), you can specify that you want to use **Dynamic PAT (Hide)** mode and then select the **outside** interface. The ASA translates the user's source IP addresses, and to the Internet it will appear that all transmitted packets (from your clients) are coming from the source address of the outside interface of the ASA. When you click **OK** and **Apply**, this configuration change is sent to the ASA. Example 16-7 shows the CLI equivalent.

Example 16-7 *CLI Equivalent for Implementing Dynamic PAT*

```
! creates a network object that refers to the 10.0.0.0/24 network
ASA1(config)# object network Inside_Hosts
ASA1(config-network-object)# subnet 10.0.0.0 255.255.255.0
```

```
ASA1(config-network-object)# description Inside_Hosts
ASA1(config-network-object)# exit
!  creates a NAT rule that says any traffic sourced from devices
!  from the Inside_Hosts object group (network the 10.0.0.0/24 network),
!  and coming in on the inside interface, as well as exiting (being routed
!  through) the outside interface (based on the routing table of the ASA),
!  it would then translate the source address of these packets,  and
!  substitute the source address of the outside interface of the ASA.
!  Additionally it would track this in a NAT/PAT  table,  that is separate
!  from the stateful  database, and the ASA would manage both of these
!  tables.
ASA1(config)# nat (inside,outside) 1 source dynamic Inside_Hosts interface
!  With the NAT on version 8.3 and newer, there are multiple options of
!  configuring the NAT, including a NAT command done within object group
!  configuration mode.  These additional options, including advanced ASA NAT
!  configuration are covered in the CCNP Security curriculum.
```

To verify the NAT configuration, navigate to the same location shown in Figure 16-13 and look at the NAT rules, as shown in Figure 16-14.

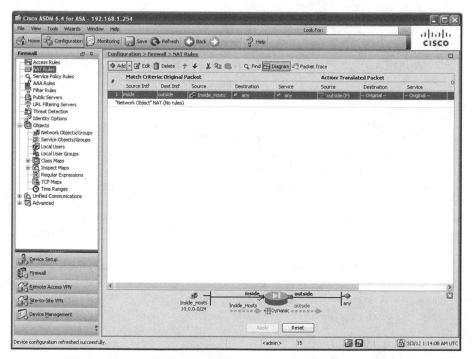

Figure 16-14 *NAT/PAT Rules Verification on the ASA*

Figure 16-14 shows that devices from the Inside_Hosts group are identified, but we do not know exactly what's in that group. On a live interface, you can hover over that group until a pop-up shows you the details of that group. Another option is to click the **Network Objects/Groups** link in the left navigation pane in Figure 16-14 to look at the details there.

One other challenge that might need to be addressed is that we can see the NAT will happen using the outside interface's IP address. But how do we know what that IP address is (on the outside interface)? Referring to Figure 16-10, we could look at the details of that interface, and even if it is DHCP-assigned for the outside interface (assigned to us by the service provider), the IP address will be revealed there, next to the interface name.

Permitting Additional Access Through the Firewall

The permissions allowing traffic sourced on higher-security interfaces and being routed through egress interfaces with lower security levels are allowed by default, and the stateful nature of the ASA dynamically allows the return traffic. If you want to apply ACLs either to filter what the inside users can initiate or to permit access that allows users on the outside to reach our DMZ resources, you can use a packet-filtering ACL. To apply an ACL, navigate to **Configuration > Firewall > Access Rules**. By default, the policy on the inside and DMZ interfaces (because they are not at security level 0) is to allow traffic sourced by devices on those interfaces to be forwarded to less-secure networks. The default policy on the outside interface is to deny everything (because the security level is 0). If you click the **Diagram** button, a diagram displays (near the bottom of the screen), which is handy to remind you which interfaces and directions you are working on within the GUI. Also down by the diagram is the option to show IPv4 and/or IPv6 access rule types, which are both supported on the ASA, as shown in Figure 16-15.

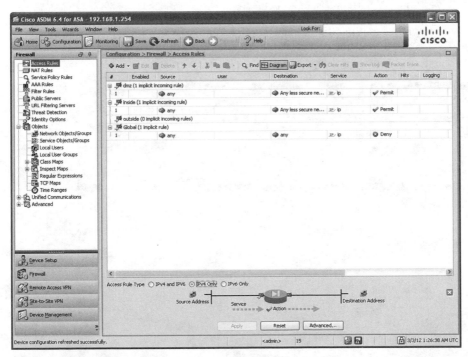

Figure 16-15 *Access Rules Configuration Page*

To create a new rule that denies Telnet traffic outbound from the inside network to the outside (regardless of source or destination IP address), you can create the rule that specifies TCP port 23 is denied, as shown in Figure 16-16.

Figure 16-16 *Adding an Access Rule*

To create a new rule, click the **Add** button. Use the drop-down list to select the interface that will be using this new rule. In the Add Access Rule dialog box, complete the form to indicate the addresses, ports, and protocols involved, and whether to permit or deny this traffic. When the configuration is as you want it, click **OK**.

You now have an ACL with one entry. Fortunately, none of this gets applied to the ASA until you click the **Apply** button. So, before you apply the changes, you also want to add a permit entry to this ACL to allow everything else, besides the Telnet traffic, through. Remember that at the end of an ACL there is an implied **deny all**.

Click **Add** once more and specify the same interface, this time specifying that you are going to permit all traffic. This then becomes the second entry in your final ACL. Figure 16-17 shows a summary.

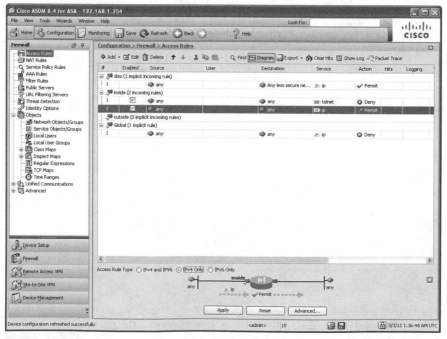

Figure 16-17 *Summary Page of Proposed Changes for the Access Rule*

The ASDM interface assumes that you will by applying the new ACL in the inbound direction to the specified interface.

After you have all the entries that you want to apply, just click the **Apply** button. Example 16-8 shows the CLI equivalent for the ACL entry (creating and applying it to the interface).

Example 16-8 *Creating and Applying an ACL at the CLI*

```
ASA1(config)# access-list inside_access_in deny tcp any any eq telnet
ASA1(config)# access-list inside_access_in permit ip any any
ASA1(config)# access-group inside_access_in in interface inside
! Note: the optional elements of line number, and extended are optional.
! The ASA assumes the ACL as an extended (if the keyword "standard" isn't
! used)
! In the absence of a "line" command, the ASA adds new entries to the end
! of the ACL
! To apply the ACL, the ASA uses a global access-group command, which is
! different than on an IOS router, where applying an ACL is done in
! interface configuration mode.
```

Using Packet Tracer to Verify Which Packets Are Allowed

Now that the firewall with interfaces has been configured and a default route has been set up and is providing NAT for the benefit of our clients, we should probably make sure that the rules that we have configured, including NAT, are performing as we want. Being able to troubleshoot a problem before it even occurs is a wonderful thing. ASA has a built-in tool called *Packet Tracer* that enables you to identify whether the ASA will forward or drop a packet, before the user even powers on her computer. Packet Tracer even indicates the reason why a packet would be dropped by the ASA.

You can launch Packet Tracer from the Tools menu, and there is an icon for Packet Tracer located on many of the configuration windows as well, including the Access Rules window shown previously in Figure 16-17. Also note that Cisco Academy has a simulator program called Packet Tracer; this is not the same tool as the Packet Tracer tool integrated into the ASAs.

After launching Packet Tracer from either the Tools menu or from an icon in the current window, you are presented with a dialog box in which you enter the specific traffic flow that you want to test or verify. Because we just placed an ACL on the inside interface that should permit everything except for Telnet traffic, we can test to see whether web traffic will be forwarded from our inside users as they make requests to web servers out on the Internet. To simulate this, we enter the source IP and port information and destination port and IP address and the interface and packet type that the packet will be using as it leaves the user and enters the firewall. Figure 16-18 shows the input for this test.

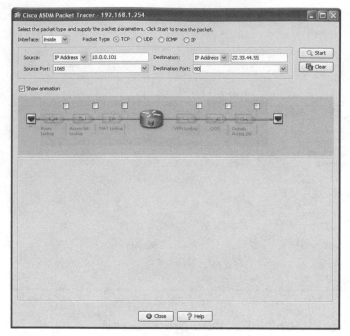

Figure 16-18   *Configuring Input for the Packet Tracer Test*

The literal IP of the source and destination do not have to be valid hosts, as the ASA is only determining, from it is current configuration, whether the firewall would allow the packet. In Figure 16-18, we use a random source port, higher than 1023, and the destination well-known TCP port of 80. The IP addresses represent a device from the inside and a server on the outside (based on the default route on the ASA). Also in the Packet Tracer, we identified that the traffic is entering the ASA on the inside interface. When we click **Start**, ASDM sends the commands to the ASA to simulate this packet.

The output in the GUI shows the final result of the packet being either allowed or denied, along with each of the individual checks that the ASA did along the way (each of which can be expanded), as shown in Figure 16-19.

From the output, we can see that the ASA performed several checks, and ultimately would have allowed this packet through the firewall. If there was any issue with ACLs, interfaces that are down, Modular Policy Framework, or any other policies or issues that would cause this ASA not to forward the packet, the result would show as a deny, including which part of the processing on the ASA caused the packet to be denied.

Behind the scenes, the ASA is really processing a CLI command and feeding the information back to ASDM. Example 16-9 shows the actual CLI for this command.

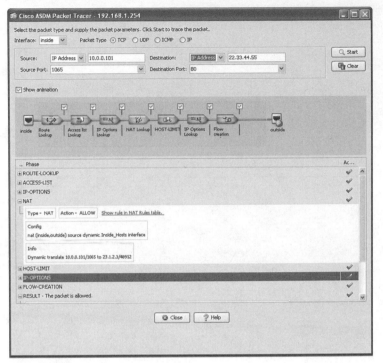

Figure 16-19 *Packet Tracer Results Screen*

Example 16-9 *Using the Packet Tracer Utility at the CLI*

```
! Checks to see if a packet, inbound on the inside interface,
! that is coming from host 10.0.0.101 and going to 22.33.44.55, and is
! TCP based and from port 1065 going to 80, and tell us if it would make
! it through the firewall
ASA1# packet-tracer input inside tcp 10.0.0.101 1065 22.33.44.55 80

! ! Here are the results of each of the tests it internally checks (based on
! the current, configured and default rules in place)
Phase: 1
Type: ROUTE-LOOKUP
Subtype: input
Result: ALLOW
Config:
Additional Information:
in    0.0.0.0        0.0.0.0         outside

Phase: 2
Type: ACCESS-LIST
Subtype: log
Result: ALLOW
Config:
```

```
access-group inside_access_in in interface inside
access-list inside_access_in extended permit ip any any
Additional Information:


Phase: 3
Type: IP-OPTIONS
Subtype:
Result: ALLOW
Config:
Additional Information:


Phase: 4
Type: NAT
Subtype:
Result: ALLOW
Config:
nat (inside,outside) source dynamic Inside_Hosts interface
Additional Information:
Dynamic translate 10.0.0.101/1065 to 23.1.2.3/5069


Phase: 5
Type: HOST-LIMIT
Subtype:
Result: ALLOW
Config:
Additional Information:


Phase: 6
Type: IP-OPTIONS
Subtype:
Result: ALLOW
Config:
Additional Information:


Phase: 7
Type: FLOW-CREATION
Subtype:
Result: ALLOW
Config:
Additional Information:
New flow created with id 1427, packet dispatched to next module


Result:
input-interface: inside
input-status: up
input-line-status: up
```

```
output-interface: outside
output-status: up
output-line-status: up
Action: allow

ASA1#
```

So, from this, we can safely say that the firewall will allow a host on the inside to initiate an HTTP session with a web server on the outside.

Verifying the Policy of No Telnet

Let's run a second test to see whether Telnet is denied (which it should be because of our ACL rule). In Packet Tracer, we input the details the same as before but change the port to 23, which is the well-known destination port for Telnet, and run the test. Figure 16-20 shows the results.

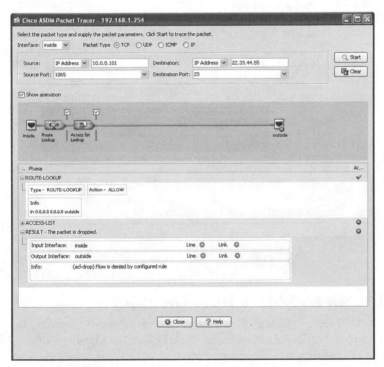

Figure 16-20 *Verifying the ACL Is Preventing Telnet Through the ASA*

This time we see that the initial route lookup took place, but when the ACL was checked, it failed and told us the result. The nice part of this is that it can assist in isolating not only that it did not work, but also the exact component (the reason) that caused it to fail.

Exam Preparation Tasks

Review All the Key Topics

Review the most important topics from this chapter, denoted with a Key Topic icon. Table 16-3 lists these key topics.

Table 16-3   Key Topics

Key Topic Element	Description	Page Number
Section	Meet the ASA Family	416
Section	ASA Features and Services	417
Section	ASA Security Levels	419
Section	The Default Flow of Traffic	420
Figure 16-2	Default Permissions and Return Traffic Allowed Because of Stateful Filtering	421
Section	Packet Filtering on the ASA	422
Section	Modular Policy Framework	424
Section	Configuring the Interfaces	435
Example 16-4	Implementing Additional Firewall Interfaces	440
Section	IP Addresses for Clients	443
Section	Basic Routing to the Internet	444
Section	NAT and PAT	445
Section	Permitting Additional Access Through the Firewall	447
Section	Using Packet Tracer to Verify Which Packets Are Allowed	449

Complete the Tables and Lists from Memory

Print a copy of Appendix C, "Memory Tables," (found on the CD) or at least the section for this chapter, and complete the tables and lists from memory. Appendix D, "Memory Tables Answer Key," also on the CD, includes completed tables and lists so that you can check your work.

Define Key Terms

Define the following key terms from this chapter, and check your answers in the glossary:

stateful filtering, security levels, SVI, Modular Policy Framework, class map, policy map, service policy

Command Reference to Check Your Memory

This section includes the most important configuration and EXEC commands covered in this chapter. To see how well you have memorized the commands as a side effect of your other studies, cover the left side of Table 16-4 with a piece of paper, read the descriptions on the right side, and see whether you remember the commands.

Table 16-4   Command Reference

Command	Description
nameif bubba	Assign the name bubba to a Layer 3 interface, done from interface configuration mode.
security-level 50	Assign a security level to an interface, done from interface configuration mode.
no shutdown	Bring an interface up out of shutdown mode.

16

This chapter covers the following topics:

IPS versus IDS

Identifying malicious traffic on the network

Managing signatures

Monitoring and managing alarms and alerts

Overview of the Cisco Next-Generation IPS solution

CHAPTER 17

Cisco IDS/IPS Fundamentals

Cisco intrusion detection systems (IDS) and *intrusion prevention systems (IPS)* are some of many systems used as part of a defense-in-depth approach to protecting the network against malicious traffic. Cisco has many different platforms and options for implementing an IPS/IDS system, but the basic concepts apply across all of these platforms. This chapter focuses on the concepts of IPS/IDS in general.

"Do I Know This Already?" Quiz

The "Do I Know This Already?" quiz helps you determine your level of knowledge of this chapter's topics before you begin. Table 17-1 details the major topics discussed in this chapter and their corresponding quiz questions.

Table 17-1 "Do I Know This Already?" Section-to-Question Mapping

Foundation Topics Section	Questions
IPS Versus IDS	1–3
Identifying Malicious Traffic on the Network	4–6
Managing Signatures	7–8
Monitoring and Managing Alarms and Alerts	9–10
Cisco Next-Generation IPS Solutions	11

1. Which method should you implement when it is not acceptable for an attack to reach its intended victim?

    a. IDS

    b. IPS

    c. Out of band

    d. Hardware appliance

2. A company has hired you to determine whether attacks are happening against the server farm, and it does not want any additional delay added to the network. Which deployment method should be used?

    a. Appliance-based inline

    b. IOS software-based inline

    c. Appliance-based IPS

    d. IDS

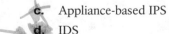

3. Why does IPS have the ability to prevent an ICMP-based attack from reaching the intended victim?

   a. Policy-based routing.

   b. TCP resets are used.

   c. The IPS is inline with the traffic.

   d. The IPS is in promiscuous mode.

4. Which method of IPS uses a baseline of normal network behavior and looks for deviations from that baseline?

   a. Reputation-based IPS

   b. Policy-based IPS

   c. Signature-based IPS

   d. Anomaly-based IPS

5. Which type of implementation requires custom signatures to be created by the administrator?

   a. Reputation-based IPS

   b. Policy-based IPS

   c. Engine-based IPS

   d. Anomaly-based IPS

6. Which method requires participation in global correlation involving groups outside your own enterprise?

   a. Reputation-based IPS

   b. Policy-based IPS

   c. Signature-based IPS

   d. Anomaly-based IPS

7. Which of the micro-engines contains signatures that can only match on a single packet, as opposed to a flow of packets?

   a. Atomic

   b. String

   c. Flood

   d. Other

8. Which of the following are properties directly associated with a signature? (Choose all that apply.)

   a. ASR

   b. SFR

   c. TVR

   d. RR

9. Which of the following is not a best practice?

   a. Assign aggressive IPS responses to specific signatures

   b. Assign aggressive IPS responses based on the resulting risk rating generated by the attack

   c. Tune the IPS and revisit the tuning process periodically

   d. Use correlation within the enterprise and globally for an improved security posture

10. What is the name of Cisco cloud-based services for IPS correlation?

   a. SIO

   b. EBAY

   c. ISO

   d. OSI

11. Which of the following is not a Next-Generation IPS (NGIPS) solution?

   a. NGIPSv

   b. ASA with FirePOWER

   c. SIO IPS

   d. FirePOWER 8000 series appliances

17

Foundation Topics

IPS Versus IDS

This section examines the platforms you can use for intrusion detection/prevention and explains the differences between IPS and IDS.

What Sensors Do

A *sensor* is a device that looks at traffic on the network and then makes a decision based on a set of rules to indicate whether that traffic is okay or whether it is malicious in some way. Because these are systems acting based on configured rules, no single system is ever 100 percent perfect. However, the objective is the same: to reduce the risk of malicious traffic, even though it cannot be completely eliminated.

Difference Between IPS and IDS

You can place a sensor in the network to analyze network traffic in one of two ways. The first option is to put a sensor inline with the traffic, which just means that any traffic going through your network is forced to go in one physical or logical port on the sensor. At the sensor, the traffic is analyzed. Then the sensor forwards out another logical or physical interface if the packet continues its journey toward its destination. If the traffic (while on its short layover at the sensor) is identified as being malicious by the sensor, the sensor (based on the rules configured) could decide that it will not forward the packet any further and drop it. Because the sensor is inline with the network, and because it can drop a packet and deny that packet from ever reaching its final destination (because it might cause harm to that destination), the sensor has in fact just prevented that attack from being carried out. That is the concept behind *intrusion prevention systems (IPS)*. Whenever you hear IPS mentioned, you immediately know that the sensor is inline with the traffic, which makes it possible to prevent the attack from making it further into the network. One negative about IPS is that because it is inline, if the sensor fails and you do not have an alternate path in your network, the entire network could fail as a result of the sensor having a problem. Depending on the platform, however, you may have the option to configure the sensor to "fail open," meaning that should the sensor fail, *all* traffic, both good and malicious, will continue to pass through the sensor. The sensor can also be configured in a "fail close" mode, which means that, should the sensor fail, *no* traffic, good or malicious, will pass through the sensor. In addition, a slight additional delay occurs as traffic is analyzed and then forwarded through the inline IPS.

So, then, what is an *intrusion detection system (IDS)*? To understand IDS, let's use the same sensor as we did previously, but instead of placing it inline in the network, we just send copies of the packets that are going through a network to the IDS sensor. When the packets arrive at the sensor in what is called promiscuous mode (because it is willing to look at anything that you send it), it can still analyze the traffic, and it can still generate alerts. However, because the original packet (that we have a copy of) is probably already on its way toward the destination, the sensor all by itself cannot deny the original packet from making its way further into the network. So, we could say that the IDS is *detecting* the attack (hence the term *intrusion detection system*) but is not *preventing* the attack. In a nutshell, that is the

IDS is

difference between IPS, which is inline, and IDS, which operates in promiscuous mode and is not inline but simply is analyzing copies of packets that were sent over to it (often by a switch configured to send it there). One benefit of IDS is that no delay is added to the original packet, and if the IDS fails, it does not hinder the network throughput because the IDS is not inline with the production network traffic. The corollary to this, however, is that an IDS solution cannot mitigate the effects of an attack directly because it does not have the capability to deny (prevent) malicious packets from entering the network.

Figure 17-1 shows a sensor implementation as an IDS versus an IPS. Also be aware that one physical sensor appliance with multiple interfaces could be configured as an IDS in one part of the network and as an IPS in a different part of the network.

Sensor in IPS (inline) mode—with the ability to drop the malicious packet before it enters the network.

Sensor "inline" IPS sees the original packet.

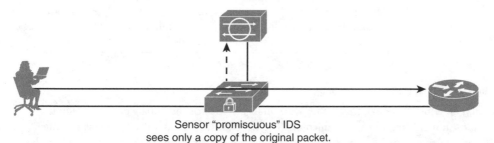

Sensor in IDS (promiscuous) mode—it gets a copy of the packet but cannot drop the malicious packet before it enters the network.

Sensor "promiscuous" IDS sees only a copy of the original packet.

Figure 17-1 *IPS Versus IDS*

The ability to compare and contrast the two implementation methods is important for both certification and the real world. Table 17-2 provides a side-by-side comparison.

Table 17-2 IDS Versus IPS

	IDS	IPS
Position in the network flow	Not inline with the flow of network traffic, the IDS is sent copies of the original packets.	Directly inline with the flow of network traffic and every packet goes through the sensor on its way through the network.
Mode	Promiscuous mode, out of band.	Inline mode.

17

	IDS	IPS
Latency or delay	Does not add delay to the original traffic because it is not inline.	Adds a small amount of delay before forwarding it through the network.
Impact caused by the sensor failing to forward packets	There is no negative impact if the sensor goes down.	If the sensor goes down, traffic that would normally flow through the sensor could be impacted. Dependent on "fail open" or "fail closed" configuration.
Ability to prevent malicious traffic from going into the network	By itself, a promiscuous mode IDS cannot stop the original packet. Options do exist for a sensor in promiscuous mode to request assistance from another device that is inline which may block future packets. An IDS can send TCP Reset packets to break (reset) malicious connections, but there is no guarantee that this will prevent an attack packet from reaching its destination.	The IPS can drop the packet on its own because it is inline. The IPS can also request assistance from another device to block future packets just as the IDS does.
Normalization ability	Because the IDS does not see the original packet, it cannot manipulate any original inline traffic.	Because the IPS is inline, it can normalize (manipulate or modify) traffic inline based on a current set of rules.

Sensor Platforms

Adding an IPS/IDS sensor to your network makes sense for the enhanced protection it provides, but this might cause a dilemma: For which of the many different areas of your network that need protection do you add a sensor? To help counter that concern, Cisco has several platforms that enable you to implement the IPS/IDS sensor functionality. Options include the following:

- A dedicated IPS appliance, such as the 4200 series
- Software running on the router in versions of IOS that support it
- A module in an IOS router, such as the AIM-IPS or NME-IPS modules
- A module on an ASA firewall in the form of the AIP module for IPS
- A blade that works in a 6500 series multilayer switch
- Cisco FirePOWER 8000/7000 series appliances
- Virtual Next-Generation IPS (NGIPSv) for VMware
- ASA with FirePOWER services

> **NOTE**   See the "Cisco Next-Generation IPS Solutions" section of this chapter for an overview of the most recent additions to Cisco's portfolio of IPS technologies and solutions.

True/False Negatives/Positives

Generally speaking, receiving accurate information (or true information) from a computer system is the desired outcome, including from an IPS/IDS looking for malicious traffic. Obviously, then, information from a computer system that is false (or inaccurate) is not a desired outcome, including from an IPS/IDS.

Positive/Negative Terminology

When working with an IPS/IDS, you will likely come across the following terms:

- False positive
- False negative
- True positive
- True negative

A *false positive* is when the sensor generates an alert about traffic and that traffic is not malicious or important as related to the safety of the network. False positives are easy to identify because alerts are generated and easily viewed. A *false negative*, however, is when there is malicious traffic on the network, and for whatever reason the IPS/IDS did not trigger an alert, so there is no visual indicator (at least from the IPS/IDS system) that anything negative is going on. In the case of a false negative, you must use some third-party or external system to alert you to the problem at hand, such as syslog messages from a network device.

The true positives and true negatives are much clearer and easier for a network administrator to understand. A *true positive* means that there was malicious traffic and that the sensor saw it and reported on it; if the sensor was an IPS, it may have dropped the malicious traffic based on the current set of rules in place. A *true negative* is also a wonderful thing in that there was normal nonmalicious traffic, and the sensor did not generate any type of alert, which is normal sensor behavior regarding nonmalicious traffic.

Identifying Malicious Traffic on the Network

Sensors can identify malicious traffic in many different ways. This section examines some of the techniques used by IPS and IDS sensors.

When the sensor is analyzing traffic, it looks for malicious traffic based on the rules that are currently in place on that sensor. There are several different methods that sensors can be configured to use to identify malicious traffic, including the following:

- Signature-based IPS/IDS
- Policy-based IPS/IDS
- Anomaly-based IPS/IDS
- Reputation-based IPS/IDS

Let's take a look at each of these options now.

Signature-Based IPS/IDS

A signature is just a set of rules looking for some specific pattern or characteristic in either a single packet or a stream of packets. A new sensor may have thousands of default signatures provided by Cisco. Not all the signatures are enabled, but the administrator can enable, disable, customize, and create new signatures to meet the needs of the current network where the sensor is operating. An example is a known attack, such as a cross-site scripting attack, where an HTTP variable contains a quote or bracket character to terminate some HTML syntax, followed by a **<SCRIPT>** tag. Cisco has written a signature (set of rules) looking for exactly that. Cisco creates additional signatures as new and significant attacks are discovered, which the administrator can implement by updating the signatures on the sensor. Signature-based IPS/IDS is the most significant method used on sensors today. For tuning purposes, if a default signature keeps triggering based on traffic that is normal for your network, that is considered a false positive for your specific network, and you could tune the sensor by either disabling that signature or setting the filter so that that signature does not generate an alert when it sees a match from specific IP addresses.

Policy-Based IPS/IDS

This type of traffic matching can be implemented based on the security policy for your network. For example, if your company has a security policy that states that no Telnet traffic should be used (for security reasons) on specific areas of your network, you can create a custom rule that states that if TCP traffic is seen destined to port 23 (which is the well-known port for Telnet) to a device in the part of the network for which Telnet is not permitted, the IPS can generate an alert and drop the packet. If this is configured as IDS, it could simply generate an alert (but cannot drop the packet on its own because IDS is in promiscuous mode, and not inline).

Anomaly-Based IPS/IDS

An example of anomaly-based IPS/IDS is creating a baseline of how many TCP sender requests are generated on average each minute that do not get a response. This is an example of a half-opened session. If a system creates a baseline of this (and for this discussion, let's pretend the baseline is an average of 30 half-opened sessions per minute), and then notices the half-opened sessions have increased to more than 100 per minute, and then acts based on that and generates an alert or begins to deny packets, this is an example of anomaly-based IPS/IDS. The Cisco IPS/IDS appliances have this ability (called *anomaly detection*), and it is used to identify worms that may be propagating through the network.

Reputation-Based IPS/IDS

If some type of global attack is propagating its way across the networks of the world but has not hit your network yet, wouldn't it be nice to know about it so that you can filter that traffic before it enters your network? The answer is yes, obviously. Reputation-based IPS collects input from systems all over the planet that are participating in global correlation; so what other sensors have learned collectively, your local sensor can use locally. Reputation-based IPS/IDS may include descriptors such as blocks of IP addresses, URLs, DNS domains, and so on as indicators of the sources for these attacks. Global correlation services are managed by Cisco as a cloud service.

Table 17-3 describes the advantages and disadvantages of these four categories of IPS/IDS detection technologies.

Table 17-3   IPS/IDS Method Advantages and Disadvantages

	Advantages	Disadvantages
Signature-based	Easy to configure, simple to implement.	Does not detect attacks outside of the rules. May need to disable signatures that are creating false positives. Signatures must be updated periodically to remain current and effective against new threats.
Policy-based	Simple and reliable, very customizable, only allows policy-based traffic that could deny unknown attacks, which by default are outside of the policy being allowed.	Policy must be manually created. Implementation of the policy is only as good as the signatures you manually create.
Anomaly-based	Self-configuring baselines, detect worms based on anomalies, even if specific signatures have not been created yet for that type of traffic.	Difficult to accurately profile extremely large networks. May cause false positives based on significant changes in valid network traffic.
Reputation-based	Leverages enterprise and global correlation, providing information based on the experience of other systems. Early-warning system.	Requires timely updates, and requires participation in the correlation process.

When Sensors Detect Malicious Traffic

Based on how the sensor is configured and which mode it is in (IPS or IDS), the sensor can implement the actions described in Table 17-4.

> **NOTE**   All of the "deny" response options in Table 17-4 apply only to a sensor that is in IPS mode.

Table 17-4   Possible Sensor Responses to Detected Attacks

Response	What It Means
Deny attacker inline	This action denies packets from the source IP address of the attacker for a configurable duration of time, after which the deny action can be dynamically removed. *Available only if the sensor is configured as an IPS.*

Response	What It Means
Deny connection inline	This action terminates the packet that triggered the action and future packets that are part of the same TCP connection. The attacker could open up a new TCP session (using different port numbers), which could still be permitted through the inline IPS. *Available only if the sensor is configured as an IPS.*
Deny packet inline	Deny packet terminates the packet that triggered the alert. *Available only if the sensor is configured as an IPS.*
Log attacker (source) packets	This action begins to log future packets based on the attacker's source IP address. This is done usually for a short duration, such as 30 seconds, after the initial alert. Log files are stored in a format that is readable by most protocol analyzers
Log victim (destination) packets	This logging action begins to log all IP packets that have a destination IP address of the victim (the destination address from the packet or packets that triggered the alert).
Log pair (source, destination) packets	This logging action begins to log IP packets if the source and destination addresses indicate that the packets from the source IP address that triggered the alert and the destination address match the destination address of the packet that triggered the alert. In essence, the sensor is only logging future packets sent between the attacker and the victim (the attacked device address).
Produce alert	An alert is the basic mechanism that is used by the IDS/IPS to identify that an event has occurred, such as a signature match indicating malicious traffic. This is the default behavior for most signatures enabled on a sensor.
Produce verbose alert	Produce verbose alert has the same behavior as produce alert; however it also includes a copy of the entire packet that triggered the alert. If both produce alert and produce verbose alert are enabled, it will still only generate a single alert and will include a copy of the triggering packet; that is, "Produce verbose alert" supercedes "Produce alert" when both are enabled.
Request block connection	Some sensor devices can ask for help to block the attacker's traffic at some point in the network. The device that connects to implement the blocking is called a blocking device, and could be an IOS router using *access control lists (ACL)*, a switch that supports *VLAN access control lists (VACL)*, or an *Adaptive Security Appliance (ASA)* firewall. This action causes the sensor to request a blocking device to block based on the source IP address of the attacker, the destination IP address of the victim, and the ports involved in the packet that triggered the alert. The difference between this option and the one that follows is that the request blocked connection gives an opportunity for the attacker to send traffic on different ports or different destination IPs and still allows connectivity for new sessions.
Request block host	This causes the sensor to request that the blocking devices (see the preceding paragraph) implement blocks based on the source IP address of the attacker (or destination IP address) regardless of the ports in use for future packets.

Response	What It Means
Request SNMP trap	This generates a *Simple Network Management Protocol (SNMP)* trap message that is sent to the configured management address for SNMP.
Reset TCP connection	This causes a sensor to send a proxy TCP reset to the attacker, with the intention of fooling the attacker into believing it is the victim sending the TCP reset. *Note: This action has an effect only on TCP-based traffic.*

Controlling Which Actions the Sensors Should Take

Many years ago, as the number of signatures kept increasing, it became very laborious to track and manage the individual actions for each and every signature on a sensor. A solution to this problem is to allow all the IPS/IDS sensors (after generating an alert) to consider how significant the risk is (related to that alert), and if the risk is high enough, then let the sensor go ahead and take appropriate countermeasure actions.

This is implemented using a calculated result called a *risk rating*. The maximum value for risk rating is 100. As the administrator, you can choose which countermeasure to take based on the risk rating that triggers an alert. There are three primary factors, or influencers, of the final risk rating value. The first is the accuracy of the signature (meaning how likely it is to not trigger false positive alerts), and this accuracy rating is known as the *signature fidelity rating (SFR)*, and it is configured as a property of a signature. The second major component that goes into calculating the risk rating is the *attack severity rating (ASR)* of the signature that triggered the alert. This property is also configured as part of the signature. The third major component that is used to calculate the risk rating is subjectively determined by the administrator of the sensor. It is called the *target value rating (TVR)*. To set the TVR, it is necessary to provide the sensor with the destination IP addresses or subnets that are the most critical. When attacks are seen going to these IP addresses, the final risk rating ends up being higher than if that same attack were going to a less-important device (that is, to an IP address or subnet that is not considered critical by the administrator). The TVR is not a property of any specific signature, but rather is a configured general parameter in the IPS. Some additional minor factors go into the risk rating, and Table 17-5 provides a summary of most relevant factors that influence the risk rating.

Table 17-5   Risk Rating (RR) Calculation Factors

Factor That Influences Risk Rating	Description
Target value rating (TVR)	The value that you, as an administrator, have assigned to specific destination IP addresses or subnets where the critical servers/devices live.
Signature fidelity rating (SFR)	The accuracy of the signature as determined by the person who created that signature. The likelihood that the signature will not result in a false positive.
Attack severity rating (ASR)	The criticality of the attack as determined by the person who created that signature.

Factor That Influences Risk Rating	Description
Attack relevancy (AR)	A signature match that is destined to a host where the attack is relevant, such as a Windows server–based attack, which is going to the destination address of a known Windows server, is considered a relevant attack, and the risk rating increases slightly as a result.
Global correlation	If the sensor is participating in global correlation and receives information about specific source addresses that are being used to implement large-scale attacks, attacks coming from these source IP addresses are also given a slightly increased risk rating value.

Implementing Actions Based on the Risk Rating

Although it is true that you can implement actions as properties of individual signatures, it makes the most sense, and it is much more scalable to manage, to configure actions based on the risk rating that is created as a result of the signature matches. For example, you can specify severe countermeasures if a risk rating is generated that is 90 or higher. (The max is 100, and if the risk rating calculation ends up with a value larger than 100, it rounds it down to that number.) A risk rating of 50 or lower may simply be configured to generate an alert but not cause a severe countermeasure, such as deny attacker, to be implemented. All of this is under administrator control.

Circumventing an IPS/IDS

An attacker has an objective, and it is likely that he does not want to be stopped or seen. So, if you have IPS/IDS in place, an attacker may try to evade detection of his activities by the IPS/IDS. Table 17-6 describes evasion methods an attacker may try to use and Cisco options to counter these evasion techniques.

Table 17-6　IPS/IDS Evasion Techniques

Evasion Method	Description	Cisco Anti-Evasion Techniques
Traffic fragmentation	The attacker splits malicious traffic into multiple parts with the intent that it will avoid detection by IPS/IDS technologies.	Complete session reassembly is performed by the sensor so that the IPS/IDS can see the entire flow of malicious traffic.
Traffic substitution and insertion	The attacker substitutes characters in the data using different formats that have the same final meaning. An example is Unicode strings, which an end station could interpret but perhaps could evade detection by IPS/IDS technologies.	Data normalization and de-obfuscation techniques. Cisco's implementation is looking for Unicode, case sensitivity, substitution of spaces with tabs, and other similar anti-evasion techniques.

Evasion Method	Description	Cisco Anti-Evasion Techniques
Protocol level misinterpretation	An attacker may attempt to cause a sensor to misinterpret the end-to-end meaning of a network protocol with the end goal of the sensor not detecting the attack in progress.	IP Time-To-Live (TTL) analysis, TCP checksum validation.
Timing attacks (for example, "low and slow" attacks)	Sending packets at a rate low enough to avoid triggering a signature (for example, a flood signature that triggers at 1000 packets per second, and the attacker sending packets at 900 packets per second).	Configurable intervals and use of third-party correlation.
Encryption and tunneling	Encrypted payloads are called encrypted for a reason. If an IPS/IDS sees only encrypted traffic, the attacker can build a Secure Sockets Layer (SSL) or IPsec session between himself and the victim and could then send private data over that virtual private network (VPN).	If traffic is encrypted and passing through the sensor as encrypted data, the encrypted payload cannot be inspected by legacy Cisco IPS solutions. For *generic routing encapsulation* (GRE) tunnels, there is support for inspection if the data is not encrypted. Starting with the latest Sourcefire version of the NGIPS solution, encrypted traffic can now be decrypted and inspected.
Resource exhaustion	If thousands of alerts are being generated by distracter attacks, an attacker may just be trying to disguise or cloak the single attack that he hopes succeeds. The resource exhaustion could be overwhelming the sensor and overwhelming the administration team who has to view the large volume of events.	Dynamic and configurable event summarization. Here is an example: 20,000 devices are all under the control of the attacker. All those devices begin to send the same attack. The sensor summarizes those by showing a few of the attacks as alerts, and then summaries at regular intervals that indicate the attack is still in play and how many thousands of times it occurred over the last interval. This is much better than trying to wade through thousands of individual alerts.

Managing Signatures

The most effective way to identify malicious traffic in the Cisco IPS/IDS systems is through the use of signature-based matching. This section covers how signatures are manipulated and managed to meet a specific network requirement.

Dealing with signatures is one of the tasks that you will perform as you tune, implement, maintain, and monitor a sensor appliance (or an IOS router running IPS in software). Cisco organizes its signatures into groups that have similar characteristics. For each of its groups, a signature micro-engine is used to govern that set of signatures. When a packet comes through the sensor, all the signatures in a specific group or micro-engine are compared simultaneously to the packet looking for matches. If you modify a signature, the micro-engine responsible for that signature is responsible for updating and implementing the changes behind the scenes. There are several signature micro-engines, and even inside of the micro-engine there are further subdivisions for the organization of the signatures. Fortunately, as administrators, we do not really have to worry too much about the specific micro-engines, but for certification you definitely want to be aware that they exist. Table 17-7 describes a few of the micro-engines.

Table 17-7   Micro-Engines (Groupings of Signatures)

Signature Micro-Engine	Signatures in This Grouping
Atomic	Signatures that can match on a single packet, as compared to a string of packets
Service	Signatures that examine application layer services, regardless of the operating system
String or Multistring	Supports flexible pattern matching and can be identified in a single packet or group of packets, such as a session
Other	Miscellaneous signatures that may not specifically fit into the previously mentioned other categories

Note that this is only a subset of the micro-engines and is presented here to introduce the concept.

Signature or Severity Levels

One of the properties of each signature is signature severity (also called *attack severity rating [ASR]*). This is a rating between 0 and 100 that indicates (in the eyes of the individual who created the signature) how severe the attack is that is covered by this particular signature. We discussed earlier the three primary factors that go into calculating the risk rating, and the ASR, which is a property of the signature, is one of those three elements. Instead of having to set a numeric value for the severity, the interface for IPS/IDS prompts us for one of four levels. Those four options are as follows:

- Informational
- Low
- Medium
- High

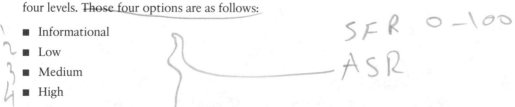

The higher the severity, the greater the number in the background that goes into the calculation for this factor into the risk rating.

The other property that is part of the signature and is a significant portion of the overall risk rating calculation is the *signature fidelity rating (SFR)*, and this value literally is a numeric value between 0 and 100 set by the person who created the signature. Both the SFR and the ASR can be tuned by the administrator regardless of what the initial value was set to by default.

Monitoring and Managing Alarms and Alerts

Cisco sensors can identify a wide range of attacks. Being aware that the attacks are happening is a big part of the IPS/IDS solution, and this section examines the options for working with the alarms and alerts generated by the IDS/IPS device.

As the sensor generates alerts, those alerts are fed real time into a monitoring system, which can display the information in beautiful color-coded formats, or you could go to the database of stored alerts, extract them, and analyze them that way, as well. Three main protocols are used in delivering alerts. They are *Security Device Event Exchange (SDEE)*, syslog, and SNMP. You can use one or all of these methods to get the alerts off of the sensor and sent to the device that you choose to use to view what is happening in the world of alerts.

SDEE is used for real-time delivery of alerts, and is the most secure method for delivering alerts. These can be sent to an application running on a server. One example is the software named *IPS Manager Express (IME)*, which can run on a workstation and be a central point of event viewing that can support up to 10 sensors simultaneously. Other management consoles, such as *Cisco Security Manager (CSM)*, can also be used and can support greater numbers of simultaneous sensors. The upper limit of what is reasonable is about 25 sensors reporting to a single manager machine.

> **NOTE** See the "Cisco Next-Generation IPS Solutions" section in this chapter for a brief overview of FireSIGHT Management Center, the most recent Cisco IPS management solution.

Security Intelligence

One thing I've noticed is that the more I work on a specific network, the more familiar I am with its behavior. This also is true with an IPS sensor. The sensor with multiple interfaces can operate in many different parts of the network at the same time, and the more visibility you have in those areas of your network, the more intelligence or information you will receive about what is going on and the greater ability you will have to establish baseline behavior patterns for those parts of the network. If you have multiple sensors in your enterprise environment, you can correlate all the events on a management station to get a better overall picture of what is happening and where the attacks are. So, in short, the more sensors you have reporting, the more granular and complete the information is going to be about the attacks and the patterns that exist in the network.

If we take this one step further and involve multiple organizations who are all reporting threats that are on global networks, such as the Internet, and we can correlate those events, we can use that information to defend our network borders against an attack that might not have reached us yet. In essence, a single sensor can give this device intelligence about that area of the network. Multiple sensors can give this enterprise intelligence about all the networks in your enterprise. The final step is global intelligence, where multiple organizations that are running sensors participate in global correlation and share information about external threats that may affect other companies, as well. With global correlation, we can increase the risk rating for specific attacks if they are from source addresses that we identified as suspect in information learned from external sensors through the global correlation process. Global correlation is available on the sensor appliances but does not have to be enabled.

Cisco offers the *Security Intelligence Operations (SIO)* service, which facilitates global threat information, reputation-based services, and sophisticated analysis for the benefit of Cisco security devices to better protect the networks they serve.

IPS/IDS Best Practices

Here are some of the recommended IPS/IDS best practices:

- Implement an IPS so that you can analyze traffic going to your critical servers and other mission-critical devices, or the "crown jewels" for your organization.

- If you cannot afford dedicated appliances, use modules or IOS software-based IPS/IDS. Appliances have better performance than modules, and modules have better performance than adding on the feature to existing IOS routers in software only.

- Take advantage of global correlation to improve your resistance against attacks that may be targeting your organization. Use correlation internally across all your sensors to get the best visibility of the network attacks that are being attempted.

- Use a risk-based approach, where countermeasures occur based on the calculated risk rating as opposed to manually assigning countermeasures to individual signatures.

- Use automated signature updates when possible instead of manually installing updates; this will assist in keeping the signatures current.

- Continue to tune the IPS/IDS infrastructure as traffic flows and network devices and topologies change. IPS tuning is mostly done on a brand new implementation but is never truly 100 percent complete.

Cisco Next-Generation IPS Solutions

Pursuant to Cisco's recent acquisition of Sourcefire, a brand new suite of IPS solutions, known as *Next-Generation IPS (NGIPS) solutions*, is now available for Cisco customers. This group of solutions consists of the following products and technologies:

- **Cisco FirePOWER 8000/7000 series appliances:** These two series of appliances make up the foundation platform for the Cisco FirePOWER NGIPS threat protection solution. These appliances provide a combination of real-time contextual awareness, full-stack visibility, and intelligent security automation. The 8000 series high-performance appliances consist of a modular design that allows security administrators to change the number and type of network interfaces as the organization's needs evolve. The 7000 series base platform provides lower throughput than the 8000 series, and it is delivered in a smaller form factor for organizations with fewer performance requirements and with more space restrictions. Threat protection with the FirePOWER 8000 and 7000 series of appliances can be extended through the purchase and installation of optional subscription licenses to provide *advanced malware protection (AMP)* along with application visibility and control.

- **Virtual Next-Generation IPS (NGIPSv) for VMware:** The virtualized offering of the Cisco FirePOWER NGIPS solution provides threat protection, real-time contextual awareness, intelligent security automation, and visibility into the entire IP stack. As with the previously described FirePOWER 8000 and 7000 series appliances, threat protection can be expanded as well for the NGIPSv through the purchase and installation of optional subscription licenses to provide AMP along with application visibility and control.

- **ASA with FirePOWER Services:** The ASA with FirePOWER services platform combines the proven and effective security protection of the existing Cisco ASA 5500-X series and ASA 5585-X firewall products with the added benefits provided by the newly released FirePOWER NGIPS and AMP technologies. ASA with FirePOWER services platforms start with the foundation of the most widely deployed stateful firewall and build on top of that features starting with the Next-Generation IPS as well as the Cisco AnyConnect Secure Mobility Client, Application Visibility and Control, URL filtering, and AMP.

- **FireSIGHT Management Center:** The Cisco ASA with FirePOWER services can be centrally managed and maintained through the use of the FireSIGHT Management Center. Use of the FireSIGHT Management Center provides automatic aggregation and correlation of network security data collected by the ASA with FirePOWER. This data brings with it visibility into the users, mobile devices, client-side applications, *virtual machine (VM)*-to-VM communications, vulnerabilities, threats, and URLs on the organization's network.

17

Exam Preparation Tasks

Review All the Key Topics

Review the most important topics from this chapter, denoted with a Key Topic icon. Table 17-8 lists these key topics.

Table 17-8 Key Topics

Key Topic Element	Description	Page Number
Table 17-2	IDS Versus IPS	461
Section	Sensor Platforms	462
List	Positive/negative terminology	463
List	The core methods for matching malicious traffic	463
Table 17-3	IPS Method Advantages and Disadvantages	465
Table 17-5	Risk Rating (RR) Calculation Factors	467
Table 17-6	IPS/IDS Evasion Techniques	468
Table 17-7	Micro-Engines (Groupings of Signatures)	470
List	IPS/IDS best practices	472
Section	Cisco Next-Generation IPS Solutions	472

Complete the Tables and Lists from Memory

Print a copy of Appendix C, "Memory Tables," (found on the CD) or at least the section for this chapter, and complete the tables and lists from memory. Appendix D, "Memory Tables Answer Key," also on the CD, includes completed tables and lists so that you can check your work.

Define Key Terms

Define the following key terms from this chapter, and check your answers in the glossary:

IPS, IDS, risk rating, attack severity rating, target value rating, signature fidelity rating, Next-Generation IPS (NGIPS)

This chapter covers the following topics:

Mitigation technology for e-mail-based threats

Mitigation technology for web-based threats

CHAPTER 18

Mitigation Technologies for E-mail-Based and Web-Based Threats

Efficient e-mail-based and web-based security requires a robust solution that is expanded beyond the traditional perimeter, as new threats are emerging on a daily basis. The Cisco *E-mail Security Appliances (ESA)* and the *Cisco Web Security Appliance (WSA)* provide a great solution designed to protect corporate users against these threats. Cisco has added *advanced malware protection (AMP)* to the ESA and WSA to allow security administrators to detect and block malware and perform continuous analysis and retrospective alerting. Both the ESA and WSA use cloud-based security intelligence to allow protection before, during, and after an attack. This chapter covers these technologies and solutions in detail. You will learn mitigation technologies such as spam and antimalware filtering, *data loss prevention (DLP)*, blacklisting, e-mail encryption, and web application filtering.

"Do I Know This Already?" Quiz

The "Do I Know This Already?" quiz helps you determine your level of knowledge of this chapter's topics before you begin. Table 18-1 details the major topics discussed in this chapter and their corresponding quiz questions.

Table 18-1 "Do I Know This Already?" Section-to-Question Mapping

Foundation Topics Section	Questions
Mitigation Technology for E-mail-Based Threats	1–4
Mitigation Technology for Web-Based Threats	5–8

1. Which of the following features does the Cisco ESA provide? (Choose all that apply.)

   a. Network antivirus capabilities

   b. E-mail encryption

   c. Threat outbreak prevention

   d. Support for remote access SSL VPN connections

2. Which of the following Cisco ESA models are designed for mid-sized organizations? (Choose all that apply.)

   a. Cisco C380

   b. Cisco C670

   c. Cisco C680

   d. Cisco X1070

3. What is a spear phishing attack?

   a. Unsolicited e-mails sent to an attacker.

   b. A denial-of-service (DoS) attack against an e-mail server.

   c. E-mails that are directed to specific individuals or organizations. An attacker may obtain information about the targeted individual or organization from social media sites and other sources.

   d. Spam e-mails sent to numerous victims with the purpose of making money.

4. Which of the following e-mail authentication mechanisms are supported by the Cisco ESA? (Choose all that apply.)

   a. Sender Policy Framework (SPF)

   b. Sender ID Framework (SIDF)

   c. DomainKeys Identified Mail (DKIM)

   d. DomainKeys Mail Protection (DMP)

5. Which of the following is the operating system used by the Cisco WSA ?

   a. Cisco AsyncOS operating system

   b. Cisco IOS-XR Software

   c. Cisco IOS-XE Software

   d. Cisco IOS Software

   e. Cisco ASA Software

6. Which of the following connectors are supported by the Cisco CWS service? (Choose all that apply.)

   a. Cisco Security Manager (CSM)

   b. Cisco ASA

   c. Cisco ISR G2 routers

   d. Cisco AnyConnect Secure Mobility Client

   e. Cisco WSA

7. Which of the following features are supported by the Cisco WSA? (Choose all that apply.)

   a. File reputation

   b. File sandboxing

   c. Layer 4 traffic monitor

   d. Real-time e-mail scanning

   e. Third-party DLP integration

8. Cisco WSA can be deployed using the Web Cache Communication Protocol (WCCP) configured in which of the following modes? (Choose all that apply.)

   a. Multiple context mode

   b. Explicit proxy mode

   c. Transparent proxy mode

   d. Virtualized mode

Foundation Topics

Mitigation Technology for E-mail-Based Threats

Users are no longer accessing e-mail from the corporate network or from a single device. Cisco provides cloud-based, hybrid, and on-premises ESA-based solutions that can help protect any dynamic environment. This section introduces these solutions and technologies explaining how users can use threat intelligence to detect, analyze, and protect against both known and emerging threats.

E-mail-Based Threats

There are several types of e-mail-based threats. The following are the most common:

- **Spam:** Unsolicited e-mail messages that can be advertising a service or (typically) a scam or a message with malicious intent. E-mail spam continues to be a major threat because it can be used to spread malware.

- **Malware attachments:** E-mail messages containing malicious software (malware).

- **Phishing:** An attacker's attempt to fool a user that such e-mail communication comes from a legitimate entity or site, such as banks, social media websites, online payment processors, or even corporate IT communications. The goal of the phishing e-mail is to steal user's sensitive information such as user credentials, bank accounts, and so on.

- **Spear phishing:** Phishing attempts that are more targeted. These phishing e-mails are directed to specific individuals or organizations. For instance, an attacker may perform a passive reconnaissance on the individual or organization by gathering information from social media sites (for example, Twitter, LinkedIn, Facebook) and other online resources. Then the attacker may tailor a more directed and relevant message to the victim increasing the probability of such user being fooled to follow a malicious link, click an attachment containing malware, or simply reply to the e-mail providing sensitive information. There is another phishing-based attack called *whaling*. These attacks specifically target executives and high-profile users within a given organization.

Cisco Cloud E-mail Security

Cisco cloud e-mail security provides a cloud-based solution that allows companies to outsource the management of their e-mail security. The service provides e-mail security instances in multiple Cisco data centers to enable high availability. Figure 18-1 illustrates the Cisco cloud e-mail security solution.

In Figure 18-1, three organizations (a large enterprise, a university, and a small- to medium-size business) leverage the Cisco hosted (cloud) environment. The solution also supports mobile workers.

18

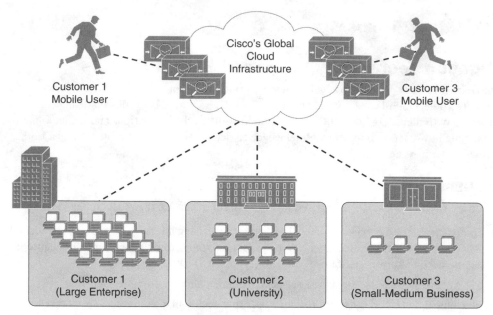

Figure 18-1   *Cisco Cloud E-mail Security Architecture*

Cisco Hybrid E-mail Security

The Cisco hybrid e-mail security solution combines both cloud-based and on-premises ESAs. This hybrid solution helps Cisco customers reduce their on-site e-mail security footprint, outsourcing a portion of their e-mail security to Cisco, while still allowing them to maintain control of confidential information within their physical boundaries. Many organizations need to stay compliant to many regulations that may require them to keep sensitive data physically on their premises. The Cisco hybrid e-mail security solution allows network security administrators to remain compliant and to maintain advanced control with encryption, *data loss prevention (DLP)*, and on-site identity-based integration.

Cisco E-mail Security Appliance

The following are the different ESA models:

- Cisco X-Series E-mail Security Appliances
  - **Cisco X1070:** High-performance ESA for service providers and large enterprises
- Cisco C-Series E-mail Security Appliances
  - **Cisco C680:** The high-performance ESA for service providers and large enterprises
  - **Cisco C670:** Designed for medium-size enterprises
  - **Cisco C380:** Designed for medium-size enterprises
  - **Cisco C370:** Designed for small- to medium-size enterprises
  - **Cisco C170:** Designed for small businesses and branch offices

The Cisco ESA runs the Cisco AsyncOS operating system. The Cisco AsyncOS supports numerous features that will help mitigate e-mail-based threats. The following are examples of the features supported by the Cisco ESA:

- **Access control:** Controlling access for inbound senders according to the sender's IP address, IP address range, or domain name.

- **Antispam:** Multilayer filters based on Cisco SenderBase reputation and Cisco antispam integration. The antispam reputation and zero-day threat intelligence are fueled by Cisco's security intelligence and research group named Talos.

- **Network Antivirus:** Network antivirus capabilities at the gateway. Cisco partnered with Sophos and McAfee, supporting their antivirus scanning engines.

- **Advanced malware protection (AMP):** Allows security administrators to detect and block malware and perform continuous analysis and retrospective alerting.

- **DLP:** The ability to detect any sensitive e-mails and documents leaving the corporation. The Cisco ESA integrates RSA e-mail DLP for outbound traffic.

NOTE   If RSA e-mail DLP is configured on a Cisco ESA that is also running antispam and antivirus scanning on inbound traffic, it can cause a performance decrease of less than 10 percent. Cisco ESAs that are only running outbound messages and are not running antispam and antivirus may experience a significant performance decline.

- **E-mail encryption:** The ability to encrypt outgoing mail to address regulatory requirements. The administrator can configure an encryption policy on the Cisco ESA and use a local key server or hosted key service to encrypt the message.

- **E-mail authentication:** A few e-mail authentication mechanisms are supported, including Sender Policy Framework (SPF), Sender ID Framework (SIDF), and DomainKeys Identified Mail (DKIM) verification of incoming mail, as well as DomainKeys and DKIM signing of outgoing mail.

- **Outbreak filters:** Preventive protection against new security outbreaks and e-mail-based scams using Cisco's Security Intelligence Operations (SIO) threat intelligence information.

NOTE   Cisco SenderBase is the world largest e-mail and web traffic monitoring network. It provides real-time threat intelligence powered by Cisco *Security Intelligence Operations (SIO)*. The Cisco SenderBase website is located at http://www.senderbase.org.

The Cisco ESA acts as the e-mail gateway to the organization, handling all e-mail connections, accepting messages, and relaying them to the appropriate systems. The Cisco ESA can service e-mail connections from the Internet to users inside your network, and from systems inside your network to the Internet. E-mail connections use *Simple Mail Transfer Protocol (SMTP)*. The ESA services all SMTP connections by default acting as the SMTP gateway.

18

> **NOTE**   Mail gateways are also known as a *mail exchangers* or *MX*.

The Cisco ESA uses listeners to handle incoming SMTP connection requests. A listener defines an e-mail processing service that is configured on an interface in the Cisco ESA. Listeners apply to e-mail entering the appliance from either the Internet or from internal systems.

The following listeners can be configured:

- Public listeners for e-mail coming in from the Internet.
- Private listeners for e-mail coming from hosts in the corporate (inside) network. These e-mails are typically from an internal groupware, Exchange, POP, or IMAP e-mail servers.

Figure 18-2 illustrates the concept of Cisco ESA listeners.

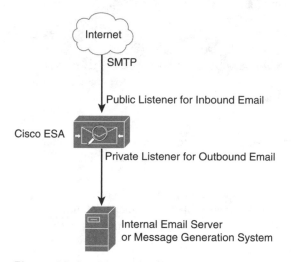

Figure 18-2   *Cisco ESA Listeners*

Cisco ESA listeners are often referred to as *SMTP daemons* running on a specific Cisco ESA interface. When a listener is configured, the following information must be provided:

- Listener properties such as a specific interface in the Cisco ESA and the TCP port that will be used. The listener properties must also indicate whether it is a public or a private listener.
- The hosts that are allowed to connect to the listener using a combination of access control rules. An administrator can specify which remote hosts can connect to the listener.
- The local domains for which public listeners accept messages.

Cisco ESA Initial Configuration

To perform the initial Cisco ESA configuration, complete the following steps:

Step 1. Log in to the Cisco ESA. The default username is admin, and the default password is ironport.

Step 2. Use the **systemsetup** command in the *command-line interface (CLI)* of the Cisco ESA to initiate the System Setup Wizard, as shown in Example 18-1.

Example 18-1   *Initial Setup with the* **systemsetup** *Command*

```
IronPort> systemsetup
WARNING: The system setup wizard will completely delete any existing
'listeners' and all associated settings including the 'Host Access Table' - mail
operations may be interrupted.
Are you sure you wish to continue? [Y]> Y


You are now going to configure how the IronPort C60 accepts mail by
creating a "Listener".


Please create a name for this listener (Ex: "InboundMail"):
[]> InboundMail


Please choose an IP interface for this Listener.
1. Management (192.168.42.42/24: mail3.example.com)
2. PrivateNet (192.168.1.1/24: mail3.example.com)
3. PublicNet (192.168.2.1/24: mail3.example.com)


[1]> 3
Enter the domains or specific addresses you want to accept mail for.
Hostnames such as "example.com" are allowed.


Partial hostnames such as ".example.com" are allowed.


Usernames such as "postmaster@" are allowed.


Full email addresses such as "joe@example.com" or "joe@[1.2.3.4]" are allowed.
Separate multiple addresses with commas


[]> securemeinc.org
Would you like to configure SMTP routes for example.com? [Y]> y


Enter the destination mail server which you want mail for example.com to be delivered.


Separate multiple entries with commas.
[]> exchange.securemeinc.org
```

18

```
Do you want to enable rate limiting for this listener? (Rate limiting defines the
maximum

number of recipients per hour you are willing to receive from a remote domain.) [Y]> y

Enter the maximum number of recipients per hour to accept from a remote domain.
[]> 4500

Default Policy Parameters
==========================
Maximum Message Size: 100M
Maximum Number Of Connections From A Single IP: 1,000
Maximum Number Of Messages Per Connection: 1,000
Maximum Number Of Recipients Per Message: 1,000
Maximum Number Of Recipients Per Hour: 4,500
Maximum Recipients Per Hour SMTP Response:
 452 Too many recipients received this hour
Use SenderBase for Flow Control: Yes
Virus Detection Enabled: Yes
Allow TLS Connections: No
Would you like to change the default host access policy? [N]> n
Listener InboundMail created.
Defaults have been set for a Public listener.

Use the listenerconfig->EDIT command to customize the listener.
*****

Do you want to configure the C60 to relay mail for internal hosts? [Y]> y

Please create a name for this listener (Ex: "OutboundMail"):
[]> OutboundMail

Please choose an IP interface for this Listener.
1. Management (192.168.42.42/24: mail3.example.com)
2. PrivateNet (192.168.1.1/24: mail3.example.com)
3. PublicNet (192.168.2.1/24: mail3.example.com)

[1]> 2

Please specify the systems allowed to relay email through the IronPort C60.

Hostnames such as "example.com" are allowed.

Partial hostnames such as ".example.com" are allowed.

IP addresses, IP address ranges, and partial IP addressed are allowed.
```

```
Separate multiple entries with commas.
[]> .securemeinc.org

Do you want to enable rate limiting for this listener? (Rate limiting defines the
maximum number of recipients per hour you are willing to receive from a remote
domain.)
[N]> n

Default Policy Parameters
==========================
Maximum Message Size: 100M
Maximum Number Of Connections From A Single IP: 600
Maximum Number Of Messages Per Connection: 10,000
Maximum Number Of Recipients Per Message: 100,000
Maximum Number Of Recipients Per Hour: Disabled
Use SenderBase for Flow Control: No
Virus Detection Enabled: Yes
Allow TLS Connections: No
Would you like to change the default host access policy? [N]> n
Listener OutboundMAil created.
Defaults have been set for a Private listener.
Use the listenerconfig->EDIT command to customize the listener.
*****

Congratulations! System setup is complete. For advanced configuration, please refer to
  the User Guide.
mail3.securemeinc.org >
```

In Example 18-1, the inside (private) and outside (public) listeners are configured. The domain name of securemeinc.org is used in this example.

To verify the configuration, you can use the **mailconfig** command to send a test e-mail containing the system configuration data that was entered in the System Setup Wizard, as shown in Example 18-2.

Example 18-2 *Verifying the Configuration with the* **mailconfig** *Command*

```
mail3.securemeinc.org> mailconfig

Please enter the email address to which you want to send
the configuration file. Separate multiple addresses with commas.

[]> admin@securemeinc.org

The configuration file has been sent to admin@securemeinc.org.

mail3.securemeinc.org>
```

In Example 18-2, the e-mail is sent to the administrator (admin@securemeinc.org).

Mitigation Technology for Web-Based Threats

For any organization to be able to protect its environment against web-based security threats, the security administrators need to deploy tools and mitigation technologies that go far beyond traditional blocking of known bad websites. Nowadays, you can download malware through compromised legitimate websites, including social media sites, advertisements in news and corporate sites, gaming sites, and many more. Cisco has developed several tools and mechanisms to help their customers combat these threats. The core solutions for mitigating web-based threats are the Cisco *Cloud Web Security (CWS)* offering and the integration of *advanced malware protection (AMP)* to the Cisco *Web Security Appliance (WSA)*. Both solutions enable malware detection and blocking, continuous monitoring, and retrospective alerting. The following sections cover the Cisco CWS and Cisco WSA in detail.

Cisco CWS

Cisco CWS is a cloud-based security service from Cisco that provides worldwide threat intelligence, advanced threat defense capabilities, and roaming user protection. The Cisco CWS service uses web proxies in Cisco's cloud environment that scan traffic for malware and policy enforcement. Cisco customers can connect to the Cisco CWS service directly by using a *proxy autoconfiguration (PAC)* file in the user endpoint or through connectors integrated into the following Cisco products:

- Cisco ISR G2 routers
- Cisco ASA
- Cisco WSA
- Cisco AnyConnect Secure Mobility Client

Organizations using the transparent proxy functionality through a connector can get the most out of their existing infrastructure. In addition, the scanning is offloaded from the hardware appliances to the cloud, reducing the impact to hardware utilization and reducing network latency. Figure 18-3 illustrates how the transparent proxy functionality through a connector works.

In Figure 18-3, the Cisco ASA is enabled with the Cisco CWS connector at a branch office. The following steps explain how Cisco CWS protects the corporate users at the branch office:

1. An internal user makes an HTTP request to an external website (securemeinc.org).
2. The Cisco ASA forwards the request to Cisco CWS global cloud infrastructure.
3. It notices that securemeinc.org had some web content (ads) that were redirecting the user to a known malicious site.
4. Cisco CWS blocks the request to the malicious site.

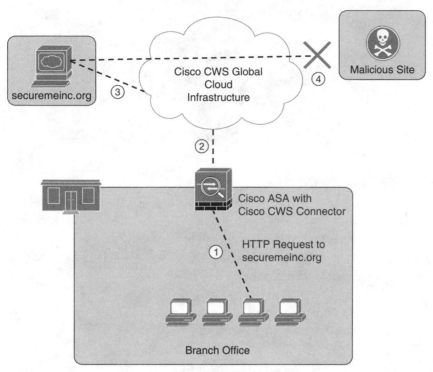

Figure 18-3   *Cisco ASA with Cisco CWS Connector Example*

Cisco WSA

The Cisco WSA uses cloud-based intelligence from Cisco to help protect the organization before, during, and after an attack. This "lifecycle" is what is referred to as the *attack continuum*. The cloud-based intelligence includes web (URL) reputation and zero-day threat intelligence from Cisco's security intelligence and research group named Talos. This threat intelligence helps security professionals to stop threats before they enter the corporate network, while also enabling file reputation and file sandboxing to identify threats during an attack. Retrospective attack analysis allows security administrators to investigate and provide protection after an attack when advanced malware might have evaded other layers of defense.

The Cisco WSA can be deployed in explicit proxy mode or as a transparent proxy using the *Web Cache Communication Protocol (WCCP)*. WCCP is a protocol originally developed by Cisco, but several other vendors have integrated it in their products to allow clustering and transparent proxy deployments on networks using Cisco infrastructure devices (routers, switches, firewalls, and so on).

Figure 18-4 illustrates a Cisco WSA deployed as an explicit proxy.

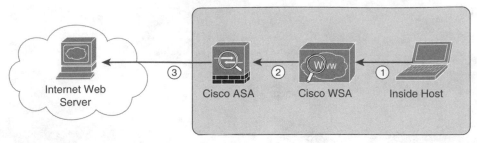

Figure 18-4 *Explicit Proxy Configuration*

The following are the steps illustrated in Figure 18-4:

1. An internal user makes an HTTP request to an external website. The client browser is configured to send the request to the Cisco WSA.

2. The Cisco WSA connects to the website on behalf of the internal user.

3. The firewall (Cisco ASA) is configured to only allow outbound web traffic from the Cisco WSA, and it forwards the traffic to the web server.

Figure 18-5 shows a Cisco WSA deployed as a transparent proxy.

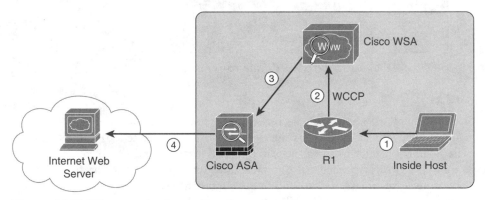

Figure 18-5 *Transparent Proxy Configuration*

The following are the steps illustrated in Figure 18-5:

1. An internal user makes an HTTP request to an external website.

2. The internal router (R1) redirects the web request to the Cisco WSA using WCCP.

3. The Cisco WSA connects to the website on behalf of the internal user.

4. Also in this example, the firewall (Cisco ASA) is configured to only allow outbound web traffic from the WSA. The web traffic is sent to the Internet web server.

Figure 18-6 demonstrates how the WCCP registration works. The Cisco WSA is the WCCP client, and the Cisco router is the WCCP server.

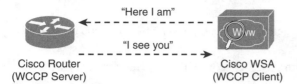

Figure 18-6 *WCCP Registration*

During the WCCP registration process, the WCCP client sends a registration announcement ("Here I am") every 10 seconds. The WCCP server (the Cisco router in this example) accepts the registration request and acknowledges it with an "I See You" WCCP message. The WCCP server waits 30 seconds before it declares the client as "inactive" (engine failed). WCCP can be used in large-scale environments. Figure 18-7 shows a cluster of Cisco WSAs, where internal Layer 3 switches redirect web traffic to the cluster.

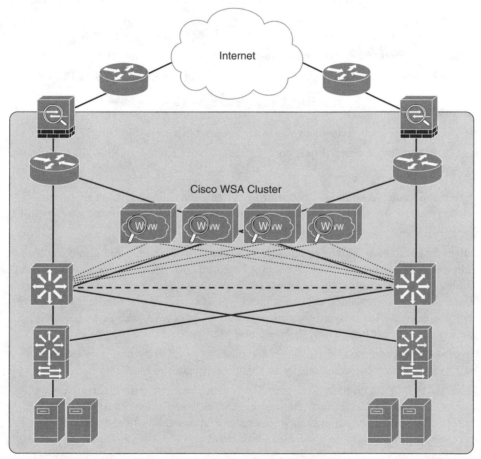

Figure 18-7 *Cisco WSA Cluster Example*

The Cisco WSA comes in different models. The following are the different Cisco WSA models:

- Cisco WSA S680
    - It is a high-performance WSA designed for large organizations with 6000 to 12,000 users.
    - A 2 *rack-unit (RU)* appliance with 16 (2 octa core) CPUs, 32 GB of memory, and 4.8 TB of disk space.
- Cisco WSA S670
    - A high-performance WSA designed for large organizations with 6000 to 12,000 users
    - A 2 RU appliance with 8 (2 octa core) CPUs, 8 GB of memory, and 2.7 TB of disk space.
- Cisco WSA S380
    - Designed for medium-size organizations with 1500 to 6000 users.
    - A 2 RU appliance with 6 (1 hexa core) CPUs, 16 GB of memory, and 2.4 TB of disk space.
- Cisco WSA S370
    - Designed for medium-size organizations with 1500 to 6000 users.
    - A 2 RU appliance with 4 (1 quad core) CPUs, 4 GB of memory, and 1.8 TB of disk space.
- Cisco WSA S170
    - Designed for small- to medium-size organizations with up to 1500 users.
    - A 1 RU appliance with 2 (1 dual core) CPUs, 4 GB of memory, and 500 GB of disk space.

The Cisco WSA runs Cisco AsyncOS operating system. The Cisco AsyncOS supports numerous features that will help mitigate web-based threats. The following are examples of these features:

- **Real-time antimalware adaptive scanning:** The Cisco WSA can be configured to dynamically select an antimalware scanning engine based on URL reputation, content type, and scanner effectiveness. Adaptive scanning is a feature designed to increase the "catch rate" of malware that is embedded in images, JavaScript, text, and Adobe Flash files. Adaptive scanning is an additional layer of security on top of Cisco WSA Web Reputation Filters that include support for Sophos, Webroot, and McAfee.
- **Layer 4 traffic monitor:** Used to detect and block spyware. It dynamically adds IP addresses of known malware domains to a database of sites to block.
- **Third-party DLP integration:** Redirects all outbound traffic to a third-party DLP appliance, allowing deep content inspection for regulatory compliance and data exfiltration protection. It enables an administrator to inspect web content by title, metadata, and size and to even prevent users from storing files to cloud services, such as Dropbox, Google Drive, and others.
- **File reputation:** Using threat information from Cisco Talos. This file reputation threat intelligence is updated every 3 to 5 minutes.

- **File sandboxing:** If malware is detected, the Cisco AMP capabilities can put files in a sandbox to inspect its behavior, combining the inspection with machine-learning analysis to determine the threat level. Cisco Cognitive Threat Analytics (CTA) uses machine-learning algorithms to adapt over time.

- **File retrospection:** After a malicious attempt or malware is detected, the Cisco WSA continues to cross-examine files over an extended period of time.

- **Application visibility and control:** Allows the Cisco ASA to inspect and even block applications that are not allowed by the corporate security polity. For example, an administrator can allow users to use social media sites like Facebook but block micro-applications such as Facebook games.

Cisco Content Security Management Appliance

Cisco *Security Management Appliance (SMA)* is a Cisco product that centralizes the management and reporting for one or more Cisco ESAs and Cisco WSAs. Cisco SMA has consistent enforcement of policy, and enhances threat protection. Figure 18-8 shows a Cisco SMA that is controlling Cisco ESAs and Cisco WSAs in different geographic locations (New York, Raleigh, Chicago, and Boston).

18

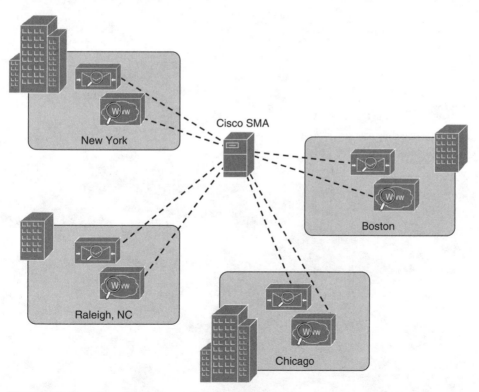

Figure 18-8 *Cisco SMA Centralized Deployment*

The Cisco SMA comes in different models. These models are physical appliances or the Cisco Content *Security Management Virtual Appliance (SMAV)*. The following are the different Cisco SMA models:

- **Cisco SMA M680:** Designed for large organizations with over 10,000 users
- **Cisco SMAV M600v:** Designed for large enterprises or service providers
- **Cisco SMA M380:** Designed for organizations with 1000 to 10,000 users
- **Cisco SMAV M300v:** Designed for organizations with 1000 to 5000 users
- **Cisco SMA M170:** Designed for small business or branch offices with up to 1000 users
- **Cisco SMAV M100v:** Designed for small business or branch offices with up to 1000 users

NOTE   Cisco also has a Cisco SMAV M000v that is used for evaluations only.

Exam Preparation Tasks

Review All the Key Topics

Review the most important topics from this chapter, denoted with a Key Topic icon. Table 18-2 lists these key topics.

 Table 18-2 Key Topics

Key Topic Element	Description	Page Number
Section	E-mail-Based Threats	479
Section	Cisco Cloud E-mail Security	479
Section	Cisco E-mail Security Appliance	480
Section	Mitigation Technology for Web-Based Threats	486
Section	Cisco CWS	486
Section	Cisco WSA	487

18

Complete the Tables and Lists from Memory

Print a copy of Appendix C, "Memory Tables," (found on the CD) or at least the section for this chapter, and complete the tables and lists from memory. Appendix D, "Memory Tables Answer Key," also on the CD, includes completed tables and lists so that you can check your work. There are no applicable tables in this specific chapter.

Define Key Terms

Define the following key terms from this chapter, and check your answers in the glossary:

antispam filters, network antivirus, advanced malware protection (AMP), file sandboxing, file retrospection

Command Reference to Check Your Memory

This section includes the most important configuration and EXEC commands covered in this chapter. To see how well you have memorized the commands as a side effect of your other studies, cover the left side of Table 18-3 with a piece of paper, read the descriptions on the right side, and see whether you remember the commands.

Table 18-3 Command Reference

Command	Description
systemsetup	Launch the System Setup Wizard to initially configure the Cisco ESA.
mailconfig	Verify the Cisco ESA configuration by sending a test e-mail that contains the system configuration data that was entered in the system setup wizard.

This chapter covers the following topics:

Antivirus and antimalware solutions

Personal firewalls and host intrusion prevention systems

Advanced Malware Protection for Endpoints

Hardware and software encryption of endpoint data

CHAPTER 19

Mitigation Technologies for Endpoint Threats

Computer viruses and malware have been in existence for a long time. However, the level of sophistication has increased over the years. This chapter provides details of the different mitigation technologies available for endpoint threats. It covers introductory concepts of endpoint threats to advanced malware protection capabilities provided by Cisco security products.

"Do I Know This Already?" Quiz

The "Do I Know This Already?" quiz helps you determine your level of knowledge of this chapter's topics before you begin. Table 19-1 details the major topics discussed in this chapter and their corresponding quiz questions.

Table 19-1   "Do I Know This Already?" Section-to-Question Mapping

Foundation Topics Section	Questions
Antivirus and Antimalware Solutions	1–3
Personal Firewalls and Host Intrusion Prevention Systems	4–5
Advanced Malware Protection for Endpoints	6–7
Hardware and Software Encryption of Endpoint Data	8

1. Which of the following are examples of the most common types of malware? (Choose all that apply.)

   a. viruses

   b. worms

   c. file encryption software

   d. Trojan horses

2. Which of the following are open source antivirus software? (Choose all that apply.)

   a. ClamAV

   b. Immunet

   c. ImuniSec

   d. ClamSoft

3. Which of the following statements is correct about back doors?

   a. Back doors are created when a buffer overflow is exploited.

   b. Back doors can open a network port on the affected system so that the attacker can connect and control such system.

   c. Back doors can open a network firewall port in the network.

   d. Back doors are used to legitimately configure system configurations.

4. Cisco AMP for Endpoints provides advanced malware protection for which of the following operating systems? (Choose all that apply.)

   a. Windows

   b. MAC OS X

   c. Android

   d. Solaris

   e. HP-UX

5. Which of the following are examples of e-mail encryption solutions? (Choose all that apply.)

   a. Secure/Multipurpose Internet Mail Extensions (S/MIME)

   b. VPNs

   c. Pretty Good Privacy (PGP)

   d. GNU Privacy Guard (GnuPG)

   e. Web-based encryption e-mail service like Sendinc or JumbleMe

6. Which of the following file types are supported by Cisco AMP for Endpoints? (Choose all that apply.)

   a. PDF

   b. ASC

   c. MSCAB

   d. ZIP

   e. MACHO

7. Which of the following are examples of full disk encryption legitimate software? (Choose all that apply.)

   a. FileVault

   b. Cisco FileEncryptor

   c. BitLocker

   d. CryptoWall

   e. CryptoLocker

8. VPN implementations can be categorized into which of the following two distinct groups?

   a. Site-to-site VPNs

   b. Free VPNs

   c. Commercial VPNs

   d. Remote-access VPNs

Foundation Topics

Antivirus and Antimalware Solutions

There are numerous antivirus and antimalware solutions on the market designed to detect, analyze, and protect against both known and emerging endpoint threats. Before diving into these technologies, you should learn what are viruses and malicious software (malware) and some of the taxonomy around the different types of malicious software. The following are the most common types of malicious software:

- **Computer viruses:** A malicious software that infects a host file or system area to perform undesirable outcomes such as erasing data, stealing information, or corrupting the integrity of the system. In numerous cases, these viruses multiply again to form new generations of themselves.

- **Worms:** Viruses that replicate themselves over the network infecting numerous vulnerable systems. In most occasions, a worm will execute malicious instructions on a remote system without user interaction.

- **Mailers and mass-mailer worms:** A type of worm that sends itself in an e-mail message. Examples of mass-mailer worms are Loveletter.A@mm and W32/SKA.A@m (a.k.a. the Happy99 worm), which sends a copy of itself every time the user sends a new message.

- **Logic bombs:** A type of malicious code that is injected into a legitimate application. An attacker can program a logic bomb to delete itself from the disk after it performs the malicious tasks on the system. Examples of these malicious tasks include deleting or corrupting files or databases and executing a specific instruction after certain system conditions are met.

- **Trojan horses:** A type of malware that executes instructions determined by the nature of the Trojan to delete files, steal data, and compromise the integrity of the underlying operating system. Trojan horses typically use a form of social engineering to fool victims to install such software in their computers or mobile devices. Trojans can also act as back doors.

- **Back doors:** A piece of malware or configuration change that allows attackers to control the victim's system remotely. For example, a back door can open a network port on the affected system so that the attacker can connect and control such system.

- **Exploits:** A malicious program designed to "exploit" or take advantage of a single vulnerability or set of vulnerabilities.

- **Downloaders:** A piece of malware that downloads and installs other malicious content from the Internet to perform additional exploitation on an affected system.

- **Spammers:** In Chapter 18, "Mitigation Technologies for E-mail-Based and Web-Based Threats"), you learned that spam is referred to as the act of sending unsolicited messages via e-mail, instant messaging, newsgroups, or any other kind of computer or mobile device communications. Spammers use the type of malware that's sole purpose is to send these unsolicited messages with the primary goal of fooling users to click on malicious links, reply to e-mails or such messages with sensitive information, or perform different types of scams. The attacker's main objective is to make money.

19

- **Key loggers:** A piece of malware that captures the user's keystrokes on a compromised computer or mobile device. It collects sensitive information such as passwords, PINs, personal identifiable information (PII), credit card numbers, and more.

- **Rootkits:** A set of tools that are used by an attacker to elevate their privilege to obtain root-level access to be able to completely take control of the affected system.

- **Ransomware:** A type of malware that compromises a system and then demands a ransom from the victim to often pay the attacker in order for the malicious activity to cease or for the malware to be removed from the affected system. Two examples of ransomware are Crypto Locker and CryptoWall. These two are malware that encrypt the victim's data and demands the user to pay a ransom in order for the data to be decrypted and accessible back to the victim.

There are numerous types of commercial and free antivirus software. The following are a few examples of commercial and free antivirus software:

- avast!
- AVG Internet Security
- Bitdefender Antivirus Free
- ZoneAlarm PRO Antivirus + Firewall and ZoneAlarm Internet Security Suite
- F-Secure Antivirus
- Kaspersky Anti-Virus
- McAfee Antivirus
- Panda Antivirus
- Sophos Antivirus
- Norton AntiVirus
- ClamAV
- Immunet

> **NOTE** ClamAV is an open source antivirus engine sponsored and maintained by Cisco and non-Cisco engineers. You can download ClamAV from http://www.clamav.net. Immunet is a free community-based antivirus software maintained by Cisco Sourcefire. You can download Immunet from http://www.immunet.com.
>
> There are numerous other antivirus software companies and products. The following link provides a comprehensive list and comparison of the different antivirus software available on the market: http://en.wikipedia.org/wiki/Comparison_of_antivirus_software.

Personal Firewalls and Host Intrusion Prevention Systems

Personal firewalls and *host intrusion prevention systems (HIPS)* are software applications that you can install on end-user machines or servers to protect them from external security threats and intrusions. The term *personal firewall* typically applies to basic software that can control Layer 3 and Layer 4 access to client machines. HIPS provides several features that offer more robust security than a traditional personal firewall, such as host intrusion prevention and protection against spyware, viruses, worms, Trojans, and other types of malware.

Today, more sophisticated software is available on the market that makes basic personal firewalls and HIPS obsolete. For example, Cisco *Advanced Malware Protection (AMP)* for Endpoints provide more granular visibility and control to stop advanced threats missed by other security layers. Cisco AMP for Endpoints takes advantage of telemetry from big data, continuous analysis, and advanced analytics provided by Cisco's threat intelligence to be able to detect, analyze, and stop advanced malware across endpoints. The following section provides details about Cisco AMP for Endpoints.

Advanced Malware Protection for Endpoints

Cisco AMP for Endpoints provides advanced malware protection for many operating systems, such as the following:

- Windows
- Mac OS X
- Android

Attacks are getting very sophisticated where they can evade detection of traditional systems and endpoint protection. Nowadays, attackers have the resources, knowledge, and persistence to beat point-in-time detection. Cisco AMP for Endpoints provides mitigation capabilities that go beyond point-in-time detection. It uses threat intelligence from Cisco to perform retrospective analysis and protection. Cisco AMP for Endpoints also provides device and file trajectory capabilities to allow the security administrator to analyze the full spectrum of the attack. Device trajectory and file trajectory support the following file types in Windows and Mac OS X operating systems:

- MSEXE
- PDF
- MSCAB
- MSOLE2
- ZIP
- ELF
- MACHO
- MACHO_UNIBIN
- SWF
- JAVA

19

NOTE   The Mac OS X connector does not support SWF files. The Windows connector does not scan Elf, Java, xar(pkg), MACHO, or MACHO_UNIBIN files at the time of writing this book.

The Android AMP connector scans APK files.

Cisco acquired a security company called ThreatGRID that provides cloud-based and on-premise malware analysis solutions.

Cisco integrated Cisco AMP and ThreatGRID to provide a solution for advanced malware analysis with deep threat analytics. The Cisco AMP ThreatGRID integrated solution analyzes millions of files and correlates them against hundreds of millions of malware samples. This provides a lot of visibility of attack campaigns and how malware is distributed. This solution provides the security administrators with detailed reports of indicators of compromise and threat scores that help them prioritize mitigations and recovery from attacks.

Hardware and Software Encryption of Endpoint Data

There are several solutions to provide hardware and software encryption of endpoint data. Several solutions provide capabilities to encrypt user data "at rest," and others provide encryption when transferring files to the corporate network. This section will cover all of those scenarios.

E-mail Encryption

There are several e-mail encryption technologies and solutions. This section explains how e-mail encryption works and describes the technologies available for e-mail encryption. When people refer to *e-mail encryption*, they often are referring to encrypting the actual e-mail message so that only the intended receiver can decrypt and read the message. However, to effectively protect your e-mails, you should make sure of the following:

- The connection to your e-mail provider or e-mail server is actually encrypted.
- Your actual e-mail messages are encrypted.
- Your stored, cached, or archived e-mail messages are also protected.

Let's talk about how to encrypt e-mail messages. There are many commercial and free e-mail encryption software programs. The following are examples of e-mail encryption solutions:

- Pretty Good Privacy (PGP)
- GNU Privacy Guard (GnuPG)
- Secure/Multipurpose Internet Mail Extensions (S/MIME)
- Web-based encryption e-mail service like Sendinc or JumbleMe

S/MIME requires you to install a security certificate on your computer, and PGP requires you to generate a public and private key. Both require you to give your contacts your public key before they can send you an encrypted message. Similarly, the intended recipients of your encrypted e-mail must install a security certificate on their workstation or mobile device and provide you their public key before they send the encrypted e-mail (so that you can decrypt it).

> **NOTE**   Chapter 5, "Fundamentals of VPN Technology and Cryptography," introduces the concept of private and public keys and how they work.

Many e-mail clients and web browser extensions for services like Gmail provide support for S/MIME. You can obtain a certificate from a certificate authority in your organization or from a commercial service such as Digicert, Verisign, and others. You can also obtain a free e-mail certificate from organizations such as Comodo.

Encrypting Endpoint Data at Rest

Much commercial and free software enables you to encrypt files in an end-user workstation or mobile device. The following are a few examples of free solutions:

- **GPG:** GPG also enables you to encrypt files and folders on a Windows, Mac, or Linux system. GPG is free.
- **The built-in MAC OS X Disk Utility:** Disk Utility enables you to create secure disk images by encrypting files with AES 128-bit or AES 256-bit encryption.
- **TrueCrypt:** A free encryption tool for Windows, Mac, and Linux systems.
- **AxCrypt:** A free Windows-only file encryption tool.
- **BitLocker:** Full disk encryption feature included in several Windows operating systems.
- **Many Linux distributions such as Ubuntu:** Allow you to encrypt the home directory of a user with built-in utilities.
- **MAC OS X FileVault:** Supports full disk encryption on Mac OS X systems.

The following are a few examples of commercial file encryption software:

- Symantec Endpoint Encryption
- PGP Whole Disk Encryption
- McAfee Endpoint Encryption (SafeBoot)
- Trend Micro Endpoint Encryption

Virtual Private Networks

Many organizations deploy *virtual private networks (VPN)* to provide data integrity, authentication, and data encryption to ensure confidentiality of the packets sent over an unprotected network or the Internet. VPNs are designed to avoid the cost of unnecessary leased lines. Many different protocols are used for VPN implementations, including the following:

- Point-to-Point Tunneling Protocol (PPTP)
- Layer 2 Forwarding (L2F) Protocol
- Layer 2 Tunneling Protocol (L2TP)

19

- Generic routing encapsulation (GRE)
- Multiprotocol Label Switching (MPLS) VPN
- Internet Protocol Security (IPsec)
- Secure Sockets Layer (SSL)

VPN implementations can be categorized into two distinct groups:

- **Site-to-site VPNs:** Enable organizations to establish VPN tunnels between two or more network infrastructure devices in different sites so that they can communicate over a shared medium such as the Internet. Many organizations use IPsec, GRE, or MPLS VPN as site-to-site VPN protocols.

- **Remote-access VPNs:** Enable users to work from remote locations such as their homes, hotels, and other premises as if they were directly connected to their corporate network. Many organizations use IPsec and SSL VPN for remote access VPNs.

In Chapter 5, "Fundamentals of VPN Technology and Cryptography," and Chapter 6, "Fundamentals of IP Security," you learned the fundamentals of VPN technologies and IPsec. In Chapter 7, "Implementing IPsec Site-to-Site VPNs," and Chapter 8, "Implementing SSL Remote Access VPNs Using Cisco ASA," you learned how to implement and configure site-to-site and remote-access SSL VPNs.

Exam Preparation Tasks

Review All the Key Topics

Review the most important topics from this chapter, denoted with a Key Topic icon. Table 19-2 lists these key topics.

Table 19-2   Key Topics

Key Topic Element	Description	Page Number
List	Endpoint-based threats and types of malware	497
List	Antivirus and antimalware solutions	498
Section	Personal Firewalls and Host Intrusion Prevention Systems	498
Section	Advanced Malware Protection for Endpoints	499
Section	Hardware and Software Encryption of Endpoint Data	500

Complete the Tables and Lists from Memory

Print a copy of Appendix C, "Memory Tables," (found on the CD) or at least the section for this chapter, and complete the tables and lists from memory. Appendix D, "Memory Tables Answer Key," also on the CD, includes completed tables and lists so that you can check your work. There are no applicable memory tables in this chapter.

Define Key Terms

Define the following key terms from this chapter, and check your answers in the glossary:

computer viruses, worms, mailers and mass-mailer worms, logic bombs, Trojan horses, back doors, exploits, downloaders, spammers, key loggers, rootkits, ransomware, ClamAV, Immunet

19

The first 19 chapters of this book cover the technologies, protocols, commands, and features required to be prepared to pass the 210-260 IINS (Implementing Cisco Network Security) exam to become certified as a CCNA Security professional. Although these chapters supply the detailed information, most people need more preparation than just reading alone. This chapter details a set of tools and a study plan to help you complete your preparation for the exam.

This short chapter has two main sections. The first section explains how to install the exam engine and practice exams from the CD that accompanies this book. The second section lists some suggestions for a study plan, now that you have completed all the earlier chapters in this book.

NOTE Appendixes C, D, and E exist as soft-copy appendixes on the CD included in the back of this book.

CHAPTER 20

Final Preparation

Tools for Final Preparation

This section lists some information about exam preparation tools and how to access the tools.

Exam Engine and Questions on the CD

The CD in the back of the book includes the Pearson Cert Practice Test engine. This software presents you with a set of multiple-choice questions, covering the topics you will likely find on the real exam. The Pearson Cert Practice Test engine lets you study the exam content (using study mode) or take a simulated exam (in practice exam mode).

The CD in the back of the book contains the exam engine. After it is installed, you can activate and download the current IINS exam from Pearson's website. Installation of the exam engine takes place in two steps:

Step 1. Install the exam engine from the CD.

Step 2. Activate and download the IINS practice exam.

Install the Exam Engine

The following are the steps you should perform to install the software:

Step 1. Insert the CD into your computer.

Step 2. The software that automatically runs is the Cisco Press software to access and use all CD-based features, including the exam engine and the CD-only appendixes. From the main menu, click the option to **Install the Exam Engine.**

Step 3. Respond to the prompt windows as you would with any typical software installation process.

The installation process gives you the option to activate your exam with the activation code supplied on the paper in the CD sleeve. This process requires that you establish a Pearson website login. You will need this login in order to activate the exam. Therefore, please register when prompted. If you already have a Pearson website login, there is no need to register again; just use your existing login.

Activate and Download the Practice Exam

After the exam engine is installed, you should then activate the exam associated with this book (if you did not do so during the installation process) as follows:

Step 1.   Start the Pearson Cert Practice Test (PCPT) software.

Step 2.   To activate and download the exam associated with this book, from the **My Products** or **Tools** tab, click the **Activate** button.

Step 3   At the next screen, enter the activation key from the paper inside the cardboard CD holder in the back of the book. Then, click the **Activate** button.

Step 4.   The activation process will download the practice exam. Click **Next**; then click **Finish**.

When the activation process is completed, the My Products tab should list your new exam. If you do not see the exam, make sure you selected the My Products tab on the menu. At this point, the software and practice exam are ready to use. Simply select the exam, and click the **Use** button.

To update a particular exam you have already activated and downloaded, simply select the Tools tab, and select the **Update Products** button. Updating your exams will ensure you have the latest changes and updates to the exam data.

If you want to check for updates to the Pearson Cert Practice Test exam engine software, simply select the Tools tab and click the **Update Application** button. This will ensure you are running the latest version of the software engine.

Activating Other Exams

The exam software installation process, and the registration process, only has to happen once. Then, for each new exam, only a few steps are required. For instance, if you buy another new Cisco Press Official Cert Guide or Pearson IT Certification Cert Guide, remove the activation code from the CD sleeve in the back of that book; you do not even need the CD at this point. From there, all you have to do is start the exam engine (if not still up and running), and perform steps 2 through 4 from the previous list.

Premium Edition

In addition to the free practice exam provided on the CD-ROM, you can purchase additional exams with expanded functionality directly from Pearson IT Certification. The Premium Edition of this title contains an additional two full practice exams as well as an eBook (in both PDF and ePub format). In addition, the Premium Edition title also has remediation for each question to the specific part of the eBook that relates to that question.

Because you have purchased the print version of this title, you can purchase the Premium Edition at a deep discount. There is a coupon code in the CD sleeve that contains a one-time use code, as well as instructions for where you can purchase the Premium Edition.

To view the premium edition product page, go to http://www.ciscopress.com/title/9781587205668.

The Cisco Learning Network

Cisco provides a wide variety of CCNA Security preparation tools at a Cisco website called the Cisco Learning Network. Resources found here include sample questions, forums on each Cisco exam, learning video games, and information about each exam.

To reach the Cisco Learning Network, go to learningnetwork.cisco.com, or just search for "Cisco Learning Network." To access some of the features/resources, you need to use the login you created at http://www.cisco.com. If you do not have such a login, you can register for free. To register, simply go to http://www.cisco.com, click **Register** at the top of the page, and supply some information.

Memory Tables

Like most Cert Guides from Cisco Press, this book purposefully organizes information into tables and lists for easier study and review. Rereading these tables can be very useful before the exam. However, it is easy to skim over the tables without paying attention to every detail, especially when you remember having seen the table's contents when reading the chapter.

Instead of simply reading the tables in the various chapters, this book's Appendixes C and D give you another review tool. Appendix C, "Memory Tables," lists partially completed versions of many of the tables from the book. You can open Appendix C (a PDF on the CD that comes with this book) and print the appendix. For review, you can attempt to complete the tables. This exercise can help you focus during your review. It also exercises the memory connectors in your brain; plus it makes you think about the information without as much information, which forces a little more contemplation about the facts.

Appendix D, "Memory Tables Answer Key," also a PDF located on the CD, lists the completed tables to check yourself. You can also just refer to the tables as printed in the book.

Chapter-Ending Review Tools

Chapters 1 through 19 each have several features in the "Exam Preparation Tasks" section at the end of the chapter. You may have used some of or all these tools at the end of each chapter. It can also be useful to use these tools again as you make your final preparations for the exam.

Study Plan

With plenty of resources at your disposal, you should approach studying for the CCNA Security exam with a plan. Consider the following ideas as you move from reading this book to preparing for the exam.

Recall the Facts

As with most exams, many facts, concepts, and definitions must be recalled to do well on the test. If you do not work with security technologies and features on a daily basis, you might have trouble remembering everything that might appear on the CCNA Security exam.

20

You can refresh your memory and practice recalling information by reviewing the activities in the "Exam Preparation Tasks" section at the end of each chapter. These sections will help you study key topics, memorize the definitions of important security terms, and recall the basic command syntax of configuration and verification commands.

Practice Configurations

The CCNA Security exam includes an emphasis on practical knowledge. You need to be familiar with switch features and the order in which configuration steps should be implemented. You also need to know how to plan a LAN switching project and how to verify your results.

This means that hands-on experience is going to take you over the edge to confidently and accurately build or verify configurations (and pass the exam). If at all possible, you should try to gain access to some Cisco Catalyst switches, Cisco IOS routers, Cisco *Adaptive Security Appliances (ASA)*, Cisco *Access Control Servers (ACS)*, and Cisco *Identity Services Engines (ISE)* and spend some time working with their security-related features.

If you have access to a lab provided by your company, take advantage of it. You might also have some Cisco equipment in a personal lab at home. Otherwise, there are a number of sources for lab access, including online rack rentals from trusted Cisco Partners and the Cisco *Partner E-Learning Connection (PEC)*, if you work for a partner. Nothing beats hands-on experience.

In addition, you can review the key topics in each chapter and follow the sample configurations in this book. At the least, you will see the command syntax and the sequence the configuration commands should be entered.

Using the Exam Engine

The Pearson Cert Practice Test engine on the CD lets you access a database of questions created specifically for this book. The Pearson Cert Practice Test engine can be used either in study mode or practice exam mode, as follows:

- **Study mode:** Study mode is most useful when you want to use the questions for learning and practicing. In study mode, you can select options like randomizing the order of the questions and answers, automatically viewing answers to the questions as you go, testing on specific topics, and many other options.

- **Practice exam mode:** This mode presents questions in a timed environment, providing you with a more exam-realistic experience. It also restricts your ability to see your score as you progress through the exam and view answers to questions as you are taking the exam. These timed exams not only allow you to study for the actual 210-260 IINS exam, they help you simulate the time pressure that can occur on the actual exam.

When doing your final preparation, you can use study mode, practice exam mode, or both. However, after you have seen each question a couple of times, you will likely start to remember the questions, and the usefulness of the exam database may go down. So, consider the following options when using the exam engine:

- Use the question database for review. Use study mode to study the questions by chapter, just as with the other final review steps listed in this chapter. Consider upgrading to the Premium Edition of this book if you want to take additional simulated exams.

- Save the question database, not using it for review during your review of each book part. Save it until the end so that you will not have seen the questions before. Then, use practice exam mode to simulate the exam.

To select the exam engine mode, display the My Products tab. Select the exam you want to use from the list of available exams, and then click the **Use** button. The engine should display a window from which you can choose study mode or practice exam mode. When in study mode, you can further choose the book chapters, limiting the questions to those explained in the specified chapters of the book.

20

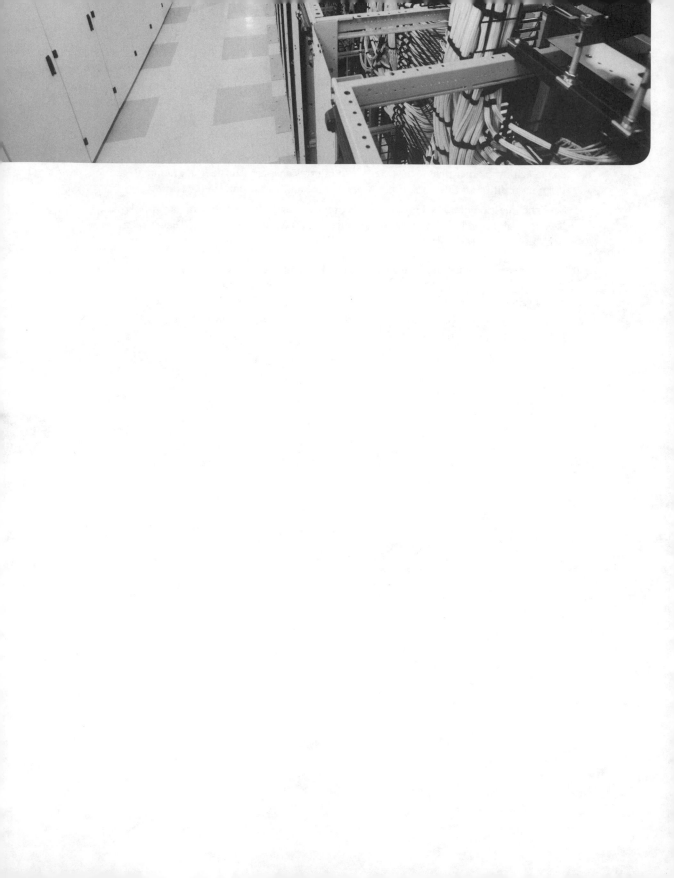

Answers to the "Do I Know This Already?" Quizzes

Chapter 1

1. B
2. D
3. B, C, and D
4. B and D
5. C
6. B
7. D
8. B and D
9. A, B, C, and D
10. B, C, and D

Chapter 2

1. B
2. B
3. C
4. B
5. C
6. C
7. C
8. C
9. C
10. B

Chapter 3

1. A and D
2. C
3. A and B
4. D
5. A
6. B and C
7. B
8. A
9. C
10. A, B, C, and D

Chapter 4

1. C
2. C
3. B
4. C
5. B
6. B
7. A
8. B
9. B
10. B

Chapter 5

1. C and D
2. D
3. D
4. B and D
5. B and D
6. A
7. B
8. A, B, C, and D
9. B
10. C
11. A
12. D
13. A, B and D
14. A
15. A, B, C, and D
16. B
17. B
18. C

Chapter 6

1. A
2. C
3. B
4. A, B, C, and D
5. D
6. D
7. A
8. A and B
9. B
10. A
11. A

Chapter 7

1. A, B, and D
2. A
3. C

4. A, B, and C
5. C
6. A
7. C
8. A
9. A
10. A, B, C, and D
11. A and B
12. C
13. A, B, C, and D
14. B

Chapter 8

1. B
2. C
3. C
4. B
5. D
6. C
7. A and B
8. B
9. A, B, and D

Chapter 9

1. C
2. B
3. D
4. A
5. A
6. A and C
7. C
8. A and D
9. A and E
10. C
11. B
12. C
13. D

Chapter 10
1. D
2. B
3. A
4. A and B
5. A and B
6. C and D
7. A, B, and C
8. B
9. A, B, C, and D
10. C

Chapter 11
1. B
2. B
3. B
4. A, B, C, and D
5. C
6. A, B, and D
7. D
8. A and D
9. B and D
10. D

Chapter 12
1. B and C
2. A
3. A
4. B
5. A, B, and C
6. A, B, C, and D
7. B and D
8. A, B, and C
9. A and B
10. D

Chapter 13
1. B
2. C
3. D
4. B
5. B
6. B
7. C
8. C
9. D
10. C

Chapter 14
1. B
2. D
3. B
4. B
5. C
6. A
7. A
8. A

Chapter 15
1. D
2. A
3. A
4. B
5. C
6. A
7. B
8. C

A

Chapter 16

1. A, B, and C
2. A and B
3. C
4. B and C
5. B and C
6. A, B, and D
7. A
8. C
9. B
10. C

Chapter 17

1. B
2. D
3. C
4. D
5. B
6. A
7. A
8. A and B
9. A
10. A
11. C

Chapter 18

1. A, B, and C
2. A and B
3. C
4. A, B, and C
5. A
6. B, C, D, and E
7. A, B, C, and E
8. B and C

Chapter 19

1. A, B, and D
2. A and B
3. A and B
4. A, B, and C
5. A, C, D, and E
6. A, C, D, and E
7. A and C
8. A and D

CCNA Security 210-260 (IINS) Exam Updates

Over time, reader feedback allows Cisco Press to gauge which topics give our readers the most problems when taking the exams. To assist readers with those topics, the authors create new materials clarifying and expanding upon those troublesome exam topics. As mentioned in the introduction, the additional content about the exam is contained in a PDF document on this book's companion website, at http://www.ciscopress.com/title/9781587205668.

This appendix is intended to provide you with updated information if Cisco makes minor modifications to the exam upon which this book is based. When Cisco releases an entirely new exam, the changes are usually too extensive to provide in a simple update appendix. In those cases, you might need to consult the new edition of the book for the updated content.

This appendix attempts to fill the void that occurs with any print book. In particular, this appendix does the following:

- Mentions technical items that might not have been mentioned elsewhere in the book
- Covers new topics if Cisco adds new content to the exam over time
- Provides a way to get up-to-the-minute current information about content for the exam

Always Get the Latest at the Companion Website

You are reading the version of this appendix that was available when your book was printed. However, given that the main purpose of this appendix is to be a living, changing document, it is important that you look for the latest version online at the book's companion website. To do so, follow these steps:

Step 1. Browse to http://www.ciscopress.com/title/9781587205668.

Step 2. Select the Updates tab.

Step 3. Download the latest "Appendix B" document.

> **NOTE**   Note that the downloaded document has a version number. Comparing the version of the print Appendix B (Version 1.0) with the latest online version of this appendix, you should do the following:
>
> Same version: Ignore the PDF that you downloaded from the companion website.
>
> Website has a later version: Ignore this Appendix B in your book and read only the latest version that you downloaded from the companion website.

Technical Content

The current version of this appendix does not contain any additional technical coverage.

GLOSSARY

3DES   Triple DES is a 168-bit (3 × 56-bit) encryption process. DES, or Data Encryption Standard, is a symmetric key encryption algorithm using a block-cipher method.

AAA   Authentication, authorization, and accounting.

AAA server   The server/host responsible for running RADIUS or TACACS services.

ACS   Access Control Server, the RADIUS and TACACS system sold by Cisco.

Advanced malware protection (AMP)   Cisco advanced malware protection (AMP) is designed for Cisco FirePOWER network security appliances. It provides visibility and control to protect against highly sophisticated, targeted, zero-day, and persistent advanced malware threats.

AES   Advanced Encryption Standard is a symmetric key encryption algorithm using a block-cipher method developed by Joan Daemen and Vincent Rijmen. Available in key sizes of 128-bit, 192-bit, or 256-bit.

amplification DDoS attacks   A form of reflected attacks in which the response traffic (sent by the unwitting participants) is made up of packets that are much larger than those that were initially sent by the attacker (spoofing the victim).

antispam filters   Multilayer filters based on Cisco's e-mail reputation and threat intelligence.

AnyConnect   Cisco's secure mobility client solution, supporting full-tunnel VPN. Requires a small client on the workstation, but then tunnels all traffic through the SSL or IPsec tunnel, allowing other nonsecure protocols to be transported and secured.

ASA   Adaptive Security Appliance firewall, such as the ASA 5510 Firewall.

asset   Property (tangible or intangible) that has value to a company, something worth protecting.

asymmetrical   Meaning both sides are not the same (not symmetrical). An asymmetrical encryption algorithm uses one key to encrypt data and a second (and different) key to decrypt the data.

attack severity rating   The amount of damage an attack can cause. It is used as one property of a signature inside an IPS/IDS.

audit   A detailed review of a network, system or collection of processes. Accounting is another word that has a similar function: collecting information about the network.

authentication method list   The list of methods to be used for authentication (RADIUS, TACACS, enable password, Kerberos, vty line, or local database).

authorization method list   The list of methods to be used for authorization (RADIUS, TACACS, Kerberos, local database, or to pass if already authenticated). Used to specify what the authenticated user is authorized to do.

back doors   A piece of malware or configuration change that allows attackers to control the victim's system remotely.

brute-force (password-guessing) attacks   A type of attack that takes place when a miscreant bombards a system with frequent guesses of a password hoping to eventually get the correct password that enables the miscreant to access the system.

BYOD (Bring Your Own Device)   BYOD refers to policies in place that enable users to connect to the corporate network using personal devices such as smartphones, tablets, and laptops.

BYOD devices   These are the corporate-owned and personally owned endpoints that require access to the corporate network regardless of their physical location.

C3PL   Cisco Common Classification Policy Language. This promotes the concept of using class maps and policy maps to identify and provide specific treatment for traffic.

CA   Certificate authority. A system that generates and issues digital certificates. This is usually a device that is trusted by both parties using certificates.

CCP   Cisco Configuration Professional. A web-based router administration tool with a GUI.

CCP communities   Groups of routers presented together in CCP as a community of devices. A way to organize the devices being managed within CCP.

CCP templates   Sections of configurations that can be reapplied to multiple devices in CCP, substituting variables (such as a hostname) that are unique to each router.

CCP user profiles   Method to restrict what CCP displays to the administrator, thus limiting what the administrator can see and change through CCP.

CDP   Cisco Discovery Protocol enables network devices to send information about the device itself to any device or application on the network that wants to listen to and collect the device information.

CERT   The CERT Division, part of the Software Engineering Institute and based at Carnegie Mellon University (Pittsburgh, Pennsylvania) is a worldwide respected authority in the field of network security and cyber security.

Cisco AnyConnect Secure Mobility Client   The Cisco AnyConnect Client provides connectivity for end users who need access to the corporate network.

Cisco AnyConnect Secure Mobility Client full-tunnel VPN   The client is designed to protect users on computer-based or mobile platforms, providing a solution to encrypt IP traffic, including TCP and UDP. Clientless SSL VPNs only provide a way to encrypt TCP-based applications, whereas the Cisco AnyConnect Secure Mobility Client provides a full-tunnel VPN capability to encrypt TCP, UDP, and other protocols.

Cisco public key   The Cisco public key is needed for the IOS-based IPS to verify Cisco's digital signature of the IPS signature package provided by Cisco.

Cisco SIO   Security Intelligence Operations. Early warning intelligence, threat and vulnerability analysis, and proven Cisco mitigation solutions to help protect networks.

ClamAV   An open source antivirus engine sponsored and maintained by Cisco and non-Cisco engineers.

class map   The portion of Modular Policy Framework (MPF) in the ASA, or C3PL on routers and switches, that defines what types of traffic belong to a certain class. Policy maps rely on class maps for the classification of traffic.

class map type inspect   This special type of class map defines specific classes and types of traffic to be used for further inspection in zone-based firewalls on IOS routers.

clientless SSL VPN   Allows for limited VPN resource access within some protocols that can natively support TLS, such as HTTPS and CIFS shared over HTTPS.

cloud-based MDM deployment   In a cloud-based MDM deployment, MDM application software is hosted by a managed service provider who is solely responsible for the deployment, management, and maintenance of the MDM solution.

computer viruses   A malicious software that infects a host file or system area to perform undesirable outcomes such as erasing data, stealing information, or corrupting the integrity of the system.

context-aware security   Security enforcement that involves the observation of users and roles in addition to things like interface-based controls. An example is an ACS providing full access to an administrator who is logged in from his local computer, but restricted access when that same user is logged in through a remote device or through a smartphone.

control plane   The control plane of a device handles packets that are generated by the device itself or that are used for the creation and operation of the network itself. Control plane packets always have a receive destination IP address and are handled by the CPU in the network device route processor.

control plane policing (CoPP)   A Cisco IOS-wide feature designed to enable users to restrict the amount of traffic handled by the route processor of their network devices.

control plane protection (CPPr)   A Cisco feature, similar to control plane policing, that can help to mitigate the effects on the CPU of traffic that requires processing by the CPU. CPPr has the capability to restrict traffic with finer granularity by dividing the aggregate control plane into three separate control plane categories known as subinterfaces.

CRL   Certificate revocation list. Used in a PKI environment to inform clients about certificates that have been revoked by the CA.

custom privilege level   Level 0 (user) and level 15 (enable) are predefined; anything in between (1–14) is custom privilege level.

data plane   The logic systems in a device that are responsible for the actual movement (post-decision) of information. End users sending traffic to their servers is one example of traffic on the data plane.

DH group   The Diffie-Hellman exchange refers to the security algorithm used to exchange keys securely, even over an unsecured network connection. Groups refer to the lengths of the keys involved in the exchange. Group 1 is a 768-bit key exchange, Group 2 is a 1024-bit key exchange, and Group 5 is a 1536-bit key exchange. The purpose of this algorithm is to establish shared symmetrical secret keys on both peers. The symmetric keys are used by symmetric algorithms such as AES. DH itself is an asymmetrical algorithm.

DHCP snooping   DHCP snooping is a security feature that acts like a firewall between untrusted hosts and trusted DHCP servers.

digital signature   An encrypted hash that uniquely identifies the sender of a message and authenticates the validity and integrity of the data received. Signing is done with the private key of the sender, and validation of that signature (done by the receiver) is done using the public key of the sender.

direct DDoS attacks   Direct DDoS attacks occur when the source of the attack generates the packets, regardless of protocol, application, and so on that are sent directly to the victim of the attack.

disabled signature   A signature that is disabled. A signature needs to be both enabled and nonretired to be used by an IPS/IDS.

downloaders   A piece of malware that downloads and installs other malicious content from the Internet to perform additional exploitation on an affected system.

dynamic ARP inspection (DAI)   DAI is a security feature that validates ARP packets in a network. DAI intercepts, logs and discards ARP packets with invalid IP-to-MAC address bindings. This capability protects the network from some man-in-the-middle attacks.

eavesdropping   Any method of listening in on other conversations, whether voice or data (sniffer).

enabled signature   A signature that is enabled. A signature needs to be both enabled and nonretired to be used by an IPS/IDS.

EUI-64   Extended Unique Identifier-64 is an IEEE standard for converting a 48-bit MAC address into a 64-bit host address in IPv6 networks. Used for stateless autoconfiguration.

exploit   A malicious program designed to "exploit" or take advantage of a single vulnerability or set of vulnerabilities.

file retrospection   After a malicious attempt or malware is detected, Cisco next-generation products (such as the Cisco ASA, Cisco WSA, and Cisco Next-Generation IPS) with AMP capabilities continue to cross-examine files over an extended period of time.

file sandboxing   If malware is detected, the Cisco AMP capabilities can put files in a sandbox to inspect its behavior, combining the inspection with machine-learning analysis to determine the threat level. Cisco Cognitive Threat Analytics (CTA) uses machine-learning algorithms to adapt over time.

hash   A unidirectional process rather than a reversible algorithm, it takes a variable-sized input and creates a fixed-size output. Common examples include MD5 and SHA.

HMAC   Hash Message Authentication Code, used to verify data integrity and authenticity of a message.

identity certificate   A digital certificate assigned to a device, host, person, or e-mail in a PKI infrastructure offering a concept of validated identity.

Identity Services Engine (ISE)   The Cisco ISE is a critical piece to the Cisco BYOD solution. It is the cornerstone of the authentication, authorization, and accounting (AAA) requirements for endpoint access, which are governed by the security policies put forth by the organization.

IDS (intrusion detection system)   Intrusion detection systems, primarily using signature matching, can alert administrators about an attack on the network, but cannot prevent the initial packet from entering the network.

IKE Phase 1   Internet Key Exchange Phase 1 negotiates the parameters for the IKE Phase 1 tunnel, including hash, DH group, encryption, and lifetime.

IKE phase 2   Internet Key Exchange Phase 2 builds the actual IPsec tunnel. This includes negotiating the transform set for the IPsec SA.

Immunet   A free community-based antivirus software maintained by Cisco Sourcefire.

IPS (intrusion prevention system)   Intrusion prevention systems, primarily using signature matching, can alert administrators about an attack on the network and can prevent the initial packet from entering the network.

IPsec   IPsec is the suite of protocols used to protect the contents of Layer 3 IP packets. ESP is the primary protocol used to encapsulate the Layer 3 packets.

key   A password or set of information used to seed other mathematical algorithms.

key loggers   A piece of malware that captures the user's keystrokes on a compromised computer or mobile device. It collects sensitive information such as passwords, PINs, personal identifiable information (PII), credit card numbers, and more.

LDAP   Lightweight Directory Access Protocol. This protocol can be used for gathering/managing information from an LDAP-accessible directory/database. An example of its use is having a AAA server use an LDAP request to Active Directory to verify the credentials of a user.

lifetime   The amount of time, in seconds or amount of data that has gone by, that a key or security association is considered valid.

LLDP (Link Layer Discovery Protocol)   LLDP was developed by Cisco and others within the Internet and IEEE community as a new, standardized discovery protocol, 802.1AB. Similar to CDP, LLDP defines basic discovery capabilities and was enhanced to specifically address the voice application.

logic bombs   A type of malicious code that is injected to a legitimate application. An attacker can program a logic bomb to delete itself from the disk after it performs the malicious tasks on the system.

mailers and mass-mailer worms   A type of worm that sends itself in an e-mail message.

malvertising   This is the act of incorporating malicious ads on trusted websites, which results in users' browsers being inadvertently redirected to sites hosting malware.

man-in-the-middle attack   A form of eavesdropping where the attacker inserts himself in the middle of a conversation, masquerading as a wireless access point, router, proxy server, and so on.

management plane   The management plane refers to traffic and technologies involved in being able to manage the network and its devices. This could include management sessions with SSH, HTTPS, and so on, and could also include information-gathering tools such as SNMP or NetFlow.

MD5   Message digest algorithm 5 is a cryptographic function with a 128-bit hash. Hashing algorithms are unidirectional. The enable secret on an IOS router is stored using an MD5 hash.

MD5 route authentication   MD5 hashing is applied to the authentication of routing updates between routers to ensure the integrity of routing protocol updates. MD5 route authentication is available for OSPF, EIGRP, RIPv2, and BGP.

method list   List of available methods for AAA to use in order (local, RADIUS, TACACS, and so on).

mobile device management (MDM)   The function of mobile device managers, also known as mobile device management (MDM), is to deploy, manage, and monitor the mobile devices that make up the Cisco BYOD solution.

MPF   Modular Policy Framework. A newer technique using the class map and policy map framework to bring about all sorts of manipulations or additional functions to a router. This is what the ASA refers to when using class maps, policy maps, and the service policy commands. On an IOS router, these are referred to as C3PL components.

NA   IPv6 neighbor advertisement. Used to communicate information from an IPv6 host to another on the same locally connected network.

named access control list (ACL)   Configured with ip access-list rather than just access-list commands, and can be defined as either standard or extended, but by name. Named ACLs are easier to edit than numbered ACLs because of the access-list configuration mode provided by the named ACL.

NAT   Network Address Translation. The process of swapping out an IP address of a packet in transit with an alternative address. An example of its use is workstations on the inside of a network using private IP addresses and having those source addresses modified by the NAT router before packets from those workstations are sent out to the Internet.

network antivirus   Antivirus capabilities in network infrastructure devices.

Next-Generation IPS (NGIPS)   The new suite of IPS solutions based on the technologies that were part of the Cisco acquisition of Sourcefire. The Cisco FirePOWER NGIPS solution provides multiple layers of advanced threat protection at high inspection throughput rates.

NFP   Network foundation protection. The concept of breaking down the network into functional components, such as control plane, management plane, and data plane, and then providing protection for each of those components.

NS   IPv6 neighbor solicitation. Used by an IPv6 speaker to make a request of one or more local IPv6 devices on the same network.

NTP   Network Time Protocol. Used to synchronize time on the network, which is important for log messages and for IPS/IDS event time stamps to correlate messages across multiple devices.

on-premises MDM deployment   In an on-premises deployment, MDM application software is installed on servers that are located within the corporate data center and are completely supported and maintained by the network staff of the corporation.

packet filtering   Packet filtering is a static check on known information such as source/destination address and source/destination port information.

parser view   Commands are available only within particular contexts (views). This is a way to implement role-based management, by creating views and associating specific administrators with those views.

PAT   Port Address Translation. This is a subset of NAT, with multiple devices being mapped to a single address. It is also referred to as a many-to-one translation.

personally identifiable information (PII)   This is the type of information that has, unfortunately, been talked about in the press all too often lately when we hear about data breaches. This information includes names, dates of birth, addresses, and Social Security numbers.

PFS   Perfect Forward Secrecy. New keys within DH are not based on seeds from previous keys when PFS is enabled, further increasing security. PFS is associated only with IKE Phase 2.

phishing   Elicits secure information through an e-mail message that appears to come from a legitimate source such as a service provider, fellow employee, or financial institution. The e-mail message might ask the user to reply with the sensitive data or to access a website to update information such as a bank account number.

PKCS#10   Public Key Cryptography Standards #10 is a file format used when sending certificate requests to a CA.

PKCS#12   Public Key Cryptography Standards #12 is a file format used to store private keys with accompanying public key certificates.

PKCS#7   Public Key Cryptography Standards #7 is used by a CA to distribute digital certificates.

PKI   Public key infrastructure. A scalable architecture that includes software, hardware, people, and procedures to facilitate the management of digital certificates.

policy map   The portion of MPF or C3PL that defines what actions occur to traffic belonging to each class.

policy map type inspect   The policy map type is associated with Zoned-Based Firewalls on the IOS. The ASA also has specific purpose policy maps for deep packet inspection.

public key   The part of a key pair that is shared with other people in a PKI exchange

qualitative   A method of risk assessment that uses a scenario model, including expert opinion.

quantitative   A method of risk assessment that uses a mathematical model based on data.

RA   IPv6 router announcement. Used by a router to inform other IPv6 devices about the local network address to which they are connected.

RADIUS   Remote Authentication Dial-In User Service. This is one method for a router or switch to communicate with a AAA server, such as ACS.

ransomware   A type of malware that compromises a system and then often demands a ransom from the victim to pay the attacker for the malicious activity to cease or for the malware to be removed from the affected system.

reflected DDoS (RDDoS) attacks   Occur when the sources of the attack are sent spoofed packets that appear to be from the victim; the sources then become unwitting participants in the DDoS attacks by sending the response traffic back to the intended victim.

regulatory compliance   Security policy created because of local/national laws or regulations (SOX, HIPAA, and so on).

retired signature   If a particular signature is deemed old and no longer a common threat, it can be retired, which reduces memory used by the IOS IPS.

risk   A measurement of the likelihood of a successful attack by measuring the level of threat against a particular vulnerability.

risk rating   A quantitative rating of your network before security measures are put in place. The IOS IPS also uses a risk rating to calculate the potential danger of an attack.

root certificate   The certificate at the top of a certificate hierarchy in PKI.

rootkits   A set of tools that an attacker uses to elevate their privilege to obtain root-level access and completely take control of the affected system.

RS   IPv6 router solicitation request. Used by an IPv6 device to obtain information from an IPv6 router on the local network.

RSA   In 1977, Rivest, Shamir, and Adleman developed a public key algorithm still used by most browsers today. This is an asymmetrical algorithm used for authentication.

SCEP   Simple Certificate Enrollment Protocol. SCEP was created to facilitate large-scale deployments of PKI, by automating the process of authenticating and enrolling with a CA that supports SCEP. This is a Cisco-sponsored protocol and is supported by some, but not all, other vendors.

secure bootset   Part of the Cisco IOS Resilient Configuration feature, preventing the erasure of IOS files from a storage device, such as flash or NVRAM.

Secure Copy (SCP)   A feature that provides a secure and authenticated method for copying device configurations or device image files.

SecureX   Cisco's security framework to establish and enforce security policies across a distributed network.

security levels   Numeric levels used in the ASA to define a relationship of more secure or less secure.

service policy   Just like in MQC for quality of service (QoS), this is the device that ties a policy to an interface (QoS) or to a zone pair (ZBF). On an ASA, this is the command element that links a policy to one or more interfaces.

SFR   Signature fidelity rating. An IPS measurement of the degree of attack certainty related to that signature correctly indicating the attack on which it is supposed to match.

SHA1   Secure Hash Algorithm 1. A successor to MD5, developed by the National Security Agency (NSA).

show ip cef command   The output of this command displays the IP prefixes of the packets that will be received and handled by the control plane (CPU) of the device.

show policy-map control-plan command   The output of this command provides the status of the policy that has been applied to the control plane.

signature files   Package of signatures that update an IDS/IPS against new attack methods. IOS IPS signature packages are similar to the signatures used on the IPS/IDS appliances.

signature micro-engines   Part of IDS/IPS that supports a group of signatures in a common category.

SNMP   Simple Network Management Protocol is used for device management, including requesting information and receiving updates from network devices.

Snort   An open source intrusion detection and prevention technology developed by the founder of Sourcefire (now a part of Cisco).

spammers   A type of malware whose sole purpose is to send unsolicited messages with the primary goal of fooling users into clicking malicious links, replying to e-mails or other such messages with sensitive information, or performing different types of scams.

spoofed address   The source address of an IP packet that has been changed to something not actually assigned or belonging to the location from which it came. Like identity theft for an IP address.

spoofing   An attack where the source pretends to be another host or user (MAC, IP, e-mail).

SSH   Secure Shell. An encrypted alternative to Telnet, for remote CLI management access to a network device.

SSL   Secure Sockets Layer is the original security method for HTTPS. Although succeeded by TLS, this term is still widely used and assumed. This is a secure alternative to HTTP.

standard/extended ACL   Access control list for packet filtering, set up by number. ACLs 1–100 are standard (source IP only), and 100–199 are extended (source and destination IP as well as port information). ACLs 1300–1999 are also standard ACLs, and 2000–2699 are also extended ACLs.

stateful filtering   More than just a simple packet-filter check, stateful inspection can determine whether a network flow exists and can look at information up to the application layer. A stateful filtering firewall dynamically allows the return traffic to the user, from the server they were accessing on the other side of the firewall. This is implemented in the ASA firewall and in the zone-based firewall feature on an IOS router.

subordinate CA   A certificate authority at a level below the root CA. Large PKIs use multiple subordinate CAs to offload the work from a single root CA.

SVI   Switched virtual interface, or "interface VLAN," on a switch.

symmetrical   Literally meaning both sides are the same, such as with pre-shared keys, where both ends have the exact same information used to encode/decode data. DH produces symmetrical keys. Symmetrical keys are used by symmetrical algorithms, such as AES, where one key encrypts the data and the same key is used to decrypt the data.

SYN flood attack   An exploit against TCP's three-way handshake opening lots of sessions via the initial SYN packet with no intent of replying to the SYN-ACK and completing the session. This leaves half-open, or embryonic, connections and can overflow a server's session table.

syslog   Logging messages can be sent to a syslog server that gathers all incoming messages into text files. Syslog server programs can sort by incoming device IP address and by severity/facility levels to make security monitoring simpler.

TACACS+   Terminal Access Controller Access Control System. This is one of the protocols that can be used to communicate between an AAA server and its client (such as between an ACS server and a router).

threat   The potential for a vulnerability to be exploited.

TLS   Transport Layer Security. Based on SSL, but more widely adopted as an IETF standard in RFC 5246.

Traffic Light Protocol (TLP)   A set of designations developed by the US CERT to ensure that sensitive information is shared with the correct audience.

transform set   A set of secure protocol parameters to be used by IPsec in IKE Phase 2. To properly peer, both sides must agree on a common set.

transparent firewall   Firewall implemented at Layer 2 of the OSI model, but still including the ability to analyze traffic at Layer 3 and higher.

Trojan horses   A type of malware that executes instructions determined by the nature of the Trojan to delete files, steal data, and compromise the integrity of the underlying operating system.

TVR   Target value rating. User-defined variable in IPS/IDS of the criticality of a particular target if attacked.

unretired   In IPS, if a new variant would cause old signatures to become valid again, the signature can be assigned as "unretired," which will make the signature available for use, and will consume memory on the IOS router.

uRPF   Unicast Reverse Path Forwarding. Comparing the entry point of a packet's source address against the routing table and making sure the ingress interface matches what the egress interface would be to reach the source of the packet. If the interface does not match, the router assumes the source address is bogus (spoofed) and can drop the packet.

VPN   Virtual private network. Used to provide encryption, authentication, data integrity, and antireplay for network traffic.

vulnerability   A flaw or weakness in a system's design or implementation that could be exploited.

worms   Viruses that replicate themselves over the network, infecting numerous vulnerable systems. In most occasions, a worm will execute malicious instructions on a remote system without user interaction.

X.509v3   The ITU standard for PKI. Version 3 typically refers more to the IETF standard (RFC 3280), which includes CRL usage.

zone pairs   The traffic flow, for initial traffic, unidirectionally between two zones. An example is a zone pair that begins in the inside zone and goes to the outside zone. Policies can then be applied to initial traffic that is moving in the direction of the zone pair (in this case, from inside to outside).

zones   The grouping of multiple interfaces under a similar security policy together, such as inside or outside.

Index

Q-R

CISCO

ciscopress.com: Your Cisco Certification and Networking Learning Resource